THE STRUCTURE OF SOVIET HISTORY

Essays and Documents

EDITED BY

RONALD GRIGOR SUNY

New York   Oxford

OXFORD UNIVERSITY PRESS

2003

Oxford University Press

Oxford   New York
Auckland   Bangkok   Buenos Aires   Cape Town   Chennai
Dar es Salaam   Delhi   Hong Kong   Istanbul   Karachi   Kolkata
Kuala Lumpur   Madrid   Melbourne   Mexico City   Mumbai   Nairobi
São Paulo   Shanghai   Singapore   Taipei   Tokyo   Toronto

and an associated company in Berlin

Published by Oxford University Press, Inc.
198 Madison Avenue, New York, New York, 10016
http://www.oup-usa.org

Oxford is a registered trademark of Oxford University Press

Library of Congress Cataloging-in-Publication Data

The structure of Soviet history : essays and documents / edited by Ronald Grigor Suny.
       p. cm.
     ISBN 1-951370-35- (cloth) — ISBN 1-951370-43- (paper)
       1. Soviet Union—History—Sources. I. Suny, Ronald Grigor.
   DK266.A3 S78 2003
   947—dc21   2002025028

9   8   7   6   5   4   3   2   1
Printed in the United States of America
on acid-free paper

To My Friend and Comrade

David Love

(1940–2002)

a man of exceptional grace and courage

CONTENTS

INTRODUCTION

Back to the Future

The history of the Soviet Union has often been interpreted as a great tragedy, a cruel deviation of a country from the general trajectory of human history. In the first decade after the collapse of the USSR, a popular consensus developed that nothing less than history itself had decisively proven the Soviet experience a dismal failure, if not an unmitigated disaster, and it was only a matter of time before the regimes that still ruled over more than a billion people in China, North Korea, Vietnam, and Cuba would come to realize that the future is knocking on a different door. For many Western analysts, the Soviet experience has demonstrated that radical social transformations proposed by intellectuals and well-meaning political reformers are doomed to failure, though not before enormous costs and burdens are suffered by ordinary people. Even more triumphantly, some have proclaimed that alternatives to capitalism have been relegated to the "trash heap of history" and that human nature and the natural world both require a social order based on markets, private property, and liberal democracy. Soviet history has been used to show that excessive state power leads to new forms of slavery, that the Left is a mirror image of the Right, and that modernity itself has within it a deep perversion. Borrowing from post-modernism, some historians have linked the Soviet program of social transformation to the Enlightenment's attempt to create a modern world through scientific study of society, careful enumeration and categorization of the population, and the application of planning and administration. In their view, these have been misguided efforts that have led to the unprecedented violence and state-initiated bloodshed that has marked the twentieth century.

Not surprisingly, then, as the funeral corteges of expired states pass by, lit up by fires of ethnic warfare, historians of Communist ancien regimes have turned to summing up the history of the recent past. The post-mortems have ranged from inspired polemics of grand theorizing, like Martin Malia's *The Soviet Tragedy*, Zbigniew Brzezinski's *The Grand Failure*, or François Furet's *Death of an Illusion* to more conventional synthetic narratives, like the many textbooks that have appeared recently.[1] The history of the Soviet Union irresistibly tugs at historians and political scientists, urging them to make some overall judgments, not merely to explain but to condemn, and it is only with great difficulty that the usual distance and detachment of scholarly analysis may be maintained. Complexity is lost as scholars join journalists to explain failure as if it were built into the story at every point. But the great puzzle remains:

---

1. Martin Malia, *The Soviet Tragedy: A History of Socialism in Russia, 1917–1991* (New York: The Free Press, 1994); Zbigniew Brzezinski, *The Grand Failure: The Birth and Death of Communism in the Twentieth Century* (New York: Scribner, 1989); François Furet, *The Passing of an Illusion: The Idea of Communism in the Twentieth Century* (Chicago: University of Chicago Press, 1999).

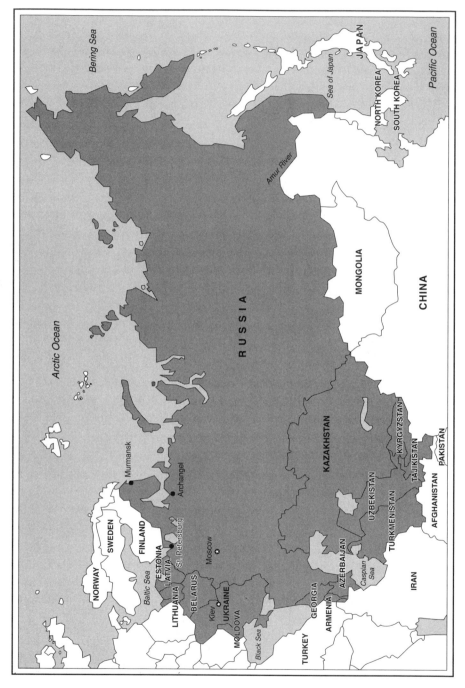

The Soviet Union, 1945–1991

How did a political project that was conceived as emancipatory, that hoped to build a new world with new kinds of humans based on equality and empowerment of ordinary people, become its opposite in actuality? How did an anti-imperialist movement became a new form of imperialism; how did national liberation turn into national oppression? Why did intellectuals and activists, who had suffered imprisonment and exile for their beliefs, turn into brutal censors and executioners? How do we explain this experiment gone wrong?

It is easy enough to begin with the observation that Russia, while part of Europe (at least in the opinion of some), has had distinguishing features and experiences that made its evolution from autocratic monarchy to democracy far more difficult, far more protracted, than it was for a few, privileged Western countries. Not only was tsarist Russia a relatively poor and over-extended member of the great states of the continent, but the new Soviet state was born in the midst of the most ferocious and wasteful war that humankind had fought up to that time. A new level of acceptable violence marked Europe in the years of the First World War. Having seized power in the capital city, the new socialist rulers of Russia fought fiercely for over three years to win a civil war against monarchist generals, increasingly conservative liberal politicians, peasant armies, foreign interventionists, nationalists, and more moderate socialist parties. By the end of the war, the new state had acquired habits and practices of authoritarian rule. The revolutionary utopia of emancipation, equality, and popular power competed with a counter-utopia of efficiency, production, and social control from above. The Soviets eliminated rival political parties, clamped down on factions within their own party, and pretentiously identified their dictatorship as a new form of democracy, superior to the Western variety. The Communists progressively narrowed the scope of those who could participate in real politics until there was only one faction in the party making decisions, and soon only one man—Joseph Stalin.

Once Stalin achieved preeminence, by the end of the 1920s, he launched a second "revolution," this one from above, initiated by the party/state itself. The ruling apparatus of Stalin loyalists totally nationalized what was left of the autonomous economy and expanded police terror to unprecedented dimensions. The new Stalinist system that metastasized out of Leninism resurrected the leather-jacket Bolshevism of the civil war and violently imposed collectivized agriculture on the peasant majority, pell-mell industrialization on workers, and a cultural straightjacket on the intelligentsia. Far more repressive than Leninism, Stalinist state domination of every aspect of social life transformed the Soviet state from a backward peasant country into a poorly industrialized and urban one, while terrorizing its people and eventually turning a massive police machine against the ruling circles of party officials. The Stalinist years were marked by deep contradictions: visible progress in industry accompanied by devastation and stagnation in agriculture; a police regime that saw enemies everywhere at a time when millions energetically and enthusiastically worked to build their idea of socialism; cultural revival and massive expansion of literacy and education coinciding with a cloud of censorship that darkened the field of expression; and the adoption of the "most democratic constitution in the world," while real freedoms and political participation evaporated into memories.

In trying to make sense of the early Soviet years, historians and political scientists have divided into two great schools. On one side are those who believe that Stalin was the logical successor and continuation of Lenin; on the other are those who, like Leon Trotsky, Stalin's defeated rival, claim that a bloody chasm separated the two. Interestingly enough, both sides see Stalinism as a social deformation, but while some link it to the original ideals and practices of the revolutionaries, others insist on the distance between the ideals and the distorted practices of the revolutionaries in power. A figure who haunts this book, Nikolai Bukharin, has been seen by some historians as a failed alternative to the traumas that followed the Great Breakthrough of the First Five-year Plan. As historians home in on Stalin's catalytic role in the Great Terror of the late 1930s, the particular costs and losses associated with his victory in the interparty struggles a decade earlier stand out even more starkly. If one thinks of Stalinism as a cancer of the revolution, then both sides may have a point. For cancer comes from the body, is impossible without the genetic makeup and life experience of that body, but need not be seen as the inevitable outcome of the life of that body. The mysteries of why cancer occurs and how it might have been treated remain, metaphorically, the same questions that continue to haunt investigators of Soviet history.

At roughly the midway point of the twentieth century, the usual account in the West about the Soviet Union was largely about men who craved power and ruthlessly worked to secure and keep it. Here there was little idealism or revolutionary romance, only the determination to cling to privilege and power with little durable support among the populace. The lack of a popular base compelled the Communists to employ terror, and once that terror dissipated and the people ceased to fear the state, the end of the regime was close at hand. This vision of the Soviet system as an artificial imposition on a recalcitrant and resistant people was challenged by a generation of social historians, beginning in the late 1960s, who turned their attention from the Kremlin and its denizens to workers, peasants, and non-Russians. First, a series of studies of the revolutions of 1917 rejected the understanding of the October Revolution as a cynical coup d'état carried out by a small revolutionary clique and showed how ordinary workers in major cities, as well as the overwhelming majority of the soldiers ("peasants in uniform"), supported local soviets and backed the most radical parties, namely the Bolsheviks and the Left Socialist Revolutionaries. "History-from-the-bottom-up," as it was sometimes called, forced a reconsideration of the popular nature of the revolution.

A second focus of attention was on the Stalinist revolution and the nature of Stalinism. Throughout the years of the Cold War, the majority of commentators on the period 1928–1953 characterized Stalinism as a quintessential example of totalitarianism, a society dominated by the state through a terroristic dictatorship by one party led by one man in which all forms of communication, organization, and public activity were controlled by the political authorities. A small number of Old Left intellectuals defended the Stalin regime as the rough but necessary modernizer of a backward peasant society. Without Stalin, collectivization, and forced industrialization, they claimed, Russia would have been defenseless against Nazi aggression.[2] Besides the few who marveled at the economic progress of the USSR, most writing at the time particularly the political science practitioners of Kremlinology, dealt almost exclusively with state actors. Few treated social actors as anything but victims, collaborators, or dupes. Into the broad, empty space left fallow by political history came a small number of social historians, most notably Moshe Lewin and Sheila Fitzpatrick, who attempted in different ways to write a history of Soviet society. With bold and

---

2. See, for example, Maurice Dobb, *Soviet Economic Development Since 1917* (New York: International Publishers, 1948).

forceful strokes, Lewin told the story of enormous processes of social movement in a "quicksand society," in which state programs had colossal, unanticipated results.[3] Fitzpatrick first turned to the world of educators and culture makers to see how writers, artists, and educational bureaucrats dealt with shifting party policies, and she later embarked on a series of historical ethnographies of peasants and workers that elaborated a pointillist picture of everyday life.[4] But the intervention of so-called "revisionists" into the historiography of Stalinism provoked bitter exchanges between the cohort that championed social history or proposed a rethinking of the Terror and a variety of other historians, some clinging to the totalitarian model, others appalled by what appeared to be apologetics for Stalinism. The sound and fury of scholarly debate degenerated at times into name-calling, and it continued after the collapse of the USSR when the newly opened archives were deployed by some to justify their own point of view.

Until quite recently, the serious study of Soviet social and political history in the West basically stopped with the outbreak of World War II. Though great studies appeared of the military campaigns, the destructiveness of the German invasion of the USSR, and the history of diplomacy both during the war and into the Cold War, only a handful of historical works dealt with domestic developments. The post-Stalin period, from 1953 to the end of the Soviet Union (1991), was for many years (and indeed to the present) largely the province of political science and, to a considerably lesser degree, sociology and anthropology. The high drama of Stalinism, with all its tragic excesses, its indiscriminate and pervasive terror, and its near-total isolation from the rest of the world remained what most people in the West associated with the Soviet system, as if there had been neither a Leninist prelude nor a long denouement. But the age of wanton terror ended with the death of Stalin in 1953, and much of the last four decades of Soviet rule was marked by fitful attempts by Khrushchev and Gorbachev to reform the system and recover, at least in part, some aspects of the original socialist inspiration. Each of these bold reformers had his own vision of what Leninism ought to be, but over time the more positive ideals of original Bolshevism faded for most of the party leadership. The name of the game for many Communists, as Gorbachev would discover to his dismay, was power and privilege, not democracy for working people or even raising the efficiency of the planned economy. Gorbachev managed to end the monopoly of power of the Communist party by 1990, that is, before his beloved union itself collapsed. But as he cautiously democratized the system, weakening the party and central state apparatus, he unleashed rival political and nationalist forces that abandoned the socialist project altogether. Gorbachev ended up the last, lonely Bolshevik on a sinking ship, as former comrades, like Boris Yeltsin, and

---

3. Moshe Lewin, *Russian Peasants and Soviet Power: A Study of Collectivization* (Evanston, Illinois: Northwestern University Press, 1968); *Political Undercurrents in Soviet Economic Debates: From Bukharin to the Modern Reformers* (Princeton: Princeton University Press, 1974), *The Making of the Soviet System: Essays in the Social history of Interwar Russia* (New York: Pantheon, 1985), and *Russia, USSR, Russia: The Drive and Drift of a Superstate* (New York: The New Press, 1995).

4. Sheila Fitzpatrick, *The Commissariat of Enlightenment: Soviet Organization of Education and the Arts Under Lunacharsky* (Cambridge: Cambridge University Press, 1970), *Education and Social Mobility in the Soviet Union, 1921–1934* (Cambridge: Cambridge University Press, 1979), *Stalin's Peasants: Resistance and Survival in the Russian Village After Collectivization* (New York and Oxford: Oxford University Press, 1994), and *Everyday Stalinism: Ordinary Life in Extraordinary Times: Soviet Russia in the 1930s* (New York and Oxford: Oxford University Press, 1999).

other leaders of the various Soviet republics, rowed away to independence and an alternative vision of democracy and the free market.

While more conservative scholars contend that the breakup of the USSR was inevitable, written into the genetic code of the revolution, others argue that the Soviet collapse was highly contingent. Russia was the most inhospitable place in the world to try to build socialism—indeed, it seems it may be the most inhospitable place to build capitalism as well! Nostalgia for the old order remains strong in Russia. In a poll a few years ago, a mere 11 percent approved the breakup of the USSR. The poet Evgenii Evtushenko has sung farewell to "our red flag/you were to us brother and enemy," but he misses the country he has lost and wistfully sighs, when "I stroke the flag . . . I cry." The Soviet Union was always in the minds of its supporters more than just another state; it was a dream. Even when dream descended into nightmare, the expectation remained that prosperity or reform would fulfill the aspirations of the founders. In the end, prosperity proved to be elusive and reform led to revolution. The casualty was socialism, which, like liberalism, was always making more promises than it could keep.

This collection of articles, essays, memoirs, and documents is an effort to offer materials that can assist a reader to reach independent judgments about the intricacies and contradictions of the Soviet past. The selected articles testify to the variety of approaches to Soviet history—political, social, and cultural history; political science and sociology; history from the bottom up and the top down. The documents reflect a variety of viewpoints—official pronouncements, dissident manifestos, memoirs, letters, and literature. By reading straight through the book, a reader can basically cover the major events and principal interpretations of Soviet history, though continuity and more complete coverage should come from reading one of the general histories of the Soviet Union now available.[5] Among the unique qualities of this particular book is that it not only covers the entire Soviet and post-Soviet period, beginning with the revolution and ending with post-Soviet Russia and the successor states, but it emphasizes the multinationality of the USSR. Selected essays and documents deal with nationality policy, repression of non-Russians, and problems of the transition to democracy by the smaller post-Soviet states.

The introductory essays and the variety of the articles and documents are designed to introduce the reader into the major historiographical controversies in the Soviet field. The assumption behind the selections is that history, as an object of study, does not exist like an object of the physical world to be checked and verified by simple empirical observation. While documents and monuments supply "facts" from which histories can be written, the act of writing a historical account is always one of human creation out of selected materials. In this sense, like a novel, a painting, or a table, history is a fabrication, and like more material things it can be made only with available ingredients and according to certain rules—in the case of history, critical examination of the evidence, relative objectivity and neutrality, emplotment in the form

---

5. Gregory Freeze (ed.), *Russia, A History* (Oxford, New York: Oxford University Press, 1997); Geoffrey Hosking, *The First Socialist Society: A History of the Soviet Union from Within* (Cambridge, MA: Harvard University Press, 1985, 1993); Peter Kenez, *A History of the Soviet Union from the Beginning to the End* (Cambridge: Cambridge University Press, 1999); Robert Service, *A History of Twentieth-Century Russia* (Cambridge, MA: Harvard University Press, 1998); Ronald Grigor Suny, *The Soviet Experiment: Russia, the Soviet Union, and the Successor States* (New York: Oxford University Press, 1998); and John M. Thompson, *A Vision Unfulfilled: Russia and the Soviet Union in the Twentieth Century* (Lexington, MA: D. C. Heath, 1996).

of a narrative, etc. History, it might be said, is two separate things with only a loose relationship between them. It is, primarily, all that actually occurred in the past but that is infinite in its manifestations and only knowable from the records it has left. For our purposes, history, or the "historical past," in distinction from all past occurrences, exists in so far as it can be re-created and imagined. History is what historians and others have written about the past. It is the literature that they have created to give us a plausible story of past experiences. Yet while it uses many of the methods of fiction and often aspires to be literary, the writing of history claims a particular relation to truth that is different from fiction. Its aspiration is to re-create a past as close as possible to what happened. History's own conventions differ from other forms of narrative writing precisely because of its self-limitation to available and verifiable evidence.

The reader of this volume is faced by the same problems that face professional historians and social scientists: how to be fair, neutral, and objective when confronted with such extraordinary events, excessive brutalities, and wrenching moral choices as presented by the Soviet past. Modern Western professional historians have been inspired by an ideal of objectivity. In the last 200 years, most of them believed that the past was real and knowable and that there was a historical truth that corresponded to that reality. Historical writing was to be factual and free of value, and this would require a sharp separation of the historian from politics or commitment to moral projects. Historical truth existed before interpretation, and the historian's task was to interpret the facts as closely as possible. As Peter Novick summed up the objectivist position, "Truth is one, not perspectival. Whatever patterns exist in history are 'found,' not 'made'."[6]

Though this ideal of a neutral, distant, and disinterested history was seldom achieved—particularly in Soviet historiography—a certain balance and fairness, openness to anomaly and contradiction, were recognized as necessary for the professional historian. Thomas Haskell suggests, in a sympathetic critique of Novick, that objectivity should not be confused with neutrality. A historian's "ascetic detachment," "self-overcoming," fairness, honesty, and openness to different perspectives in a search for more complete understandings are closer to the sense of objectivity with which most practicing historians work.[7] It is that kind of neutrality that this volume seeks to make available to its readers. This collection invites them to think of themselves as historians and to begin to create their own history of the Soviet Union.

A NOTE ON THE TEXT

There are two kinds of footnotes in this collection. Numbered footnotes denote commentary by the editor of this volume. Footnotes designated by symbols are those taken from the source material credited.

---

6. Peter Novick, *That Noble Dream: The "Objectivity Question" and the American Historical Profession* (Cambridge: Cambridge University Press, 1988), p. 2.

7. Thomas Haskell, "Objectivity is Not Neutrality: Rhetoric Versus Practice," *History and Theory* XXIX (1990), pp. 129–57.

Acknowledgments

As in all of my previous work, the debt to fellow scholars is enormous. Here I would like to thank in particular those who read my original proposal and made suggestions as to selections. First, my colleague at the University of Chicago, Sheila Fitzpatrick, has generously shared with her students and associates her expert knowledge of Soviet history, particularly the era of Stalinism. A pioneer in the archival study of the darker regions of the Soviet past, at a time when other explorers were too timid to venture far beyond the revolution, Sheila has become a mentor to much of the profession, and one of my joys of the last years has been working closely with her in workshops and conferences at Chicago. No less a debt is owed to my close friend, collaborator, and comrade, Lewis H. Siegelbaum, whose passion for Soviet history is matched by his deep knowledge and wide reading. He is often a critic of what I write, but always with a shared interest in making what we both do better. Philip C. Skaggs, my student at the University of Michigan and already emerging as a scholar of the revolution in his own right, was enthusiastic about this project from the beginning and not only contributed many suggestions but infected me with his own energy for our common field of study. A special thanks goes to Andrei Doronin, a friend and indispensable facilitator, who has made my visits to the Russian Center for Preservation and Study of Documents of Modern History (RTsKhIDNI; now the Russian State Archive for Social and Political History (RGASPI), both productive and personally pleasant. My gratitude as well to my editors at Oxford. Gioia Stevens guided the book through the shoals of readers, board members, and production, all while handling the early years of her first child, while Linda Jarkesy and Peter Coveney facilitated the final stages of production. And finally, a special debt of gratitude to those closest to me, who share my life and put up with my work—to Armena, Sevan, and Anoush.

Transliteration and Dating

Transliteration is based on a modified Library of Congress system. Most names and places are given in the Russian form, except for a few of the most familiar. So, for example, Alexander Kerensky is rendered Aleksandr Kerenskii, but Moscow is given, not Moskva. In most instances the word "soviet" will be used with no capitalization to mean the councils formed during the revolution and established as part of the USSR system of legislatures. If capitalized, Soviet refers to the central government, the state, or the system of the USSR. This general rule does not apply to selections quoted from other sources.

Dates are given in the Julian calendar, used in Russia up to February 1918, for documents up to that date, unless otherwise noted. That calendar was thirteen days behind the Western Gregorian calendar in the twentieth century. So, for example, the "October Revolution," took place on October 25, 1917, in Petrograd, which was November 7, 1917, in Ann Arbor, Michigan.

1

REVOLUTION AND CIVIL WAR

CHAPTER ONE

The Revolution of 1917

For all the heat that discussions of Russia, Marxism, and the revolution generated among intellectuals and activists, there was surprisingly little self-conscious historiography, that is discussions of competing historical views, by professional Western historians. The first topic to attract speculation about possible interpretations was the revolution itself: Why did tsarism fall? How did the Bolsheviks manage to take power? And what was the meaning of the revolution more universally? Ronald Suny's essay reviews the controversies over February and October and reflects on the challenge that a revisionist social history presented to an older orthodox political history. From roughly the fiftieth anniversary of the Russian Revolution (1967) through the early 1990s, a steady series of monographs, most of them based on archival sources and informed by at least some appreciation of social historical approaches, reintroduced the workers and soldiers back into the story of 1917. Older works, informed by participants' memoirs, a visceral anti-Leninism, and a steady focus on political maneuvering and personalities, had dealt with the Bolsheviks as rootless conspirators representing no authentic interests of those who foolishly followed them. The new historiography argued that a deep and deepening social polarization between the top and bottom of Russian society radicalized the lower classes, prevented the consolidation of a political consensus, so desired by moderate socialists and liberals, and thus undermined the Provisional Government. Rather than being dupes of radical intellectuals, workers articulated their own concept of autonomy and lawfulness at the factory level, while peasant soldiers developed a keen sense of what kind of war (and for what regime) they were willing to fight. More convincingly than any of their political opponents, the Bolsheviks pushed for a government of the lower classes institutionalized in the soviets and advocated workers' control over industry and an end to the war. By the fall of 1917, a coincidence of lower-class aspirations and Lenin's program resulted in elected Bolshevik majorities in the soviets of both Petrograd and Moscow and the strategic support of soldiers on the northern and western fronts. Yet after a relatively easy accession to power, the Bolsheviks, never a majority movement in peasant Russia, were faced by dissolution of political authority, complete collapse of the economy, and disintegration of the country along ethnic lines. As Russia slid into civil war, the Bolsheviks embarked on a program of regenerating state power that involved economic centralization and the use of violence and terror against its opponents.

The social-historical interpretation was in turn challenged by Harvard University's Richard Pipes, who, in a mammoth multivolume work, attempted to dismantle much of this "revisionist" paradigm and breathe new life into older conceptions.[1] Once again, for Pipes, the major players were politicians and intellectuals, the former mostly weak-willed, the latter obsessed with power and reshaping human beings. The ancien regime, Pipes argues, was a patriarchal or patrimonial despotism, the appropriate government for Russia's peasants, who did not crave civil or political rights. This autocratic state, dependent on its landed nobility and bureaucracy, both initiated and restrained capitalist development, which proved subversive to it. The revolution might have been avoided, he claims, if the state had opened up to society, but the monarchy failed to reform because of the social threats to unity and stability. Disloyal intellectuals were matched by unpatriotic peasants who tended toward primitive anarchism, until by the second decade of the century, the tsar had lost all support from society. For Pipes, only the February overthrow of the tsar was a genuine revolution; October was a classic coup d'état engineered cynically by power-hungry conspirators, led by the cowardly Lenin. Once in control of the state, the Bolsheviks ruthlessly used all their instruments to realize the imperatives of Marxist ideology, which included the destruction of multiparty democracy and the market system, the introduction of compulsory labor, and a war against the peasantry. Pipes's work offended many scholars, who were appalled by his failure to discuss almost any of the new scholarship in the field and by his cavalier disregard for the mass actors in the revolution. But his argument that the Bolshevik regime was unpopular and illegitimate from its inception found a ready audience both among those in the West celebrating the demise of what they understood to have been socialism and among those in the Soviet Union who believed that their recent past could be completely expunged.

Social history became the dominant mode of doing early Soviet history and seemed destined for a long hegemony over the field. But outside of Russian studies, the writing of history was already taking a new turn. Early in the 1970s, a series of influential books did nothing less than subvert the confidence of social scientists in the objectivity of the social categories with which they had been working, as well as the possibility of objective research itself. The examination of history as a form of fiction by Hayden White, the interpretive study of culture as a web of significations by Clifford Geertz, and the focus on discourse by Michel Foucault were like a series of explosions that undermined the foundations of a social science built on social causation. Instead of looking for explanations of human motivation in social structures, social positions, and environments alone, attention was given to the realm of culture, the meanings that people give to phenomena, and the need to look at artifacts, documents, and histories as humanly created texts.

In the classic moment of social history, historians of 1917 tended to see class formation or the generation of political identities as located squarely in the real economic and social world, the world of deprivations and disadvantages, which became the primary site from which perceptions of differences arose. Whether it was within the factories themselves or while participating in strikes and demonstrations, work-

1. Richard Pipes, *The Russian Revolution* (New York: KNOPF, 1990) and *Russia Under the Bolshevik Regime* (New York: KNOPF, 1993). For discussions of the changing approaches to the Russian Revolution, see the historiographical reviews by Ronald Grigor Suny, "Toward a Social History of the October Revolution," *American Historical Review*, LXXXI, 1 (February 1983), pp. 31–52, "Revision and Retreat in the Historiography of 1917: Social History and its Critics," *The Russian Review*, LIII, 2 (April 1994), pp. 165–182; and R. G. Suny and Arthur Adams (eds.), *The Russian Revolution and Bolshevik Victory: Visions and Revisions* (Lexington, MA: D. C. Heath, 1990).

ers' experience primarily at the level of economic conflict was seen as both creating and reinforcing identities. Following the pioneering work in other historiographies by Edward P. Thompson, William H. Sewell, Jr., Gareth Stedman Jones, Joan Wallach Scott, and others, Russian historians began to pay growing attention to language, culture, and the available repertoire of ideas.[2] Investigating class formation in the post-Thompsonian period involved not only exploring the structures of the capitalist mode of production or the behavior of workers during protests and strikes—all of which remained important sites for investigation—but also the discourses (the universes of available meanings) in which workers expressed their sense of self, defined their "interests," and articulated their sense of power or, more likely, powerlessness. Representations in the socialist and bourgeois press, which shaped and reinforced social identities and the sense of social distance, were extraordinarily influential in forming the workers' (and others') understanding of the way the world worked. Whatever the experience of workers might have been, the availability of an intense conversation about class among the intellectuals closest to them provided images and language with which to articulate and reconceive their position. Now, suspicious of explanations from structure or "the material," explanations that easily descended into a kind of social or economic determinism, social historians of Russia began to consider both "material," environmental elements and more subjective experiences, like discrimination, humiliation, and a sense of social justice.

Without retreating to a political history with society left out, a number of Western and post-Soviet historians were influenced by this so-called "linguistic" or "cultural turn" that scholars in other fields had made. Class was a category insistently present in 1917, yet the story of class formation of workers had often been told without reference to the class formation of the "bourgeoisie" and other social "others." Since the politics of forming class is a matter of inclusions and exclusions, of politically eliminating some distinctions between "us" and "them" and constructing others, the story of the working class was only partially told when treated in isolation from its allies and its enemies. Classes are political coalitions of diverse elements, and in 1917, the formation of class in Russia occurred on the basis of a broad conception of the demokratiia (the "democracy," the lower classes) that included workers, soldiers, peasants, and others, but excluded people of property. Through 1917, myriad groups began to believe and articulate that they shared a cluster of "interests" and that those "interests" could not be reconciled with the existing political and social order. Among waged workers, all kinds of distinctions and antagonisms between women and men, younger and older workers, skilled and unskilled, those in "hot" shops and "cold," had to be overcome until a new community was imagined and created through political understandings and activities.

How the boundaries of the lower classes were negotiated between soldiers, artisans, the petit bourgeois, and the white-collar population, as the concept of demokratiia evolved, could already have been inferred from the works of the social historians of the 1970s and 1980s. But a sense of "class" solidarity could not be deduced simply from shared experiences, however intensely felt, or the elimination of internal differ-

---

2. E. P. Thompson, *The Making of the English Working Class* (London: Victor Gollancz, 1963); Gareth Stedman Jones, *Languages of Class: Studies in English Working Class History, 1832–1982* (Cambridge: Cambridge University Press, 1983); William H. Sewell, Jr., *Work and Revolution in France: The Language of Labor from the Old Regime to 1848* (Cambridge: Cambridge University Press, 1980); Joan Wallach Scott, *Gender and the Politics of History* (New York: Columbia University Press, 1988).

ences, but only as people gave particular meanings to activities in which they were engaged. Here the approaches associated with discursive analyses, with concepts of political culture, and with ideas of cultural hegemony and cultures of resistance provided the necessary links to bring structure, experience, and the generation of meaning together. In this volume, the young Russian historian Boris Kolotnitskii engages precisely in such a study of discourse, of the ways in which people spoke about the bourgeoisie and created a discursive geography into which they, their allies, and their opponents fit. Whether marching in a demonstration, participating in a strike, or voting for a deputy to the factory committee, the choice for a worker to participate or not did not arise simply from his or her social position but was already imbedded in all kinds of understandings about the nature of society, who one was, what would result from such action, and who the enemy was.

Just as in its "deconstructive" phase social history undermined and expanded the old political history, so two decades later it was itself challenged by the discursive investigations of meanings and the rejection of simple referential recordings of "realities." No longer could social categories or identities be taken as given, as fairly stable, or as expressing clear and objective interests emanating from their essential nature. Though historians of Russia and the Soviet Union had long been suspicious of the available social categories, only recently have they questioned their objectivity and essentialism and highlighted the provisional, subjective, and representational character of estate, class, nationality, generation, and gender.[3] In the post-Soviet years, historians of Russia and the Soviet Union amplified their investigations by bringing in culture, discourse, and language, and with their new tools they discovered new sites, like festivals and rituals, posters and poems, sexual practices and popular entertainment, in which to dig.

TOWARD A SOCIAL HISTORY OF THE OCTOBER REVOLUTION

Ronald Grigor Suny

. . . Historians have understandably had difficulty separating their political preferences for or abhorrence of the Soviet Union from their treatment of the complexities of the revolutionary years. Frequently, history has been written backwards, beginning with the knowledge of the single-party dictatorship, Stalin, collectivization, and the Great Purges and retreating in time toward the heady days of 1917 to find what went wrong. Western interpretations of the Russian Revolution are arrayed all

---

3. See, for example, Gregory L. Freeze, "The Soslovie (Estate) Paradigm and Russian Social History," *American Historical Review,* XCI, 1 (February 1986), pp. 11–36; Leopold H. Haimson, "The Problem of Social Identities in Early Twentieth Century Russia," *Slavic Review,* XLVII, 1 (Spring 1988), pp. 1–20, and the discussion that followed with William G. Rosenberg and Alfred J. Rieber, pp. 21–38; Sheila Fitzpatrick, "L'usage bolchevique de la 'classe': Marxisme et construction de l'identite individuelle," in *Actes de la recherche en sciences sociales,* no. 85 (November 1990), pp. 70–80; "Ascribing Class: The Construction of Social Identity in Soviet Russia," *Journal of Modern History,* LXV, 4 (December 1993), pp. 745–770; Ronald Grigor Suny, "Nationality and Class in the Revolutions of 1917: A Re-examination of Categories," in Nick Lampert and Gabor T. Rittersporn (eds.), *Stalinism: Its Nature and Aftermath. Essays in Honour of Moshe Lewin* (London: Macmillan, 1992), pp. 211–242.

along the political spectrum, from nostalgic reactionary views regretting the passage of the tsarist regime to radical apologia for the necessity of violence and terror. But none are free, or ultimately can be free, from explicit or unconscious value judgments about the benefits or costs of this revolution.

Although history is never entirely free of ideological preconditioning and cannot be completely "objective," historians are still obligated to be clear about their values and preferences and their politics and to attempt, within these limits, to be as sensitive and fair to the evidence as possible. Not surprisingly, most Western historians of the Russian Revolution come to the study of 1917 committed to an evolutionary, democratic political and social system and are highly suspicious of the possibility of creating a noncapitalist, socialist economic order—particularly out of whole cloth, as the Bolsheviks attempted to do. Despite frequent claims of detachment and objectivity, scholars often make their judgments about the revolution and the Soviet Union against the standard of quite different European and American experiences. It is helpful, therefore, to explore the connection between conscious and unconscious ideological intrusions and the approach to a historical problem, for a particular angle of vision may illuminate some aspects while obscuring others.

Not unconnected to political values brought to the study of the revolution are the kinds of analyses preferred by most Western historians. Up until the last decade, Western historiography of 1917 has been concerned primarily with political explanations, emphasizing the importance of governmental forms and ideas but underestimating the more fundamental social and economic structures and conflicts in Russian society. Approaching the revolution from the top down, these writers have been concerned with the politics of the tsarist and provisional governments, with parties and revolutionary organizations, and with the dynamic personalities of Lenin, Trotsky, and Kerensky as well as with ideological questions. . . .

Russian history in general and the study of the revolution in particular have been latecomers to social history. This might seem anomalous to people outside the field, given that scholars in the Soviet Union write exclusively in a Marxist tradition. But during the Stalinist years Soviet Marxist historiography of the revolution was limited to explorations of the role of the party and key party leaders, and only recently have there been more broadly gauged investigations of workers, peasants, the soviets, and other mass organizations and movements. In the West, the sociohistorical approach has also long been hindered by the inaccessibility of Soviet archives, but in the last decade the picture has changed dramatically. Scholars have turned away from the most visible participants in the revolution to look at the rest of Russian society and to outlying regions and have produced a number of sociohistorical studies—of workers (by Mark David Mandel, William G. Rosenberg, Diane Koenker, Stephen A. Smith, Ziva Galili), of revolution in the provinces (by Donald J. Raleigh, Roger Pethybridge, Ronald Grigor Suny, Andrew Ezergailis), of the soldiers (by Allan K. Wildman), of the sailors (by Norman E. Saul, Evan Mawdsley), and the whole array of spontaneous mass organizations (by Marc Ferro, Oskar Anweiler, Rex A. Wade. John L. H. Keep, Tsuyoshi Hasegawa). The Russian peasantry, hitherto largely neglected in the revolutionary period, is now the subject of a monograph by Graeme J. Gill.

The debate about social and political history has been both fruitful and divisive within the profession—fruitful in that it has forced more conscious appreciation by all historians of the tasks in which they are engaged, but divisive in that it has hardened positions and distorted the dialogue between Marxist and non-Marxist social historians. The study of the Russian Revolution has been spared the sparring that has divided European social historians, in part because Russian scholars have neglected or consciously avoided theoretical and methodological issues and in part because they have not written much nonnarrative, quantitative, apolitical social history of the sort done by some family historians. Russian social history has been more concerned with the movement and movements of social groups and classes than with patterns of fertility or mortality and has emphasized those moments of intense conflict, such as 1905 and 1917. That focus has always demanded some attention to politics. An appreciation of the estate (*soslovie*) structure of Russian society and the emergence of classes has long been a part of this tradition of historical writing. Yet there have been influential examples of histories written without much concern with the underlying social context as well as studies that have dealt almost exclusively with social movements without adequate consideration of political issues. And, perhaps most surprisingly, the October Revolution has often been studied without taking into account the sociopolitical developments of the late tsarist period, particularly the crucial last years of constitutional impasse and rising urban unrest.

The overthrow of the tsar, accomplished by workers and soldiers in Petrograd, was the product of largely spontaneous action by thousands of hungry, angry, and war-weary women and men who had lost all confidence in the government of Nicholas II. But, along with the political revolution aimed at autocracy, a deeply rooted social antagonism, particularly on the part of certain groups of workers, against the propertied classes (the so-called *tsenzovoe obshchestvo*) was evident. This social cleavage was not simply a product of the war years but antedated that conflict, as Leopold H. Haimson showed in a two-part, seminal article published more than a decade ago. Haimson argued that a dual polarization had been taking place in urban Russia in the last years before the war. As all but the most conservative strata of society moved away from the bureaucratic absolutist regime, the working class—or, more precisely, workers in large firms, such as the metallurgical plants—was pulling away from the liberal intelligentsia, from moderates in the Social Democratic party, and from Duma politicians. "By 1914," Haimson stated, "a dangerous process of polarization appeared to be taking place in Russia's major urban centers between an *obshchestvo* ["society"] that had now reabsorbed the vast majority of the once-alienated elements of its intelligentsia—and that had even begun to incorporate many of the "workers' own intelligentsia"—"and a growing discontented and disaffected mass of industrial workers, now left largely exposed to the pleas of an embittered revolutionary minority."

In contrast to the usual picture of the Bolsheviks as an isolated clique among a working class generally concerned with economic issues, the workers became steadily and increasingly radicalized in the metal industry and in St. Petersburg particularly such that Bolshevik influence grew at the expense of the Mensheviks and Socialist Revolutionaries (SRs). Haimson's work of the last decade demonstrates that workers had an increasing sense of class unity and separation from the rest of society as well as an awareness that they could solve their own problems. Ever more militant and far-reaching demands were put forth, most notably by St. Petersburg metalworkers, and the high incidence of defeat in their economic strikes only propelled them further toward a revolutionary opposition to the regime and the industrialists. "Given the even more precise correspondence between the image of the state and society that the Bolsheviks advanced and the instinctive outlook of the laboring masses, the Bolshevik party cadres were now able to play a significant catalytic role. They succeeded

. . . in chasing the Menshevik 'Liquidators' out of the existing open labor organizations." By 1914 the key labor unions were in the hands of the Bolsheviks, and working-class discontent exploded in a sharp increase in the number and duration of strikes and political protests.

While the war years demonstrated the fragility of the Bolsheviks' newly conquered positions within the working class and arrests and patriotism ate into their influence, the potential for a renewal of militance remained intact. Much more visible than the exiled Bolshevik leaders were those more moderate socialists who remained in the capital and worked in the legal and semilegal institutions permitted by the autocracy. With the collapse of tsarism, timing and geography promoted even the less-prominent Mensheviks and Socialist Revolutionaries into positions of enormous power and influence. Although in the first month of revolution workers were neither unified around any one program nor tightly tied to any one party, there was a striking consensus among most Petrograd workers on the question of power in both the state and the economy. Except for the most militant, the metalworkers of the Vyborg district, the workers were not yet anxious either to take state power or to run the factories themselves. Thus, there was a strategic parallel between their conditional support of the Provisional Government—*poskol'ko, postol'ko* ("insofar as") their policies corresponded to the interests of the Soviet—and the notion of *rabochii kontrol'* ("workers' control"), which at this time meant merely the supervision of the owners' operations by representatives of the workers, not the organization of production directly by the workers. Both the political and economic policies favored by active workers in the first months of revolution entailed watching over and checking institutions that continued to be run by members of propertied society.

Yet the social polarization that Haimson has noted was already evident even in the euphoria of February and early March, as the workers and soldiers set up their own class organizations—factory committees, soldiers' committees, militia, and, most importantly, the soviets—to articulate and defend their interests. From the beginning of the revolution they registered a degree of suspicion toward the Duma Committee and the Provisional Government, even though significant concessions were made to the representatives of educated society. Among the rank-and-file soldiers the sense of distance and distrust toward their officers led them to form their own committees and draft the famous Order Number One, which both legitimized the committees and placed the Petrograd garrison under the political authority of the Soviet. Among the sailors of the Baltic Fleet, a force in which workers were much more heavily represented than in the peasant-based army, the hatred of the crewmen toward the officer elite resulted in an explosion of summary "executions." The genuine suspicions of the *demokratiia* ("lower classes") were reflected by their leaders, who rejected any notion of a coalition government with the bourgeoisie and maintained that the Soviet should remain a separate locus of power critical of but not actively opposing the government. Thus, *dvoevlastie* ("dual power") was an accurate mirror of the real balance of forces in the city and the mutual suspicion that kept them from full cooperation.

The irony of the February Revolution was that the workers and soldiers had effectively overthrown the old government, but neither they nor their leaders were yet confident enough of their abilities to form their own government or to prevent a counterrevolutionary challenge if the propertied classes were excluded. At the same time that soldiers and workers were reluctant to be ruled by their old class enemies, they realized that without agreement with the Temporary Duma Committee the loyalty of the army at the front was problematic. The Duma leadership, for its part, understood that real power—the power to call people into the streets, defend the city, make things work or fall apart—was in the hands of the Soviet, not the government. Moderate leaders in both the government and the Soviet were willing to play down the conflict within society in the face of a possible reaction from the right. Realism and caution through March and early April allowed a brief period of cooperation and conciliation that at first convinced many of the possibility of collaboration between the top and bottom of society but that ultimately created, when collaboration failed, a bitter and divisive aftermath.

As early as March 10 the Soviet and the Petrograd Society of Industrialists agreed to introduce an eight-hour working day in the factories. This victory for the workers on an issue that had caused deep hostility in the prewar period was achieved with surprising ease, and the conciliatory attitude of industrialists like Konovalov seemed to predict further concessions. Demands for higher wages were met with sympathy, and during the first three months of the revolution nominal wages rose on the average of 50 percent in Russia. Although there was greater resistance to the idea of a minimum wage, it too was finally approved by the industrialists on April 24. In a sense workers were trespassing on prerogatives traditionally held by capitalists when they demanded the removal of unpopular administrative personnel, but early in the revolution even such desires as these were satisfied.

As Ziva Galili y Garcia has convincingly shown, workers' expressions of suspicion toward the "bourgeoisie" declined substantially in March, but significant groups within the industrial class began to express their opposition to the "excessive demands" of the workers. Even Konovalov, an advocate of cooperation with the workers, held that the overthrow of tsarism should rightly result in the establishment of the commercial-industrial bourgeoisie as the dominant force in Russia's social and economic life. Although this notion seems to coincide with the Menshevik conception of the revolution as "bourgeois-democratic," serious tactical differences emerged between the Progressist leaders, representing powerful industrialists, and the Revolutionary Defensists, who led the Soviet. Whereas the First Congress of Trade and Industry called for restoration of "free trade" and the placing of food supply in the hands of the "experienced commercial-industrial class," the Menshevik economists favored price regulation and state control of the economy. But the issue that brought the fragile dual-power arrangement down was not the emerging economic issue but the conflict between the upper and lower classes over the war.

Initially, the soldiers were suspicious of dual power and even of the Soviet to some extent, but Allan K. Wildman has demonstrated that, as a result of a campaign by the "bourgeois" press to turn the army against workers struggling for the eight-hour day and of a successful propaganda effort by Soviet agitators directed at the lower ranks, soldiers began to perceive the Provisional Government as a "class" instead of a "national" institution. One by one the soldiers' congresses held at the various fronts came out in support of Soviet control over the government and a "democratic peace without annexations or contributions"—the positions taken by the Revolutionary Defensists. The April crisis marked the end of the futile attempt by Miliukov and his closest associates to maintain a foreign policy independent of the Soviet. The same cleavage that was visible in Petrograd between the *demokratiia* and the *tsenzovoe obshchestvo* on the questions of power, the economy, and the war was also reflected within the army between the soldiers and their officers.

The dependence of the Provisional Government on the Soviet, clear from the first days of their coexistence, required in the view of the members of the government the formation of a coalition. At first resistant to joining a government of the bourgeoisie, the Mensheviks reluctantly agreed in order to bolster the government's authority. For the Revolutionary Defensist leader Irakli Tsereteli, coalition meant the unification of the workers with other "vital forces of the nation" in an effort to end the war and fight social disintegration. The successful collaboration of the bourgeoisie and the Soviet in the first months of the revolution had lulled the Mensheviks into a belief that class hostility could be overcome, but almost simultaneously with the formation of coalition the economic situation grew worse. Inflation forced more demands for wage increases, but industrialists who had recently been so generous now were resistant to further raises. In May and June workers began to suspect that factory shutdowns were deliberate attempts at sabotage by the owners. Economic difficulties, so intimately tied to the war, turned workers against the industrialists and the government. Although some workers supported coalition, the great bulk of Petrograd's factory workers grew increasingly suspicious both of the government and of those socialists who collaborated with the bourgeoisie. The beneficiaries of this suspicion and distrust were those parties that opposed the coalition and advocated a government composed of the representatives of the working people—that is, the Bolsheviks.

The association of the Menshevik and SR leaders of the Soviet with the coalition government—and, consequently, with the renewed war effort in June—placed a stark choice before the workers and soldiers: either cooperation and collaboration with the upper classes, who were increasingly perceived as enemies of the revolution, or going it alone in an all-socialist soviet government. The first efforts of the demokratiia were directed at convincing the Soviet leaders of the necessity of taking power in their own hands. The erosion of lower-class support for the government was already quite clear on May 31 when the workers' section of the Petrograd Soviet voted for the Bolshevik resolution calling for "All Power to the Soviets!" Even more dramatic was the demonstration of June 18, in which hundreds of thousands of workers marched carrying slogans such as "Down with the Ten Capitalist Ministers!" By early July, with the distressing news of the failure of the June offensive filtering into the city, the more militant soldiers, sailors, and workers attempted through an armed rising to force the Soviet to take power. Emblematic of the paradox of the situation is that famous scene when sailors surrounded the SR leader Chernov and yelled at him, "Take power, you son-of-a-bitch, when it is given to you."

But, as is well known, the Soviet did not take power, and a series of weak coalition governments followed the July crisis until their forcible overthrow in October. The brief eclipse of the Bolsheviks in July and their rapid rise from isolation and persecution through the summer to state power in October have been the object of an enormous amount of historical study, but in their search for explanations historians have tended to overemphasize the role of political actors, like Lenin and Trotsky, and to underestimate the independent activity of workers and soldiers. Before setting out a new sociopolitical interpretation of the Bolshevik victory emerging from recent and ongoing research, I shall consider the limitations exhibited by several influential works that focus too exclusively on either the political or the social aspects of the revolution.

About a decade and a half ago, one of the most stimulating views of the October Revolution was what might be called the "conservative-accidentalist" interpretation shared by Sergei Petrovich Melgunov and Robert V. Daniels. Melgunov, who was a minor participant in the events he described, revealed his approach in his opening quotation from Kerensky: "By the will of men, not by the force of the elements, did October become inevitable." To Melgunov, the October Revolution was in no sense inevitable; indeed, he made clear from the beginning his disagreement with those historians for whom "social processes almost fatalistically predetermined the course of events. . . . 'October' was not the realization of 'February.'" Melgunov deliberately distinguished his approach from his notion of the Marxist approach to history—inevitability, social determinism, and the idea that revolutions, like societies, march lock step through a series of succeeding stages.

Melgunov emphasized instead the power and persuasiveness of Lenin, who singlehandedly was able to turn the central committee of the Bolshevik party from moderation to the radical alternative of seizing power by force. Melgunov treated Lenin as if he had been mad: "With the stubbornness of a maniac under self-hypnosis, he insisted *now or never.* . . . The uprising had become an obsession with Lenin." Lenin was "still raving" on page 7, made "hysterical demands" on page 9, and fell "into a complete fit of rage" on page 16. Moreover, the government was lulled to sleep. With the exception of the energetic prime minister, Kerensky, the cabinet had, in Melgunov's terminology, become "spineless." No adequate measures were taken to stop the Bolsheviks until it was too late. There was a false sense of confidence that the government with the support of the garrison could put down a Bolshevik uprising. Thus, in Melgunov's treatment the Bolshevik seizure of power appears to have been a matter of competing wills—the determined will of Lenin to take power by any means before the Second Congress of Soviets, the misguided will of Kerensky to allow the Bolsheviks to make a move so that they could be exposed and crushed, and the vacillating wills of cabinet officers and the military who did not take resolute action in time. Once the Bolsheviks began their occupation of government buildings, the Kerensky government found no one in Petrograd willing to defend the Winter Palace, except some military cadets and the famous Women's Battalion of Death.

The Kerensky government's inability to mobilize military and popular support in the moment of crisis is well known and indisputable, but Melgunov argued further that the Bolsheviks, too, lacked mass support in the October Days. The garrison, on the whole, remained neutral; "only individual soldiers or sub-regimental units—at best"—came out into the streets at the call of the Military Revolutionary Committee. Workers and their Red Guard units participated in the uprising only sporadically. The decisive force on the Bolshevik side were the sailors of Kronstadt and Helsinki, who arrived in Petrograd on the afternoon of October 25. Here, then, was the extent of mass backing for the Bolsheviks: a few strategically placed armed units of soldiers, sailors, and workers. "The Russian public was almost completely absent on that tragic day."

Melgunov conceded that the Bolsheviks did manage to have enough force at the right place to win the day in October, and he quoted Lenin in seeming agreement: "To have an overwhelming superiority of forces at the decisive moment at the decisive point—this law of military success is also a law of political success." With their "powerful backing in the capital cities," the Bolsheviks were able to take over the rest of the country. Melgunov did not explain how the Bolsheviks received the backing that they managed to mobilize in October, nor did he explain why the "revolutionary democracy proved impotent," except to note that the forces in the center had no unity of will. This, of course, begs the question why there was no unity of will among the moderates in the face of their impending loss of power. Why were the Bolsheviks capable of the necessary will and determination and not Kerensky or the moderate socialists? Indeed, the moderates had leaders of determination and will, most notably the Menshevik Tsereteli and the conservative General Kornilov. Yet their attempted political solutions failed. Ultimately, the momentous events in October require more than explanations based on such accidental qualities as personality and mood.

In his *Red October,* published to mark the fiftieth anniversary of Lenin's seizure of power, Robert Daniels portrayed the revolution as a "veritable orgy of democracy," "galloping chaos," and "violent political struggle." Although Daniels acknowledged early in his book that the workers of Petrograd "played a decisive role in the flow of events because they were the strongest social force in the deciding center of the country, the capital city," he did not provide much in the way of an explanation for their leftward shift; indeed, the body of his book essentially ignores the role of the workers. Daniels's view echoes that of Melgunov: the people in power were indecisive, and one party—the Bolsheviks—was able and willing to take decisive action. The October insurrection, largely the product of Lenin's determination, "succeeded against incredible odds" and was a "wild gamble, with little chance that the Bolsheviks' ill-prepared followers could prevail against all the military force that the government seemed to have. . . . To Lenin, however, it was a gamble that entailed little risk, because he sensed that in no other way and at no other time could he have any chance at all of coming to power."

Daniels's idea that Lenin produced the October crisis, that he "singlehandedly polarized Russian political life in the fall of 1917," is crucial to what followed:

> If the revolution had not occurred as it did, the basic political cleavage of Bolsheviks and anti-Bolsheviks would not have been so sharp, and it is difficult to imagine what other events might have established a similar opportunity for one-party Bolshevik rule. Given the fact of the party's forcible seizure of power, civil violence and a militarized dictatorship of revolutionary extremism followed with remorseless logic.

But Lenin's victory was neither inevitable nor necessitated by social causes. Lenin was personally responsible for and indispensable to the Bolshevik victory; if he had been kept out of Russia in 1917 or had been "recognized by the cadet patrol" that stopped him on the way to Smolny on the very eve of the October Revolution, "his followers could not have found a substitute." Thus, for Daniels, October is a historical accident contingent upon just the right, somewhat arbitrary elements, present at just the right moment. There is no sense here, except for a few sentences in the first pages, of the great social and economic forces at play in 1917, the movements of workers and soldiers, that made Lenin's success possible and Kerensky's defeat a near certainty. Such a sense, of course, cannot be gained from a largely biographical or political approach to the revolutionary events of 1917.

Useful as a corrective to the approach of Melgunov and Daniels is the work of Alexander Rabinowitch, a meticulous student of the Bolshevik party in 1917, who has attacked the cliché that the key element in Bolshevik success was the party's superior leadership and organization. This stereotype of Bolshevism stems from a reading of Lenin's 1902 tract, *Chto delat'?* ("What Is to Be Done?"), in which Lenin put forth an image of a centralized, disciplined party of underground, professional revolutionaries. Such a party was the crucial instrument, it is often argued, that brought off the *coup d'état* of October and established order in the midst of anarchy. Rabinowitch has argued instead that this stereotype is overdrawn, that "the party's internally relatively democratic, tolerant, and decentralized structure and method of operation, as well as its open and mass character," made possible a flexible, dynamic relationship between the party hierarchy and its potential supporters.

On the question of mass backing for the Leninists, Rabinowitch has convincingly established that in the aftermath of the July Days the Bolsheviks did not lose as much support, particularly among workers, as many contemporaries and later historians believed. Their recovery was swift, thanks to "worsening economic conditions and the unpopular policies of the government and the majority of socialists." The shift to the right by the Soviet was unpopular in many workers' districts, and the re-establishment of the death penalty at the front alienated the soldiers of the Petrograd garrison. The attempt by Kornilov to establish a military dictatorship raised industrial workers and soldiers from their summer lethargy to come out against the "counterrevolution." Kerensky was discredited in the eyes of the left and the masses for his involvement with Kornilov. . . . After the Kornilov Affair the possibility of collaboration with the liberals and upper classes, especially with the compromised Kadet party, had become anathema to the lower strata of the Petrograd population.

Rabinowitch's treatment of 1917 is still primarily political history, though not of the state but of an intermediate political organization with effective links to the lower classes. He has clearly demonstrated that the Bolshevik—Left SR positions on the war, opposition to the coalition government, and advocacy of a government by soviets were consonant with the aspirations of the lower classes in Petrograd. Most interestingly of all, he emphasized that the actual conquest of power in Petrograd by the Military Revolutionary Committee occurred a week before the fall of the Winter Palace. The question of who ruled in Petrograd was resolved by answering who had real control over the army in the city, and the decisive moment arrived when the Petrograd Soviet, in Bolshevik hands from early September, challenged the government's authority over the garrison. In the week before the Bolshevik insurrection, "the Military-Revolutionary Committee of the Petrograd Soviet took control of most Petrograd-based military units, in effect disarming the Provisional Government without a shot." Once again, as in the first months of the revolution, the Soviet made it clear to the government that real power, the power to call troops into the streets and implement decisions, belonged to the Soviet. Formal power fell to the Soviet with the capture of the Winter Palace and the ratification by the Second Congress of Soviets.

Rabinowitch also took issue with the exaggeration of Lenin's role, so dominant a theme in the work of Melgunov and Daniels:

> early on the morning of October 24, Kerensky initiated steps to suppress the Left. Only at this point, just hours before the scheduled opening of the Congress of Soviets and in part under the continuous prodding by Lenin, did the armed uprising that Lenin had been advocating for well over a month actually begin. . . . Only in the wake of the government's direct attack on the Left was an armed uprising of the kind envisioned by Lenin feasible. For . . . the Petrograd masses, to the extent that they supported the Bolsheviks in the overthrow of the Provisional Government, did so not out of any sympathy for strictly Bolshevik rule but because they believed the revolution and the congress to be in imminent danger.

Thus, although Lenin was instrumental in preparing the armed uprising, the actual social and political constellation of forces on October 24—most importantly the provocation by Kerensky—was responsible for the move into the streets.

Clearly, to isolate Lenin or his party from this rich and contradictory social context in which they operated not only distorts an understanding of the events of 1917
but may lead to unwarranted conclusions about the artificial, unorganic, manipulated
nature of October and to the more general view that great revolutions, like more
modest acts of political protest, are the creations of outside agitators. Although Rabinowitch has left many questions unanswered, including the critical one of the sources
of the Bolsheviks' mass support, he has provided a persuasive reassessment of the personal and political factors that led to the October Revolution.

At the other pole of historical writing on October is *The Russian Revolution* (1976),
the massive work of John Keep, a well-known specialist on Russian social democracy.
Keep has focused on the mass organizations of the Russian people—the soviets, factory committees, trade unions, peasant committees, Red Guard units, and so forth
rather than on political parties or the government. Indeed, the book is quite difficult
to follow if the reader does not have a firm grasp of the basic historical events of the
period. There is, for example, no discussion whatsoever of the "April crisis" or the
"July Days" and only the most cursory allusions to the *Kornilovshchina*. His approach
seems, at first, to be diametrically opposed to the personality-dominated views of
Melgunov and Daniels and also to the close political analysis of Rabinowitch. Yet the
hundreds of pages spent on looking at the bottom of society reflect a peculiarly condescending view of the lower classes and reinforce the more traditional interpretations of the revolution.

Like so many other works on the Russian Revolution, Keep's book is history
written backwards, from the results to their causes. He stated, "Any evaluation of this
revolution's place in history must proceed from an awareness of the consequences to
which it led: namely, the world's first experiment in totalitarian rule." And he sought
material for this type of evaluation not so much in Leninist ideology or Bolshevik organization, though both clearly play a role, but in the methods and effects of mass mobilization. Keep has claimed that revolutions begin as anarchistic movements against
the bureaucratic state but end up by setting up new bureaucratic organizations.
"Chaos and anarchy . . . best describe the state of Russia during 1917." Categories
such as class interests or ideologies are not helpful, in Keep's view, in understanding
the complexity of these events. More important is "instinct"! Of the crowds of workers in October. Keep noted, "the mob followed its instincts" in destroying things of
value that it did not understand, or, later on, "the crowds followed a logic all their
own, in which instinct was more important than reason."

The subrational, spontaneously generated political behavior of the workers is
even more typical of the peasantry. "The agrarian movement," for Keep, "was neither
a product of external agitation nor a manifestation of class struggle. It was a phenomenon *sui generis*—plebian, anarchic and anti-centralist." At times Keep showed little regard for the capacity of peasants and workers to understand the events and programs of 1917, as, for example, in his discussion of a gathering of trade unionists,
where he stated, "Such intellectual subtleties were beyond the grasp of many delegates
to the conference, let alone to their rank-and-file supporters." Or—"it is scarcely
suprising that to the politically untutored Russian masses this propaganda [of the Bol-
sheviks] had a strong appeal." Yet, despite their lack of comprehension, workers in
Keep's portrait were able, without intellectual leadership, to acquire some political
consciousness, to arrive eventually at "a new awareness of their dignity as human be-

ings, their rights as citizens and consumers." Indeed, "a class-oriented viewpoint came naturally to Russia's industrial workers," but Keep never explained why such a class outlook "came naturally."

Underlying and informing all of Keep's preferences and conclusions is a bedrock belief that ideological solutions to social and political problems are utopian, dangerous, and doomed to failure, that moderation and a spirit of compromise are the desired and most pragmatic political postures, that checks and balances are needed in government just as conciliation and cooperation are required in the economic conflicts between employers and employees. His great regret is that political democracy could not weather the storms of 1917, and his sympathies clearly lie with the right wing of the Soviet leadership, with men like Gots, Tsereteli, and Kerensky, rather than with Chernov, Martov, or Lenin. Yet in passages that echo Oliver Radkey, Keep castigated even these Russian socialist intellectuals, who were "brought up in a tradition that was ideological rather than pragmatic. . . . By instinct they were hostile to governmental authority even if the regime in question was one with which they themselves were associated." And, by their own manipulation of the working masses, Soviet moderates prepared the ground for the cruder direction of workers' affairs by the Bolsheviks.

Keep's explanation of the demise of soviet democracy is subtle and intriguing. The seizure of power was only one moment in a long process that began earlier in the revolution as real power shifted within the soviets from the plenary assemblies to cadre elements in executive positions. Autonomous soviets representing workers, soldiers, and peasants merged and were increasingly subjected to control from above. These tendencies "were in part spontaneous in origin and in part the deliberate outcome of official Bolshevik policy." As early as

> the end of September the several hundred delegates attending meetings of the plenum could feel that they were shaping the country's destiny. Their aspirations seemed to accord so closely with the directives they received that they were scarcely conscious of being guided at all. The plenum of the Petrograd soviet became a genuine revolutionary assembly, a resonator automatically echoing the signals emitted from above.

Keep explained "this state of affairs . . . in terms not merely of crowd psychology but also of institutional mechanics." By the end of his analysis, the Soviet plenum becomes the chorus in a Greek tragedy: "blind instruments of fate, [the members] could scarcely follow the intricate maneuvers of their leaders upon which they were called to pronounce." The Military Revolutionary Committee of the Petrograd Soviet was "in essence a *junta* whose powers were defined solely by the ambitions of its leaders."

Three factors doomed the moderate socialists. First, the radicalism of many workers, especially metalworkers, which Keep has explained as the product of "their eagerness to renounce their close involvement in what seemed to them a disastrous and senseless war," played into the hands of the Leninists. Second, "the weakness of the Provisional Government obliged [the moderate socialists] to assume joint responsibility for direction of the nation's affairs, yet by doing so they inevitably became ever more isolated from their popular following." And, third, the skills of the Bolsheviks in conquering the working class and the soldiers through the soviets: "the soviets had never been conceived as organs reflecting the full range of their members' opinions; they were cadre organizations, whose purpose was to mobilize support for their leaders' policies. The Bolsheviks were simply more ruthless and systematic than their rivals in eliminating dissent by their long-familiar manipulative techniques." Thus, radicalism from below, the class-oriented views of workers and others, and Bolshevik manipulation combined to turn the soviets into directors of popular affairs rather than reflectors of popular interests.

John Keep's "study in mass mobilization" is, in actuality, a study of mass manipulation by the radical intelligentsia. Evidently the Leninists, who "sought a complete monopoly of power for their own party," were the best of the manipulators. And this study of history at the bottom returns us full circle to the Melgunov-Daniels perspective. The mass organizations were simply the means through which the Bolsheviks worked to secure power; as "the soviets were converted from means of mass mobilization into instruments of party dictatorship," the masses of revolutionary Russia were shown to be the first dupes of the communists.

In describing at a distance the shift to the left of Petrograd's masses, Keep did not provide much of an explanation for their radicalization, except—as did Melgunov and Daniels—through an appreciation of the superiority of Bolshevik will and skill. What seems at first to be a "social history with the politics left out" might be characterized more accurately as "political history disguised as social history," for there is no feel in *The Russian Revolution* for the coincidence of workers' aspirations and Bolshevik ideals in the context of deepening social polarization. For this aspect of the picture we must turn to those historians who have studied the working class, the army, and the navy. Although the works under review do not individually present a complete synthesis of social dynamics and political developments, through such works Western historians are providing the raw material for a new paradigm to explain the "deepening of the revolution" and the victory of the Bolsheviks in October.

Several western historians have made much of the workers' instinctive rebelliousness or propensity for anarchy; but the real and incipient violence in the revolution does not necessitate concluding, as John Keep has argued, that workers were instinctively distrustful of authority in any form. Given their long and painful experience with arbitrary authority under the Romanovs, workers were understandably concerned about the proper exercise of power, and they searched for forms of self-organization and demanded authorities responsive to their needs. The growing feeling that the Provisional Government, even in its coalition variant, was not a responsive authority led to workers gravitating to soviet power. This sense by workers of their own interests being frustrated by hostile middle and upper classes can be seen both as a revival of prewar attitudes of the most militant workers and as a reaction to perceived counterrevolutionary attitudes and actions by industrialists, intellectuals (both liberal and socialist), and, in time, the government.

Among historians who have looked most closely at workers' activities, the superficial impression of chaos has been superseded by the realization that workers' actions in 1917 demonstrate a "cautious and painful development of consciousness" that was "an essentially rational process." After distinguishing three principal strata of workers—the politically aware skilled workers (primarily the metalworkers of the Vyborg district), the unskilled workers (largely women textile workers), and the "worker aristocracy" (characterized best by the pro-Menshevik printers)—David Mandel has shown that the metalworkers were most radical in the political sphere, calling for the early establishment of soviet power, while the unskilled workers, who tended to be more moderate on political issues, showed the greatest militancy in the struggle for higher wages. The contours of worker activity are complex but not chaotic. Stephen Smith has broken down the metalworkers into shops and carefully delineated between "hot" shops, such as foundries, where most newly arrived peasant-workers were located, and "cold" shops, such as machine shops, where highly skilled and literate workers were most receptive to social democratic activists. In examining the Putilov Works, Smith found that workers there moved more slowly toward Bolshevism than in other metalworking plants and that "shopism" and "conciliationism" remained stronger there than elsewhere. Both Smith and Mandel have presented pictures of growing worker suspicion of the upper levels of society, especially after the formation of the coalition government—a suspicion that translated into struggles for control in the factories and increased opposition to those moderate socialists who were backing the government.

Although the rapidity of labor radicalization in Petrograd is certainly distinctive, similar processes, marked by growing class cohesion and consciousness, were evident in other parts of the country, as my own work on Baku and Donald Raleigh's study of Saratov demonstrate. By engaging in a detailed quantitative analysis of the dynamics of labor activity in Moscow, Diane Koenker has also reached a similar conclusion . . .

To Koenker, the radicalization of workers in the first year of the revolution was an "incremental process, which took place in response to specific economic and political pressures." Her conclusion is supported in other studies as well. Galili, for example, has noted the delayed radicalization of the less politically conscious, unskilled workers in the second quarter of 1917, observing that these less well-organized workers had not benefited from the initial round of wage raises in March and April. By the time they made their bid for higher pay, the industrialists had adopted a more intransigent attitude. By mid-May there were already forty thousand unemployed workers in Petrograd, and as real wages began to plummet and mass dismissals accelerated, more and more less-skilled workers joined the "proletarians" in a commitment to soviet power. By June–July a majority of Petrograd workers were already opposed to the coalition government and shared a sense of separate and antagonistic interests between workers and the propertied classes. A greatly heightened sense of class was apparent among the mass of workers by the summer.

The studies of Mandel, Galili, Koenker, and others provide the specifics of the economic and political stimuli that led to radicalization, and for the first time it has become possible to understand how individual grievances within the larger context of social polarization combined to create class antagonisms. Given that Russia's workers had long been closely involved with a radical, socialist intelligentsia anxious to forge a Marxist political culture within the urban labor force, it is hardly surprising that workers in 1917 should "naturally" come to a "class-oriented viewpoint." . . .

The perception by workers of common interests with fellow workers and of shared antagonisms toward the rest of society was complemented by a growing sense of hostility from the upper levels of society toward the lower classes. William G. Rosenberg has illustrated this shift to the right by the Kadets as the liberals' growing identification with commercial and industrial circles changed them from a party of liberal professionals and intellectuals into Russia's party of the bourgeoisie. Even as they persisted in maintaining their "nonclass" ideology, the Kadets emerged as the de facto defenders of a capitalist order and the determined opponents of the approaching social revolution desired by the more militant of the *nizy* ("lower classes"). Their isolation from the socialist workers and soldiers led the liberals to turn to the military as a source of order and power. Rosenberg has argued, as had the Left Kadets in 1917, that the only hope for a democratic political outcome in Russia was lost when the Kadets failed to work effectively with the moderate socialists in the coalition government and to make significant concessions to the lower classes. "The very coalition with moderate socialists that Miliukov and the new tacticians strove for so persistently in emigration [after the Civil War] *was* possible in the summer of 1917." The failure to form such a liberal-socialist alternative to Bolshevism might be seen as the consequence of the Kadets' lack of "true liberal statesmanship," but Rosenberg's analysis permits an alternative explanation. As the Kadet party evolved into the principal spokesman for propertied Russia, it was increasingly unlikely to compromise the interests of the privileged classes that backed the party in order to form a dubious alliance with the *demokratiia,* whose ever more radical demands threatened the very existence of privilege and property. *Nadklassnost'* (the Kadet notion of standing above class considerations) was simply a utopian stance in a Russia that was pulling apart along class lines.

Against this background of deepening social cleavage with all its inherent fear and suspicion, hope and despair, the question of power was posed in the summer and fall of 1917. Underestimating the extent of the social polarization, the growing intensity of class hostility, and the perceived irreconcilability of the interests of the *demokratiia* and the *tsenzovoe obshchestvo* within the constraints of the February regime leads historians away from any satisfactory explanation of the failure of the moderates and the victory of the Bolsheviks, forcing them to rely on accidental factors of will and personality. Only through a synthesis of political and social history in which the activity and developing political consciousness of workers, soldiers, and sailors is taken seriously can the Bolsheviks' success be adequately explained.

By the summer of 1917 there were four possible solutions to the problem of who would rule Russia. The first solution was that advocated by Tsereteli and Kerensky, by the Menshevik Revolutionary Defensists and the Right Socialist Revolutionaries: a continuation of the coalition government, a policy of social unity and class collaboration to defend Russia against her enemies and prevent civil war. But such a solution was doomed in the face of the deepening social crisis and political paralysis. Given the hostility between classes and their mutually antagonistic aspirations and interests, a coalition government could move neither to the left nor to the right without stirring up opposition. It could neither satisfy the demands of the peasants for the land nor attempt to protect the landlords' rights to private property. Paralyzed between its competing constituencies, all movement looked like vacillation, the product of a lack of will or determination, but was in fact the result of the real political bind faced by a government stretched between the extremes of a splintering society.

A second solution was a government made up of the upper classes alone—that is, a dictatorship of the center and the right. The Kadet leader Miliukov had desired such a government at the beginning of the revolution, but, without a base of support in the population, that hope collapsed finally in the April crisis. Real power was in the hands of the Soviet; as Stankevich quipped, "The soviet could make the Provisional Government resign with a telephone call." The only possible way for the upper classes to rule—and the liberals as well as the right came to this conclusion by mid-summer—was to establish a military dictatorship. Kerensky and Kornilov worked toward that goal in August, but it ended in Kornilov's ill-fated grasp for power, thwarted not just by his disagreement with Kerensky over the final disposition of power but by the actions of workers, soldiers, and soviets. With the failure of the military *coup d'état,* the only possibilities remaining were for a government by one or several of the Soviet parties.

The third solution—and probably the one most desired by the lower classes in urban Russia—was an all-socialist regime (*odnorodnoe sotsialisticheskoe pravitel'stvo*), a government representing the workers, soldiers, and peasants of Russia but excluding the *tsenzovoe obshchestvo*. A broader variant of this solution, the *odnorodnoe demokraticheskoe pravitel'stvo,* would have included nonsoviet "democratic" elements such as municipal and government workers, people from cooperatives, and small shopkeepers. Historians seem to agree that, when workers and soldiers voted for soviet power, they were in fact opting for a multiparty government of the leftist parties. This solution was never really implemented because of the serious divisions between the moderate socialists and the Bolsheviks, and there is legitimate doubt that the former defenders of coalition and the advocates of working-class rule could have lasted long in an all-socialist coalition.

In October 1917 the Bolsheviks came to power in the name of the soviets. The coalition government had been completely discredited, and almost no one would defend it in its last hours. The Military Revolutionary Committee merely completed the process of political conquest of the population of Petrograd that the Bolsheviks had begun months earlier. Bolshevik policy, alone among the political programs, corresponded to and reflected the aspirations and perceived interests of workers, soldiers, and sailors in Petrograd. Even without much direct participation in the October Days, the workers acquiesced in and backed the seizure of power by the soviets. Lenin and a few others had seen the potential in 1917 for a government of the lower classes. He, earliest among almost all of the political leaders, had understood that in this revolution—marked by deep, long-standing social tensions and stoked by a seemingly endless war—unification of "all the vital forces of the nation" became increasingly unlikely. By late spring an all-class or nonclass government was no longer possible, and by linking his party's fortunes with the real social movement in Petrograd he was able to destroy the flimsy coalition of liberals and moderate socialists and to facilitate a seizure of power in the name of the soviets.

Instead of soviet power or socialist democracy, however, the Russian people eventually received a dictatorship of the Bolshevik party. This was the fourth possible solution to the question of power. Why it succeeded over the more democratic third solution is a question that goes beyond the limits of this essay, for the answer in this instance lies not so much in the events of 1917 as in the long years of the Civil War. But again, the answer cannot be provided by resorting to personal and ideological influences or by extending the analysis based on politics alone; rather, it lies in an examination of the intense class struggle that was carried beyond the limits of the city of Petrograd into the countryside and all the provinces of Russia.

As historians have shifted their attention away from the political elites that formerly dominated explanations of the Russian Revolution and to the people in the streets, the victorious Bolsheviks have appeared less like Machiavellian manipulators or willful conspirators and more like alert politicians with an acute sensitivity to popular moods and desires. Without forgetting the authoritarian traits in Lenin, Trotsky, and other Bolshevik leaders or the power of the image of the party outlined in *Chto delat'?*, we can move on to a new paradigm for understanding 1917 that reduces the former reliance on party organization or personal political skills so central to older explanations. The key to a new paradigm is an appreciation of the deepening social polarization that drew the upper and middle classes together and away from the workers, soldiers, and peasants. The *tsenzovoe obshchestvo*, after an initial period of compromise in the early spring of 1917, began to resist encroachments on its prerogatives in the economy and in foreign policy and, faced by growing militancy among workers and soldiers, developed a clearer and more coherent sense of its own political interests. Likewise, the workers and soldiers, confronted by lockouts, falling wages, a renewal of the war effort, and perceived sabotage of the revolution as they hoped it to be, evolved their own sense of class interests. In time, both parts of Russian society found their interests to be incompatible, and those parties that tried to stand "above class" or to unite "all the vital forces of the nation" were either compelled to take sides with one major force or abandoned by their former supporters.

For Russians in 1917, the revolution was a struggle between classes in the inclusive sense of the *verkhi* ("upper classes") versus the *nizy* ("lower classes"). Those broad, antagonistic "classes" coalesced in the course of 1917. This heightened feeling of class was forged in the actual experience of 1917 and contained both social hostilities bred over many years and intensified under wartime and revolutionary conditions and a new political understanding that perceived government by soviets as a preferable alternative to sharing power with the discredited upper classes. The Bolsheviks had since April been advocating such a government by the lower classes. With the failure of the coalition and its socialist supporters to deliver on the promise of the revolution, the party of Lenin and Trotsky took power with little resistance and with the acquiescence of the majority of the people of Petrograd. The Bolsheviks came to power not because they were superior manipulators or cynical opportunists but because their policies as formulated by Lenin in April and shaped by the events of the following months placed them at the head of a genuinely popular movement. Sadly for those who had overthrown autocracy and turned to the Bolsheviks to end the war and alleviate hunger, that solution based on a government by soviets evolved inexorably through a ferocious civil war into a new and unforeseen authoritarianism.

WORKS CITED

Oskar Anweiler, *The Soviets: The Russian Workers', Peasants', and Soldiers' Councils* (New York, 1974).

Robert V. Daniels. *Red October* (New York, 1967).

Andrew Ezergailis, *The 1917 Revolution in Latvia* (Boulder, CO, 1974).

Marc Ferro, *The Russian Revolution of February 1917* (London, 1972), and *October 1917: A Social History of the Russian Revolution* (London, 1980).

Ziva Galili, *The Menshevik Leaders in the Russian Revolution: Social Realities and Political Strategies* (Princeton, 1989).

Graeme Gill, *Peasants and Government in the Russian Revolution* (London, 1979).

Leopold H. Haimson, "The Problem of Social Stability in Urban Russia, 1905–1917." *Slavic Review* XXIII, 4 (December 1964), pp. 619–642; XXIV, 1 (March 1965), pp. 1–22.

Tsuyoshi Hasegawa. *The February Revolution: Petrograd 1917* (Seattle, 1981).

George Katkov, *Russia 1917: The February Revolution* (New York, 1967).

John H. L. Keep, *The Russian Revolution: A Study in Mass Mobilization* (New York and Toronto, 1976).

Diane Koenker, *Moscow Workers and the 1917 Revolution* (Princeton, 1981).

David Mandel, *The Petrograd Workers and the Fall of the Old Regime* (New York, 1983), and *The Petrograd Workers and the Soviet Seizure of Power* (New York, 1984).

Evan Mawdsley, *The Russian Revolution and the Baltic Fleet: War and Politics, February 1917–April 1918* (London, 1978).

Sergei Melgunov, *The Bolshevik Seizure of Power* (Santa Barbara, CA, 1972).

Roger Pethybridge, *The Spread of the Russian Revolution: Essays on 1917* (London, 1972).

Alexander Rabinowitch, *Prelude to Revolution: The Petrograd Bolsheviks and the July 1917 Uprising* (Bloomington, 1968), and *The Bolsheviks Come to Power: The Revolution of 1917 in Petrograd* (New York, 1976).

Oliver H. Radkey, *The Agrarian Foes of Bolshevism* (New York, 1958), and *The Sickle Under the Hammer* (New York, 1963).

Donald J. Raleigh, *Revolution on the Volga: 1917 in Saratov* (Ithaca, N.Y., 1986).

William G. Rosenberg, *Liberals in the Russian Revolution: The Constitutional Democratic Party, 1917–1921* (Princeton, 1974).

Norman E. Saul, *Sailors in Revolt: The Russian Baltic Fleet in 1917* (Lawrence, KN, 1978).

Steve A. Smith, *Red Petrograd: Revolution in the Factories, 1917–1918* (Cambridge, 1983).

Ronald Grigor Suny, *The Baku Commune, 1917–1918: Class and Nationality in the Russian Revolution* (Princeton, 1972).

Rex A. Wade, *Red Guard and Workers' Militias: Spontaneity and Leadership in the Russian Revolution* (Stanford, 1983).

Allan K. Wildman, *The End of the Russian Imperial Army*, 2 vols. (Princeton, 1983, 1987).

Ronald Grigor Suny, "Toward a Social History of the October Revolution," *American Historical Review*, LXXXVIII, 1 (February 1983), pp. 31–52.

Antibourgeois Propaganda and Anti- *"Burzhui"* Consciousness in 1917

Boris I. Kolonitskii

The central question in the study of any revolution is that of power. A mere description of power and authority, however conscientiously done, would not be sufficient to answer that question. D. S. Merezhkovskii has called revolution a "governmental meltdown" and underscored the instability, mobility and "provisionality" of all structures of authority during such revolutionary periods. Accordingly, the direct influence of political cultures and subcultures on the formation and activities of institutions of authority is extraordinarily great during revolutionary eras. During a revolution, the peculiarities of political cultures that have taken shape over decades and even centuries become manifest. It is impossible to penetrate the riddle of "the secret of power" without exploring the forms of consciousness and culture of revolutionary eras.

Inherent in revolutionary eras are specific forms and methods of exercising power that differ greatly from those practiced during "normal" times. The operation of laws,

Translated from Russian by Kurt S. Schultz

for example, is rather limited: the old juridical order weakens, while new centers of "revolutionary law-making" appear. Several legal systems begin to operate within a country and in fact neutralize each other; as they resolve their conflicts, the opposing sides rule not by juridical acts but by their own revolutionary (or counterrevolutionary) morality.

In such circumstances, the role of *force* as an instrument for exercising authority grows significantly. But this leads to the state's loss over the monopoly on the legitimate use of force. Both the old and new centers of authority must constantly persuade "their" military and police supporters that their right to use force is justified. In a period of revolution, therefore, that *authority* acquires significance which employs certain structures for inspiring respect: they must literally daily re-conclude the "social contract" with the masses that support them. And, accordingly, the role of ideology and propaganda as instruments for exercising authority in such periods also grows significantly. Any study of the Russian Revolution of 1917 must give special attention to the ideologies and propaganda of the socialist parties.

The peculiarity of dual power was manifest in the ability of the centers of authority to rely on their "own" propaganda apparatus. For one thing, the soviets and soldiers' committees themselves were effective propaganda structures, serving as channels for distributing literature, centers for lecturing and so on. For another, the various soviets and soldiers' committees already had begun to function as political censors by the spring of 1917. The Bolsheviks were the first to experience pressure— from many soviets controlled by moderate socialists. But the blows of "soviet" censorship fell most often upon the so-called bourgeois publications, something that appeared most graphically during the Kornilov affair. And, finally, the socialist parties, using their influence in the soviets and committees, were able to establish control over a large number of presses, paper supplies and other printing establishments. Thanks to this they could quickly create their own propaganda structures. In July–August 1917, for example, the total press run of daily "bourgeois" newspapers in Petrograd was 1.5–1.6 million; for SR-Menshevik papers it was 640,000 to 740,000; while for the Bolsheviks it was approximately 80,000 (from 7 to 24 July the Bolsheviks were unable to publish their daily paper in Petrograd). The moderate socialists, however, led in the publication of brochures on sociopolitical themes: in Petrograd, presses of that orientation put out no less than 500 titles with an overall press-run of more than 27 million. "Bourgeois" presses published over 250 titles with a total run of over 11 million. And the Bolshevik press "Priboi" put out no less than 50 brochures, its overall run exceeding 1.5 million.

The Bolsheviks' and moderate socialists' propaganda did have points in common. Soviet historiography as a rule did not touch on this matter: it viewed the Bolshevik party as a single force struggling for socialism, a view in keeping with the well-known diagram of the "two camps." But the Bolsheviks by no means had a monopoly over anticapitalist propaganda. Take, for example, the unusual "best-seller" of 1917, a brochure by Wilhelm Leibknekht called *Pauki i mukhi*. It went through over twenty editions and was published by Bolshevik, SR and Menshevik presses, including G.V. Plekhanov's publishing group "Edinstvo." The brochure, which was widely distributed even before 1917 by the revolutionary underground, vividly sketched an "enemy image"—the class enemy:

> The spiders are the gentlemen, the money-grubbers, the exploiters, the gentry, the wealthy, and the popes, pimps and parasites of all types! . . . The flies are

the unhappy workers who must obey all those laws the capitalist happens to think up—must obey, for the poor man has not even a crumb of bread. The spider is the factory-owner earning five or six rubles every day from each of his workers and impertinently giving them a paltry wage as if it were a kindness.

The brochure, which during the First World War was often attributed to Karl Liebknecht rather than Wilhelm Liebknecht, enjoyed widespread popularity before February 1917. A participant in the Revolution subsequently recalled that

> I always had an excellent memory and earned only high marks in school. But I began to see things clearly in 1915, after I read *Pauki i mukhi* by the truly ardent revolutionary Karl Liebknecht. It ignited in me the spark of revolutionary disagreement with existing affairs. And what had I been before my "encounter" with this torchbearer of reason? A country lad, the son of a poor woman.

Liebknecht's brochure had a similar effect on many readers in 1917:

> The brochure was most interesting. It exposed the bourgeoisie and its role in capitalist society. The exposition was so popular that, after a brief explanation, even a semiliterate soldier understood: the bourgeoisie holds all the nation's wealth in its hands and has de facto power. Through merciless exploitation it sucks out the juices of the toilers like a spider. The brochure was very useful for soldiers in the trenches. It helped to raise their consciousness and became, as they say, our first political textbook.

Obviously, such a perception did not depend on which press—Bolshevik, Menshevik, SR—had published the copy of the brochure in the reader's hands.

S. R. Dikshtein's brochure, *Kto chem zhivet,* also went through many editions—no less than eleven in 1917—and was published by Bolshevik, Menshevik and SR presses. Both Liebknecht's and Dikshtein's brochures were among the most popular publications of the Russian revolutionary underground, and several young generations of revolutionaries were raised on them. It is not surprising that they were reprinted in much greater numbers when the legal circumstances were favorable.

The various expositions of party programs, published most often by party committees and organizations, also deepened the antibourgeois orientation of mass consciousness. *Za chto boriutsia sotsialisty-revoliutsionery,* a brochure that went through at least seven editions, announced that

> people who previously had enjoyed equal rights in everything have been divided into classes: a class of property-owning capitalists; and a class of toilers that has been deprived, or practically deprived, of property and that has been forced to feed a small group of effete drones. As a result of this state of affairs, people who have worked indefatigably their entire lives live in dirty hovels, in need, suffering from hunger and cold, while the drones, the capitalists and property-owners, enjoy all the best of life without lifting a finger.

It seems that the moderate socialists' propaganda contained a deep contradiction: *countervailing the strategic programmatic goal—the negation of capitalism—was the tactical task of the moment—reaching agreement with the "bourgeoisie."*

The Socialists, however, often conducted concrete political campaigns as if they were class-based, antibourgeois acts. On the eve of elections in Kiev for local offices, for example, they distributed the leaflet *Get' burzhuev,* which called upon people to vote for the Ukrainian slate.

The influence of the socialist political subculture also could be seen in revolutionary symbols: the red flag became the de facto banner of post-February Russia and flew above the Winter Palace when A. F. Kerenskii occupied it. New revolutionary symbols arose as well: the hammer and sickle appeared as early as the spring of 1917. The liberals could not offset the socialists with their own political symbols.

The influence of the socialist subculture also manifested itself in all sorts of renamings. On 19 April, for example, the transport ship *Nikolai II* became the hospital ship *Tovarishch.* The socialist movement's holidays became official governmental holidays in the new Russia. On the eve of May Day, G. E. L'vov received a telegram stating that "the entire Fourth Cavalry Division, at full battle strength, greets you as representative of the first responsible ministry of free Russia on this great international workers' holiday."

It was not only the socialist parties, however, which conducted various types of socialist propaganda. The Union of Evolutionary Socialism, founded in part by N. O. Losskii, propounded an ethical socialist ideal. The Union's position, "Through a people's Great Russia—to socialism," won support among the Provisional Government's propaganda officials, who financed the publication of brochures carrying a corresponding message. Several members of the Petersburg Religious-Philosophical Society also adhered to a socialist orientation. All sorts of organizations propagandizing the ideals of Christian Socialism appeared. Advocates of a radical reform of the Church utilized "antibourgeois" rhetoric in their arguments: "Is it not a disgrace when the overfed bourgeois, with their fat bellies and fine garments, talk of a worldwide Christian brotherhood and pray for peace on earth?"

Several clergymen of the Orthodox Church also took an anticapitalist position. A. A. Vvedenskii, the future founder of the "Living Church," wrote on behalf of "socialist clergymen":

> How great a love for the Church we have seen from even the most inveterate Bolsheviks! We have appeared in factories, in military units, on cruisers and so on. We have not made unfeasible promises, but we have said that the Gospels and the holy fathers are not deaf to societal evils, that Christianity has long condemned capitalism, and that [Christianity] "stands behind the sorrowful and those left out." I would dare to maintain that many [Bolsheviks] have come to terms with the Church. . . . The struggle on behalf of the poor is the basic principle of socialism, and it is our own Christian struggle.

It stands to reason that the author of those lines was one of the most radical clergymen, and it is not surprising that he was elected to the Petersburg Soviet by the "democratic clergy." But it is indicative that even the editor of the Holy Synod's newspaper was fairly sympathetic to the sort of critique of capitalism leveled by the socialist parties. Subsequently, the Local Council of the Russian Orthodox Church created a special "Commission on Bolshevism in the Church." From its sessions came the admission that "Bolshevism has captured a significant number of clergymen."

The "fashion for socialism" had already spread widely before the February Revolution. Attesting to its further spread is the appearance of a variety of socialist organizations, even a Socialist Union of Deaf-Mutes. They demanded that nonsocialist groups precisely define their attitudes toward socialism. The executive organ of the Kadet Party, for example, received a letter which in part read:

Why are the Kadets not socialists? Why do they say nothing about this? What other ways for a better life or better economic arrangement are there besides socialism? Only capitalism or socialism? Or is there something else? Do tell us. After all, you are not socialists yet you admit that we cannot go on like this. How, then, should things be?

When he examined this "fashion for socialism" the well-known historian A. A. Kizevetter took note of "the general aspiration of a huge mass of Russians to declare themselves, no matter what, to be absolute socialists, to the amazement of foreigners." It stands to reason that various models of socialism and various tactical approaches for achieving the socialist ideal countervailed each other at this time. *But they all helped to shape antibourgeois attitudes.* Thus, the numerous examples of political mimicry are revealing: the efforts to paint oneself "in the protective color of socialism"; the desires to conduct propaganda "with a socialist stamp"; and, as A. S. Izgoev ironically noted, "even *Birzhevye vedomosti* did not deny itself the pleasure of wounding 'the bourgeoise' and laughing at 'bourgeoisness.'" The Interregional Group's journal wrote indignantly about the same phenomenon: "The yellow street press calls itself nonparty socialist. The financial newspapers repaint themselves with the protective color of 'realistic socialism,' while banks try to protect themselves by raising the red banner of revolution over their buildings."

One of the most vivid examples of political mimicry can be found in Petrograd's *Malen'kaia gazeta,* which was widely read well before February. This was a lively urban chronicle (covering the criminal scene for the most part), with a religious moralizing tone and a position as a defender of the weak against "the powers-that-be" and "rich men"—all of which made it the Petrograd plebians' "own" newspaper. *Malen'kaia gazeta*'s political line, meanwhile, was decidedly chauvinistic, anti-Semitic and militaristic. After February, the paper's publishers, with a fine sense of the political competition, decorated the paper with the subheading: "The paper of nonparty socialists." "Our ideal," it informed its readers, "is working humanity. The first stage toward this lies in the ideals of the proletariat, the liberation of labor."

Malen'kaia gazeta took an anti-Bolshevik stance, interestingly, while several ultra-right publications welcomed October. The Black Hundred organ *Groza,* for example, wrote that

> the Bolsheviks have prevailed: they have swept that servant of the English and the bankers, the Jew Kerenskii, who insolently arrogated the high title of supreme commander and minister-chairman of the Orthodox Russian realm, from the Winter Palace, where his very presence defiled the repose of the Tsar-peacemaker Alexander III. On 25 October the Bolsheviks united around themselves all those regiments who refused to obey the government of Jew-bankers, traitorous generals and landowners, and robbing merchants.

There also were several attempts to use antibourgeois propaganda to start pogroms. On 26 June, for example, leaflets of the "Free Association of Anarchists and Communists" appeared in Kiev: "Down with the Provisional Government, smash the bourgeoisie and the Jews."

It is rather curious that the enemy tried to make use of the Russian soldier's antibourgeois moods. *Russkii vestnik,* a newspaper published in Berlin, had invariably denounced the "English vampires" even before the Revolution. After the Revolution

similar denunciations became tinged with an antibourgeois tone. "The Russian people has not freed itself in order to replace tsarism with the capitalist yoke of the English and their friends," the German paper proclaimed in late April. It continued in this
vein throughout the spring, writing in early June that "the government officials in
Petrograd are paying in blood, the blood of their compatriots, to receive money
which in turn flows into the pockets of English and French capitalists." The paper also
printed similar letters from Russian soldiers: "We do not want millions of people like
us to perish because of the whims of our capitalists." Austro-Hungarian propaganda
used similar arguments. The Vienna-based *Vestnik* wrote that "Russian soldiers must
continue to sacrifice their lives for the fantastic plans of the Entente; in reality they
are fighting for England's mercenary aims and on behalf of French capitalists."

Efforts to engage in counterpropaganda also attest to the prevalence of antibourgeois sentiment, one example being a brochure put out by the Petrograd Union of
Trade and Industry. Curiously, the cover of this brochure carried a revolutionary soldier with his rifle and a worker with a hammer, itself an indication of how widespread
symbols of the socialist subculture had become. I should note that such counterpropaganda appears to have been counterproductive. It often happened, for example, that
entrepreneurs refused to refer to themselves as "bourgeois," preferring to be part of
the "trade and industry class." At other times they preferred moralistic tracts: any
greedy and egotistical man, regardless of his social class, was "bourgeois." In both cases
the negative connotations of the term not only was not called into question but rather
was confirmed. Finally, the fact that the "bourgeoisie" as a thematic subject began to
appear in folklore, satire and parodies indirectly testifies to the broad diffusion of antibourgeois attitudes.

While conducting their antibourgeois propaganda, various parties and organizations set out definitions of the term "bourgeoisie" that were markedly different. On
the level of mass consciousness, however, antibourgeois propaganda led to the appearance of new appraisals that at times were quite different from the "correct" evaluations given by the parties. Often, for instance, all property-owners, even those just
living comfortably, were called "bourgeois." The term was often used to describe a
person's social status: the soldier considered officers to be "bourgeois"; soldiers at the
front regarded soldiers in the rear as "bourgeois"; and the infantry looked upon ar-
tillerymen as "bourgeois." Then again, the naval officer who was infuriated with the
demands of his sailors would call them "bourgeois."

The frequent utilization of this understanding of the term facilitated the rise of
sociocultural conflict. "Who isn't called bourgeois these days?" asked a contemporary.
"Workers call all nonworkers bourgeois; peasants—all 'gentlemen,' including anyone
dressed in city clothes." In reality, the "term" helped reveal an anti-Western, anti-
urban mood: "Don't you believe the newspapers," a peasant admonished a schoolteacher. "The bourgeoisie writes them." It is not surprising that outward appearances
often determined membership in the "bourgeoisie": "There are some who think that
anyone who wears a hat and has a 'seigniorial face' is bourgeois"; "The word 'bourgeois' sticks to anyone whose clothes are clean or who wears a starched collar and
cuffs"; "Many people often are called bourgeois because they are educated, live
cleanly, wear a gentleman's suit instead of a worker's blouse, even though they barely
make ends meet and live solely through their own labor"; "Soon it will be dangerous
to put on a collar, tie, hat or decent suit without being called 'bourgeois.' " Sociocultural conflicts arose in innumerable everyday arguments:

The masses do not see an abstract "bourgeoisie" or social class, but real, living people whom they call *burzhui* [bourgeois], *barzhui* [barge-owners] and *birzhui* [stockbrokers], and they feed their anger not against some imaginary class of "bourgeoisie" but against living people whom they meet on the streets, trams and trains.

A similar sociocultural conflict influenced the outcome of political campaigns. When analyzing the results of local elections in Moscow, which the SRs won, A. A. Kizevetter wrote:

The shawls and peaked caps voted against the fur hats, regardless of what sort of world view—bourgeois or non-bourgeois—filled those hat-covered skulls. . . . To be sure, the masses have mastered the "prevailing" terminology of "socialist" and "bourgeois," but while using these terms quite boldly and confidently they have infused them with their own meanings that have nothing in common with the programs of the [Social Democrats] or SRs.

"Bourgeois" was used as a swear-word. "From 1 March a new swear word has appeared in party newspapers," the well-known publicist A. Iablonovskii wrote: "Bourgeois. It seems that this word, with its abusive meaning, occupies a position between 'scoundrel' and 'swine,' and its wide usage is explained, apparently, by its polemical convenience."

Finally, the term was utilized as a type of ethical category. "A genuine 'bourgeois' is not bourgeois because he is rich, owns a factory, is educated, or is not a Socialist," wrote N. Kabanov. "Rather, he is bourgeois because he places his interests and those of his class highest of all." And N. Kadmin declared:

A bourgeois is someone who thinks only of himself, of his belly. It is someone who is aloof, who is ready to grab anyone by the throat if it involves his money or food. A bourgeois is a person who leads an egotistical, meaningless and aimless life unilluminated by the vivid and wonderful goals of any cherished, spiritual labor. . . . Such people, regardless of their class identity—be they rich merchants, kulaks or a skilled worker whose only goal is his paycheck—all are in such cases identically bourgeois.

In line with such an interpretation, egoism and cupidity also were signs of "bourgeoisness." As noted above, this was the plane on which the polemic with the socialists often was conducted. In criticizing a Bolshevik leaflet, for example, a provincial newspaper wrote: "You say that our Provisional Government is 'bourgeois.' But it consists of honest, intelligent citizens who fervently love their country." Such arguments somehow implied that the "bourgeoisie" lacked honesty, intellect and patriotism.

Accusations of "bourgeoisness," moreover, were often a way of attaching political labels. The socialists considered all other parties to be "bourgeois"; however, the term also was used in the polemic between the various socialist groupings. As A. Izgoev noted with malicious glee:

The Social Democrats call the Socialist Revolutionaries a bourgeois party; the Socialist Revolutionaries do not recognize as true socialists either the Populist Socialists or those in their own party who call for war until victory over the Germans. The Social Democrats also are riven by internecine strife: the Bolsheviks curse the Mensheviks as bourgeois, while the Mensheviks try to prove that the Bolsheviks are a petit bourgeois party.

The Moscow Soviet numbered G.V. Plekhanov's group among the "bourgeoisie" and called upon people not to vote for it in local elections. The question of "bourgeois" identity, moreover, at times was decided according to various criteria even within a single military unit. In April, for example, both the 2d Company and a detachment of young soldiers from the Petrograd Electro-technical battalion listed *Edinstvo* as one of the socialist newspapers and contrasted it with "bourgeois" papers, which were to be boycotted. At the same time, however, the battalion's 3d Company demanded that the "bourgeois" *Edinstvo* be boycotted.

Antibourgeois ideas also colored the antimilitary mood that had spread: the "bourgeoisie" was regarded as primarily responsible for the war. Thus, on 25 May a meeting of workers from the Moscow factory "Dinamo" adopted a resolution declaring that "the cause of all the destruction is a war that no one needs but the greedy capitalists." Tellingly, the text of the resolution was put forward by the SRs; the Bolshevik resolution (which we should assume was more radical) was rejected.

On the other hand, even the advocates of "revolutionary defensism" utilized antibourgeois arguments. On 19 April the Kolomna Garrison Soviet declared itself in favor of "laying down weapons only after that lair of global militarism—the German ruling classes—has been destroyed and all peoples have reached the threshold of general disarmament and liberation from the excessive weight of arms that is ravaging nations on behalf of the interests of dynasties and capital." While trying to demonstrate the need for continuing the war, I. G. Tsereteli noted that "we have declared to all the world's people what Russian democracy has done, what is the sole way out of this murderous situation in which, on behalf of the interests of a few bourgeois, millions of people must shed blood. . . . Trying to end the possibility of war is senseless as long as personal property and bourgeois states, even the most democratic ones, still exist." Such declarations obviously aided in the spread of antibourgeois feelings.

In socialist propaganda, "bourgeois" was often counterposed to democracy—"revolutionary democracy." At the same time, repression of the bourgeoisie was not considered to be contradictory to democracy. In one and the same resolution the Slutskii Soviet, for example, demanded the restoration of a free press and the closing of the counterrevolutionary press. And a resolution to the "Central Soviet" from workers at the Baltic Factory in Petrograd demanded that "our socialist newspapers, regardless of the party, be circulated freely and no arrests be made." At the same time, however, it wanted "decisive measures to close all counterrevolutionary newspapers of the hateful and dirty bourgeoisie."

In practice, groups that were considered "bourgeois" were placed beyond the pale of the democratic process, making repressive measures against them justifiable. On 7 September the Min'iarskii Soviet of Workers' Deputies urged postal workers to deliver only socialist newspapers; "bourgeois" papers should be taken to the Soviet, which would "sell them for wrapping paper, if possible." The Sobinsk Factory Soviet, meanwhile, called for "halting the importation and trade of bourgeois newspapers and placing them under strict control: subscribers will receive them after the lapse of one month."

It stands to reason that it was the Bolsheviks and their political allies who most frequently introduced such resolutions. But the moderate forces also called for political discrimination against the "bourgeoisie." A resolution of greetings to Kerenskii also contained a call for "curbing the bourgeois press, which is disseminating vile slander." And the influential SR-Menshevik paper *Golos soldata* proclaimed "the need to stop the piles of bourgeois newspapers, which no one reads, from clogging up the postal system." It seems to me that such a broad dissemination of "antibourgeois" attitudes, differing in their form, depth and content, left an imprint on the development of the political situation in 1917.

It is well known that many viewed the February Revolution as a "resurrection of our beloved motherland from death." The theme of "resurrection"—a rebirth of the country, the nation, and the people—is fairly characteristic of many revolutionary eras. But the theme seems to have played a special role in the circumstances of the Russian Revolution of 1917.

Memoirists frequently compared February to the Easter holiday: "It was an all-round holiday. The crowd rushed into the street. Everyone greeted one another, as on Easter Sunday"; "In both Moscow and Petrograd the people strolled as they do on Easter. Everyone praised the new regime and the Republic." Contemporary diaries also recorded the "Easter" mood: "The streets were so lively, as if it were the Easter Holiday," wrote one Petrograd resident on 28 February. Periodicals of various political leanings also compared the Revolution to Easter. One reader wrote to the editors of *Malen'kaia gazeta*: "I do not know what will happen next, but if everything they write, say and promise comes true, then I can only say that this is the second coming of Christ on earth; He will not come in order to descend to the Hell of tormented, offended and oppressed people but rather to resurrect them to a new, joyous and free life." Prominent cultural figures also gave their blessing to such an interpretation. Merezhkovskii wrote that "perhaps since the time of the Christian martyrs there has been no phenomenon in history more Christian, more Christ-like, than the Russian Revolution."

Society, which was quickly—explosively—being politicized under revolutionary conditions, at times utilized traditional and significant religious images and rituals in place of empty political symbols, concepts, slogans and clichés. This explains the constant comparison of the Tauride Palace with the "Temple of Revolution" and the universal "rite" of kissing soldiers: "There are times when one wants to embrace the whole world in joyful ecstasy and kiss everyone without end," *Soldatskoe slovo* exclaimed. It is not surprising, then, that the workers' campaign to collect Easter gifts for front-line soldiers was conducted under the slogan, "Send red revolutionary eggs to the trenches."

This political consciousness, however, was rational only in form. In essence it was a quasi-religious consciousness; the symbols and institutions of the Revolution had become an object of worship. People expected the Revolution to bring not merely social and political changes but also a miracle—a rapid and universal purification and "resurrection." The path toward this "bright future," this "resurrection," had been opened thanks to the miraculous elimination of the "dark forces."

The term "internal enemy" (or, sometimes, the "internal German"), which had been borrowed from the old army lexicon, was used rather frequently in the spring of 1917 to describe the old regime. But quite soon after February a well-known phrase from the era of the French Revolution came into use—"enemy of the people"—and included at times among the number of "enemies" that spring was the "bourgeoisie." An appeal from a factory committee of the Russian Society for the Production of Shells and Ammunition for the Soldiers proclaimed:

Comrades! We are very pleased that you have understood us and now fully realize who the enemies of the people are. You have seen that you could not and
cannot find such an enemy among workers, particularly among the workers of
our factory. For the worker and the soldier represent a single entity, one army
of labor ruthlessly and pitilessly exploited by a small group of bloodthirsty capitalists, headed by Nicholas and Rasputin, which built its happiness upon our
ignorance.

A few months after February, not many people retained the sense of a "revolutionary holiday" or a "miracle of the revolution": the war dragged on, the supply situation worsened, inflation rose, and crime grew threatening. The Revolution had not
lived up to the hopes of the "little man": his life became more dangerous, hungrier
and unpredictable. By the autumn of 1917 the euphoria and hyperpoliticization of
the February days had been replaced by political despondency and disappointment.
For many, meanwhile, "deepening the revolution" offered an escape from the situation. Mass consciousness explained the rush of crises as a "bourgeois plot." In describing such attitudes, N. A. Berdiaev wrote that "our social problem has turned into
a problem of searching for those 'scoundrels' and 'blackguards'—those 'bourgeois'—
from whose ideas flows all evil. Exclusive moralism is leading to morally ugly results."
Mass consciousness has been inclined during many different eras to find the "reasons" for critical situations in the plots of sabotaging minorities (be it the myths about
Jewish, Masonic, or Jesuit plots, for example). The logical "way out," then, was to expose and cut short the plot. In Russian circumstances, the idea of needing to suppress
the counterrevolutionary and antipopular "bourgeois plot" became an important element of political consciousness. A certain Petr Okurikhin, who wrote "A Message
from the Sailors of the Baltic Fleet to the Oppressed of the World," proposed an eloquent recipe for saving the Revolution: "Let all those bloodthirsty butchers who oppress the people perish in the storm of social revolution. Smash to smithereens the
skull of capital, the skull of bloody despotism, which for centuries has darkened the
working people's sepulchral lives, the lives of honest working people." (It is instructive to note that here, as in many other cases, "capital" and "working people" were
portrayed as eternally opposed oppressors and oppressed.) In the mass consciousness
of 1917, the "bourgeoisie" was not so much an economic, social or political category;
rather, it was an infernal, insidious and powerful force standing in the way of the great
and holy resurrection promised by the Revolution. The image of the "bourgeoisie"
was made diabolical.

The Bolsheviks' and their political allies' propaganda took such moods into account and made good use of them. It stands to reason that in the autumn of 1917 various entrepreneurs, bankers and like-minded political figures would participate in secret enterprises that genuinely could be called "plots against the Revolution." But
both mass consciousness and leftist propaganda explained everything as a grandiose
and overarching "bourgeois conspiracy": an ideological metaphor began to take on a
life of its own, becoming an important factor in the political process and giving shape
to, provoking and strengthening conflicts between structures of authority.

The manifestation of "antibourgeois" sentiments, understandably, was not provoked solely by socialist propaganda: the latter fell on fertile soil. The anti-urbanist antibourgeois attitudes of the intelligentsia, the anti-burgher position of the gentry, the
anti-Western rhetoric of Russian nationalists, and the egalitarian tradition of the
Russian peasantry, rooted in the ancient *obshchina* tradition—over the decades they all

prepared the way for an "antibourgeois" explosion. Because of this, the Russian Revolution could not help but be antibourgeois in tone, although the concrete forms of the Revolution's development could of course have been different.

It seems to me that the significance of this factor (along with others) must be taken into account when discussing potential alternatives of social development in 1917. The spread of "antibourgeois" sentiments, in the formation of which the most varied and at times conflicting political forces took part, hampered the chances for a workable and durable agreement between moderate socialists and liberals. All other alternatives, including a "unified socialist government," scarcely could have averted civil war.

Boris I. Kolonitskii, "Antibourgeois Propaganda and Anti-'*Burzhui*' Consciousness in 1917," *The Russian Review,* LIII, 2 (April 1994), pp. 183–196.

Order No. 1

In the first volume of his splendid study of the soldiers in the revolution, the late Allan K. Wildman referred to Order No. 1 as "the terse document that more than any other permanently institutionalized a new order of things and finalized the distribution of power in Petrograd at the front, and throughout the country at large."[1] An eyewitness to the events, the radical lawyer N. D. Sokolov, understood immediately what had transpired: "With the publication of Order no. One the situation of the Soviet of Workers' Deputies sharply changed for the better. The Soviet suddenly perceived it was of a great magnitude, supported by a genuinely existing force—the Petrograd garrison."[2] Real power backed by soldiers now lay with the soviet, and the same kinds of suspicions and divisions that alienated workers from their bosses were expressed by soldiers toward their officers. From the earliest days, the revolution in Petrograd was marked by this social distance between the "top" and "bottom" of society. With the soldiers essentially siding with the workers, restoration of the old political order became almost impossible—at least without bloody civil war. The regret at what had happened is evident in the account given by the conservative politician, M. V. Rodzianko, former chairman of the last tsarist Duma and head of the Temporary Committee of the Duma from which the new Provisional Government would be formed.

RODZIANKO'S VERSION OF
THE GENESIS OF ORDER NO. 1

On the evening of March 1, an unidentified soldier came, on behalf of the elected representatives of the Petrograd Garrison, to the Military Commission created under the chairmanship of member of the State Durna Engel'hardt of the Temporary Committee. He demanded that an order should be elaborated which would regulate the mutual relations between officers and soldiers on a new basis; Engel'hardt replied with a sharp rebuff, indicating that the Temporary Committee considered the publication of such an order inadmissible.

1. Allan K. Wildman, *The End of the Russian Imperial Army: The Old Army and the Soldiers' Revolt (March-April 1917)* (Princeton: Princeton University Press, 1983), p. 183.
   2. Cited in ibid., p. 188.

Then the soldier declared to Colonel Engel'hardt: "If you don't want to, then we can dispense with you."

During the night of March 1–2, the Order was printed in a huge number of copies by order of the Soviet of Workers' and Soldiers' Deputies whom the workers of all the printing houses of Petrograd implicitly obeyed; by an order unknown to the Temporary Committee the Order was sent to the front.

When the matter came to the knowledge of the Temporary Committee, while the Provisional Government did not as yet exist, the Committee decided that the Order should be considered invalid and unlawful.

A sharp discussion with the Soviet of Workers' and Soldiers' Deputies took place, and as a result the latter published in one of the issues of its *Izvestiia* another order which declared for the information of all that Order No. 1 was obligatory only for the Petrograd Garrison and the troops of the Petrograd District.

But, of course, the wrong had already been done.

M. V. Rodzianko, "Gosudarstvennaia duma i fevral'skaia revoliutsiia," *Arkhiv Russkoi Revolutsii,* VI (1922), pp. 74–75.

THE VERSION OF THE EXECUTIVE COMMITTEE OF THE PETROGRAD SOVIET

In view of the fact that during the past days the content of "Order No. 1" of the Petrograd Soviet and the circumstances that accompanied its publication were reported and interpreted incorrectly in various institutions and meetings, the Executive Committee thinks it necessary to reprint this Order, by way of reference, and to state in the most condensed form the history of the appearance of this document which, in the opinion of the Committee, played a beneficial role in the matter of organizing the Russian army under the conditions of revolution.

The Order was issued (by agreement between the Temporary Committee of the State Duma and the Executive Committee of the Soviet) on March 1, that is, prior to the creation of the Provisional Government, and consequently cannot be considered as an order competing with the authority of the latter.

The Order was addressed exclusively to the Petrograd Garrison.

The Order was signed by the "Petrograd Soviet of Workers' and Soldiers' Deputies" and was drawn up at the first session of the Soviet in full membership, that is, with the participation not only of workers but of its soldiers' section as well.

The deputies of the Petrograd Garrison wished at the very first meeting to formulate the bases of the social organization of the soldiers and introduced during the conference a number of suggestions on regimental and company committees, on abolishing the compulsory salute, on soldiers' civil rights, etc. And it was these suggestions in their sum total that comprised "Order No. 1."

Neither the Executive Committee, as such, nor its individual members (as seen from the minutes of the meetings printed in *Izvestiia* for March 2) introduced at the meeting either the draft of the Order or even the draft of its individual points. . . .

The Order was published on the third day of the revolution, when its military-technical period had not yet been completed. And a "notice" was published on the first page of *Izvestiia* for March 1 about the necessity of bringing to the Mikhailov Riding School all the machine guns in order to "liquidate the shooting from roofs."

The alarm was increased by rumors that in some regiments officers were beginning to disarm the soldiers. . . .

It is natural, therefore, that the representative organ of the Petrograd soldiers wanted, on the one hand, to calm the soldier masses and, on the other, to protect the Russian revolution in a critical period by [preventing] the disarming of the basic military force. This desire was expressed in point 5 of the Order.

On March 4 the War Department, reporting through General Potapov that Order No. 1 was in some instances incorrectly interpreted, appealed to the Executive Committee with the request to issue an explanation of the Order that would remove the possibility of any false interpretations. Moreover, General Potapov requested that this explanation also be published in the form of an "order" to give it greater authority.

To edit the requested explanation the Committee appointed a Commission which worked out, together with the Military Commission [of the Duma], under the presidency of General Potapov, an explanatory "Order No. 2."

["Order No. 2" was signed by] Acting President M. I. Skobelev, for the President of the Executive Committee of the Soviet of Workers' and Soldiers' Deputies; General M. Potapov, President of the Military Commission of the Temporary Committee of the State Duma: and War Minister A. Guchkov.

In conclusion, the Executive Committee points out that most of the points in Order No. 1 have already been enforced as law, in part during the time when Minister of War A. I. Guchkov was in office and in part under A. F. Kerensky. As for regimental, detachment, and other committees, the thought about which was first expressed in Order No. 1, their role was regarded as sound and organizing, not only by public institutions but also by many representatives in the high command.

The Executive Committee of the Petrograd Soviet of Workers' and Soldiers' Deputies *Izvestiia*, No. 125, July 23, 1917, p. 6

ORDER NO. 1

To the garrison of the Petrograd District, to all the soldiers [and sailors] of the guard, army, artillery, and navy, for immediate and strict execution, and to the workers of Petrograd for their information:

The Soviet of Workers' and Soldiers' Deputies has resolved:

1. In all companies, battalions, regiments, parks, batteries, squadrons, in the special services of the various military administrations, and on the vessels of the navy, committees from the elected representatives of the lower ranks of the above-mentioned military units shall be chosen immediately.

2. In all those military units that have not yet chosen their representatives to the Soviet of Workers' Deputies, one representative from each company shall be selected, to report with written credentials at the building of the State Duma by ten o'clock on the morning of the second of this March.

3. In all its political actions, the military branch is subordinated to the Soviet of Workers' and Soldiers' Deputies and to its own committees.

4. The orders of the Military Commission of the State Duma shall be executed only in such cases as do not conflict with the orders and resolutions of the Soviet of Workers' and Soldiers' Deputies.

5. All kinds of arms, such as rifles, machine guns, armored automobiles, and oth-

ers, must be kept at the disposal and under the control of the company and battalion committees, and in no case should they be turned over to officers, even at their demand.

6. In the ranks and during their performance of the duties of the service, soldiers must observe the strictest military discipline, but outside the service and the ranks, in their political, general civic, and private life, soldiers cannot in any way be deprived of those rights that all citizens enjoy. In particular, standing at attention and compulsory saluting, when not on duty, is abolished.

7. Also, the addressing of the officers with the titles "Your Excellency," "Your Honor," etc., is abolished, and these titles are replaced by the address of "Mister General," "Mister Colonel," etc. Rudeness toward soldiers of any rank, and especially, addressing them as "thou" [*ty*] is prohibited, and soldiers are required to bring to the attention of the company committees every infraction of this rule as well as all misunderstandings occurring between officers and privates.

The Order itself was drafted by N. D. Sokolov, who described the events in *Ogonek*, no. 11 (1927). These documents were translated and reprinted in *The Russian Provisional Government 1917: Documents*, selected and edited by Robert Paul Browder and Alexander F. Kerensky, vol. II (Stanford: Stanford University Press, 1961), pp. 846–849.

<hr style="width:30%">

A. F. Kerenskii's Statement in the Soviet of Workers' Deputies,
March 2, 1917

Alexandr Kerenskii (1881–1970) was a moderate socialist associated with the pro-peasant Socialist Revolutionary Party. Famed as a eloquent orator and a lawyer ready to defend opponents of tsarism, Kerenskii was elected to the Fourth State Duma in 1912, a member of the Trudovik (Labor) faction. With the outbreak of the February Revolution he maneuvered himself to be both in the new Provisional Government, as its first minister of justice, and a member of the Petrograd Soviet, even though those two organs of power were highly suspicious of each other. In May he became minister of defense in the Coalition Government and launched the June Offensive, which turned out to be a military disaster. Nevertheless, in the ensuing political crisis in July he became prime minister, a position he held until his overthrow in the October Revolution. Historians have identified Kerenskii as a democratic alternative to the more authoritarian strains in Russian socialism, yet his histrionic personal style and the hostility that radical socialists, liberals, and conservatives felt for him contributed to his increasing political isolation through the late summer of fall of 1917.

After the organization of the new Government, A. F. Kerenskii, the Minister of Justice, appeared at the meeting of the Soviet of Workers' Deputies [March 2] and asked permission to make a statement out of order. He was immediately given the floor, and A. F. Kerenskii addressed the following words to the Soviet of Workers' Deputies:

"Comrades! Do you trust me? (*Cries from the whole audience:* "We trust you, we trust you.") I am speaking from the depths of my heart; I am ready to die if need be. (*General stir in the audience. A. F. Kerenskii is greeted with prolonged applause, turning into a long ovation.*) Comrades, in view of the formation of a new Government, I had to give an immediate answer, without waiting for your formal approval, to the offer I received of accepting the portfolio of the Ministry of Justice. *(Storm of applause, general enthusiasm.)* Comrades, the representatives of the old regime were in my hands and I could not bring myself to let them [slip] out of my hands. *(Storm of applause and cries: "Right!")* I accepted the offer extended to me and entered the new Provisional Government in the capacity of Minister of Justice. *(General applause and shouts: "Bravo!")* My first step was an order to release immediately all political prisoners, without any exceptions, and to send here from Siberia, with special honors, our fellow deputies of the Social Democratic faction. *(A thunder of applause, general enthusiasm.)* In view of the fact that I assumed the duties of the Minister of Justice prior to receiving your formal authorization for this, I resign from the office of Vice-President of the Soviet of Workers' Deputies. But I am ready to accept this title from you once again, if you find this necessary. *(Storm of applause and cries from the audience: "We ask, we ask.")* Comrades, in entering the new Provisional Government, I remain, as I always have been, a republican. *(Loud applause.)* I declared to the Provisional Government that I am a representative of the democracy and that the Provisional Government should look upon me as a spokesman for the demands of the democracy and must be particularly considerate of those views which I shall uphold in the capacity of a representative of the democracy by whose efforts the old regime was overthrown. Comrades, time does not wait, every minute is precious, and I call upon you to organize, to [maintain] discipline, to support us, your representatives, who are ready to die for the people and who have dedicated their whole lives to the people."

A. F. Kerenskii's speech, which was delivered with great animation, was drowned in a storm of applause. It is difficult to convey the enthusiasm which gripped the audience. Isolated voices which tried to protest against the fact that A. F. Kerenskii acted without the formal consent of the Soviet of Workers' Deputies were drowned by the unanimous cries of the overwhelming majority of the Soviet of Workers' Deputies, who accorded A. F. Kerenskii a stormy ovation such as never was heard within the walls of the Tauride Palace.

Izvestiia revoliutsionnoi nedeli, no. 7, March 3, 1917, p. 1; translated and reprinted in *The Russian Provisional Government 1917: Documents,* selected and edited by Robert Paul Browder and Alexander F. Kerensky, vol. I (Stanford: Stanford University Press, 1961), pp. 128–129. For more on Kerenskii, see Richard Abraham, *Alexander Kerensky, The First Love of the Revolution* (New York: Columbia University Press, 1987; and his memoirs, Alexander Kerensky, *Russia and History's Turning Point* (New York: Duell, Sloan, and Pearce, 1965).

═══ Iraklii Tsereteli's Speech on Returning from Siberian Exile ═══
March 20, 1917

One of the least well-known, yet central figures, in the Russian Revolution, was the Georgian Social Democrat (Menshevik) Iraklii Tsereteli (1881–1959). Elected to the Second State Duma in 1906, he emerged as a leader of the parliamentary left before the tsar dissolved the Duma. Arrested and exiled to Siberia, Tsereteli returned to Petrograd only after being liberated by the revolution. From his arrival in the capital, he articulated a centrist political program for the soviet known as "revolutionary defensism," which called for the soviet to work with the progressive bourgeoisie ("unity of all the vital forces of the nation") and military defense of the revolution until a "democratic peace" could be concluded among all the belligerents. He opposed Lenin's call for "all power to the soviet" and supported the formation of a

*Coalition Government of soviet and "bourgeois" representatives in May, joining that govern-
ment as Minister of Posts and Telegraphs. His coalition policy was backed by his own Menshevik Defensist party and their allies the Right Socialist Revolutionaries but opposed by the
Bolsheviks, the Menshevik Internationalists, and the Left Socialist Revolutionaries.*

Comrades-workers, on behalf of your faction in the State Duma, which was liberated
by you, I want to express my deep gratitude to you for the welcome [you have given
us] . . . We came here to join your ranks, and, comrades, before we take our place
once again in the kindred ranks of the working class, we would like to share with you
our reactions to this victory and our understanding of the tasks that now confront the
revolutionary working class and all the popular movements as a result of recent events.
It is in the name of these tasks that we are ready to fight together with you until victory or death. Thus we have a natural need to share with you everything that we have
experienced during these days and to outline together with you the tasks for which
we will fight and the paths which we will follow. Comrades-workers, it was arm in arm
with all the living forces of the country that you cast the autocracy into oblivion; it was
together with the revolutionary army, the peasantry, and all the progressive bourgeoisie.
Your achievement is great, comrades-workers, but the greatness of this achievement is
equaled by your other achievement; having overthrown the old regime, you weighed
the circumstances from the point of view of the interests of the great people, you understood that the time has not yet come for achieving the ultimate aims of the proletariat, the class aims which have nowhere as yet been achieved, but [you understood]
that the hour had struck for the complete triumph of democracy, the triumph which
the working class and all the living forces of the country are interested in. And you,
having no opportunity fully to realize all those lofty ideals which will be realized by
the combined efforts of the world proletariat, you did not want to assume the responsibility for the collapse of the movement [which would have occurred] had you in a
desperate attempt decided to force your will on the events at that time. You understood
that a bourgeois revolution is taking place, that it represents a state of the social revolution, and that, first of all, you must strengthen your position at this stage in order to
accelerate the progress of all Russia, the progress of all mankind toward the bright ideals
of socialism. The power is in the hands of the bourgeoisie. You transferred this power
to the bourgeoisie, but at the same time you have stood guard over the newly gained
freedom—you control the actions of the bourgeoisie, you push it into the fight, you
support its resolute measures in the fight against the old order. And in order to fulfill
this task, you, together with the revolutionary army, have created a powerful bulwark
of freedom, standing guard over new Russia.

. . . The Provisional Government must have full executive power in so far as this
power strengthens the revolution, in so far as it is overthrowing and breaking down the
old order. The proletariat represents the prime moving force behind these decisions; the
proletariat dictates these decisions; the proletariat supports them with all its strength.
But in order to apply its revolutionary tactics it is imperative to have organization and
strict discipline in the ranks of the proletariat itself. I know, comrades, that at the present moment you are occupied with the problem of improving your organization in
view of the fact that the Petrograd Soviet of Workers' and Soldiers' Deputies, having assumed the leadership of the all-Russian revolutionary movement, has now expanded
to such an extent that it technically cannot cope with all the tasks that confront it. We

believe that the question of reorganizing the revolutionary vanguard of Russia is a basic, cardinal question: will we succeed in organizing a workers' representation and a representation of the revolutionary army on such principles as would enable them actually to subject the bourgeoisie to their control, actually to dictate revolutionary measures to the bourgeoisie, and at the same time to exert all their authority in support of those actions of the executive power which are essential to free Russia?

But should the moment arrive when this government renounces the revolutionary path and chooses the path of negotiations, the path of compromises, then you and we together, comrades, will march dauntlessly against this government and together we will cast it into oblivion in the same way as we did the old regime. But as long as this government, under the impact of revolutionary events, is following the revolutionary path, as long as the interests of the bourgeoisie are embodied in acts which coincide with the common national interests of the democracy, as long as the Provisional Government carries the banner of the Constituent Assembly . . . , and as long as its measures are directed toward the liquidation of the old order, we, together with you, will support it . . .

Comrades, allow me to close my speech with that national cry with which all speeches at public meetings are brought to a close. "Long Live Free Russia! Long Live the Constituent Assembly! Long Live the Democratic Republic!" *(Stormy applause.)*

Following Tsereteli, other Social Democratic comrades returning from exile delivered speeches. When the speeches were over, the soldiers' deputies stood up and sang "Eternal Glory" to the fallen fighters.

Izvestiia, no. 20, March 21, 1917, pp. 2–3:translated and reprinted in *The Russian Provisional Government 1917: Documents,* selected and edited by Robert Paul Browder and Alexander F. Kerensky, vol. III (Stanford: Stanford University Press, 1961), pp. 1219–1221.

V. I. Lenin, "The Tasks of the Proletariat in the Present Revolution ('April Theses')"
April 7, 1917

Vladimir Il'ich Lenin (born Ulianov) (1870–1924) was the leader of the Bolshevik wing of Russian Social Democracy and the principal opponent of those socialists who supported the Provisional Government and a "bourgeois revolution." From his arrival in Petrograd (from exile in Switzerland) in April, Lenin staked out a clear position of opposition to compromise with the propertied classes, a call for an immediate end to the war, and the transfer of political power to the soviets, which represented exclusively the lower classes. His "April Theses" shocked even his fellow Bolsheviks, some of whom, like Joseph Stalin, were prepared (until Lenin's arrival) to compromise with the government. Lenin managed to rally his party comrades around his program, and the Bolsheviks, though still a minority party within the soviets, emerged from the early political clashes with a clear profile as uncompromising revolutionaries opposed to collaboration with the liberals, landlords, and industrialists.

I did not arrive in Petrograd until the night of April 3, and therefore at the meeting on April 4 I could, of course, deliver the report on the tasks of the revolutionary proletariat only on my own behalf, and with reservations as to insufficient preparation.

The only thing I could do to make things easier for myself—and for honest opponents—was to prepare the theses in *writing*. I read them out, and gave the text to Comrade Tsereteli. I read them twice very slowly: first at a meeting of Bolsheviks and then at a meeting of both Bolsheviks and Mensheviks.

I publish these personal theses of mine with only the briefest explanatory notes, which were developed in far greater detail in the report.

THESES

1. In our attitude towards the war, which under the new government of Lvov and Co. unquestionably remains on Russia's part a predatory imperialist war owing to the capitalist nature of that government, not the slightest concession to "revolutionary defensism" is permissible.

The class-conscious proletariat can give its consent to a revolutionary war, which would really justify revolutionary defensism, only on condition: (a) that the power pass to the proletariat and the poorest sections of the peasants aligned with the proletariat; (b) that all annexations be renounced in deed and not in word; (c) that a complete break be effected in actual fact with all capitalist interests.

In view of the undoubted honesty of those broad sections of the mass believers in revolutionary defensism who accept the war only as a necessity, and not as a means of conquest, in view of the fact that they are being deceived by the bourgeoisie, it is necessary with particular thoroughness, persistence and patience to explain their error to them, to explain the inseparable connection existing between capital and the imperialist war, and to prove that without overthrowing capital *it is impossible* to end the war by a truly democratic peace, a peace not imposed by violence.

The most widespread campaign for this view must be organized in the army at the front.

Fraternization

2. The specific feature of the present situation in Russia is that the country is *passing* from the first stage of the revolution—which, owing to the insufficient class-consciousness and organization of the proletariat, placed power in the hands of the bourgeoisie—to its *second* stage, which must place power in the hands of the proletariat and the poorest sections of the peasants. This transition is characterized, on the one hand, by a maximum of legally recognized rights (Russia is now the freest of all the belligerent countries in the world), on the other, by the absence of violence towards the masses, and, finally, by their unreasoning trust in the government of capitalists, those worst enemies of peace and socialism.

This peculiar situation demands of us an ability to adapt ourselves to the *special* conditions of party work among unprecedentedly large masses of proletarians who have just awakened to political life.

3. No support for the Provisional Government; the utter falsity of all its promises should be made clear, particularly of those relating to the renunciation of annexations. Exposure in place of the impermissible, illusion-breeding "demand" that *this* government, a government of capitalists, should *cease* to be an imperialist government.

4. Recognition of the fact that in most of the soviets of workers' deputies our

party is in a minority, so far a small minority, as against a *bloc of all* the petty-bourgeois opportunist elements, from the Popular Socialists and the Socialist-Revolutionaries down to the OK (Chkheidze, Tsereteli, etc.), Steklov, etc., etc., who have yielded to the influence of the bourgeoisie and spread that influence among the proletariat.[1]

The masses must be made to see that the soviets of workers' deputies are the only *possible* form of revolutionary government, and that therefore our task is, as long as *this* government yields to the influence of the bourgeoisie, to present a patient, systematic, and persistent *explanation* of the errors of their tactics, an explanation especially adapted to the practical needs of the masses.

As long as we are in the minority we carry on the work of criticizing and exposing errors and at the same time we preach the necessity of transferring the entire state power to the soviets of workers' deputies, so that the people may overcome their mistakes by experience.

5. Not a parliamentary republic—to return to a parliamentary republic from the soviets of workers' deputies would be a retrograde step—but a Republic of Soviets of Workers', Agricultural Laborers' and Peasants' Deputies throughout the country, from top to bottom.

Abolition of the police, the army and the bureaucracy.[2]

The salaries of all officials, all of whom are elective and displaceable at any time, not to exceed the average wage of a competent worker.

6. The weight of emphasis in the agrarian program to be shifted to the soviets of agricultural laborers' deputies.

Confiscation of All Landed Estates

Nationalization of all lands in the country, the land, to be disposed of by the local soviets of agricultural laborers' and peasants' deputies. The organization of separate soviets of deputies of poor peasants. The setting up of a model farm on each of the large estates (ranging in size from 100 to 300 *desiatiny,* according to local and other conditions, and to the decisions of the local bodies) under the control of the soviets of agricultural laborers' deputies and for the public account.[3]

7. The immediate amalgamation of all banks in the country into a single national bank, and the institution of control over it by the soviets of workers' deputies.

8. It is not our immediate task to "introduce" socialism, but only to bring social production and the distribution of products at once under the control of the soviets of workers' deputies.

9. Party tasks:

   (a) Immediate convocation of a party congress;

   (b) Alteration of the party program, mainly:

---

1. The Popular Socialists were the most moderate of the pro-peasant parties, a right-wing faction that broke off from the Socialist Revolutionaries in 1906 and gave its support to the Provisional Government. The Socialist Revolutionaries remained through 1917 the most popular party among the peasantry, who were the overwhelming majority of the Russian population. The OK or Organizational Committee was the central committee of the Menshevik wing of Social Democracy from 1905 until August 1917, when at the so-called "Unification Congress" the Mensheviks elected a Central Committee for their organizations.

2. Lenin added: "i.e., the standing army to be replaced by the arming of the whole people."

3. *Desiatina* is a Russian unit of land measurement equal to 2.7 acres.

(1) On the question of imperialism and the imperialist war;

(2) On our attitude towards the state and our demand for a "commune state;"[4]

(3) Amendment of our out-of-date minimum program.

(c) Change of the party's name.[5]

10. A new International.

We must take the initiative in creating a revolutionary International, an International against the *social-chauvinists* and against the "Center."[6]

Pravda, no. 26, April 7, 1917; translated in V. I. Lenin, *Collected Works*, XXIV(London: Laurence and Wishart, 1964), pp 21–24.

Tsereteli and Lenin's Exchange of Words During the First All-Russian Congress of Soviets of Workers' and Soldiers' Deputies"
June 3–4, 1917

Early in June, representatives of the workers' and soldiers' councils (soviets) from all over Russia gathered in Petrograd to discuss the current political situation and to show support for the Provisional Government. Lenin's Bolsheviks were a small minority at the congress but already represented the most effective and influential party opposed to the Government. In this brief exchange, Lenin distinguished between the "reformist democracy" of Tsereteli and the Mensheviks and his own conception of "revolutionary democracy," which would be based in the soviets and would represent only "the toiling classes," the peasants, soldiers, and workers.

TSERETELI: At the present moment, there is not a political party in Russia which would say: hand the power over to us, resign, and we will take your place. Such a party does not exist in Russia. (Lenin: "It does exist.") . . . They [the Bolsheviks] say—When we have a majority, or when the majority comes over to our point of view, then the power should be seized. Comrade Lenin, you said that. At least the Bolsheviks and you with them say it in their official statements.

Gentlemen, until now, there has not been a single party in Russia which has come out openly for getting for itself all power at once, although there have been such cries by irresponsible groups on the Right and the Left. . . . The Right says, let the Left run the Government, and we and the country will draw our conclusions; and the Left says, let the Right take hold, and we and the country will draw our conclu-

4. Lenin added: "i.e., a state of which the Paris Commune was the prototype."
5. Lenin added: "Instead of 'Social Democracy', whose official leaders *throughout* the world have betrayed socialism and deserted to the bourgeoisie (the 'defensists' and the vacillating 'Kautskyites'), we must call ourselves the *Communist Party*."
6. Lenin added: "The 'Center' in the international Social Democratic movement is the trend which vacillates between the chauvinists (= 'defensists') and internationalists, i.e., Kautsky and Co. in Germany, Longuet and Co., in France, Chkheidze and Co. in Russia, Turati and Co. in Italy, MacDonald and Co in Britain, etc."

sions. . . . Each side hopes that the other will make such a failure, that the country will turn to it for leadership.

But, gentlemen, this is not the time for that kind of a play. . . . In order to solve the problems of the country, we must unite our strength and must have a strong Government . . . strong enough to put an end to experiments dangerous for the fate of the revolution. . . . experiments that may lead to civil war. . . .

This, gentlemen, is our policy. . . .

LENIN: Comrades! In the short time allotted to me, I am able—and I deem it more advisable—to dwell only on those questions of fundamental principle that have been brought up by the speaker from the Executive Committee and by the speakers that followed him.

The first fundamental question we have been confronted with is this: *Where* are we? What are these soviets that have assembled here in an All-Russian Congress?. . . . The soviets are an institution that does not and cannot exist within, or alongside of, the ordinary bourgeois-parliamentary state. . . .

It is one thing or the other: either we have an ordinary bourgeois government— then there is no need for peasants', workers', soldiers', or any other kind of soviets, then they will be dispersed by the generals, the counter-revolutionary generals, who control the army, paying no heed whatever to Minister Kerensky's oratory, then they will die an ignominious death otherwise—or we have a real government of the soviets. There is no other way open for these institutions; they can neither go backward nor remain in the same place if they are to live; they can only exist going forward. Here is a type of state not of the Russians' invention but created by the revolution itself which could not be victorious in any other way. Friction, party struggle for power within the All-Russian Soviet are inevitable. But that will mean that the masses themselves are overcoming possible errors and illusions through their own political experience (*noise*) and not through reports by Ministers who quote what they said yesterday, what they are going to write tomorrow and what they are going to promise the day after tomorrow. This, comrades, is ridiculous, if one looks at things from the point of view of this institution which sprang from the revolution itself and is now facing the question: to be or not to be. The soviets cannot continue to exist as they exist now. Adult people, workers and peasants, must come together, pass resolutions, listen to reports, without being able to verify them by studying the original documents! Institutions of this kind are a transition to a republic which, in deeds, not in words, will establish a firm power without police, without a standing army—the kind of power that cannot as yet exist in Europe, that is, however, indispensable for a victory of the Russian Revolution if we mean by it a victory over the landowners, a victory over imperialism. . . .

If you wish to refer to *"revolutionary"* democracy, then please differentiate between this conception and that of *reformist* democracy under a capitalist cabinet, for it is high time we passed from phrases about "revolutionary democracy," from mutual congratulations upon "revolutionary democracy," to a class characterization as taught by Marxism and scientific socialism in general. What we are offered is a reformist democracy under a capitalist cabinet. This may be excellent from the point of view of the ordinary patterns of Western Europe. Now, however, a number of countries are on the verge of ruin, and those practical measures, which, according to the preceding orator, citizen–Minister of Posts and Telegraphs, are so complicated that it is difficult to introduce them, that they need special study those measures are perfectly clear. He said that there is no political party in Russia that would express willingness to take all state power into its hands. I say: "Such a party exists! No party has a right to refuse power, and our party does not refuse it. Our party is ready at any moment to take all power into its hands." *(Applause, laughter)*

You may laugh, but if the citizen–Minister confronts us with this question side by side with a party of the Right, he will receive the proper reply. No party has a right to refuse power. At the present time while we still have freedom, while the threats of arrest and Siberian exile, made by the counter-revolutionists with whom our near-socialist ministers sit in one cabinet, are only threats as yet—at this moment each party should say: give us your confidence, and we shall give you our program. . . .

The passing of power to the revolutionary proletariat supported by the poorest peasants means passing to as safe and painless a form of revolutionary struggle for peace as the world has ever known, passing to a situation where the power and the victory of the revolutionary workers will be made secure in Russia and throughout the whole world. *(Applause from a part of the audience.)*

Tsereteli's speech: *Izvestiia*, no. 84, June 6, 1917, pp. 6–9; translated in Frank Alfred Golder, *Documents of Russian History* (New York, 1927), pp. 361–363; Lenin's speech: *Pravda*, nos. 82, 83, June 15, 16, 1917; translated in *Collected Works of V. I. Lenin: The Revolution of 1917*, XX (New York: International Publishers, 1929), book 2, pp. 195–205.

"Report of the Commissar of the Novoaleksandrovsk *Uezd*, Kovno *Guberniia*"[1]
June 14, 1917

Already by the late spring and summer of 1917, the situation in villages across Russia was becoming unpredictable. The mobilization of peasants against the old order in the countryside was, in the words of Orlando Figes, chronicler of the agrarian movement in the Volga region, "decisive."

> *Without the simultaneous rising of the peasants, the workers' revolution could not have been accomplished. By undermining the old agrarian order, upon which the political and military supports of the Tsarist state had been based, the peasants enabled the Bolsheviks, with the support of only a minority of the population, to consolidate their power in the capital and the other major cities.[2]*

Breaking out sporadically and with little coordination, peasant risings fed into each other, as the confidence of the villagers grew and the panic of the landowners spread. Without a powerful state behind them, protecting their estates and enforcing their rights, landlords faced the raw power of peasants who wanted to hold the land and run their own affairs. Inspired by the words of pro-peasant intellectuals, peasants elected committees that became the real local power in the villages. The Provisional Government tried to set up its own volost' authorities, provisions committees, and land committees (zemel'nye komiteti), but they were unable to compete with

---

1. *Guberniia* is a province; *uezd* is a district within a province; and *volost'* is a township within an *uezd*.

2. Orlando Figes, *Peasant Russia, Civil War: The Volga Countryside in Revolution, 1917–1921* (Oxford: Oxford University Press, 1989), p. 30.

the elected peasant committees. While the government and moderates tried to delay resolution of the land question until the convening of the Constituent Assembly, peasants simply took matters into their own hands and created their own economic and political system, a rough, localized democracy, in the vast spaces outside of the cities.

June 14, 1917, No. 204

A congress of peasants of the Vil'na *guberniia* and part of Novoaleksandrovsk *uezd*, administratively joined to it, was called by the *guberniia* commissar in the city of Disna, Vil'na *guberniia*, on June 4. Approximately 400 delegates, peacefully disposed peasants, assembled. Speakers of the most extreme left-wing parties (Socialist Revolutionaries) spoke at the congress. And they stirred up the entire assembly [by the following appeals]: All land is yours, and now you can, in accordance with the resolutions of the *volost'* committees, take everything you need—fields, meadows, forests, lakes, pastures, and so forth. And in order to legalize all this and not regard it as seizure, you must pay, not to the owner but to the *volost'* committees, at least a minimum price per *desiatina*. They advised that all foresters be replaced by their own men in privately owned and government forests. The fixed price for milling the grain is most insignificant, and the millers, unwilling to suffer further losses, refuse to mill at this price. The mills are consequently to be taken over by the *volost'* committees and placed at their disposal. All waterways, lakes, and rivers are to be placed at once at the disposal of *volost'* committees, which are preparing to seize them and draw up new agreements, discontinuing old tenants. Private owners are given only up to July 10 to gather in the hay necessary for their own needs. And the owners are to gather in the hay themselves and not with the aid of hired hands. In a word, private owners and tenants are, in accordance with the resolutions of this congress, completely denied the management of their lands. Everything passes into the hands of *volost'* and village committees. Persons are elected to the *volost'*, not on the basis of fitness for their posts, but because they promise the peasants to confiscate at once the privately owned lands and turn them over to the peasants. Private owners have a right only to the land they can cultivate themselves. Prior to this resolution of the congress I was able, although with difficulty, to restrain the peasants in the Novoaleksandrovsk *uezd*, entrusted to me, from extensive seizures, damages to fields caused by cattle, felling of trees, etc. At present, however, I am powerless [to do anything]. Because, after their return from the congress, the peasant deputies, discussing the speeches they have heard, pay no attention to my reasonings; they say that they have heard something entirely different at the congress. Two days after the congress I received the following telegram: "I request you to take personally and through the *volost'* executive committees the strictest measures to prevent seizures, damages to and destruction of meadows and fields, regardless of whom they may belong to. No. 10129. Vil'na-Kovno *Guberniia* Commissar, Balai." I was confused by this telegram. At the congress in the city of Disna, Mr. Balai and other speakers were saying something entirely different. And on the heels of [those speeches] they authorize me to restrain the population from seizures. I was the more confused because at the congress the role of the *uezd* commissars and *uezd* executive committees was reduced to zero. Not once was it suggested that [the people] refer to the *uezd* commissar for any explanations. And all resolutions of the *volost'* committees were passed with no participation whatsoever of the *uezd* commissar. Consequently, on receipt of the above-mentioned telegram, I made the following telegraphic inquiry: "To the Vil'na Guberniia Commissar. Disna. In compliance with the protocol of the peasant congress in Disna on June 4, the *volost'* and village committees remove the owners, take charge of privately owned meadows, forests, pastures, etc., as if they were their own property. They hire laborers, issue permits to individuals, as well as to troop units and organizations for grazing of cattle in meadows, on fields of mowed clover, and other places. Notify me how to act. Novoaleksandrovsk *Uezd* Commissar Montvil'." This telegram was prompted by the fact that members of the village committee of Ozhovsk *volost'*, on their return from Disna, came to the landowner of the estate of Mekian, Mr. Bortkevich, and announced that they had rented the mowed clover to the army to graze the horses. One hundred horses were sent out to graze and only after strenuous efforts in the headquarters of the regiment did Mr. Bortkevich succeed in having the horses removed. Moreover, they came to the estate, told the workers to leave, and those who wished to remain had to be paid by the *pomeshchik* [landlord] at the rate of not less than 5 rubles a day. Several such complaints about the actions of *volost'* and village committees come to me daily. And I am powerless to restrain [the offenders] since they refer to the resolutions of the congress and the addresses of the speakers in Disna. The role of the elected *uezd* commissars is extremely difficult. At the *volost'* meetings, in answer to my efforts to restrain the peasants from seizures and my explanations of the evil [consequences] of such [acts], they shout: "We elected you, and if you won't go with us, we will throw you out." Moreover, each *volost'* committee, in passing any kind of resolution, does not submit it for approval by the *uezd* commissar. And the resolutions are immediately carried out. I request the Ministry to make public as soon as possible the rights and obligations of the *volost'* executive committees; [I further request] that no resolution of the *volost'* committee be made effective without the approval of the *uezd* commissar or *uezd* committee. All money for confiscated lands go for safekeeping to the *volost'* committees, so that the private owners are even unable to pay for the labor of their workers. Army units are forced to pay the *volost'* committees for the [use of] pastures of private owners. According to them, the money will be held in safekeeping by the committee, pending the decision of the Constituent Assembly.

Montvil', Novoaleksandrovsk *Uezd* Commissar

M. Martynov, "Agrarnoe dvizhenie v 1917 godu po dokumentam Glavnogo Zemel'nogo Komiteta," *Krasnyi arkhiv*, XIV (1926), pp. 225–226; translated and reprinted in *The Russian Provisional Government 1917: Documents*, selected and edited by Robert Paul Browder and Alexander F. Kerensky, vol. II (Stanford: Stanford University Press, 1961), pp. 587–588.

===== **V. I. Lenin, "Letter to Central Committee Members"** =====
October 24, (November 6), 1917

Though Lenin's place in the history of the revolution has often been exaggerated, as if he alone were responsible for the radicalization of workers, soldiers, and peasants, one of the moments when his personal intervention was particularly important occurred in the weeks before the October insurrection, when he urged his followers to seize power. By early September, the Bolsheviks had majorities in both the Petrograd and Moscow soviets and, along with their allies, the Left Socialist Revolutionaries, were likely to dominate the forthcoming Second All-

Russian Congress of Soviets due to open in late October. With workers and soldiers evidently
moving increasingly toward support of Soviet power and voting for the Bolsheviks, many Bol-
sheviks believed that an armed seizure of power was unnecessary. Among Lenin's chief lieu-
tenants, Lev Trotsky advocated waiting for the opening of the Congress, which would confer le-
gitimacy on a new Soviet government. When the party's Central Committee voted to launch
an insurrection (October 10), Lev Kamenev and Grigorii Zinoviev went further and revealed
the Bolshevik intentions to the press. Lenin was outraged and called for their expulsion from
the party. Fearing that Kerenskii would act first and carry out his own action against the Bol-
sheviks, Lenin pressed ever harder for decisive action. On the very eve of the insurrection, as
the delegates to the Congress of Soviets gathered in the capital, Lenin wrote this frantic letter
to the Central Committee.

Comrades,

I am writing these lines on the evening of the 24th. The situation is critical in the extreme. In fact it is now absolutely clear that to delay the uprising would be fatal.

With all my might I urge comrades to realize that everything now hangs by a thread; that we are confronted by problems which are not to be solved by conferences or congresses (even congresses of soviets), but exclusively by peoples, by the masses, by the struggle of the armed people.

The bourgeois onslaught of the Kornilovites and the removal of Verkhovsky show that we must not wait. We must at all costs, this very evening, this very night, arrest the government, having first disarmed the officer cadets (defeating them, if they resist), and so on.[1]

We must not wait! We may lose everything!

The value of the immediate seizure of power will be the defense of the *people* (not of the congress, but of the people, the army and the peasants in the first place) from the Kornilovite government, which has driven out Verkhovsky and has hatched a second Kornilov plot.

Who must take power?

That is not important at present. Let the Military-Revolutionary Committee do it, or "some other institution" which will declare that it will relinquish power only to the true representatives of the interests of the people, the interests of the army (the immediate proposal of peace), the interests of the peasants (the land to be taken immediately and private property abolished), the interests of the starving.[2]

All districts, all regiments, all forces must be mobilized at once and must immediately send their delegations to the Military-Revolutionary Committee and to the Central Committee of the Bolsheviks with the insistent demand that under no cir-

---

1. Kornilovites refers to those who supported the military mutiny and march on Petrograd of the authoritarian General Lavr Kornilov in August 1917. General Aleksandr Verkhovskii was the Minister of War in Kerenskii's so-called "Directory," a short-lived government from September 1 to 25, and in his Third, and last, Coalition. On October 20, Verkhovskii stated that the army was not capable of fighting the Germans. Two days later, he took a leave of absence after being publicly accused of advocating a separate peace with the Germans.

2. The Military-Revolutionary Committee was formed by the Petrograd soviet to defend the city, but in the second half of October it effectively took over the Petrograd garrison and held de facto power in the city. Headed by Lev Trotsky, then chairman of the Petrograd soviet, the Committee was the general headquarters of the military effort to overthrow the Provisional Government.

cumstances should power be left in the hands of Kerensky and Co. until the 25th—not under any circumstances; the matter must be decided without fail this very evening, or this very night.

History will not forgive revolutionaries for procrastinating when they could be victorious today (and they certainly *will* be victorious today), while they risk losing much tomorrow, in fact, they risk losing everything.

If we seize power today, we seize it not in opposition to the soviets but on their behalf.

The seizure of power is the business of the uprising; its political purpose will become clear after the seizure.

It would be a disaster, or a sheer formality, to await the wavering vote of October 25. The people have the right and are in duty bound to decide such questions not by a vote, but by force; in critical moments of revolution, the people have the right and are in duty bound to give directions to their representatives, even their best representatives, and not to wait for them.

This is proved by the history of all revolutions; and it would be an infinite crime on the part of the revolutionaries were they to let the chance slip, knowing that the *salvation of the revolution,* the offer of peace, the salvation of Petrograd, salvation from famine, the transfer of the land to the peasants depend upon them.

The government is tottering. It must be *given the deathblow* at all costs.

To delay action is fatal.

This letter was first published in 1921. V. I. Lenin, *Collected Works,* XXVI (Moscow: Progress Publishers, 1964), pp. 234–235.

CHAPTER TWO

CIVIL WAR, SOCIALISM, AND NATIONALISM

The period of the Russian Civil War was without doubt foundational for what became the Soviet system. By seizing power, the Bolsheviks helped precipitate war between the supporters of Soviet power and those who opposed either the February or October revolutions. Once the war broke out, those in power in Moscow no longer could contemplate building a social order along the decentralized, democratic lines that many socialists had envisioned in 1917. The exigencies of war, social disintegration, nationalist conflict, and foreign threat pushed the Bolsheviks relentlessly toward greater concentration of power in the center, greater authoritarian direction from above, and a general militarization of the polity and economy. The tendencies in Marxist thought and Leninist practice toward organizing, disciplining, and molding society, even creating a new human nature, reinforced and justified the reliance on state power and the willful intervention of the party into autonomous spheres of peasants' and workers' lives. Socialists in power became more dismissive of the spontaneous, self-generated preferences of their erstwhile constituents and employed the power of the state to lay the groundwork for a modern, industrial, urban society that they believed would lead to human emancipation.

The story of the civil war has often been told from the point of view of warring armies, military victories and defeats, as if superior tactics or supplies won the war. But the years 1918–1921 were a time of social dislocation, famine, and mass death, in which rival political forces competed for the loyalties of the great peasant majority. In some ways the Bolsheviks proved to be more flexible ideologically than their opponents. To survive as rulers of Russia the Bolsheviks rapidly adapted to the needs of the moment. For example, though they were traditionally suspicious of professional, standing armies and preferred popular militias, key leaders quickly adjusted to the necessities of war and agreed to form a professional army.

Along with the new army, the Communist party also underwent significant changes. In his study of the Bolsheviks and the Red Army, Francesco Benvenuti argues that one kind of party was transformed into another. A fissiparous party of free-thinking, cantankerous individuals was molded into a disciplined machine. "The communist," a party document declared late in 1918, "must be a model of discipline, submission, and the ability to execute orders. If your commander gives an order, validated by the commissar, your duty is to submit to it without question, however senseless it may seem to you."[1] As the war progressed, the internal democracy in the party was curtailed. Party organizations remodeled themselves along military lines. Appointment replaced election; orders and reports replaced resolutions. "The party increasingly acquired the characteristics of a state apparatus."[2] Opposition to these changes grew within the party. Many Bolsheviks remained opposed to a regular army and especially against the use of the so-called "military specialists" (tsarist officers). They resisted subordination of party organizations to the military, contended with the "political departments" (*politotdely*) appointed from above, and proposed a return to a more democratic militia-type army. The opposition crystallized at the Eighth Party Congress (March 1919), and Trotsky's supporters were forced, briefly, to compromise. The resolutions promised greater party autonomy and influence, but in fact the military specialists remained powerful, as did the *politotdely*.

Marxist ideology shaped and was shaped by the world in which the Bolsheviks found themselves. At times certain options were precluded by the commitment to socialism, but at other times ideological preferences gave way to more pragmatic requirements, as can be seen in the way the civil war was won. In the historians' debate over whether ideology or social circumstances played the greater role in determining the outcome of the revolution, some analysts have concluded that the two cannot be cleanly, surgically separated. Rather than seeing the degeneration from democratic aspirations of 1917 to the authoritarian party/state of the early 1920s as either the working out of ideology or the product of social determination, ideology is seen as influential, providing a template or frame through which the world is understood, but also as something that either adapts to lived experience or withers away. The activity and thoughts of key people and social groups affect political and social circumstances profoundly, but those people and groups must also work within the constraints of the environment they have been given. Marx's succinct summary of the structure/agent problem still rings clearly:

> People make their own history, but they do not make it just as they please; they do not make it under circumstances chosen by themselves, but under circumstances directly encountered, given, and transmitted from the past. The tradition of all the dead generations weighs like a nightmare on the brain of the living, and just when they seem engaged in revolutionizing themselves and things, in creating something that has never yet existed, precisely in such periods of revolutionary crisis, they anxiously conjure up the spirits of the past to their service and borrow from them names, battle cries and costumes in order to present the new scene of world history in this time-honored disguise and this borrowed language.[3]

But fatefully, sometimes fatally, once certain decisions are made or actions taken, for whatever personal, ideological, or expedient reason, they determine the further development of circumstances. Prior choices affect later choices in what political scien-

---

1. Francesco Benvenuti, *The Bolsheviks and the Red Army, 1918–1922* (Cambridge: Cambridge University Press, 1988), p. 64.

2. Ibid., p. 62.

3. Karl Marx, *The Eighteenth Brumaire of Louis Napoleon*.

tists call "path dependency."Certain options are eliminated; others become more possible, likely, or acceptable. In the new situation, particular aspects of ideology are reinforced, others become irrelevant. In other words, one can follow the post-structuralist insight and conclude that circumstances themselves are constructed by actors, ideas, perceptions, ideologies, and operative discourses. Circumstances never exist completely outside the relevant actors and toss them to and fro like a violent storm. Environments and structures do not determine outcomes in a hard, direct way, but are always mediated by how people understand who and where they are, what they want to be and where they want to go, by their idea of the good and how much effort and pain are worth expending to achieve it.

Peter Holquist raises the discussion of ideas and ideology to a new level. Rather than focus on Marxism or Leninism, he places Bolshevism within the wider context of modernity and proposes that practices of surveillance were related not to anything specifically Russian but to a post-Enlightenment approach to the disciplining of society. His attack on Russian exceptionalism forces us to rethink the relationship of the Soviet project of modernization to developmentalist projects of other European states, both on the continent and in the colonies.

"INFORMATION IS THE ALPHA AND OMEGA OF OUR WORK": BOLSHEVIK SURVEILLANCE IN ITS PAN-EUROPEAN CONTEXT

Peter Holquist

Information is the alpha and omega of our work.
Our work should concentrate on the information apparatus, for only when the Cheka is sufficiently informed and has precise data elucidating organizations and their individual members will it be able . . . to take timely and necessary measures for liquidating groups as well as the individual who is harmful and dangerous.
—CHEKA CIRCULARS, 1920–21

With the opening of the Russian archives, scholars finally have open access (more or less) to materials generated by the Soviet regime. One particular kind of document has sparked interest more than any other: reports by surveillance organs in the form of summaries of popular moods, excerpts made from intercepted letters, and accounts of overheard conversations. The reasons for such interest are not far to seek. These reports promise answers to a question scholars in this field had been asking for several decades: What did people really think about the Soviet order? (While I cannot examine the question itself here, it should be noted that this problematic operates with assumptions drawn from our own society, assumptions that may not have been operative in Soviet Russia.). . . .

In addition to providing raw data on people's moods, then, these eagerly sought-after surveillance materials should cause us to ponder what kind of system would produce information in such amounts and in this manner. A reevaluation of this type requires comparative study, if only to avoid considering what may be general, pan-European features as something specific either to Russia or to its incarnation of socialism (both of which have been invoked to account for Soviet Russia's "exceptionalism" or sui generis nature).

This article seeks, first, to describe the underlying ethos that motivated the Soviet state to engage in surveillance, that practice responsible for generating the materials which now so interest historians, and, second, to situate surveillance within its broader, pan-European context. It contends that the desire to generate such material is in fact of far greater significance than the material itself. For, as Robert Gellately has shown for Nazi Germany, a regime that is deeply concerned about what the population thinks and feels does not necessarily seek or even require the support of all or most of its citizens. For Nazi Germany, and no doubt for Stalinist Russia as well, "the crucial factor was not the 'popularity' of the system." And "popularity" and "public opinion" (or, rather, these terms as they are understood in late twentieth-century America) were certainly not the primary factors motivating surveillance. The Soviet and Nazi regimes did not collect such information to determine which policy to pursue in conformity with public opinion or to win support. The attitudes described in surveillance reports did not operate within systems that recognized popular support or public opinion (again, as we understand the terms today). These systems were concerned instead with sculpting and "gardening" (to use Zygmunt Bauman's evocative term) a better, purer society while simultaneously molding society's human material into a more emancipated, conscious, and superior individual—the "new man." Surveillance, then, was not designed to uncover popular sentiments and moods, nor was it intended merely to keep people under control; its whole purpose was to act on people, to change them. So the surveillance project encompasses both the attempt to gather information on popular moods and the measures intended to transform them.

Surveillance may be best understood, then, not as a Russian phenomenon but as a subfunction of the modern form of politics, of which totalitarianism is one expression. From this perspective, Bolshevism can indeed be seen as distinct. But this distinctiveness was historically conditioned within its particular European context. So, while Bolshevism was a specific type of civilization, it was hardly unique or sui generis.

The Don territory (a province in southern Russia) in the period of the Russian Revolution and Civil War provides an ideal locus for a study of surveillance as a political practice, for it permits comparative analysis. (By "political practices" I mean the repertoire of measures a state employs to realize the goals it has set for itself.) The Don territory did not merely pass under intermittent Red and White military control but alternated for long periods under the civil control of each side. In addition, all sides left behind an extensive and diverse source base documenting their activities. This is important, for analyses of the Soviet experience have often argued for the absolute primacy of "ideology." Yet few studies have sought, in any rigorous way, to identify what was specific to Bolshevism. Often it is a case of "what the Bolsheviks did was Bolshevik because it was the Bolsheviks who did it"—that is, a tautology. Bolshevism's specificity is often asserted but seldom demonstrated. One gets a very different view by examining how some Soviet practices elaborated on actions of the tsarist regime (particularly in its total war manifestation) and paralleled similar measures by contemporaneous anti-Soviet movements.

What is surveillance? As used here, surveillance refers to information gathering and handling of a particular type: that which observes the population's attitudes, in aggregate, for political purposes (politics being understood as the endeavor intended par excellence to transform the world). That is, surveillance is the collection of information for the purpose not of reporting the population's collective mood but of managing and shaping it. As such, surveillance must be seen as part and parcel of a larger shift in the goal of ruling, a shift from a territorial concept to a governmental one. A governmental state seeks to manage populations, not just to rule territories. Of course, the people who made up "the population" had always existed, but they had not always been conceptualized as a discrete, aggregate object. A governmental state seeks to manage its population not so much legitimately or righteously as effectively and economically. Once the Russian political elite began to conceptualize the body politic in terms of a "population" (instead of, say, a divinely established order of estates), its duty became serving the aspirations and needs of this new focus of legitimacy. In the process of investigating these needs through varied mechanisms (censuses, agricultural studies, statistics), the political elite summoned "the population" (as a discrete entity) into being.

In Russia, the Revolution brought into sharp focus this shift from an administrative, territorial state to a governmental one. Nicholas II had been emperor of "all the Russias, Tsar of Poland, Grand Duke of Finland, etc., etc., etc." He ruled territorial entities rather than a collectivity of citizens. After 1917 all political movements (the Provisional Government, the Constituent Assembly, the Soviet Council of People's Commissars, and nearly all anti-Soviet movements in the Civil War) claimed to represent not a territory, but the people living within it. And to engage the population most productively, states required a new discipline of popular attitudes: surveillance.

It is important to note that the concept of surveillance is not something thought up, after the fact, by historians. Contemporaries, by the terms they used, distinguished policing (reporting on delinquents, malcontents, and even revolutionaries as individuals in order to protect an established order) from surveillance (reporting on the whole population to amass aggregate rather than individual data on attitudes in order better to act upon society). Policing was concerned with maintaining public order: its goal was to protect people from exposure to contaminants, be they heresies, books, or ideas. While it continued to have a policing function, surveillance went far beyond this purely negative agenda. The governmental ideal was for the state, armed with the proper information and employing it correctly, to transform both society and individual citizens for the better. Where policing sought to order society, surveillance, as part of the governmental project, sought to transform it.

The state went about collecting the knowledge it required to meet this newly conceived task through two primary mechanisms. First, it constructed surveillance bureaucracies to conduct regularized reporting on the population's attitudes. And second, the state engaged in the routine perlustration of correspondence (perlustration being the interception and reading of mail for the express purpose of discovering what people were writing and thinking—in contrast to censorship, which has as its goal the control of content). The creation of organs for the express purpose of quantifying and analyzing the population's attitudes (be they progovernment, antigovernment, or indifferent) was a qualitatively new endeavor. Indeed, categories such as "popular support" and especially "apathy" simply were not part of the mental universe of tsarist bureaucrats (at least until early in the twentieth century). Subjects were either obedient or not. The administrative goal was compliance rather than belief. In sharp contrast to this, Soviet officials expressed a burning interest not so much in people's behavior as in what they thought and believed. . . .

I.   SURVEILLANCE IN 1913 AND IN 1920

To demonstrate the explosive emergence of surveillance as a practice of governing, one can simply compare how it was practiced at two points in time, first under the Imperial and then under the Soviet regime. In 1913 the tsarist regime most definitely engaged in perlustration, practiced in so-called Black Offices. However, the autocracy limited the opening and perusing of mail to the correspondence of suspected revolutionaries and opponents of the regime (plus, of course, diplomatic correspondence). That is, the autocracy practiced perlustration for purposes of policing and intelligence. The number of surveillance technocrats serving in such Black Offices throughout the entire Empire came to a grand total of forty-nine people.

Seven years later, in 1920, we find a very different type of surveillance being practiced. The Soviet regime was intercepting and reading not just the letters of individual suspects but nearly all correspondence passing through the post. The goal of this massive effort was not simply to destroy those letters reflecting poorly on the regime or even to identify dissidents: it was in addition to compile "summary reports" complete with extensive excerpts from representative letters. To this end, the Soviet regime, in the midst of a civil war contesting its very existence, was employing somewhere in the neighborhood of ten thousand officials—ten thousand trusted and trained officials—for opening and analyzing citizens' mail. And when the Civil War ended in 1921, responsibility for perlustration passed from military postal boards to Cheka and OGPU information departments. Throughout the 1920s the regime continued to scrutinize letters passing through the mail, making ever more extensive extracts and ever more detailed summaries.

We see an identical picture regarding surveillance bureaucracies. In Imperial Russia, governors' reports and secret police reports intermittently touched on the population's general moods. But the Imperial administration evinced little interest in what the population thought, so long as it did not support the revolutionary movement. Needless to say, the tsarist autocracy did not feel it necessary to have anything akin to the Soviet state's OGPU information subsections (in the 1920s) or the NKVD secret political departments (in the 1930s), whose primary purpose was to compile regular reviews of the population's political sentiments.

The Soviet regime's desire for information was so voracious and all-encompassing that it came to establish "information networks" (*osvedomitel'naia set'*) to keep track of shifting moods even among inhabitants of the GULAG and POW camps. The extent of these networks is truly stunning. According to one report, by 1944 the information network in the GULAG camp system came to encompass nearly 8 percent of the total detained population. According to another report, every third German being held in the postwar POW camps contributed at some point to the information network. In this case, "information" was obviously not needed to identify potential enemies (these populations had already been deemed hostile) or even to forestall their actions (they were already under detention). These figures testify instead to the regime's intense desire to have all-encompassing (one is tempted to say total) information on "political moods"—not in order to control people or to protect itself, but to put it to use in refashioning even these detained—but still redeemable—people.

Moreover, the regime valued equally information about those determined to be incorrigible. The Soviets massacred the Polish detainees at Katyn in 1940, but they retained the judicial proceedings and other material on these people until 1959. Likewise, when the Soviets retreated before the German Army in 1941, they deliberately removed many files on the people they were holding. Many of the prisoners whom the files documented they simply shot. One cannot escape the conclusion that the information about these people was more important to the regime than the people themselves. And here again this information had no prophylactic use whatsoever, as the people who were documented were already dead. For the Soviet state, then, surveillance and information-gathering cannot have been primarily a defensive endeavor.

In any case, figures such as forty-nine bureaucrats occupied with opening citizens' mail in 1913 versus ten thousand of them in 1920 would seem to suggest a convenient and simple explanation: that it is Bolshevism (however one may define it) that accounts for the institutionalization of surveillance. Indeed, scholars have frequently invoked surveillance as the classic manifestation of totalitarianism and a marker of Bolshevik Russia's uniqueness.

This view of Russia's exceptionalism is in fact quite widespread, although there exist many different explanations for it. Most frequently this exceptionalism has been traced to purported anomalies in certain areas of Russia's development, be they economic, social, political, or cultural. Recently, an emergent orthodoxy has argued that socialism, not Russia, made the Soviet experience unique. Yet it makes little difference here whether scholars find the origins of Bolshevik specificity in Russia's backwardness or in its socialism. Depending on the scholar, surveillance testifies either to how a hopelessly decrepit autocratic political order perverted technology to retain its control over society (the Russian *Sonderweg* argument), or to surveillance as the inevitable product of the modern if surreal project of realizing socialism in practice (the Marxist *Sonderweg* thesis). Whether it involves some form of backwardness or its unique attempt to implement socialism, Soviet Russia is portrayed as exceptional. And surveillance testifies to the exceptional nature of this Bolshevik—or, at the very most, totalitarian—system.

II.   SURVEILLANCE IN 1915 AND IN 1920

A very different picture emerges, however, merely by selecting different years for comparison. Instead of contrasting the Imperial regime of 1913 and its Soviet successor, it is instructive to compare Soviet Russia with the Imperial order in its total war configuration. Surveillance aspirations did not begin with socialism, nor did they emerge only during the war period. In the years preceding the outbreak of the First World War, both the Imperial regime and zemstvo society had begun their own halting steps in the direction of governmental surveillance. The autocracy moved from concern only about court opinion and the revolutionary movement and increasingly sought to probe the "mood" of zemstvo and industrial circles through a network of secret reporting. Yet the tsarist state held no monopoly on such aspirations. Zemstvos in the Ufa region, for instance, took up a project on the eve of the war to establish an entire network of "reading huts" (*izba-chital' nia*) at the village level—all, of course, in order to transform benighted peasants into enlightened citizens.

So prior to 1914 Russian officials had certainly conceived of surveillance as a project, and they had even taken some tentative steps to realize their aspirations. However, it was during the First World War that these embryonic plans for social management were massively translated into practice. Thirteen months into a war that was rapidly becoming total, the Imperial administration reevaluated its conduct of the war and came to the conclusion that it could no longer rely only on commands but must instead seek to harness the country's "vital forces." Accordingly, in October 1915 the Russian interior minister ordered provincial and district officials to compile regular monthly reports on the population's "moods" and issued a standardized set of questions to be addressed ("attitude of workers and peasants to the war and any changes in their mood"; "mood of zemstvo personnel and officials"; "mood of pedagogic personnel and students"; and so on). Due to the different nature of their previous institutional culture, local officials proved to be ill prepared for such concerns. Officials somewhat laconically noted that "the mood is satisfactory" and thereafter merely submitted updates noting that "no changes have occurred" month after month, right up to the February 1917 Revolution. But the bureaucracy's unfamiliarity with its new task should not cause us to overlook a significant shift: the government was now concerned with the collection of such information and was pursuing institutional measures to secure it. . . .

But it was in the Russian Army that the practice of surveillance was most advanced. By 1915, the army began compiling its own "summaries on the mood" (*svodki o nastroenii*) of soldiers in the ranks as well as among the population in general. But its main source of information on popular moods came from the military postal censorship departments (*voenno-tsenzurnye otdeleniia*). At the beginning of the First World War, the army established postal censorship departments to open all mail passing through the post. This was a major task. A single field postal censorship office in one army corps opened, read, and analyzed over thirteen thousand letters in the course of two weeks. Postal censorship boards opened, read, and evaluated fifty thousand letters per day from Russian POWs alone (and this figure does not even cover the regular internal post). To meet demand, authorities pressed postal employees and interior ministry officials into service as censors. Things got so desperate that, after more than two years of war, the authorities finally relented and in April 1916 permitted women to perform this sensitive duty.

The task of these organs was not to control content but to describe and, insofar as possible, explain people's attitudes. On the basis of literally tens of thousands of perused letters, officials in every army formation and each military district throughout the Russian Empire compiled "summaries" (using mimeographed forms) and categorized (in statistical percentages) all correspondence as "patriotic," "depressed," and "indifferent." One such summary from 1916, with comic precision, recorded 30.25 percent of all letters "patriotic," 2.15 percent "depressed," and 67.6 percent "indifferent." And, like their associates in Britain, authorities in Russia sought not only to record but also to shape soldier-correspondents' means of self-expression—and indeed their identities—through standardized form letters and postcards. . . .

Tellingly, postal censorship departments were not abolished with the February 1917 Revolution but continued their activity throughout 1917 under the Provisional Government. They were abolished only with the Soviet Revolution in October 1917. Yet the Soviets found they could not do without the information generated by postal censorship organs, and in 1918 they reintroduced these organs in the Red Army. This is not to say that there were not important differences. The Soviet regime, with its larger definition of the political sphere, was concerned with a much broader spectrum of issues than the tsarist regime had been. But the task and structure of the Soviet organs did not fundamentally differ from that of their prerevolutionary predecessors. Again, the purpose was less to forestall unrest than to measure opinion so as to act on it. Soviet military censors copied out excerpts from all letters indicating in any way—positive, negative, or apathetic—the author's political attitudes. These excerpts were then codified and served as the source for regular bimonthly thematic and regional reports. There were desertion summaries, supply summaries, summaries on abuse of office—but the most prevalent was the political summary.

It is not difficult to demonstrate the Soviet concern for surveillance. It became suffused throughout virtually the entire Soviet apparatus. In the course of the Civil War, every major Soviet institution—the army, the Party, the Soviet civil apparatus, the Cheka—generated "summaries on the population's mood" (*svodki o nastroenii naseleniia*). The Cheka not only demanded regular summaries; it also circulated critiques of incomplete or unsatisfactory reports, indicating the specific error and what was expected in the future. In particular, the Cheka sternly admonished its officials that it was not enough merely to describe attitudes; they should also "indicate what *explains*" these attitudes. Similarly, the postal censorship departments not only issued "summaries" but also invariably included interpretative analyses of their contents in an accompanying cover letter. These ubiquitous "summaries on the population's mood" and the standardized categories drawn up to typify those moods (categories which historians now employ so casually) became a virtual genre in Soviet administrative literature and represent the classic artifacts of surveillance.

Yet this "Soviet" practice merely extended aspirations that had been prevalent during the First World War and that had already been institutionalized in state structures. The practices of the autocracy's total war regime thus stood not so much in stark contrast to Soviet ones, but rather at midpoint along a continuum between the prewar Imperial administrative order and the Soviet governmental state. Hence comparisons of Soviet surveillance practices with those of the tsarist secret police (particularly its Black Offices), while fashionable, are misguided. In terms of purview, extent, and even genealogy, Soviet surveillance should be set against the practices of World War I. Indeed, throughout the 1920s, the Soviets themselves recognized the First World War as the relevant context for discussing their elaboration of techniques in political work and economic planning.

III.   RED SURVEILLANCE, WHITE SURVEILLANCE

. . . If surveillance was somehow intrinsically Bolshevik (even if one admits that its origins lay earlier), one would expect that Bolshevism's opponents would not have resorted to it, or at least would not have employed it as extensively.

Here one is confronted with a major surprise, however. Recalling Stalin's explicit claim that the Bolsheviks aspired to be engineers of the human soul, scholars are prepared for the fact that the Soviet regime would seek knowledge of people's inner lives. Yet how is one to explain entire caches of reports on the populace's moods generated by surveillance bureaucracies of the anti-Soviet movements?

It could be argued that the Whites merely sought to counter Soviet surveillance activities. Certainly this was a consideration. But White movements embarked on surveillance projects of their own even before the Soviets got their apparatus up and running. In the Don territory, for instance, even localized anti-Soviet insurgencies felt it necessary to form their own surveillance organs. And the Whites evinced an identical concern for knowing about and fostering the population's consciousness (not "public opinion" or "popular support"). This was the goal, after all: one couldn't act on people's consciousness (however that consciousness might be defined) unless one had first determined at what level it already stood. All political movements had passed through the experience of the First World War and all had emerged from it thinking of surveillance as indispensible to governing. For while the various movements in the Civil War all appealed to different constituencies and sought to realize different views of the world, they all operated within the governmental paradigm. That is, they all practiced a form of politics predicated on the social theory of representation and deriving legitimacy from the idea of popular sovereignty. And while they differed significantly over the precise form the world should take, they all viewed politics as a tool for both sculpting society and operating on populations to realize this blueprint.

For the anti-Soviet movements surveillance was just as routinized and well-established as it was for the Bolsheviks. Among the very first acts of the anti-Soviet Don government was to establish a "Don Information Agency" (what I shall only half-facetiously term the DIA). In informing the population about the new agency, the authorities described its task as twofold. First, it was to inform the population "about the military and political situation and also about the government's activity"; and second, it was to inform the government about "life, events and sentiments in the territory." This agency came to encompass a network of roughly two hundred sub-centers, sixty centers, and nine district departments, in addition to the central administration. The DIA's network for a single province was thus comparable in numbers and extent to what the tsarist secret police had had for the entire Empire. And this was so not because the Whites had more resources to commit than the tsarist regime, but because the White surveillance organs served a fundamentally different purpose than the tsarist security divisions.

"Information"—the coin of the new political realm—was meant to circulate in two directions: from the authorities to the population, and from (or rather about) the population to the authorities. The first task, informing the population, was meant to engage citizens and, ultimately, to aid in transforming them. To this end, the DIA published several of its own newspapers, controlled the content of all other press reporting, and established a network of information subcenters throughout the region. Most intriguing, however, was another tool for keeping the population abreast of the government's activity: the reading hut (*izba-chital' nia*), a humble cabin in some small, out-of-the-way community equipped with newspapers and political pamphlets. This intended redoubt of political knowledge in the benighted countryside has hitherto been identified only with the Bolsheviks. As we have seen, however, zemstvo activists before the First World War and Whites in the course of the Civil War also established information networks for enlightening the population. And, very significantly, both Reds and Whites described their task not as "propaganda" but as "enlightenment." The propaganda state—or more accurately, the Enlightenment state—was not solely a Bolshevik ideal.

But information was equally meant to flow in the other direction, informing the government of the population's "mood." For this task, the DIA established an entire network of secret informers and set up special courses to train them. These agents then traveled undercover throughout the Don territory in the guise of actors,

refugees, students, railway workers, teachers, and even obstetricians. It was from the
regular reports of these agents and employees working in its subcenters that the central administration compiled its own daily summaries. These summaries were organized topically, with each topic assigned a letter. It is no coincidence that the first letter of the alphabet was reserved for reports "on the population's mood."

Nor did the Whites share only the practice of surveillance. White surveillance
technocrats also shared a concern about people's "consciousness" (a condition that officials in the late tsarist period had increasingly also sought to foster). Thus the project of transforming ignorant subjects into emancipated and enlightened citizens derived not from socialism alone, but also from a much larger tectonic shift in the nature
of politics (from territorial to governmental), of which socialism was merely the most
successful and forceful representative.

The White surveillance project, like its Red counterpart, was concerned at least
as much with thought as with action. For instance, a White report on one recently
liberated region reads, "Most of the rural population quite sincerely submit to the
lawful Russian authority, but remain primarily in a state of obedience and sympathy.
The broad masses in the village welcomed [our] units, since with their arrival they
were delivered from the Bolsheviks' arbitrary rule and violence . . . but now they
relate to their liberators entirely passively. . . . One often hears in conversations
among peasants: 'your guys [vashi] did so and so, and the Bolsheviks did such and such.'
They don't say 'our guys [nashi].'" What this official bemoans is precisely the attitude
earlier tsarist officials would have desired most: obedient, sympathetic submission. But
the concern now is with people's beliefs, not just with how they behave. . . .

And people could not avoid knowing that the authorities had a newfound interest in what they thought, felt, and said. Not all welcomed the incessant gaze of this
new mechanism of governing. One DIA report noted that in Chernyshevskaia stanitsa "the entire population has been mobilized"; that the "mood is firm"; that "relations between Cossacks and outlanders are strained"; and, inter alia, that "the attitude
of both the stanitsa ataman and the stanitsa members to the formation of an information office is negative." Many became increasingly reticent to express their opinions. The DIA (as would later the OGPU-NKVD) of course found significance even
in people's reluctance to express themselves, and therefore duly reported that the population "fears to express its views openly"; "engages in political discussions only very
reluctantly"; "expresses itself very reservedly, unwillingly, cautiously." Such reports do
not mean that people had ceased to talk about politics, only that they now had to
temper their expressions with the knowledge that the authorities—Red and White—
were listening.

Although White and Red shared some common practices, there were also significant differences. Without doubt, the Soviets had a much broader definition of
the political sphere, and their surveillance endeavor was correspondingly more all-
encompassing. However, the aspirations for surveillance and the concrete institutionalization of this desire cannot be chalked up to Bolshevism alone. Bolshevism was
more important in determining the ends to which surveillance would be used. . . .

V. SURVEILLANCE AND THE NATIONAL SECURITY STATE

Thus surveillance was hardly unique to Russia or to its socialist revolution. Denounced as one of the most pernicious manifestations of a totalitarian mindset, sur-

veillance is not a specifically Bolshevik, Marxist, or even totalitarian practice—it is a modern one. By the comparisons I have chosen, I obviously see the First World War as a major watershed in the methods states used to govern their populations.

In addition to the introduction of mass, industrial killing, the Great War also saw the institutionalization of a particular type of modern governmental politics in the form of the national security state. While this governmental concept certainly did not originate at the beginning of the twentieth century, the period of the First World War and its aftermath permitted its implementation, both on a large scale and in state form. These aspirations to manage society, and the practices to implement them, were most certainly not simply a response to wartime exigencies, summoned forth by the exceptional circumstances of war. But, significantly, war was the context within which states massively implemented these practices. For the first time, populations unavoidably experienced the political consequences of this governmental style of ruling in its statist manifestation, in actual policies and concrete institutions, day in and day out. Populations, however they felt about it, simply could not avoid the state's new pretensions. States imposed themselves in ever newer spheres and on ever greater numbers of people through their aspirations to organize large sectors of the economy and society (whether this be called *Kriegswirtschaft*, War Communism, or "Defense of the Realm Act" [DORA]); through their universal tendency to deploy the population itself as a resource (reflected in the use of terms such as *Menschenmaterial*, the Russian "human power" (*liudskaia sila*), or the British government's concept of an "economy of manpower"); and, most tellingly, through various states' attempts to engage the population not just as an object but also as a subject in its own right by managing a newly conceived resource—the national will or psyche, as quantified and described through a new endeavor, surveillance.

Nor did these measures pass into history with the end of the war. Surveillance was by no means geographically limited to Russia and its revolution nor chronologically circumscribed by the Great War. National security states that emerged to manage the practices of total war did not pass from war to peace, but from war to preparation for future wars. National security states throughout Europe found the measures implemented during war to be equally useful in managing their populations in peace . . .

Throughout Europe, as Michael Geyer has noted, the "encompassing and comprehensive mobilization of the nation for war was a common feature of all the major belligerents in World War One. . . . All the nations resorted to a tangled web of compulsion and suasion, developed national forms of management." The First World War was the matrix within which states nurtured their own particular aspirations and developed the mechanisms to realize them. And Geyer's observations on Europe in general apply fully to Russia. In Russia's case, however, the 1917 Revolution has obstructed our view of the changes that took place in the course of the war. Indeed, if the Russian Civil War is seen as an extension of Europe's general 1914–18 deluge, the Russian Revolution, far from ending the war in 1918 at Brest-Litovsk, might instead be seen as having extended Russia's own deluge experience until 1921, three years longer than for the rest of Europe. That extension is significant because it provided a rationale for the continued existence of a wartime national security (total war) regime that carried Russia through the Revolution: Russia now had a different ex post facto explanation for the changes it had undergone along with other European societies. That is, the 1917 Revolution suggested that Russia's national security style of state modernization—a style of modernization common to many other European powers—originated not in the shared experience of the Great War but in the unique experience of Russia's Revolution. In discussing the changed world, Europe and Russia now had different short answers to describe the deluges they had undergone. Europe ascribed the changed world to the Great War; Russia, to its Revolution.

What then of ideology? Was Bolshevik Russia like every other European state in the post-1918 period? Clearly it was not. And the difference between Russia's and Europe's political and institutional development was not just a matter of the rhetorical explanation attached to some generic form of modernization. Russia's institutionalization of modernity, in its statist form, was conceptually telescoped into the Revolution—and the Revolution (in its Bolshevik configuration, of course) then came to shape the conceptual ends to which these practices were directed. Instead of operating on nation-states (both its own and others) and seeking national security, the Soviet Union employed these common tools on classes (outside but especially within its own borders) in an attempt to bring about socialism. "The Revolution" simultaneously became the matrix for the development of, as well as the explanation for, all the novel features that had arisen in the 1914–21 period. Hence it is not just historians who came to treat reading huts and reportage on moods as products of the Revolution; contemporaries too identified such developments as "revolutionary."

But a comparative study of state practices demonstrates that what is specific to Bolshevism is not that which is frequently claimed for it: the use of particular practices, as in the Friedrich-Brzezinski model of totalitarianism, for instance. Rather, Bolshevism was distinct in how and to what ends it used these practices. For example, the Soviets' broader definition of the political sphere—a definition that ultimately encompassed virtually all others—led to a much broader spectrum of surveillance interests than that of the Whites (or of their French, German, and English counterparts, for that matter).

If the Bolsheviks shared a common governmental sensibility that the state could shape the world and defined revolutionary politics as the tool par excellence for this project, Marxism as ideology furnished the specific articulation of that world. It established a particular moral urgency for changing it. More concretely, Marxism provided the precise goals of political action and described both who the beneficiaries and who the targets of state activity were to be. And, perhaps of particular significance, it delineated a time frame for its proclaimed goal, the creation of a socialist society and the making of a new man (and this was a highly gendered model). What particularly distinguished the Soviet project was its use of a common repertoire of practices in its endeavor to perfect citizens in a fundamental manner and within a specified time span. That is, Bolshevism had a closed, rather than open, model of historical progress.

And this Marxist outlook influenced how the Bolsheviks deployed practices of governing. In the area of food supply, for instance, both the Red and White camps sought to manage the economy and rationalize the market through planning and control (just as the Russian Empire and other European powers had done during World War I). The Bolshevik regime's specificity lay not in its pretension to manage the economy (an aspiration it shared with many others), but in how it sought to do so. For, unlike other states, the object of Soviet practices in food supply was not so much to manage the actual shortfall itself as to deal with the individual who had failed to meet his assignment. Given the belief that people who so desired could, as Stalin later put it, "storm any fortress," failure necessarily testified to one's unwillingness rather than to one's inability to do so. A greater sense of human agency brought with it greater (and often nearly unrealizable) responsibilities. In the regime's eyes, any shortfall testified not to a shortage of grain but to a shortage of will: it presumed recalcitrant farmers were choosing not to turn over their grain, not that the grain was simply not there. Hence, during the 1920–21 food supply campaign the Soviet state simply refused to accept drought as a legitimate cause for a farmer's inability to hand over grain to the state, hauling such people before revolutionary tribunals and often shooting them for this "crime." Attempting to manage the economy and market was common at the time; to do so in this way was not. So the Soviet system was not distinct because of its practices, its technical tools, or even its aspirations. It was distinct because of the particular configuration those aspirations took: to move society toward socialism while seeking simultaneously to mold humanity, both as a collective and as individuals. Surveillance then was only part of the larger project to build communism and the new man simultaneously.

. . . The collection of information was not an end in itself: surveillance was not primarily intended to reflect public opinion, nor was it meant merely for the preventive, protective task of forestalling any possible opposition (although it was most certainly put to that use, too). Surveillance was an instrumental endeavor, aimed at reshaping society and transforming every individual in it. And it was only as part of this larger project of transforming each and every individual that surveillance was used to recognize the recalcitrant (so they could be singled out for special attention) and, later, to identify those impervious to improvement (so they could be eliminated and no longer pollute the body politic). Thus, using surveillance materials only for data on popular moods (significantly, the documents themselves do not describe their general object of inquiry as either "opinion" or "support") neglects the purposes for which this information was collected and the context in which it was generated. This is not a minor or semantic distinction. Soviet citizens knew surveillance was instrumental. They knew (though how extensively most could not guess) that, through surveillance, the state was not only reporting what they said and wrote but also seeking to use this information to change and correct them and their views. Surveillance was not a passive, observational endeavor; it was an active, constructivist one.

But this article has also sought to show that such measures, and the projects they served, cannot be treated as an anomaly unique to Russia, or even to totalitarian regimes in general. For better or for worse, scholars are simply not confronted with good states that refrained from using surveillance versus bad states that resorted to it. Throughout the interwar period all states employed surveillance. We confront instead differences—crucial differences—in how and to what ends all regimes practiced surveillance. And these differences in practice were profound, both for the historian and even more for the citizens who were subject to them. There was a vast difference between being under surveillance by British Mass Observation or by the NKVD's secret political departments. But to determine how different it was, and in what ways, one must situate the Bolshevik surveillance project both in the current of Russian history and within its more general pan-European context. . . .

In Soviet Russia we see neither some unique socialist case nor a Russian exception to European norms, but instead a highly specific manifestation of a new governmental modality of politics. This article has emphasized the significance of the First World War, which provided the context within which many of these features took on their particular forms. What set the Soviet regime apart was not "ideology" in a general sense, nor some totalitarian essence, but the intersection of a particular ideology with the simultaneous implementation of a particularly modern understanding of politics—put succinctly, an understanding that views populations as both the means and the goal of some emancipatory project. This vantage point can serve to shift the focus of debate away from all-or-nothing propositions about totalitarian regimes to a study of how states might (or might not) employ certain practices in a totalitarian manner. The task, then, is not to seek reasons to dismiss Russia as anomalous but to identify what was specific about Russia's particular constellation of more general European features. The Soviet experience cannot be limited either to a case of Russian backwardness or to some surreal attempt to build socialism in practice. Insofar as Soviet Russia represents a problem, it is a problem of the modern project itself.

Peter Holquist, "'Information Is the Alpha and Omega of Our Work': Bolshevik Surveillance in Its Pan-European Context," *The Journal of Modern History*, LXIX, 3 (September 1997), pp. 415–450.

First Decrees of the New Soviet Government

Lenin and the Bolsheviks came to power with little initial resistance and immediately embarked on a radical program of political transformation. Their first decree called for an end to the world war and denounced the agreements to divide and share the spoils among the "imperialist" powers. The Soviets antagonized Russia's former allies by publishing the secret agreements that the tsarist and provisional governments had signed with the West. They followed with a decree seizing the land of the landlords and turning it over to the use of the peasants. This idea was essentially borrowed from the land program of the peasantist Socialist Revolutionary party, which had delayed implementing it while tied to the more moderate policies of the Provisional Government. As a result of the general breakdown of order in the country and the new permissiveness approved by the Soviet government, peasants rapidly appropriated noble lands, abolished private property in the countryside, and redistributed the land among themselves. In a few months, Russia's peasants themselves had carried out one of the most extensive land reforms in history.

Fearing a counter-revolutionary offensive from their opponents, the Bolsheviks suppressed newspapers, arrested liberal politicians, and created a political police, the Extraordinary Commission to Suppress Counter-Revolution (Cheka). Yet in his first six months in power, Lenin's objective "was emphatically not the capture and consolidation of state power but rather the dissolution of the state itself."[1] His unrealized hope was that ordinary workers and peasants would substitute themselves for the repressive apparatus of the old order. The revolution was supposed to be about emancipation, equality, and freedom. "You are the power," he told the workers, "do all you want to do, but take care of production, see that production is useful. Take up useful work, you will make mistakes but you will learn."[2] But as Neil Harding notes, "His advent to power swiftly disabused him of the utopian vision of an immediate transition to popular participation in and control over what he discovered to be exceedingly complex structures."[3] By April 1918, he was clearly replacing the idea of a "commune state" run by working people with a concept of a "dictatorship of the proletariat," reviving another strain of Marxism that would prove to be have a much longer and darker tenure.

1. Neil Harding, *Lenin's Political Thought. Vol. 2. Theory and Practice in the Socialist Revolution* (New York: St. Martin's Press, 1981), p. 178.
2. V. I. Lenin, *Collected Works*, vol. XXVI (Moscow, 1960–1970), p. 468.
3. Harding, *Lenin's Political Thought*, vol. 2, p. 126.

LENIN'S DECREE ON PEACE,
OCTOBER 26 [NOVEMBER 9], 1917

The workers' and peasants' government created by the revolution of October 24–25 and relying on the Soviets of Workers', Soldiers', and Peasants' Deputies calls upon all the belligerent peoples and their governments to start immediate negotiations for a just, democratic peace. By a just or democratic peace, for which the overwhelming majority of the working and toiling classes of all the belligerent countries, exhausted, tormented and racked by the war, are craving—a peace that has been most definitely and insistently demanded by the Russian workers and peasants ever since the overthrow of the tsarist monarchy—by such a peace the government means an immediate peace without annexations (i.e., without the seizure of foreign lands, without the forcible incorporation of foreign nations) and without indemnities.

This is the kind of peace the government of Russia proposes to all the belligerent nations to conclude immediately, and expresses its readiness to take all the resolute measures immediately, without the least delay, pending the final ratification of all the terms of such a peace by authoritative assemblies of the people's representatives of all countries and all nations. In accordance with the sense of justice of the democracy in general, and of the toiling classes in particular, the government conceives the annexation or seizure of foreign lands to mean every incorporation into a large or powerful state of a small or weak nation without the precisely, clearly and voluntarily expressed consent and wish of that nation, irrespective of the time when such forcible incorporation took place, irrespective also of the degree of development or backwardness of the nation forcibly annexed to, or forcibly retained within, the borders of the given state, and irrespective, finally, of whether this nation resides in Europe or in distant, overseas countries.

If any nation whatsoever is forcibly retained within the borders of a given state, if, in spite of its expressed desire—no matter whether expressed in the press, at public meetings, in the decisions of parties, or in protests and uprisings against national oppression—it is not accorded the right to decide the forms of its state existence by a free vote, taken after the complete evacuation of the troops of the incorporating or, generally, of the stronger nation and without the least pressure being brought to bear, such incorporation is annexation, i.e., seizure and violence. The government considers it the greatest of crimes against humanity to continue this war over the issue of how to divide among the strong and rich nations the weak nationalities they have conquered, and solemnly announces its determination immediately to sign terms of peace to stop this war on the conditions indicated, which are equally just for all nationalities without exception. At the same time the government declares that it does not regard the above-mentioned terms of peace as an ultimatum; in other words, it is prepared to consider any other terms of peace, but only insists that they be advanced by any of the belligerent nations as speedily as possible, and that in the proposals of peace there should be absolute clarity and the complete absence of all ambiguity and secrecy.

The government abolishes secret diplomacy, and, for its part, announces its firm intention to conduct all negotiations quite openly under the eyes of the whole people. It will immediately proceed to the full publication of the secret treaties endorsed or concluded by the government of landlords and capitalists from February to October, 25, 1917. The government proclaims the absolute and immediate annulment of everything contained in these secret treaties in so far as it is aimed, as is mostly the case, at securing advantages and privileges for the Russian landlords and capitalists and at the retention, or extension, of the annexations made by the Great Russians. . . . In proposing an immediate armistice, we appeal to the class-conscious workers of the countries that have done so much for the development of the proletarian movement. We appeal to the workers of England, where there was the Chartist movement, to the workers of France, who have in repeated uprisings displayed the strength of their class consciousness, and to the workers of Germany, who waged the fight against the Anti-Socialist Law and have created powerful organizations.

In the manifesto of March 14, we called for the overthrow of the bankers, but, far from overthrowing our own bankers, we entered into an alliance with them. Now we have overthrown the government of the bankers.

That government and the bourgeoisie will make every effort to unite their forces and drown the workers' and peasants' revolution in blood. But the three years of war have been a good lesson to the masses: the Soviet movement in other countries and the mutiny in the German navy, which was crushed by the Junkers of Wilhelm the hangman. Finally, we must remember that we are not living in the wilds of Africa, but in Europe, where news can spread quickly.

The workers' movement will triumph and will pave the way to peace and socialism.

V. I. Lenin, *Selected Works in Two Volumes* (Moscow: Foreign Languages Publishing House, 1952), II, Part 1, pp. 328–330, 332–333.

DECREE ON THE LAND, OCTOBER 26 [NOVEMBER 8], 1917

Landlord ownership of land is abolished forthwith without any compensation. The landed estates, as also all crown, monasterial and church lands, with all their livestock, implements, buildings and everything pertaining thereto, shall be placed at the disposal of the *volost* [township] land committees and the *uezd* [district] soviets of peasants' deputies pending the convocation of the Constituent Assembly. . . .

4. The following peasant mandate, compiled by the *Izvestia* of the All-Russian Soviet of Peasant's Deputies from 242 local peasant mandates and published in No. 88 of *Izvestia* (Petrograd, no. 88, August 19, 1917), shall serve everywhere to guide the implementation of the great land reforms until a final decision on the latter is taken by the Constituent Assembly.

5. The land of ordinary peasants and ordinary Cossacks shall not be confiscated.

Peasant Mandate on the Land

'The land question in its full scope can be settled only by the popular Constituent Assembly.

'The most equitable settlement of the land question is to be as follows:

"1) Private ownership of land shall be abolished forever; land shall not be sold, purchased, leased, mortgaged, or otherwise alienated.

"All land, whether state, appanage, crown, monasterial, church, factory, primogenitary, private, public, peasant, etc., shall be alienated without compensation and become the property of the whole people, and pass into the use of all those who cultivate it.

"Persons who suffer by this property revolution shall be deemed to be entitled to public support only for the period necessary for adaptation to the new
conditions of life.

"2) All mineral wealth, e.g., ore, oil, coal, salt, etc., as well as all forests and
waters of state importance, shall pass into the exclusive use of the state. All the
small streams, lakes, woods, etc., shall pass into the use of the communities, to be
administered by the local self-government bodies.

"3) Lands on which *high-level scientific* farming is practiced, e.g., orchards,
plantations, seed plots, nurseries, hot-houses, etc. *shall not be divided up, but shall be
converted into model farms,* to he turned over for exclusive use *to the state* or *to the
communities,* depending on the size and importance of such lands.

"Household land in towns and villages, with orchards and vegetable gardens
shall be reserved for the use of their present owners, the size of the holdings, and
the size of tax levied for the use thereof, to be determined by law. . . .

"6) The right to use the land shall be accorded to all citizens of the Russian
state (without distinction of sex) desiring to cultivate it by their own labor, with
the help of their families, or in partnership, but only as long as they are able to
cultivate it. The employment of hired labor is not permitted. . . .

"7) Land tenure shall be on an equality basis, i.e., the land shall be distributed among the toilers in conformity with a labor standard or a consumption
standard, depending on local conditions.

"There shall be absolutely no restriction on the forms of land tenure: household, farm, communal, or cooperative, as shall be decided in each individual village and settlement.

"8) All land, when alienated, shall become part of the national land fund. Its
distribution among the toilers shall be in charge of the local and central self-government bodies, from democratically organized village and city communities, in
which there are no distinctions of social rank, to central regional government
bodies.

"The land fund shall be subject to periodic redistribution, depending on
the growth of population and the increase in the productivity and the scientific
level of farming. . . .

V. I. Lenin, *Selected Works in Two Volumes* (Moscow: Foreign Languages Publishing House, 1952), II, Part 1,
pp. 338–343.

DECREE ON SUPPRESSION OF HOSTILE NEWSPAPERS, OCTOBER 27 [NOVEMBER 9], 1917

In the serious decisive hour of the revolution and the days immediately following it
the Provisional Revolutionary Committee was compelled to adopt a whole series of
measures against the counter-revolutionary press of all shades.

Immediately on all sides cries arose that the new socialistic authority was violating in this way the essential principles of its program by an attempt against the freedom of the press.

The Workers' and Soldiers' Government draws the attention of the population to
the fact that in our country behind this liberal shield there is practically hidden the

liberty for the richer class to seize into their hands the lion's share of the whole press and by this means to poison the minds and bring confusion into the consciousness of the masses.

Everyone knows that the bourgeois press is one of the most powerful weapons of the bourgeoisie. Especially in this critical moment when the new authority, that of the workers and peasants, is in process of consolidation, it was impossible to leave this weapon in the hands of the enemy at a time when it is not less dangerous than bombs and machine guns. This is why temporary and extraordinary measures have been adopted for the purpose of cutting off the stream of mire and calumny in which the yellow and green press would he glad to drown the young victory of the people.

As soon as the new order will be consolidated, all administrative measures against the press will be suspended; full liberty will be given it within the limits of responsibility before the laws, in accordance with the broadest and most progressive regulations in this respect.

Bearing in mind, however, the fact that any restrictions of the freedom of the press, even in critical moments, are admissible only within the bounds of necessity, the Council of People's Commissaries decrees as follows:

General rules on the press.

The following organs of the press shall be subject to be closed: (a) those inciting to open resistance or disobedience towards the Workers' and Peasants' Government; (b) those sowing confusion by means of an obviously calumniatory perversion of facts; (c) those inciting to acts of a criminal character punishable by the penal laws.

The temporary or permanent closing of any organ of the press shall be carried out by a resolution of the Council of People's Commissars.

The present decree is of a temporary nature and will be revoked by special *ukaz* [governmental order] when the normal conditions of public life will be reestablished.

Chairman of the Council of People's Commissars,
Vladimir Ulianov (Lenin)

English translation in *Bolshevik Propaganda: Hearings before a Subcommittee of the Committee on the Judiciary, U. S. Senate, 65th Congress, 3rd Session, Feb.* 11, 1919 to Mar. 10, 1919 (Washington, Government Printing Office, 1919), p. 1243.

DECLARATION OF THE RIGHTS OF THE PEOPLES OF RUSSIA, NOVEMBER 2 [15], 1917

The October revolution of the workmen and peasants began under the common banner of emancipation.

The peasants are being emancipated from the power of the landowners, for there is no longer the landowner's property right in the land—it has been abolished. The soldiers and sailors are being emancipated from the power of autocratic generals, for generals will henceforth be elective and subject to recall. The workingmen are being emancipated from the whims and arbitrary will of the capitalists, for henceforth there will be established the control of the workers over mills and factories. Everything living and capable of life is being emancipated from the hateful shackles.

There remain only the peoples of Russia, who have suffered and are suffering oppression and arbitrariness, and whose emancipation must immediately be begun, whose liberation must be effected resolutely and definitely.

During the period of tsarism the peoples of Russia were systematically incited against one another. The results of such a policy are known—massacres and programs on the one hand, slavery of peoples on the other. There can be and there must be no return to this disgraceful policy of instigation. Henceforth the policy of a voluntary and honest union of the peoples of Russia must be substituted.

In the period of imperialism, after the February revolution, when the power was transferred to the hands of the Kadet [leading liberal party] bourgeoisie, the naked policy of instigation gave way to one of cowardly distrust of the peoples of Russia, to a policy of fault-finding and provocation, of "freedom" and "equality" of peoples. The results of such a policy are known: the growth of national enmity, the impairment of mutual trust.

An end must be put to this unworthy policy of falsehood and distrust, of fault-finding and provocation. Henceforth it must be replaced by an open and honest policy which leads to complete mutual trust of the people of Russia. Only as the result of such a trust can there be formed an honest and lasting union of the peoples of Russia. Only as the result of such a union can the workmen and peasants of the peoples of Russia be cemented into one revolutionary force able to resist all attempts on the part of the imperialist-annexationist bourgeoisie.

Starting with these assumptions, the First Congress of Soviets, in June of this year, proclaimed the right of the peoples of Russia to free self-determination. The Second Congress of Soviets, in October of this year, reaffirmed this inalienable right of the peoples of Russia more decisively and definitely. The united will of these congresses, the Council of the People's Commissaries, resolved to base its activity upon the question of the nationalities of Russia, as expressed in the following principles:

The equality and sovereignty of the peoples of Russia.

The right of the peoples of Russia to free self-determination, even to the point of separation and the formation of an independent state.

The abolition of any and all national and national-religious privileges and disabilities.

The free development of national minorities and ethnographic groups inhabiting the territory of Russia.

The concrete decrees that follow from these principles will be immediately elaborated after the setting up of a Commission on Nationality Affairs.

Chairman of the Council of People's Commissars,
V. Ulianov (Lenin)
People's Commissar of Nationality Affairs,
Iosef Jugashvili (Stalin)

English translation in *The Nation,* December 28, 1919.

The Dissolution of the Constituent Assembly

The convening of the Constituent Assembly, something like a constitutional convention, had long been the goal of liberal and socialist opponents of tsarism. The Provisional Government had delayed calling it because of the war, and many fundamental reforms were thereby postponed. The Bolsheviks supported the convening of the Assembly, and elections took place in mid-November, but the results were disappointing to the Leninists. Although the overwhelming majority of the population had voted for socialist parties, the largest number of votes went to the Socialist Revolutionaries (SR) (40 percent), while the Bolsheviks came in second (24 percent). The SRs won most of the rural districts, while Bolsheviks did better than any other single party in most major cities of Russia, including Moscow and Petrograd, and among the soldiers at the various fronts.

Before the Assembly opened its first session on January 5, Red Guards fired on an un-armed demonstration of its supporters. Ten people were killed. The Assembly met for only one day before Red Guards prevented the delegates from reconvening. In a session of the Central Executive Committee of the Soviets, Lenin presented his view that the country stood before a stark choice: Soviet power and socialism, or the Constituent Assembly and bourgeois democracy. Historians, who have long debated whether the October Revolution was an authentic expression of popular will or a coup d'état, have far less disagreement about the events of January 5–6. A minority party, the Bolsheviks, with considerable strength among soldiers and workers, overthrew the democratically elected Constituent Assembly through the use of force. That dissolution marked an indisputable coup d'état and opened the way to civil war. A country deeply divided between those who wished to preserve the victories of the February Revolution and those anxious to move on to Soviet power settled their political differences with violence and terror.

DISSOLUTION OF THE CONSTITUENT ASSEMBLY IS DISCUSSED AT THE ALL-RUSSIAN CENTRAL EXECUTIVE COMMITTEE OF SOVIETS. TWENTY-FIFTH SESSION 6 JANUARY 1918

Chairman: Sverdlov   11.30 p.m.

I.   Shooting of Persons Demonstrating in Support of the Constituent Assembly

SVERDLOV: [Bolshevik]: Today's emergency session has been called to consider the dissolution of the Constituent Assembly. I propose the following agenda: confirmation of the CPC's decree on the dissolution; incorrect compilation of party lists in the Constituent Assembly elections.

RYAZANOV: [Bolshevik], on a point of order: I protest in the strongest terms against yesterday's bloodshed, when peaceful demonstrators were fired upon. I demand that the CEC suspend its sessions until the Third Congress of Soviets, which should consider whether the CPC acted correctly in permitting such excesses, and I further demand that a commission be set up at once to investigate these events.

SHTEYNBERG: [Left SR]: As PC of Justice, I support this proposal for a commission of inquiry. Yesterday's incident has made everyone rather excited. When I went round all the places where clashes occurred I discovered that only minor injuries had been caused. However, this morning [in the CPC] I insisted that an investigating commission be set up, and I repeat this demand now.

The proposal is adopted unanimously. The commission is to consist of seven persons, chosen by the fractions, to whom trade-union representatives are to be added. It is to be organized by the Presidium.

2. *Dissolution of Constituent Assembly*

LENIN: [Bolshevik] (*Sustained applause*): The conflict between soviet power and the Constituent Assembly was foreshadowed by the whole history of the Russian revolution, faced as it is with the unheard-of problems of reconstructing society on socialist lines. After the events of 1905 there could be no doubt that tsarism was at its last gap. Only the backwardness and ignorance of the countryside allowed it to climb back from the abyss. In the 1917 revolution the party of the imperialist bourgeoisie [i.e. the Kadet party] has been turned by force of circumstance into a republican one, and democratic organizations have emerged in the form of soviets. These were created as early as 1905: already then socialists realized that their appearance signified something entirely new in the history of world revolution. The soviets, created by the people entirely on their own [initiative], are a form of democracy that has no equal in any other country.

The [February] revolution brought forth two forces: the masses, who united for the purpose of overthrowing tsarism, and the organizations of labouring people. When I hear enemies of the October revolution crying how impossible of realization, how utopian, the ideas of socialism are, I generally put to them the simple and obvious question: 'what are the soviets?', 'what led to the emergence of these popular organizations, which have no parallel in history . . . ?' And to this question none of them has ever given me, or could ever give me, a definite answer. Their stubborn defence of the bourgeois order leads them to oppose these mighty organizations, the like of which no revolution hitherto ever witnessed.

Whoever is fighting the landlords joins the soviets of peasants' deputies. The soviets are made up of all those who want to engage in creative work instead of idling. A network of them has spread over the whole country. The denser this network becomes, the less chance there will be for exploitation of working people, for the existence of soviets is incompatible with a flourishing bourgeois order. This explains all the contradictions into which bourgeois representatives fall. They are struggling against our soviets solely in order to advance their own interests.

The transition from capitalism to socialism involves a long and bitter struggle. Having overthrown tsarism, the Russian revolution has inevitably gone further. It could not limit itself to ensuring the victory of a bourgeois [order], for the war imposed untold sufferings upon the people, and their exhaustion created conditions in which social revolution could break out. There is accordingly nothing more ridiculous than to assert that the deepening of the revolution, the growing indignation of the masses, has been stimulated by a single party, by a single individual, or—as [our enemies] scream—by the will of some 'dictator'. The revolutionary conflagration has come about exclusively as the consequence of the incredible sufferings to which Russia has been subjected by the war. This relentlessly forced working people to choose: either to take a bold, desperate and fearless step [forward] or else to perish, to die a hungry death. (*Applause.*)

The revolutionary [impulse] expressed itself in the creation of soviets, bastions of the revolution of labour. The Russian people have made a gigantic leap from tsarism to soviets. This is an incontestable and unprecedented fact. At a time when in all [other] countries bourgeois parliaments, inhibited by the limitations of capitalism and [respect for] property, have never given any support to the revolutionary movement, the soviets, stoking the fires of revolution, are imperiously telling the people to fight, to take everything into their hands, to organize themselves.

No doubt all manner of mistakes and blunders will be made in the course of deepening this revolution, called into being by the mighty soviets. But it is no secret that every revolutionary movement is invariably accompanied by chaos, destruction, and disorder. Bourgeois society involves war and slaughter too, and it is this which has so accentuated the conflict between the Constituent Assembly and the soviets.

Those who keep on telling us that we used to defend the assembly but are now 'dissolving' it have no sense and are just uttering empty phrases. Formerly, we preferred the Constituent Assembly to tsarism, to the republic of Kerensky, but as the soviets developed [we saw that] they, as revolutionary organs of the entire people, were incomparably superior to all parliaments anywhere in the world. I stressed this point already in April. The soviets, by effecting a radical breach in bourgeois and landlord property, by assisting the insurrection which finally swept away all traces of the bourgeois order, pushed us on to the course which led the people to build their lives for themselves.

We have set about this great [task of] construction, and we are right to have done so. The socialist revolution cannot be served up to the people in a neat, smooth package. It is inevitably accompanied by civil war, by sabotage and resistance. Those who assert the contrary are either lying or blind. (*Stormy applause.*)

The events of 20 April, when the people—independently, without any orders by 'dictators' or parties—manifested their opposition to the compromisers' government, demonstrated already then the feeble basis on which bourgeois [power] rested. The masses sensed their own strength, and to please them, or rather to deceive them, there began that celebrated ministerial leapfrog [of the first coalition]. But the people saw through this, especially once Kerensky, who had in his pockets the secret robber treaties with the imperialists, launched the offensive. The people gradually came to understand that they were being deceived by everything the compromisers were doing. Their patience began to run out, and the result of all this was the October revolution. The people learned from their experience of tortures, death sentences and mass shootings. It is no use assuring them that the revolt of the labouring people is the work of the Bolsheviks, or of some kind of 'dictators'. This is clear from the schism apparent among the masses at their various congresses, conferences, meetings and so on. As yet the people have not finally assimilated the [lessons of the] October revolution.

This revolution showed in practice how they should proceed in taking the land, the natural resources, the means of transport and production, into their hands, into the hands of the workers' and peasants' state. 'All power to the soviets!' was our slogan. That is what we are fighting for. The people wanted the Constituent Assembly convoked—and so we convoked it. But they at once realized what this notorious Constituent Assembly amounted to. And now we have fulfilled the people's will by [transferring] all power to the soviets. We shall crush the saboteurs.

When I left Smolny, pulsating with vitality, and went to the Tauride Palace I felt as though I were amidst corpses and lifeless mummies. The enemies of socialism used every available means in their fight. They resorted to violence and sabotage; they even exploited knowledge, humanity's great pride, against the labouring people. They were able to delay the advance towards socialist revolution, but they could not halt it and they never shall. For the soviets are too strong: they have begun to smash the antiquated foundations of the bourgeois order, not in a gentlemanly fashion but in the [rough] manner of proletarians and peasants.

The transfer of all power to the Constituent Assembly [would be] another compromise with the pernicious bourgeoisie. The Russian soviets place the interests of the toiling masses much higher than the interests of the treacherous conciliators, who have donned a fresh disguise. The speeches of Chernov and Tsereteli gave off a mouldy smell. These politicians of bygone times are still whining about stopping the civil war. But so long as Kaledin exists, so long as the slogan 'All power to the Constituent Assembly!' masks the slogan 'Down with soviet power!', civil war is inevitable, for we shall not for anything in the world surrender soviet power! (*Stormy applause.*)

And when the Constituent Assembly announced its readiness to postpone once again [decisions on] all the urgent issues presented to it by the soviets, we answered: there is not a moment to lose. And so by the will of the Soviet government the Constituent Assembly, which refused to recognize the people's power, has been dissolved. The general staff of the Ryabushinskys has been defeated. If the latter resists, this will only lead to a new upsurge of civil war. The Constituent Assembly is dissolved and the revolutionary Soviet Republic will triumph, cost what it may. (*Stormy applause, turning into a prolonged ovation.*)

STROYEV: for the United SDs [Mensheviks]: The dissolution of the Constituent Assembly seems to me a dizzying jump into the unknown. I remind the Left SRs that not long ago they were numbered among defenders of the assembly. Too soon have they shed this 'illusion', and in so doing also their [allegiance to their] red banners and to political liberty. On the basis of the Constituent Assembly it would have been possible to unite the whole of revolutionary democracy. This course is no longer possible. As late as November the Bolsheviks were also in favour of broadening the basis of the revolution, but now they have betrayed this principle.

Yesterday red banners were being snatched from the worker's hands. One more illusion is being done away with. The respect for socialist banners reddened with proletarian blood . . . (*Cries of 'That's enough!' Uproar.*) I am used to speaking against noises like these. I made speeches despite [interruptions] by the Black Hundreds . . . and should like to think that now I am under the protection of the red flag. (*Tremendous uproar. The chairman calls on the speaker to refrain from such comparisons.*) The Bolsheviks who control the government failed to carry out the will of the Second Congress of Soviets, . . . which resolved to call the Constituent Assembly, not to dissolve it . . . (*Cries and hisses in the hall.*)

Amidst the commotion Stroyev tries to continue his speech but is forced to leave the tribune. [Before doing so he reads a resolution which ends as follows:]

> . . . The Constituent Assembly alone is capable of uniting all parts of Russia to end the civil war which is accelerating the country's economic ruin and to solve all the essential questions raised by the revolution . . . In view of this the CEC resolves that the CPC shall enable the Constituent Assembly to continue its labours without interference, and that a new government shall be formed in agreement with the assembly's socialist majority.

SELIVANOV: for the [Left] SR Maximalists: Once again we have heard from this tribune the whining of the United SDs. We still remember what they said about our

October revolution, and then about nationalization of the banks. They keep on re-peating themselves and threatening us with every kind of misfortune. I call on the as-sembly to ignore the whining of these petty-bourgeois intellectuals and to carry on with the revolution. Now that the Constituent Assembly has at last been closed down, Russia will march ahead rapidly to a Soviet Republic of Labour (*Applause.*)

RYAZANOV: Explaining his vote: We are taking an extremely serious step which affects not just Russia but the whole world proletariat. I never made a fetish of the Constituent Assembly but I believe that, having convoked it, we should have given it time to show its true face. This was not done. In a single day the people could not as-sess its [value] or compare their own opinions with its performance. Before dissolv-ing the assembly we should have shown that it had to be dissolved by confronting it with the Third Congress of Soviets and letting the people decide between them. For this reason I shall vote against the [motion approving] dissolution of the Constituent Assembly.

AVILOV: [Menshevik Internationalist]: Lenin talked exclusively about the supe-riority of the soviet form of organization but failed to say why the Constituent As-sembly did not reflect the people's will . . .

KARELIN: [Left SR] greeted by stormy applause, reads the text of the decree.

SUKHANOV: [Menshevik Internationalist] given the floor for an amendment: It is false to assert that the Constituent Assembly refused to acknowledge the conquests of the October revolution, and I suggest that this passage be omitted from the reso-lution—as well as the immediately following passage, namely the approval given to the dissolution. (*Cries of indignation; laughter.*)

LOZOVSKY: [Bolshevik] supporting the amendment: The CEC has committed a tremendous mistake, indeed a crime, in voting in favour of the decree, for in so doing it has assumed the function of the [rightful] legislative organ. It is also wrong to say that the people have seen the assembly's real face, since not even Petrograd, let alone Russia, has had a chance to take proper stock of it.

The amendment is rejected. The resolution is put to the vote and passed with 2 dissentients and 5 abstentions.

3. *Incorporation of Radical Constituent Assembly Deputies into the CEC*

As Karelin ascends the tribune KRAMAROV: [Menshevik Internationalist] calls out: 'Bolshevik lackey!' Storm of indignation in the hall. The chairman demands that he retract the expression. When he merely modifies it the chairman excludes him from the session, adding that the Presidium will consider his misconduct.

KARELIN: Kramarov's remark applies to the whole Left SR fraction, not just to myself, and I bear him no personal grudge—although it was ill-mannered. I oppose his exclusion since in a class organization such as the CEC we should preserve com-radely relations.

I propose that those Bolshevik and Left SR deputies to the Constituent Assembly who walked out of that body be invited to take part in the work of the CEC, as this will improve our liaison with the provinces.

An UNIDENTIFIED member moves that the same right be extended to the na-tional-minority deputies who walked out.

Resolution adopted unanimously, except for the United SDs, who take no part in the vote.

John L. H. Keep (trans. and ed.). *The Debate on Soviet Power: Minutes of the All-Russian Central Executive Committee of Soviets, Second Convocation, October 1917–January 1918* (Oxford: Oxford University Press, 1979), pp. 260–267.

I. N. Steinberg, "The Cheka is Cheated"

I. N. Steinberg was a Left Social Revolutionary who was appointed People's Commissar of Justice on December 12 [25], 1917 in what became the Soviet coalition government of Bolsheviks and Left SRs. He had already protested in the Central Executive Committee of Soviets against the Bolshevik outlawing of the Kadet party, and throughout his tenure as Commissar of Justice he struggled against the extralegal exercise of power by the Bolsheviks. He frequently confronted Feliks Dzerzinskii, the head of the Cheka, the security police established in December, and its use of political terror. Steinberg resigned from the government, along with his fellow Left SRs, in March 1918 over the signing of the Brest-Litovksk Treaty with Germany, and a year later he himself became a prisoner of the Cheka. He left Russia for Germany in 1923 and eventually became an American citizen. With the death of Stalin in 1953, I. N. Steinberg was the last surviving member of the first and only Soviet coalition government.

The decree against the Kadets, which had been passed on December 1, 1917, was, of course, a formidable obstacle in the path of justice. Although it had not been ratified with the enthusiasm the Bolsheviks had anticipated, we could not deny the effect it might have on the aroused emotions of the masses. It was, after all, almost an invitation to terror issued by the most authoritative institution in the country. Once the idea of impunity toward supposed counter-revolutionaries penetrated the minds of irresponsible individuals, one could expect lynching incidents to spread among the population.

But during the first few weeks of the new coalition Soviet Government, both parties strained to prevent such acts of spontaneous "mob justice." Characteristic, in this sense, was a sudden and sober conflict with the garrison at the Peter and Paul Fortress in Petrograd. This fortress had become a dual symbol of ruthless czarist reaction and sublime revolutionary martyrdom. Inside one of the thick walls of the fortress, the Troubetzkoy Bastion, hundreds of courageous revolutionaries had been held prisoner. Many did not leave the fortress alive. For decades men had dreamt of the day when the Russian "Bastille" would be destroyed forever.

I want to record here in melancholy remembrance that, within a few days of my appointment as Commissar of Justice, Maria Spiridonova, the spiritual leader of our movement, came to see me. Spiridonova herself had experienced revolutionary martyrdom in Siberian prisons from the time she was twenty-one. Her soul was saturated not only with the pain which she had felt, but with the suffering of thousands of prisoners she had known. In their name she came to me demanding that we blow up the Peter and Paul Fortress, the infamy of the shattered regime. Unfortunately it proved impossible to accede to her noble demand because—expert engineers informed us—

this prison was no more than one wall in the fortress as a whole. And in the fortress itself huge quantities of dynamite were stored which could not be exploded.

Dozens of leaders from the Liberal camp were now imprisoned in the fortress— they had been arrested immediately after the October revolt. The prison was under the supervision of a commandant and of the council of the fortress's military garrison.

During the night of January 2, 1918, I received word of a resolution passed by the garrison council which would deprive the prisoners of visits by relatives and food from outside. The soldiers wanted to restrict the life of their high-born captives whom they regarded as their class enemies. This resolution had all the symptoms of terrorist intent. I got in touch with Lenin at once and he willingly agreed to send a joint, urgent letter to the garrison. Because this was an unusual document, it is worth quoting the text in full:

"To the commandant and the garrison council of the Peter and Paul Fortress:

"We have learned that, during the night of January 2, the garrison council voted to deprive prisoners of their right to visits and to provisions. While we respect the revolutionary ardor of the representatives of the garrison, we consider such action against individuals, who are already deprived of their freedom, unnecessary. Since the general supervision of all prisons in Petrograd is the function of the People's Commissariat of Justice, separate action on the part of individual groups can only hamper its work.

"We therefore suggest that you review your decision and keep us informed of developments.

Chairman of the Council of People's Commissars:
V. Lenin
People's Commissar of Justice:
I. Steinberg"

Unusual in this letter is its style. In those days even the supreme Government authorities spoke to the rank and file in the form of "requests" and "suggestions." They issued no orders; instead they asked them to "review the decision" of the soldiers. The tone proved effective and the dangerous resolution was withdrawn.

Unfortunately this kind of co-operation between ourselves and the Bolsheviks did not last long. The poisonous effect of open or overt propaganda in favor of "revolutionary ardor" became evident soon both in the popular psychology and in the leading circles of the new rulers. Two dramatic incidents illuminated this trend of events.

The first concerned an unknown officer by name of Rutkovsky, who was then a prisoner in a Petrograd jail. The second incident ended tragically for two former Liberal ministers of the Kadet Party, imprisoned in the Peter and Paul Fortress.

It was bitterly cold in Petrograd that February day. The People's Commissars were engaged in the dramatic contest between the Russian Republic and the German military empire, taking place in the city of Brest-Litovsk. The Soviet Government, which had risen to power on the promise of ending the war on international democratic terms, had made intensive efforts to induce the Western powers (United States, Britain and France) to begin joint negotiations for peace. We knew that the peoples of those countries also wished for an end of the bloodshed that was now in its fourth year. But their official spokesmen did not respond to the call of the new Russia. And so the Soviet Government was left alone at the diplomatic table in Brest-Litovsk face to face with its greatest enemy—the German militarists.

The Soviet delegation, led by the Bolsheviks Leon Trotsky and Adolph Yoffe, included also representatives of the Left Social-Revolutionaries. For weeks the bitter struggle went on between the spokesmen of Russia—armed only with the moral prestige of liberation triumphant—and the Kaiser's Germany, displaying on the battlefields the full strength of its armed forces. Small wonder that the People's Commissars were harassed by thoughts of the future: Would Russia have to succumb to the armed fist of the Kaiser? And would such submission save the revolution?

But in the offices of the People's Commissariats the day to day work continued. On that cold morning I, too, sat in my office answering a constant stream of telephone calls.

Smirnov, a Left Social-Revolutionary and chairman of the prison commission at the Kresti jail, was on the line. His voice quivering, he told me that Dzershinsky, chief of the Cheka, was at the prison. He wanted, he said, to investigate the cases of several counter-revolutionaries imprisoned there and ordered their cells searched. In one of them, the Chekists found a revolver, whereupon Dzershinsky ordered the guilty officer into solitary confinement under special guard whence he was eventually to be taken to the Cheka and shot.

"Shot?" I interrupted. "You're mad!"

"It's true. Dzershinsky suspects a plot. Comrade Commissar, we can't let this happen."

"Certainly not. But why did you let him have his way?"

"We protested, but it didn't help. Comrade Commissar, you must do something at once, or it will be too late."

"Comrade Smirnov," I said firmly. "I forbid you to let the prisoner be moved. You will be personally responsible for his safety. In the meantime, I'll see about this situation."

Smirnov was satisfied with my order, which strengthened his position with the Cheka. But I was far from certain that Dzershinsky would respect it. I knew the temper of the Bolsheviks. They were frantic because of the imminent disgrace of their succumbing to the German imperialists, and sought to compensate for it by retaliating against their enemies at home. I felt that more than the life of a man was at stake: it was the whole character of the new era.

But what could I do? No use telephoning Dzershinsky. He would stall, promise to submit our conflict to the Council of People's Commissars—and, in the meantime, present us with a *fait accompli*. Should I speak to Alexandrovitch, the Left Social-Revolutionary in the Cheka? But where would I find him?

Perhaps I should go to the prison and defend the officer personally against the would-be executioners? But would I be in time? And what if Dzershinsky remained stubborn? The confusion in my mind lasted only a few moments—decisions in those days had to be made quickly.

I called Alexander Schreider, a Left Social-Revolutionary and my deputy at the Commissariat. With all the fire of his youth, Schreider was waging a ceaseless battle against the Cheka. I told him to proceed at once to the prison and, in my name, stop the removal of the prisoner by any means he thought fit, and to await further instructions from me. I wrote out an order and handed it to him without waiting for it to be typed. It read:

"This will serve as authority for my deputy, Alexander Schreider, to resort to any measures in preventing the execution or removal of any prisoner in the Kresti jail. If necessary, Comrade Schreider is instructed to use force on orders from the People's Commissar of Justice. The officials of the Kresti, including the prison Commissioner, are in duty bound to assist him to the full.   March 3, 1918."

There could be no misinterpreting this message; it meant that we were ready to pit our strength against the Cheka. Schreider ran down the stairs and jumped into a car, while I set out as hurriedly for the Smolny Institute, where Lenin lived.

I had no illusions about Lenin's attitude in matters of this kind. I knew, also, that he was impatient with my continuous protests against the Cheka, mainly because they were continuous. Still, he was the only authority for Dzershinsky; he alone could call off the execution.

It was four o'clock in the afternoon. No official meetings of the Government were scheduled, and I hoped to find Lenin in his office. As I ran up the broad staircase of the Smolny, I met Prosh Proshyan, another Commissar and a member of our party. I seized him by the arm and told him what had occurred. He indignantly exclaimed, "This mustn't happen. Kill a prisoner without trial, a man who is already in our power? I'll come with you."

Lenin was at a meeting of the Central Committee of the Bolshevik Party. We sent word asking him to come out for a minute and see us. But the work of his Central Committee—planning Bolshevik program and disciplinary measures—was most important to Lenin, and it was some time before he joined us.

Proshyan immediately plunged into the story, telling it with suppressed emotion and demanding that the projected execution be halted at once. Lenin, preoccupation with other matters obvious in his face, asked in some bewilderment why we were so excited. Proshyan explained again, this time with anger in his voice:

"All right, so they found a gun on the prisoner. Of course that's against regulations. But you cannot execute a helpless man for that! Let him be tried, but restrain Dzershinsky. Telephone at once and have the execution stayed. Then we'll decide what to do. . . ."

When Lenin realized what it was all about, his face became distorted. Never before had I seen him like that. At public meetings, during sessions of the cabinet, and on all other occasions, his features were calm, showing utter self-confidence, close concentration and, now and then, a faint ironic smile. Now, however, his face was neither calm nor ironical.

"Is this the important matter for which you called me from serious business?" he demanded furiously. "You perpetually worry about trifles. Dzershinsky wants to shoot an officer? What of it? What else would you do with these counter-revolutionaries?"

Our protests were of no avail. Lenin was adamant. At that moment a sentry called me to the telephone. Alexandrovitch, representative of the Left Social-Revolutionaries in the Cheka, was on the line.

"Don't worry," he said calmly. "Nothing is going to happen."

"But how do you know about it already?" I asked.

"Dzershinsky came back to the office from the prison and demanded official confirmation from the Cheka Council for the shooting of the prisoner. But in line with our party instructions, I refused to vote for it—and so there will be no execution. In the meantime, his fury has abated somewhat and the case will take its normal course."

Alexandrovitch, the man who had once begged the Central Committee of the Left Social-Revolutionaries not to appoint him to the Cheka Council, had managed to turn the blade of Dzershinsky's sword. Proshyan and I left the Smolny Institute wondering whether this alone was not worth our "co-operation" with the Bolsheviks in the Government.

But it was only the beginning—the beginning of the Red Terror. We had saved the life of one man; only one. What of the future?

A few years later, one of the participants in this drama was forcibly reminded again of this incident. It was not in Russia, but in Poland—inside the headquarters of the Polish political police.

A prisoner was brought in—none other than Alexander Schreider. In 1919, our party had been declared illegal by the Bolsheviks and Schreider was using a forged passport to escape to Germany through Poland. When his papers were examined and his true identity discovered, the Poles decided to impress him with the power of the new Polish republic and to imprison him. At this gloomy moment an officer approached Schreider and asked if he did not recognize him, smiling as he spoke.

"I am Rutkovsky, the officer whom Dzershinsky ordered shot. You and your friends saved my life then, as I shall help you now. You can rely on the word of a Polish officer."

Nothing is lost in the world—neither a good deed nor an evil one. Back in Petrograd we had fought the Bolsheviks for an abstract principle: the sanctity of human life. A humane voice had once been heard in the Russian Cheka and its echo vibrated in the headquarters of the Polish police.

I. N. Steinberg, *In the Workshop of the Revolution* (New York and Toronto: Rinehart and Co., 1953), pp. 65–73.

Iulii Martov's Letter to A. N. Stein

June 16, 1918

Iulii Martov (1873–1923) was a founder of the Russian Social Democratic Workers' Party and had been a close associate of Lenin's until the second party congress in 1903, when he emerged as a leader of the Menshevik wing. Whereas Lenin wanted a tightly organized party of professional revolutionaries, Martov had a broader conception of a workers' party. He saw the Russian Revolution as essentially a "bourgeois revolution," but unlike the Menshevik Defensists Martov and his fellow Menshevik-Internationalists opposed the Coalition Government of socialists and the propertied classes. In July 1917, he shifted to the left and favored a broad socialist government of the "democracy," a "homogeneous democratic government" based on the soviets but including other lower-class representatives as well. He and his followers walked out of the Second Congress of Soviets during the October insurrection, but during the civil war he recognized the Communist government as the "defender of the revolution" against the Whites. Nevertheless, with Mensheviks being persecuted throughout the country, driven into hiding, exile, or prison, Martov decided to leave Russia in 1920. His correspondent here, A. N. Stein, was a member of the German Independent Social Democratic Party, a close sympathizer of Martov's, through whom Martov reported on Russian events to European Social Democracy.

16 June 1918

Dear Comrade . . .

I am writing to furnish you with as much material as possible about conditions in Russia for your useful work in making this information public. To a certain extent, we are informed of your efforts. I am writing immediately after a small Bolshevik coup d'état. On June 14, the All-Russian CEC [Central Executive Committee of Soviets], with the votes of the Bolsheviks against those of the Left SRs [Socialist Revolutionaries], decreed to expel the opposition, that is to say us [the Mensheviks] and the Socialist Revolutionaries, from the CEC and suggested that all other soviets do the same. The resolution was passed on the grounds that we were counterrevolutionaries and that we were taking part in the conspiracies and uprisings of the Czechoslovaks and so on.

As far as we are concerned, it is a consciously false accusation on the Bolsheviks' part because the numerous attempts to link our organizations with such actions have been laid bare quickly and clearly. Bolshevik investigators themselves could not succeed in implicating even one Menshevik in the conspiracy trials. (Some SRs were, though.) Lack of evidence for the decree, as far as we are concerned, was made up for by a proposition that our campaigning against Soviet power made possible the rise of the counterrevolution.

With our expulsion from the soviets, the very foundation of the Soviet constitution is destroyed because the soviets have ceased to represent all workers. In those places where we are in the majority, the soviets will be liquidated. This decree summarizes the process that has been going on *everywhere* during the last few months. Everywhere the workers demanded new elections to those soviets that were elected before the October coup. The Soviets have stubbornly resisted this demand. As a result, struggle over this question often escalated to workers' strikes and the suppression of workers' demonstrations by armed forces (Tula, Yaroslavl, etc.). In some places the workers succeeded in forcing the authorities to hold new elections. Everywhere the returns from these elections either strengthened the opposition or brought a majority to the Mensheviks and SRs once again. In all these cases, by order of the MRCs [military revolutionary councils], the soviets were disbanded by armed force or the opposition delegates were *expelled* as "counterrevolutionaries" from the soviets.

The first method, that is, disbanding the soviet, was used in the following places: Zlatoust, Yaroslavl, Sormovo, Orel, Vyatka, Roslavl, Tambov, Gus-Mal'tsevo, (the center of the textile industry in Vladimir province), Bogorodsk (the center of the leather industry in Nizhnii Novgorod province), and other places. During the last few days, this method has also been applied to the *uezd* congresses of peasant soviets. . . . For example, they disbanded the congresses in Rzhev, Novotozhsk (Tver province), Yegoryevsk (Ryazan province), and elsewhere.

The second method, that is, expulsion of the opposition from the soviets, took place in the following soviets: Rostov-na-Donu (before the German occupation), Saratov, Kronstadt, Kaluga, and in many smaller towns. The struggle for new elections has led to unending arrests of workers. Protest strikes against all kinds of violent acts perpetrated by the authorities took place repeatedly in Sormovo, Tula, Yaroslavl, Lugansk, Sestroretsk, Kostroma, Kolomna, Bogorodsk, Kaluga, Kovrov, Rybinsk, Arkhangelsk, Tver, Orekhovo-Zuyevo, and at some factories in Moscow and Saint Petersburg. At present, a one-day strike has been declared simultaneously for June 18 in

Nizhnii Novgorod and Vladimir provinces in protest against the disbanding of a workers' conference that assembled in Sormovo and represented forty thousand workers from those provinces. It is also a protest against the shooting of workers who had staged a rally in support of this conference (one worker was killed and four wounded). . . . A general strike is scheduled for June 17 in Tula to protest the arrest of a number of workers there. . . . Yesterday, one factory (Gustav List's) was on strike in Moscow, and tomorrow there will be more strikes in protest of the arrest of the entire [intercity] workers' conference, where delegates from a number of factories had gathered in order to discuss the political and economic crisis. Saint Petersburg is in commotion because representatives of the Saint Petersburg workers took part in that conference as well.

Such "independent assemblies without party affiliation" have lately sprung up in all those places where Bolshevik Soviets do not permit new elections or where they disband the newly elected soviets. These assemblies are elected on the model of the soviets. They consist of delegates elected by all the workers, yet they oppose the "state bureaucratic soviets" because the latter, as institutions of the state, are subordinate to the CPC [Council of People's Commissions]. (Since October 1917 an uninterrupted process of centralization has been going on that is increasingly robbing the local soviets of their independence.) These assemblies consider themselves "independent working class organizations" whose role is to defend the interests of the proletariat vis-à-vis the pseudoworkers' government. Already in January, such an assembly appeared in Saint Petersburg. Now it unites all the factories and the majority of workers so that the Saint Petersburg soviet is completely isolated from the masses right now.

The expulsion of the opposition from the soviets is going to speed up the expansion of the assemblies and strengthen the influence of their bureaus, whereas the soviets are turning into institutions of the Bolshevik party. That party is progressively acquiring the character of high- and low-ranking functionaries of the Bolshevik government. Because the process of centralization and bureaucratization of the state apparatus has gone a long way since October, this army of functionaries has turned into a machine ready to carry out any order of the central government. We hope that the formation of these assemblies, which are unconnected with the soviets, will make it possible to prevent the dispersion of the proletariat. Conditions are approaching when counterrevolution prevails, and we hope the assemblies will preserve for the proletariat revolutionary cadres capable of exerting influence on the development of political events when the pseudoproletarian dictatorship is liquidated (provided the revolutionary situation remains such that the existence of these organizations, expressing the will of the masses, is thinkable at all).

During all this struggle over the soviets, persecution of our party became much more relentless. They have shut down our newspapers almost everywhere. Our official newspapers, *Novyi Luch'* [New Ray] in Saint Petersburg and *Vpered* [Forward] in Moscow, have been banned. In Moscow, we are allowed to publish only a "private" daily, *Nash Golos* [Our Voice]. In the provinces, only five or six papers survived in some out-of-the-way places. The closing down of our newspapers caused political strikes as well (Tula, Ekaterinodar, Lugansk). Attempts to put the editorial boards of newspapers on trial [usually for discrediting Soviet power in the eyes of the masses] likewise brought about stormy protests and rallies (Novonikolaevsk in West Siberia, Kharkov, Odessa).

In Odessa, the trial of the editorial board of *Iuzhnyi Rabochii* [Southern Worker] (editors, Tuchapskii and Garvi) turned into a powerful demonstration of the entire proletariat. Workers' delegations from factories arrived in court with declarations of solidarity with the accused. The trial ended with an acquittal. In Kharkov, the trial of editors F. Kon and Ber of *Sotsial Demokrat* did not materialize because the threatening posture of thousands of workers assembled there made the judges run away. After this the authorities decided not to try us anymore, but to close newspapers by administrative order. The trials here against me, Dan, Martynov, and other comrades remain unfinished.

They make arrests for "counterrevolutionary activity" or for "agitation against Soviet power" and the like. In Kolomna, Bogorodsk and Tver, the workers succeeded by means of political strikes, forcing the Bolsheviks to release those who had been arrested. In Tyumen, on the other hand, the general strike, which broke out when seventeen Social Democrats were arrested, remained fruitless. In Lugansk a workers' political strike saved the life of A. Nesterov, formerly a workers deputy in the Second Duma. He was sentenced to death without trial and had already been put up against the wall.

Many of our comrades were executed. A gang of Red Guards seized a miner, I. Tuliakov, formerly a deputy in the Fourth Duma, and executed him not far from Sulin (Taganrog area). This was before the Germans marched in. Just a few days ago in Bogorodsk (Nizhnii Novgorod province), they shot and killed Emel'ianov, a Menshevik, after disorders broke out in response to the Bolsheviks' disbanding the soviet. Four Bolshevik commissars were killed by the crowds. (According to the testimony of the Bolsheviks themselves, comrade Emel'ianov was shot in revenge. He was not accused of taking part in the disorders.) In Rostov-na-Donu, after their victory over Kaledin, the Bolsheviks shot an old Menshevik worker, Kalmykov, even though throughout Kaledin's rule in Rostov, the Menshevik party had selflessly protested against annihilation of the Bolsheviks by the Cossacks.

These are only a few examples out of many. Now, in connection with our expulsion from the CEC, we expect that the terror against us will reach its highest degree. During the CEC session, the necessity of taking me, Dan, and other comrades as "hostages" has already been discussed. So far under arrest are two members of the Central Committee, Kuchin and Troianovskii; two members of the Moscow committee, Egorov and Malkin (workers); as well as Kamermakher, an influential worker from Saint Petersburg, a printer, and a number of party functionaries in the provinces.

I have listed all these facts to demonstrate the true relationship between the proletariat and the Bolshevik party. It should be added here that this government relies on the apparatus of factory committees, which likewise [like the Bolshevik Soviets] refuse to hold new elections and likewise have been turned into a hired bureaucracy. The factory committees hold the masses on the threat of hunger. They fire those who are recalcitrant (especially during curtailment of production). They impose fines on workers if they strike. They disband workers' meetings by armed force, prohibit the selling of opposition papers on the factory premises, and so on. This is what our Paraguayan communism looks like.

The workers' economic dependency on the state inhibits them from breaking with the Bolsheviks. Nevertheless, this process has made substantial headway. In big cities it advances under the slogan of the restoration of civil liberties and the Constituent Assembly, and in the provinces it takes on stormy forms. There the workers' masses are dissolved in the petit bourgeois masses whose frame of mind is either Orthodox Russian or bourgeois. In Saint Petersburg, Nizhnii Novgorod, Tula, Yaroslavl, the Bryansk-Mal'tsevo industrial region, as well as in large parts of Vladimir, Kostroma, and Moscow provinces, the workers have completely abandoned the Bolsheviks. In Kazan, Samara, and other areas on the Volga, the workers' movement away from the Bolsheviks is also very strong. In the Urals, a former bastion of bolshevism, one plant after another has turned its back on it. In the entire South (before the Germans marched in), except for a part of the Donets Basin, the masses have completely given up bolshevism. Generally speaking, at present Bolshevism relies primarily on the lumpen proletariat, Latvian riflemen, detachments of prisoners of war, and the Chinese. They also rely on some Red Army detachments insofar as those are not demoralized to such an extent as to pose a threat to the Bolsheviks themselves. In other words, the Bolsheviks rely on a hired gendarmerie.

In the countryside the Bolsheviks have relied for a long time on soldiers returning home from the front. In the chaotic conditions prevailing during the elections to the village soviets, these soldiers seized the soviets, terrorized the peasants (small property holders), and became the privileged group in the countryside. Because summer was approaching, these ex-soldiers were returning to their original peasant way of life. Submitting to the "power of the land," their sansculotte communism was fading away. Now the Bolshevik government, in its fight for power, has taken a number of steps that will inevitably lead to a total break with the peasants. To feed the starving population in the cities, they began to preach a "crusade against the village" to take away grain from peasants by force. The peasants did not want to sell grain at the fixed price (which is, by the way, ridiculously low in view of the devaluation of paper money).

Aiming first and foremost at broadening their base in the Civil War. Lenin and his comrades have turned this crusade into a punitive expedition [*dragonada*]. They hire the lumpen proletarians and send them with unlimited authority into the villages to requisition grain. A number of bloody clashes have already taken place. At present, this measure is being supplemented by another. In addition to the village soviets, they will create "committees of the poor," whose task will be to take away any "surplus" grain from the well-to-do peasants and deliver part of it to urban detachments. The other part they can keep for themselves. One can easily imagine the kind of carnage that will break out because of this.

At the present moment, according to all indications, we find ourselves at a turning point. The Czechoslovak uprising, apparently endorsed by the Allies, has every chance of not being quickly suppressed by the Bolsheviks. Encouraged by this uprising, various social groups—the bourgeoisie, the petit bourgeois intelligentsia, and the active part of the middle peasantry—have begun to rally around on the Volga, in the Urals, and in Siberia. The convocation of the Constituent Assembly remains their slogan. For how long is hard to say. The danger is that a new government may be formed on Russian territory, a government backed by the Allies and maybe even by the Japanese or some other expeditionary force. This danger will make the Germans either broaden their occupation [of Russia] or offer Lenin an "honest alliance" for the preservation of his power and suppression of enemies on the Volga and in Siberia. It is also possible that the Skoropadsky affair will be replayed in Saint Petersburg and Moscow as well. Or a final "Bonapartism" of Lenin's dictatorship will take place if he decides to break with the ideology of "communism" in one stroke and to form a government of pro–German orientation as a counterpart to the democratic or Kadet-Octobrist government in the East [Siberia] with a pro–Allied orientation. . . .

Greetings to all friends,
your
L. Martov

Translated in Vladimir N. Brovkin (ed. and trans.), *Dear Comrades: Menshevik Reports on the Bolshevik Revolution and Civil War* (Stanford, CA: Hoover Institution Press, 1991), pp. 96–103.

Lenin's Letter to V. V. Kuraev, E. B. Bosh, and A. E. Minkin
August 11, 1918

This letter to three local Bolsheviks in Penza was discovered by researchers in a closed fund of Leniniana in the archive of the Communist party and only published after the fall of the Soviet Union. Though at times, particularly in the first months of the revolution, many Bolsheviks were wary of using political terror against their opponents, Lenin, Trotsky, and Dzerzinskii in particular were among those who believed that violence against enemies of and insurgents against Soviet power was essential in the current civil war. A little over a month after coming to power, Lenin told the Central Executive Committee of Soviets:

> We are reproached for persecuting the Kadet party. But one cannot distinguish between class struggle and [the struggle against] political opponent[s]. When it is said that the Kadet party is not a strong force, this misrepresents the facts. The Kadet Central Committee is the political staff of the bourgeoisie. The Kadets have absorbed all the possessing classes; elements to the right of the Kadets have merged with them and support them. . . .
>
> When a revolutionary class is waging war against the possessing classes that resist it, then it must suppress this resistance; and we shall suppress the possessors' resistance by all the methods which they used to suppress the proletariat; other methods have not yet been invented. . . .
>
> The bourgeoisie is using its capital to organize counter-revolution and to this there can be but one reply: prison! That is how [the Jacobins] acted in the great French Revolution: they declared the bourgeois parties outside the law.[1]

Trotsky went even further:

> There is nothing immoral in the proletariat finishing off a class that is collapsing: that is its right. You [the Left SRs] wax indignant at the naked terror which we are applying against our class enemies, but let me tell you that in one month's time at the most it will assume more frightful [groznye] forms, modeled on the terror of the great French revolutionaries. Not the fortress but the guillotine will await our enemies.[2]

Whereas at the end of 1917, Lenin spoke of prison for political opponents and Trotsky spoke

---

1. John L. H. Keep (trans. and ed.), *The Debate on Soviet Power: Minutes of the All-Russian Central Executive Committee of Soviets, Second Convocation, October 1917-January 1918* (Oxford: Oxford University Press, 1979), pp. 174–176.

2. Ibid., pp. 177–178.

of the guillotine, a year later, after months of fighting civil war and peasant resistance to grain requisitioning, Lenin wrote of mass executions—without trials—of class enemies.

11 August 1918

To Penza

To Comrades Kuraev, Bosh, Minkin, and other Penza Communists

Comrades! The uprising of the five kulak districts should be **mercilessly** suppressed. The interests of the **entire** revolution require this, because now "the last decisive battle" with the kulaks is under way **everywhere.** One must give an example.

1. Hang (hang without fail, so **the people see) no fewer than one hundred** known kulaks, rich men, bloodsuckers.

2. Publish their names.

3. Take from them *all* the grain.

4. Designate hostages—as per yesterday's telegram.

Do it in such a way that for hundreds of versts[3] around, the people will see, tremble, know, shout: **they are strangling** and will strangle to death the bloodsucker kulaks. Telegraph receipt and **implementation.**

Yours, Lenin

Translated in Richard Pipes (ed.), *The Unknown Lenin: From the Secret Archive,* with the assistance of David Brandenberger, trans. by Catherine Fitzpatrick (New Haven and London: Yale University Press, 1996), p. 50.

Lev Trotskii, "Report on the Red Army" to the First Congress of the Communist International
March 2, 1919

Initially the Bolsheviks created a democratic army, voluntary, loyal to the soviets, largely made up of workers who elected their officers. With the dissolution of the Imperial Army the Red Guard filled this bill and, in January 1918, became the nucleus of the new Red Army. But when in March 1918, Lev Trotsky became People's Commissar of War, he began implementing new principles of military organization. Against the resistance of those dedicated to the idea of a voluntary army, Trotsky pushed for a conscripted, professionally trained army that employed former Imperial officers. To assure loyalty of the old officers, political commissars were to be attached, as agents of the soviets, to army units, and given power over the formerly decisive soldiers' committees.

This radical reorganization of a "socialist" army into a professional force took the better part of a year to achieve. Trotsky presented himself as the defender of officers' rights, and given the widespread distrust of the old officers, particularly at the front, the Commissar of War be-

___

3. A verst (*versta*) is a Russian measurement of distance equal to 3,500 feet.

came politically isolated. Thanks to support from Lenin and to the impressive victories of his new army, however, his prestige and influence remained high. The Red triumph at Kazan in early September 1918 confirmed Trotsky's program as the more effective, and in the coming months the influence of elected party organizations in the army declined as appointed "political departments" (politotdely) became dominant.

Trotsky's military policies were crowned by success, but his single-mindedness in pursuing his positions created enemies both among top party leaders and rank-and-file members. His willingness to use terror against commanders and political commissars created fear and hostility among many. Besides alienating those who embraced the anti-militarist tendencies of the socialist tradition, Trotsky engendered opponents among many of the leading military officials, including Mikhail Frunze and Mikhail Tukhachevskii, who favored developing a "single military doctrine" based on Marxist analysis. He fought with Stalin and Voroshilov over tactics in the defense of Tsaritsyn (later Stalingrad, still later Volgagrad). Finally, he stirred up great discontent with his proposal at the end of the civil war to militarize labor. Even as his greatest triumph, the five-million-man Red Army, appeared to present a base for a personal bid for power, Trotsky was politically quite vulnerable by 1920–1921.

More than most of their comrades, Lenin and Trotsky opted for pragmatic solutions to immediate problems, hopeful that historic processes and the Western proletariat would eventually come to their aid. Their expectations were not fulfilled, and the full consequences of their improvisations were understood only once the civil war had come to an end. Lenin in particular constantly referred to the collapse of the economy, shortages of fuel and food, the erosion of the social base of the party, and the isolation of the republic from the outside world as necessitating compromises and retreats. While both men seriously rethought the nature of the postrevolutionary political order in the early 1920s, the new structures of the disciplined, undemocratic party that were in place by the end of the civil war provided an opportunity to another, unexpected contender for power.

It is clear from Comrade Albert's[1] report that the question of the Red Guard has become the talk of the town in Germany, and if I understood him correctly, the thought of a possible incursion of our Red Guard into the territory of East Prussia is causing Messrs. Ebert and Scheidemann[2] to suffer nightmares and sleepless nights. On this score Comrade Albert may reassure the rulers of Germany: they have nothing to fear. Fortunately or unfortunately—and this is, of course, a matter of taste—affairs have not yet reached that stage. On the other hand, as far as the threat of intervention against us is concerned, we can say boldly that we are in an incomparably better position than the one we were in last year at the time of the conclusion of the Brest-Litovsk Treaty. It is hardly necessary to dwell on that.

At that time we were still wearing diapers so far as the construction of both the Red Army and the Soviet government as a whole was concerned. The Red Army was

---

1. Max Albert was the pseudonym of Hugo Eberlein (1887–1944), a German Communist, who was a delegate to the founding congress of the Comintern, but ended up arrested in 1937 in Stalin's purges and died in a Soviet prison.

2. Friedrich Ebert (1871–1925) and Philipp Scheidemann (1865–1939) were the leading centrist Social Democrats in Germany, founders of the Weimar Republic, and involved in the suppression of the Spartacist and Communist insurrections of 1918–1919.

then actually called the Red Guard, but that name has long since dropped out of circulation among us. The Red Guard was the name given to the first partisan detachments, improvised groups of revolutionary workers who, prompted by revolutionary zeal, spread the proletarian revolution from Petrograd and Moscow throughout the country. This phase lasted until the first clash between the Red Guard and the regular German regiments, when it became quite obvious that such improvised detachments, while able to conquer the Russian counter-revolution, were impotent before a disciplined army and in consequence could not serve as the real shield of the revolutionary socialist republic.

That moment was the turning point in the attitude of the working masses toward the army. From that time on, we began to scrap the old methods of army organization. Under the pressure of events we proceeded to the creation of a healthy army, organized on principles dictated by military science. It is true that our program calls for a "people's militia." But it is impossible even to talk of a people's militia—this demand of political democracy—in a country where the dictatorship of the proletariat is in power, for an army is always intimately bound up with the character of the reigning power. War, as old Clausewitz says, is the continuation of politics by other means. The army is the instrument of war, and it must therefore correspond to politics. Since the government is proletarian, therefore the army, too, must be proletarian in its social composition.

For this reason we introduced a set of restrictions into the army. Since May of last year, we passed from a volunteer army, from the Red Guard, to an army based on compulsory military service, but we accept into our army only workers and peasants who do not exploit the labor of others.

The impossibility of seriously considering a people's militia in Russia becomes even clearer if we take into account that within the boundaries of the former tsarist empire there were and still are to be found simultaneously several armies from classes hostile to us. In the Don region there is even a monarchist army consisting of bourgeois elements and rich Cossacks, commanded by Cossack officers. Furthermore, in the Volga and Ural regions, there was the army of the Constituent Assembly. Now, this army was also designed as a "people's army" and took this name, but it quickly fell apart. The honorable members of the Constituent Assembly were left with empty hands. They found it necessary—entirely against their will—to leave the Volga province and to accept the hospitality of our Soviet government. Admiral Kolchak[3] simply placed the government of the Constituent Assembly under arrest, and the army was converted into a monarchist army. We thus observe that in a country involved in a civil war, the army can be built only according to class principle; we did exactly that, and we got results.

The formation of a commanding staff presented us with great difficulties. Our primary concern, naturally, was to train Red officers from among the workers and the most advanced peasant youth. This is a job we tackled from the outset, and here at the doors of this hall you can see not a few Red cadets who will shortly enter the army as Red officers. We have quite a number of them. I do not want to specify the exact figure, since military secrets should always remain military secrets. This number, I re-

---

3. Admiral Aleksandr Kolchak (1873–1920) led the White Forces in Siberia and became their Supreme Commander in November 1918, after overthrowing the Directory, a government of Socialist Revolutionaries and liberals, in Omsk. He was captured and executed by the Communists.

peat, is rather large. But we could not bide our time until Red generals arose out of our Red cadets; the enemy did not give us such a breathing spell. We had to turn to the old commanding personnel and find capable people among these reserves; this too was crowned with success. Naturally, we did not seek our officers amid the glittering salons of military courtesans, but we did find in more modest circles people who were quite capable and who are now helping us in the struggle against their own former colleagues. On the one hand, we have the best and the most honest elements among the old officer corps, whom we surround with sensible Communists in the capacity of commissars; and on the other, the best elements from among the soldiers, workers, and peasants in the lower commanding posts. This is the way we formed our Red commanding staff.

From the moment the Soviet republic arose in our country, it was compelled to wage war, and it is waging war to this very hour. Our front extends more than 8,000 kilometers—from the south to the north, from the east to the west—everywhere the struggle is being waged against us arms in hand, and we must defend ourselves. Why, Kautsky[4] has even accused us of cultivating militarism! But it seems to me that if we wish to preserve the power in the hands of the workers, then we must show them how to use the weapons they themselves forge. We began by disarming the bourgeoisie and by arming the workers. If that is called militarism, so be it. We have created our own socialist militarism, and we shall not renounce it.

Our military position in August of last year was extremely precarious; not only were we caught in a ring of steel, but this ring surrounded Moscow rather tightly. Since then we have widened this ring more and more, and in the course of the last six months the Red Army has reconquered for the Soviet republic an area of not less than 700,000 square kilometers, with a population of some 42,000,000—sixteen provinces with sixteen large cities, the workers of which conducted and continue to conduct an energetic struggle. Even today, if you draw a straight line on the map radiating from Moscow in any direction, you will find everywhere at the front a Russian peasant, a Russian worker standing in this cold night, gun in hand, at the frontiers of the socialist republic and defending it. And I can assure you that the worker-Communists who comprise the hard core of this army feel that they are not only the elite troops of the Russian socialist republic, but also the Red Army of the Third International. . . .

And although it does not even enter our minds at present to attack East Prussia—on the contrary, we would be extremely satisfied if Messrs. Ebert and Scheidemann left us in peace—one thing is nonetheless unquestionable: should the hour strike and our Western brothers call upon us for aid, we shall reply:

"We are here! We have in the meantime become skilled in the use of arms; we are ready to struggle and die for the world revolution!

Translated in John Riddell (ed.), *Founding the Communist International: Proceedings and Documents of the First Congress: March 1919* (New York: Pathfinder Press, 1987), pp. 85–89.

4. Karl Kautsky (1854–1938) was a leading German Social Democratic theorist, who had been very popular among the Russian radicals until World War I. When he declined to condemn German participation in the war and later came out against the October Revolution and Bolshevik use of political terror, Kautsky became a favorite target for the polemics of the Communists.

2

RETREAT AND REBUILDING

CHAPTER THREE

POLITICS, SOCIETY, AND CULTURE IN THE 1920s

When journalists and historians first looked at the Soviet Union of the 1920s, they were fascinated by the personal and political struggles of the big Bolsheviks—Trotsky and Stalin, Zinoviev, Kamenev, and Bukharin. The most intriguing question was how a relatively unknown (at least to the journalists) figure like Stalin could emerge from being a "grey blur" (Sukhanov's phrase) to the dominant leader in the party in just a few years. The longer and deeper analysts looked into the political conflicts, however, the more often they turned away from personality (important as that was) toward broader social explanations. The great biographer of Stalin and Trotsky, Isaac Deutscher, was among the first to note how early Stalin had accumulated power and the irony of how it had happened:

> Two years after the civil war Russian society already lived under Stalin's virtual rule, without being aware of the ruler's name. More strangely still, he was voted and moved into all his positions of power by his rivals . . . But the fight began only after he had firmly gripped all the levers of power and after his opponents, awakening to his role, had tried to move him from his dominant position. But then they found him immovable."[1]

Three successive political contests took place in the 1920s: the isolation and defeat of Trotsky by the triumvirate of Zinoviev, Kamenev, and Stalin (1923–1925); the defeat of Kamenev and Zinoviev by the diumvirate of Bukharin and Stalin (1925–1927); and Stalin's victory over Bukharin and the so-called "Right" in the party (1928–1929). The struggle against Trotsky was largely artificially devised because the triumvirs feared his prominence and were determined to prevent him from donning the mantle of Lenin. Personal ambition certainly played a role, but the various participants in the struggle also represented different trends in the party and articulated different visions of how the country should be governed and socialism built. Deutscher saw the Bolshevik dilemma arising from the fact that the working class, small as it was in peasant Russia, had disintegrated, dispersed, largely disappeared during the civil war. The Communists represented only themselves, not the class in whose name they had seized power. "[T]he Bolshevik party maintained itself in power by usurpation.

---

1. Isaac Deutscher, *Stalin, A Political Biography* 2nd edition (New York: Oxford University Press, 1967), p. 228.

Not only its enemies saw it as a usurper—the party appeared as a usurper even in the light of its own standards and its own conception of the revolutionary state."[2] For Deutscher—a Marxist and a Trotskyist—the revolution had been derailed in a backward, peasant country. An authentically socialist revolution was impossible without a strong, conscious working class. Bolsheviks substituted their party for the working class, and in turn the party itself changed.

> In the early stages of the revolution the proletarian-democratic strand was preeminent in the Bolshevik character. Now the bent towards authoritarian leadership was on top of it. . . . As the party substituted itself for the proletariat, it substituted its own dictatorship for that of the proletariat. 'Proletarian democracy' was no longer the rule of the working class which, organized in the Soviets, had delegated power to the Bolsheviks but was constitutionally entitled to depose them or 'revoke' them from office. Proletarian dictatorship had now become synonymous with the exclusive rule of the Bolshevik party. The proletariat could 'revoke' or depose the Bolsheviks as little as it could 'revoke' or depose itself.[3]

Deutscher's contemporary, Edward Hallett Carr, was himself, not only the prodigious chronicler of the early Soviet years (producing fourteen volumes covering the period 1917 to 1929), but also a philosopher of history. In his work, he subordinated politics to the great economic and social processes that shaped the environment in which historical actors could operate. Even great revolutions, he argued, could not obliterate the constraints imposed by history's legacy. "The mere act of transforming revolutionary theory and practice into the theory and practice of government involves a compromise which inevitably breaks old links with the revolutionary past and creates new links with a tradition of governmental authority."[4] Russia's tradition of government was, of course, authoritarianism and reform (or revolution) from above. For Carr, the key to understanding the paths the Bolshevik revolution took lay in "the problem of Russia's backwardness in comparison with western Europe." Backwardness led to envy and fear of the West; the need to use state power to develop Russia rather than rely on initiatives from society; and a pattern of development marked by fits and starts rather than a smooth, sustained, orderly transition into modernity.[5] Stalin's idea of building "socialism in one country," his playing down of Trotsky's internationalist and revolutionary appeals to foreign militants, was for Carr a reassertion of a traditional Russian pattern of national development. Stalin was central to this turn inward, but only because he reflected his environment and embodied "the wills and aspirations of his contemporaries."[6]

> Stalin rose to power through his skill in hitching his fortunes at precisely the right moment to policies that were about to win acclaim, and extricating himself in time from commitments to lost causes.[7]

---

2. Isaac Deutscher, *The Prophet Unarmed: Trotsky: 1921–1929* (New York: Vintage Books, 1959), pp. 9–10.
3. Ibid., pp. 14–15.
4. E. H. Carr, *Socialism in One Country, 1924–1926*, I (New York: Macmillan, 1958), pp. 5–6.
5. Ibid., pp. 8–11.
6. Ibid., p. 137.
7. Ibid., p. 138.

Trotskii, on the other hand, "had much of the common failing of the intellectual in politics: intolerance of the crude realities of the exercise of political power."[8] Stalin had "few claims as a thinker" but was "an outstanding organizer and administrator."[9]

Stalin's great achievement—the industrialization of Russia—validated one aspect of Marxist theory, seeming to prove that modernization did not require markets and capitalism. But even as he "laid the foundations of the proletarian revolution on the grave of Russian capitalism," he did so "through a deviation from Marxist premises so sharp as to amount almost to a rejection of them."[10] Personal character, rather than principle, combined with the political and social climate to raise some up to the pinnacles of power and dash others down to destruction. Soviet politics in the interwar years was harsh and unforgiving. Those who fell almost never rose again.

With the explosion of social history in the 1970s and 1980s, historians began to sketch in the social environment in which the Communists of the 1920s operated. Besides the withering away of the working class and general industrial and urban collapse, widespread famine in the countryside and peasant disaffection because of the forced requisitions of grain by the regime all narrowed the options open to the Soviet leaders. Either the Communists would hold on to power and establish a party dictatorship or they would open up the political process and risk losing power. They never seriously considered the second choice. Rival political parties were eliminated, and the party itself tightened up internally, condemning the various "oppositions" that had appeared within it. The Soviet regime emerged from the civil war with some powerful resources—a battle-hardened Red Army of five million; a loyal, enthusiastic, militarized party membership of 600,000, most of them recent recruits; and possession of a formidable state apparatus.[11] Its social support may have shrunk during the civil war, but now the party was armed and its enemies defeated. Even with debilitating divisions in its ranks, in the ruined landscape of 1920–1922, the Communist party was one of the few institutions left intact.

Moshe Lewin personally experienced the Soviet system when as a young man he fled his native Lithuania as Hitler's army advanced. He worked on a farm and in a factory before joining the Red Army. His lifelong intellectual effort had been to understand "the system," how it evolved, its changes and constancies. Lewin sees the system as emerging from the civil war in ways unintended by the Bolshevik leaders, something "improvised under the pressure of constant emergencies, although ideologies and programs of the previous era did play their role."[12] The party changed in the course of the war from a revolutionary opposition to rulers of a state. The "party became militarized and highly centralized, in a state of almost permanent mobilization and disciplined action. Its cadres were moved around where necessary by a newly created department, the *uchraspred*. Elections to secretarial positions ended, not to reappear in any meaningful way until Gorbachev . . ."[13] In the next half decade the party divided, unequally, between an "old guard" of prerevolutionary and revolution-

---

8. Ibid., p. 147.

9. Ibid., p. 177.

10. Ibid., pp. 185–186.

11. For the social consequences of the civil war, see the essays in Diane P. Koenker, William G. Rosenberg, and Ronald Grigor Suny (eds.), *Party, State, and Society in the Civil War: Explorations in Social History* (Bloomington: Indiana University Press, 1989), particularly Sheila Fitzpatrick, "The Legacy of the Civil War," pp. 385–398, and Moshe Lewin, "The Civil War, Dynamics and Legacy," pp. 399–423.

12. Ibid., p. 399.

13. Ibid., p. 412.

ary veterans, and a new majority that came in during the New Economic Policy (NEP) years. With the peasant redistribution of land in 1918 and the sanctioning of the status quo in the NEP period, the archaic features of peasant Russia re-emerged to dominate the countryside. Outside the villages, a coercive state edifice became a permanent feature of Soviet political life. "Authoritarianism," Lewin writes, "was an unavoidable feature in these conditions—the question was, what type of authoritarianism was it going to be."[14] One of the most longlasting and pernicious legacies of the civil war, he concludes, was the identification in Bolshevik minds of socialism with statization.

The theme of "the revolution betrayed" (the phrase is Trotsky's) that featured in the work of Deutscher, Carr, and Lewin stood in stark contrast to more conservative authors who proposed that even if the revolution did not fit an orthodox Marxist agenda, Bolshevik practice, and particularly Stalinism, was "the revolution fulfilled" (this phrase is Adam Ulam's). A unique position was taken by Sheila Fitzpatrick who, instead of evaluating whether the revolution fulfilled or betrayed Marxism, elaborated the actual relation of the party/state to the class it purported to represent. Rather than a severing of the Bolshevik-worker connection, Fitzpatrick noted: "By recruiting party members primarily from the working class for fifteen years after the October Revolution, the Bolsheviks did a good deal to substantiate their claim to be a workers' party."[15] Workers became party members and managers, moved up through the ranks, and ended up the chief beneficiaries of the revolution. Upward social mobility, rather than proletarian democracy, was the real outcome of 1917. Socialism came to mean economic development and modernization, laying the foundations of an industrial society, and Stalin's choices were usually in favor of workers and the towns and against peasants and the villages. "The party's new orientation was expressed in Stalin's slogan 'Socialism in One Country'. What this meant was that Russia was preparing to industrialize, to become strong and powerful, and to create the preconditions of socialism by its own unaided efforts."[16] This practical and patriotic program had great resonance in a significant segment of the party and the urban population. Years later, even after they had fled the USSR, Soviet emigrants could agree that the one great achievement of the Communists was the industrialization of a backward peasant society.

For most of the leading Communists, the NEP was a retreat from the forward movement toward socialism, a period of transition fraught with dangers of a capitalist restoration. That fear, as well as anxiety about Stalin's accumulating power, led Zinoviev and Kamenev to break with the General Secretary. Stalin sided with Nikolai Bukharin, who envisioned NEP as an evolutionary road to socialism in which the state socialist sector would bring "the seething, unorganized economy under socialist influence."[17] Bukharin, one of the most popular, even beloved members of the Politburo, emphasized the potential for class collaboration, rather than violent conflict, under the dictatorship of the proletariat. Central to Bukharinism was the unity of the

14. Ibid., p. 418.

15. Sheila Fitzpatrick, *The Russian Revolution,* 2nd edition (Oxford and New York: Oxford University Press, 1994), p. 11.

16. Ibid., p. 114.

17. Stephen F. Cohen, *Bukharin and the Bolshevik Revolution: A Political Biography, 1888–1938* (New York: Alfred A. Knopf, 1973), p. 197.

peasant and worker, the *smychka* symbolized in the sickle and hammer, and a rejection of the coercive tradition of the civil war militants. His policies were mild and reflected Bukharin's own nature. A genial, lively man known to have been a personal favorite of Lenin's, Bukharin did not possess the ruthlessness of his political partner. When the NEP economy soured at the end of 1927, and peasants withheld grain needed for the cities, Stalin was prepared to adopt radical, violent measures against the villages. He now castigated Bukharin's pro-peasant lenience as a "right deviation." Steadily, Stalin and his closest comrades moved to crush the better-off peasants, the so-called "kulaks," and eventually to drive the peasants into collective farms. Instead of concessions to society, most importantly to the mass of peasants who made up the majority of the population, a new political order arose that ruled by the abundant application of terror on society. The crisis that had led to the end of political moderation and the Stalin-Bukharin diumvirate opened the way for the radicals to end NEP and establish a quite different socioeconomic system—one that would pass into history as Stalinism.

Terry Martin was one of the first Western researchers using the newly opened Soviet archives in the early 1990s to investigate the nationality policies of the Communist party. His work shows that in its first decade, Soviet policy aimed at the eradication of nationalism by paradoxically promoting national cultural autonomy in hundreds of territorial units. A policy of "affirmative action" for non-Russians coexisted with imperial political relations between the center and the national peripheries. Hence Martin coins the phrase "Affirmative-Action Empire" to describe the peculiar program that discriminated against the largest nationality, the Russians, who were susceptible to "Great Russian Chauvinism," while both fostering and limiting the national expression of non-Russians.

An Affirmative-Action Empire: The Emergence of the Soviet Nationalities Policy, 1919–1923

Terry Martin

When the Bolsheviks seized power in October 1917, they did not possess a coherent nationalities policy. They had only a slogan, which they shared with Woodrow Wilson, of the right of all peoples to self-determination. This slogan, however, was designed to recruit ethnic support for the revolution, not to provide a model for the governing of a multiethnic state. The strength of nationalism as a mobilizing force during the revolution and civil war greatly surprised and disturbed the Bolsheviks. They expected nationalism in Poland and Finland, but the numerous nationalist movements that sprung up across most of the former Russian empire were not expected. In particular, the strong nationalist movement in Ukraine, which most Bolsheviks felt differed little from Russia, was particularly unnerving. This direct confrontation with nationalism compelled the Bolsheviks to formulate a new nationalities policy.

THE LOGIC OF THE SOVIET NATIONALITIES POLICY

Nationalities policy was not on the agenda when the Eighth Communist Party Congress convened in March 1919. However, during a discussion of the Party Program, a polemic arose over the Bolsheviks' traditional support for the right of national self-determination. Piatakov argued that "during a sufficiently large and torturous experience in the borderlands, the slogan of the right of nations to self-determination has shown itself in practice, during the social revolution, as a slogan uniting all counter-revolutionary forces." Once the proletariat had seized power, Piatakov maintained, national self-determination became irrelevant: "it's just a diplomatic game, or worse than a game if we take it seriously." Piatakov was supported by Bukharin, who argued that the right to self-determination could only be invested in the proletariat, not in "some fictitious so-called 'national will'."

Lenin had clashed with Piatakov and others on this issue both before and during the revolution, and he answered this new challenge with characteristic vigor. Nationalism had united all counter-revolutionary forces, Lenin readily agreed, but it had also attracted the Bolsheviks' class allies. The Finnish bourgeoisie had successfully "deceived the working masses that the Muscovites (*Moskvaly*), chauvinists, Great Russians want[ed] to oppress the Finns." Arguments such as Piatakov's served to increase that fear and therefore strengthen national resistance. It was only "thanks to our acknowledgement of [the Finns'] right to self-determination, that the process of [class] differentiation was eased there." Nationalism was fueled by historic distrust: "the working masses of other nations were full of distrust (*nedoverie*) toward Great Russia, as a kulak and oppressor nation." Only the right to self-determination could overcome that distrust, Lenin argued, but Piatakov's policy would instead make the party the heir to Tsarist chauvinism: "scratch any Communist and you find a Great Russian chauvinist . . . He sits in many of us and we must fight him."

The congress supported Lenin's position and retained the right of national self-determination. Of course, the majority of the former Russian empire's nationalities were forced to exercise that right within the confines of the Soviet Union. The period from 1919 to 1923, therefore, was devoted to working out what exactly non-Russian "national self-determination" could mean in the context of a unitary Soviet state. The result was the Soviet nationalities policy: a strategy aimed at disarming nationalism by granting the forms of nationhood. This policy was based on a diagnosis of nationalism worked out largely by Lenin and Stalin. Lenin had addressed the national question repeatedly from 1912 to 1916, when he formulated and defended the slogan of self-determination, and again from 1919 to 1922, after the alarming success of nationalist movements during the civil war. Stalin was the Bolsheviks' acknowledged "master of the nationalities question": author of their standard pre-revolutionary text—*Marxism and the Nationalities Question,* Commissar of Nationalities from 1917 to 1924, and official spokesman on the national question at party congresses. Lenin and Stalin were in fundamental agreement on both the logical rationale and the essential aspects of this new policy, though they came into conflict in 1922 over important issues of implementation.

Their diagnosis of the nationalities problem rested on three premises. First, the point on which Piatakov and Lenin agreed, nationalism was a uniquely dangerous mobilizing ideology because it had the potential to forge an all-class alliance for national goals. Lenin called nationalism a "bourgeois trick," but recognized that like the

hedgehog's, it was a good one. It worked because it presented legitimate social grievances in a national form. At the Twelfth Party Congress in 1923, Bukharin, now a fervid defender of the party's nationalities policy, noted that "when we tax [the non-
Russian peasantry], their discontent takes on a national form, is given a national
interpretation, which is then exploited by our opponents." Ernest Gellner has paro-
died this argument as the "Wrong-Address Theory" of nationalism: "Just as extreme
Shi'ite Muslims hold that Archangel Gabriel made a mistake, delivering the Message
to Mohammed when it was intended for Ali, so Marxists basically like to think that
the spirit of history or human consciousness made a terrible boob. The wakening
message was intended for *classes,* but by some terrible postal error was delivered to
nations."

The Bolsheviks viewed nationalism, then, as a masking ideology. Masking
metaphors recur again and again in their discourse about nationality. Stalin was particularly fond of them: "the national flag is sewn on only to deceive the masses, as a
popular flag, a convenience for covering up (*dlia prykrytie*) the counter-revolutionary
plans of the national bourgeoisie." "If bourgeois circles attempt to give a national tint
(*natsional'naia okraska*) to [our] conflicts, then it is only because it is convenient to hide
their battle for power behind a national costume." This interpretation of nationalism
as a masking ideology helps explain why the Bolsheviks remained highly suspicious
of national self-expression, even after they adopted a policy explicitly designed to encourage it. For example in 1934, in justifying a wave of national repression, Stalin
characteristically invoked a masking metaphor: "The remnants of capitalism in
the people's consciousness are much more dynamic in the sphere of nationality than
in any other area. This is because they can mask themselves so well in a national
costume."

This understanding of nationalism led Piatakov to support the only apparently
logical response: attack nationalism as a counter-revolutionary ideology and nationality itself as a reactionary remnant of the capitalist era. Lenin and Stalin, however,
drew the exact opposite conclusion. They reasoned as follows: By granting the forms
of nationhood, the Soviet state could split the above-class national alliance for statehood. Class divisions, then, would naturally emerge, which would allow the Soviet
government to recruit proletarian and peasant support for their socialist agenda. Lenin
argued that Finnish independence had intensified, not reduced, class conflict. National self-determination would have the same consequences within the Soviet
Union. Likewise, Stalin insisted it was "necessary to 'take' autonomy away from [the
national bourgeoisie], having first cleansed it of its bourgeois filth and transformed
it from bourgeois into Soviet autonomy." A belief gradually emerged, then, that
the above-class appeal of nationalism could be disarmed by granting the forms of
nationhood.

This conclusion was buttressed by a second premise: National consciousness was
an unavoidable historic phase that all peoples must pass through on the way to internationalism. In their pre-revolutionary writings, Lenin and Stalin argued that nationality emerged only with the onset of capitalism and was itself a consequence of capitalist production. It was not an essential or permanent attribute of mankind. Piatakov
understandably interpreted this as meaning that under socialism nationality would be
irrelevant and therefore should be granted no special status. However, both Lenin and
Stalin insisted that nationality would persist for a long time even under socialism. In
fact, national self-awareness would initially increase. Already in 1916, Lenin stated that

"mankind can proceed towards the inevitable fusion (*sliianie*) of nations only through a transitional period of the complete freedom of all oppressed nations." Stalin later explicated this paradox as follows: "We are undertaking the maximum development of national culture, so that it will exhaust itself completely and thereby create the base for the organization of international socialist culture."

Two factors appear to have combined to create this sense of the inevitability of a national stage of development. First, the collapse of the Austro-Hungarian empire and, second, the surprisingly strong nationalist movements of 1917 to 1921 within the former Russian empire, which greatly increased the Bolsheviks' respect for the power and ubiquity of nationalism. Stalin was particularly impressed by the process of national succession in the formerly German cities of Austro-Hungary. At the 1921 party congress, he pointed out that just fifty years ago, all cities in Hungary were predominately German, but had now become Hungarian. Likewise, he maintained, all Russian cities in Ukraine and Belorussia would "inevitably" be nationalized. Opposing this was futile: "It is impossible to go against history (*nel'zia itti protiv istorii*)." Elsewhere Stalin called this pattern "a general law of national development in the entire world." National consolidation, then, was unavoidable even under socialism.

Moreover, this national stage of development took on a more positive connotation as it became associated not only with capitalism, but with modernization in general. In his rebuttal of Piatakov and Bukharin, citing the example of the Bashkirs, Lenin had stated that "one must await the development of a given nation, the differentiation of proletariat from bourgeois elements, which is unavoidable . . . the path from the medieval to bourgeois democracy, or from bourgeois to proletarian democracy. This is an absolutely unavoidable path." As Lenin focused Bolshevik attention on the Soviet Union's eastern, "backward" nationalities, the consolidation of nationhood became associated with historical progress. This trend reached its climax during the Cultural Revolution, when Soviet propaganda would boast that in the Far North, the thousand-year process of national formation had been telescoped into a mere decade. The formation of nations, then, came to be seen as both an unavoidable and positive stage in the modernization of the Soviet Union.

A third and final premise asserted that non-Russian nationalism was primarily a response to tsarist oppression and was motivated by an historically justifiable distrust (*nedoverie*) of the Great Russians. This argument was pressed most forcefully by Lenin, who already in 1914 had attacked Rosa Luxembourg's denial of the right of separation as "objectively aiding the Black Hundred Great Russians. . . . Absorbed by the fight with nationalism in Poland, Rosa Luxembourg forgot about the nationalism of the Great Russians, though it is exactly this nationalism that is the most dangerous of all." The nationalism of the oppressed, Lenin maintained, had a "democratic content" which must be supported, while the nationalism of the oppressor had no redeeming feature. He ended with the slogan: "fight against all nationalisms and, first of all, against Great Russian nationalism."

Bolshevik conduct between 1917 and 1919 convinced Lenin that the All-Russian Communist party had inherited the psychology of Great Power chauvinism from the tsarist regime. In non-Russian regions, the Bolshevik party, relying almost exclusively on the minority Russian proletariat and colonists, had frequently adopted an overtly chauvinist attitude toward the local population. This attitude alarmed Lenin and prompted his harsh words for Piatakov in March 1919, as Piatakov had supported an anti-Ukrainian line in Kiev. In December 1919, Lenin again launched a fierce denunciation of Bolshevik chauvinism in Ukraine. His anger climaxed during the notorious Georgian affair of 1922, when he denounced Dzerzhinskii, Stalin, and Ordzhonikidze as Great Russian chauvinists. (Russified natives, he maintained, were often the worst chauvinists.) Bolshevik chauvinism inspired Lenin to coin the term "*rusotiapstvo*" (mindless Russian chauvinism), which then entered the Bolshevik lexicon and became an invaluable weapon in the national republics' rhetorical arsenals.

Lenin's concern over Great Russian chauvinism led to the establishment of a crucial principle of the Soviet nationalities policy. In December 1922, he reiterated his 1914 position with an admonition that one must "distinguish between the nationalism of oppressor nations and the nationalism of oppressed nations, the nationalism of large nations and the nationalism of small nations . . . in relation to the second nationalism, in almost all historical practice, we nationals of the large nations are guilty, because of an infinite amount of violence [committed]." This concept entered formulaic Bolshevik rhetoric as the distinction between offensive (*nastupitelnyi*) Great Power nationalism and defensive (*oboronitelnyi*) local nationalism, the latter being accepted as a justifiable response to the former. This belief in turn led to the establishment of the important 'Principle of the Greater Danger': namely, that Great Power (or Great Russian) chauvinism was a greater danger than local nationalism.

Lenin's extremely categorical expression of this principle led to one of his two differences of opinion with Stalin over nationalities policy in late 1922. They also disagreed about the structure of the Soviet Union. . . . Stalin had supported the Principle of the Greater Danger prior to 1922–23, reiterated his support in 1923, and supervised a nationalities policy based on that principle from 1923 through 1934. Nevertheless, Stalin was uncomfortable with the insistence that *all* local nationalism could be explained as a response to Great Power chauvinism. Based on his experience in Georgia, Stalin insisted that Georgian nationalism was also characterized by Great Power exploitation of their Ossetine and Abkhaz minorities. Stalin, therefore, always paired his attacks on Great Russian chauvinism with a complementary attack on the lesser danger of local nationalism. This difference in emphasis led Stalin, in September 1922, to jocularly accuse Lenin of "national liberalism." This difference of emphasis was also evident in Lenin and Stalin's terminology. Lenin always referred to Russian nationalism as Great Power chauvinism, which distinguished it from other nationalisms, while Stalin preferred the term Great Russian chauvinism. Still, this was a difference in emphasis, not content. Stalin consistently supported the Principle of the Greater Danger.

These three premises, then, combined to form the theoretical rationale for the nationalities policy that Lenin and Stalin successfully imposed on the Bolshevik party through a series of resolutions at the 1919, 1921, and 1923 party congresses. Their reasoning can be summarized as follows. Nationalism is a masking ideology that leads legitimate class interests to be expressed, not in an appropriate class-based socialist movement, but rather in the form of an above-class national movement. National identity is not a primordial quality, but rather an unavoidable by-product of the modern capitalist *and* early socialist world, which must be passed through before a mature international socialist world can come into being.

Since national identity *is* a real phenomenon in the modern world, the nationalism of the oppressed non-Russian peoples expresses not only masked class protest, but also legitimate national grievances against the oppressive Great Power chauvinism of

the dominant Russian nationality. Neither nationalism nor national identity, therefore, can be unequivocally condemned as reactionary. *Some* national claims—those
confined to the realm of national form—are in fact legitimate and must be granted
in order to split the above-class national alliance. Such a policy will speed the emergence of class cleavages, and so allow the party to recruit non-Russian proletarian and
peasant support for its socialist agenda. Nationalism will be disarmed by granting the
forms of nationhood.

I have thus far ignored one other factor, foreign policy concerns, that did play a
role in the formation of the Soviet nationalities policy. Already in November 1917,
Lenin and Stalin issued an "Appeal to all Muslim Toilers of Russia and the East," which
promised to end imperial exploitation within the former Russian empire and called
upon Muslims outside Russia to overthrow their colonial masters. This link between
domestic nationalities policy and foreign policy goals in the East was quite common
during the civil war period. After the Treaty of Riga fixed the Soviet-Polish border in
1921, this concern shifted westward. The Soviet Union's western border now cut
through the ethnographic territory of Finns, Belorussians, Ukrainians, and Rumanians, and it was hoped that a generous treatment of those nationalities would attract support from their ethnic brethren in neighboring countries. This foreign policy goal,
however, was never the primary motivation of the Soviet nationalities policy. It was
seen as an exploitable benefit of a domestically driven policy that affected the intensity of implementation in sensitive regions, but not the content of the policy itself.

THE CONTENT OF THE SOVIET NATIONALITIES POLICY

An authoritative account of the actual content of the Soviet nationalities policy was
finally delineated in resolutions passed at the Twelfth Party Congress in April 1923
and a special TsK conference on nationalities policy in June 1923. These two resolutions, along with Stalin's speeches in defence of them, became the standard Bolshevik
proof texts for nationalities policy and remained so throughout the Stalinist era. Prior
to April 1923, nationalities policy had been debated repeatedly at important party
meetings. After June 1923, this public debate ceased. The 1923 resolutions affirmed
that the Soviet state would maximally support those forms of nationhood that did not
conflict with a unitary central state. This meant a commitment to support the following national forms: national territories, national cultures, national languages, and
national elites.

National territories had in fact already been formed for all the large Soviet nationalities. The 1923 resolutions merely reaffirmed their existence and denounced all
plans to abolish them. . . . The 1923 resolutions also reiterated the party's recognition of distinct national cultures and pledged central state support for their maximal
development. . . . The primary focus of the 1923 resolutions was on national languages and national elites. In each national territory, the language of the titular nationality was to be established as the official state language. National elites were to be
trained and promoted into positions of leadership in the party, government, industry,
and schools of each national territory. While these policies had been articulated as early
as 1920, and officially sanctioned at the 1921 party congress, next to nothing had actually been accomplished. These two policies came to be called *korenizatsiia*. . . .

Korenizatsiia is best translated as indigenization. It is not derived directly from the
stem *koren*–("root"—with the meaning "rooting"), but from its adjectival form *ko-*

rennyi as used in the phrase *korennyi narod* (indigenous people). The coining of the word *korenizatsiia* was part of the Bolsheviks' decolonizing rhetoric, which systematically favored the claims of indigenous peoples over "newly arrived elements" (*prishlye elementy*). . . .

The 1923 resolutions established *korenizatsiia* as the most urgent item on the Soviet nationalities policy agenda. In keeping with the Bolshevik interpretation of nationalism, *korenizatsiia* was presented in psychological terms. It would make Soviet power seem "native" (*rodnoi*), "intimate" (*blizkii*), "popular" (*narodnoi*), "comprehensible" (*poniatnyi*). It would address the positive psychological needs of nationalism: "The [non-Russian] masses would see that Soviet power and her organs are the affair of their own efforts, the embodiment of their desires." It would likewise disarm nationalism's negative psychological anxiety: "Soviet power, which up to the present time [April 1923] has remained Russian power, [would be made] not only Russian but international, and become native (*rodnoi*) for the peasantry of the formerly oppressed nationalities." Native languages would make Soviet power comprehensible. Native cadres who understood "the way of life, customs, and habits of the local population" would make Soviet power seem indigenous rather than an external Russian imposition.

. . . Soviet nationalities policy. . . . did not involve federation. In 1923, Ukraine, led by Khristian Rakovskii, pressed very aggressively for the devolution of meaningful federal powers to the national republics. Stalin rebuffed Rakovskii's proposals scornfully as amounting to confederation. Although the 1922–23 constitutional settlement was called a federation, it in fact concentrated all decision-making power in the center. National republics were granted no more powers than Russian provinces. Prior to June 1917, both Lenin and Stalin denounced federation and advocated a unitary state with "oblast autonomy" for national regions. This meant the formation of national administrative units and the selective use of national languages in government and education. In June 1917, Lenin abruptly rehabilitated the term federation, but used it to describe what amounted to a much more ambitious version of oblast autonomy. As Stalin noted coyly in 1924, federation "turned out to be not so nearly in contradiction with the goal of economic unification as it might have seemed earlier." Soviet federation did not mean devolution of political power, but rather the promotion of national forms: national territories, cultures, elites, and languages.

Economic equalization occupied a much more ambiguous place in the Soviet nationalities policy. The 1923 resolutions called for measures to overcome "the real economic and cultural inequality of the Soviet Union's nationalities." One economic measure proposed was transferring factories from the Russian heartland to eastern national regions. This policy was adopted but then almost immediately discontinued. This proved typical of economic equalization programs. In contrast to cultural and national equalization, there were almost no bureaucratic institutions to supervise and implement economic equalization. Economic equalization programs belonged to an all-Union economic policy sphere, where they had to compete with other economic goals, rather than a privileged nationalities policy sphere. National republics could and often successfully did use the 1923 resolutions and their "backward" national status to lobby all-Union agencies for privileged economic investment. However, they could make no absolute claim to investment based on nationalities policy. One prominent exception to this rule in the 1920s was the preferential redistribution of land in favor of titular nationalities, which did become a systematic part of the Soviet nationalities policy.

AN AFFIRMATIVE-ACTION EMPIRE

If the Soviet Union cannot accurately be described as a federation, then how should it be categorized? Its distinctive feature was the systematic support of national forms: territory, culture, language, and elites. These were not original choices. They are the primary domestic concerns of most newly formed nation-states. In Georgia and Armenia, for instance, the Soviet government boasted that it had deepened the national work begun by the governments it deposed in 1920–21. Soviet policy was original in that it supported the national forms of minorities rather than majorities. It decisively rejected the model of the nation-state and replaced it with a plurality of nation-like republics. The Bolsheviks attempted to fuse the nationalist's demand of national territory, culture, language, and elites, with the socialist's demand for an economically and politically unitary state. In this sense, we might call the Bolsheviks international nationalists.

To develop this idea, I will compare Soviet practice with Miroslav Hroch's famous three-phase model for the development of nationalism among the "small" stateless peoples of Eastern Europe: first, elite non-political interest in folklore and popular culture (Phase A); second, the consolidation of a nationalist elite committed to the formation of a nation-state (Phase B); third, the emergence of a nationalist movement with mass popular support (Phase C). Hroch largely ignored the existing multiethnic state, reflexively assuming it would oppose these developments. The Soviet state, instead, literally seized leadership over all three phases: the articulation of a national culture, the formation of national elites, and the propagation of mass national consciousness. It went still further and initiated even "Phase D" (my term now, not Hroch's) measures typical of newly formed nation-states: establishing a new language of state and a new governing elite. To use more familiar Bolshevik terminology, the party became the vanguard of non-Russian nationalism. Just as party leadership was needed to lead the proletariat beyond trade-union consciousness to revolution, the party could also guide national movements beyond bourgeois nationalism to Soviet international nationalism.

This policy represented a dramatic shift from 1913, when Lenin had argued that the party should only support ending all national discrimination and warned that "the proletariat cannot go further [than this] in the support of nationalism, for going further means the 'positive' (*pozitivnaia*) affirmative action (*polozhitel'naia deiatel'nost'*) of the bourgeoisie which aims at strengthening nationalism." In the same spirit, Zinoviev told a Ukrainian audience in 1920 "that languages should develop freely. In the end, after a period of years, the language with the greater roots, greater life and greater culture will triumph." Dmitrii Lebed, Secretary of the Ukrainian Tsk, called this theory "The Battle of Two Cultures" in which, "given a party policy of neutrality, the victory of the Russian language will be guaranteed due to its historic role in the epoch of capitalism."

By the 1923 party congress, neutrality had become anathema. Zinoviev himself now stated: "We should first of all reject the 'theory' of neutralism. We cannot adopt the point of view of neutralism . . . we should help [the non-Russians] create their own schools, should help them create their own administration in their native languages . . . Communists [should not] stand to the side and think up the clever phrase 'neutrality'." Neutrality, Zinoviev insisted, was simply a cover for Great Russian chauvinism.

The 1923 resolutions supported this position. Not only was Piatakov's call for a positive fight against nationalism denounced as Great Power chauvinism, so was Lenin's pre-revolutionary policy of neutrality. Lebed's "Battle of Two Cultures" was condemned in 1923 as was a similar "leftist" position in Tatarstan and Crimea.

The Communist party had now embraced Lenin's "positive affirmative action of the bourgeoisie." However, as the Hroch comparison illustrated, Soviet affirmative action supported national minorities, not majorities. The Bolsheviks now scorned bourgeois governments for supporting only formal "legal equality," instead of taking positive action to achieve "actual (*fakticheskoe*) equality." This extreme suspicion of neutrality explains one of the most striking features of the Soviet nationalities policy: its resolute hostility to even voluntary assimilation. Neutrality meant voluntary assimilation due to the historic strength of Russian national culture. Positive action, therefore, was needed in order to defend non-Russian national culture against this unjust fate. No one denounced neutrality and assimilation more categorically than Stalin:

> We are undertaking a policy of the maximum development of national culture . . . It would be an error if anyone thought that in relation to the development of the national cultures of the backward nationalities, central workers should maintain a policy of neutrality—'O.K., fine, national culture is developing, let it develop, that's not our business.' Such a point of view would be incorrect. We stand for a protective (*pokrovitel'stvennuiu politiku*) policy in relation to the development of the national culture of the backward nationalities. I emphasize this so that [it will] be understood that we are not indifferent, but actively protecting (*pokrovitel'stvuiushchie*) the development of national culture.

Of course, positive action on behalf of one nationality implies negative action toward others. In the Soviet case, where all non-Russians were to be favored, Russians alone bore the brunt of positive discrimination. Bukharin stated this fact bluntly: "As the former Great Power nation, we should indulge the nationalist aspirations [of the non-Russians] and place ourselves in an unequal position, in the sense of making still greater concessions to the national current. Only by such a policy, when we place ourselves artificially in a position lower in comparisons with others, only by such a price can we purchase for ourselves the trust of the formerly oppressed nations." Stalin, who was more sensitive to Russian feelings, rebuked Bukharin for the crudeness of his statement, but did not and could not dispute its content. As we shall see, Soviet policy did indeed call for Russian sacrifice in the realm of nationalities policy: majority Russian territory was granted to non-Russian republics; Russians had to accept extensive affirmative-action programs for non-Russians; they were asked to learn non-Russian languages; and traditional Russian culture was stigmatized as the culture of oppression.

New phenomena merit new terminology. As a national entity, I believe the Soviet Union can best be described as an Affirmative-Action Empire. I am, of course, borrowing the contemporary American term for policies that give preference to members of ethnic groups that have suffered from past discrimination. Such policies are common internationally and go by various names: compensatory discrimination, preferential policies, positive action, affirmative discrimination. I prefer the term Affirmative Action because, as the above paragraphs have shown, it describes precisely the Soviet policy choice: affirmative action (*polozhitel'naia deiatel'nost'*) instead of neutrality. The Soviet Union was the first country in world history to establish affirmative-action programs for national minorities and no country has yet approached the vast scale of Soviet affirmative action. The Soviet Union also adopted even more extensive class-based affirmative-action programs and considerably less assertive gender-based programs. As a result, the vast majority of Soviet citizens were eligible for some sort of preferential treatment. Affirmative action permeated the early Soviet Union and was one of its defining features.

However, the existence of such programs alone does not justify calling the Soviet Union an Affirmative-Action Empire, since I am proposing this term as an ideal-type to distinguish the Soviet Union *as a national entity* from alternative ideal-types: nation-state, city-state, federation, confederation, empire. I am using affirmative action here to refer not only to programs on behalf of members of a given ethnic group, but primarily to Soviet state support for the national forms of those ethnic groups. As noted in the Hroch comparison above, the Communist party assumed leadership over the usual process of national formation, and took positive action to construct Soviet international nations (nations in form not content) that would be content to be part of a unitary Soviet state. Positive support of the forms of nationhood was the essence of Soviet nationalities policy. The formation of the Soviet Union in 1922–23 established the territorial form of nationhood, not a federation of autonomous national territories. Therefore, the constitutional form of the Soviet Union was itself an act of affirmative action. . . .

. . . Modern empires, however, are not usually associated with affirmative action. They were typically divided into a center and periphery with different legal, political, and economic norms. The Soviet Union was a unitary state. In modern empires, the periphery was economically exploited by the center. This was not at all the case in the Soviet Union. Most importantly, modern empires had a privileged state-bearing people (Lenin's Great Power Nation), with whom the empire was identified and whose interests the empire served. The Soviet Union explicitly renounced the idea of a state-bearing people. Despite this fact, in an important sense the Russians did remain the Soviet Union's state-bearing people. Only the Russians were not granted their own territory and their own Communist party. Instead, the party asked the Russians to accept a formally unequal *national* status in order to further the cohesion of the multinational state. The hierarchical distinction between state-bearing and colonial peoples was thus reproduced, but reversed, as the new distinction between the formerly oppressed nationalities and the former Great Power nation.

. . . In Hroch's model, the imperial state acts only negatively (and futilely) to prevent the emergence of national movements. The Soviet state instead adopted the opposite strategy. It acted positively in support of this decolonizing movement with the aim of co-opting and diverting it away from the goal of independent statehood. Soviet affirmative action, then, was a radical strategy for imperial maintenance. As the state-bearing people, Russians were now literally asked to bear the burden of empire by suppressing their national interests and identifying with a non-national Affirmative Action Empire. Had Lenin lived to write a theoretical account of his creation, he might have called it: *The Soviet Union, as the Highest Stage of Imperialism.*

Terry Martin, "An Affirmative-Action Empire: The Emergence of the Soviet Nationalities Policy, 1919–1923," unpublished essay; a fuller version will appear in his *The Affirmative-Action Empire: Nations and Nationalism in the Soviet Union, 1923–1939* (Ithaca, NY: Cornell University Press, 2001).

Aleksandra Kollontai, *The Workers' Opposition*
1921

Robert V. Daniels, the historian of oppositions within the Communist party, wrote that this pamphlet by Kollontai "could well represent man's (sic.) highest ascent toward faith in the proletariat."[1] Written just before the Tenth Congress of the RKP (b) (March 1921), the pamphlet expresses the views of a fervent group of left Communists, formed loosely the year before in the famous "trade union controversy." As party leaders fought over what role the trade unions should play in the economy and the degree of control of the unions by the party, the Workers' Opposition, which included Aleksandr Shliapnikov, the first Soviet commissar of labor, came out clearly for empowering the working class, organized into trade unions, with autonomous control over industry. Lenin condemned this tendency as a "syndicalist" or "anarchist deviation" that hides behind the back of the proletariat but is actually not proletarian but petty bourgeois. He was furious at the Opposition's attack on what he considered the prerogatives of the party, the leading role in directing both the state and the economy. In the name of party unity, the congress ordered the dispersal of all organized factions, thus establishing a dangerous practice of the majority squelching the views of minorities. Lenin pushed for the expulsion of the faction from the party but failed to obtain the necessary two-thirds majority in the Central Committee by a single vote (August 9, 1921).

Kollontai and Shliapnikov took their case to the Executive Committee of the Communist International, where Trotsky argued the party's position and had the appeal dismissed. The next year, the Eleventh Party Congress upheld the condemnation of the Workers' Opposition, rejecting its view that the Soviet government was promoting the interests of kulaks and a new bourgeoisie. For the Workers' Opposition, NEP stood for 'New Exploitation of the Proletariat." Kollontai left the Opposition in the mid-1920s, but other veterans joined Trotsky's and later Zinoviev's oppositions. But pressure from the Stalinist majority convinced Shliapnikov and others to repent their errors and denounce the opposition. Though they were granted a pardon at the time, almost all of the oppositionists disappeared in the great purges of the 1930s. Only Kollontai, who had become a career diplomat, indeed the first female ambassador of any state, survived.

The first main basic cause is the unfortunate environment in which our party must work and act. The Russian Communist Party must build communism and carry into life its programme:

    a. in the environment of complete destruction and breakdown of the economic structure;

    b. in the face of a never diminishing and ruthless pressure of the imperialist states and White Guards;

    c. to the working class of Russia has fallen the lot of realising communism, creating new communist forms of economy in an economically backward coun-

---

1. Robert Vincent Daniels, *The Conscience of the Revolution: Communist Opposition in Soviet Russia* (Cambridge, MA: Harvard University Press, 1960), p. 128.

try with a preponderant peasant population, where the necessary economic prerequisites for socialisation of production and distribution are lacking, and where
capitalism has not as yet been able to complete the full cycle of its development
(from the unlimited struggle of competition of the first stage of capitalism to its
highest form: the regulation of production by capitalist unions—the trusts).

It is quite natural that all these factors hinder the realisation of our programme
(particularly in its essential part—in the reconstruction of industries on the new basis)
and inject into our Soviet economic policy *diverse influences and a lack of uniformity.*

Out of this basic cause follow the two others. First of all, the economic backwardness of Russia and the domination of the peasantry within its boundaries create
that diversity, and inevitably detract the practical policy of our party from the clear-
cut *class direction, consistent in principle and theory.*

Any party standing at the head of a heterogeneous Soviet state is compelled
to consider the aspirations of peasants with their petty-bourgeois inclinations and
resentments towards communism, as well as lend an ear to the numerous petty-
bourgeois elements, remnants of the former capitalists in Russia and to all kinds of
traders, middlemen, petty officials etc. These have very rapidly adapted themselves to
the Soviet institutions and occupy responsible positions in the centres, appearing in
the capacity of agents of different commissariats etc. . . .

These are the elements—the petty-bourgeois elements widely scattered through
the Soviet institutions, the elements of the middle class, with their hostility towards
communism, and with their predilections towards the immutable customs of the past,
with resentments and fears towards revolutionary acts. These are the elements that
bring decay into our Soviet institutions, breeding there an atmosphere *altogether re-
pugnant to the working class.* They are two different worlds and hostile at that. And yet
we in Soviet Russia are compelled to persuade both ourselves and the working class
that the petty-bourgeoisie and middle classes (not to speak of well-to-do peasants)
can quite comfortably exist under the common motto: "All power to the Soviets",
forgetful of the fact that in practical everyday life, the interests of the workers and
those of the middle classes and peasantry imbued with petty-bourgeois psychology
must inevitably clash, rending the Soviet policy asunder, and deforming its clear-cut
class statutes.

Beside peasant-owners in the villages and burgher elements in the cities, our
party in its Soviet state policy is forced to reckon with the influence exerted by the
representatives of wealthy bourgeoisie now appearing in the form of specialists, technicians, engineers and former managers of financial and industrial affairs, who by all
their past experience are bound to the capitalist system of production. They cannot
even imagine any other mode of production, but the one which lies *within the traditional bounds of capitalist economics.*

The more Soviet Russia finds itself in need of specialists in the sphere of technique and management of production, the stronger becomes the influence of these
elements, foreign to the working class, on the development of our economy. Having
been thrown aside during the first period of the revolution, and being compelled to
take up an attitude of watchful waiting or sometimes even open hostility towards the
Soviet authorities, particularly during the most trying months (the historical sabotage
by the intellectuals), this social group of brains in capitalist production, of servile,

hired, well-paid servants of capital, acquires more and more influence and importance in politics with every day that passes.

Do we need names? Every fellow worker, carefully watching our foreign and domestic policy, recalls more than one such name.

As long as the centre of our life remained at the military fronts, the influence of these gentlemen directing our Soviet policy, particularly in the sphere of industrial reconstruction, was comparatively negligible.

Specialists, the remnants of the past, by all their nature closely, unalterably bound to the bourgeois system that we aim to destroy, gradually began to penetrate into our Red Army, introducing there their atmosphere of the past (blind subordination, servile obedience, distinction, ranks, and the arbitrary will of superiors in place of class discipline, etc.). But their influence did not extend to the general political activity of the Soviet Republic.

The proletariat did not question their superior skill to direct military affairs, fully realising through their healthy class instinct that in military matters the working class as a class cannot express a new world, is powerless to introduce substantial changes into the military system—to reconstruct its foundation on a new class basis. Professional militarism—an inheritance of past ages—militarism and wars will have no place in communist society. The struggle will go on along other channels, will take quite different forms inconceivable to our imagination. Militarism lives through its last days, through the transitory epoch of dictatorship, and therefore it is only natural that the workers, as a class, could not introduce into the forms and systems anything new and conducive to the future development of society. Even in the Red Army, however, there were innovating touches of the working class. But the nature of militarism remained the same, and the direction of military affairs by the former officers and generals of the old army did not draw the Soviet policy in military matters away to the opposite side sufficiently for the workers to feel any harm to themselves or to their class interests.

In the sphere of national economy it is quite different however. Production, its organisation—this is the essence of communism. To debar the workers from the organisation of industry, to deprive them, that is, their individual organisations, of the opportunity to develop their powers in creating new forms of production in industry through their unions, to deny these expressions of the class organisation of the proletariat, while placing full reliance on the "skill" of specialists trained and taught to carry on production under a quite different system of production—is to jump off the rails of scientific marxist thought. That is, however, just the thing that is being done by the leaders of our party at present.

Taking into consideration the utter collapse of our industries while still clinging to the capitalist mode of production (payment for labour in money, variations in wages received according to the work done) our party leaders, in a fit of distrust in the creative abilities of workers' collectives, are seeking salvation from the industrial chaos. Where? In the hands of scions of the bourgeois-capitalist past. In businessmen and technicians, whose creative abilities in the sphere of industry are subject to the routine, habits and methods of the capitalist system of production and economy. They are the ones who introduce the ridiculously naïve belief that it is possible to bring about communism by bureaucratic means. *They* "decree" where it is now necessary to create and carry on research.

The more the military front recedes before the economic front, the keener becomes our crying need, the more pronounced the influence of that group which is not only inherently foreign to communism, but absolutely unable to develop the right qualities for introducing new forms of organising the work, of new motives for increasing production, of *new approaches to production and distribution*. All these technicians, practical men, men of business experience, who just now appear on the surface of Soviet life, bring pressure to bear upon the leaders of our party through and within the Soviet institutions by exerting their influence on economic policy.

The party, therefore, finds itself in a difficult and embarrassing situation regarding the control over the Soviet state. It is forced to lend an ear and to adapt itself to three economically hostile groups of the population, each different in social structure. The workers demand a clear-cut, uncompromising policy, a rapid, forced advance towards communism; the peasantry, with its petty-bourgeois proclivities and sympathies, demands different kinds of "freedom", including freedom of trade and non-interference in their affairs. The latter are joined in this demand by the burgher class in the form of "agents" of Soviet officials, commissaries in the army etc. who have already adapted themselves to the Soviet régime, and sway our policy towards petty-bourgeois lines.

As far as the centre is concerned, the influence of these petty-bourgeois elements is negligible. But in the provinces and in local Soviet activity, their influence is a great and harmful one. Finally, there is still another group of men, consisting of the former managers and directors of the capitalist industries. These are not the magnates of capital, like Ryabushinsky or Rublikov, whom the Soviet republic got rid of during the first phase of the revolution, but they are the most talented servants of the capitalist system of production, the "brains and genius" of capitalism, its true creators and sponsors. Heartily approving the centralist tendencies of the Soviet government in the sphere of economics, well realising all the benefits of trustification and regulation of production (this, by the way, is being carried on by capital in all advanced industrial countries), they are striving for just one thing—they want this regulation to be carried on, not through the labour organisations (the industrial unions), but by themselves—acting now under the guise of Soviet economic institutions—the central industrial committees, industrial centres of the Supreme Council of National Economy, where they are already firmly rooted. The influence of these gentlemen on the "sober" state policy of our leaders is great, considerably greater than is desirable. This influence is reflected in the policy which defends and cultivates bureaucratism (with no attempts to change it entirely, but just to improve it). The policy is particularly obvious in the sphere of our foreign trade with the capitalist states, which is just beginning to spring up: *these commercial relations are carried on over the heads of the Russian as well as the foreign organised workers.* It finds its expression, also, in a whole series of measures restricting the self-activity of the masses and giving the initiative to the scions of the capitalist world.

Among all these various groups of the population, our party, by trying to find a middle ground, is compelled to steer a course which does not jeopardise the unity of the state interests. The clear-cut policy of our party, in the process of identifying itself with Soviet state institutions, is being gradually transformed into an upper-class policy, which in essence is nothing else but an adaptation of our directing centres to the heterogeneous and irreconcilable interests of a socially different, mixed, population. This adaptation leads to inevitable vacillation, fluctuations, deviations and mistakes. It is only necessary to recall the zigzag-like road of our policy towards the peasantry, which from "banking on the poor peasant", brought us to placing reliance on "the industrious peasant-owner". Let us admit that this policy is proof of the political soberness and "statecraft wisdom" of our directing centres. But the future historian, analysing without bias the stages of our domination, will find and point out that in this is evident "a dangerous digression" from the class line toward "adaptation" and a course full of harmful possibilities or results. . . .

As long as the working class, during the first period of the revolution, felt itself to be the only bearer of communism, there was perfect unanimity in the party. In the days immediately following the October revolution, none could even think of "ups" as something different from "downs", for in those days the advanced workers were busily engaged in realising point after point in our class-communist programme. The peasant who received the land did not at the time assert himself as a part of and a full-fledged citizen of the Soviet republic. Intellectuals, specialists, men of affairs—the entire petty-bourgeois class and pseudo-specialists at present climbing up the Soviet ladder, rung by rung, under the guise of "specialists", stepped aside, watching and waiting but meanwhile giving freedom to the advanced working masses to develop their creative abilities.

At present, however, it is just the other way. The worker feels, sees, and realises at every step that specialists and (what is worse) untrained illiterate pseudo-specialists, and unpractical men, throw out the worker and fill up all the high administrative posts of our industrial and economic institutions. And the party, instead of putting the brakes on this tendency from the elements which are altogether foreign to the working class and communism, encourages it. The party seeks salvation from the industrial chaos, not in the workers but in these very elements. Not in the workers, not in their union organisations does the party repose its trust, but in these elements. The working masses feel it and instead of unanimity and unity in the party, there appears a break.

The masses are not blind. Whatever words the most popular leaders might use in order to conceal their deviation from a clear-cut class policy, whatever the compromises made with the peasants and world capitalism, and whatever the trust that the leaders place in the disciples of the capitalist system of production, the working masses feel where the digression begins.

The workers may cherish an ardent affection and love for such personalities as Lenin. They may be fascinated by the incomparable flowery eloquence of Trotsky and his organising abilities. They may revere a number of other leaders as leaders. But when the masses feel that they and their class are not trusted, it is quite natural that they say: "No, halt! We refuse to follow you blindly. Let us examine the situation. Your policy of picking out the middle ground between three socially opposed groups is a wise one indeed, but it smacks of the well-tried and familiar adaptation and opportunism. Today we may gain something with the help of your sober policy, but let us beware lest we find ourselves on a wrong road that, through zigzags and turns, will lead from the future to the débris of the past."

Distrust of the workers by the leaders is steadily growing. The more sober these leaders get, the more clever statesmen they become with their policy of sliding over the blade of a sharp knife between communism and compromise with the bourgeois past, the deeper becomes the abyss between the "ups" and the "downs", the less understanding there is, and the more painful and inevitable becomes the crisis within the party itself.

The third reason enhancing the crisis in the party is that, in fact, during these three years of the revolution, the economic situation of the working class, of those who work in factories and mills, has not only not been improved, but has become more unbearable. This nobody dares to deny. The suppressed and widely-spread dissatisfaction among workers (*workers,* mind you) has a real justification.

Only the peasants gained directly by the revolution. As far as the middle classes are concerned, they very cleverly adapted themselves to the new conditions, together with the representatives of the rich bourgeoisie, who had occupied all the responsible and directing positions in the Soviet institutions (particularly in the sphere of directing state economy, in the industrial organisations and the re-establishment of commercial relations with foreign nations). Only the basic class of the Soviet republic, which bore all the burdens of the dictatorship as a mass, ekes out a shamefully pitiful existence.

The workers' republic controlled by the communists, by the vanguard of the working class, which, to quote Lenin, "has absorbed all the revolutionary energy of the class", has not had time enough to ponder over and improve the conditions of all the workers. . . .

The trouble is that Lenin, Trotsky, Bukharin and others see the functions of the trade unions not as control over production or as the taking over of the industries, but merely as a school for bringing up the masses. During the discussion it seemed to some of our comrades that Trotsky stood for a gradual "absorption of the unions by the state"—not all of a sudden, but gradually and that he wanted to reserve for them the right of ultimate control over production, as it is expressed in our programme. This point, it seemed at first, put Trotsky on a common ground with the Opposition at a time when the group represented by Lenin and Zinoviev, being opposed to the "absorption of the state", saw the object of union activity and their problem as "training for communism". "Trade unions," thunder Trotsky and Zinoviev, "are necessary for the rough work" . . . Trotsky himself, it would seem, understands the task somewhat differently. In his opinion, the most important work of the unions consists in organising production. In this he is perfectly right. He is also right when he says, "Inasmuch as unions are schools of communism, they are such schools not in carrying on general propaganda (for such activity would mean they were playing the part of clubs), not in mobilising their members for military work or collecting the produce tax, but for the purpose of all-round education of their members on the basis of their participation in production" . . . All this is true, but there is one grave omission: *the unions are not only schools for communism, but they are its creators as well.*

Creativeness of the class is being lost sight of. Trotsky replaces it by the initiative of "the real organisers of production", by communists inside the unions . . . What communists? According to Trotsky, by those communists appointed by the party to responsible administrative positions in the unions (for reasons that quite often have nothing in common with considerations of industrial and economic problems of the unions). Trotsky is quite frank. He does not believe that the workers are ready to create communism, and through pain, suffering and blunder still seek to create new forms of production. He has expressed this frankly and openly. He has already carried out his system of "club education" of the masses, of training them for the role of "master" in the Central Administrative Body of Railways, adopting all those methods of educating the masses which were practised by our traditional journeymen upon their apprentices. It is true that a beating on the head by a boot-stretcher does not make an apprentice a successful shopkeeper after he becomes a journeyman. And yet as long as the boss teacher's stick hangs over his head, he works and produces.

This, in Trotsky's opinion, is the whole essence of shifting the central point "from politics to industrial problems". To raise, even temporarily, productivity by every and all means is the whole crux of the task. The whole course of training in the trade unions must be, in Trotsky's opinion, also directed towards this end.

Comrades Lenin and Zinoviev, however, disagree with him. They are "educators" of "a modern trend of thought". It has been stated many a time that the trade unions are schools for communism. . . .

Wide publicity, freedom of opinion and discussion, the right to criticise within the party and among the members of the trade unions—such are the decisive steps that can put an end to the prevailing system of bureaucracy. Freedom of criticism, right of different factions freely to present their views at party meetings, freedom of discussion—are no longer the demands of the Workers' Opposition alone. Under the growing pressure from the masses, a whole series of measures that were demanded by the rank and file long before the party conference are now recognised and officially promulgated. One need only read the proposals of the Moscow Committee in regard to party structure to be proud of the great influence that is being exerted on the party centres. If it were not for the Workers' Opposition, the Moscow Committee would never have taken such a sharp "turn to the left". However, we must not overestimate this "leftism", for it is only a declaration of principles to the Congress. It may happen, as it has many a time with decisions of our party leaders during these years, that this radical declaration will soon be forgotten. As a rule, these decisions are accepted by our party centres only just as the mass impetus is felt. As soon as life again swings into normal channels, the decisions are forgotten. . . .

Inequality in the party still persists, in spite of repeated resolutions passed on this subject. Comrades who dare to disagree with decrees from above are still being persecuted. There are many such instances. If all these various party decisions are not enforced, then it is necessary to eliminate the basic cause that interferes with their enforcement. We must remove from the party those who are afraid of publicity, strict accountability before the rank and file, and freedom of criticism.

Non-working-class members of the party, and those workers who fell under their influence, are afraid of all this. It is not enough to clean the party of all non-proletarian elements by registration or to increase the control in time of enrolment, etc. It is also necessary to create opportunities for the workers to join the party. It is necessary to simplify the admission of workers to the party, to create a more friendly atmosphere in the party itself, so that workers might feel themselves at home. In responsible party officials, they should not see superiors but more experienced comrades, ready to share with them their knowledge, experience and skill, and to consider seriously workers' needs and interests. How many comrades, particularly young workers, are driven away from the party just because we manifest our impatience with them by our assumed superiority and strictness, instead of teaching them, bringing them up in the spirit of communism?

Besides the spirit of bureaucracy, an atmosphere of officialdom finds a fertile ground in our party. If there is any comradeship in our party it exists only among the rank and file members.

The task of the party congress is to take into account this unpleasant reality. It must ponder over the question: why is the Workers' Opposition insisting on introducing equality, on eliminating all privileges in the party, and on placing under a stricter responsibility to the masses those administrative officials who are elected by them.

In its struggle for establishing democracy in the party, and for the elimination of all bureaucracy, the Workers' Opposition advances three cardinal demands:

1. Return to the principle of election all along the line with the elimination of all bureaucracy, by making all responsible officials answerable to the masses.

2. Introduce wide publicity within the party, both concerning general questions and where individuals are involved. Pay more attention to the voice of the rank and file (wide discussion of all questions by the rank and file and their summarising by the leaders; admission of any member to the meetings of party centres, except when the problems discussed require particular secrecy). Establish freedom of opinion and expression (giving the right not only to criticise freely during discussions, but to use funds for publication of literature proposed by different party factions).

3. Make the party more a workers' party. Limit the number of those who fill offices, both in the party and the Soviet institutions at the same time.

This last demand is particularly important. Our party must not only build communism, but prepare and educate the masses for a prolonged period of struggle against world capitalism, which may take on unexpected new forms. It would be childish to imagine that, having repelled the invasion of the White Guards and of imperialism on the military fronts, we will be free from the danger of a new attack from world capital, which is striving to seize Soviet Russia by roundabout ways to penetrate into our life, and to use the Soviet Republic for its own ends. This is the great danger that we must stand guard against. And herein lies the problem for our party: how to meet the enemy well-prepared, how to rally all the proletarian forces around the clear-cut class issues (the other groups of the population will always gravitate to capitalism). It is the duty of our leaders to prepare for this new page of our revolutionary history.

It will only be possible to find correct solutions to these questions when we succeed in uniting the party all along the line, not only together with the Soviet institutions, but with the trade unions as well. The filling up of offices in both party and trade unions not only tends to deviate party policy from clear-cut class lines but also renders the party susceptible to the influences of world capitalism during this coming epoch, influences exerted through concessions and trade agreements. To make the central committee one that the workers feel is their own is to create a central committee wherein representatives of the lower layers connected with the masses would not merely play the role of "parading generals", or a merchant's wedding party. The committee should be closely bound with the wide non-party working masses in the trade unions. It would thereby be enabled to formulate the slogans of the time, to express the workers' needs, their aspirations, and to direct the policy of the party along class lines.

Such are the demands of the Workers' Opposition. Such is its historic task. And whatever derisive remarks the leaders of our party may employ, the Workers' Opposition is today the only vital active force with which the party is compelled to contend, and to which it will have to pay attention.

Is the Opposition necessary? Is it necessary, on behalf of the liberation of the workers throughout the world from the yoke of capital, to welcome its formation? Or is it an undesirable movement, detrimental to the fighting energy of the party, and destructive to its ranks?

Every comrade who is not prejudiced against the Opposition and who wants to approach the question with an open mind and to analyse it, even if not in accordance with what the recognised authorities tell him, will see from these brief outlines that the Opposition is useful and necessary. It is useful primarily because it has awakened slumbering thought. During these years of revolution, we have been so preoccupied with our pressing affairs that we have ceased to appraise our actions from the standpoint of principle and theory. . . .

The Workers' Opposition has said what has long ago been printed in The Communist Manifesto by Marx and Engels: the building of communism can and must be the work of the toiling masses themselves. The building of communism belongs to the workers.

Finally, the Workers' Opposition has raised its voice against bureaucracy. It has dared to say that bureaucracy binds the wings of self-activity and the creativeness of the working class; that it deadens thought, hinders initiative and experimenting in the sphere of finding new approaches to production; in a word that it hinders the development of new forms for production and life.

Instead of a system of bureaucracy, the Workers' Opposition proposes a system of self-activity for the masses. In this respect, the party leaders even now are making concessions and "recognising" their deviations as being harmful to communism and detrimental to working class interests (the rejection of centralism). The Tenth Congress, we understand, will make another series of concessions to the Workers' Opposition. Thus, in spite of the fact that the Workers' Opposition appeared as a mere group inside the party only a few months ago, it has already fulfilled its mission. It has compelled the leading party centres to listen to the workers' sound advice. At present, whatever might be the wrath towards the Workers' Opposition, it has the historical future to support it.

Just because we believe in the vital forces of our party, we know that after some hesitation, resistance and devious political moves, our party will ultimately again follow that path which has been blazed by the elemental forces of the proletariat. Organised as a class, there will be no split. If some groups leave the party, they will not be the ones that make up the Workers' Opposition. Only those will fall out who attempt to evolve into principles the temporary deviations from the spirit of the communist programme that were forced upon the party by the prolonged civil war, and hold to them as if they were the essence of our political line of action.

All those in the party who have been accustomed to reflect the class viewpoint of the ever-growing proletariat will absorb and digest everything that is wholesome, practical and sound in the Workers' Opposition. Not in vain will the rank-and-file worker speak with assurance and reconcilation: "Ilyich (Lenin) will ponder, he will think it over, he will listen to us. And then he will decide to turn the party rudder toward the Opposition. Ilyich will be with us yet".

The sooner the party leaders take into account the Opposition's work and follow the road indicated by the rank-and-file members, the quicker shall we overcome the crisis in the party. And the sooner shall we step over the line beyond which humanity, having freed itself from the objective economic laws and taking advantage of all the richness and knowledge of common working-class experience, will consciously begin to create the human history of the communist epoch.

Translated and first published in Sylvia Pankhurst, *Workers Dreadnought* (April 22–August, 19, 1921; later reprinted in *Solidarity* (London, 1961; 1968); and in *Selected Writings of Alexandra Kollontai* (ed. Alix Holt) (New York: W. W. Norton, 1977), pp. 159–200.

Resolutions of the Tenth Congress of the Russian Communist Party, "On Party Unity" and "On the Syndicalist and Anarchist Deviation in Our Party"
March 1921

It is not too much of an exaggeration to claim that March 1921 was as significant a turning point in Russian/Soviet history as October 1917. The long years of revolution and civil war were coming to an end; the extravagant hopes of exporting revolution to Europe and the "East" had been laid to rest; and Soviet Russia was making its first important agreements with the capitalist states of the West. At a moment of economic collapse, the Communist party abandoned the militant statist policies that would become known as "war communism" and at the Tenth Party Congress adopted a "new economic policy" (NEP) that would allow a degree of marketization of the economy. But the turn toward economic moderation was not complemented by a turn toward political pluralism. Fearing opposition both within the party and among the peasant masses, Lenin tightened the political order, clamping down on factions within the party and steadily moving against oppositional parties. When sailors at the Kronstadt naval base near Petrograd mutinied against the anti-democratic practices of the Communists, calling for soviets without the party, the Communists responded with a swift military campaign that crushed the revolt and graphically demonstrated the new limits on political expression.

"ON PARTY UNITY"

1. The Congress calls the attention of all members of the Party to the fact that the unity and solidarity of the ranks of the Party, ensuring complete mutual confidence among Party members and genuine team work, genuinely embodying the unanimity of will of the vanguard of the proletariat, are particularly essential at the present juncture when a number of circumstances are increasing the vacillation among the petty-bourgeois population of the country.

2. Notwithstanding this, even before the general Party discussion on the trade unions, certain signs of factionalism had been apparent in the Party, viz., the formation of groups with separate platforms, striving to a certain degree to segregate and

create their own group discipline. Such symptoms of factionalism were manifested, for example, at a Party conference in Moscow (November 1920) and in Kharkov, both by the so-called "Workers' Opposition" group, and partly by the so-called "Democratic-Centralism" group.

All class-conscious workers must clearly realize the perniciousness and impermissibility of factionalism of any kind, for no matter how the representatives of individual groups may desire to safeguard Party unity, in practice factionalism inevitably leads to the weakening of team work and to intensified and repeated attempts by the enemies of the Party, who have fastened themselves onto it because it is the governing Party, to widen the cleavage and to use it for counterrevolutionary purposes.

The way the enemies of the proletariat take advantage of every deviation from the thoroughly consistent communist line was perhaps most strikingly shown in the case of the Kronstadt mutiny, when the bourgeois counterrevolutionaries and Whiteguards in all countries of the world immediately expressed their readiness to accept even the slogans of the Soviet system, if only they might thereby secure the overthrow of the dictatorship of the proletariat in Russia, and when the Socialist-Revolutionaries and the bourgeois counterrevolutionaries in general resorted in Kronstadt to slogans calling for an insurrection against the Soviet government of Russia ostensibly in the interest of Soviet power. These facts fully prove that the Whiteguards strive, and are able, to disguise themselves as Communists, and even as the most Left Communists, solely for the purpose of weakening and overthrowing the bulwark of the proletarian revolution in Russia. Menshevik leaflets distributed in Petrograd on the eve of the Kronstadt mutiny likewise show how the Mensheviks took advantage of the disagreements and certain rudiments of factionalism in the Russian Communist Party actually in order to egg on and support the Kronstadt mutineers, the Socialist-Revolutionaries and Whiteguards, while claiming to be opponents of mutiny and supporters of the Soviet power, only with supposedly slight modifications.

3. In this question, propaganda should consist, on the one hand, of a comprehensive explanation of the harmfulness and danger of factionalism from the point of view of Party unity and of achieving unanimity of will among the vanguard of the proletariat as the fundamental condition for the success of the dictatorship of the proletariat; and, on the other hand, of an explanation of the peculiar features of the latest tactical devices of the enemies of the Soviet power. These enemies, having realized the hopelessness of counterrevolution under an openly Whiteguard flag, are now doing their utmost to utilize the disagreements within the Russian Communist Party and to further the counterrevolution in one way or another by transferring power to the political groupings which outwardly are closest to the recognition of Soviet power.

Propaganda must also teach the lessons of preceding revolutions, in which the counterrevolution supported that opposition to the extreme revolutionary party which stood closest to the latter in order to undermine and overthrow the revolutionary dictatorship and thus pave the way for the subsequent complete victory of the counterrevolution, of the capitalists and landlords.

4. In the practical struggle against factionalism, every organization of the Party must take strict measures to prevent any factional actions whatsoever. Criticism of the Party's shortcomings, which is absolutely necessary, must be conducted in such a way that every practical proposal shall be submitted immediately, without any delay, in the

most precise form possible, for consideration and decision to the leading local and central bodies of the Party. Moreover, everyone who criticizes must see to it that the form of his criticism takes into account the position of the Party, surrounded as it is by a ring of enemies, and that the content of his criticism is such that, by directly participating in Soviet and Party work, he can test the rectification of the errors of the Party or of individual Party members in practice. Every analysis of the general line of the Party, estimate of its practical experience, verification of the fulfilment of its decisions, study of methods of rectifying errors, etc., must under no circumstances be submitted for preliminary discussion to groups formed on the basis of "platforms," etc., but must be exclusively submitted for discussion directly to all the members of the Party. For this purpose, the Congress orders that the *Discussion Bulletin* and special symposiums be published more regularly, and that unceasing efforts be made to secure that criticism shall be concentrated on essentials and not assume a form capable of assisting the class enemies of the proletariat.

5. Rejecting in principle the deviation towards syndicalism and anarchism, to the examination of which a special resolution is devoted, and instructing the Central Committee to secure the complete elimination of all factionalism, the Congress at the same time declares that every practical proposal concerning questions to which the so-called "workers' opposition" group, for example, has devoted special attention, such as purging the Party of nonproletarian and unreliable elements, combating bureaucracy, developing democracy and the initiative of workers, etc., must be examined with the greatest care and tried out in practical work. The Party must know that we do not take all the measures that are necessary in regard to these questions because we encounter a number of obstacles of various kinds, and that, while ruthlessly rejecting unpractical and factional pseudo criticisms, the Party will unceasingly continue—trying out new methods—to fight with all the means at its disposal against bureaucracy, for the extension of democracy and initiative, for detecting, exposing and expelling from the Party elements that have wormed their way into its ranks, etc.

6. The Congress therefore hereby declares dissolved and orders the immediate dissolution of all groups without exception that have been formed on the basis of one platform or another (such as the "workers' opposition" group, the "democratic-centralism" group, etc.). Nonobservance of this decision of the Congress shall involve absolute and immediate expulsion from the Party.

7. In order to ensure strict discipline within the Party and in all Soviet work and to secure the maximum unanimity in removing all factionalism, the Congress authorizes the Central Committee, in cases of breach of discipline or of a revival or toleration of factionalism, to apply all Party penalties, including expulsion, and in regard to members of the Central Committee to reduce them to the status of alternate members and even, as an extreme measure, to expel them from the Party. A necessary condition for the application of such an extreme measure to members of the Central Committee, alternate members of the Central Committee and members of the Control Commission is the convocation of a plenum of the Central Committee, to which all alternate members of the Central Committee and all members of the Control Commission shall be invited. If such a general assembly of the most responsible leaders of the Party, by a two-thirds majority, deems it necessary to reduce a member of the Central Committee to the status of alternate member, or to expel him from the Party, this measure shall be put into effect immediately.

"ON THE SYNDICALIST AND
ANARCHIST DEVIATION IN OUR PARTY"

1. In the past few months a syndicalist and anarchist deviation has been definitely revealed in our Party, and calls for the most resolute measures of ideological struggle and also for purging and restoring the health of the Party.

2. The said deviation is due partly to the influx into the Party of former Mensheviks and also of workers and peasants who have not yet fully assimilated the communist world outlook; mainly, however, this deviation is due to the influence exercised upon the proletariat and on the Russian Communist Party by the petty-bourgeois element, which is exceptionally strong in our country, and which inevitably engenders vacillation towards anarchism, particularly at a time when the conditions of the masses have sharply deteriorated as a consequence of the crop failure and the devastating effects of war, and when the demobilization of the army numbering millions releases hundreds and hundreds of thousands of peasants and workers unable immediately to find regular means of livelihood.

3. The most theoretically complete and formulated expression of this deviation (*or:* one of the most complete, etc., expressions of this deviation) are the theses and other literary productions of the so-called "workers' opposition" group. Sufficiently illustrative of this is, for example, the following thesis propounded by this group: "The organization of the administration of the national economy is the function of an All-Russian Producers' Congress organized in industrial trade unions, which elect a central organ for the administration of the entire national economy of the Republic."

The ideas at the bottom of this and numerous analogous statements are radically wrong in theory, and represent a complete rupture with Marxism and Communism as well as with the practical experience of all semiproletarian revolutions and of the present proletarian revolution.

Firstly, the concept "producer" combines proletarians with semiproletarians and small commodity producers, thus radically departing from the fundamental concept of the class struggle and from the fundamental demand for drawing a precise distinction between classes.

Secondly, banking on the non-Party masses, flirting with them, as expressed in the above-quoted theses, is no less a radical departure from Marxism.

Marxism teaches—and this tenet has not only been formally endorsed by the whole of the Communist International in the decisions of the Second (1920) Congress of the Comintern on the role of the political party of the proletariat, but has also been confirmed in practice by our revolution—that only the political party of the working class, i.e., the Communist Party, is capable of uniting, training and organizing a vanguard of the proletariat and of the whole mass of the working people that alone will be capable of withstanding the inevitable petty-bourgeois vacillations of this mass and the inevitable traditions and relapses of narrow craft unionism or craft prejudices among the proletariat, and of guiding all the united activities of the whole of the proletariat, i.e., of leading it politically, and through it, the whole mass of the working people. Without this the dictatorship of the proletariat is impossible.

The wrong understanding of the role of the Communist Party in relation to the non-Party proletariat, and in the relation of the first and second factor to the whole mass of working people, is a radical, theoretical departure from Communism and a deviation towards syndicalism and anarchism, and this deviation permeates all the views of the "workers' opposition" group.

4. The Tenth Congress of the Russian Communist Party declares that it also regards as radically wrong all attempts on the part of the said group and of other persons to defend their fallacious views by referring to point 5 of the economic section of the program of the Russian Communist Party which deals with the role of the trade unions. This point says that "the trade unions must eventually actually concentrate in their hands the entire administration of the whole of national economy as a single economic unit" and that they will "ensure in this way indissoluble ties between the central state administration, the national economy and the broad masses of the working people," "drawing" these masses "into the direct work of managing economy."

This point in the program of the Russian Communist Party also states that a condition precedent to the trade unions "eventually concentrating" is that they must "to an increasing degree free themselves from the narrow craft spirit" and embrace the majority "and gradually all" the working people.

Lastly, this point in the program of the Russian Communist Party emphasizes that "according to the laws of the R.S.F.S.R. and by established practice the trade unions already participate in all the local and central organs of administration of industry."

Instead of studying the practical experience of participation in administration, and instead of developing this experience further, strictly in conformity with successes achieved and rectified mistakes, the syndicalists and anarchists advance as an immediate slogan "congresses or a Congress of Producers" "which elect" the organs of administration of economy. Thus, the leading, educational and organizing role of the Party in relation to the trade unions of the proletariat, and of the latter to the semi-petty-bourgeois and even wholly petty-bourgeois masses of working people, is utterly evaded and eliminated, and instead of continuing and correcting the practical work of building new forms of economy already begun by the Soviet state, we get petty-bourgeois-anarchist disruption of this work, which can only lead to the triumph of the bourgeois counterrevolution.

5. In addition to theoretical fallacies and a radically wrong attitude towards the practical experience of economic construction already begun by the Soviet government, the Congress of the Russian Communist Party discerns in the views of these and analogous groups and persons a gross political mistake and a direct political danger to the very existence of the dictatorship of the proletariat.

In a country like Russia, the overwhelming preponderance of the petty-bourgeois element and the devastation, impoverishment, epidemics, crop failures, extreme want and hardship inevitably resulting from the war, engender particularly sharp vacillations in the moods of the petty-bourgeois and semiproletarian masses. At one moment the wavering is in the direction of strengthening the alliance between these masses and the proletariat, and at another moment in the direction of bourgeois restoration. The whole experience of all revolutions in the eighteenth, nineteenth, and twentieth centuries shows with utmost and absolute clarity and conviction that the only possible result of these vacillations—if the unity, strength and influence of the revolutionary vanguard of the proletariat is weakened in the slightest degree—can be the restoration of the power and property of the capitalists and landlords.

Hence, the views of the "workers' opposition" and of like-minded elements are not only wrong in theory, but in practice are an expression of petty-bourgeois and anarchist wavering, in practice weaken the consistency of the leading line of the Communist Party, and in practice help the class enemies of the proletarian revolution.

6. In view of all this, the Congress of the Russian Communist Party, emphatically rejecting the said ideas which express a syndicalist and anarchist deviation, deems it necessary.

Firstly, to wage an unswerving and systematic ideological struggle against these ideas;

Secondly, the Congress regards the propaganda of these ideas as being incompatible with membership of the Russian Communist Party.

Instructing the Central Committee of the Party strictly to enforce these decisions, the Congress at the same time points out that space can and should be devoted in special publications, symposiums, etc., for a most comprehensive interchange of opinion among Party members on all the questions herein indicated.

V. I. Lenin, *Selected Works in Two Volumes* (Moscow: Foreign Languages Publishing House, 1952), II, Part 2, pp. 497–501, 502–506.

Lenin's Letter to Stalin
July 17, 1922

From their first days in power, the Bolsheviks had a difficult relationship with the Russian intelligentsia. Teachers refused to teach; journalists attacked them in the press; and many writers, artists, and professors preferred liberals, moderate socialists, or even monarchists to the Bolsheviks. With the economic liberalization of the New Economic Policy, intellectual life revived. New publications appeared, and various professionals, like doctors and academics, began to organize themselves. Extraordinarily fearful of the revival of the "bourgeois" intelligentsia, Lenin called for "a systematic offensive against bourgeois ideology, philosophical reaction, and all forms of idealism and mysticism." In May 1922, he wrote to Feliks Dzerzhinskii, the head of the Cheka, to consider deporting those "writers and professors helping the counterrevolution." Ironically Soviet Russia, which had been a haven a few years earlier for anarchists and other radicals forcibly deported from the United States, now drove hundreds of non-Communist socialists and liberals out of the country. Tens of thousands of other people, well over a million altogether, emigrated from the new Soviet republic, either as defeated White Guardists, disenfranchised bourgeois, or the growing numbers of those defined by the Bolsheviks as enemies of the revolution.

Comrade Stalin!

On the matter of deporting Mensheviks, Popular Socialists [*NS*], Constitutional Democrats [Kadets], etc. from Russia, I would like to ask a few questions, since this operation, which was started before my leave, still has not been completed.

Has the decision been made to "eradicate" all the *NS*s? Peshekhonov, Miakotin, Gornfel'd, Petrishchev *et al.?*

As far as I'm concerned, deport them all. [They're] more harmful than any *SR* [Socialist Revolutionary]—because [they're] more clever.

Also A. N. Potresov, Izgoev and *all* the *Ekonomist* contributors (Ozerov and *many, many* others). The Mensheviks Rozanov (a physician, cunning), Vigdorchik, (Migulov or something like that), Liubov' Nikolaevna Radchenko and her young daughter (rumor has it they're the vilest enemies of Bolshevism), N. A. Rozhkov (he has to be

deported, incorrigible), S. A. Frank (author of *Metodologiia*). The commission supervised by Mantsev, Messing et al. should present lists and several hundred such ladies
and gentlemen must be deported without mercy. Let's purge Russia for a long while.

As for Lezhnev (former[ly associated with] *Den'*), let's think it over: shouldn't we
deport him? He will always be the wiliest sort as far as I can judge based on his articles I have read.

Ozerov as well as all the *Ekonomist* contributors are the most ruthless enemies. All
of them—out of Russia.

This must be done at once. By the end of the *SRs'* trial, no later. Arrest a few hundred and *without a declaration* of motives—get out, ladies and gentlemen!

Deport all authors of *Dom literatorov, Mysl'* from Piter [Petrograd]; ransack
Kharkov, *we do not know it,* for us it is a "foreign country." We must purge *quickly, no
later* than the end of the *SRs'* trial.

Pay attention to the writers in Piter (addresses, *Novaia Russkaia Kniga,* No. 4,
1922, p. 37) and to the list of private publishers (p. *29*).

With communist greetings   Lenin

RTsKhIDNI [Rossiiskii Tsetr Khraneniia i Izucheniia Dokumentov Noveishei Istorii] [now RGASPI
(Rossiiskii Gosudarstvennyi Arkhiv Sotsial'noi i Politicheskoi Istorii)], f. 2 op. 2. d. 1338, l. 1, lob, 2–4:
translated in Diane P. Koenker and Ronald D. Bachman (eds.), *Revelations from the Russian Archives: Documents in English Translation* (Washington, D.C.: Library of Congress, 1997), p. 232; and in Richard Pipes
(ed.), *The Unknown Lenin: From the Secret Archive,* with the assistance of David Brandenberger, trans. by
Catherine Fitzpatrick (New Haven and London: Yale University Press, 1996), pp. 168–169.

V. I. Lenin, "Letter to the Congress"
[Lenin's "Testament"]
December 23–31, 1922

*Incapacitated by a series of strokes, Lenin dictated a letter to the forthcoming Twelfth Party
Congress in which he expressed his fears about the infighting among the top party leaders. His
criticism was particularly harsh against Stalin, with whom he had deep differences over nationality policy and the form that the future Union of Soviet Socialist Republics would take.
He called for Stalin's removal from his position as General Secretary. Lenin's notes on the nationality question were read to delegates of the congress in closed session, but it was not until
a year later, after Lenin's death, that delegates to the Thirteenth Party Congress read the notes
on Stalin and other party leaders. The Politburo had decided that Stalin should stay in his job
and that Lenin's notes should not be published. The congress went along. An American Trotskyist, Max Eastman, was the first to reveal the "testament" in his Since Lenin Died in
1925, but Trotskil was forced to renounce Eastman and claim that his account was fabricated.
Not until the early 1960s were these documents published in the Soviet Union.*

Continuation of the notes.

December 24, 1922. . . .

Our Party relies on two classes and therefore its instability would be possible and
its downfall inevitable if there were no agreement between those two classes. In that

event this or that measure, and generally all talk about the stability of our C.C., would be futile. No measures of any kind could prevent a split in such a case. But I hope that this is too remote a future and too improbable an event to talk about.

I have in mind stability as a guarantee against a split in the immediate future, and I intend to deal here with a few ideas concerning personal qualities.

I think that from this standpoint the prime factors in the question of stability are such members of the C.C. as Stalin and Trotsky. I think relations between them make up the greater part of the danger of a split, which could be avoided, and this purpose, in my opinion, would be served, among other things, by increasing the number of C.C. members to 50 or 100.

Comrade Stalin, having become Secretary-General, has unlimited authority concentrated in his hands, and I am not sure whether he will always be capable of using that authority with sufficient caution. Comrade Trotsky, on the other hand, as his struggle against the C.C. on the question of the People's Commissariat for Communications has already proved, is distinguished not only by outstanding ability. He is personally perhaps the most capable man in the present C.C., but he has displayed excessive self-assurance and shown excessive preoccupation with the purely administrative side of the work.

These two qualities of the two outstanding leaders of the present C.C. can inadvertently lead to a split, and if our Party does not take steps to avert this, the split may come unexpectedly.

I shall not give any further appraisals of the personal qualities of other members of the C.C. I shall just recall that the October episode with Zinoviev and Kamenev was, of course, no accident, but neither can the blame for it be laid upon them personally, any more than non-Bolshevism can upon Trotsky.

Speaking of the young C.C. members, I wish to say a few words about Bukharin and Pyatakov. They are, in my opinion, the most outstanding figures (among the youngest ones), and the following must be borne in mind about them: Bukharin is not only a most valuable and major theorist of the Party; he is also rightly considered the favourite of the whole Party, but his theoretical views can be classified as fully Marxist only with great reserve, for there is something scholastic about him (he has never made a study of dialectics, and, I think, never fully understood it).

December 25. As for Pyatakov, he is unquestionably a man of outstanding will and outstanding ability, but shows too much zeal for administrating and the administrative side of the work to be relied upon in a serious political matter.

Both of these remarks, of course, are made only for the present, on the assumption that both these outstanding and devoted Party workers fail to find an occasion to enhance their knowledge and amend their one-sidedness.

Lenin

December 25, 1922

Taken down by M.V.

———

Addition to the Letter

Of December 24, 1922

Stalin is too rude and this defect, although quite tolerable in our midst and in dealings among us Communists, becomes intolerable in a Secretary-General. That is why

I suggest that the comrades think about a way of removing Stalin from that post and appointing another man in his stead who in all other respects differs from Comrade Stalin in having only one advantage, namely, that of being more tolerant, more loyal, more polite and more considerate to the comrades, less capricious, etc. This circumstance may appear to be a negligible detail. But I think that from the standpoint of safeguards against a split and from the standpoint of what I wrote above about the relationship between Stalin and Trotsky it is not a detail, or it is a detail which can assume decisive importance.

Lenin

Taken down by L. F.
January 4, 1923

———

Continuation of the notes.
December 30, 1922

THE QUESTION OF NATIONALITIES OR "AUTONOMISATION"

I suppose I have been very remiss with respect to the workers of Russia for not having intervened energetically and decisively enough in the notorious question of autonomisation, which, it appears, is officially called the question of the union of Soviet socialist republics.

When this question arose last summer, I was ill; and then in autumn I relied too much on my recovery and on the October and December plenary meetings giving me an opportunity of intervening in this question. However, I did not manage to attend the October Plenary Meeting (when this question came up) or the one in December, and so the question passed me by almost completely.

I have only had time for a talk with Comrade Dzerzhinsky, who came from the Caucasus and told me how this matter stood in Georgia. I have also managed to exchange a few words with Comrade Zinoviev and express my apprehensions on this matter. From what I was told by Comrade Dzerzhinsky, who was at the head of the commission sent by the C.C. to "investigate" the Georgian incident, I could only draw the greatest apprehensions. If matters had come to such a pass that Orjonikidze could go to the extreme of applying physical violence, as Comrade Dzerzhinsky informed me, we can imagine what a mess we have got ourselves into. Obviously the whole business of "autonomisation" was radically wrong and badly timed.

It is said that a united apparatus was needed. Where did that assurance come from? Did it not come from that same Russian apparatus which, as I pointed out in one of the preceding sections of my diary, we took over from tsarism and slightly anointed with Soviet oil?

There is no doubt that that measure should have been delayed somewhat until we could say that we vouched for our apparatus as our own. But now, we must, in all conscience, admit the contrary; the apparatus we call ours is, in fact, still quite alien to us; it is a bourgeois and tsarist hotch-potch and there has been no possibility of getting rid of it in the course of the past five years without the help of other countries and because we have been "busy" most of the time with military engagements and the fight against famine.

It is quite natural that in such circumstances the "freedom to secede from the union" by which we justify ourselves will be a mere scrap of paper, unable to defend the non-Russians from the onslaught of that really Russian man, the Great-Russian chauvinist, in substance a rascal and a tyrant, such as the typical Russian bureaucrat is. There is no doubt that the infinitesimal percentage of Soviet and sovietised workers will drown in that tide of chauvinistic Great-Russian riffraff like a fly in milk.

It is said in defence of this measure that the People's Commissariats directly concerned with national psychology and national education were set up as separate bodies. But there the question arises: can these People's Commissariats be made quite independent? and secondly: were we careful enough to take measures to provide the non-Russians with a real safeguard against the truly Russian bully? I do not think we took such measures although we could and should have done so.

I think that Stalin's haste and his infatuation with pure administration, together with his spite against the notorious "nationalist-socialism", played a fatal role here. In politics spite generally plays the basest of roles.

I also fear that Comrade Dzerzhinsky, who went to the Caucasus to investigate the "crime" of those "nationalist-socialists", distinguished himself there by his truly Russian frame of mind (it is common knowledge that people of other nationalities who have become Russified overdo this Russian frame of mind) and that the impartiality of his whole commission was typified well enough by Orjonikidze's "manhandling". I think that no provocation or even insult can justify such Russian manhandling and that Comrade Dzerzhinsky was inexcusably guilty in adopting a light-hearted attitude towards it.

For all the citizens in the Caucasus Orjonikidze was the authority. Orjonikidze had no right to display that irritability to which he and Dzerzhinsky referred. On the contrary, Orjonikidze should have behaved with a restraint which cannot be demanded of any ordinary citizen, still less of a man accused of a "political" crime. And, to tell the truth, those nationalist-socialists were citizens who were accused of a political crime, and the terms of the accusation were such that it could not be described otherwise.

Here we have an important question of principle: how is internationalism to be understood?★

Lenin

December 30, 1922
Taken down by M.V.

———

★ After this the following phrase was crossed out in the shorthand text: "It seems to me that our comrades have not studied this important question of principle sufficiently."—*Ed.*

Continuation of the notes.

December 31, 1922

THE QUESTION OF NATIONALITIES
OR "AUTONOMISATION" (CONTINUED)

In my writings on the national question I have already said that an abstract presentation of the question of nationalism in general is of no use at all. A distinction must
necessarily be made between the nationalism of an oppressor nation and that of an
oppressed nation, the nationalism of a big nation and that of a small nation.

In respect of the second kind of nationalism we, nationals of a big nation, have
nearly always been guilty, in historic practice, of an infinite number of cases of violence; furthermore, we commit violence and insult an infinite number of times without noticing it. It is sufficient to recall my Volga reminiscences of how non-Russians
are treated; how the Poles are not called by any other name than Polyachishka, how
the Tatar is nicknamed Prince, how the Ukrainians are always Khokhols and the
Georgians and other Caucasian nationals always Kapkasians.

That is why internationalism on the part of oppressors or "great" nations, as they
are called (though they are great only in their violence, only great as bullies), must
consist not only in the observance of the formal equality of nations but even in an inequality of the oppressor nation, the great nation, that must make up for the inequality which obtains in actual practice. Anybody who does not understand this has not
grasped the real proletarian attitude to the national question, he is still essentially petty
bourgeois in his point of view and is, therefore, sure to descend to the bourgeois point
of view.

What is important for the proletarian? For the proletarian it is not only important, it is absolutely essential that he should be assured that the non-Russians place the
greatest possible trust in the proletarian class struggle. What is needed to ensure this?
Not merely formal equality. In one way or another, by one's attitude or by concessions, it is necessary to compensate the non-Russians for the lack of trust, for the suspicion and the insults to which the government of the "dominant" nation subjected
them in the past.

I think it is unnecessary to explain this to Bolsheviks, to Communists, in greater
detail. And I think that in the present instance, as far as the Georgian nation is concerned, we have a typical case in which a genuinely proletarian attitude makes profound caution, thoughtfulness and a readiness to compromise a matter of necessity for
us. The Georgian who is neglectful of this aspect of the question, or who carelessly
flings about accusations of "nationalist-socialism" (whereas he himself is a real and
true "nationalist-socialist", and even a vulgar Great-Russian bully), violates, in substance, the interests of proletarian class solidarity, for nothing holds up the development and strengthening of proletarian class solidarity so much as national injustice;
"offended" nationals are not sensitive to anything so much as to the feeling of equality and the violation of this equality, if only through negligence or jest—to the violation of that equality by their proletarian comrades. That is why in this case it is better to overdo rather than underdo the concessions and leniency towards the national
minorities. That is why, in this case, the fundamental interest of proletarian solidarity,
and consequently of the proletarian class struggle, requires that we never adopt a formal attitude to the national question, but always take into account the specific atti-

tude of the proletarian of the oppressed (or small) nation towards the oppressor (or great) nation.

Lenin

Taken down by M.V.

December 31, 1922

_____

Continuation of the notes.

December 31, 1922

What practical measures must be taken in the present situation?

Firstly, we must maintain and strengthen the union of socialist republics. Of this there can be no doubt. This measure is necessary for us and it is necessary for the world communist proletariat in its struggle against the world bourgeoisie and its defence against bourgeois intrigues.

Secondly, the union of socialist republics must be retained for its diplomatic apparatus. By the way, this apparatus is an exceptional component of our state apparatus. We have not allowed a single influential person from the old tsarist apparatus into it. All sections with any authority are composed of Communists. That is why it has already won for itself (this may be said boldly) the name of a reliable communist apparatus purged to an incomparably greater extent of the old tsarist, bourgeois and petty-bourgeois elements than that which we have had to make do with in other People's Commissariats.

Thirdly, exemplary punishment must be inflicted on Comrade Orjonikidze (I say this all the more regretfully as I am one of his personal friends and have worked with him abroad) and the investigation of all the material which Dzerzhinsky's commission has collected must be completed or started over again to correct the enormous mass of wrongs and biased judgements which it doubtlessly contains. The political responsibility for all this truly Great-Russian nationalist campaign must, of course, be laid on Stalin and Dzerzhinsky.

Fourthly, the strictest rules must be introduced on the use of the national language in the non-Russian republics of our union, and these rules must be checked with special care. There is no doubt that our apparatus being what it is, there is bound to be, on the pretext of unity in the railway service, unity in the fiscal service and so on, a mass of truly Russian abuses. Special ingenuity is necessary for the struggle against these abuses, not to mention special sincerity on the part of those who undertake this struggle. A detailed code will be required, and only the nationals living in the republic in question can draw it up at all successfully. And then we cannot be sure in advance that as a result of this work we shall not take a step backward at our next Congress of Soviets, i.e., retain the union of Soviet socialist republics only for military and diplomatic affairs, and in all other respects restore full independence to the individual People's Commissariats.

It must be borne in mind that the decentralisation of the People's Commissariats and the lack of co-ordination in their work as far as Moscow and other centres are concerned can be compensated sufficiently by Party authority, if it is exercised with sufficient prudence and impartiality; the harm that can result to our state from a lack of unification between the national apparatuses and the Russian apparatus is infinitely less than that which will be done not only to us, but to the whole International, and to the hundreds of millions of the peoples of Asia, which is destined to follow us on to the stage of history in the near future. It would be unpardonable opportunism if, on the eve of the debut of the East, just as it is awakening, we undermined our prestige with its peoples, even if only by the slightest crudity or injustice towards our own non-Russian nationalities. The need to rally against the imperialists of the West, who are defending the capitalist world, is one thing. There can be no doubt about that and it would be superfluous for me to speak about my unconditional approval of it. It is another thing when we ourselves lapse, even if only in trifles, into imperialist attitudes towards oppressed nationalities, thus undermining all our principled sincerity, all our principled defence of the struggle against imperialism. But the morrow of world history will be a day when the awakening peoples oppressed by imperialism are finally aroused and the decisive long and hard struggle for their liberation begins.

Lenin

December 31, 1922
Taken down by M.V.

V. I. Lenin, *Collected Works,* 4th ed. (Moscow: Progress Publishers, 1966), XXXVI, pp. 594-596, 605-611.

Bukharin and Dzerzhinskii Disagree About the Nature of Revolutionary Government
December 1924

There was no formal debate at party conferences on the nature of Soviet government or the internal party regime, but the issues of democracy and dissent, the powers of the police and censorship, were constantly discussed. The next two documents illustrate the range of views, all within an acceptance of "the dictatorship of the proletariat" and single-party rule, that leading Communists expressed in the mid-1920s. At the height of his power, Nikolai Bukharin, then a member of the Politburo and editor of the party newspaper, Pravda, *wrote to Feliks Dzerzhinskii (1877–1926), head of the GPU,[1] in December 1924 to express his view that Soviet power should soon move toward "a more liberal form of rule." Dzherzhinskii conveyed this letter to his deputy, Viacheslav Menzhinskii (1874–1934), expressing grave doubts about the concessions that some Communists were willing to make.*

LETTER FROM NIKOLAI BUKHARIN TO FELIX DZERZHINSKII, DECEMBER 1924

Dear Feliks Edmundovich,

I was not at the last meeting of the executive group. I heard that you, by the way, said there that I and Sokol'nikov are "against the *GPU*" etc. I was informed about the

---

1. The GPU [*Gosudarstvennoe politicheskoe upravlenie*] was the political police, the successor to the Cheka.

argument that took place the day before yesterday. And so, dear Feliks Edmundovich, lest you have any doubt, I ask you to understand *what* I do think.

I believe that we should move *more rapidly* toward a more liberal form of rule: fewer acts of repression, more rule by law, more discussion, self-government (under the direction of the party, naturally) and so on. In my article in *Bolshevik,* which you *approved,* I laid out the theoretical underpinnings of this course. *Therefore,* I occasionally come out against proposals that expand the powers of the *GPU* and so on. Understand, dear Feliks Edmundovich (you know how fond I am of you) that you do not have *the slightest* reason to suspect me of any sort of ill will, either toward you personally or toward the *GPU* as an institution. It's a question of *principle*—that is what is at issue.

Because you are a man deeply passionate about politics but at the same time [one who] can be impartial, you will understand me.

I warmly embrace you, warmly press your hand, and wish you a speedy recovery.

Yours,
N. Bukharin

RTSKhIDNI, fond 76, opis 3, delo 345, listy 2, 2ob; translated in Diane P. Koenker and Ronald D. Bachman (eds.), *Revelations from the Russian Archives: Documents in English Translation* (Washington, D.C.: Library of Congress, 1997), pp. 18–19.

LETTER FROM DZERZHINSKII TO V. R. MENZHINSKII, DECEMBER 24, 1924

To Comrade Menzhinskii   For your eyes only
(copying forbidden)

Here attached is Bukharin's letter to me which I would like you to return to me after reading.

We have to take into consideration that such attitudes exist among the Central Committee members, and [we have] to think it over. It would be the greatest political blunder if the party yielded on the fundamental question of the *GPU* and gave "new life" to the Philistines—as a line, as a policy, and as a declaration. It would mean a concession to Nepmanism, Philistinism, and tending toward a rejection of bolshevism; it would mean a victory for Trotskyism and a surrender of our positions. To counteract these attitudes we need to review our practices, our methods and eliminate everything that can feed such attitudes. That means that we (the *GPU*) must become quieter, more modest. We should use searches and arrests more carefully, with better incriminating evidence; some categories of arrests (Nepmanism, official misconduct) should be limited, and carried out under pressure, or by mobilizing popular party support for us; we must better inform the Moscow committee about all matters, more closely involving the party organization in these affairs. We need to review our policy on granting permission to go abroad and on visas. We must pay attention to the struggle for popularity among peasants, organizing help for them in the struggle against hooliganism and other crimes. And in general, we need to plan measures to gain support among workers and peasants and mass party organizations.

In addition, once again, we need to pay attention to our information summaries so that they provide the members of the Central Committee an accurate picture of our work in brief, very specific terms. Our information summaries are presenting a one-sided picture, completely black, without the proper perspective and without describing our real role. We must compile accounts of our work.

December 24, 1924 F. Dzerzhinsky

[Stamp, upper left corner:] Archive of F. Z. Dzerzhinsky

RTSKhIDNI, fond 76, opis 3, delo 345, listy 1, 1 ob; translated in Diane P. Koenker and Ronald D. Bachman (eds.), *Revelations from the Russian Archives: Documents in English Translation* (Washington, D.C.: Library of Congress, 1997), p. 19.

Joseph Stalin, "The October Revolution and the Tactics of the Russian Communists"
December 17, 1924

Stalin was not only a master politician but an effective, if dull, political writer. In 1924, he promoted the cult of Lenin, who soon was regarded as an infallible theorist and practitioner of revolution. The party was changing from a collection of intellectuals and professional revolutionaries, in which debate and divisions prevailed, into a mass party whose members were required to subscribe to a set of orthodox ideas. Obedience steadily replaced discussion, and in this new political arena the didactic, simplified prose of Stalin provided clear guidance through the thickets of theory. In this article, Stalin contrasted Trotsky's theory of "permanent revolution" with his own idea of "socialism in one country" and gave the latter a Leninist pedigree. Stalin argued that socialism could be built in the USSR without the aid of foreign revolutions, while Trotsky believed, like Lenin, that socialism in peasant Russia required aid from abroad. In his sermonic manner, with little regard for the nuances of his opponent's theory, Stalin distorted Trotsky's notion of "permanent revolution" for polemical purposes. Trotsky in 1905, had developed a hypothesis that the bourgeois revolution in Russia would inevitably grow over into a socialist revolution (an approach that Lenin found persuasive); Stalin, in 1924, depicted the theory as one that eliminated the role for the peasantry that Lenin favored. He found a quotation from Lenin that spoke of socialism in one country, took it out of context, and deployed it for his argument. To many rank-and-file party members, Stalin appeared to be pragmatic and patriotic, a loyal follower of "that unquestioned Marxist" Lenin, while Trotsky seemed to be an impractical adventurer ready to gamble the USSR's future on dreams of international revolution.

There are two specific features of the October Revolution which must be understood first of all if we are to comprehend the inner meaning and the historical significance of that revolution.

What are these features?

Firstly, the fact that the dictatorship of the proletariat was born in our country as a power which came into existence on the basis of an alliance between the proletariat and the labouring masses of the peasantry, the latter being led by the proletariat. Secondly, the fact that the dictatorship of the proletariat became established in our country as a result of the victory of socialism in one country—a country in which capitalism was little developed—while capitalism was preserved in other countries where capitalism was more highly developed. This does not mean, of course, that the October Revolution has no other specific features. But it is precisely these two specific features that are important for us at the present moment, not only because they distinctly express the essence of the October Revolution, but also because they brilliantly reveal the opportunist nature of the theory of "permanent revolution." . . .

One of the specific features of the October Revolution is the fact that this revolution represents a classic application of Lenin's theory of the dictatorship of the proletariat.

Some comrades believe that this theory is a purely "Russian" theory, applicable only to Russian conditions. That is wrong. It is absolutely wrong. In speaking of the labouring masses of the non-proletarian classes which are led by the proletariat, Lenin has in mind not only the Russian peasants, but also the labouring elements of the border regions of the Soviet Union, which until recently were colonies of Russia. Lenin constantly reiterated that without an alliance with these masses of other nationalities the proletariat of Russia could not achieve victory. In his articles on the national question and in his speeches at the congresses of the Comintern, Lenin repeatedly said that the victory of the world revolution was impossible without a revolutionary alliance, a revolutionary bloc, between the proletariat of the advanced countries and the oppressed peoples of the enslaved colonies. But what are colonies if not the oppressed labouring masses, and, primarily, the labouring masses of the peasantry? Who does not know that the question of emancipating the colonies is *essentially* a question of emancipating the labouring masses of the non-proletarian classes from the oppression and exploitation of finance capital?

But from this it follows that Lenin's theory of the dictatorship of the proletariat is not a purely "Russian" theory, but a theory which necessarily applies to all countries. Bolshevism is not only a Russian phenomenon. "Bolshevism," says Lenin, is "*a model of tactics for all*". . . .

Lenin speaks of the *alliance* between the proletariat and the labouring strata of the peasantry as the basis of the dictatorship of the proletariat. Trotsky sees a "*hostile collision*" between "the proletarian vanguard" and "the broad masses of the peasantry."

Lenin speaks of the *leadership* of the toiling and exploited masses by the proletariat. Trotsky sees "*contradictions* in the position of a workers' government in a backward country with an overwhelmingly peasant population."

According to Lenin, the revolution draws its strength primarily from among the workers and peasants of Russia itself. According to Trotsky, the necessary strength can be found *only* "in the arena of the world proletarian revolution."

But what if the world revolution is fated to arrive with some delay? Is there any ray of hope for our revolution? Trotsky offers no ray of hope, for "the contradictions in the position of a workers' government . . . could be solved *only* . . . in the arena of the world proletarian revolution." According to this plan, there is but one prospect left for our revolution: to vegetate in its own contradictions and rot away while waiting for the world revolution. . . .

What difference is there between this "theory of permanent revolution" and the well-known theory of Menshevism which repudiates the concept of dictatorship of the proletariat?

Essentially, there is no difference.

There can be no doubt at all. "Permanent revolution" is not a mere underestimation of the revolutionary potentialities of the peasant movement. "Permanent revolution" is an underestimation of the peasant movement which leads to the *repudiation* of Lenin's theory of the dictatorship of the proletariat.

Trotsky's "permanent revolution" is a variety of Menshevism. . . .

It goes without saying that for the *complete* victory of socialism, for a *complete* guarantee against the restoration of the old order, the united efforts of the proletarians of several countries are necessary. It goes without saying that, without the support given to our revolution by the proletariat of Europe, the proletariat of Russia could not have held out against the general onslaught, just as without the support given by the revolution in Russia to the revolutionary movement in the West the latter could not have developed at the pace at which it has begun to develop since the establishment of the proletarian dictatorship in Russia. It goes without saying that we need support. But what does support of our revolution by the West-European proletariat imply? Is not the sympathy of the European workers for our revolution, their readiness to thwart the imperialists' plans of intervention—is not all this support, real assistance? Unquestionably it is. Without such support, without such assistance, not only from the European workers but also from the colonial and dependent countries, the proletarian dictatorship in Russia would have been hard pressed. Up to now, has this sympathy and this assistance, coupled with the might of our Red Army and the readiness of the workers and peasants of Russia to defend their socialist fatherland to the last—has all this been sufficient to beat off the attacks of the imperialists and to win us the necessary conditions for the serious work of construction? Yes, it has been sufficient. Is this sympathy growing stronger, or is it waning? Unquestionably, it is growing stronger. Hence, have we favourable conditions, not only for pushing on with the organising of socialist economy, but also, in our turn, for giving support to the West-European workers and to the oppressed peoples of the East? Yes, we have. This is eloquently proved by the seven years' history of the proletarian dictatorship in Russia.

J.V. Stalin, *Works* (Moscow: Foreign Languages Publishing House, 1953), pp. 378–386, 388–389, 391–392.

Lev Kamenev, "Speech to the Fourteenth Party Congress"
December 1925

Lev Borisovich Kamenev (1883–1936) was one of Lenin's closest confidants and worked closely with Stalin from 1917 until their falling out in 1925. He was the long-serving chairman of the Moscow soviet and was linked with Grigorii Zinoviev, the chairman of the Leningrad soviet, in opposition to Stalin's notion of "socialism in one country." His speech at the Fourteenth Party Congress was a vain call to curtail Stalin's power. The General Secretary controlled the overwhelming majority at the congress, which supported Stalin and Molotov's reports by a vote of 559 to 65. Kamenev was dropped from the Council of People's Commissars (Sovnarkom) and demoted to candidate status in the Politburo. The next year, he and Zinoviev joined Trotsky in the so-called "United Opposition," but that year they lost their chairmanships of the city soviets. Expelled from the party in December 1927, Kamenev became one of the first victims of Stalin's great purges. Forced to confess to crimes he had not committed, tried in the first of the major "show trials" in Moscow, he was executed in August 1936.

I turn to intraparty questions. To these questions I give three answers.

The first concerns the organizational forms of our intraparty life. Comrade

Bukharin has said that we bought the controversy with Comrade Trotsky at the price, as he expressed it, of a convulsion in intraparty life. You must resolve this question in the sense that in the background of a general enlivening and heightening of the activity of all strata of the population, intraparty democracy is essential, its further development is essential. According to the testament of Lenin this has now become possible precisely because the de-classing of the proletariat has ceased.

In the contrary case with this background you will inevitably have a new convulsion in intraparty life. This will be a phenomenon on a catastrophic order. I appeal to you not to choose this path, but the other path.

The things you hear about that path at the congress—about defeatists, liquidators, Axelrodists, etc.—cannot be true; such things had not entered the party's head even after it assembled at the congress. *This must be avoided. This can be avoided only if the minority, which is not made up of newcomers, which you know about fully—if this minority is given an opportunity to defend its views in the party, of course with the full responsibility which the party and the dictatorship impose upon us.*

Second: Besides the invigoration of party discussion, besides granting the minority an opportunity to express its views to the whole party, as becomes Bolsheviks, within those limits which are set by the party statutes and the dictatorship of the party and the proletariat—it seems to me that you must *resist this new tendency in the party which I have tried to sketch out to you.* I am sure that if you find it impossible to do this now because of some organizational consideration or another—the facts of life, the course of the class struggle in our country, the growth of differentiation in the village will compel you to do this, and to say that the school which Bukharin has established is based on a departure from Lenin. What we need right now is in the slogan, back to Lenin! (Voice from a seat: "Why back?") Because this is going forward. Comrades, I know that in the first part of my speech you tried to attribute the matter to malice. We see that the matter is not one of malice, and I hope you will say this after a few months.

And finally, the third point: *We are against creating a theory of the "Duce,"*[1] *we are against establishing a "Duce."* We are against the Secretariat, which has in practice combined both policy and organization, standing over the political organ. *We are for our upper level being organized in such a fashion that there would be a really all-powerful Politbureau, bringing together all our party's policies, and at the same time the Secretariat would be subordinate to it and execute the technical aspects of its decisions.* (Noise) We cannot consider it normal but think it harmful to the party, if such a situation is continued where the Secretariat combines both policy and organization, and in fact predecides policy. (Noise) Here, Comrades, is what we need to do. Everyone who does not agree with me will draw his own conclusions. (Voice from a seat: "You should have begun with this.") The speaker has the right to begin with what he wants. You think I ought to have begun with what I have said, that personally I assert that our General Secretary is not the kind of figure that can unite the old Bolshevik staff around himself. I don't consider this a basic political question. I don't consider this question more important than the question of the theoretical line. I feel that if the party adopted (Noise) a definite political line which was clearly marked off from those deviations which part of the Central Committee is now supporting, this question would not now be on the agenda. But I must say this out to the end. Precisely because I more than once told Comrade Stalin this, precisely because I more than once told a group of Leninist

---

1. Russian *vozhd*—"leader," in a then derogatory sense—Ed.

comrades, I repeat it here at the congress: *I have arrived at the conviction that Comrade Stalin cannot fulfill the role of unifier of the Bolshevik staff.* (Voices from the audience:"Untrue!" "Nonsense!" "So that's what it is!" "He's shown his cards!" Noise. Applause by the Leningrad delegation. Shouts: "We won't surrender the commanding heights to you." "Stalin! Stalin!" The delegates stand and cheer Comrade Stalin. Stormy applause. Shouts: "Here's where the party has become united. Now the Bolshevik staff must be united.")

(Yevdokimov, from his seat) "Long live the Russian Communist Party! Hurrah! Hurrah!" (The delegates stand and shout "Hurrah!" Noise. Stormy, long-sustained applause)

(Yevdokimov, from his seat) "Long live the Central Committee of our party! Hurrah!" (The delegates shout "Hurrah!") "The party above all! Right!" (Applause and shouts, "Hurrah!")

(Voice from a seat) "Long live Comrade Stalin!" (Stormy, continued applause, shouts) "Hurrah!" (Noise)

(Chairman) "Comrades, I beg you to quiet down. Comrade Kamenev will now finish his speech."

I began this part of my speech with the words, "We are against the theory of individual preëminence, we are against creating a Duce!" With these same words I end my speech. (Applause by the Leningrad delegation)

(Voice from a seat) "And who do you propose?"

(Chairman) "I declare a ten minute recess." . . .

Translated in Robert V. Daniels (ed.), *A Documentary History of Communism,* vol. 1 (New York: Alfred Knopf, 1960), pp. 277–279.

The Code of Laws on Marriage and Divorce, the Family and Guardianship
November 19, 1926

For a whole year, from the fall of 1925 to November 1926, a countrywide debate on the draft law on family, marriage, and divorce raged in the Soviet Union. Left reformers saw the new law as a model for socialist relations, but pro-peasant Communists, like Mikhail Kalinin, as well as the bulk of the peasantry itself, opposed the law's provisions on alimony, simple declaration of divorce, and de facto, unregistered marriages. The Left complained that if such important laws are made "solely on the basis of a majority vote in the villages, in the skhod *[village gatherings], then we are taking the leadership of our country away from the party, away from the vanguard, and turning it over to the backward, long-bearded village elders." Kalinin, on the other hand, wanted to draw in "the workers and peasants to participate in the legislative project." And Aron Solts, a Communist member of the Soviet Supreme Court, agreed: "We write laws not for Communists, but for the entire country. It is impossible to build socialism with only one socialist hand."[1] Peasants feared that de facto marriage would undermine the peasant household, the very basis of their society and economy.*

The law code was liberationist in its aim, the product of intellectuals and jurists reconceiving gender and generational relations. But its effect on impoverished Russian society was

1. Wendy Z. Goldman, *Women, the State, and Revolution: Soviet Family Policy and Social Life, 1917–1936* (Cambridge: Cambridge University Press, 1993), pp. 215, 221.

far from positive. The divorce rate almost doubled. People refused to pay alimony, and punishment for neglecting child support was rare. Though the chronic problem of homeless children (bezprizornost') was somewhat ameliorated by the legalization of adoption, only a dedicated state campaign reduced the number of children on the streets from 125,000 to about 10,000 in the late 1920s. With the coming of the First Five-Year Plan and the massive flow of women into the industrial workforce, the party leaders shifted their views on family stability and abortion. What had begun as a commitment to "the withering away" of the family ended with the Stalinist reversion to its strengthening. "By 1944 the reversal in family law was complete," writes Wendy Z. Goldman; "the Family Edict of that year repudiated the remaining traces of the legislation of the 1920s by withdrawing recognition of de facto marriage, banning paternity suits, reintroducing the category of illegitimacy, and transferring divorce back to the courts. . . . Stalinist policy toward the family was a grotesque hybrid: Rooted in the original socialist vision, starved in the depleted soil of poverty, and ultimately deformed by the state's increasing reliance on repression."[2]

Decree of the All-Russian Central Executive Committee passed at the Third Session of its Twelfth Election Period on November 19, 1926

PART I. MARRIAGE AND DIVORCE

Chapter 1. *General Principles*

1. The registration of marriages is introduced in the interest of the State and society as well as for the purpose of facilitating the protection of the personal and property rights and the interests of husband and wife and of children. A marriage is contracted by registration at a Civil Registrar's Office in the manner prescribed by Part IV of the present code.

2. The registration of a marriage at a Civil Registrar's Office is conclusive evidence of the existence of the state of matrimony. Documents attesting the celebration of marriage according to religious rites have no legal effect.

Note.—Marriages celebrated according to religious rites prior to December 20, 1917, or which were celebrated in localities occupied by the enemy prior to the establishment of the Civil Registrar's Offices, have the same effect as registered marriages.

3. Where *de facto* conjugal relations exist between persons which relations have not been registered in the manner prescribed such persons are entitled at any time to regularize their relation by registration, stating when so doing the period of their actual cohabitation.

Chapter 2. *Conditions Governing the Registration of Marriages*

4. The following conditions are required for the registration of a marriage: (*a*) there must be mutual consent to register the marriage; (*b*) both parties must be of marriageable age. . . .

5. The marriageable age is fixed at eighteen years.

---

2. Ibid., pp. 340, 342.

Note.—The Presidiums of the Central Executive Committees of the Autonomous Republics, the Presidiums of the Executive Committees of the Autonomous Regions, Regional Executive Committees and also those of Town and District Soviets in towns may, in exceptional cases, and acting upon individual petitions, lower the marriageable age fixed for women in the present section, but not by more than one year. . . .

6. It is unlawful to register the following marriages: (*a*) between persons one or both of whom is or are already married either with or without registration; (*b*) between persons one or both of whom has or have been adjudged weak-minded or insane, in the manner prescribed by law; (*c*) between relatives in the direct line of descent; also between brothers and sisters, whether of the full blood or the half blood.

Chapter 3. *Rights and Duties of Husband and Wife*

7. On registering a marriage the contracting parties may declare it to be their wish to have a common surname, either that of the husband or of the wife, or to retain their antenuptial surnames.

8. On the registration of a marriage between a person who is a citizen of the R.S.F.S.R. and a person who is a foreign citizen, each party retains his or her respective citizenship. Change in citizenship of such persons may be effected in the simplified manner provided for by the Union laws. . . .

9. Both husband and wife enjoy full liberty in the choice of their respective trades and occupations. The manner in which their joint household is conducted is determined by the mutual agreement of the two contracting parties. A change of residence by either husband or wife does not oblige the other marriage partner to follow the former.

10. Property which belonged to either husband or wife prior to their marriage remains the separate property of each of them. Property acquired by husband and wife during continuance of their marriage is regarded as their joint property. The share belonging to either husband or wife shall, in case of dispute, be determined by the court. . . .

11. Section 10 of the present code extends also to the property of persons married *de facto* though not registered, provided such persons recognize their mutual status of husband and wife, or their marital relationship is established as a fact by a court on the basis of the actual conditions under which they live.

12. Proof of joint cohabitation is sufficient for the court to establish marital cohabitation in cases where the marriage has not been registered, provided that in addition to proof of joint cohabitation proof of a common household be adduced and that statements have been made to third persons either in personal correspondence or in other documents tending to prove the existence of marital relations, taking also into consideration such circumstances as the presence or absence of mutual material support, joint raising of children, and the like.

13. The husband and wife may enter into any contractual relations with each other regarding property provided they are lawful. Agreements between husband and wife intended to restrict the property rights of the wife or of the husband are invalid and are not binding on third parties or on the husband or wife who may at any time refuse to carry them out.

14. When either husband or wife is in need and unable to work he or she is entitled to receive alimony from the other conjugal partner, if the court finds that the latter is able to support the former. A husband or wife in need of support but able to work is likewise entitled to alimony during the period of his or her unemployment.

15. The right of a husband or wife in need and unable to work to receive alimony from the other conjugal partner continues even after the dissolution of the marriage until there has been a change in the conditions which according to Section 14 of the present code serve as a basis for the receipt of alimony, but not or a period exceeding one year from the time of the dissolution of the marriage. The amount of alimony to be paid to a needy unemployed husband or wife in case of dissolution of the marriage is fixed by the court for a period not exceeding six months and shall not exceed the corresponding amount of Social Insurance relief.

16. The right to receive alimony both during marriage and after its dissolution extends also to persons who are married *de facto,* though not registered, provided they fall within the purview of Sections 11 and 12 of the present code.

Chapter 4. *Dissolution of Marriage*

17. A marriage is dissolved by the death of one of the parties to it or by a declaration of the presumptive death of either the husband or the wife through a notary public or court. . . .

18. During the lifetime of both parties to a marriage the marriage may be dissolved either by the mutual consent of both parties to it or upon the *ex parte* application of either of them.

19. During the lifetime of both parties, the dissolution of a marriage (divorce) may be registered at the Civil Registrar's office, whether the marriage was registered or unregistered, provided that in the latter case it had been established as a fact by the court in accordance with Section 12 of the present code.

20. The fact that a marriage has been dissolved may also be established by a court, if the divorce was not registered.

21. When registering the dissolution of their marriage the husband and wife indicate what surname each of them wishes to use. In the absence of an agreement between the parties on this point, each resumes his or her antenuptial surname.

22. When registering the dissolution of a marriage it is the duty of the Registrar to consider the question of which child or children, if any, shall be entrusted to the custody of each parent to what extent each parent is to bear the expense of raising the children, and the amount of alimony to be paid to a husband or wife unable to work. In case the husband and wife arrive at an understanding on these points, such agreement is recorded in the register of divorces and a corresponding extract from the book is handed to both husband and wife; this agreement does not deprive either the husband or wife, or the children, of the right subsequently to present, by way of an ordinary lawsuit, a claim for alimony in a sum exceeding that stipulated in the agreement.

23. If the obligations set forth in the agreement have not been carried out, the persons interested may apply at the office of a notary public for a writ of execution in accordance with Clause B Section 47, of the regulations governing the State notaries public.

24. In the absence of an agreement the question of the amount of alimony to be awarded to children is settled by an ordinary lawsuit; the court at the time the statement of claim was filed renders a decision, after careful consideration of the circumstances of the case and the interests of the children, specifying which of the parents, and to what extent, he or she must, pending the decision of the lawsuit, provisionally bear the expense of the maintenance of the children, and who is to have provisional custody of the children.

The amount of alimony awarded to a husband or wife in need and unable to work must in the absence of an agreement likewise be decided by the court upon the institution of an ordinary lawsuit.

PART II. MUTUAL RELATIONS BETWEEN PARENT AND CHILD AND BETWEEN OTHER RELATIVES

Chapter 1. *General Principles*

25. The mutual rights of children and parents are based on consanguinity. Children whose parents are not married possess the same rights as children born in wedlock.

26. The father and mother of a child are recorded in the register of births.

27. If no record is made of the parents, or if the record made is incorrect or incomplete, the parties interested are entitled to prove or disprove paternity or maternity by recourse to the court.

28. In order to protect the interests of the child, the mother is granted the right, during the period of her pregnancy or after the birth of the child, to file a declaration of paternity with the local Civil Registrar's Office according to her place of residence, stating the name, patronymic, surname and residence of the father of the child.

29. The Civil Registrar's Office informs the person alleged in the declaration to be the father, of the filing of such declaration. If the putative father, within a month after receiving this notification, does not raise any objection, he is recorded as the father of the child. The person alleged to be the father may within one year after the date of the receipt of the notification institute a suit, against the mother of the child contesting the truthfulness of her statement.

30. The mother of the child has also the right to institute a paternity suit in court after the birth of the child.

31. If the court is satisfied that the person stated in the declaration (Sections 28 and 30 of the present code) is the father of the child, it enters a finding to that effect and imposes on the father the duty of contributing to the expenses connected with her pregnancy, lying-in, childbirth and maintenance of the child, also to the expenses of the mother during the period of her pregnancy and for six months after childbirth.

32. In case the court during the trial of the paternity case finds as a fact that the mother of the child at or about the time of conception had sexual intercourse not only with the person referred to in Section 28 of the present code, but also with other persons, the court enters a decree which recognizes one of these persons as the father of the child and imposes on him the duties set forth in Section 31 of the code.

Chapter 2. *Rights and Duties of Relatives*

33. Parental rights are to be exercised exclusively in the interests of the children and in case they are improperly exercised the court is authorized and empowered to deprive the parent of their rights.

34. If the parents have a common surname, that surname is also given to the children. If the parents have not a common surname, the surname of the children is determined by agreement between the parents. In the absence of an agreement between the parents on the question of the surname of their children, the surname of the children is decided upon by the Office of Guardians and Trustees. If the father is unknown the child takes the name of the mother. In the case of a dissolution of the marriage, the children retain the surname given them at birth.

35. If the citizenship of the parents is not the same, but at least one of them at the time of the birth of the child is a citizen of the R.S.F.S.R., and at least one of the parents at the time of the birth of the child was living on U.S.S.R. territory, the child will be deemed a citizen of the R.S.F.S.R. If one of the parent was a citizen of the R.S.F.S.R. at the time of the child's birth but at that time both parents lived outside the territory of the U.S.S.R., the citizenship of the child is determined by agreement between the parents.

36. A change in the citizenship of either husband or wife where both are citizens of the R.S.F.S.R. and living on U.S.S.R. territory, does not affect the citizenship of their children. The citizenship of children in cases where one of the parents, citizens of the R.S.F.S.R. but who live outside the territory of the U.S.S.R., loses his R.S.F.S.R. citizenship, is determined by agreement of the parents.

37. Agreement between the parents that their children adhere to any particular religion is of no legal effect.

38. All steps in regard to children are taken by both parents jointly. . . .

43. The protection of the interests of minors, whether they pertain to their persons or their property, is incumbent upon the parents, who act as guardians *ad litem* of the children in courts and other institutions.

44. The parents are entitled to sue in court for the return of their children from any person detaining the children on his premises without warrant of law and not in pursuance of any court decree; in such case the court is not bound by the formal rights of the parents but decides according to the merits of each case with due regard only for the welfare of the children.

45. Parents are granted the right to entrust their children to other persons to have them brought up and educated. They also enjoy the right, with the consent of the children, to make contracts of apprenticeship and work for wages in the cases and in the manner permitted by the labour legislation in force at the time.

Children may not be entrusted for purposes of being brought up and educated to persons who under Section 77 of the present code may not act as guardians and trustees. . . .

46. In the event of non-fulfilment of their duties on the part of the parents or in case they do not properly exercise their rights with respect to their children, or if they treat their children cruelly, the court issues a decree to the effect that the children be taken away from the parents and handed over to the care of the Office of Guardians and Trustees, and the court is authorized to decree at the same time that both parents contribute to the support of their children.

Note.—The Office of Guardians has the right pending the decision of the court to issue orders to take the children away from their parents or from other persons in whose custody they are, if the continuance of their stay with these persons constitutes a menace to the children.

47. In the event of the court issuing a decree depriving parents of their parental rights, the Office of Guardians and Trustees must allow parents to see their children except in cases where such meetings may prove injurious to the children.

48. The duty to support children rests upon both parents; the extent of their contributions towards their support depends upon their respective means.

49. Children must support their needy incapacitated parents.

50. When parents are unwilling to support their children, or children their parents, in the cases provided for in Sections 42 and 49 of the present code, the persons entitled to support may sue for such support in court.

Note.—In case of any change in the material position of the parents or children, the court decree may be modified by instituting a lawsuit in the usual way.

51. The deprivation of parental rights does not relieve parents of the duty to support their children.

52. Persons who are jointly liable to contribute support are liable in equal shares, except where the court in view of the unequal means of the persons liable to contribute or in view of the absence of one of them, or for some other cogent reason, finds it necessary to fix other ratios for the discharge of this duty.

53. The rights of parents and children with regard to the property of a peasant household (*Dvor*) are determined by the pertinent sections of the Land Code.

54. Needy brothers and sisters, if minors, are entitled to obtain support from their brothers and sisters who possess efficient means if the former brothers and sisters are unable to obtain alimony from their parents because the parents are not a party to the action or because they are impecunious.

55. A needy, incapacitated grandfather or grandmother is entitled to alimony from his or her grandchildren if the latter possess sufficient means, provided such alimony cannot be obtained from the conjugal partner or the children. Similarly needy grandchildren who are either under age or incapacitated are entitled to alimony from their grandfather or grandmother who possess sufficient means, provided they are unable to obtain such alimony from their parents.

56. Children born of members of a peasant household (*Dvor*) are recognized as members of the *Dvor* to which their father or mother belongs, irrespective of whether their parents are married with or without registration.

Where parents belong to different peasant households, their children may be registered as members of one of these households at the option of the parent with whom the children are living.

Disputes concerning the place where a child is to be recorded as a member of a peasant household are decided by the court which is guided by the interests of the child. . . .

56 (1) Where the fatherhood of a member of a peasant household (*Dvor*) has been established, the court fixes at the same time the quantity of food products which the *Dvor* of the father must contribute to the support of the child.

Children born of a member of a peasant household (Sec. 56) retain the right to alimony out of the personal means of the father and out of the personal means of the mother over and above the rights which they possess as members of the peasant household on the general principles laid down in Sections 48 and 50 of the present code. . . .

Chapter 3. *Adoption*

57. Adoption is allowed only in the case of young children and persons under age, and exists exclusively in the interests the children.

58. Persons deprived of the right to act as guardians in accordance with Section 77 of the present code have no right to adopt.

59. Adoption is effected by order of the Office of Guardians and Trustees and must be registered in the usual manner in the Civil Registrar's Office.

Note.—The adoption of children of Soviet citizens by foreign citizens (subjects) residing on U.S.S.R. territory is allowed provided the rules laid down in the present chapter are observed and provided further that special permission be obtained in each individual case from the Presidium of the Executive Committee of the respective Gubernia, Okrug, or other respective administrative area.

60. At the time of adoption, the adopted child may be given the surname of the adopter, and with the consent of the adopted child, also the adopter's patronymic.

61. If the parents of the adopted child are living, or if it is under the care of a guardian or trustee, adoption can take place only with the consent of the parents, if they have not been deprived of their parental rights; or of the respective guardians or trustees.

62. Where the adopter is married, adoption can only take place with the consent of the other conjugal partner.

63. No children above the age of 10 may be adopted without their own consent.

64. Adopted children and their offspring have the same personal and property rights and duties with regard to their parents by adoption, and the latter with regard to their children by adoption and their offspring, as have the corresponding relatives by consanguinity.

65. Adoption effected in the absence of, or without the consent of, the parents of the adopted child, may be annulled by the Office of Guardians and Trustees at the request of the parents, the child's return to them is in the interests of the child. In order to annul the adoption of a minor over 10 years of age his own consent is required.

66. Any person or institution may institute a suit in court or the annulment of an adoption if such annulment is necessary in the interests of the child. . . .

Translated in Rudolf Schlesinger (ed.), *The Family in the U.S.S.R.: Documents and Readings* (London: Routledge & Kegan Paul, 1949), pp. 154–165.

═══ Kamenev-Bukharin Exchange ═══
July 11, 1928

Early in 1928, the alliance of Stalin and Bukharin fell apart. The "extraordinary measures" taken by Stalin and his agents in collecting the grain that past fall, and his intention to move beyond individual peasant agriculture to collective farms, stood in sharp contrast to Bukharin's desire to rely on peasants and the market to develop the Soviet economy. When Kliment Voroshilov, Stalin's old comrade from the civil war campaigns, and Kalinin, both of whom had wavered in the economic debate, joined the Stalinists, Stalin had a majority on his side in the Politburo. He then used his powers as General Secretary to replace Bukharin's men throughout the bureaucracy with his own. At a Central Committee plenum in July, Bukharin tried to convince the party leaders that there could be no sustained industrialization without a prosperous peasant sector. Stalin answered him by calling for greater class warfare and the extraction of "tribute" from the peasantry. A few days later, on July 11, Bukharin met secretly with his old opponent Kamenev and lamented that Stalin was out to destroy the revolution. The fact that Bukharin had met with an expelled party member leaked out, and Stalin used it as another weapon against the Right.

KAMENEV: Is the struggle really serious?

BUKHARIN: That's just what I wanted to talk about. We feel that Stalin's line is ruinous for the whole revolution. We could be overthrown on account of it. The disagreements between us and Stalin are many times more serious than the disagreements which we used to have with you. Rykov, Tomsky and I agree on formulating the situation thus: "It would be much better if Zinoviev and Kamenev were in the Politbureau instead of Stalin." I have spoken with Rykov and Tomsky about this quite frankly. I have not spoken with Stalin for several weeks. He is an unprincipled intriguer, who subordinates everything to the preservation of his own power. He changes his theory according to whom he needs to get rid of. In the "seven"★ our arguing with him reached the point of saying, "false," "you lie," etc. Now he has made concessions, so that he can cut our throats. We understand this, but he maneuvers so as to make us appear to be the schismatics. . . . This is the line which he pronounced at the plenum: 1) Capitalism grew either on account of colonies, or loans, or the exploitation of the workers. We have no colonies, we can get no loans, therefore our basis is tribute from the peasantry. You understand that this is just what Preobrazhensky's theory is. 2) The more socialism grows, the greater will be the resistance [to it]. . . . This is idiotic illiteracy. 3) Since tribute is necessary and resistance will grow, we need firm leadership. Self-criticism must not apply to the leadership, but only to those who carry out orders. Self-criticism is in fact aimed at Tomsky[1] and Uglanov.[†] As a result we are getting a police regime. This is not a "cuckoo" matter, but will really decide the fate of the revolution. With this theory everything can perish. . . .

The Petersburg [Leningrad] people are in general with us, but they got scared when the talk got to the possibility of removing Stalin. . . . Our potential forces are vast, but 1) the middle-ranking Central Committee member still does not understand the depth of the disagreements, 2) there is a terrible fear of a split. Therefore, when

---

★   The informal leadership group, including most of the Politbureau—Ed.
1. Tomsky, head of Soviet trade union and an ally of Bukharin;
†   Uglanov: pro-Bukharin secretary of the Moscow party organization, removed in the fall of 1928—Ed.

Stalin conceded on the extraordinary measures, he made it difficult for us to attack him. We don't want to come forth as schismatics, for then they would slaughter us. But Tomsky in his latest speech showed clearly that Stalin is the schismatic. . . .

Kamenev–Bukharin exchange, July 11, 1928, from Trotsky archive; translated in Robert V. Daniels (ed.), *A Documentary History of Communism*, vol. I (New York: Alfred Knopf, 1960), pp. 308–309.

Kliment Voroshilov's Letter to "Sergo" Orjonikidze
June 8, 1929

Voroshilov was one of Stalin's closet comrades. Together they had been active on the southern front in the civil war, and Stalin promoted Voroshilov's fortunes through the 1920s and 1930s, when he served as People's Commissar of Military Affairs. A legendary soldier, he was distinguished politically primarily by his loyalty to Stalin. Orjonikidze was also a long-time friend of Stalin. A fellow Georgian, he was closely associated with the defeat of Georgian "national-communists" in 1922–1923 and enthusiastically supported Stalin's plan for a federal union of the Transcaucasian republics and a more centralized Soviet Union. Voroshilov's letter to Orjonikidze reveals the depth of personal animosity that divided the Politburo by 1929. His letter gives a sense of the violence in language that marked Soviet politics. It would be less than a decade before Voroshilov, as part of the dominant faction led by Stalin, would sign the death warrants for the defeated oppositionists. Voroshilov not only survived the Stalinist purges but actively denounced many of his army officers. Despite arousing Stalin's suspicions in the late 1940s and suffering an ignominious fall from power in 1957, Voroshilov died a natural death in 1969. Orjonikidze, however, was troubled by the purges, and after a violent disagreement with Stalin early in 1937, he shot himself.

Moscow, 8 June 1929

Dear Friend,

I am extremely glad to hear about your general condition and that your wound is healing well. Everything is going well and the sun will make up for what the "old bod" finds difficult to handle. I know that you're mad at me for being silent. Please note, however, my great friend, that neither Unshlikht nor [S. S.] Kamenev (my deputies) are here, and I am taking the rap all alone. Of course this circumstance is no justification, but still you must be more indulgent with me. What's going on with our affairs? I think you know everything that's interesting and important from Koba [Stalin], and the rest is being reported fairly accurately by the newspapers. It will hardly be news to you that Bug-arin★ has been appointed to the Scientific-Technical Administration of the Supreme Economic Council. The information was published in the newspapers. The newspapers just don't know the details that accompanied this "act." The correspondents of the bourgeois European newspapers explain Bukharin's

---

★ Literally *Bukhashka,* a play on Bukharin's name with the Russian word *bukashka,* or insect—Trans.

appointment as his removal from politics, as his dismissal from the leadership. There are quite a few people in our country who think the same thing. But in reality Bukharin begged everyone not to appoint him to the Commissariat of Education and proposed and then insisted on the job as administrator of science and technology. I supported him in that, as did several other people, and because we were a united majority we pushed it through (against Koba). Now I somewhat regret my vote. I think (I fear) that Bukharin will directly or indirectly support the idea that this was a removal from power. Mikhail [Tomskii] is still at loose ends. For the time being, he has been nominated to the Central Union of Consumer Organizations, but neither Tomskii nor Liubimov is especially sympathetic to that idea. There is now talk of nominating Liubimov commissar of finance, and if that goes through, then it is quite likely that Tomskii will have to go to the Central Union of Consumer Organizations.

At the last Politburo meeting, a rather nasty affair broke out between Bukharin and me. The Chinese affair was being discussed. Some favored a demonstration of military force on the Manchurian border. Bukharin spoke out sharply against this. In my speech I mentioned that at one time Bukharin had identified the Chinese revolution with ours to such an extent that the ruin of the Chinese revolution was equivalent to our ruin. Bug-arin said in reply that we have all said different things at different times, but only you, Voroshilov alone, had advocated support for Feng and Chiang Kai-shek, who are presently slaughtering workers. This unpardonable nonsense so infuriated me that I lost my self-control and blurted out in Nikolashka's [Bukharin's] face, "You liar, bastard, I'll punch you in the face," and other such nonsense and all in front of a large number of people. Bukharin is trash and is capable of telling the most vile fabrications straight to your face, putting an especially innocent and disgustingly holy expression on his everlastingly Jesuitical countenance; this is now clear to me, but, still, I did not behave properly.

But the trouble is my nerves. The damned things get me into trouble. After this scene, Bukharin left the Politburo meeting and did not return. Tomskii did not react at all. Rudzutak, who was chairman, should have called me to order, I think, but got by with just mumbling something.

RTsKhIDNI, f. 85, op. 1/s, d. 110, 11. 1–2ob; translated in Lars T. Lih, Oleg V. Naumov, and Oleg V. Khlevniuk (eds.), *Stalin's Letters to Molotov, 1925–1936,* trans. by Catherine A. Fitzpatrick (New Haven and London: Yale University Press, 1995), pp. 148–150.

══ Stalin's Letter to Molotov, Voroshilov, and Orjonikidze ══
September 30, 1929

Stalin, then vacationing as he often did in the Black Sea resort Sochi, wrote in anger to his closest associates, upbraiding them for their tolerance of Aleksei Rykov (1881–1938), the chairman of the Sovnarkom (the Council of People's Commissars). Rykov had served as head of the government since Lenin's death and was known to be a very frank, even blunt, man of great intelligence. An ardent supporter of NEP and a close associate of Bukharin, Rykov had offended Stalin by proclaiming, "Your policy does not even smell of economics!" Two months after this letter was written, Stalin denounced Rykov and Bukharin in a long speech at a meeting of the Central Committee, and the "Right deviationists" were removed from their governmental positions. Rykov and Bukharin were tried in a great "show trial" in 1938 and executed.

[30 September 1929]

To Molotov, Voroshilov, Ordzhonikidze:★

1) Did you read Rykov's speech? In my opinion, it's the speech of a nonparty soviet bureaucrat pretending to take the tone of a "loyal" person, "sympathizing" with the soviets. But not a single word about the party! Not a single word about the right deviation! Not a single word to say that the party's achievements, which Rykov underhandedly ascribes now to himself, were attained in struggle with the rightists, including Rykov himself! All our officials who give speeches usually consider it their duty to speak about the rightists and to call for struggle against the rightists. But Rykov, it seems, is free from such an obligation! Why?—I might ask—on what basis? How can you tolerate (meaning *covering up* as well) this political hypocrisy? Don't you understand that in tolerating such hypocrisy, you create the *illusion* that Rykov has separated from the rightists and you thus *mislead* the party, because everyone can see that Rykov has never had a thought of leaving the rightists? Shouldn't you give Rykov an alternative: either disassociate openly and honestly from the rightists and conciliators, or lose the right to speak in the name of the Central Committee and Council of Commissars. I think this should be done because it's the least the Central Committee can demand—less than that and the Central Committee ceases to be itself.

2) I learned that Rykov is still chairing your meetings on Mondays and Thursdays.[†] Is that true? If it's true, why are you allowing this comedy to go on? Who is it for and for what reason? Can't you put an end to this comedy? Isn't it time?

3) I think I'll stay in Sochi another week. What's your opinion? If you say so, I can return immediately.

Greetings,
Stalin
9/30/29

RTsKhIDNI, f. 558, op. 1, d. 5388; translated in Lars T. Lih, Oleg V. Naumov, and Oleg V. Khlevniuk (eds.). *Stalin's Letters to Molotov, 1925–1936,* trans. by Catherine A. Fitzpatrick (New Haven and London: Yale University Press, 1995), p. 181.

===== **Lev Kopelev, from *To Be Preserved Forever*** =====

In this memoir, Lev Kopelev remembers his involvement both with the Trotskyist opposition and the secret police (GPU). Later he would become, in his own words, "a true believer" and participate in the grain collection campaigns during collectivization in Ukraine. After studying

---

★ In the upper left-hand corner is Molotov's note:
Totally agree with everything said. Didn't read Rykov's speech, but only skimmed the headings. Will read. I do see now, however, that Stalin is right. Just don't agree that we're "covering" for Rykov. We have to fix things in the way Stalin proposes, however. V. Molotov. 10/3.
[†] The reference is to Rykov's chairing of Politburo sessions.

German at the Institute for Foreign Languages, Kopelev worked as a translator with the Red Army during the Second World War. He was arrested in 1945 after protesting Soviet treatment of German civilians and spent nine years in Soviet prison camps. There he met the young Aleksandr Solzhenitsyn, who later fictionalized Kopelev as Lev Rubin in The First Circle. *After his release, Kopelev joined the dissident intellectuals who fought restrictions on political and cultural freedoms in the Brezhnev years. From a fervent Stalinist he had evolved into a humanist Marxist. When they vacationed together in Sukhumi in the 1970s, the Nobel laureate and dissident Andrei Sakharov remembered Kopelev as a "big strong, kindly man, with his enormous dark eyes gazing at the world with childlike wonder."[1] Along with his wife and fellow memoirist and dissident, Raisa Orlova, Kopelev later emigrated to the West.*

I was sixteen, in Kharkov, and looking for work. The juvenile labor exchange didn't have much to offer, and I spent most of my days reading: Marx, Engels, Plekhanov, Lenin, Kautsky, Bukharin, Trotsky, Lunacharsky, Zinoviev, Stalin, Preobrazhensky; minutes of Party congresses; the memoirs of Clemenceau, Noske and Denikin; various magazines—all this and more used to be published in those days. Politically, I was one of the 'unorganized.' At the age of fourteen I had been thrown out of the Pioneers for smoking, drinking vodka and keeping company with 'bourgeois' girls who smoked, painted their lips and wore high-heeled shoes. And in the technical school where I studied electrical engineering, my application for membership in the Komsomol was rejected because of my past sins, compounded by new offenses: I had taken part in a fistfight with pupils of another school, and, at a Komsomol meeting, I had spoken up against the Comintern line in China, condemning the alliance with the Kuomintang. With a repetition of the fistfight, I was expelled from the school.

Now and then the labor exchange would find me work unloading trucks or delivering messages or selling subscriptions, and I would spend the money on cigarettes, movies and beer. Evenings I liked to spend at the debates and poetry readings at the local writers' club. My friends and I would also meet there to read each other our verses, some of which would be published on the literary page of *The Kharkov Proletarian*.

One morning in February 1929 my cousin Mark Polyak came to see me. Looking mysterious, he said he had been waiting out in the street for my parents to leave for work and for my brother to leave for school. Taking two large packages wrapped in newspaper and tied with string out of his briefcase, he said, 'Hide this. They may search my place. And not a word to anyone.'

Mark was seven years older than I was, and his family considered him a genius. He had graduated with a degree in biology, had published a pamphlet called 'Dreams and Death,' and gave lectures in various clubs on such topics as 'What Is Life?' and 'The Beginnings of Man.' I looked up to him as a scholar and the possessor of a fabulous library—the entire half of a large bookcase. His desk was always piled high with books and brochures: philosophy, biology, history, political science (but no literature). He scoffed at my literary pretensions and attempts at poetry. 'Read Kant and Hegel, Plekhanov, Lenin, Freud. Verses are romantic piffle—nineteenth century—good for

---

1. Andrei Sakharov, *Memoirs,* trans. Richard Lourie (New York: Alfred A. Knopf, 1990), p. 485.

girls' albums, nothing else. And a smart, modern girl will prefer science, philosophy and serious political writing. To waste time on some tail-wagger, some silly goose with an album, is even more stupid than to write verses. Don't tell me you can be attracted to even a pretty girl if all she can talk about is, "Do you believe in love? Whom do you like better, Pushkin or Nadson? Ah, Lermontov—how lovely!" Better practice onanism—it's less harmful than killing time that way.'

He gibed at me but wasn't offended when, snapping back, I would call him a withered husk, a bookworm, a Laputan, a wart. And he gave me wonderful books to read.

One morning he told me confidentially that he was an active member of an underground group of 'Bolshevik-Leninists'—the political opposition, which the Stalinist bureaucracy had stigmatized as Trotskyist and Zinovievist. He let me read pamphlets about Trotsky's exile, the platform of the 'united Leninist opposition' of 1927, the 'Notes of a conversation between Bukharin and Kamenev in August 1928,' etc. Even before that, I had pored over the records of the 14th and 15th Party congresses, the Party conferences, the plenary meetings of the Comintern executive committee, and *Pravda*'s 'discussion papers.' Reading all this often had an unsettling effect on me. The speeches and articles of the oppositionists had a compelling revolutionary logic and ardor: they spoke out against the NEPmen, the kulaks, the bureaucrats; against deals with the international bourgeoisie; for a world proletarian revolution. Yet I knew that they had been rejected by the Party majority, and, for a Bolshevik, the will of the majority was the highest law. Besides, with the country a besieged fortress, it was no time for schisms.

Mark contradicted me on that score. He reminded me that Lenin too had opposed the majority when it came to issues of principle, fundamentals and the fate of the Revolution—when he split with the majority over the Brest-Litovsk peace treaty, for instance, or over his introduction of NEP. And the situation then had been much more difficult than now. He had me meet 'Comrade Volodya,' our contact with 'the Center'—the opposition leadership. This was Ema Kazakevich, who was later to win the Stalin Prize for literature. As far as I know, this role of his in the 1920s was known throughout his life only to a few of his closest friends. One day Mark took me along 'on business'—we took a droshky and brought home a trunk containing a small hand printing press, dubbed *Amerikanka*. Several times later I had to disassemble it and hide it, piece by piece, with my friends.

Mark was arrested in March, leaving me with two packages, which he had said were 'part of the Center's archives, particularly conspiratorial in nature.' I gave them to Vanya Kalyanik to hide. Vanya's father was a factory director and a staunch Stalinist, but Vanya was for the opposition, though he was more interested in poetry. Yet his was the home they searched. Apparently one of our crowd was an informer. Vanya behaved splendidly—didn't divulge a single name. The father was stunned when a cache of opposition literature, including texts of political appeals, reports, resolutions, planned announcements, figures, lists of political prisoners, and so on, was found in the space between the top of the Dutch stove and the ceiling. Vanya insisted that he had had no idea how this terrible material had gotten there—that he didn't even remember who had been to his house, since he had been blind drunk all week. His father, to his credit, didn't volunteer any information, although he knew of our political sentiments, having often argued with us.

Vanya was ordered to report to the GPU the next day. Naturally, I decided to go with him and confess. Being sure that I would be arrested, I said good-bye to the girl I was then in love with, wrote a farewell note to my parents (which she was to deliver if I did not return), and took along a supply of cigarettes. At the GPU, I said that I had hidden the packages in Vanya's house without telling him or anyone else and without knowing what was in them (which, strictly speaking, was true). I also declared that as a convinced Communist-Bolshevik-Leninist, even though not a member of the Komsomol, I was duty-bound not to reveal who had asked me to hide the packages, since I believed that the GPU in this case was following an incorrect line, persecuting genuine Leninists.

The interrogator at first twitted me: 'Some conspirator! When did you stop playing cops and robbers?' Then they let Vanya go, and two of them proceeded to 'educate' me. I, in turn, sought to indoctrinate them, quoting Lenin and Trotsky, citing facts, pointing out that before adopting the policy of 'building Socialism in one country'—the U.S.S.R.—Stalin himself had written in the first edition of *Problems of Leninism* that to believe in that goal was to believe in utopia. They let me go, making me sign a promise not to leave town. I was almost disappointed: The good-bye scene had been so moving; she had kissed me for the first time; I had felt like a gallant revolutionary, heir to the Old Bolsheviks and the People's Will movement, and here they had sent me out of the room like a naughty schoolboy!

At the labor exchange they had a whole week's work for me, collecting subscriptions for newspapers and magazines. In the process I took to distributing opposition leaflets. I even pasted some of them up in a locomotive factory, and I couldn't resist boasting about it to the very friend I had earlier told about the packages. The next night I was arrested.

It was curious, after my imprisonment in 1945, to recall the ten days I spent in Kharkov's House of Corrective Labor (the word 'prison' had been relegated to the vocabulary of the old regime). A clean cell, for three people; a sunny window; the voices of other inmates, arrested for ordinary crimes, raised in cheerful bickering or in their hoarse, underworld songs. They let us keep several rubles in cash, and with this money we could buy newspapers and magazines and complement our tasteless but plentiful meals (meat, noodles, gruel) with bread, sausage, cheese and candy. We could even order books from a woman librarian who came around every other day. The guards addressed us as 'comrades.'

They released me on April 9, my seventeenth birthday. My father was made responsible for my good behavior. Still true to my convictions, I attended several underground meetings and read and passed on a number of pamphlets. But by May of 1929, with the 'unmasking' of Bukharin, Rykov and Tomsky, the opposition movement began to disintegrate. There were letters in the newspapers by people announcing that they were leaving the opposition; one such letter, signed by Preobrazhensky, Radek and Smilga—all three highly respected figures and longtime friends of Trotsky's—had a particularly strong effect. A secret underground meeting was held in a wood outside the city; a certain 'Comrade Alexander' from Moscow delivered a report on 'the current situation and the problems of the Leninist opposition.' He explained that the Party's Central Committee had, in effect, adopted the opposition's program of industrialization; that the danger of a kulak comeback was over; that Stalin himself had destroyed the sociological and theoretical base of his usurped power by appropriating the concepts and proposals of Preobrazhensky, Piatakov, Zinoviev, Kamenev, Rakovsky, Zalutsky and the other Leninists.

There were questions from the audience; debates sprang up; I found myself among those who argued against the need for any further opposition. The rightists had been exposed; an era of construction was beginning; the Party's general line was basically sound—why continue with the underground struggle against the Central Committee? To argue about who had appropriated whose thoughts—this was petty squabbling. The main thing now was to build factories and electric power plants, strengthen the Red Army. Let Trotsky in exile take care of the world revolution—we at home had to work with the Party and the working class, instead of widening the split and undermining the authority of the Central Committee and the Soviet government.

Soon after this meeting, Mark returned from 'political isolation' in the Urals; he too had left the opposition. Won over by newspaper articles, by the example of people like Mark, and, most of all, by Nadia, whom I had by then met and fallen deeply in love with (we registered as man and wife a year later), I went to the Komsomol and announced my resignation from the opposition.

The joyous welcome for the prodigal son that I had half-imagined when I wrote out my long declaration did not take place. A sharp-faced fellow who was chairman of the control commission met me with a dry and businesslike air.

'Hmm. Finally realized your comrades are full of bull, huh? Better late than never. Here. Here's a piece of paper. Write down all their names—everyone you knew. Which of them were Trotskyists, which were Zinovievists, and so on. If you don't remember the surname, write down the first name or the nickname—who, where from, where you met. What do you mean—why? Are you baring yourself before the Party and the Komsomol or just throwing dust in our eyes?'

I sat down and made a rather long list. I wanted to be frank; I believed that nothing should be kept hidden from the Party and the Komsomol. All the same, I held back a dozen or so names—people who had never been arrested or expelled from the Komsomol and who weren't in any kind of trouble. Sitting there under the portraits of Lenin, Dzerzhinsky, Chubar, Petrovsky,* I was embarrassed to know that I was deceiving them. But I knew full well that if I added the names of Tanya A., Zina I., Kima R., Zoya B., Ilya B., Kolya P. and some others, I would be identifying people whom I myself had drawn into the opposition, who now thought differently (as I did), and who could never be enemies of the Party or do anything to damage Soviet interests. I would feel more ashamed naming even one of them than I did in holding back the whole list. And yet, if they found me out? Then I would say that I had forgotten these names, that I attached no importance to them—I'd think of something. But now I wouldn't write them down.

The official looked over my list. 'Fine. You didn't forget anyone? Sure? Good. That means you're baring yourself before the Party. Now, about you—what are you doing? Well, the labor exchange isn't for you. You're not a country boy; you're an educated sort. So educated that you got mixed up with the opposition. You've been using your education against us. Now you must try to use it to help us. The whole country is caught up in this liquidation of illiteracy business. The construction of Socialism requires literate cadres. You go to your labor exchange and tell them you want to be sent where you can combat illiteracy. Show what you can do—then apply to the Komso-

---

* Vlas Chubar and Grigori Petrovsky, then members of the Central Committee of the Ukrainian Communist Party.

mol. Words—let them be as pretty as you like, as revolutionary as you like—are still only words. With the Party and the Komsomol what counts is deeds.'

They sent me to a railroad depot in a nearby village, where I was made director, no less, of a night school for semi-illiterates. A year later, in 1930, I was working for the newspaper of the local locomotive factory. Renewing my application for Komsomol membership, I gave a detailed account of my past 'Trotskyist connections,' exaggerating them, if anything. How exciting for an eighteen-year-old to see himself as a man 'with a past.'

They took their time with my application. The secretary of the Komsomol committee at the factory, a tall, thin fellow with a tubercular flush, would say to me, 'You seem to think you're a pretty deserving comrade—all those books and Party documents you read, all those discussions you had with the Trotskyists. Maybe you think we ought to say "Thank you" and bring you a Komsomol card on a tray, with musical accompaniment? Well, we're not saying thank you. Because I don't get the feeling that you've thought it all through. I don't seem to feel you know the reasons, the class reasons, for all your deviations. Here's Pashka—he's about your age. Pashka, did you ever sympathize with the opposition? No, he says, And you, Nikola, did you ever speak up for Trotsky or Bukharin at any meetings? Never—you were more interested in soccer. And you, Anya, did you always agree with the Central Committee? Always.

'You see—these are working lads, proletarians like their fathers and grandfathers. They laugh at your waverings and your doubts, your twists and turns. There's real class instinct for you! So you go think about it. Go on the production line. Show what you can do as a shock worker. And then we'll say, "Welcome to the Komsomol."'

For almost a year, I worked at a lathe during the day and for our newspaper at night. We took turns writing, editing and proofreading, and I didn't get more than three or four hours' sleep before day shift on the production line. After I became a full-fledged member of the Komsomol, they put me in charge of a paper at a tank shop. Leaving my lathe, I worked at my new job virtually around the clock, sleeping on piles of newsprint. The GPU representative at the factory, a stern but good-natured veteran of the Cheka, would often visit us in the evenings, asking us to take note of the workers' attitudes, keep an eye out for kulak propaganda and expose any remnants of Trotskyist and Bukharinist thoughts. I wrote several reports on conditions at the plant, although there was little I told him that I had not already said at meetings or written in our paper. My editorial colleagues did the same. The GPU man would chide us for our frankness in public. 'Don't you see, now they'll hide things from you—they'll give you a wide berth. No, fellows, you've got to learn Chekist tactics.' These words didn't jar us. To be a Chekist in those days seemed worthy of the highest respect, and to cooperate secretly with the Cheka was only doing what had to be done in the struggle against a crafty foe.

How could there be anything to be ashamed of in that? Yet I found it more than trying, because of my makeup. I was an enthusiast, I was hot-tempered, I lacked self-control, and I didn't know how to pretend or hide things from my friends (of which I had quite a number). The GPU representatives (another one came on the scene soon after) had to keep impressing me with the need for secrecy. It was a problem for them: They had some full-fledged undercover agents working for them at the factory, whom they saw only at special meeting places, but they were also dependent on more or less open cooperation with Party and Komsomol activists like us.

In the winter of 1932–33, our editorial brigade took part in forced collection of grain in the countryside. The GPU representative, in full uniform, with a Mauser in a wooden holster, accompanied us to meetings with the peasantry and in our search for buried grain. We saw him as a true comrade and helped him compile the reports that led to the arrest and exile of 'malicious hoarders.'

In 1933 I enrolled in a history course at the local university and wrote him several reports on political conditions at the school. When Kirov was assassinated, Mark was arrested again (this time to perish in a labor camp several years later), and a week after he was picked up I was expelled from the Komsomol and the university for 'maintaining relations with a Trotskyist relative,' though I had not seen Mark for quite a while. With the GPU man's help, I obtained a character reference from the factory which said: 'He did not hide his family ties, or the gross political mistakes he had committed before joining the Komsomol. . . . At the factory he proved himself as a worker . . . and he struggled actively against Trotskyism and other forms of hostile ideology.' A month later I was reinstated in the Komsomol, with a reprimand for a 'lapse in vigilance,' inasmuch as I had not known about my cousin's arrest.

In 1936—by then I was in Moscow, studying at the Institute of Foreign Languages—I was called in for a number of interviews with some serious-looking men, who explained that the class struggle was becoming more acute than ever and that there was no telling how many enemies of the people were still in hiding in the very bosom of the Party, spying, wrecking and hatching plots. They told me to join an Esperanto study group and find out who its members were and what mail it received from abroad. They also wanted reports on some of the teachers and foreign students. I wrote only what I knew to be true. For instance, when one of the instructors, Fritz Platten, was arrested, I wrote that he was a considerate and demanding pedagogue, a good athlete and an excellent raconteur, fascinating in his account of how he had accompanied Lenin in the sealed car of the famous train from Switzerland, and a man who spoke of Lenin with fondness and admiration.

My interrogators were often dissatisfied with me: 'You ought to be a lawyer. You're too trusting. If it turns out that you have given a clean bill of health to an enemy, it will be a blot on your record.' But I was sure that in telling the truth and only the truth, I was doing my duty as a Komsomol patriot.

Today I realize that a truthful police report on someone is still a police report. Today I don't see any substantial moral difference between an informer who invents and an informer who sticks to the facts. And it is painful and humiliating for me to recall those assignments I had carried out and my rationalizations of them. As Pushkin wrote,

> *I read my life, the painful sum of years;*
> *I shudder and I curse—but nay:*
> *For all my grief, for all my bitter tears,*
> *No wretched line is washed away.*

Lev Kopelev, *To Be Preserved Forever,* trans, and ed. by Anthony Austin (Philadelphia: J. B. Lippincott, 1977), pp. 105–113.

3

STALINISM

CHAPTER FOUR

THE STALIN REVOLUTION

No other period of Soviet history has been as fraught with historical controversy as the era of Stalinism. Earlier justification for Stalin's harsh rule by Communist or sympathetic writers was challenged by both Left critics, like Menshevik émigrés or Trotsky and his followers, and the proponents of the "totalitarian model," who were prominent during the Cold War. While the Left saw Stalinism as a perversion of socialism, the "totalitarians" argued that fascism (particularly Hitler's "national socialism") and Stalinism were essentially variants of a single political system. This model building went on in the absence of field work or deeply empirical studies (with some notable exceptions), for the Soviet Union was closed to serious foreign investigators. Western writers disagreed about the role of the dictator, the scale and purpose of the Great Purges, and the nature of the Stalinist state. The imagery associated with totalitarianism obscured the differences between Nazism and Stalinism. The two economies, for all the importance of the state, were fundamentally different. Stalin obliterated the capitalist market economy, while Hitler essentially preserved the market and established a form of state capitalism. The ideologies of the two regimes were quite distinct. Stalinism inherited (and perverted) a secular humanist doctrine of human liberation based on equality and the empowerment of the working class. While Soviet socialism failed to live up to its ideology, Nazism lived up to its only too well. Hitler and the fascists proudly proclaimed the inequality of people and the right of designated races or supermen to rule over (and exterminate) their social and racial inferiors. The launching of the Second World War and the physical elimination of Jews, Gypsies, homosexuals, the handicapped, Communists, and others were all too consistent with the original doctrine of Nazi party.

As a school of analysis within Russian/Soviet studies the totalitarian approach began to dissipate in the late 1960s and through the 1970s, as some historians moved from the study of personalities, parties, and the state to look more deeply at society, social movements, and the ways of life of ordinary people. A divide developed between social historians, on the one hand, and more traditional political historians and political scientists, on the other. While many of those writing in the totalitarian vein neglected the sources of resistance and autonomy within Soviet society, some social historians overreacted by diminishing the role of Stalin or searching for sources of support from below for collectivization or playing down the purges to the point that they were accused of being Stalinist apologists. At times, an apolitical social history denied the need to look at the state and politics altogether. But after initial excesses, the social history of the Soviet Union began to reap new insights from its wider source base. Collectivization, hailed by the Soviets as the "Great Breakthrough" and regarded by many on the Left as necessary for the survival of the Soviet Union, was seriously challenged by social historical research. From a victorious march toward a new form of agricultural production, collectivization has in more recent years been condemned as a vicious and costly war of the ruling elites (and part of the urban classes) against the great peasant majority of the country. One of the first scholarly works to challenge the rationality of the war on the peasants was Moshe Lewin's study, *Russian Peasants and Soviet Power,* first published in French in 1966. The Soviet economic historian A. A. Barsov and the American economist James Millar unraveled the old certainties about collectivization as contributing to economic growth by showing that agriculture actually did not provide resources to industry but, just the opposite, required resources from other sectors. Collectivization proved to be the Achilles' heel of the Soviet economy, a great drain into which the sweat and hopes of the peasants flowed with little real return. For all the real achievements of the Soviet system—in education, art and culture, health care, industrialization and urbaniza-tion—the methods and forms with which Stalin's state drove its people into its imag-ined future produced devastating effects on the environment, the quality of goods and services, and the lives of millions of ordinary people.

Ideology and intentions certainly affect historical outcomes, but sadly for histo-rians, facile deductions from individual or even collective motivations cannot explain fully where human actions might end up. Lewin proposes that the fate of the Russian Revolution might be likened to a train that confident Bolsheviks boarded and began to drive "from Station Promise to Station Hope."

> But as the train moved it became clear to growing numbers of the erstwhile founders that the train was moving, inexorably, somewhere else, in some un-wanted direction, but could not be stopped, nor could anyone get off. We can give many of the Bolsheviks credit for having tried, opposition after opposition, to correct the course of their train, but nothing seemed to work.[1]

Lenin himself complained, "I doubt very much whether the Communists are the ones who are leading. I believe rather that they are the ones who are being led." The train his comrades were on "traveled to an unknown destination, a destination which, for about a generation, was to earn the name 'Stalinism'."[2]

The great divide between Leninism and Stalinism may lie less in theoretical dif-ferences than in the experience and consequences of what has come down to us as "the revolution from above," the violent upheaval that ended traditional peasant agri-culture, collectivized the peasants, and moved millions from the land into industry. The years in which Stalin ruled unchallenged, roughly 1928 to 1953, were when the foundations of the system of government and economy that would last essentially until the 1990s were solidified. Lenin's revolution had established the one-party state and eliminated all non-Communist political rivals within the country, but it ended up with the transitional regime of the New Economic Policy (NEP). However ef-fective NEP was in restoring the economy and providing some social support for the

---

1. Moshe Lewin, *The Making of the Soviet System: Essays in the Social Hisory of Interwar Russia* (New York: Pantheon Books, 1985), p. 9.
2. Ibid.

Soviet government, Communists saw it as a moment of passage rather than the final goal of the revolution. They understood socialism to be a non-market system, the abolition of private property in the means of production. How the economy and state would function within such a system remained vague and subject to radically different interpretations. Stalin appropriated the aspiration toward socialism, linked it to his state-initiated drive to industrialize Russia, and declared confidently in 1936 that socialism had been essentially achieved. Rival ideas of what Marx or Lenin might have meant could no longer be expressed. And in the mind of Stalinists (as well as many liberals and conservatives in the West), socialism was what existed in Stalin's Soviet Union.

How that "socialism" worked in daily life, how it affected ordinary citizens, has been the subject of two extraordinary works by Sheila Fitzpatrick.[3] She begins by noting that collectivization was not something that came out of the villages but was brought to it "by outsiders—Soviet rural officials, supplemented by tens of thousands of urban Communists, workers, and students whom the regime sent out into the countryside for that purpose.[4] It began with an act of robbery—the seizure by the state of the peasants' livestock—and was aimed at increasing state grain procurements and preventing peasants from withholding grain from the market.[5] Peasants resisted both actively and passively, but in time they learned to live with the new order, to accommodate to it, and to bend its rules so that they might survive. In the decade after collectivization "the dominant mood among peasants seemed to be a mixture of resentment, malice, and lethargy."[6] The young and energetic left for the towns or the new building sites springing up all over the Soviet Union. The great mass of the Soviet population was traumatized by the cataclysmic blow that the state delivered, by the repression of a way of life, the suppression of their religion, and the forced or voluntary departure of many of the most able. Even the political terror of 1937–1938 did not have the devastating effect on the countryside that the famine and dekulakization of the early 1930s had had.

"Judging by police reports, Russian peasants strongly disliked Stalin, blamed him personally for collectivization and the famine, and regarded his every subsequent overture to them with deep suspicion, always looking for the hook hidden in the bait."[7] Nevertheless, they shared certain values with the regime and complained about the state's failure to carry out its obligations. Fitzpatrick says that "it was beyond dispute for many kolkhozniks [collective farmers] that the state had welfare obligations towards its peasants. 'The state ought to feed and clothe us,' one peasant stated simply."[8] Peasants also absorbed the party/state's enthusiasm for education, which was vastly extended into the villages in the 1930s. Over time "virtually all peasants seem to have acquired this perception. Education was the ticket out of the kolkhoz."[9] Ironically, with all the pressure from above, the Communist party had only a very weak presence in rural areas, and after a few years most of the kolkhoz [collective farm]

3. Sheila Fitzpatrick, *Stalin's Peasants: Resistance and Survival in the Russian Village After Collectivization* (New York and Oxford: Oxford University Press, 1994); *Everyday Stalinism: Ordinary Life in Extraordinary Times, Soviet Russia in the 1930s* (New York and Oxford: Oxford University Press, 1999).

4. Fitzpatrick, *Stalin's Peasants*, p. 3.

5. Ibid., p. 4.

6. Ibid., p. 14.

7. Ibid., p. 17.

8. Ibid., 151.

9. Ibid., p. 231.

chairmen were recruited from the local peasants.[10] The villages remained cut off to a considerable degree from urban society. Peasants resented the state and its agents but also directed much of their anger and malice toward members of their own village society. Feuds and family squabbles, resentments toward the new inequalities in the village (managers, officeholders, and machine operators lived much better than ordinary field hands) all tore at any peasant solidarity. In many ways the collectives led to a growth in individualization for many peasants, many of them anxious to get ahead either through schooling or leaving peasant life for the factories.

But when migrants came to the towns they found crowded communal apartments, stores without goods, and the pervasive presence of the state. Shortages were ubiquitous; even vodka was hard to find until Stalin ordered an increase in its production to pay for military expansion. Yet living in such dire material conditions was often accompanied by the development of a particularly Stalinist mentality, a kind of socialist realism. "Ordinary citizens also developed the ability to see things as they were becoming and ought to be, rather than as they were. An empty ditch was a canal in the making; a vacant lot where old houses or a church had been torn down, littered with rubbish and weeds, was a future park."[11] Shortages and industrial breakdowns led to a search for scapegoats, for "wreckers" and "class enemies." As many people moved up from peasant to worker to manager to party boss, others experienced a downward mobility, to the margins of Soviet society, to unrelieved poverty, or prison camp. Stalinism reversed many of the egalitarian trends of earlier Soviet periods and instituted a system of privileges and advantages for those more skilled, better placed politically and economically, or personally well connected. But those nearer the top had the greater distance to fall, and the purges of the late 1930s disproportionately decimated Communists, intellectuals, army officers, and state officials.

BUILDING STALINISM

After the fury of the first Five-Year Plan and "Cultural Revolution" years (1928–1931), Soviet society experienced a brief period of relative calm before a second storm. A few more consumer goods appeared—though shortages of most necessities remained the norm. Certain excessive powers of the police were curtailed. Peasants who had been driven into collective farms, their livestock taken from them, were permitted to sell some produce at farmers' markets and to possess a few animals—cows and chickens, but not horses. Writers at their first Soviet congress proclaimed a new literary tolerance. In foreign policy, the USSR took a milder line toward capitalist countries, allying with democracies against fascism, and the Comintern declared the Popular Front in which socialists and Communists would work together against the threat from the radical Right. A new constitution in 1936, said by its authors to be "the most democratic in the world," claimed to guarantee political, civil, and social rights for the Soviet people. Technicians and engineers regained privileges, but ordinary workers fell under the greater power of managers and were disciplined under harsh labor laws. One party member reported, "A proletarian in the proletarian state

---

10. Ibid., p. 186.
11. Fitzpatrick, *Everyday Stalinism,* p. 9.

is suspect, and any hypocritical bastard turned into a proletarian by the will of the Revolution can drown you in a teaspoon of water at any given moment."[12]

This period of relative calm and moderation was given the name "the Great Retreat" by Nicholas Timasheff, a Russian sociologist who had left Soviet Russia in 1921 to avoid political persecution. In the 1930s he worked with the distinguished émigré sociologist Pitirim Sorokin, lecturing at Harvard University and eventually joining the faculty at Fordham University. His concept of "the Great Retreat" was based on his observations that the USSR had abandoned its original revolutionary élan and internationalist mission in the mid-1930s and become a more traditional Great Power. For Timasheff, the Russian revolutionary process began as a phase of Marxist radicalism (1917–1921), moved on to the first retreat of NEP (1921–1928), which undid some of the reforms of the revolutionary period, turned radical once again with "the New Communist Offensive" (1928–1934), and ended with the Great Retreat (beginning in 1934) which marked the abandonment of utopia and the regime's accommodation to reality. The Great Retreat was manifest in politics (with the establishment of the Stalin dictatorship), in foreign policy (with the policy of collective security), in economics (with the concessions to the peasants after collectivization), and in social policy (with the reinstatement of the family, traditional schooling, and the softening of attitudes toward the church). In the selection here, Timasheff examines how the Stalinist state reconsidered history and moved from proletarian internationalism to a more traditional form of national patriotism.

But even in this period of "the Great Retreat," Soviet officials were not fully committed to a more modulated, gradualist evolution to a new society. Fearful of the consequences of the war on the peasants, aware that crime and banditry were rampant, and unable to tolerate high levels of social disruption, the party/state felt vulnerable, unprepared "to protect the forced expansion of state power over the economy."[13] Instead of class warfare, the Communists were faced by an enormous wave of crime, particularly crime directed against the state and its officials. Social disobedience was seen as a threat to the revolution and to the stability of the new, fragile political order. As historian David R. Shearer puts it,

> party and state officials no longer saw themselves engaged in a revolutionary struggle for power, allied with one class against other classes. Instead, they saw themselves as the established protectors of order and discipline against the whole of an unruly society . . . [Officials, however, were divided by] disputes over bureaucratic power and jurisdiction and differences in strategies about how best to defend state interests and authority. All believed, rightly or wrongly, that the state was involved in nothing less than a social struggle to extend its power, and that the whole of the state's legal and repressive infrastructure must be deployed in the protection of the state's authority and its goals.[14]

More and more activities of ordinary people were seen as criminal, and it was extremely easy for Soviet citizens to fall afoul of the law. Not only was more behavior

---

12. Lewis H. Siegelbaum, *Stalinism as a Way of Life* (New Haven: Yale University Press, 2000), document no. 43.

13. David R. Shearer, "Crime and Social Disorder in Stalin's Russia: A Reassessment of the Great Retreat and the Origins of Mass Repression," *Cahiers du Monde russe,* XXXIX (1–2) (January-June 1998), pp. 130–131.

14. Ibid., p. 139.

criminalized, but crimes were seen as political.[15] A worker could be fired and lose her housing if she were twenty minutes late three times in a month or four times in two months. So harsh were Stalin's laws that many managers and judges would not fully enforce them. Such "softness" could itself get the lenient official into trouble. Although there was little overt political opposition to the Stalinist state, social unrest and discontent, often expressed in "crimes" against property, was widespread, and the police apparatus grew to confront it. That repressive machine was then turned loose on the political and intellectual elite in the Great Terror of 1937–1938, as well as on kulaks and other "alien elements" in the last years before the war.

The Stalinist regime was feared, even by those who supported it. "Hence, the normal posture of a Soviet citizen was passive conformity and outward obedience. . . . [T]he ordinary 'little man' in Soviet towns, who thought only of his own and his family's welfare, was 'dissatisfied with Soviet power,' though in a somewhat fatalistic and passive manner."[16] Stalin's greatest support came from "the young, the privileged, office-holders and party members, beneficiaries of affirmative action policies, and favored groups like Stakhanovites [champion workers]."[17] The working class, now swelled by millions of peasants, was not the coherent and conscious class of the revolutionary years, but "many workers retained a residual feeling of connection with the Soviet cause, especially in cities with a strong revolutionary tradition like Leningrad . . . [T]his constituted passive support for the regime."[18] Stalin managed to associate the Soviet project with the most progressive efforts of humankind, with national liberation, socialism, and modernity. "Whether or not the Soviet regime had broad legitimacy with the population, its modernizing (civilizing) mission appears to have done so."[19]

Building Stalinism was not only about the extension of the power of the state over society. It was also about the construction of a new Soviet culture and view of the world in which citizens were supposed to believe and participate. Historians have turned to exploring the celebrations and rituals, heroes and celebrities of the new Stalinist order. Pilots and polar explorers, Stakhanovite workers and exemplary collective farmers, great soccer players and film stars were raised to the rarified heights of Soviet celebrity.[20] The essay by Sheila Fitzpatrick in this volume shows how a new "imagined community" based on class was envisioned by the Bolsheviks even as old social classes dissolved in the aftermath of the revolution. Given their Marxist vision, Communists worked hard at establishing new lines of class division, in a sense "inventing" classes where they had not existed in exactly that way.[21] James Van Geldern

15. Peter H. Solomon, Jr., *Soviet Criminal Justice Under Stalin* (Cambridge: Cambridge University Press, 1996), pp. 450–451.

16. Fitzpatrick, *Everyday Stalinism,* pp. 222, 224.

17. Ibid., p. 224.

18. Ibid., pp. 224–225.

19. Ibid., p. 225.

20. See, for example, Lewis H. Siegelbaum, *Stakhanovism and the Politics of Productivity in the USSR 1935–1941* (Cambridge: Cambridge University Press, 1990); Robert Edelman, *Serious Fun: A History of Spectator Sports in the USSR* (New York: Oxford University Press, 1993); John McCannon, *Red Arctic: Polar Exploration and the Myth of the North in the Soviet Union, 1932–1939* (New York: Oxford University Press, 1998); and Karen Petrone, *Life Has Become More Joyous, Comrades: Celebrations in the Time of Stalin* (Bloomington: Indiana University Press, 2000).

21. Fitzpatrick borrows the language of imagination and invention from Benedict Anderson, *Imagined Communities. Reflections on the Origin and Spread of Nationalism* (London: Verso, 1983; 1991); and Eric J. Hobsbawm and Terrence Ranger, eds., *The Invention of Tradition* (Cambridge: Cambridge University Press, 1983).

deals evocatively with the Stalinist culture of the 1930s, proposing that as the center, Moscow, extended its sway over the periphery of the USSR, it simultaneously integrated the diverse citizenry of the vast country into passive participants in a new stability. A new mental geography linked the many nationalities in the Soviet Union into a single multinational family based on "friendship of the peoples." The very expanse of the country, its sweep from Europe to the Pacific, was a matter of pride and confidence, and in the films and mass songs of the period the dark, gray, mundane realities of socialist construction were painted over in the glorious colors of an anticipated future.

MAKING A SOVIET PEOPLE

How did Stalin rule? How did he maintain his authority while establishing a personal autocracy? His extraordinary and brutal political achievement was to act in the name of the Communist party and its central committee against that party and central committee, while remaining the unchallenged head of party and state and, evidently, a vastly popular leader. At the end of the process, his absolute grip on power allowed him to declare black white and completely reverse the foreign policy of the Soviet Union and the line of the Comintern by embracing Nazi Germany in a non-aggression pact. The colossal and costly destruction he brought upon the country on the eve and in the early days of the Second World War gave rise to no organized opposition, and the centralized apparatus of control that he had created was not only able to weather the Nazi invasion but to organize a victory that would preserve the essence of the system he forged for another half century.

The simplest, though inadequate, answer to the question, would be that Stalin's power was maintained through the exercise of terror and monopolistic control of the means of communication throughout society. Though terror is certainly an important part of the answer, it cannot explain how Stalin won his authority within the party in the 1920s and maintained it among his own supporters even before the advent of the Great Terror. Once initiated, terror operated through collaboration, and Stalin's associates almost never attempted to free themselves from the source of their fears. Terror was supported by many within and outside the party who believed that extraordinary means against vicious and hidden enemies were required. Tens of millions regarded Stalin as the indispensable leader of the "socialist" camp, perhaps someone to be feared, as was Ivan *groznyi*, a leader who filled the hearts of enemies with awe.[22]

The naked exercise of unrestrained power was key to Stalin's monopolization of power, but his regime simultaneously worked to create authority and acceptance, borrowing from and supplementing the repertoire of justifications from Lenin's day. While appropriating the mantle of Lenin and much of the rhetoric of Bolshevism, however, Stalin revised, suppressed, and even reversed much of the legacy of Lenin. Internationalism turned into nationalism; the *smychka* (union) between the workers and the peasants was buried in the ferocity of collectivization; radical transformation of the family and the place of women ended with reassertion of the most conservative "family values." And in the process, almost all of Lenin's closest associates fell victim to the self-proclaimed keeper of the Leninist flame.

---

22. Michael Cherniavsky, "Ivan the Terrible as Renaissance Prince," *Slavic Review,* XXVII, 2 (June 1968), pp. 195–211.

Within ten years of his dispute with Lenin, Stalin transformed nationality policy from a series of concessions to non-Russians into a powerful weapon of imperial state-building. He reversed Lenin's focus on "Great Russian chauvinism" as the principal danger in nationality relations and emphasized instead the dangers from the nationalism of non-Russians. In 1923, he turned on M. Kh. Sultan-Galiev, a former associate in Narkomnats (People's Commissarist of Nationalities' Affairs) and a spokesman for the aspirations of Muslim Communists, accused him of "national deviationism," had him "tried" before a party conference, arrested, and expelled from the party. Five years later, the state police "discovered" a new plot, the "Sultan-Galiev counter-revolutionary organization," and in the next decade the OGPU and its successor, the NKVD, "unmasked" dozens of conspiratorial groups promoting nationalism, from Ukraine to Central Asia. In a letter to Levon Mirzoian, the Armenian first secretary of the Kazakh *kraikom,* in 1933, Stalin called for intensifying the struggle against local Kazakh nationalism "in order to create the conditions for the sowing of Leninist internationalism." Five years later, after having carried out purges against Kazakh intellectuals and "deviationist" party members, Mirzoian himself was arrested and executed.

The ultimate man of the political machine, Stalin was one of the least likely candidates for the title of charismatic hero. Short in stature, reticent in meetings and on public occasions, neither a talented orator like Trotsky or Zinoviev, nor an attractive and engaging personality, like Lenin or Bukharin, Stalin did not himself project an image of a leader—until it was created for him (and by him) through the cult. First the promotion of a cult of Lenin, which Stalin actively encouraged, then his identification as a loyal Leninist, and eventually the substitution of his own image for that of Lenin were important props for Stalin's authority both within the party and in society.[23] All this was accomplished in a political culture based on the prerevolutionary Bolshevik traditions to which emphasis on personality, the exaggerated importance of the leader, and the attendant sacral notions of infallibility were all alien.

The ideological props of the Stalin dictatorship were both a radically revised Marxism and a pro-Russian nationalism and étatism. Class warfare was seen as inevitable and intensifying rather than diminishing as the country approached socialism. As long as the country was surrounded by hostile capitalist states, it was claimed, state power had to be built up. When the Soviet Union was declared to be socialist by Stalin in 1936, the positive achievement of reaching a stage of history higher than the rest of the world was tempered by the constant reminders that the enemies of socialism existed both within and outside the country, that they were deceptive and concealed, and must be "unmasked." Repeated references to dangers and insecurity and to the need for "vigilance" justified the enormous reliance on the "steel gauntlets of Ezhov," arguably the most vicious of Stalin's policemen.

TERROR

As Stalin narrowed the oligarchy that had carried out the Stalin revolution and effectively closed the party to debate and consideration of alternatives, there were smoldering expressions of dissatisfaction within the party. The popular enthusiasm for in-

23. Robert C. Tucker, "The Rise of Stalin's Personality Cult," *American Historical Review,* LXXXIV, 2 (April 1979), pp. 347–366.

dustrialization was tempered by much less support for Stalin's agrarian revolution. The open (and later passive) resistance to collectivization among the peasants was reflected in less dramatic form by quiet forms of opposition within the party. The evident failures and costs of implementing these policies of rapid industrialization and full collectivization and dekulakization fueled discontent with the General Line. In his own statements, Stalin refused to accept any blame for the economic chaos or the famine. In his view "the last remnants of moribund classes," some of whom had "even managed to worm their way into the party," were actively sabotaging the building of socialism. The remedy was more repression.

> The abolition of classes is not achieved by the extinction of the class struggle, but its intensification. . . . We must bear in mind that the growth of the power of the Soviet state will intensify the resistance of the last remnants of the dying classes."[24]

A broad, inchoate disgruntlement with Stalin's rule permeated political and intellectual circles but could not be openly expressed. Several loyal Stalinists, like Kaminskii, Kosior, Vareikis, and Bauman, harbored serious doubts about Stalin's agricultural policies. Others, like Mykola Skrypnyk, a co-founder of the Ukrainian Communist party who had sided with Stalin in the 1920s and early 1930s, were critical of the growing pro-Russianness of Stalin's nationality policies.[25] Perhaps most ominously, tensions arose between the Red Army commander, Mikhail Tukhachevskii, who called, in 1930, for expansion of the armed forces, particularly aviation and tank armies, and Stalin and Voroshilov, who opposed what they called "Red militarism."[26] During the famine in Ukraine, high military officers, like Iona Iakir, angered Stalin by reporting their upset at peasant resistance, which, they felt, could spread to the troops, and demanding that more grain be kept in the region.[27] Even among Stalin's closest supporters there were fractures, but Stalin still represented for the majority of party members the militant turn toward socialism—collectivization, rapid industrialization, and the destruction of organized political opposition. To some, however, his personal proclivity toward the use of force seemed to have gone beyond the broad bounds of Bolshevik practice.

On December 1, 1934, Stalin's lieutenant in Leningrad, Sergei Kirov, was assassinated. Some historians have tried to pin the murder on Stalin himself, but there is no conclusive evidence to support such a claim.[28] After some hesitation, the regime blamed the murder on the former oppositionists, Zinoviev and Kamenev, and a cascade of accusations, confessions, grand trials, and executions followed. By the end of the decade, more than 1,700,000 people had been arrested; 1,345,000 sentenced; and about 700,000 executed. Millions sat long years in prison or toiled in labor camps;

---

24. Originally this was an idea put forth by Trotskii. I.V. Stalin, "Itogi pervoi piatiletki: Doklad 7 ianvaria 1933 g.," *Sochineniia*, XII, pp. 211–212.

25. Skrypnyk committed suicide in 1933, as Ukrainian national Communists were systematically being purged.

26. R.W. Davies, *The Industrialisation of Soviet Russia, 3: The Soviet Economy in Turmoil, 1929–1930* (Cambridge, MA: Harvard University Press, 1989), pp. 446–447. In May 1932 Stalin apologized to Tukhachevskii and endorsed some of his proposed reforms.

27. Eventually some grain was sent to Ukraine in January 1933 along with the new party boss, Postyshev.

28. For the case against Stalin, see Robert Conquest, *Stalin and the Kirov Murder* (New York: Oxford University Press, 1989); and Amy W. Knight, *Who Killed Kirov? The Kremlin's Greatest Mystery* (New York: Hill and Wang, 1999).

hundreds of thousands died from exposure, disease, and hunger. Why this enormous self-destruction of party members, intellectuals, simple workers and peasants, most of them loyal to the regime, happened has remained controversial. There is no consensus among scholars as to the motivations behind the purges. Interpretations range from the idea that purging was a permanent and necessary component of totalitarianism in lieu of elections (Zbigniew Brzezinski) to seeing the Great Terror as an extreme form of political infighting (J. Arch Getty).[29] Dissatisfaction with Stalin's rule and with the harsh material conditions was palpable in the mid-1930s, and the regime had trouble controlling the "family circles" of high-placed officials and powerful local bosses, particularly in the union republics, who thwarted the plans of the center. One of the effects of the purges was the replacement of an older political and economic elite with a younger, potentially more loyal one.[30] Great numbers of promoted workers, party rank-and-file, and young technicians rose rapidly up through the state and party bureaucracy. These men (and they were primarily men) would make up the Soviet elite through the post-Stalin period until the early 1980s.[31]

Yet neither arguments from social context nor functionalist deductions from effects to causes have successfully eliminated the principal catalyst to the Terror, the will and ambition of Stalin. The Great Purges have been seen traditionally as an effort "to achieve an unrestricted personal dictatorship with a totality of power that [Stalin] did not yet possess in 1934."[32] Stalin guided and prodded forward the arrests, show trials, and executions, aided by the closest members of his entourage: Molotov, Kaganovich, Voroshilov, Zhdanov, Malenkov, Mikoyan, and Ezhov.[33] Here personality and politics merged, and the degree of excess repression was dictated by the peculiar demands of Stalin himself, who could not tolerate limits on his will set by the very ruling elite that he had brought to power.[34]

Stalin remains the central mystery within the Soviet enigma, and the Great Terror the most opaque episode of his reign. His biographer, Robert C. Tucker, employed the insights of the psychologist Karen Horney to probe the psychic formation of the dictator, while "revisionist" historians tried to deconstruct explanations derived from a

---

29. J. Arch Getty, *Origins of the Great Purges, The Soviet Communist Party Reconsidered, 1933–1938* (New York: Cambridge University Press, 1985), p. 206. For a range of views on the purges, particularly of the so-called "revisionists," see J. Arch Getty and Roberta T. Manning (eds.), *Stalinist Terror: New Perspectives* (Cambridge: Cambridge University Press, 1993).

30. A. L. Unger, "Stalin's Renewal of the Leading Stratum: A Note on the Great Purge," *Soviet Studies*, XX, 3 (January 1969), pp. 321–330; Kendall E. Bailes, *Technology and Society under Lenin and Stalin: Origins of the Soviet Technical Intelligentsia, 1917–1941* (Princeton: Princeton University Press, 1978), pp. 268–271, 412–413; Sheila Fitzpatrick, "Stalin and the Making of a New Elite, 1928–1939," *Slavic Review*, XXXVIII, 3 (September 1979), pp. 377–402.

31. Bailes criticizes Fitzpatrick for not distinguishing between those who rose into the intelligentsia through formal education, many of whom were workers (the *vydvizhentsy*), and the *praktiki*, who were elevated through their work experience. ["Stalin and the Making of a New Elite: A Comment," *Slavic Review*, XXXIX, 2 (June 1980), pp. 286–289.]

32. Robert C. Tucker, "Introduction," Tucker and Stephen F. Cohen (eds.), *The Great Purge Trial* (New York: Rosset & Dunlap, 1965), p. xxix. This is essentially the argument of the second volume of his Stalin biography, as well as the view of Robert Conquest in *The Great Terror: Stalin's Purge of the Thirties* (New York: Macmillan, 1968); Robert Conquest, *The Great Terror: A Reassessment* (New York: Oxford University Press, 1990).

33. Boris A. Starkov, "Narkom Ezhov," in Getty and Manning (eds.), *Stalinist Terror*, pp. 21–39.

34. Stalin's personal involvement in the details of the terror have been indisputably demonstrated by archival documents released in the late 1980s and early 1990s. One such note to Ezhov will suffice to give the type of intervention that the *vozhd'* engaged in. In May 1937, he wrote: "One might think that prison for Beloborodov is a podium for reading speeches, statements which refer to the activities of all sorts of people but not to himself. Isn't it time to squeeze this gentleman and make him tell about his dirty deeds? Where is he, in prison or in a hotel?" [*Dialog* (Leningrad), no. 4 (1990), p. 21; cited in Starkov, "Narkom Ezhov," p. 29]

single purpose by a single man. Revisionists elaborated a picture of unrelieved confusion, contradiction, false starts, improvisation, and swings from policies of negotiation and reconciliation to desperate resorts to repression, violence, and terror.[35] Though there was general agreement that Stalin intended to create a powerful state able to carry out a radical program of social transformation and defend the country against "imperialism," the revisionists held that there were no blueprints pre-existing in Stalin's mind, that other players had significant, even if subordinate roles, and that Stalin's personal power was not as great as usually imagined.[36] Gabor Rittersporn, one of the boldest of the revisionists, argued that the purges were "a fierce internal battle within the state apparatus [that] arose from the need to ensure regular functioning of the administrative, economic and political mechanisms, though they were by their very nature uncontrollable. . . . Stalin, for all he played an important role, was in fact far from being always able to dictate the course of the turbulent events of the 1930s and that in fact his personal position on the top of the party-state emerged shaken rather than strengthened from the 'Great Purge'."[37] The contribution of social history in general and of the revisionists (the two groups may overlap but are not synonymous) was to broaden the historical canvas in the Soviet field. The landscape of the 1930s was drawn in greater detail and color than ever before. But some of the more controversial conclusions of the 1980s had to be revised once more when the Soviet archives were unexpectedly opened. As the work of Oleg Khlevniuk, both in his collections of documents and his monographs, has shown, Stalin dominated the state and party from the early 1930s and grew so powerful in the period of the purges that even the Politburo was diminished as an organ of power.[38] Historians had to surrender the notion that a group of Communist moderates tried to ameliorate the political repression but lost out to radicals led by Stalin and Molotov once no archival evidence could be found to support it. Stalin has essentially been restored to the "symbolic and real" center that he had occupied in more traditional political histories, but the social context in which he acted could now be understood and appreciated in ways that had been impossible earlier.

Whatever his authentic political aspirations, Stalin was marked by his deep suspiciousness and insecurity. As Bukharin told the old Mensheviks Fedor and Lydia Dan,

> Stalin is even unhappy because he cannot convince everyone, and even himself, that he is greater than everyone, and this is his unhappiness, perhaps the most

---

35. Robert C. Tucker, *Stalin as Revolutionary, 1879–1929: A Study in History and Personality* (New York: W. W. Norton, 1973), *Stalin in Power: The Revolution from Above, 1928–1941* (New York: W. W. Norton, 1990). For a discussion of the "new cohort" of revisionist historians, see Sheila Fitzpatrick, "New Perspectives on Stalinism," *Russian Review,* XLV, 4 (October 1986), pp. 357–373; the replies by Stephen F. Cohen, Geoff Eley, Peter Kenez, and Alfred G. Meyer, with a reply by Fitzpatrick, in ibid., pp. 375–413; and by Daniel Field, Daniel R. Brower, William Chase, Robert Conquest, J. Arch Getty, Jerry F. Hough, Hiroaki Kuromiya, Roberta T. Manning, Alec Nove, Gabor Tamas Rittersporn, Robert C. Tucker, and Lynne Viola, in ibid., XLVI, 4 (October 1987), pp. 375–431.

36. "Evidence of high-level confusion, counterproductive initiatives, and lack of control over events has not supported the notion of a grand design." (Getty, *Origins of the Great Purges,* p. 203)

37. Gabor Tamas Rittersporn, *Stalinist Simplifications and Soviet Complications: Social Tensions and Political Conflicts in the USSR, 1933–1953* (Chur, Switzerland: Harwood Academic Publishers, 1991) [Translation of *Simplifications Staliniennes et Complications Soviétiques: Tensions sociales et conflits politques en URSS, 1933–1953* (Paris: Editions des archives contemporaines, 1988)], p. 184.

38. See, for example, O. V. Khlevniuk, A. V. Kvashonkin, L. P. Kosheleva, and L. A. Rogovaia (eds.), *Stalinskoe Politbiuro v 30-e gody. Sbornik dokumentov* (Moscow, 1995); O. V. Khlevniuk, *In Stalin's Shadow: The Career of "Sergo" Ordzhonikidze,* ed. Donald J. Raleigh, trans. David J. Nordlander (Armonk, New York and London: M. E. Sharpe, 1995); O. V. Khlevniuk, *Politbiuro: Mekhanizmy politicheskoi vlasti v 1930-e gody* (Moscow: Rosspen, 1996).

human feature in him, perhaps the only human feature in him, but already not human. Here is something diabolical: because of his great "unhappiness" he cannot but avenge himself on people, on all people, but especially on those who are somehow higher, better than he . . .[39]

The purges destroyed primarily those in power. "It is one of the mysteries of Stalinism," Lewin summarizes,

> that it turned much of the fury of its bloody purges against this very real mainstay of the regime. There were among the *apparaty,* probably, still too many former members of other parties or of the original Leninist party, too many participants and victors of the civil war who remembered who had done what during those days of glory. Too many thus could feel the right to be considered founders of the regime and base on it part of the claims to a say in decisions and to security in their positions. Probably, also letting the new and sprawling administration settle and get encrusted in their chairs and habits could also encourage them to try and curtail the power of the very top and the personalized ruling style of the chief of the state—and this was probably a real prospect the paranoid leader did not relish.[40]

Stalin's initiation and personal direction of the purges gave the green light to thousands of smaller settlings of scores.[41] In the context of deep and recurring social tensions, the state stoked resentments against the privileged, the intelligentsia, other ethnicities, and outsiders. The requirement to find enemies, to blame and punish, worked together with self-protection and self-promotion (and plain sadism) to expand the purges into a political holocaust. At the end, the Soviet Union resembled a ruined landscape, seriously weakened economically, intellectually, and militarily, but at the same time dominated by a towering state apparatus made up of new loyal *apparatchiki,* disciplined by the police, and presided over by a single will.

HIGH STALINISM, 1945–1953

Scholarly writing on Soviet society during the period of "High Stalinism" began in earnest only in the 1990s, with the opening of the Russian archives, but earlier, an imaginative reconstruction of Soviet society in the post-war years had been attempted by the literary historian Vera S. Dunham. Through a careful reading of the middle-brow literature of the late Stalin years, Dunham elaborated a conception of Soviet values and of a deliberate policy of the state toward the most influential members of society—what she suggestively called "the Big Deal." Dunham concluded that the Soviet regime had not only retreated from its earlier revolutionary ideals in the late 1930s and 1940s, but had made a pact with those in society it needed most—managers, intellectuals, skilled workers, and white-collar employees—granting them a degree of material comfort in exchange for acquiescence in the party's rule and support in its economic and social campaigns.

---

39. "On Pozhret Nas," from the archive of L. O. Dan in the Institute of Social History, Amsterdam, published in Kh. Kobo (ed.), *Osmyslit' Kul't Stalina: Perestroika—Glasnost', Demokratiia, Sotsializm* (Moscow: Progress, 1989), p. 610.

40. Moshe Lewin, "Grappling with Stalinism," *The Making of the Soviet System,* pp. 308–309.

41. Sheila Fitzpatrick, "How the Mice Buried the Cat: Scenes from the Great Purges of 1937 in the Russian Provinces," *Russian Review,* LII, 3 (July 1993), pp. 299–320.

The Stalinist system was restored and consolidated after the devastation of the war years. As a single, political cultural synthesis became hegemonic and the more disruptive violence of the prewar period receded, pervasive fear, which disciplined people into obedient silence, co-existed with genuine acceptance of the system. The figure of Stalin stood symbolically for ideal behavior in an ideal society. Enemies were still said to be omnipresent, and the country was radically cut off from the outside world by strict restrictions on travel and a heavy censorship. Before his sudden death at the end of August 1948, Andrei Zhdanov, party chief of Leningrad and Stalin's cultural tsar, launched a series of attacks on writers, cinematographers, and musicians, condemning "formalism" in art and calling for a return to plot, melody, wholesomeness, and optimism. The late Stalinist years were marked by an intense Russo-Soviet nationalism and anti-Western isolationism. Official propaganda convincingly identified the victory over Nazism with the superiority of the Soviet system, its organic link with *rodina* (the motherland), and the personal genius of Stalin. The triumph over fascism provided the Communists with another source of legitimation and authority. Now Russia and the Soviet Union were melded into a single image. Patriotism and accommodation with established religious and national traditions, along with the toning down of revolutionary radicalism, contributed to a powerful ideological amalgam that outlasted Stalin himself. In the post-war decades, the war became the central identifying moment of Soviet history, eclipsing the revolution and the "Great Breakthrough" of the early 1930s.[42] Each decade of Soviet history had its own hardships, but the 1940s was perhaps the harshest of all. The catastrophe of the German invasion was followed by the "hungry years," 1946–1947, when drought hit central Russia, Ukraine, and Moldavia. Yet another famine tore through Russia and Ukraine, with an estimated two million deaths. Peasant life was particularly brutal. Collective farms received no income at all in 1946, and letters from the villages expressed a general despair about their future. People voted with their feet and left the farms. Between 1949 and 1953, the number of peasants on collective farms fell by 3,300,000.[43]

The Soviet Union put on a brave face for the outside world, posing as a Great Power and the most "advanced," "progressive" state in the world, humanity's future in the present. All the while it was in actuality poor and paralytic. Whatever benefits accrued to the Soviet system from the unity of decision-making at the top had to be weighed against the costs of over-centralization and the resultant paralysis lower down in the apparatus. In the years of the Cold War, as Stalin deteriorated physically and mentally, the entire country—its foreign policy, internal politics, cultural life, and economic slowdown—reflected the moods of its leader and were affected by his growing isolation, arbitrariness, and inactivity. Vicious anti-Semitic campaigns culminated in the infamous "Doctors' Plot" of 1952–1953, in which Kremlin doctors, most of them Jewish, were arrested for allegedly attempting to poison Soviet leaders. The ruling elite was concerned with plots, intrigues, the rivalries among Stalin's closest associates, the rise and fall of clients and patrons. No one could feel secure. "All of us around Stalin," writes Khrushchev, "were temporary people. As long as he trusted us to a certain degree, we were allowed to go on living and working. But the moment

    42. Nina Tumarkin, "The Great Patriotic War as Myth and Memory," *Atlantic Monthly,* CCLXVII, 6 (June 1991), pp. 26, 28, 37, 40, 42, 44; Amir Weiner, *Making Sense of War: The Second World War and the Fate of the Bolshevik Revolution* (Princeton: Princeton University Press, 2001).
    43. Elena Zubkova, *Russia After the War: Hopes, Illusions, and Disappointments, 1945–1957,* trans. Hugh Ragsdale (Armonk, N.Y.: M. E. Sharpe, 1998), p. 66.

he stopped trusting you, Stalin would start to scrutinize you until the cup of his distrust overflowed."[44] In his last years, Stalin turned against Molotov and Mikoyan and grew suspicious of Beria, Voroshilov, Kaganovich, and Malenkov. Khrushchev overheard him say, "I'm finished. I trust no one, not even myself."[45]

THE BOLSHEVIK INVENTION OF CLASS: MARXIST THEORY AND THE MAKING OF "CLASS CONSCIOUSNESS" IN SOVIET SOCIETY

Sheila Fitzpatrick

The "imagined communities" for which revolutionaries fight are often nations. But the Bolshevik revolutionaries who took power in Petrograd in October 1917 were exceptions to the rule. They did not at first "imagine" a new Russian or even Soviet nation. Instead, being Marxist internationalists, they imagined a class—the international proletariat, whose revolution, begun in Russia, would soon sweep Europe. The international revolution failed to materialize, however, and the Bolsheviks were left with the unexpected task of building a previously unimagined socialist nation. Their commitment to the international proletariat became increasingly tenuous, finally disappearing, perhaps, with the formal dissolution of the Comintern during the "Great Patriotic War" against Nazi Germany. . . .

It will be argued in this essay that the Bolsheviks, cherishing an imagined class community yet inheriting a shattered and fragmented class structure in Russia after the revolution, found themselves obliged to invent classes on the basis of Marxist theory . . . in that most obvious and yet least expected place, the Union of Soviet Socialist Republics.

CLASS AND THE BOLSHEVIK REVOLUTION

Marxism, a Western import of the late nineteenth century, quickly won great popularity among Russian intellectuals, particularly but not exclusively those on the revolutionary left. The industrial proletariat and capitalist bourgeoisie were important concepts in political discourse some time before they became actual socio-economic entities in Russia. By the first decades of the twentieth century, however, thanks to an energetic program of state-sponsored industrialization initiated in the 1890s, reality was catching up with Marxist imagination. The industrial working class of Russia in the immediate prewar years was small but highly concentrated and politically active. Petersburg and Moscow workers created the first soviets in 1905, and played a crucial role in bringing down the Tsarist regime in February 1917.

Though intelligentsia-led (like all other revolutionary groups), the Bolsheviks became a mass party with broad working-class support in 1917. They profited from the progressive radicalization of workers and conscript soldiers and sailors in the

---

44. *Khrushchev Remembers,* trans. and ed. by Strobe Talbott (Boston: Little, Brown and Co., 1970), p. 307.
45. Ibid.

months after the February Revolution, having distinguished themselves from other socialist parties by their intransigent stand against the war and the politics of coalition and compromise. By the fall of 1917, the Bolsheviks' claim to be "the party of the proletariat" seemed justified by a run of electoral successes, and it is at least arguable that they had a popular mandate in October for their seizure of power in the name of the workers' soviets.

One of the great strengths of Marxism in Russia had been its success in predicting the future. In the 1880s, Marxists and Populists had argued about the inevitability of capitalist industrialization in Russia—and in less than a decade the Marxist prediction had come to pass. Marxism had accurately identified the urban working class as a revolutionary force in Russia. It had asserted that class conflict was the basis of politics—thus in effect predicting the collapse of the February coalition between "bourgeois liberalism" (the Provisional Government) and "proletarian socialism" (the Petrograd soviet). To the Bolsheviks, and even to many of their political opponents, the October victory seemed only the latest proof that in Russia, at least, history was on the Marxist side.

But, as it turned out, this was to be not just the latest but also the last Russian proof of Marxist axioms. No sooner had the proletarian revolution occurred than, by a spectacular irony, history abruptly disowned the Russian Marxists, mocking their theories by destroying the class structure of Russian society and the class basis of revolutionary politics.

Consider the following:

• During the Civil War years, Russia's urban proletariat disintegrated and dispersed because of hunger in the towns and industrial closures. Many workers returned to their native villages—where, contrary to earlier assertions by Marxist intellectuals, it appeared that they still had land and an available alternative (non-proletarian) identity.

• A significant segment of the remaining working class turned against the Bolsheviks, as was dramatically demonstrated to the world by the 1921 Kronstadt revolt.

• The landowning nobility was expropriated by the peasants, the capitalists were expropriated by the new Soviet regime, and a large part of both formerly privileged classes retreated with the White Armies and ended up in emigration.

• The class differentiation of the Russian peasantry associated with Stolypin's prewar agrarian reforms was halted and in large part reversed as a result of the revolution and the resurgence of the peasant commune.

The result was that in 1921, when the Bolsheviks emerged victorious from the Civil War, they found themselves in a truly new world—one in which class and class conflict had become irrelevant. The class that had made the revolution was dispersed and fragmented, and the classes that had opposed it no longer existed. There were no further guidelines for political action in Marxist theory, and no Marxist basis for understanding an amorphous and essentially classless (but not yet, alas, socialist) society. The Bolsheviks' revolutionary imagination of class had reached an impasse. At this point, the Bolsheviks had the choice of repudiating Marxist theory and the legitimacy of their own revolution, or soldiering on regardless. Not surprisingly, they chose the latter. But that choice led them inexorably to reinvent the class base of Russian politics and society that history had so capriciously denied them.

THE REINVENTION OF CLASS IN THE 1920S

For the Bolsheviks, society was divided into two antithetical class camps. The two camps revolved around the proletariat, on the one side, and the bourgeoisie, on the other. The "proletariat" consisted of the industrial working class (very small at the beginning of the 1920s, but growing with the revival of industry under the New Economic Policy) and its landless and poor—peasant allies in the villages (although poor peasants were unfortunately difficult to distinguish as a stable socio-economic group). Cast as symbolic leader of the proletariat was the Bolshevik party, self-identified as the vanguard of the dictator-class.

The "bourgeoisie" was an amalgam of pre- and post-revolutionary social groups, including the remnants of the old nobility and capitalist classes, urban Nepmen (private traders and entrepreneurs, whose activity was legalized with the advent of NEP in 1921), and kulaks (the more prosperous peasants, whom the Bolsheviks regarded as potential capitalists). This composite class had, in fact, little coherence and no leadership. But the Bolsheviks were inclined to cast the old Russian intelligentsia—now collectively labelled the "bourgeois" intelligentsia, in contrast to its miniscule Communist counterpart, and individually known as "bourgeois specialists"—as its symbolic leader. This conveyed recognition that the intelligentsia had been one of the pre-revolutionary elites (a proposition many of its members vehemently denied), was the only such group to survive the revolution more or less intact, and constituted the Bolsheviks' main potential rival for authority and leadership.

Large segments of the society were neither clearly proletarian nor clearly bourgeois. But they nevertheless had to be associated with one or the other camp and given a precise social location and class analysis. The Bolsheviks devoted much energy and ingenuity to the task of identifying the class tendencies of such groups as "middle peasants" (those who were neither exceptionally poor nor exceptionally prosperous: that is, the great majority of the peasantry), artisans, and white-collar state employees (*sluzhashchie*).

A whole Soviet statistical industry sprang up in the 1920s around the problem of identifying classes and strata, quantifying them, and determining the exact "class composition" of particular demographic and institutional groups, ranging from members of peasant cooperative organizations to Red Army inductees, Communists, and senior civil servants. Even the 1926 national population census made a valiant attempt to classify respondents by class as well as occupation.

But the Bolshevik reinvention of class involved more than passive record-keeping and data collection. They actively developed the concept of class by creating legislative and bureaucratic structures that were class sensitive, that is, discriminated in favor of the proletariat and against the bourgeoisie. This list of such structures in the 1920s included schools, universities, the Communist party, the Komsomol, and the Red Army (which discriminated in favor of proletarians and against kulaks and other "bourgeois elements" in admissions and recruitment), taxation departments, law courts, municipal housing bodies, and rationing boards (which gave preference to proletarians and penalized the bourgeoisie), and local electoral committees (which kept lists of residents who were ineligible to vote in soviet elections because they were "class aliens".[1] The Bolsheviks' class-discriminatory policies had both a social-justice

---

1. The 1918 constitution of the RSFSR withheld the right to vote from persons who were not "toilers," i.e., kulaks, rentiers, priests, former Tsarist gendarmes, and White officers. This remained in force for almost two decades, until the introduction of the Stalin constitution.

and a social-engineering aspect. In the cause of social justice, they aimed to redistribute resources and opportunities, giving preferential treatment to those who had been excluded from privilege under the old regime and denying it to those who came from the old privileged classes. In the cause of social engineering, they aimed to "proletarianize" recruitment to key institutions and elites in order to consolidate the position of the new regime and secure the gains of the revolution.

In addition, Bolshevik policies and perceptions created entirely new "classes," that is, collective social entities whose members had not previously had a common identity, status, or consciousness, but acquired them through their experience as Soviet citizens. One such group consisted of *byvshie:* "former people," who had once had high position and privilege in society, but lost it as a result of the revolution. An overlapping group, more of a juridical entity, was that of *lishentsy,* i.e., persons deprived of voting rights because of their class background and affiliation with the old regime. Deprivation of voting rights carried with it other civil disabilities such as lack of entitlement to housing, rations, and higher education. At the end of the 1920s, the total number of *lishentsy* increased sharply, and so did the authorities' thoroughness in imposing other civil disabilities on *lishentsy* and their immediate families.

So far, our discussion has assumed that the Bolsheviks were rational actors whose reinvention of class served specific and definable purposes. But of course this is an expository convention that conveys only a partial truth. In fact, the Bolsheviks were generally irrational on the question of class in the 1920s because it was their collective obsession. Class was the universal referent, the touchstone of political and personal identity. Intuitive perceptions of class were valued and cultivated: for example, that village blacksmiths were proletarians, that women in all social strata tended to be petty-bourgeois, that Jews were "a bourgeois nation." Elaborating such class cosmologies was a favorite pastime of Bolshevik autodidacts in the 1920s.

However, it was the question of class enemies that was central for most Bolsheviks. The idea of class could not be separated from the idea of struggle. Bolshevik "class consciousness" was above all an awareness of the need for vigilance and ruthlessness in the face of the threat of bourgeois counter-revolution. Working-class Bolsheviks kept a keen watch for signs of "bourgeois liberalism" and faintheartedness on the part of the party's intellectuals. Bolsheviks of intelligentsia background abased themselves before the toughminded "proletarian instincts" of their lower-class confrères. Although it was the party leadership's policy during NEP not to "fan the flames of class war," the party's rank and file accepted this message only unwillingly and imperfectly. Uncompromising intolerance of Nepmen, kulaks, and "bourgeois" intellectuals was always considered to be a sign of Bolshevik principle.

A second premise of our argument so far has been that the Bolsheviks were sole authors of the Soviet discourse of class. But this too needs to be qualified. The imagination of class became a societal preoccupation as well as a Bolshevik one after the revolution. Indeed, it may be said that the Bolsheviks' invention of class produced in all strata of Soviet society a degree and intensity of class consciousness—in the literal sense of consciousness of class as an issue and a problem—that has rarely been equalled.

Social groups and individual citizens struggled to assimilate and improve the class identities available to them. They learned the new public language of class. This language was not simply, as is sometimes suggested, an Orwellian ClassSpeak that existed in Soviet newspapers but was shunned by ordinary people. On the contrary, ordinary people—not to mention intellectuals—were often fascinated by it. By the mid 1920s, the use of class language was de rigueur for many groups of young city dwellers: Komsomols, high-school pupils, and young industrial workers. It was as alluring and chic as *blatnoi iazyk,* the jargon of the criminal world, which came into fashion at the same time. It was, indeed, part of urban youth's popular culture, as well as Communist political culture in the 1920s.

In other circles, class discourse might be used ironically, like the new acronyms by which Soviet institutions were known. But even this was a form of societal acceptance. The centrality of the discourse can be gauged by its suddenly dominant position in Russian humor and satire: from the time of the revolution (and for many decades thereafter), the wittiest jokes and funniest anecdotes in circulation revolved around class. The use and misuse of class language in everyday life was a stock-in-trade of satirical journalists, caricaturists and writers in the 1920s and 1930s, from Zoshchenko and Ilf and Petrov to Platonov. A somewhat different response to class discourse is recorded in peasant milieux in the 1920s. Peasants were more puzzled than city dwellers by the new class jargon, and therefore generally less amused. But they appreciated its potential for invective, and the word "*burzhui,*" virtually unknown in the villages before the revolution, though well established in urban slang, reportedly became popular as a term of abuse in village arguments in the early 1920s.

Individual Soviet citizens were deeply involved in the invention of class because they had to have personal class identities. Obviously there were fortunate individuals whose class identity was clear and unambiguous. But there were also large numbers who were not in that position. Because of the chaotic and amorphous condition of the society and the high degree of social and occupational mobility in the revolutionary period, the social position of a great many citizens was ambiguous. Such people had to "invent" social and class identities—not in the sense of making them up out of whole cloth, but it in the sense of selecting and interpreting their own biographical data in such a way as to produce an optimal (in terms of personal security and career opportunities) result.

The necessity of creativity in the definition of individual class identity was all the greater because of the lack of clarity about the rules. It was generally accepted that both class origin and current social (occupational) position were or might be relevant to an individual's class status. But there were no hard-and-fast guidelines about the relative importance of the two criteria. Additional complications were introduced by the prevalent opinion that an individual's social position in October 1917 was of particular importance in determing his "real" or essential class. As a result of these complexities of classification, no class identification could be regarded as iron-clad. Even apparently solid social identities could crumble when challenged; and in such cases the individual was said to have been "unmasked." Thus, from the standpoint of individual citizens, especially those of ambiguous background and circumstances, it was necessary not only to create a class identity but also to put some effort into maintaining and protecting it.

It has already been pointed out that the class position officially ascribed to individuals had important practical implications in the society of the 1920s. A "good" class identity could get you into higher education, or into the Komsomol and the Communist party, with all the career advantages that implied. A "bad" class identity could result in loss of an apartment or compulsory *uplotnenie* (when the local soviet settled another family in your living space), special taxes, refusal of unemployment benefits or other social services, and, if you found yourself before a court, increased likelihood of conviction and a heavy sentence.

There was, therefore, a considerable temptation for persons with "bad" social origins to disguise them, i.e., to invent a class identity in the literal sense, especially if they had career or educational ambitions. . . .

Take the case of the peasant woman Sarbunova of Sviiazhsk village, for example. After the dekulakization of her husband and the confiscation of their household property, Sarbunova appealed to the courts unsuccessfully for the return of the property. Then, having divorced her husband, she

> submitted a petition to the Procurator of the [Tatar] Republic stating that her husband really was a kulak, and deprived of voting rights, but for the whole period of their marriage, about twenty years, she had been nothing but a hired female laborer (*batrachka*).

The court regarded the divorce as fictitious, but who can tell? No doubt Sarbunova mainly blamed Soviet power for the disaster that had befallen her and her husband. But sometimes she probably blamed her husband as well—using for that purpose the "Soviet" language of class exploitation with which she addressed the court.

IMAGINING CLASS WAR:
THE PROLETARIAT'S BID FOR HEGEMONY

. . . In an atmosphere of extreme social and political tension at the end of the 1920s, the Communist party called for an intensification of class war, motivating this by the external challenge of an allegedly imminent danger of military attack by the encircling capitalist powers and the internal challenges of collectivization and the First Five-Year plan. The proletariat, it was said, was now ready to settle once and for all with its class enemies. This "proletariat" was clearly virtually synonymous with the state and Communist party.

In the new phase of imagined class war and actual state aggression against segments of the society, an important symbolic role was played by the cultural revolution of the First Five-Year Plan period. Cultural revolution was a process through which the proletariat allegedly cast off bourgeois hegemony in culture and claimed hegemony for itself. It may be understood as a symbolic expropriation of the old intelligentsia—which was collectively brought under suspicion through the show trials of some leading "bourgeois specialists" on charges of treason and sabotage—and its renewal as a class by an infusion of new proletarian and Communist cadres. Other class enemies, notably kulaks and Nepmen, were less fortunate, since their "liquidation as a class" was more than symbolic. The kulaks experienced actual expropriation in the dekulakization campaign accompanying collectivization, and the Nepmen suffered the same fate in connection with the abolition of the urban private sector of the economy and the introduction of the First Five-Year Plan.

The impact on society of Stalin's "revolution from above" can be summarized as follows:

• Kulaks were expropriated, evicted from their homes, and in many cases deported and resettled in distant areas of the Soviet Union, or arrested and sent to GULAG. About half of the deported kulaks and their families became wage-earners working in industry and construction in their new places of residence.

• In addition to the deported and arrested kulaks, a very large number of peasants—perhaps ten million peasants in all—left the village voluntarily during collectivization and entered the urban labor force.

• Urban Nepmen were expropriated and forced to find other occupations.

• Self-employed artisans in the towns, regarded with suspicion by the Bolsheviks as a backward and "petty-bourgeois" group, were pushed to join newly organized urban cooperatives. Many preferred to give up their artisan status and become factory workers.

• Rural craftsmen, also an object of suspicion to the authorities, mainly stopped practising their crafts during collectivization because of the danger of being dekulakized. Many left the villages and became urban wage-earners.

• As a result of state policies of "proletarian promotion," together with the opportunities for upward mobility created by rapid industrialization, hundreds of thousands of young workers and peasants were sent to technical schools and colleges, or moved into white-collar, professional, and administration work.

In rhetorical terms, the outcome of the grand confrontation of proletariat and bourgeoisie at the end of the 1920s was, needless to say, a victory for the proletariat. Proletarian hegemony was firmly established. The bourgeoisie as a class was annihilated. From the standpoint of Marxist theory, even the possibility of its resurgence was precluded by the changes in the underlying economic structure and modes of production, namely from traditional-cum-small-capitalist peasant farming to collective farming and from partially private trading and manufacturing in the towns to complete state ownership and control of urban production, distribution, and exchange. The proletarian state was strengthened, the proletariat grew vastly in size as a result of industrialization, and workers were freed forever from the danger of being held to ransom by hoarding peasants or economically exploited by Nepmen.

But which proletariat was the victor? As we have already seen, the term "proletarian" was applied both to the industrial working class and to the Communist party in the early Soviet period. In the early 1930s, however, the two aspects of the concept started to diverge. Increasingly, the word "proletarian" (*proletarii, proletarskii*) was kept for formal and ceremonial purposes, and the words "worker" and "working-class" (*rabochii*) were preferred in other contexts.

One reason for the shift in usage was that the Soviet working class had changed as a result of Stalin's revolution. During the rapid industrial expansion of the First Five-Year Plan, it had been flooded by new peasant recruits, who constituted a majority of all workers in many branches of the economy in the early 1930s. It was hard to see these peasants—fresh from the farm, many of them fleeing collectivization and dekulakization, inexperienced, aggrieved—as a proletarian in consciousness or class essence. Furthermore, the industrial working class had simultaneously lost many of its most capable and "conscious" young cadres via "proletarian promotion," which took them away from the factory bench and launched them on new administrative and professional careers. This trajectory raised all kinds of theoretical problems. Could the proletariat still be the center of the Communist cosmos if it was possible and desirable to "promote" workers outwards and upwards?[2] Indeed, the whole concept of

2. The Russian terms used for proletarian promotion—"*vydvizhenie*" or, with reference to a specific policy objective, "*vydvizhenchestvo*"—literally convey only movement outward, but their usage in practice had strong connotations of upward movement as well.

"proletarian promotion" was difficult to square with the bipolar or dialectical class structure of early Soviet imagination. Its implications were all hierarchical.

THE RETREAT FROM CLASS WAR IN THE 1930s

The phase of intensified imagination of class war lasted only a few years. This was not because Communist cadres lacked enthusiasm; however, all the evidence suggests that hunting class enemies was an extremely popular activity in the Communist party and the Komsomol, and that low-level cadres and activists much preferred it to more mundane administrative and organizational tasks. It was the party leadership that backed off in the second quarter of the 1930s, evidently satisfied that major objectives like dekulakization and collectivization had been achieved, and perhaps also worried by the degree of disruption, the rapidly expanding size of the GULAG and prison population, and the economic and social costs incurred.

By the mid 1930s, the party leadership had firmly put on the brakes, and a series of initiatives had been taken to redress the balance and move away from class discrimination.

New rules on educational admissions, designed to move away from a class basis of selection to either an academic or egalitarian one, began to be introduced as early as 1931, but it took several years fully to implement and codify them. At the end of 1935, rules on entry to higher and secondary technical educational institutions were changed to allow admission of "all citizens of both sexes who pass the examinations." This removed all trace of proletarian priority and lifted the earlier ban on admission of "social aliens" and children of kulaks and other disenfranchised persons.

In general, kulaks' children (though not kulaks themselves) had recovered most of their civil rights, including the right to vote, by the middle of the 1930s. The new stance towards kulaks' children was publicized in dramatic form at the end of 1935 at a conference of Stakhanovite tractorists and combine-drivers. One of the delegates, combine-driver Tilba, described his travails as the son of a dekulakized kulak, complaining that, despite his fine record as a Stakhanovite, local party officials had tried to prevent him attending the conference because of the disgrace of his class background. At this point, Stalin interjected the momentous words: "A son does not answer for his father."

The previous rule that sons did answer for their fathers had been enforced with particular zeal by the Komsomol, whose successive leaders in the 1920s and early '30s cherished its reputation for proletarian vigilance. The Komsomol had always used class criteria in admitting new members to the organization. These criteria were routinely incorporated in the draft of a new Komsomol constitution prepared for the Tenth All-Union Congress of the Komsomol, which was to meet in the spring of 1936. Stalin, however, amended the draft to eliminate class discrimination in admissions, recommending that the Komsomol should no longer consider itself "primarily a proletarian organization" but rather as "an organization of all progressive Soviet youth—workers, kolkhozniki, employees, and students."

The Communist party's admission procedures were amended not long after the Komsomol's. After several years of intensive (and intensively class-biased) recruitment that had greatly increased the numbers and proportional weight of worker and peasant members, the party had imposed a temporary moratorium on admission of new members in 1933. In 1936, it announced new rules on admissions which would come into force in 1937. In future, the emphasis would be on recruitment of "the best people" in Soviet society rather than, as before, proletarian recruitment. "The best people" was a new concept in Soviet discourse. It implied a status hierarchy along a continuum (though without defining the axis), and it clearly represented a departure from the two-camp, Manichean approach to class that had been characteristic of the 1920s. In practice, the new admissions rules opened the way to intensified recruitment from the white-collar, professional, and administrative group whose new collective name was "the Soviet intelligentsia."

The culmination of the retreat from class war came with the adoption of a new constitution of the USSR, known as "the Stalin constitution." This was promulgated in 1937, after extensive preparation and public debate. It provided for juridical equality, including voting rights and the right to be elected as soviet deputies, for all citizens. This restored voting rights to former *lishentsy*, kulaks, priests, and others formerly in the category of "class aliens."

It was in connection with the forthcoming constitution that Stalin articulated a new theory of class in Soviet society, appropriate to circumstances in which proletarian dictatorship was giving way to the "building of socialism." In a speech on the draft constitution in November 1936, Stalin said that Soviet society had grown beyond the initial revolutionary phase of class war. It still contained classes, but these were nonantagonistic, that is, not liable to class conflict among themselves. As Stalin subsequently developed this concept:

> The distinctive thing about Soviet society at the present time, in contrast to any capitalist society, is that there are no longer antagonistic, hostile classes. The exploiting classes have been liquidated, and workers, peasants and intelligentsia, which comprise Soviet society, live and work on a basis of friendly cooperation . . . Soviet society . . . does not know [class] contradictions; it is free of class conflicts . . .

According to Stalin's famous "two-and-a-half" formula, Soviet society in the current phase of the building of socialism consisted of two main classes, the working class and the kolkhoz peasantry, together with a "stratum" (*prosloika*), the intelligentsia. This "new" or "Soviet" intelligentsia subsumed both the old bourgeois intelligentsia (a term that was no longer used) and the new group of working-class and peasant *vydvizhentsy*, promoted since the late 1920s. For most purposes, it also included white-collar employees (*sluzhashchie*). By calling the intelligentsia a "stratum," Stalin evidently wanted to detach it from a class context and minimize any connotations of hierarchy. Nevertheless, a sense of social hierarchy—peasants, workers, and intelligentsia, in an ascending sequence—was definitely creeping in to the Communist discussions of the second half of the 1930s. In his speech to the Eighteenth Party Congress, for example, Stalin rebuked those comrades who were still in the grip of the "old theory" that workers or peasants who moved up into the intelligentsia were "second-rate people" compared with those who remained in the proletariat. How could they be second-rate people, Stalin asked, when they belonged to that still, alas, relatively small proportion of the population that was "cultured and educated?" In time, culture and education would be accessible to all workers and peasants. But until that time, he implied, members of the "new Soviet intelligentsia" were the first-rate people, superior in social worth to the less-cultured workers and peasants.

CLASS AND PERSONAL IDENTITY IN THE 1930s

. . . The meaning of class may have changed in the 1930s, but class nevertheless remained a basic aspect of the formal identity of the Soviet citizen. In fact, this aspect of identity became fully institutionalized only in 1933, when all Soviet citizens (except peasants) received internal passports. These gave the basic Soviet coordinates of personal identity, namely age, sex, social position (class), and nationality.[3] The normal entries under "social position" in the 1930s were reportedly worker (*rabochii*), white-collar employee (*sluzhashchii*), *kolkhoznik*,[4] and, for members of the Soviet intelligentsia, a designation of profession, such as doctor, engineer, teacher, or factory director. . . .

The "social position" entry in Soviet passports had its prerevolutionary counterpart in the "estate" (*soslovie*) entry in the Tsarist passports. This in turn suggests a possible function: that of identifying a citizen in terms of his rights, privileges, and obligations vis-à-vis the state. In Imperial Russia, the rights and obligations of different *sosloviia* with regard to such matters as taxation, state service, liability for military conscription, the right to own serfs or engage in trade, and so on were formally codified as well as informally recognized. The Soviet Union never developed an elaborated formal system of this kind. Nevertheless, certain institutional tendencies of the 1930s seemed to point in such a direction. For example, the kolkhoz peasantry acquired special obligations and rights in the early 1930s that set it apart from other groups of the population: these included a *corvée*[5] obligation (*trudguzhpovinnost'*), restrictions on mobility, the right to collective use of land, and the right to engage in trade at peasant markets. By contrast, the urban population (divided into the quasi-"estates" of workers, *sluzhashchie,* and intelligentsia) lacked the right to trade, but possessed the right to internal passports and freer mobility. Moreover, different urban social groups (for example, workers, *sluzhashchie,* ITR [engineering-technical personnel], and *otvetrabotniki* [senior cadres] had their own separate "closed distribution" systems for rationed goods in the first half of the 1930s; and, later in the decade, *otvetrabotniki* acquired a range of special privileges including access to "closed" stores and government dachas. It is reasonable to suggest that in Soviet society of the 1930s, class was acquiring *soslovie* overtones and becoming for some purposes an ascriptive category that defined a citizen's relationship to the state.

But there was another important aspect of class and social identification in Stalinist society. This might be called the "then and now" perspective. In the 1930s, as in the 1920s, the Soviet approach to class involved an important retrospective dimension. Even more significant than an individual's current social position was his class origin. A true class identification required that both factors be considered. It was not enough to know that an individual was a worker: was he a "cadre" (*kadrovyi*) or "hereditary" (*potomstvennyi*) worker or a worker "from the peasantry?" Similarly was

---

3. It was not until the 1974 Statute on the Passport System (28 August 1974) that social position was dropped as a passport entry.

4. Peasants were not routinely issued with passports, but could receive them on application if they were making an approved trip out of the village for paid employment. In the 1930s, the usual designations for peasants were "kolkhoznik" and "edinolichnik" (non-collectivized peasant). The categories of class differentiation in use in the 1920s ("kulak", "middle peasant," "poor peasant") were no longer used after collectivization.

5. Obligatory physical labor

a member of the intelligentsia "from the old intelligentsia" or "from the workers?" Was a kolkhoznik a former poor peasant or a former kulak? . . .

There was no specific term for social mobility in Stalinist discourse, but the idea was very familiar to Soviet citizens of the 1930s. One trajectory in particular was often described and offered for emulation. This was the Soviet version of the Horatio Alger story, in which a young man rises from the working class or peasantry by dint of hard work and commitment to the revolution, is helped by the party to acquire an education, and becomes a member of the "new Soviet intelligentsia," that is, the professional and administrative elite. A typical example is the short autobiographical sketch offered by the rising young politician P. S. Popkov when he ran as a candidate in the 1938 elections for the Russian Supreme Soviet:

> My life is the life of an ordinary warrior of the party of Lenin and Stalin. The son of a landless poor peasant, I worked as a shepherd from 9 years of age. Then I was a laborer, a carpenter, a rabfak student, a university student. In 1937, I became an engineer . . .

Popkov, a peasant's son who had worked for a few years as a young man in various blue-collar occupations before receiving his "proletarian promotion," was of lower-class origin, but clearly his actual working-class affiliations were marginal. His proletarian roots were in the invented class of the 1920s, and that class was in process of conceptual evolution in the latter part of the 1930s. It was becoming an imagined community that existed only in the past tense—a place people came from, but not a place they currently inhabited.

In the spectrum of "then and now" trajectories, not all were as benign as Popkov's. A second trajectory that frequently attracted attention in the 1930s was that of the apparently harmless Soviet citizen, usually a *sluzhashchii* or worker, who had successfully concealed his "alien" origins. In legal terms, such people always had the right to employment, and from 1936 even had the right to vote. In practice, however, their presence in the workforce, when discovered, was almost invariably regarded as undesirable, and a sinister interpretation was put on their attempts to "pass" as normal citizens.

The common "alien" origin of such persons was, of course, the invented bourgeoisie of the 1920s. Like its antithesis, the invented proletariat, this class underwent evolution. But its evolution was different: instead of being reimagined in a new form, it had actually made the transition from imagination to substance. Part of the original invented bourgeoisie split off and assumed concrete form in the 1920s as *byvshie* (people who had lost their former privileged status because of the revolution) and *lishentsy* (people who were disenfranchised as social aliens). In the 1930s, the same process occurred with peasants expropriated as kulaks during collectivization, who formed a new social class of the dekulakized (*raskulachennye*).

This is one of the most interesting examples of Soviet invention of class, since it can be seen as a second attempt to invent a kulak class after the first attempt had failed to win universal acceptance. The concept of a kulak class of peasants, defined by its exploitative relationship to other peasants, was very attractive to Communists in the 1920s. But peasants were not readily convinced that such a class existed in their midst, and Communist officials often found it difficult to define the criteria for kulaks or say exactly which peasants in a given community they fitted. This ambiguity was completely resolved by dekulakization. There might previously have been room for argument about whether peasant X—with his two cows, an orchard, and an uncle in

trade in a nearby town—was or was not a kulak. Once he had been formally dekulakized, however, there was no room for further argument about his status. He was a
raskulachennyi, that is, by definition a former (dekulakized) kulak. Thus, the Soviet liquidation of the kulak class could even be regarded as the final, definitive step in its
invention.

SHADOWS OF OLD CLASS ENEMIES

According to Marxist theory, transformation of the Soviet Union's economic base
and the relations of production had not only removed the last remnants of capitalism
but also guaranteed against the possibility of resurrection. Yet Communists could still
sense the presence of those class enemies that had been consigned to the dustheap of
history; and it turned out to be almost more terrible to fight them as ghosts.

This had been somberly predicted by Stalin in 1929 when he first formulated the
theory that the more certain the defeat of the class enemy, the more desperate and
uncompromising would be his resistance. The theory had then seemed implausible
and un-Marxist to many Communist intellectuals. Five years later, however, after
practical experience of the "liquidation as a class" of kulaks and Nepmen, the paradox may have acquired broader resonance. Stalin, in any case, had developed his
thought more fully. His remarks on the subject in 1934 were paraphrased thus by State
Prosecutor Krylenko:

> How does the question [of class enemies] stand today? Is the landowning class in
> existence or not? No, it has been annihilated, destroyed. The capitalists? No, de-
> stroyed, annihilated. Merchants? . . . annihilated. Where are the [old exploit-
> ing] classes? It seems there are none! Wrong! Thrice wrong! Th[os]e people
> exist . . . We did not physically destroy them, and they have remained with all
> their class sympathies, antipathies, traditions, habits, opinions, world views and so
> on . . . The class enemy, despite the annihilation of the class of landlords, has
> remained in the person of living representatives of those former classes. . . .

An entrenched Communist mentalité of suspicion of class enemies meant that the
policies of class conciliation introduced in the mid 1930s were neither wholeheart-
edly recommended by party leaders nor systematically implemented by lower-level
party officials. There was a basic ambivalence on the class issue in the 1930s that
swung over towards genuine relaxation only at the end of the decade, in the period
of exhaustion and hungover sobriety that followed the bacchanalia of the Great
Purges. Before that time, it was always likely that a Communist's head and his heart
(including, no doubt, Stalin's) would be at odds on questions of class and the class
enemy. The rational man might accept that class-discriminatory policies had outlived
their day and the class enemy was no longer a real threat, but the intuitive man remained dubious and fearful. . . .

[N]ot only were citizens inclined to inform on hidden "class enemies" in their
midst, but Communist officials continued to dignify these accusations by investigating them seriously and conscientiously. Huge numbers of bureaucratic man-hours
were spent on careful on-site investigations of whether kolkhoz brigade-leader Y was
really married to the daughter of a former priest, or Komsomol Z had tried to conceal the fact that his uncle had been dekulakized. . . .

A sense of similar indecisiveness is associated with Stalin's interjection at the
Stakhanovite Congress of 1935 that "A son does not answer for his father." Unchar-

acteristically, this remark was left almost without commentary in the Soviet press of 1935. Several newspapers even published editorials and articles shortly afterwards that reaffirmed the party's commitment to vigilance against class enemies, as if to mitigate its impact. Moreover, Stalin himself did not repeat the thought in any more formal context or include it in any of his published works, and, uncharacteristically, it was only rarely cited by his colleagues. As a result, although the remark seems instantly to have entered Soviet folklore and was firmly attributed to Stalin, a certain mystery surrounded it. Was it Stalin's opinion, but not that of others in the leadership, that "A son does not answer for his father?" Had Stalin really said it? Or was the persistent rumor that he had said it put about by enemies for the confusion of Communists?

In each successive political crisis of the 1930s, Communists hastened to round up "the usual suspects," knowing instinctively that the class enemy must be somehow to blame. This happened during the 1932–3 famine, when the NKVD expelled hundreds of thousands of "class aliens" and *lishentsy* from Moscow, Leningrad, and other cities at the time of the introduction of passports. There were similar mass expulsions from Leningrad in 1935 after Kirov's murder; and a local newspaper reporting them scarcely even bothered to explain why a connection might be suspected between Kirov's assassin and *byvshie* such as "former Baron Tipolt [who had] got himself a job in an industrial meal-service as an accountant, General Tiufiasev [who] was a teacher of geography, former politsmeister Komendantov [who] was a technician at a factory, [and] General Spasskii, [who] was a cigarette seller in a kiosk."

The pattern was repeated even in the Great Purges, whose primary target was "enemies of the people" (construed primarily as highly-placed Communist cadres by the press and other sources of public instruction) rather than the now somewhat faded "class enemies."

While Communist cadres did indeed comprise the main category of victim, the Great Purges clearly inflicted significant damage on the old category of class enemies as well. In Leningrad in the autumn of 1937, Zakovskii, head of the NKVD, identified university students who were sons of kulaks and Nepmen as a particular category of "enemies of the people" who should be exposed and rooted out. At the same period, the Smolensk Komsomol expelled dozens and probably hundreds of its members on grounds of alien social origin, connection by marriage with class aliens, concealment of such origins and connections, and so on. (A large number of these victims were formally reinstated in the Komsomol in 1938 after appealing their expulsions.) In Cheliabinsk, former class enemies were among those executed as counter-revolutionaries in 1937–8.

In the GULAG labor camps system, according to recently published data from NKVD archives, the number of prisoners classified as "socially-harmful and socially-dangerous elements" grew from just over 100,000 in 1937 to close to 300,000 two years later. This implies that a substantial contingent of former class enemies fell victim to the Great Purges, even if it was less than half the size of the contingent of "counter-revolutionaries" that arrived in GULAG over the same period.

CONCLUSION

The Bolshevik "invention of class" in the 1920s probably served at least some useful organizational and restructuring functions. But there was a price to be paid. In the first place, the notion of enemies became inseparable from the idea of class. That introduced a corrosive chemical into the Bolsheviks' social cement. In the second place, individual class identities that had to be "invented" were liable to contain elements of deception. That increased the regime's distrust of its citizens and citizens' distrust of each other.

In the 1930s, there were signs that Russia was domesticating the foreign import, adding a *soslovie* overtone to the Marxist categories of class and arranging them in more decorous and traditional hierarchical sequence. Stalin provided a theoretical underpinning when he redefined classes in Soviet society as social entities that interacted with the state, not with each other. Soviet citizens became completely accustomed to the idea that class was part of their public identity; as the authors of the postwar Harvard Interview Project reported (with a touch of perplexity!), their Soviet refugee respondents had no difficulty, identifying themselves in terms of class, despite the fact that they "showed only a modest degree of class hostility or conflict" and thus presumably possessed "only mild class consciousness."

The corrosive element was still present, however, as the Great Purges demonstrated. The bewilderingly vague accusations against "enemies of the people" become fully comprehensible only if we remember the light in which Bolshevik imagination cast their precursors, the "class enemies." A class enemy was potentially harmful to society regardless of his specific actions or individual intentions, and often wore a mask concealing his true identity. He was a member, whether he knew it or not, of an imagined community of class whose interests were inimical to those of Soviet power. It was only a small conceptual step from being part of an imagined class community to being part of an imagined conspiracy. One step further, and the imagined class basis of the conspiracy would fall away.

Sheila Fitzpatrick, "The Bolshevik Invention of Class: Marxist Theory and the Making of 'Class Consciousness' in Soviet Society," was published as "L'Usage bolchevique de la 'Classe': Marxisme et construction de l'Identité individuelle," in *Actes de la Recherche en Sciences sociales,* no. 85 (November 1990), pp. 70–80; published here for the first time in English.

THE CENTRE AND THE PERIPHERY: CULTURAL AND SOCIAL GEOGRAPHY IN THE MASS CULTURE OF THE 1930S

James Von Geldern

In the mid-1930s, Soviet society struck a balance that would carry it through the turmoil of the purges, the Great War and reconstruction. The coercive policies of the Cultural Revolution were replaced or supplemented by the use of inducements. Benefits were quickly apparent: education opened professional opportunities; a stable countryside improved dietary standards; increased production and income encouraged consumerism. A lightened mood swept the nation. Women wore make-up; young people revived ballroom dancing. Life, as Stalin said, and Lebedev-Kumach's popular song repeated, had become better and happier.

The stability gave some groups, for example, the new 'middle class', a measure of economic and social security that encouraged them to identify with the Soviet system. Yet it was not founded solely on a rational, if short-sighted, perception of personal advantage. Consumer shortages continued throughout the 1930s; agricultural and housing supplies stayed below 1928 levels. The regime maintained its support during the purges, not only with prospering bureaucrats, but amongst those who fell. The feeling survived the Great War and the years after, when comfort and security were noticeably absent. The most permanent support of Stalinist society was a sense of pride and participation, shared by many social groups, that weathered the gravest tribulations. Society forged a new identity that integrated citizens excluded by the Cultural Revolution.

The nature of this new identity is best sought in mass culture, produced for the people by the state-controlled media. To consider the mass media a reflection of popular attitudes is, of course, problematic. Popular taste was often overriden by political considerations. Discussion was one-sided, dominated by the state; popular participation was limited to the consumer option. Yet the mass media were part of the social fabric. By the mid-1930s, informal social discourse from unofficial gatherings to neighbourly gossip had been subverted. Bilateral forms of communication were cut off, creating a void. If there was a national consciousness, it was informed by the mass media. The party squelched the Cultural Revolution's sectarianism and created a culture shared by the whole country. Restrictions placed on the makers of culture actually opened it to most of the audience: mass culture spoke the language of most people, and used them as its heroes. It represented socialist society in ways that allowed for popular identification.

Media culture was not limited to its political messages which often invited scepticism. Beneath them were less formalized beliefs that help explain the social dynamic. During the mid-1930s, power was centralized; society became increasingly hierarchical; citizens were deprived of many rights. Yet the dissatisfaction aroused by these measures coexisted with a sense of participation. The Cultural Revolution's aggressive political demands had excluded most people from the category of contributing citizens. The mid-1930s redrew the national identity to include them. This chapter will look at the mass media's cultural geography—its representation of relations between centre and periphery, and its ability to integrate parts of the country into the whole—for reflections of the social geography. The attitudes underlying them suggest one cause for popular identification with Soviet society in the mid-1930s: the consolidation of the centre did not exclude those outside, it aided their integration.

The centralization of power, a process observable throughout revolutionary history, was accelerated by the Great Leap. The mid-1930s saw a continuation of the trend, but in ways that often contradicted earlier policies. Investment was shifted from the periphery—the hero projects in the Urals and elsewhere—to the centre. Magnitogorsk found desperately needed funds moving back to Moscow, and fewer projects outside the capital were initiated. Resources were diverted to nonproductive construction in an overcrowded capital. Some projects were economically justified (the Moscow Metro, the Moscow-Volga Canal), but others were not: the Exhibition of Economic Achievements and several Lenin monuments among them. An economically sound project like the Moscow Metro mocked utility with its stations clad in semiprecious stone.

Rebuilding Moscow bolstered its symbolic role as centre of the country. It was the capital, focus of political and economic life, and the visible face of the Soviet Union, representing it to Soviet citizens and the world. The plan for a new Moscow had cultural implications beyond its economic consequences. It acted as a model for the state, where power radiated out from the centre to the periphery. The city was to be rebuilt from a medieval to a modern pattern, its crooked alleys replaced by straight thoroughfares. The plan showed the ambiguities of mid-1930s Soviet taste: it facilitated linear communications, but it also preserved a circular structure marking the centre of the city (and thus the country) in the Kremlin. Modern concepts of city planning: the decentralized 'green' city of Barshch and Ginzberg's 1930 Moscow plan, or the linear city of Leonidov's Magnitogorsk plan, were passed over for the ancient model of concentric circles radiating from a fortress centre. The symbolic emphasis on the centre overrode economic need. Removing the Chinatown Wall and Iberian Chapel could have channelled transport efficiently through the city, yet instead the space was devoted to expanding Red Square, an impediment to traffic. Red Square is the ritual centre of the Soviet Union, where May Day and 7 November are celebrated, a role enhanced by the new space.

Moscow centralism was not new to the 1930s; its cultural definition, however, was. The shift of investment from the periphery to the capital signalled a new hierarchy of values, by which society's attention shifted from the many to the one outstanding representative. It was neither democratic nor egalitarian; yet the media encouraged the people to identify with the projects. Grandiose projects in the centre were a source of pride shared by all. The Moscow Metro, for instance, was a constant topic of mass culture, and it was a source of national, not Muscovite pride. The theme ran from newspaper campaigns to children's books. Muscovite youth used the subway as a meeting place for dates; provincial visitors toured the facility as a national landmark. It was incorporated into the culture of the masses.

The strengthening of the centre was to the advantage of all, as was evident in depictions of the centre's counterpart: the periphery. From its inception, Soviet power struggled with huge territorial expanses: by military means during the Civil War, by electrification during NEP, with factories and dams during the industrial revolution. These were, for the most part, lands untouched by civilization. The media showed various attitudes towards the hinterland. The Cultural Revolution typically saw the periphery as savage and hostile. It gained value only when subjugated by the socialist order, that is, when it was industrialized. The cultural geography of the time saw cities—industrial, socialist, the centre of power—as benevolent, and the hinterland malevolent, a place of dark forests, raging rivers, retrograde traditions and socially hostile elements. To the engineer Margulies in Kataev's *Time Forward!,* the great expanses were 'cumbersome'. Nature had no autonomous value; it was neither romantic nor beautiful. If for another age the phrase 'nocturnal spectres, pathless forest . . . marshy miasmas' would have evoked mystery, in Leonov's *Sot'* (Soviet River) it concealed a hermitage bent on sabotaging the pulp-mill project. The outer regions, with their dark peasants and elemental nature, provided the villains of industrial novels like *Sot'* (1930) and Gladkov's *Energiia* (Energy, 1933). They had to be conquered, usually by representatives of the centre, Komsomol members and workers sent by Moscow.

Hostility to the periphery had softened by the mid-1930s. The mastery of Soviet man over nature was deemed as important as ever in songs, essays and movies. Even the 'March of the Jolly Fellows' (1934) proclaimed *My pokoryaem prostranstvo i vremya, My molodye khozyaeva zemli!* (We conquer space and time, We are young masters of the land!). Yet the attitude was supplemented by a great pride in the vast frontier, which, as it had for nineteenth-century Americans, provided a new source for the national identity. There was consonance between Soviet man and the periphery. The outer bounds of the national identity had shifted from the West, where internationalism had once pointed, to the eastern regions of Soviet Russia. The *Internationale,* the national anthem since the revolution, was replaced unofficially by 'Song of the Motherland' (1936). Its refrain proclaimed the new-found benevolence of uncharted spaces:

> Broad is my native land
> It has many forests, fields and rivers
> I don't know of any other country
> Where man breathes so freely.

The new consciousness helped redefine Soviet notions of heroism, which had often been tied to territorial expansion. Heroes of the Cultural Revolution had been conquerors of open space: the young builders of Magnitogorsk, the collectivizers of virgin lands. Cultural geography mapped the Soviet Union as a set of socialist islands—progressive cities, industrial projects, *kolkhozes*—immersed in a sea of hostile influences—the open spaces. By the mid-1930s the periphery no longer seemed alien or hostile. The map was redrawn to include the great expanses, all in one way or another considered 'Soviet' (in the cultural as well as political sense). The demarcation was not by points—the islands—but by the great outer boundary enclosing the country. There was a new and powerful consciousness of the border. Socialist conflict arose not when the centre penetrated the periphery, but when outsiders (foreigners) violated the outer boundary. For earlier revolutionaries, the border had been a symbol of enlightenment and sanctuary, but by the mid-1930s it became a symbol of hostility. The border was inviolable, and its sanctity gave mass culture a new adventure hero: the border guard (NKVD *pogranichnik*).

For the mid-30s, heroism lay not so much in subjugating the hinterland as in discovering and exploiting its riches. Mass culture found a new type of hero in geologists searching Siberia and the Arctic for natural resources. They became stock figures in adventure films like *The Bold Seven* (1936), *Gold Lake* (1935), *Moon Stone* (1935), *In the Far East* (1937) and *The Golden Taiga* (1937). The change in attitude touched new industrial projects. Ivan Kataev's account of the building of Khibinogorsk treated open space as a *tabula rasa* for the new socialist culture. As he wrote (in an assumed dialogue with the Second Revolution), 'it turns out that not only historically inhabited regions are fit to be cultivated for socialism, but also regions previously untouched by human hands'. The periphery was no longer hostile; and its affinity to Moscow was represented in the concluding paragraph, when the narrator's gaze travelled over the expanses to the Kremlin Chimes—symbol of Moscow centralism.

The most prominent variations on the pioneer-hero were pilots and polar explorers. The development of an advanced aviation industry and a generation of capable designers had put Soviet aircraft among the world's best; and with them came a generation of daring pilots. Soviet pilots set world records for flight altitude, endurance and distance, and they competed with athletes and movie stars for celebrity status. At the top of the aviation elite was the arctic pilot; in fact the highest Soviet medal, Hero of the Soviet Union, was first awarded to seven fliers who rescued the crew of the Cheliuskin from ice floes. Pilots such as Babushkin provided a new model for the Soviet hero: brave, modest, taciturn—and non-party. The most famous flyer, Valerii Chkalov, became an international hero by leading two flights over the North Pole. A darling of the mid-30s mass media was Professor Otto Schmidt, leader of the Cheliuskin expedition. Schmidt became the subject of newsreels, newspaper essays, even comics.

Aviators and explorers had also earned renown during the Cultural Revolution. What was different about the mid-30s was how they earned celebrity, and how it was described in the media. The Cultural Revolution saw practical purposes for exploration and aviation: opening land for mining and industry, building an air defence against the hostile capitalist world. By the mid-30s, the foremost purpose was national prestige: Chkalov's flight from Moscow to Alaska had marginal military value, but it brought glory to the Soviet Union. A new attitude toward nature could also be seen in the Arctic explorations and flights. Nature remained something to be conquered; yet conquest demanded not subjugation or destruction, but the ability to live in harmony with the elements. Moscow was no longer alien to the periphery.

For Soviet mass culture, as has been true of many other cultures, nature and the periphery stood as metaphors of society. The pattern of classification and association observable in cultural geography, by which consolidating the centre helped reintegrate the periphery, was also applied to social groups. Society became stratified; power and attention were focused on a new elite. Yet coincident with the consolidation of the elite was an attitude of social inclusivity. Classes and institutions deemed hostile by the Cultural Revolution once again found a place in Soviet society.

The evolution of a geographical hierarchy, with Moscow on top, coincided with the stiffening of social hierarchy. Its upper rungs, on the model of Moscow, monopolized attention and investment. The new emphasis on hierarchy was most evident in a tendency to praise leaders of all kinds. Bards wrote paeans to Stalin; films presented him as Lenin's closest comrade. Leadership itself, regardless of its politics, became an object of praise in films like *Peter the Great* (1937–1939), *Alexander Nevsky* (1938) and *Suvorov* (January 1941). The tendency was not limited to political life. Ranks and uniforms, already a norm for the military, were re-introduced to the civil administration, the foreign service, even the railroad. Outstanding workers, artists and scientists were singled out for praise and given economic privileges. The Stakhanovite movement restructured production processes on the model of Moscow centralism: a balanced distribution of responsibilities and privileges was replaced by hierarchy, under which many workers supported the efforts of one. In sports, mass participation, emphasized by the revolution and the Cultural Revolution, was eclipsed by outstanding achievement; investment shifted from mass sports clubs to elite central institutions such as Moscow Spartak. Old sports like production gymnastics and non-competitive mass games were replaced by competitive sports, which called for winners and losers, and thus hierarchy. Athletes were strictly ranked by titles (e.g. Master of Sport), with corresponding uniforms, badges and privileges.

The introduction of hierarchical centralism might have weakened the social position of the average citizen. But closer inspection of the mass media suggests that the new values offered something to all levels of the population. Social legitimacy was concentrated in the centre not as a monopoly, but as a point of distribution. There was a new understanding of Soviet citizenship that allowed for the symbolic distribution of status from the centre to the periphery. The model was mirrored by the cultural geography. Moscow centralism had included greater respect for the periphery. The hierarchy of places was not so much a deprivation of the periphery as a concentration of efforts from all directions on one spot. Elevating Moscow elevated the entire Soviet Union. This vicarious pride was repeated with the accomplishments of the new elite. Soviet citizens basked in the glory of achievements in which they had no direct part. The daring of pilots, the strength of athletes and the productivity of Stakhanovite workers were the effort of an entire nation, and every citizen could justly feel pride in them. Stakhanov was expressing a common sentiment when he said:

> every improvement in the work of the individual contributes to the general wel-
> fare. The Soviet people know, they see and realize, that the better work pro-
> gresses, the wealthier the country becomes . . . Loving their homeland, they
> love their machines, their factories, their work.

Elite status and its attendant celebrity were available to groups excluded by the Cultural Revolution. For the revolution, the path to heroism and celebrity had been through the party. One had first to declare allegiance, then paths were opened. The mid-30s offered celebrity to broader range of citizens; the unspoken guidelines had changed. While the party was still a path to celebrity, celebrity was also a path to the party. The new heroes were not always party members, and their accomplishments were often apolitical. The new success story was fictionalized in the poor shepherd Kostya in *Jolly Fellows,* or the title character of *The Flying Painter* (1936), and it found real-life models in newly celebrated pilots, athletes and workers. Yet the broadening of political standards did not imply a loosening of discipline. The new nonparty heroes expressed a stronger appreciation of social hierarchy and political guidance than previous heroes had. The headstrong, politically correct and sometimes arrogant heroes of the Cultural Revolution—Communists and Komsomols—had, despite their acceptance of party discipline, been allowed to resist its restraints. A party organizer sent to the hinterlands to build an industrial complex could act without orders from Moscow, or even ignore them; collectivizers worked independently, and could outdo the political centre in enthusiasm. Heroes of the mid-30s acknowledged the centre's primacy more clearly than their predecessors; it was, in fact, a condition of their celebrity. Citizens were encouraged to pursue and realize their individual potential provided that, in the end, they gave proper credit to the social system. The system condemned those who, after attaining their goals, tried to rise above the collective. The protagonist of the movie *Goalie* (1936) rose from factory-floor worker to star soccer player; yet his final ambition, to represent the Soviet Union in international play, was satisfied only after returning to the team he had abandoned on his rise to the top.

Celebrity in the mid-30s could only be attained with the hierarchy, and it was conferred by the hierarchy. Hierarchy was expressed in a series of personal relationships: leader and people, director and worker, parents and children. Social roles were, in essence, personalized; the apex of the hierarchy was embodied in the person of Stalin. Stalin's personalization of social hierarchy offered average citizens a way to identify with the political system. It bolstered a belief in direct contact between the top of the social order and the masses that institutionalized power had weakened. Even in the most imposing rituals of order, like the Red Square demonstrations, the myth of direct contact was maintained. The event, it must be remembered, was not seen directly by most of the population (entrance was strictly controlled), but through newsreels, which could include a clip of Stalin atop the mausoleum waving to the crowd and acknowledging marchers with a finger or a wink of the eye.

The personalization of politics also contributed to a belief in the direct and immediate transmission of legitimacy and celebrity. Unknown but worthy citizens like Stakhanov or the *kolkhoz* activist Pasha Angelina could win instant recognition from the centre. Mass culture offered countless examples of how the centre—Stalin and the Kremlin—was aware of what was happening throughout the country, and would reward commendable efforts. The transition was always sudden: Stakhanov went straight from simple coal-miner to national hero, the peasant Angelina was given all the trappings of power—from transport in a luxurious Lincoln sedan to election to the Supreme Soviet. Fictional models were provided by Grigorii Alexandrov's popular films, *Jolly Fellows* (1934) and *Volga-Volga* (1938). These were stories of simple musicians living in small towns on the Russian periphery. Local authorities do not recognize their talents; but by a series of fortuitous circumstances, they make their way to Moscow. There they are recognized—the hero of *Fellows* ends up in the Bolshoi Theatre.

The direct transmission of status bolstered the hierarchy by acknowledging its prerogatives. Legitimacy and celebrity were passed on person to person in a mentor-student (*pitomets* or *vospitannik*) relationship; the old notion of party discipline was translated into a new value system. The system was used by Stalin himself in the *Short Course,* which claimed party leadership had been passed on to him by Lenin; the claim was supported and acted out in sculptures, paintings and movies. A ritual evolved in the mid-30s to represent the transfer of status: individual heroes came to the Kremlin to be acknowledged by the leadership. Stakhanov was called to the Kremlin for a congress of Stakhanovites, Pasha Angelina for a *kolkhoz* workers' congress. Chkalov's famous flights were consecrated by a similar ritual. The flight plans were drawn up by the country's foremost experts, and prepared by a team of pilots and engineers. Yet the flights could not begin until permission was given by Stalin. This moment, when Chkalov's crew was summoned to the Kremlin and granted approval, became a central moment in the retelling of the story. Stalin offered a few words of fatherly advice:

> I explained I fly valuable experimental planes that must be preserved no matter what. During a test flight my thoughts are directed toward bringing the plane back to earth safely.
> 'Your life', said Comrade Stalin, 'is more important to us than any plane. Make sure to use a parachute if needed.'

When social roles were embodied by people rather than collectives, individual lives seemed more valuable.

The ritual of acknowledgement conferred instant status; it allowed average citizens to bypass the middle ranks of society on their way to the top. According to the mass media, the centralization and personalization of power in the mid-30s offered greater opportunities to the masses; it was the middle of the hierarchy that suffered. The defeat of oafish local bureaucrats by popular initiative, usually assisted by the centre, was a standard part of mid-30s success stories: Alexandrov's films, the mythology of Stakhanovism. The middle ranks were a source of mass culture villains, as in *A Great Citizen* (1937); and they were the constant target of media campaigns. Amateur theatre groups attacked bureaucratic ineptitude; satirists like Zoshchenko, Ilf and Petrov, Koltsov mocked institutional inertia. They were free to skewer the bureaucracy as long as they did not attack the centre. The strictures they worked under, which seem obvious to the present-day reader, were not necessarily evident to their audience, who saw satire as a needed avenue of petition. The pattern, as has been observed many times, was a revival of the pre-revolutionary myth of the good tsar and bad civil servants: there was a strong popular fealty to Moscow unshaken by local bungling. In fact it was strengthened by mass media revelations: the belief went that, if only Stalin knew what was going on, the problems would be corrected.

One of the assumed roles of the 1930s mass media was to facilitate direct communication between the leadership and the population in a way that bypassed the bureaucratic middle. One interpretation of the role is consonant with the totalitarian model of Soviet society: the mass media were a transmission belt of party policy to the obedient people. Yet communication ran in two directions: relying on existing institutions, the media published information on middle-level abuse of bureaucratic power. Theatre groups, 'sketch-writers' and worker-correspondents acted as government agents; but they were agents of the centre directed at the middle. They were intermediaries representing the little man and ensuring the just operation of Soviet power. Their work was aided by a remarkable institution, the letter to the editor. Citizens could use this channel of communication to petition higher authorities against the local abuse of power. Extensive publicity was given to instances when justice was served, and people were encouraged to report all abuses.

The centralization of Soviet society in the mid-30s opened a new range of passive roles, like the vigilant letter-writer, to the masses. Mass action in the Cultural Revolution had been a matter of *doing:* collectivizing the countryside and industrializing the periphery, doing mass calisthenics, writing poetry in workers' clubs. For the mid-30s, it was a matter of seeing. The mass media had become the dominant model of social intercourse, and their ability to frame the citizen as a passive viewer penetrated other aspects of social life. The passive spectator became, in many ways, a model of the Soviet citizen. Political and social discourse was redefined by the spectator-performer relationship. During the first decade of the revolution, political communication often occurred where audience participation was encouraged—mass rallies, newspaper readings, mock trials. Contact between performer and audience was direct. A new set of institutions and practices evolved in the mid-30s to accommodate the citizen-spectator. An expensive show-place for the economy, Moscow's VDNKh, was built; voting was ritualized, recorded on newsreel and distributed about the country; show trials afforded a purging of alien elements. The Constitution of 1936 was presented in folk poems and stage tableaux; and, on special occasions, the leaders viewed and were viewed by the nation from atop Lenin's Mausoleum. The leadership took measures to assure citizens that their needs as spectators were given proper weight—even as their passive role was being underlined. Plans for important monuments were exhibited for public review, the Constitution and other legislative acts were subjected to public comment. The public had no more influence in the decision-making process than did a Supreme Soviet ballot, but it was nevertheless an essential ritual of participation.

The role of Soviet citizen found increasingly circumscribed models. When a society stabilizes citizen roles, it also limits social mobility and activism. The mid-30s saw the model Soviet citizen's attention shift from public roles—the workplace and political activism—to private roles, particularly those centred in the family. The family, sorely buffeted by the first fifteen years of Soviet power, was stabilized. Divorce, formerly a matter of one party signing a register, was granted only at the consent of both, and a stiff fee was charged for the proceeding; bigamy, which had been encouraged by light laws and lax prosecution, became subject to stiff penalties. The strongest measure was the controversial 1936 law abolishing abortion.

The revision of marital customs eliminated cherished rights. What was gained in the deal? If the media were to be believed, the life of a model Soviet citizen during the late 1920s and early 30s had been emotionally unrewarding. It seemed that satisfying one's ambition, whether through greed or socialist altruism, impeded personal fulfilment. Communist activists sacrificed their private lives for the good of a society that often distrusted or despised them. What was worse, they could not depend on their families, an institution that they themselves had weakened, for emotional support. One of the stock figures of NEP and the Cultural Revolution was the Communist who sacrificed love for the cause. The prototype was Gleb Chumalov of Gladkov's *Cement* (1925), but the figure was repeated in the engineer Uvadaev of Leonov's *Sot'*; in the heroes of *Time, Forward!,* whose wives leave them or give birth while they break construction records; the loveless Communist of Glebov's *Inga,* who in her devotion to duty ceases to be a woman. The apex of the trend was Pavlik Morozov, who sacrificed his family in the battle for collectivization.

By the mid-30s, this stock figure was an object of condemnation or mockery in films like *The Enthusiasts* (1934) or *A Chance Meeting* (1936). The revolutionary ideal of free sexual relations gave way to monogamous relations. Monogamy was not only encouraged by the government for various policy considerations, it became fashionable. 'Show' marriages were featured in the press. Love and marriage were in effect de-ideologized; romantic love became a standard plot mechanism for films such as *The Rich Bride* (1937). Documents of earlier times were even translated to fit the new tastes; when Furmanov's novel *Chapaev* (1923) was filmed in 1934, a love motif (Petka and Anka the Machine-Gunner) was added.

The new family was cast in the image of the state. The Soviet Union was a great family, in an over-used metaphor of the time. The values of patriotism and family went hand in hand: each assigned similar hierarchical roles and responsibilities. In 1934, the word *rodina,* the country as mother, was revived. Citizens were children, expected to give obedience and loyalty, and to receive parental care and support in return; Stalin was of course the father. The family, like the state, was held together by respect, supported by a hierarchy of obligations extending from the bottom up and the top down. Both parents and children had defined roles. Children were encouraged to respect their parents; hero pioneers of the 30s, like Timur of Gaidar's *Timur and his Squad,* were always considerate of their elders. In return, the duty of parents was to care for their children and raise them as healthy members of the collective. High state officials gave living demonstrations of the ideal: Stalin paid a visit to his old mother in Tiflis; the story of Lenin's New Year visit to a children's colony was revived and given broad publicity.

Women were the mainstay of the new family. They were given new obligations that focused their identity on the roles of wife and mother. The most important role a woman could play was to marry and have children; mass media of the thirties showed these women to be the happiest. Motherhood was the most cherished desire of even the zealous tractor driver Pasha Angelina. Sex roles were increasingly differentiated by the mass media. Rights given by the revolution were taken away, paths to social recognition were cut off. Heroines like the hardened commissar of Vishnevsky's *Optimistic Tragedy* (1933) were replaced by the heroines of *Girl-Friends* (1936), whose contribution was in filling the female role of nurse. A woman's path to recognition was through her unique feminine qualities, as Lebedev-Kumach's 'Merry Girl-Friends' (1937) made clear:

> *Let's go, let's go, my merry girl-friends!*
> *Like a mother, our country calls and loves us!*
> *Caring hands are needed everywhere*
> *As is our warm and overseeing women's eye.*

Well now, girls! Very well, my beauties!
Let the country sing about us
And may our names in sonorous song
Be glorified among the heroes!

To compensate for the loss of active participation, Soviet society acknowledged passive contributions to the national welfare, and transferred social status to these new roles. Mass culture offered women a path to social recognition inactive since the revolution: tangential status—status awarded for the merit of another. Secondary contributions (similar to the spectator-citizen) to the country were acknowledged. When a famous man was honoured, the supporting role of his wife, which had previously been ignored, was highlighted and commended. The wives of the pilot Chkalov and the shock-worker Stakhanov were used as models for Soviet womanhood; there was a congress of wives of industrial managers in the Kremlin. Wives sacrificed their careers for their husbands, accepted their essential family roles, and freed their husbands for their great exploits.

The role of motherhood received growing recognition. Building a strong family and raising healthy children was a contribution to the state. The child reared in the new Soviet family was a prepared citizen. The most famous child-rearing primer of the Cultural Revolution, Anton Makarenko's *Road to Life* (1933), emphasized the role of the social unit in rearing children. In his second important work, *A Book for Parents* (1937), Makarenko emphasized family roles as the foundation of society. Poorly-raised children could not be good citizens; raising a family depended on mutual love and respect between parents, and the freely given obedience of children. The man who was a good husband and father, and the woman who was a good wife and mother, were making a valued contribution to Soviet society.

The mid-30s redefined the ways a citizen could be integrated into Soviet society. The tendency was evident in changes to a theme prominent since the revolution: redemption. Socialism, it was believed, offered worthless individuals a chance to remake themselves, to give their lives some purpose. For the Cultural Revolution, salvation came from a change of environment. Wreckers and thieves were removed from old associates and brought to the White Sea Canal Project, homeless waifs were resettled in Makarenko's colony. To become a model citizen, a 'Soviet person', one had to surrender one's background and the identity attached to it. Prominent figures like Levinson of Fadeev's *Rout* or Pavel Korchagin of Ostrovsky's *How the Steel was Forged* found an exit from personal difficulties through their social or professional identities. Man was remade by labour, by surrendering personal comfort for the communal welfare; he could, in a most extreme metaphor, become a machine.

Towards the mid-30s the process by which an individual becomes a Soviet person changed. The exclusive standards that kept many groups outside the pale were weakened. Perhaps the most remarkable return was the peasant, who had disappeared from the mass media as a positive image. The typical peasant of the twenties and early thirties was, at best, ignorant: the peasant mother of the literacy campaign's 'Mama, if only you could read, you could help me' poster (1923), or the peasant of *smychka* posters gratefully accepting proletarian tutelage. The peasant heroes of Pogodin's *Tempo* (1929), Avdeenko's *I Love* (1933) or Dovzhenko's film *Ivan* (1932) saved themselves by leaving the countryside and becoming proletarians. A peasant could be saved, but only by ceasing to be a peasant.

Cultural Revolution attitudes towards the peasantry resembled attitudes towards the hinterland: industrial activists felt their duty was to destroy nature when it stood in their way; collectivizers believed they were right to crush kulaks. With the consolidation of the *kolkhoz* movement in the mid-30s, the peasantry was rehabilitated, both in law and culture. The 1936 Constitution provided for the equal representation of workers and peasants in the legislature (as opposed to a 1:5 ratio). With new rights came new duties: peasants were subject to civil military training from 1937. Films of the period showed *kolkhoz* peasants defending the frontier alongside border guards. Collectivization created a new range of positive images for female peasants. The outstanding example was Alexandra Sokolova of *Member of the Government* (1939), but the type could be found elsewhere. The figure was a curious amalgam of traditionally feminine qualities and new Soviet ways. Using her fine human understanding and perseverance, she was able to convert the countryside to the Soviet system and win Moscow's recognition. Yet she did not lose her rural identity.

Hybrid identities allowed Soviet society to assimilate folk cultures. The process resembled the redefining of the geographic periphery: the map was redrawn to include most of the population through the intermediacy of the centre. The state patronized the return of folk creativity to national attention; by doing so, it ensured its own primacy. Russian folk culture had been a *bête noire* of the Cultural Revolution. It was seen, like the geographic periphery and the family, as a repository of values antithetical to the Soviet state: patriarchality, the private property instinct, religion. Groups dedicated to its preservation, like the Andreev Orchestra of Russian Folk Instruments or the Piatnitsky Folk Chorus, came in for harsh criticism. The Cultural Revolution saw only one possibility for peripheral cultures: to undergo radical change and accept the ways of the centre.

Hostility towards peripheral cultures eased by the mid-30s. Peasants and nationalities no longer had to surrender their unique identities to become part of the Soviet nation. Folk culture was accepted for a number of reasons, the most obvious being that it supported the surge in nationalist sentiment. Yet it must be remembered that the folk cultures of the nationalities, which were rehabilitated at the same time, did not support great Russian nationalism. Perhaps the only common feature of all Soviet folk cultures, and the one most commonly exploited by the mass media, was that they provided a rhetoric of hierarchy and patriarchality absent in other cultural traditions. Russian and Central Asian bards sang songs in praise of Lenin, Stalin, even the Constitution, in which the Soviet state and its leaders were shown to be benevolent patriarchs creating and distributing benefits to the people—the little children of the Soviet Union. The duties of Soviet citizens were modelled on the family: they demanded a hierarchical system of loyalties, and allowed for status by association. Praise of the state and its leaders was, by association, praise of oneself. Folk poetry represented a social system in which leaders and people were joined by a direct, personal and hierarchical relationship, and it was this relationship that ushered folk culture back into Soviet society.

Once the primacy of the centre was acknowledged, folk culture was no longer contrary to Soviet citizenship. The acknowledgement had its obvious manifestations in paeans to Stalin and Soviet power, but its less obvious and more important facet was that Moscow, represented by the mass media (radio, film, recordings) was now the disseminator of folk culture. Like so many other parts of Soviet culture, folk culture became a spectator entertainment. Traditional folk culture was a local phenomenon:

it was transmitted orally within a community, with direct contact between performer and audience. The 1930s assimilation of folk culture was initiated not by the local community, but by the centre. Scholars were sent to the countryside to find outstanding folk performers. They collected anthologies, published them in Moscow, and sent them back to the countryside. Folk performers like Lidia Ruslanova and Maria Kriukova won a nationwide audience for the first time, but their celebrity was won at the expense of removal from the folk community. The centre's ability to control relationships within media culture (which folk culture had become) was demonstrated by a ritual we have already seen: acknowledgement by the Kremlin.

Revived interest in folk culture in 1935 led to a burst of activity. Stalin visited a Bolshoi Theatre performance of popular song and dance on the October anniversary; there was a Moscow Olympiad of folk music; folk companies discovered by researchers were brought to Moscow to perform. Russian folk culture was celebrated, but so were Ukrainian, Transcaucasian and other minority cultures.

The social stability struck in the mid-30s was not dependent on prosperity and opportunity alone; it lasted through times of dire economic need. Its cultural foundations rested on a rethinking of the Soviet national identity. Geographical and social boundaries shifted to include vast expanses of the country excluded by the Cultural Revolution. Previously, the Soviet population had been divided into the small group of faithful and the great grey masses. Now, Soviet citizenship in its ideal sense was extended to the masses, whose support of the state was not always active and not always political, but still valued. New classes and groups were given access to the ranks of the elite without the need to surrender cherished personal and cultural identities. The rights and duties of social initiative were concentrated in the hands of a few, but the acknowledgement of passive contributions and tangential status allowed average citizens to feel they were contributing to the national welfare. They were acknowledged by the state, and were in turn ready to acknowledge its primacy.

James Von Geldern, "The Centre and the Periphery: Cultural and Social Geography in the Mass Culture of the 1930s," in Stephen White (ed.), *New Directions in Soviet History* (Cambridge: Cambridge University Press, 1992), pp. 62–80.

"WORLD REVOLUTION OR RUSSIA," FROM *THE GREAT RETREAT*

Nicholas S. Timasheff

The logical counterpart to the program of World Revolution was an antinational program within Russia. In the course of the first few years after the Revolution, the famous sentence from the Communist Manifesto, "proletarians have no fatherland," was repeated as often as possible, and such words as fatherland and patriotism disappeared from the vocabulary. The Russian national sentiment, both the moving spring in the building of the Empire and the product of its successful expansion, was called "chauvinism," and denied the right to exist. In teaching and in official speeches, membership in the First Socialist State was emphasized just because of the socialist character of that community, not because of its national individuality. Members of that community were invited to become citizens of the World Republic of the Proletariat, no longer citizens and patriots of an historically given State,

In 1923, Lunacharski, the people's commissar for education, said:

> The teaching of history which would stimulate the children's national pride, their nationalistic feeling, and the like must be banned, as well as such teaching of the subject which would point at stimulating examples in the past for imitation in the present. For I do not know what kind of thing is a healthy love for one's fatherland. Let us look at things objectively and recognize that we need internationalistic, all-human education.

In accordance with such ideas, the teaching of Russian history and of the history of Russian literature was discontinued. The official thesis was that up to Lenin's birth and the rise of the labor movement, Russian history had been all chaos, darkness, and oppression and not worth being memorized. The pre-Revolutionary culture was rejected to the limit of possibility, since this was a typically bourgeois culture. Perhaps a few bright spots could be found in the darkness, pointing to the Revolution to come. Symptomatic was the treatment of Pushkin: a few poems, mainly written when the author was young and in which he praised liberty and insurrection against tyranny, or professed superficial atheism in the style of the French Encyclopedists, were selected for study and imitation. The others, the great works which made him the national poet of Russia, were ignored.

In 1922–3, the designation of the First Socialist State as Russia was officially discontinued and replaced by the impersonal term, "Union of Socialist Soviet Republics."* Around 1930, the idea of abandoning the Cyrillic alphabet and shifting to the Latin one was seriously pondered upon. . . .

The Communist leaders ascribed great value to their dominance over Russia, but for them, Russia was still primarily an excellent springboard for the forthcoming International Revolution, and not a value in itself.

Then, in 1934, . . . the trend suddenly changed, giving place to one of the most conspicuous phases of The Great Retreat, which in the course of a few years transformed Russia into a country with much more fervent nationalism than she ever had before the attempt of international transfiguration. The process started this way.

In June, 1934, "treason against the nation" was made a capital offense; actually it always had been one, but this time it was emphasized that the greatest villain was one who helped the enemies of the nation, not one who was the enemy of socialism. In July, an editorial published in *Izvestia* startled quite a few readers: it was stated that every Soviet citizen ought to love his fatherland. A little later on, the leader of the Young Communist League declared that one of the League's duties was to foster the love of their motherland among the youth so that they would consider it an honor to die for it.

In 1936, Levin's play, *Fatherland,* was highly applauded by officials. When interviewed by representatives of Moscow papers, the author remarked: "The theme is immense; if I have succeeded in developing one-tenth of it, I am very happy." A few days later, a group of engineers condemned in 1934 and later pardoned wrote a letter to the editor of *Pravda* in which they said that they were proud to belong to their "happy fatherland" and were willing to apply all their strength to serve it. Later in the year, a

---

* The term Russian (Socialist Soviet) Republic continued designating the senior partner of the Union.

film entitled, *We, the Russians,* was produced. A few months earlier, the title would have been considered impossible by the Kremlin authorities. In 1937, these statements by high authorities could be found:

> The word "fatherland" has become a fundamental political concept . . . The most important condition [of success] is the fighting patriotism of our nation, its unlimited faithfulness to the mother country . . .

First of all, Russia's past was rediscovered by Russia. More exactly, after many years of denial of any value inherent in the past, Russia's people were given a spiritual vision of one thousand years of glory and national achievements surpassing those of any other nation. History, which for many years had been taught only in terms of mass activity, reappeared as a sequence of magnificent deeds performed by Russia's national heroes, no longer the few rebels such as Pugachev and later on Lenin, but the princes of Kiev, the Tsars of Moscow, the dignitaries of the Church, the generals and admirals of the Empire.

Naturally, Peter the Great was one of the first among the national heroes of Russia to be restored in their dignity—the indomitable reformer, considered by many as a precursor of Bolshevism, and also a great and victorious military leader. As great masters in the art of propaganda, the Communists asserted that Peter was being worshiped by the class which, according to the Doctrine, is infallible. They said:

> The workers of the Putilov factory (Leningrad) display great interest in the past of our fatherland. They are especially interested in the epoch of Peter the Great, in his war with Sweden, and in the great deed which was the creation of the Russian navy.

After Peter the Great, the founders of the Moscow State, out of which the Russian Empire evolved, were reintroduced into the gallery of national heroes, especially Alexander Nevsky, the victor over the Swedes and Germans, and Dmitri Donskoy, the victor over the Tartars. Later on, even Prince Vladimir the Saint, under whom Russia had been Christianized, was added. The famous film, *Alexander Nevsky,* was first shown on the eve of the twenty-first anniversary of the Communist revolution (November 6, 1938). The next day the following words appeared in one of the leading papers of Moscow:

> The youth, especially the members of the Young Communist League, enthusiastically applauded the deeds of the great Russian leader who lived 700 years ago. They did it because the Russian nation is imbued with flaming patriotism and had been imbued with it throughout her history.

As to Dmitri Donskoy, the paper of the Red Army inserted the following comment:

> The victory at the Kulikovo Pole opened the way for the growth of the national Russian State. The Russian people realize that only unity gives strength and secures a glorious future to the fatherland.

It is noteworthy that all the leaders just mentioned had been canonized by the Russian Orthodox Church. A few years earlier, expressing reverence to one of them would have been judged almost a symptom of counterrevolution. Now it was explicitly stated that:

Despite the fact that Alexander Nevsky is considered a saint by the Orthodox Church and that many churches and monasteries have been dedicated to him, atheists have to avoid any defamation of his memory; they must remember that he is a beloved hero of the people and that he merited the gratitude of later generations by his patriotism and military prowess. The Church canonized him in consideration of the love of the people; the Militant Atheists League has failed to pursue an equally wise policy.

Somewhat earlier a comic opera in the best style of the early 'thirties, ridiculing Prince Vladimir, was withdrawn from the repertoire, and the significance of the action was emphasized in a declaration of one of the highest governmental agencies:

> It is well known that the Christianization of Russia was one of the principal factors in the rapprochement of the backward Russian people with the people of Byzantium and later with the peoples of the West, namely with peoples of higher culture. It is also well known what a big part clergymen, particularly Greek clergymen, played in promoting literacy in the Russia of the Kiev period; thus, from a historical standpoint Byedny's libretto is an example not only of an anti-Marxist, but also of a frivolous attitude towards history and a cheapening of the history of our people.

Then came the turn of the great generals of the heroic epoch of Catherine the Great and Alexander I. Suvorov was honored in a film which, according to the paper of the Red Army, was enthusiastically received by the audience. The following order was directed to the Red Commanders: "You must fully understand the aggressive strategy of such remarkable Russian generals as Suvorov and his pupil Kutuzov."

Professor Tarle, a great historian exiled in the course of the Socialist Offensive, was invited to glorify Kutuzov and the magnificent performance of the Russian nation in 1812. He did this in two brilliant books and, among other things, refuted the derogatory statements of Clausewitz about Kutuzov. It is noteworthy that Clausewitz had been one of the few authorities recognized by Lenin, so that a departure from Clausewitz was necessarily a departure from Lenin. Said *Pravda:*

> In the hearts of the Russian people the memory of Kutuzov will live forever, as the head of a victorious army which liberated the beloved fatherland from foreign invaders.

Once more, to make the departure from previous evaluations as inconspicuous as possible, the government used a spokesman, this time a military man. He was directed to say:

> It is incorrect that in 1812 Napoleon was defeated by cold and hunger. The Russian armies operated correctly, in full accordance with the situation. The Russian soldier has always displayed unsurpassed stubbornness and aggressiveness and a number of Russian military leaders (Bagration, Rayevsky, and others) showed great courage and skill. They had behind them the experience of the great wars of the late eighteenth and early nineteenth centuries, an experience second to none, even to that of the French marshals.

To strengthen the impression, unnamed professors of the Military Academy were scolded for their inability to describe correctly the patriotism of the Russian Nation in the course of the War of 1812. In this way, a whole series of military heroes were given a place in the Communistic Pantheon. Among them Prince Bagration, another disciple of Suvorov, an army commander killed in the great battle of Borodino, was selected for special worship.

"It is time to rehabilitate the memory of Bagration," said *Krasnaya Zvezda,* "and to recognize in him a national hero, beloved by the army and having sacrificed his life to the independence of his fatherland."

Then came the time to glorify the military leaders of Russia on the eve of the Revolution. This was the more surprising, as one of the justifications of the Revolution had been the alleged corruption and incompetence of the Russian generals in the course of the First World War. Now one could read:

"The Warsaw-Ivangorod operation (October, 1914) showed the world that the Russian army was as good as the German. Once more it displayed the courage and endurance of the Russian soldier."

Up to that time all reforms enforced by the Imperial government were interpreted as dupery; thus, the Emancipation Act of 1861 which abolished slavery in Russia had been "unveiled" as "no reform at all," maintaining slavery in disguise. "This interpretation must be abandoned," declared the Commissariat of Education in its official paper: "the reform of 1861 actually was the beginning of a new epoch, that of bourgeois Russia."

Another feature of Russian history to be reinterpreted was the Popular Army of 1611–13 which put an end to the Time of Trouble, liberated Moscow from the Poles, and opened the way to the election of the first Tsar of the Romanov dynasty. "A book by Professor Lubomirov on the Popular Army had been suppressed for many years," wrote one of the Soviet papers. "Now, it must be rehabilitated; the Popular Army was not at all a creature of the landed gentry and the merchants, but actually a popular army." In the course of the war the names of the leaders of that army, Minin and Pozharsky, were often invoked as symbols of the traditional unity of the Russian nation in the face of foreign aggression.

Much later came the rehabilitation of the memory of Ivan the Terrible. Alexis Tolstoy, the most acclaimed of the then living Russian authors, was granted the honor of performing this deed. In an interview he said: "Ivan the Terrible was one of the most remarkable figures in Russian history. He represents Russia in all his grandiose ambitions, his fervid will, and his inexhaustible possibilities and power."

In the course of the war quite a few figures were added to the neo-Communist Pantheon, among them Admiral Kornilov, a hero of the Crimean war, and Prince Gorchakov, foreign minister under Alexander II. On both occasions Tarle served as the government's spokesman.

The choice of the heroes and deeds was not chronological. Russia's past has been revealed to the Russian nation neither by looking backward, nor by looking forward. By trial and error, personalities and events were picked here and there which would appeal to the Russians of the 'thirties and 'forties of the twentieth century and which, in addition to this, could well symbolize the traditional attachment of the Russians to their soil, and their willingness to sacrifice everything for its protection. Finally, an almost uninterrupted series of heroes and heroic deeds emerged, beginning with Russia's Christianization and finishing with Russia's participation in the First World War.

Three heroes were selected during that time to receive the highest rank. These were Alexander Nevsky, Suvorov, and Kutuzov. Orders of military merit were created bearing their names. In 1943, schools were opened in which children of the heroes of this war were to be prepared for the glorious career of a Red Army officer; they were given the name of "Suvorov schools." Early in 1944, the first pupils of these schools wrote letters to Soviet papers: their central theme was: "We want to be like Suvorov."

The rehabilitation of Russian history met some resistance in Stalin's inner circle, as shown by the following story. On January 27, 1936, Bukharin, then editor of *Izvestia,* said that laziness was the most universal trait of the Russian nation and that Oblomov, a famous "hero" from Goncharov's novel, was its chief symbol. On February 1, *Pravda,* without mentioning Bukharin, assailed those who asserted that Russia had been organized by foreigners, especially Germans, and enumerated the reasons why the Russians ought to be proud of their past. Bukharin did not understand the seriousness of his blunder and the next day published an article in which he obstinately defended his position. On February 10, a philippic against Bukharin appeared in *Pravda* in which, by numerous citations, it was "proved" that the slanderous distortion of the Russian past had nothing to do with Marxism. Now Bukharin had to apologize:

> The theory making Russian history a lasting darkness is historically wrong and politically harmful. Russian history knew periods of great progress and tremendous displays of energy. Russian science has given a number of brilliant names, Russian literature is entitled to occupy one of the first places in universal literature. I never shared that erroneous theory, but having made the unfortunate reference to Oblomov, I unwillingly deceived many. I am sorry that I have done so.

Official statements inducing the Russians to worship their past were insufficient. It was necessary to inculcate the new ideas, and still more the associated sentiments, into the minds of the younger generation. The study of Russian history was restored in schools of all levels. Great difficulties arose. First of all, no appropriate textbook was available. Naturally, when the government made it clear that it wanted a textbook on Russian history written from the standpoint of reviving nationalism, quite a few authors tried to do it. But it appeared that the competitors did not realize the magnitude of the swing of the pendulum. The first drafts introduced into an official committee, headed by Stalin himself, proved to be too "sociological," in other words, written according to the rejected pattern of "mass activity" and not emphasizing enough the positive value of such facts as the unification of Russia by the Grand Dukes of Moscow, the reforms of Peter the Great, and the emancipation of the serfs. Finally, a revised version of one of the drafts was selected and permitted to become the official textbook. The author, Professor Shestakov, has probably received tremendous royalties, and the students have received a rather dull textbook, lacking in any scientific value but well adapted to the new program.

Many years must pass before the young generation of the period of The Great Retreat reaches that age which gives access to high positions and honors. But the change in mentality, the reorientation of the nation towards national values was urgent. Therefore, all the means of mass adult indoctrination, this time with nationalism, were used. Thus, for instance, a series of pamphlets on the national heroes of Russia was published and distributed among the soldiers of the Red Army. Naturally, the film and the radio were amply used. Those on Suvorov and Alexander Nevsky have already been mentioned; there have been others, such as on Peter the Great and Pushkin. The theater was also used. In this field, an almost incredible performance is worthwhile mentioning: the remodeling of Glinka's opera, *The Life for the Tsar,* which under the old regime was used to re-enforce monarchical sentiments. In the original opera the hero, Ivan Sussanin, saves the young Tsar Michael from capture by Poles. It was first planned to make him save Minin, the head of the Popular Army, but this was rejected as contrary to history. Finally, he was made to save Moscow. The final hymn (addressed to the Tsar) was reworded to celebrate the glory of Russian arms, the might and indomitable character of the Russian nation.

As a further means to re-enforce the national sentiment, historical exhibitions were organized. In 1936, Kutuzov's and Napoleon's carriages were exhibited. In 1938, the Naval Academy organized an exhibition of Russian naval victories under Peter the Great and Catherine the Great, as well as the exploits of the Russian navy in the course of the Japanese war and the First World War. In 1939, an exhibition of Russian historical paintings was opened in Moscow. This exhibition was visited daily by thousands of people. It was on this occasion that *Pravda* began to rehabilitate the memory of Ivan the Terrible. *Pravda* wrote:

> The interpretation of some periods of Russian history, namely, of the time of Ivan the Terrible, is wrong. Only a few painters and sculptors, among them Antokolsky, have been able to grasp his greatness.

About the same time, in Kiev, an exhibition to celebrate the half-millennium of Russian artillery was organized. Wrote the paper of the Red Army:

> The exhibition shows that a number of inventions wrongly attributed to Western nations were made in Russia. Among other things, the exhibition shows the skill of the Russian artillery in the course of the Napoleonic wars, especially at the battle of Borodino.

In the cathedral of St. Basil in Moscow, an exhibition of the history of the Red Square (on which the cathedral is located) was opened. From 500 to 1,000 visitors were registered daily.

It is well known that monuments of the past are of high symbolic value in re-enforcing the national sentiment. Such a device could not be neglected by the masters in the art of managing public opinion. Naturally, the great battlefields came first, such as Poltava (Peter's victory over the Swedes, 1709) and Borodino (glorious resistance of Russian armies against Napoleon, 1812). The government had to insist on this new tool, so entirely different from the practice of the previous years. Thus, one of the Moscow papers triumphantly reported that the monuments on the battlefield of Borodino had been completely restored. However, a few days later another paper asserted that in actuality nothing had been done, and on this occasion revealed the evil deeds of the previous years. In 1932, the monument to Bagration was sold as scrap iron. Reliefs on the monument to Kutuzov were destroyed. The church on the battlefield was demolished. On the wall of a former monastery, a board was placed with the following inscription: "We need not take care of the remnants of the accursed past." *Pravda* naturally explained these evil deeds by intrigues of the "enemies of the people," who knew that they hurt the dignity of a great nation and provoked hostility towards the Party and the Soviet government. This, by the way, is an acknowledgment of tremendous importance: the destructions were carried out in complete accordance with the antinational policy of the first seventeen years of the Revolution, under the sponsorship of the high leaders. Their activity had provoked hostility to the regime; or, to put it in still other words: so long as the Communist rulers insisted on their antinational policy, they were considered as enemies by the people.

Among other items in the historical heritage of Russia restored under The Great Retreat were: the monument on the Kulikovo Pole where Dmitri Donskoy defeated the Tartars; the famous Trotsko-Sergyevsky cloister, the center of resistance against the Poles in the seventeenth century; the residences of the Moscow Tsars; the Petrinian Academy of Sciences in Leningrad; the Peterhof palaces; the Kutuzov hut where the famous general made the historical decision to surrender Moscow and thus preserve the army, as the instrument of coming victory; Yasnaya Polyana, the seat of Leo Tolstoy. . . .

Not only were monuments restored and exhibitions organized, but pilgramages to them fostered. Names already mentioned recurred on the list: Poltava, Borodino, Kulikovo Pole, Yasnaya Polyana and, in addition to this, a score of places where Pushkin lived or worked.

On some occasions, the political purpose behind the rediscovery of Russia's past comes to the fore. Thus, for instance, a keen observer reports:

> On a poster which I can observe from my room there appears underneath a por-
> trait of Kutuzov a quotation from Stalin in flaming letters reading: "Let the dar-
> ing spirit of our ancestors inspire you in this war."

What a contrast with the inscription of the Borodino monument executed in 1932!

A colorful feature of the historical tradition was restored relating to the Cossacks. For centuries they had formed semimilitary communities on the frontier and served the Tsars well against foreign and internal foes. For the latter they were hated by the revolutionists, and under the Communist regime their communities were disbanded. Then, later in 1935, letters from Don and Kuban Cossacks to Voroshilov (then war commissar) appeared in Soviet papers in which they declared their ardent desire to serve the fatherland as their fathers had done. Very soon, Cossack regiments were formed and quite a few special usages were permitted to revive. Thus, fathers resumed transmitting hereditary swords to their sons and this was done in ceremonies per- formed before big audiences. Young men returning from service in the Red Army re- sumed being received by similar assemblies. Cossack choirs were restored and invited to come to Moscow and perform before Stalin in their colorful folk costumes.

The rediscovery of Russia's past was supplemented by the rediscovery of the cul- tural heritage accumulated by generations but, because of its incompatibility with the Doctrine, ignored for many years. . . . Pushkin's centennial (1937) was used to or- ganize a kind of Festival of Russian Culture. A special Committee was created, and on this occasion Pushkin was called "the great Russian poet, the creator of the liter- ary language, and the originator of our great Russian literature." A few months later it was noteworthy that the country of the Soviets had rediscovered Pushkin.

> We have dropped the silly attempts to make of Pushkin a revolutionist, a pre-
> cursor of Bolshevism. But we declare war on those who dare to say that
> Pushkin's poetry does not mean anything for the proletarian. Pushkin is a genius
> who discovered the music of the mother tongue. He is the guiding star of Rus-
> sian poetry. He is alive in the people's hearts.

Never were the leaders closer to the truth than when making these statements.

The places where Pushkin had lived and worked were restored and opened for pilgrimage. Tens of thousands used this opportunity to display their deep attachment to the man who had given its highest expression to Russian culture. His works were published in millions of copies, and a few days after their appearance in individual cities all the copies available were sold out, in contrast with Marx and Lenin, whose works stood in solid masses on the shelves of the bookstores or were used to wrap herrings. One of the slogans of the centennial days was: "Russia is a great nation because she gave Pushkin and Lenin to the world."

The Russian language, Pushkin's instrument, became a special object of worship. While the tendency under the Communist Experiment was to contaminate the language with slang, foreign words, and cacophonic abbreviations of official terms, the tendency under The Great Retreat turned towards its purification. A famous writer, Chukovsky, acknowledged that twenty years earlier it had been necessary to shake everything, even the language, but that since then things had changed, and it was not desirable to get rid of the awkward forms prevailing in literature, especially in poetry.

A few years later this proud statement could be read in a Soviet paper:

The Russian language has resisted the strain of the revolutionary years very well. The tendency to use official abbreviations has disappeared; as of September 1, 1938, the post offices have been forbidden to distribute mail if the addressee is designated by abbreviation. The number of foreign words in use is now smaller than before the Revolution. For many words of this type Russian counterparts have been found and accepted by everybody. The Russian language is more Russian than ever.

It was only natural that, in the course of the war, efforts were made to link the present with the glorious past. "Stalingrad reminds us of Kulikovo Pole," one could read a few weeks after the decisive victory of the Red Army. When the battlefield of Borodino was liberated from the enemy, this statement was made: "The Russians think of Borodino as a prophetic symbol of this war." The restoration of the monuments on the battlefield torn down by the Germans was immediately ordered. A letter to Stalin from a group of peasants was given great publicity; in this letter the peasants said that they were proud of their sons, who were worthy great-grandsons of men who, in 1812, had valiantly fought under the banner of Kutuzov.

In an article entitled *The Russian Soldier* these qualities are ascribed to him: greatness of soul, strength of will, clearness of mind. To confirm such statements, the authors have always gone far back into history; Russia has obviously proven to be more solid ground than Communist Utopia.

As to culture in general, statements like these are typical of the war period: "The Russians look with pride on their past and with hope on their future"; "The Russian people has been granted the highest gifts. It has created a rich culture, it possesses a rich heritage in art and science, it has given birth to two of the greatest military men known to history, Peter the Great and Suvorov." Apropos Derzhavin's bicentennial, the role of Russian literature in the formation of Russia's national spirit was stressed. This literature, it was said, always reflected the heroic deeds of the Russian people correctly and brilliantly.

"We are proud of our science, literature, music, and painting," exclaimed Shostakovich, the leading Russian composer of our day. In the course of a special conference held at the University of Moscow, it was resolved that the great achievement of Russian, science had not yet been fully recognized and that all textbooks minimizing these achievements should be rewritten.

In summing up, it can be said that in all realms of cultural activity, great achievements of the past have been shown to the peoples of the Soviet Union, young and old, advanced and backward. All the strength of the propaganda machine was now used to reawaken the national sentiment, the same machine which for seventeen years had been used to uproot this sentiment. The results have been quite different. In the earlier period, the propaganda machine worked against the natural aspirations of human beings and their cultural tradition. The result was not very edifying. Perhaps the tradition was weakened, but nothing did replace it in the hearts of the Russians. Enthusiasts of the International Proletarian culture could be found in books only, not in actuality.

Since 1934, the propaganda machine worked in the same direction as the national aspirations and culture tradition. No wonder that this time the effect was striking: not only was the national sentiment reawakened, but it grew overwhelming, perhaps stronger than desired by those in power. . . .

The character of this new nationalism is apparent in these statements:

The Russians can be exterminated up to the last man, but they cannot be conquered . . . In this struggle we ought to be inspired by the images of our glorious ancestors, Alexander Nevsky, Dmitri Donskoy, Minin, and Pozharsky, Suvorov, Kutuzov, and by the victorious banner of Lenin . . . The readiness of the present generation to give everything to protect the Russian country from invaders and struggle for its independence has deep historical roots. It began with the Tartar invasion and Alexander Nevsky and continued through Dmitri Donskoy, Minin, and Pozharsky, the battle of Poltava, and the Patriotic War of 1812. Soviet patriotism is national and historical. Also historical and national is the Russian Revolution which continues the tradition of the Russian nation. National consciousness is in the air of our time. The cosmopolitanism of the nineteenth century is a thing of the past, the dreamers who were patriots of time and space have died out. Love for one's own village has been resurrected. But this is not a reversion. Can one love mankind without loving one's own people? We have not lost faith in the brotherhood of nations, but love of our motherland has made it a living faith . . . Patriotism is love of one's country. What is one's country? My mountains, my trees, my history, the history of my people, my brothers and sisters, my beloved ones . . . Our love of the motherland has conquered all other sentiments. Human faces, human eyes, human language—this is our Russia, and we are their guardians in this age of calamity. Motherland: this is a stream of people from the remote past to the future in which we believe and which one builds up for himself and the next generation. In some remote future, these individual streams will combine into Humanity. But for our age this is a dream. Our age is an age of struggle for freedom, independence, and the right to construct society according to a nation's own laws . . . We love Russia not because other lands are less admirable, but because Russia is our country . . . We are proud of our people, and there is no purer sentiment in the world. The value of Russia has stood the test. We look at this value with calm and firmness. We have become the greatest nation in the world, because our ideals are human ideals.

The definitions of patriotism just reproduced already belong to the war period. In the light of such definitions, it is understandable that the annexation of eastern Poland (September, 1939) was officially motivated by historical and racial reasons, as a kind of reunion of estranged brothers, and that no word was said about the fraternity of all toilers throughout the world, which certainly would have been mentioned if the annexation had taken place in 1920, in the course of the Russo-Polish war. It is also understandable that war propaganda has been entirely national; people have fought for their motherland, for the Russian soil which from time immemorial was tilled by their ancestors, and not for the realization of the initial blueprint of the Revolution.

In this line of development the climax was reached when on December 20, 1943, the government decided to drop the "International" as the national anthem and chose a new national anthem, which better than anything else expresses the compromise structure of the new society created under The Great Retreat. The Soviet Union and the great Russian country are used as interchangeable terms; Lenin and Stalin appear as heroes of the glorious fatherland which, in 1917, they hoped to see disappearing in the framework of the anonymous World Society of Toilers.

Nicholas S. Timasheff, *The Great Retreat: The Growth and Decline of Communism in Russia* (New York: E. P. Dutton & Co., 1946), pp. 165–181.

THE BIG DEAL

Vera S. Dunham

IT DID NOT CRUMBLE

. . . The assault of the German armies on the unprepared Soviet Union was so sudden and devastating that the system might well have crumbled altogether. But it did not. Stalin's wartime dictatorship, more absolute than before or after; the mobilization of mammoth economic resources by draconic labor laws; the vastness of the country and the enormous size of its human resources; the "Napoleonic" frost; the contribution of the Allies to the Soviet war effort and their stake in it—all these enmeshed into a formidable bulwark. Moral factors must be considered as well. Love of country, old and new (that is, a residual national cohesiveness in the older people and Soviet patriotism among the young); the Russian military tradition and its Soviet version, created by the war; anger, pride, despair, compassion blending into a new social solidarity; the bestiality and stupidity of the Nazis; the perplexing balance between the system's reprisals against disaffection, slackness, fatigue on the one hand and the wartime concessions made to the people on the other—these are the forces that worked in an intricate pattern to support the system.

Even when the occupied borderlands seemed lost, the core remained solid and Soviet society held together. There was sizable defection among minorities. Unquestionably, in Odessa the Rumanians were greeted with flowers by some Soviet citizens. Yet the inhabitants of Leningrad behaved heroically during two years of siege, and the way they lived and died said much for the morale of the nation as a whole.

The mechanisms of survival called forth by the war enhanced the system's ability to face its postwar difficulties. And Stalin, the victor, profited in a particularly dizzying manner. Victory gave him *carte blanche* and legitimated his rule as nothing had previously done, which in turn brought new hardships. The twenty million dead spoke from their mass graves for the maimed and bereaved, for an adequate acknowledgment of the people's sacrifice. While praising verbosely national heroism, Soviet leaders were less clear on the matter of rewards.

Potential conflict between the people and the regime was nothing new. But, by 1944, its social base had widened. The people knew who had won the war and how. Defeat was averted by mass exertion. So when, now in the name of peace, Stalin continued to make harsh demands of the citizens, they were resisted as they had not been during the war. And one new protagonist on the social scene proved hard to handle, the returning front-line soldier. Stalin's savagery, however, met this challenge like any other. In the early postwar years a policy of stepped-up coercion, intimidation, terror and the proliferation of concentration camps proved effective tools of control. Yet it is unlikely that these alone explain how the system managed to maintain itself. For these controls were merely negative, doing nothing to attain the goals of the system, doing nothing to satisfy popular hopes, aroused during the war, for a building of better lives. Other controls—positive controls—had to be made operative for, if next to Stalin's throne there stood Beria, Malenkov stood close by as well. Thus new policies came to be adopted, and these were policies of mediation, of concession, of internal alliances, of conflict resolution. One such major alliance during the period from the end of the war to Stalin's death will be examined [here]. I call it the "Big Deal."

A tacit concordat was formed by the Soviet leadership with the resilient middle class. This middle class had managed to increase the ground won in the thirties and, at the close of the war, had come into its own. "Middle class" can have different meanings. It can indicate a statistical entity in the stratification of the society by income, wealth, or occupation. In a society with a dichotomous and extreme class division, it can identify a stratum between these two antagonistic extremes. But it can also be applied to an attachment to specific values, to a way of life which partly crosscuts differences of position, of occupation and of income and which is, therefore, somewhat amorphous and difficult to anchor in any one sharply defined social group. It is this last meaning that the term middle class has here. Symbolically, in a somewhat perverse way, it expresses the embourgeoisement of Soviet manners, values, and attitudes. These are not confined to one demographic statistical zone. Their very diffusion, their wide resonance and appeal became a strong social force, and in it stalinism found its firm anchorage.

Despite the perils of imposing terms from the language of one culture on another, I want to suggest that the Soviet middle class does consist of many Soviet Babbitts and organization men, as well as of white-collar and mid-culture men and women. They are the solid citizens in positions and style of life below the top officials and the cultural elite, yet above the world of plain clerks and factory workers, of farm laborers and sales girls. This middle class did not weaken in the period of national devastation. On the contrary, it managed to add to the gains it had made in the thirties as a result of the country's modernization.

Two seemingly contradictory processes must be taken into account. One impeded modernization, the other worked in its favor. The wartime fatigue of the people, the devastation of the country, the infinite strain on the economy had seriously disrupted the prewar economic pace and its goals. The leadership had been forced to put a premium on skill, on productivity, on performance, instead of on political adroitness and ideological orthodoxy and, just as in the military, where the bungling mustachioed civil-war heroes were replaced by up-to-date professionals (the Zhukovs and Rokossovskys), so too in the civilian sphere the need for a new legion of productive engineers, organizers, administrators, and managers became pressing. The middle class was there to furnish it. And the very need for this class consolidated its base, encouraged its proliferation, and insured further modernization. Without the enormous middle class this would have been impossible.

This indicates the story I will try to tell. It is one of settlement and of realignment of the effective forces within the system itself. . . .

POSTWAR CHALLENGE

. . . [A]fter the war [Stalin] had to face the terrible devastation of the land. The last resources had been used up. Literally nothing was left. Minorities were showing signs of disaffection. Repatriates had to be reintegrated. The whole social order was in disarray. The population was exhausted.

During the war the party itself, moreover, had undergone a disturbing change. An unprecedented increase in the military and peasant had taken place within the party's ranks and those were the very elements that had saved the country. Mass admission of the military at the front had effectively enacted the policy of national unification. New members had been inducted on the ground of valor in combat rather than for service in the bureaucracy. This alone made party membership less a reflection of the official establishment than before and made it insufficiently reliable for postwar reconstruction. Stalin had, of course, needed massive popular support during the critical phase of the war. But with victory assured, he needed to reaffirm the primacy of his civilian and political bureaucracy, because mutual distrust between the people and the regime could not be drowned by the trumpet blasts of official patriotism.

But conflicts divided the citizenry also. There grew, for instance, a wearisome, if muted, quarrel between those who had risked their lives at the front and those who were allegedly safe in the rear. The hungry workers—to say nothing of the legions involved in forced labor—did not always approve of the privileged, army officers or officials. The cleavage between the haves and the have-nots had grown wider during the war. Lateral social stresses also became pervasive. Husbands asked some account for the years of separation from their wives, and wives, who at thirty had turned into old women, asked the same of their husbands. War casualties left so many widows, orphans, and spinsters behind that the entire population mourned. The sorrow of women marks Soviet life to this day.

Even wartime patriotism left explosive residues. Among the Russians, nationalism tended to move into chauvinism, stimulating in turn the underground separatism of minorities. Other developments, which had been useful for the war effort, now became disruptive. The dogged partisan movement in occupied territories, which had at first been wooed by the regime, later became difficult to handle after its anarchical tendencies surfaced.

Many centrifugal impulses accompanied the dislocation of the population both eastward and westward. Contact with the West created unforeseen difficulties. Defection took place in numbers that could not be disregarded. Those civilians and soldiers who had seen the West, who had come in contact with other norms, had to be repatriated. This, however, is a euphemism. They were liquidated or quarantined. Those who were permitted some modicum of normal existence were watched. In another category, some intellectuals now craved contact with their Western counterparts, as did Soviet Jews and Armenians and Ukrainians, citizens with kinsfolk outside Soviet borders. The main point of it all is that it was difficult to batten down the hatches that had been opened for the waging of a war in which the Soviet Union had to cooperate with allies. And if the Orthodox Church had lent staunch support, its usefulness after the war had become dubious. For the revival of religion pulled people away from the established norms.

Some obstreperous elements, then, took hold in the population. They derived from divided loyalties; from social differentiation; and, increasingly, from what the rulers considered heresy. They took hold by default and by the tear and pull of human experience *in extremis*. In the transition from war to peace, when so much seemed possible, popular hopes of democratization of the system ran deep. In part, these hopes went back to the dissident intelligentsia's revulsion against stalinism. But a different consequence of war also pulled in the same direction. Corruption of mores, from the elite to the poor, contributed not only to an alarming growth of crime. It also helped the spread of antiauthoritarian attitudes.

The bereaved and exhausted population was prone to disaffection. Pauperization reached tragic proportions. And at the base of it all, the war-torn family showed strain. The regime rightly feared dissent. The fear was immediate and it triggered draconian measures that swelled the size of the concentration camp population.

But the regime's need for support, on the other hand, had all the features of a long-range problem. So the regime faced those two problems differently. Decisions made to prevent dissent had little in common with the steps taken to seek new popular support.

The immediate problem of popular discontent brought the short-term response: the repair and use of its coercive powers. The challenge of social and economic betterment, however, brought forth the regime's long-term response, which was to search for new and reliable allies in the population.

In Stalin's time—and even in Stalin's worst times—the regime was supported by more than simple terror, a truism still overlooked from time to time. The system did possess regenerative powers, and it was capable of responding to the pressures of postwar reconstruction. Accommodation and settlement were being used at the same time that millions suffered because of Stalin's paranoia. Despite the spread of terror, the dictatorship had to decide whether to honor wartime promises to the people—some stated, but most implicit. The risky alternative was to tear up the wartime treaty with the people. The regime chose instead a long-term middle course, and this course was that it modified its wartime treaty with *all* the people in favor of a new treaty with *some* of the people.

Soviet political leadership had chosen and nurtured certain allies in the past. It had relied in those earlier days on the workers. It had appealed, too, to the intelligentsia. But this time it looked for a new force, sturdy and pliable. And it was the middle class which offered itself as the best possible partner in the rebuilding of the country. The middle class had the great advantage of being "our own people": totally stalinist, born out of Stalin's push for the industrialization, reeducation, and bureaucratization of the country, flesh of the flesh of Stalin's revolutions from above in the

thirties, and ready to fill the vacuum created by Stalin's Great Purge and by the liquidation of the leninist generation of activists.

So it was with the middle class that the regime entered a concordat. This particular response to the long-term challenge of reconstruction—this particular social accommodation—I call the beginnings of the post-war Big Deal. On the surface it is
true that neither big nor small accommodations with any part of the population
seemed probable. This was, after all, the very time when Stalin was at the height of his
prestige, determined to make his power in postwar Russia secure, and when he had
all the means to do it. The pressure on the population as a result of Stalin's determination had a leveling effect. No one was safe. Still, the coercive maintenance mechanism of the regime was only one of its key devices. More positively, it also sought a
stabilizing accommodation with middleclass values. Thus in an inconspicuous, ingen-
uous, and natural way the Big Deal was concluded.

One can see this rapprochement in part as a calculated policy of the stalinist dictatorship. But the policy grew out of spontaneous, cumulative processes where the development of the new Soviet middle class was paralleled by the transformation of the
Soviet political regime from a revolutionary bolshevik force into an essentially conservative establishment, intent on preserving the status quo. This dual process brought
closer together the preferences and aspirations of the political establishment and those
of the middle class. It made the establishment's appeal to middleclass hopes and sen-
sitivities a reflection not only of the manipulative policies of the regime but also of its
own preferences and values. Given the staggering size of the job to be done, the old
mystique of the collective lost its popular appeal and its economic usefulness. What
was now urgently needed was a wide range of individually hardworking and individually committed citizens.

The war had rapidly accelerated social change. Class differentiation had become
more palpable, if only because the survival rate differed. In wartime conditions, naturally, the military structure reflected new class distinctions more strikingly than the
civilian one. The infantry soldier, still wrapping his feet in the primordial strips of
cloth and craving home-grown tobacco to be rolled in a shred of newspaper, had to
be dazzled by the accoutrements and deportment of his refurbished commanders. The
gap between the various classes of the classless society was symbolized by the newly
introduced sumptuousness of the gold and velvet trim, the épaulettes, and insignia of
rank and distinction of the new comrade generals and marshals, and the generalissimo
himself.

The average citizen, too, had changed. Demands on the system, as with the rapidly advancing wartime official, expressed awareness of a newly acquired status. It
seemed that those citizens' commitment to the system could now best be made secure through the ties of a mutual agreement, a bargain that would give both sides the
most important things they wanted. The nature of that special agreement had already
been worked out by Stalin in the thirties, when he had discredited the egalitarian
myth by attacking the concept of "leveling" (uravnilovka); by masterminding the
movement of stakhanovism—that takeover by the competitive eager beavers, hated
by their coworkers for their individualistic effort and individual reward. It made citizens believe that in Stalin's country they were not invited to work for themselves, for
their self-interest, even for their own selfish good.

The relationship between what I call the Big Deal and the thirties lent solid
strength to the transaction. But what was new in this accommodation was as important as its roots in the past. The fact that, for example, the worker was now excluded

was central and strikingly new. The offer of partnership markedly shifted toward the professional groups. A new support of the system was being built with a new partner on a new basis of mutual satisfaction—a new tacit alliance between the regime and the middleclass ethos.

Of course, such an alliance was not an easy matter. Nor was it one for unabashed public display. The pressing of claims took special forms. Because Soviet society is ideology laden, it must be constantly asserted that all is just and well at all times. This makes public disclosure of significant change difficult. Also, by definition, no one can make competitive and discordant claims, nor can opposing value systems be said to exist. Throughout those years, while it strengthened its bonds with the middle class, the regime paid lip service to other themes and values. Because of the potency of its centralized, unitary, public mythology, the ruling group itself acted out this ambiguity. It did so most conspicuously in its language, for the new accommodation required the use of old language. So whatever really took place continued to be expressed in old clichés. No wonder, then, that the Big Deal called for much manipulation of the doctrine. The regime had two objectives; to obscure the Big Deal in its form, and to induce a conversion of official public values in substance.

CONVERSION OF PUBLIC VALUES

. . . the Soviet party oligarchy—whatever its social blend—is not so much a class as it is an organization. In the language of nineteenth-century literature, its members are the twentieth-century *raznochintsy*—a conglomerate of people of "various ranks." The varying social origins of Lenin, Trotsky, and Stalin help make exactly this point. Sharing no common social traditions and defending no common historical patrimony, the membership of this organization has been marked not only by its fratricidal propensity but by extraordinary flexibility. This last may have been a blessing in the initial turbulent revolutionary period. With the advent of bonapartism, however, the oligarchy sought its own social base, that legitimization which comes only from identifiable social roots. Obviously, a slow, covert change had been taking place from the twenties onward. The intoxication of the revolution faded. Gradually there came the canonization of revolutionary "traditions"—a telling contradiction in terms. Stalinist dictatorship, bolstered by its self-generated traditional mythology of Great and Old Russia, looked around for sturdy class roots. . . .

It is true that the Great Purges led to a radical decline of the heterogeneity of the social origins of the party leaders and militants. In the wake of this calamity, the ranks of the middle and higher leadership were filled by *arrivistes*. These mostly second-generation people rose from the komsomol, or from the industrial bureaucracy, or were recruited from technical institutes. Having made their careers and having reached positions of leadership, they deliberately disengaged themselves from their social roots. They did not consider that their social heritage provided a fitting base for their newly acquired life-style, for their wider horizons. So the upper party echelons remained unanchored, yet feeling the need for a solid base.

By uniting now, after the war, with its own indigenous middle class, the stalinist dictatorship was able finally to acquire class roots and it did this by fostering the interests it shared with the middle class. It did not, let it be noted, choose to turn to the peasant, to better his lot, to increase his social mobility, to alter significantly the institutional workings of collective agriculture. Indeed, on the contrary, experimental measures such as Khrushchev's idea of "agro-towns" of 1949, which showed some active interest in the lot of the peasant, were abrogated. Neither did the regime really turn to the mass of the workers, for labor laws remained harsh, physical mobility curtailed, wages low and housing very bad, and the educational system in its lower regions and its vocational branches impeded, rather than encouraged, the upward mobility of industrial youth by pinning adolescents to the shop. Nor did the regime choose to offer the central advantages of the Big Deal to the stakhanovites; for all their ideological affinity these people had the necessary zeal but lacked the expertise required for optimum partnership. As finally for the intelligensia, it was treated for a tragic period as little short of an internal enemy. If it was unresponsive to the claims of the peasants and workers, the regime was punitive toward the cultural intelligentsia. Wanting such diverse things as the right to privacy, on one hand, and the right to participate in a substantive reshaping of the ideological realm on the other, wanting the right to err and at the same time the right to be right, the intellectuals, in short, wanted freedom. Complex and dangerous, this did not make for stabilization of the internal status quo. That was clear enough. And the regime was simply not prepared to settle for such.

Instead, the kind of social arrangement the regime was looking for was one which was capable of producing contented citizens who, in turn, would be eager to pass on the contentment to their children. It badly needed durable and reliable support and this was defined in terms of one central social group's apolitical, instrumental commitment to the system's maintenance and growth. The regime's primary demands, beyond apolitical conformism, were loyalty to the leader, unequivocal nationalism, reliable hard work, and professionalism.

The middle class, too, craved contentment. And if the regime looked for a new and broad stabilizing base, essential to the staggering job of social and economic reconstruction, it was primarily the middle class that was ready to offer it. The possibilities of rapprochement between the regime and the middle class went deep. Primarily material values were laid on the bargaining table. But this was done neither crassly nor exclusively. The regime courted its new partner in a special way and not without sophistication. What made the Big Deal strong was the fact that it worked at more than the material level. It appealed to the partner's complex of self-interests, involving his prestige, involving his pride in his work, the satisfaction derived from his professionalism, and from his apolitical conformism.

What the partners shared turned out to be more weighty than what divided them. Specifically, what did they want? The middle class wanted careers backed by material incentives—housing, consumer goods, luxuries, and leisure time. Neither the regime nor the middle class was interested in ideology or further revolutionary upheavals. Neither objected to a stratified society. Both proposed to build on the basis of what was there already. Both were interested in stabilization, normalization, and material progress. Both were interested in social mobility. The new careerism satisfied the upwardly mobile individual, who was then expected to be loyal to those who permitted him to be such. Both partners were interested in affluence; one, as an incentive to ensure that work be done; the other as reward. Above all, both were interested in security.

The advantages of the rapprochement were natural. There were, it is true, difficulties. For a start, canonized bolshevik tenets abhor everything to do with the middle class, a hatred which, dating from before 1917, had given the revolution some of its thrust. The old language of bolshevik formulae remains to this day the foundation of the legitimacy of Soviet political power and proclaims the system's public rationale and, since these bolshevik tenets could be neither explicitly abandoned nor adhered to, the Big Deal had to be accompanied by an ambivalence in the ways it was explained to the people. In the end, as we shall see, it was spelled out in a quite perplexing manner. A process of translation of one set of values into another was imperceptibly initiated and it was this manipulation which served as a solution to the ideological dilemma. Instead of *doing away* with its traditional canons, the regime simply *accommodated* them to those preferences of its new partner, the middle class.

The transformation was largely semantic; it endeavored to minimize the standard bolshevik invective against private aspirations and to make certain private values legitimate. In the end, it reflected the embourgeoisement of the entire system.

Established doctrine underwent a curious change which, though difficult and subtle, carried no risk. It introduced no new ideas and no extrinsic ideological material. Yet an ideological conversion, formidable in its implications, was nevertheless accomplished. Without it the settlement probably would not have worked.

The basis of it was that, wherever possible, private values were converted into public values. The result of this is particularly vivid if set against the model hero of earlier days. From child to pensioner, the classic prewar bolshevik heroes both supported public values and were indeed their incarnation. Selflessness, devotion to the party, asceticism, quixotic courage—these were the main virtues. Heroism other than public was inconceivable. Public commitment in those early days was pitched with unequivocal shrillness against primary loyalties and private values. The canonized martyr, the "boy-scout" Pavlik Morozov, is an example. At the age of fourteen, at the peak of the collectivization campaign in 1932, he was murdered by relatives for denouncing his own parents to the authorities. He had reported them because he thought their attempt to help some outcast kulaks subversive. Choosing the state before his parents, this archetypal Soviet youth personified the then lethal confrontation between private and public loyalties.

As against such extremism, things now mellowed. A new concept of happiness formed the bridge where fraternization took place between the private and the public. A model citizen was saddled with the moral and political obligation to be happy as a person, in his private life as well as in his job. A rich home life began to be praised; self-sacrificing, ascetic satisfactions were losing ground. No hero could now claim leadership if he denied private needs. It was no longer his business to be concerned about society as a whole and still less to be dogmatic about it. In every way, moderation was emerging as a supreme virtue. Too much selflessness was as discreditable as excess of pride. There was, though, one thing where no limits, at least in fiction, were imposed. And that was work, work, work; but it was still not to interfere with the hedonistic enjoyment of material rewards. Slowly, the paragon of the forward-striding communist took on a new form. Someone resembling a middleclass careerist replaced the revolutionary saint of the twenties and the party vigilante of the thirties. He appeared now in the form of a vigorous manager. He progressed rapidly in his career. He was content in his family life. He aspired to a private house and perhaps to a dacha. He drove his own private car. He was disinterested in touchy matters of ideology and higher policy.

In large part, this conversion of public values is what the Big Deal was all about.

MESHCHANSTVO AND INTELLIGENTSIA
WITH A NOTE ON KULTURNOST

The term middle class, even in a broad sense, lacks substantive meaning in Russian. There is, however, a richly evocative term—*meshchanstvo*—not a synonym but a cogent relative. It denotes a style of life or a personality structure. In origin, meshchanstvo in seventeenth-century Muscovy referred to a class or estate; it encompassed the lower economic bracket of urban dwellers—peddlers, servants, some artisans. One might call them burghers, except that this curious administrative classification included dislocated peasants but excluded big merchants. In any event, whatever the peculiarity of this humble urban conglomerate, the word carried no pejorative overtones at first. With the growth of the urban population, however, the word changed its meaning, and acquired a figurative one. In the late nineteenth century two connotations became current. In literary terms, meshchanstvo turned into a near equivalent of petty bourgeoisie and, in a looser usage, evolving from the snobbism of the educated few, the term became derogatory. This usage has persisted, and as a target, meshchanstvo helped to stimulate the revolution. But it not only managed to survive but indeed managed, too, to overcome and flourish.

This claim may sound peculiar, given that whatever else survived 1917, the prerevolutionary middle class did not. But in due time, and through the modernization the revolution brought to a backward country, the soil was prepared for a new middle class, public in employment but private and inner-directed in its strivings. And with this development, meshchanstvo got a chance to locate itself again on a solid social base. It represents today, as it did before, a middleclass mentality that is vulgar, imitative, greedy, and ridden with prejudice. Both deficiency of spirit and the defensive mechanisms of philistinism are implicit in the term. Some equivalent can be found in the German word *Spiessbürgertum,* which also emphasizes stagnation rather than the class origin of a social group. "Petty bourgeois" is not as derogatory. The American "Babbitt," although also both aggressive and complacent, seems actually weaker than the Russian *meshchanin.*

In the Soviet world, meshchanstvo appears at every rung of the social scale. In one aspect it refers to the social climbing and careerism of the newly rich; in another to complacent vegetation. A vice admiral of the Soviet navy may be a meshchanin, and a professor may as easily be seen wallowing in meshchanstvo as a post-office clerk or party official, to say nothing of their wives. In many ways in fact, meshchanstvo is a familial and feminine affair, and its pretentiousness expresses itself in the number and size of material acquisitions, by which the newly arrived aim to impress. Fervor for possessions is a key trait. Significantly, meshchanstvo can be satisfied.

Literary descriptions of prerevolutionary meshchanstvo made it appear more stifling but less pompous than the Soviet kind. Material acquisitions weighed heavily in pre-1917 Moscow suburbia, in the kingdom of stolid semi-literate merchants—from Ostrovsky's genre picture to Blok's visionary revulsion. But they did not stand for anything beyond themselves. Goods, wares, fat-bellied chests of drawers, bank accounts, were not extolled as incentives for emulation. They were despised or admired for what they were—despised certainly by the satirists of meshchanstvo from Saltykov-Shchedrin, in the second half of the last century, to the great Zoshchenko who in the twenties left behind the record of early Soviet meshchanstvo; this disdain for meshchanstvo is a venerable tradition at least a century old. With the advent of stalinism, however, and especially during its last phase, ambivalence toward meshchanstvo became noticeable. If the great writers upheld the tradition, the servants of the establishment took on an increasingly ambiguous tone.

Meshchanstvo's natural and historical antagonist is the intelligentsia. In this study those two terms are used not so much as class or social group designations, but as cultural terms and as modal personalities. Meshchanstvo, as has been shown, resists translation as a word: it is singularly focused and compact as a cliché and a derogation. By contrast, "intelligentsia" has several meanings, and lacks a focus. The official Soviet usage of the term intelligentsia was, until recently, statistical and administrative. It embraced everyone who was neither a peasant nor an industrial worker. A substantial category, it covered all persons engaged in nonmanual work, and meaningless use of the term is still common in official Soviet writings.

Peter I established the foundation for social mobility, for industrialization, commerce, and urbanization. Both meshchanstvo and intelligentsia are connected with the first steps toward modernization undertaken by the administrative and social reforms of the eighteenth century. Both are urban phenomena, detached from peasant culture as well as from that of the landed gentry. And both underwent considerable changes, before the revolution of 1917 and after. What is constant is the intrinsic hostility between the meshchanin and the intellectual, shown amply in prerevolutionary literature, and spilling over into Soviet literature from its very inception.

The intelligentsia, despite its historical transmutations, is capable of remembering its past. At times, it is inclined to do so openly, causing friction with the rulers. In this respect, meshchanstvo is happily blind. It knows no past. It sprouts anew at each juncture of social stabilization. Eminently visible, it does not plot. It has nothing to conceal. It is, therefore, manageable.

Meshchanstvo does not fret except about private matters. On the contrary, effectively or not, the intelligentsia, in its old form and its new reincarnation, has always been mainly preoccupied with fretting over social wrong. If it were to stop worrying, it would stop existing. It cannot be satisfied; dissatisfaction is its condition. It is true that the more, at times, it has fretted, the less capable it was of social action. Intellectually and spiritually, however, it dedicated itself to the humanist propositions that salvation was corporate, that tyranny was evil, that freedom was meaningless unless it was universal. It glorified self-sacrifice, personal purity, public service. It stubbornly dreamed of an ideal society. Idealism in this moral sense of self-sacrifice and of devotion to the cause of the enslaved and underprivileged was enacted in the relentless critique of the status quo.

There was a time when ideas were taken seriously to the extent that blood was amply and ruthlessly shed on their behalf. And the Russian intelligentsia has been responsible for violence. One might say that, tragically, commitment to ideas, incited by the tornado of utopianism, became the intelligentsia's overcommitment. The spirit of the revolution was nurtured by relentless fretting.

In Stalin's time, however, the regime has managed to divide the intelligentsia and to seduce part of it. So the intelligentsia cannot be considered a homogeneous entity, and it might be useful to try to distinguish at least its "pure" from its "impure" elements. This is to say that a special type has emerged from it, powerful and vocal. He is a hybrid *par excellence:* a meshchanin, enjoying the material privileges (and the materially underpinned pretentions) of an intellectual who has been hoisted by the regime to leadership. The comfortable life-style of the prominent Soviet *homo academicus* makes the point, as do his striving emulators. Such hybrids put the less learned and sophisticated meshchanstvo to shame, and make the intelligentsia's splintering into "pure" and "impure" palpable and painful. It is one more peril that the princi-pled intelligentsia must endure. For, deep down in everyday life itself, these hybrids help the conversion of public values. The conversion, in turn, etiolates just those val-ues the regime had shared in the revolutionary past with the revolutionary intelli-gentsia, the purest of the pure and the most foolish.

Although purist idealism had provided the supreme rationale for the revolution, the stalinist regime undertook finally to obscure it. What was done was done; the past belonged to the past. The lingering of certain prerevolutionary and, for that matter, revolutionary memories spelled trouble, and because the memory cells of the Soviet intelligentsia hold the quixotic drive toward social equity and intellectual freedom, they represented a source of conflict with the system. On the other hand, mesh-chanstvo is entirely free of such aspirations. It thrives viscerally on distrusting the in-telligentsia and shares with the regime a dislike of people who take ideas seriously. From the thirties on, when the new middle class emerged, Soviet society has been making room for meshchanstvo; the very ambiance, the underlying mood and feel of the postwar Big Deal thus had been in gestation for sometime.

The regime's shift in the public realm from the revolution to stalinism determines the curious relationship of two additional words, eminently untranslatable, *kultura* and *kulturnost*. Akin in etymology, substantively they stand at odds with each other. *Kul-tura* is the achievement of the intelligentsia in the sense of higher culture, a synthesis of ideas, knowledge, and memories. The other, *kulturnost,* is its alternative: a deriva-tive, second-hand notion. Having nothing to do with a spiritual legacy, it is instead a mere program for proper conduct in public. Conforming with prescribed prefer-ences, it blends with the aspirations of meshchanstvo. The regime, especially after the chaos of war, cared a lot about the manageable, predictable, and "proper" manners of its citizens. It also cared that conduct be impeccable, inside as well indeed as outside Soviet borders. Kulturnost was thus given a weighty foreign political responsibility. Soviet representatives, with military boots as well as diplomatic footwear polished to the highest gloss; with chests covered with sparkling decorations; with hands mani-cured and gloved according to etiquette; with grandiose titles, and with well-groomed and stiff entourages entered the political arena as emissaries of a Great Power. Kul-turnost represents, both at home and abroad, a refurbished, victorious, conservative force in Soviet postwar life, embodying a slick decorum and a new kind of self-righteousness—stable, prudent, heavy. Its special function is to encode the proper re-lationship between people through their possessions and labels; between mores and artifacts, to put it more fancifully. (It might even shake the individual's grip on his pos-sessions: for instance, a strategic abstinence from acquisitiveness for the sake of dis-playing "good taste"; the occasional "generous" sharing of coveted earthly goodies for the sake of show and future profit.)

Strictly and minimally, kulturnost turns into a fetish notion of how to be indi-vidually civilized. In the panoramic view of Soviet society, there is much more to it. Kulturnost, admonitory and educative, and at first denoting little more than personal hygiene, expanded into a commodious umbrella under stalinism. It began to mean more important things than clean nails, abstinence from cursing and spitting, a re-quired minimum of good manners. It began to mean the only desirable conduct, the self-image of dignified citizens. Those alone could now be models. The notion of kul-turnost had grown out of mores; in turn, it began to shape them, in accord with the regime's predilection for ponderous, monumental meshchanstvo.

The usefulness of kulturnost to the regime, which exhorted the people to implement it, was manifold. Like ideological orthodoxy, it became a device for control. As a purpose shared by both the regime and the middle class, it lent support to the relationship between them. As a prescription for proper conduct, it helped build a clearing house where middleclass ways were recommended by the regime to everybody.

The artifacts of the postwar middleclass culture must be seen through the prism of kulturnost for, after the war, it was kulturnost which helped to channel the direction of sanctioned aspirations. Most of all, kulturnost helped to bestow on material possessions attributes of dignity and of virtue.

Vera S. Dunham, *In Stalin's Time: Middleclass Values in Soviet Fiction* (Durham: Duke University Press, 1990), pp. 3–5, 11–23.

Joseph Stalin, "Dizzy with Success: Concerning Questions of the Collective Farm Movement"
March 2, 1930

The vicious onslaught of party workers and activists, policemen and even the army, against the peasants heightened in the first months of 1930. That year alone, peasants fought back in more than 13,000 instances of mass protest or armed resistance. In a superb book on this last-ditch fight of Russian villagers, Lynne Viola tells how peasants used everything from killing livestock, murdering officials, to spreading rumors of the coming of the Antichrist to resist the seizure of grain and the destruction of their traditional way of life. Though other historians have accentuated the lack of cohesion and class ties among peasants. Viola emphasizes the cultural elements and the shared social position of peasants that empowered them to act as a class. At a moment when the economic survival of the peasantry was at stake, women in particular emerged as initiators and principal participants in thousands of so-called bab'i bunty *(women's uprisings). By March, the stability of the state itself was threatened, and Stalin issued his famous article, "Dizzy with Success," in which he called for a halt to the rush to collectivize and blamed lower officials for the very excesses that his policies had allowed. Peasants rejoiced, read the article aloud in villages, and even used it to justify further resistance when collectivization efforts resumed. Ultimately, at a slower pace but with relentless determination, the state collectivized almost all of peasant agriculture. The peasant war was over, and the state was the victor. "In the end," Viola concludes,*

> *peasant rebels were no match for the vast police powers of the state, and, like most other peasant rebellions, this one was destined to fail. The main element in the peasantry's defeat was state repression. Millions of peasants were arrested, imprisoned, deported, or executed in the years of collectivization. The state dismantled existing authority structures in the village, removing and replacing traditional elites. The economy of scarcity complemented state repression, first robbing peasants of their grain and then depriving millions of their lives in the famine that followed collectivization.[1]*

1. Lynne Viola, *Peasant Rebels under Stalin: Collectivization and the Culture of Peasant Resistance* (New York and Oxford: Oxford University Press, 1996). pp. 238–239.

The Soviet government's successes in the sphere of the collective-farm movement are now being spoken of by everyone. Even our enemies are forced to admit that the successes are substantial. And they really are very great.

It is a fact that by February 20 of this year 50 per cent of the peasant farms throughout the U.S.S.R. had been collectivised. That means that by February 20, 1930, we had *overfulfilled* the five-year plan of collectivisation by more than 100 per cent. . . .

What does all this show?

That a *radical turn of the countryside towards socialism may be considered as already achieved*.

There is no need to prove that these successes are of supreme importance for the fate of our country, for the whole working class, which is the directing force of our country, and, lastly, for the Party itself. To say nothing of the direct practical results, these successes are of immense value for the internal life of the Party itself, for the education of our Party. They imbue our Party with a spirit of cheerfulness and confidence in its strength. They arm the working class with confidence in the victory of our cause. They bring forward additional millions of reserves for our Party.

Hence the Party's task is: to *consolidate* the successes achieved and to *utilise* them systematically for our further advancement.

But successes have their seamy side, especially when they are attained with comparative "ease"—"unexpectedly," so to speak. Such successes sometimes induce a spirit of vanity and conceit: "We can achieve anything!", "There's nothing we can't do!" People not infrequently become intoxicated by such successes; they become dizzy with success, lose all sense of proportion and the capacity to understand realities; they show a tendency to overrate their own strength and to underrate the strength of the enemy; adventurist attempts are made to solve all questions of socialist construction "in a trice." In such a case, there is no room for concern to *consolidate* the successes achieved and to *utilise* them systematically for further advancement. Why should we consolidate the successes achieved when, as it is, we can dash to the full victory of socialism "in a trice": "We can achieve anything!", "There's nothing we can't do!"

Hence the Party's task is: to wage a determined struggle against these sentiments, which are dangerous and harmful to our cause, and to drive them out of the Party.

It cannot be said that these dangerous and harmful sentiments are at all widespread in the ranks of our Party. But they do exist in our Party, and there are no grounds for asserting that they will not become stronger. And if they should be allowed free scope, then there can be no doubt that the collective-farm movement will be considerably weakened and the danger of its breaking down may become a reality.

Hence the task of our press is: systematically to denounce these and similar anti-Leninist sentiments. . . .

Clearly, the principle of taking into account the diversity of conditions in the various regions of the U.S.S.R. is, together with the voluntary principle, one of the most important prerequisites for a sound collective-farm movement.

But what actually happens sometimes? Can it be said that the voluntary principle and the principle of taking local peculiarities into account are not violated in a number of areas? No, that cannot be said, unfortunately. We know, for example, that in a number of the northern areas of the consuming zone, where conditions for the immediate organisation of collective farms are comparatively less favourable than in the grain-growing areas, attempts are not infrequently made to *replace* preparatory work for the organisation of collective farms by bureaucratic decreeing of the collective-farm movement, paper resolutions on the growth of collective farms, organisation of collective farms on paper—collective farms which have as yet no reality, but whose "existence" is proclaimed in a heap of boastful resolutions.

Or take certain areas of Turkestan, where conditions for the immediate organisation of collective farms are even less favourable than in the northern regions of the consuming zone. We know that in a number of areas of Turkestan there have already been attempts to "overtake and outstrip" the advanced areas of the U.S.S.R. by threatening to use armed force, by threatening that peasants who are not yet ready to join the collective farms will be deprived of irrigation water and manufactured goods. . . .

Who benefits by these distortions, this bureaucratic decreeing of the collective-farm movement, these unworthy threats against the peasants? Nobody, except our enemies!

What may these distortions lead to? To strengthening our enemies and to discrediting the idea of the collective-farm movement.

Is it not clear that the authors of these distortions, who imagine themselves to be "Lefts," are in reality bringing grist to the mill of Right opportunism?

Such is the line of the Party at the present moment.

Can it be said that this line of the Party is being carried out without violation or distortion? No, it cannot, unfortunately. We know that in a number of areas of the U.S.S.R., where the struggle for the existence of the collective farms is still far from over, and where artels are not yet consolidated, attempts are being made to skip the artel framework and to leap straight away into the agricultural commune. The artel is still not consolidated, but they are already "socialising" dwelling houses, small livestock and poultry; moreover, this "socialisation" is degenerating into bureaucratic decreeing on paper, because the conditions which would make such socialisation necessary do not yet exist. One might think that the grain problem has already been solved in the collective farms, that it is already a past stage, that the principal task at the present moment is not solution of the grain problem, but solution of the problem of livestock- and poultry-breeding. Who, we may ask, benefits from this blockheaded "work" of lumping together different forms of the collective-farm movement? Who benefits from this running too far ahead, which is stupid and harmful to our cause? Irritating the collective-farm peasant by "socialising" dwelling houses, all dairy cattle, all small livestock and poultry, when the grain problem is still *unsolved,* when the artel form of collective farming is *not yet consolidated*—is it not obvious that such a "policy" can be to the satisfaction and advantage only of our sworn enemies?

One such overzealous "socialiser" even goes so far as to issue an order to an artel containing the following instructions: "within three days, register all the poultry of every household," establish posts of special "commanders" for registration and supervision; "occupy the key positions in the artel"; "command the socialist battle without quitting your posts" and—of course—get a tight grip on the whole life of the artel.

What is this—a policy of directing the collective farms, or a policy of *disrupting* and *discrediting* them?

I say nothing of those "revolutionaries"—save the mark!—who *begin* the work of organising artels by removing the bells from the churches. Just imagine, removing the church bells—how r-r-revolutionary!

How could there have arisen in our midst such block-headed exercises in "socialisation," such ludicrous attempts to overleap oneself, attempts which aim at bypassing classes and the class struggle, and which in fact bring grist to the mill of our class enemies?

They could have arisen only in the atmosphere of our "easy" and "unexpected" successes on the front of collective-farm development.

They could have arisen only as a result of the block-headed belief of a section of our Party: "We can achieve anything!", "There's nothing we can't do!"

They could have arisen only because some of our comrades have become dizzy with success and for the moment have lost clearness of mind and sobriety of vision.

To correct the line of our work in the sphere of collective-farm development, *we must put an end to these sentiments.*

That is now one of the immediate tasks of the Party.

The art of leadership is a serious matter. One must not lag behind the movement, because to do so is to lose contact with the masses. But neither must one run too far ahead, because to run too far ahead is to lose the masses and to isolate oneself. He who wants to lead a movement and at the same time keep in touch with the vast masses must wage a fight on two fronts—against those who lag behind and against those who run too far ahead.

Our Party is strong and invincible because, when leading a movement, it is able to preserve and multiply its contacts with the vast masses of the workers and peasants.

Pravda, no. 60, March 2, 1930; translated in J.V. Stalin, *Works* (Moscow: Foreign Languages Publishing House, 1955), XII, pp. 197–205.

Lev Kopelev, "The Last Grain Collections"
1933

Kopelev, whom we met before as a young Trotskyist, had become a "true believer" in Stalin by the time of the "revolution from above." Without questioning the wisdom of forced requisitioning of grain from hungry, even starving, peasants, he and his comrades swept into the Ukrainian countryside at a moment of widespread famine. The famine in Ukraine was one of the great unplanned misfortunes that followed collectivization and the removal of the most productive peasants, the so-called "kulaks." It is estimated that five million people died from starvation. This catastrophe has become an iconic event in Ukrainian national history, and many historians, most notably Robert Conquest, argue that the famine was a deliberate state policy designed to eradicate Ukrainian nationalism by weakening Ukraine's peasants.[1] The famine was certainly the result of the state's absurd calculations that Ukrainian peasants were sabotaging the grain collections and could contribute more, but it was more the result of government incompetence than a clear plan to kill ethnic Ukrainians. German, Jewish, and Russian villages in Ukraine also suffered, and far from Ukraine, in the Volga region, the North Caucasus, and Kazakhstan, similar policies led to horrendous loss of life.

1. Robert Conquest, *The Harvest of Sorrow: Soviet Collectivization and the Terror-Famine* (New York and Oxford: Oxford University Press, 1986).

The grain front! Stalin said the struggle for grain was the struggle for socialism. I was convinced that we were warriors on an invisible front, fighting against kulak sabotage for the grain which was needed by the country, by the five-year plan. Above all, for the grain, but also for the souls of these peasants who were mired in unconscientiousness, in ignorance, who succumbed to enemy agitation, who did not understand the great truth of communism. . . .

We did not consider them opponents or feel like hostile aliens among them. For in every village we found comrades, like-minded people.

In Petrivtsy our mentor was the head of the village soviet, Vashchenko. He had served in the German war to the rank of noncommissioned officer and had won two Saint George decorations, and in the Civil War he had commanded a company.

"It was easier then. Believe it or not, but it was lots easier. Everything was clear as clear could be. Say right here was your unit, your position. Then there was the enemy—the Cadets, the Petlyurans, the Makhno rabble. They were bad, the rats, the counterrevs! So you light 'em up, like from one cigarette to the next. Blast 'em with machine guns and rifles. And then wiggle like a snake around the side, or rush 'em head on, one after the other. Hurrah! Stick 'em with the bayonet! Butt 'em in the chops! If they don't raise their hands, pack 'em off to the graveyard! And keep going—march, march! Take the Crimea! Take Warsaw! Clear as clear can be. But now the enemy, maybe, is sitting next to you, maybe he's shaking your hand and saying hello. I've got my Nagan revolver on me, you can be sure, but I got to keep it in my pocket. You can pull it out only in dire emergency: for self-defense or for show. To shake up some real rat. But even this ain't often. And still the front is all around you. I figure the grain sacked up and buried in Petrivtsy alone must amount to over seventy thousand pounds. Those dirty turkeys hid it. [Individual farmers were derided as "turkeys, gobblers, hoaxers."] They themselves eat only makukha. Some of 'em got kids with bloated bellies already. But they don't open up their underground stores. The hoaxer hopes he can sit out the grain collection, we'll give up, and then he'll dig it up and stuff himself silly. Or else he's afraid we'll find the hoard, take away the grain. And then his family'll be hungry again, and he'll be cooling his heels with the polar bears. What kind of hayseeds are they, anyway? Cunning as cunning can be, but stupid. I know them real good. I'm from the same stock. Born here, ten kilometers away. At the age of six I was already working for the kurkuls. My mother was a farm girl, a widow. I was her only son. Hadn't grown as high as the table, but I tended the master's geese. Then I went to school, onct or twict a week. And all the other days and all the mornings and all the evenings I was moiling and toiling with the master's cows, pigs and sheep. And I plowed and cut. . . . And only when I was fourteen did I get my first few coins. Two, then three rubles a month they gave me. Before that everything was 'natural payment': grub, living expenses. Summer in the threshing barn, winter in the hut, keeping one side to the stove, the other to the cowshed. For clothes—the master's worn-out rags. . . . Mama worked herself to death as a farm girl. Caught cold one spring. She had shoes only for going to church, strolling on a holiday. So in the winter she wore bast sandals with leg wrappings; the rest of the time, always barefoot. Through the cut fields, through the forest, through all the sticker bushes . . . Mama used to say her feet were hard as oak, no worse than hoofs. But the sandals got soaked, and Mama caught cold. Got a fever. She was like a drunk or someone with typhus—said all sorts of things, sang songs. Then she died in the cold barn, on the straw. The master didn't even send for the village doctor. Didn't give any horses to go for him. 'It's nothing,' said he. 'She'll pull through. That woman's stronger than them all. But right now we need the horses to pull the manure. What a spring this is—all the snow has washed away in one week. The ground's already soft.' He carted the manure. Mama died. And I had to go bowing and scraping to him, so he'd give me a couple rubles for the priest and the coffin. He didn't give it outright, he took it off our pay. This kurkul had a rule: farm hands are paid only in the autumn, after the harvest. I got so worked up over Mama and this kurkul greediness that I grabbed a wood-chopper and went at 'im. If the lads hadn't caught holt of me, I would've hacked 'im in two. And gone to hard labor without regret. He got real scairt then, gave me all his small change and chased me away. 'Go wherever you wish, just so it's far from the village. Or else I'll tell the village elder and the mounted police that you're a Gaidamak, a rebel, a murderer.' I left and walked through all the Ukraine, from one end to the other. Worked for the kurkuls and worked for the pans. Both in the city and in the mines. Until I got made into a soldier. . . .

"So you see, I've hated the kurkuls since childhood. They're worse than any pan landowners, any Prussian gentry, any officers. They're your worst enemies. You can see the pan's white bones a mile away, you know who he is. And some of 'em are even good people. Who did Lenin come from? And there were others too. But these princes who climbed out of the mud, who curled the bulls' tails themselves—they grew up in manure! They've got no learning and no respect. They're so heartless to the farm hand, to the poor man, that they're worse than all pans. Even if it's their own blood, their own kin, they'll tear out his throat for a kopeck. They begrudge a starving man his last crumb. You could be dying—they wouldn't give you a drop of water. Because they can't make a profit out of someone who's dying."

He spoke without raising his voice. His little, deep-set, slightly slanted eyes had no glint. His big "goat's leg"—a roll-your-own cigar with a turned-down end, made from a quarter page of the district newspaper—let off a steady stream of smoke. Only his broad hands balled into fists and showed white knuckles.

He spoke just as quietly, evenly and distinctly at the meeting held every evening in the "corners." The big village was divided into several sections (or "corners") enclosing fifty to one hundred farms. The village executives and kolkhoz activists invited/induced into the hut all those who had not fulfilled the grain quota, and then they made sure that no one left without special permission.

Usually Vashchenko began. He would tell how much grain the village had given, how much more remained to be given. He would name the malefic holdouts and report in detail who had hidden grain and where it had been found.

"He thought he was so smart. Buried it in a distant field. Only he didn't outsmart the mice. They found his hoard. And the fox found them. And our lads there, who love hunting, noticed that the fox was always in the same place, mousing in the same field. So that's how they found that smart hoard. It was filled up—half with grain and half with mouse shit. Well, farmers, of course the NKVD took 'im. Now he's going where the sun ain't seen all winter. And his family is left without grain. Turns out he's not only an enemy to the empire, but the worst enemy to his own children."

Then the new arrivals had their say: the district grain collectors, Volodya and I, the local Komsomol activists, the kolkhoz crew leaders.

All the speakers sat at a table under the icons. On the white wall you could see big dark frames stuffed with different-sized photographs. Nikolai soldiers in visorless hats, cocked rakishly. Girls in ribbon garlands. Red Army men in Budyenny helmets. Hayseeds standing petrified before the camera in stiff visored hats or sheepskin caps, in embroidered shirts and city jackets. And right alongside them, color pictures from old journals, postcards with mustachioed Zaporozhian Cossacks dancing the hopak.

On the benches and simply on the floor by the stove sat huddled together scowling bearded men, mustachioed men in fur jackets, in gray caftans, young lads dreamily indifferent or sullen with contempt. The womenfolk clustered in separate groups, wearing dark kerchiefs tied up cleverly like cabbages or spread like tents over bright bandannas, and also half-length cloth coats called yupkas, embroidered along the collar and breast with bright strips of sheep fur.

The blue-gray smoke of the makhorka tobacco formed thick clouds in the shifting half light. There was little illumination from the home-made candles, the burning sticks, the occasional kerosene lamp. Villages which did not fill their grain quota were put on the "blacklist" and subjected to a "trade boycott." The shops were closed. It became impossible to obtain either kerosene or nails.

Every time I began to speak I wanted to prove to these people that they were making a serious mistake by hiding the grain, that they were harming the entire country and themselves. I tried to repeat myself as little as possible, though I was called upon to make a speech at several meetings a day. I told them how hard was the life of workers in the cities and at construction sites. They worked two and sometimes three shifts in a row, without a day off. Their wives stood in line because our country was threatened on all sides by mortal enemies. And that meant we had to muster up our strength in order to fulfill the plans on time. And therefore grain was needed. . . .

I told them about the worldwide crisis (we didn't know then that it had already subsided). I spoke of the German fascists, the Japanese troops in Manchuria, the craftiness of the Polish pans. They were all getting ready to pounce on us, they wanted to master, enslave, rob us.

I said only what I definitely believed. And every time I got carried away, screamed, waved my arms. They listened, it seemed to me, attentively. The women stopped whispering. No one left to have a smoke, exchanging curses with the officials at the door who held back those suspected of intending to sneak away. . . . And to be sure, I reviled and cursed the kulaks and their hangers-on every which way. And all those who out of malice or lack of social conscience were concealing grain I threatened with the people's contempt and the proletariat's avenging sword.

Our superior also went to such meetings, several times to the same ones as we. He never sat at the table with us and never made a speech, but found himself a seat somewhere in the back.

Vashchenko time and again would make the appeal:

"Who wants to stand up and state voluntarily that he will do his duty?"

Sometimes a hand was raised. A young lad or a spry peasant woman.

"Tomorrow maybe I can. A relative promised me a bag or two. Then I'll cart it in."

Such conscientious people were resoundingly praised and permitted to go home to sleep. And the next day our news sheet would come out: "Bravo to the honest villager who has taken the path to the fulfillment of his duty before the people. Follow his example!"

But usually after a number of determined appeals, Vashchenko would start calling the holdouts to the table by name.

"Well, citizen Dubyna, Stepan, how many times is it we've sawed the same old saw here with you? Why the tight lip? The Soviet power is asking you—how many times have we already called you up?"

"Don' know. Din' reckon."

"Eh, so you're still cracking wisecracks. Joking jokes. Well, I'm telling you seriously, very seriously, that this is the fourteenth—no, wait—the fifteenth time we have asked you this. When will you fill your quota?"

"Ah han't e'en a pound a grain. . . . Ma kids already eating makukha."

"So you want to play it smart? How much did you plant? Five and a half hectares. It's known for a fact: you had two hectares of wheat and one and a half of spring wheat. And then the peas and barley and oats and sunflowers and corn make up two more hectares. Don't hand me any bull; I know your fields. They didn't lie fallow. So how much did you harvest? How many ricks? Don't play smart, don't hand me any bull, how many? . . . You don't remember anymore? What kind of sorry farmer are you that you don't remember your own harvest? Well, I'm just going to remind you. There wasn't some other sun shining on your field. And the rains didn't pass you by. That means you took in twenty-four metric centners of wheat. Well, say twenty-two. And how much did you hand over? Eight metric centners in all, and that's including the corn and barley! Hardly forty percent of your quota. And your quota is hard and fast. We know who you are, citizen Dubyna, Stepan. The Soviet power knows everything. I didn't come here from far away, from Kharkov, from Moscow. I can still remember how you got married. The same year the lightning burned down the pan's barn. You didn't even have new boots then. Had to borrow them from your older brother Taras for the wedding. We know: you come from poor people. Only you shunned your own class. Now right here in front of everybody I'm going to figure out how much grain you need for your family. We'll allow one pood [thirty-six pounds] a month for each soul. Let's count up all of you, the young and old, and the grandkids on the tit. In all—nine souls. We'll count up the tsarist way—nine poods a month. That's one and a half metric centners. Now, during the winter you would have been hard put to eat up six centners. You have both barley and corn. So where are they, all the other centners? Don't know? If you didn't stash them away, it means you sold them. Broke the law! Didn't fill your grain quota, but speculated instead. You're undermining our plan and secretly passing grain to resellers. You know the penalty for that?"

"Chop off ma head! Ah don' have a pound! No' a bit a grain."

These were exactly the words heard most often in such nightly exchanges: "Chop off my head!" Some uttered them gloomily, furiously, some tearfully, heartrendingly, some fatalistically, wearily, almost indifferently.

"Chop off my head. There's nothing in the hut. Not a pound."

The women often cried, screamed, ranted.

"May I neva see ma kids again! May ma eyes roll out of ma head. I won't budge from the spot if I'm fibbing! May I be struck down with paralysis, may ma arms and legs shrivel up! May I see no good till I die! I'm not fibbing and neva fibbed as long as I lived! I swear it to God, I don' have no grain, not an itsy-bitsy bit! Chop off ma head, right here on the threshold!"

Vashchenko banged his fist heavily on the table, but spoke just as calmly and evenly as before:

"Hold it! Enough! Sit down there and don't get up until you think of something! Until you promise what you're supposed to. Sit there and don't ask to go home; we won't let you."

So it went, night after night. Some meetings continued straight through two or three days and nights. The activists took turns at the table. We relieved one another, went out or slept right there in snatches, leaning back against the wall, in the stifling smoke. Many peasants also slept, sitting and lying on the floor.

Vashchenko was the most indefatigable. Again and again he took charge, interrogated the next holdout to the end. The others sitting around seconded him, nodding or straining not to doze off. They asked the same questions, some more calmly, some in a shout. They repeated the same appeals and threats.

And I, too, confronted more than once some downcast, sleepy peasants, stupefied by the insistent clamor, stuffiness and lack of sleep.

"Do you really fail to understand? Just think about it: the workers are your brothers, your sons, after all. They are waiting for grain, asking for grain, so they can live, so they can work. Come on, think about it."

I pleaded with a woman wiping her cheeks—which were wet with sweat and tears—with the ends of a fringed kerchief tied cabbagewise around her head:

"You yourself are a mother, you love your own children. Now just imagine how the mothers in the cities are crying now. They don't know what to feed their little ones. Have pity on them and on your own. Because the grain you've hidden you have taken away from your own children. And if they punish you, what will happen? Your children will be left hungry, without a mother." . . .

It was the rule not to "detain" peasants in the village soviet cooler longer than a week. After that the detained were either released or dispatched to the district.

The only policeman in the village, Vasil the Copper, a former master sergeant, wide-shouldered, red-snouted, a sot and a letch, would wave his Nagan pistol around. Two guards with sticks would lead out the benumbed, dirty-faced people wrapped up in ragged fur jackets and sackcloth. At the porch they were put in the sled. The drivers were often their relatives, holdouts like themselves.

Vasil took charge with a stentorian voice:

"Sit down, you lousy mob! Sit closer together! So you'll keep warm and we'll keep farther away from your lice!"

And Vashchenko would go into the cooler and tell those remaining:

"Let's go, off to your huts. And make sure you fill your quota! Else it'll be worser next time. It might be cold here, but it's in your own village. But you get sent from the district and you'll be minding polar bears. There it'll be a bit colder."

The highest measure of coercion on the hard-core holdouts was "undisputed confiscation."

A team consisting of several young kolkhozniks and members of the village soviet, led as a rule by Vashchenko himself, would search the hut, barn, yard, and take away all the stores of seed, lead away the cow, the horse, the pigs.

In some cases they would be merciful and leave some potatoes, peas, corn for feeding the family. But the stricter ones would make a clean sweep. They would take not only the food and livestock, but also "all valuables and surpluses of clothing," including icons in their frames, samovars, painted carpets and even metal kitchen utensils which might be silver. And any money they found stashed away. Special instructions ordered the removal of gold, silver and currency. In a few cases they found tsarist gold coins—five-ruble, ten-ruble coins. But usually the hidden treasures turned out to be paper: old bonds with Peter and Catherine, horribly faded Kerensky notes, Hetman and Petlyura "paces," Denikin "bells," and likewise Soviet "lemons" (million rubles) and "lemonards" (billion rubles). They also came across Soviet silver rubles, half rubles and even copper five-kopeck pieces. "Coins minted and legal before the kolkhozes."

Several times Volodya and I were present at such plundering raids. We even took part: we were entrusted to draw up inventories of the confiscated goods.

"The comrade chiefs from Kharkov can check to make sure everything was as it should be. Give the weights. We'll reweigh all your wheat in pounds. We won't take a grain of wheat for ourselves."

The women howled hysterically, clinging to the bags.

"Oy, that's the last thing we have! That was for the children's kasha! Honest to God, the children will starve!"

They wailed, falling on their trunks:

"Oy, that's a keepsake from my dead mama! People, come to my aid, this is my trousseau, never e'en put on!"

I heard the children echoing them with screams, choking, coughing with screams. And I saw the looks of the men: frightened, pleading, hateful, dully impassive, extinguished with despair or flaring up with half-mad, daring ferocity.

"Take it. Take it away. Take everything away. There's still a pot of borscht on the stove. It's plain, got no meat. But still it's got beets, taters 'n' cabbage. And it's salted! Better take it, comrade citizens! Here, hang on, I'll take off my shoes. They're patched and repatched, but maybe they'll have some use for the proletariat, for our dear Soviet power."

It was excruciating to see and hear all this. And even worse to take part in it. No, it was worse to be present without taking part than when you tried to persuade someone, to explain something. . . . And I persuaded myself, explained to myself. I mustn't give in to debilitating pity. We were realizing historical necessity. We were performing our revolutionary duty. We were obtaining grain for the socialist fatherland. For the five-year plan.

Our only worry was to make sure that there were no "gratuitous" cruelties, that no overeager Komsomol activist used his fists on a woman lying across her trunk and saying, "I won't give it up!" And to make sure that the confiscated goods were accurately described, in two copies. Because the condition of such confiscation was this: hand over the grain and we'll return everything we took.

Some sort of rationalistic fanaticism overcame my doubts, my pangs of conscience and simple feelings of sympathy, pity and shame, but this fanaticism was nourished not only by speculative newspaper and literary sources. More convincing than these were people who in my eyes embodied, personified our truth and our justice, people who confirmed with their lives that it was necessary to clench your teeth, clench your heart and carry out everything the party and the Soviet power ordered. . . .

When I recovered from my illness, I rode out to the protectorate villages only on short official trips, for several days, for a week.

A murky gray foggy morning. The snow still on the ground. Whitish spots and strips on the thatched roofs. Snow turned gray, with bluish pockmarks and bruises, lying on both sides of the street, alongside the hedges, alongside the huts. It was mixed with brownish-yellow muddy slush in the middle of the street, frozen in some places, melted in others. The ruts were dark brown, though there were few people riding through the village.

Two sleds plowed ahead, drawn unsteadily by sagging nags with their ribs showing. Three drivers made their way on foot. They had tied something over their caps like hoods—not exactly sackcloth, nor women's kerchiefs. Their grimy reddish caftans were tightly fastened with the typical braided cord. They strode along deliberately, placing their bundled-up feet carefully.

In one sled lay two stretched-out mat sacks, covered over with a bag and bast matting. The other sled was empty.

They passed by the blinded huts, whose windows were stuffed up or boarded over. In others the windows were untouched, but the doors hung open on their hinges. It was obvious no one lived there.

They lumbered up to a hut with a smoking chimney. The chief driver rapped on the window.

"Got 'ny?"

"Nh-uh, thank God, n'n."

At the next hut, the same question. The same answer. And at another.

They came to a little hut with peeling stucco and no smoke from the chimney.

"Priskilla w's alive yestyday."

"Yestyday. But there's n' fire t'day, dad."

The young driver, wrapped up like an old man, goes up to the hut. The horses are led to the hedges. They gnaw some twigs. The lad returns.

"Still breathing. Lying on th' stove. Gave 'er water."

They pass by two more homes.

A large cottage with clean, recently whitewashed walls. And the straw on the roof is bright, barely beginning to darken.

"Got 'ny?"

From the window a faint, tearless woman's voice.

"Ye'. Pop died las' night."

"Bring 'im."

"I don' have the strength. It's jus' me and the kids."

The drivers glance at each other. The three go in. They carry out a skinny body on a sack. The face covered with a towel.

The woman leans on the doorjamb. Her kerchief hangs askew, her gaze is burned out. She slowly crosses herself.

They put the body in the second sled. Cover it up. Another stretched-out mat sack.

Beyond the village, a cemetery. At the edge of the forest, a long ravine, half covered with earth and snow—a mass grave. No cross. . . .

In the spring the village shops and kolkhoz storehouses distributed relief once or twice a week: little bags of flour, peas, groats, preserves, sometimes baked bread.

Women with kerchiefs wrapped over their fur and velvet jackets stood and sat in line. They were still cold, even on sunny days. Edematose faces, dull, apparently unsighted eyes. The men were fewer. Skinny, bent, they looked even more emaciated next to the swollen, wrapped-up women.

The silence of these lines was frightening. Both old and young conversed little, with weak voices. Even the most shrewish squabbled quietly and somehow without passion.

The chairman of the village soviet, very skinny, pale yellow, a mummy come to life, tried to buck up his spirits as he related to the big shots:

"For today we have a reverse improvement. Neither yesterday, nor the day before, was there any fatality. All this week only four were buried, and two of them were from various illnesses. They caught cold, and they were old people besides. But those from insufficiency of nourishment—that's definitely down to a few. And you could even say some of them are doing it from lack of social conscience. Soon as they started getting relief, soon as the first grass came up, the first green shoots, they started eating like mad. But their health is weak. You have to do it a little at a time, go slow. But some of 'em, even though they're full-grown daddies, they're worse than kids. Soon as they saw borscht or kasha, be it a potful or a bucketful, they wouldn't leave off till they had downed the whole thing. And then their guts don't turn over the way they're supposed to. Just like a horse: if it eats too much clover or drinks too much cold water, it gets a belly like a mountain and kicks out its hoofs for good. . . . Or it happens that the old boy got fresh-baked bread for the whole family, a loaf and a half, or twice as much, and while he's carrying it home he gobbled it all up. The kids cry with hunger, and he's clutching his belly, groaning his groan. And then he ain't breathing no more. That's how they're dying—not from hunger, but from stupidity. This is mostly the muzhiks. The women—they're more conscientious, you could say, about nourishment. Or more patient. And of course, they're sorrier for the kids. The women don't die that way."

Not that way, but all the same the women died too. Even in May, when the weeding of the vegetables began. The work best suited for women.

A hot afternoon in May. The women weeders move down the dark furrows between the rows of bright green young leaves. They take heavy steps. Bend over slowly. Even more slowly stand back up. Some can only crawl on all fours. Dark and dingy clumps amid the fresh, gay greenery.

One has stopped. She didn't exactly lie down, didn't exactly sit down. An hour later someone notices.

"Oy, woe, Auntie Odarka, she's up and died! And I thought her's just taking a rest."

But in the spring they were able to bury them in separate graves. And in coffins.

They were dying less and less often. In the second half of May there were no burials for weeks.

A day in June. The district agit brigade drove in to the kolkhoz field camp. Young lads in embroidered shirts, wide blue trousers; young lasses in ribboned garlands, blouses with even more variegated embroidery, multicolored skirts with petticoats, fancy dress boots.

Lunch break. Women behind wooden tables spooning up thick gruel from earthen pots. Cauldrons steaming on the fireplace under a canopy. The rich aroma of cooked millet.

The women are hot: they are wearing white kerchiefs, bright jackets or linen undershirts. And therefore their faces and hands, blackened by the smoke, become even darker. No edematose faces. Almost all the women are thin, dried up, hardened, like old bark on logs.

And they are no longer silent: even though they have worked since sunup—

"checked" the sugar beets, banked the potatoes, burned off the weeds in the cabbage field. The young people laugh to one another, looking at the rigged up visitors.

The agitators lined up in front of a table. The musical director, in a little pea jacket, announced in a rather hoarse tenor:

"In honor of the shock workers of the socialist fields, our choir will perform folk songs."

. . . I gaze at the heavens
Their riddle to ponder . . .

They sang full volume, in one voice. And right away you could tell they were not from the city. They sang not in neatly rounded melodies, as on the stages and music hall platforms, but way up high, in long, drawn-out, sonorous phrases. The way they sing in the villages—at friendly get-togethers, at weddings.

The women leave the pots, put aside the spoons. Stand fixed to the spot. Some lean on each other, press into little clusters.

And suddenly one breaks out crying. And then another. Crying softly. Covering their faces with their bandannas.

The choir falters. The director looks around. Whispers. A slender young woman in a garland strikes up a merry tune:

Oy, beyond the grove,
Grove so green, so green . . .

The choir picks it up quickly, in a slapdash manner:

There plowed a little lassie
With bull so keen, so keen . . .

But the women keep crying. And another. And now another. First those who are older, then the young ones. And now they are crying openly, sobbing out loud.

She plowed, she plowed,
Worked till she could scream,
So she hired a little Cossack
To play on his violin . . .

The singers begin to lose their places. The dressed-up girls in the choir wipe their eyes and wet cheeks. The director looks around anxiously.

"What is this, good women, comrades? What's wrong? Who's making you sad? We're trying to make things more merry."

The women's crying is broken by a shout:

"It's not you, not you! Oy, good people! It's we ourselves. We will never sing again. . . . Oy, how we used to sing! We don't even hear those songs in our sleep anymore. . . . We've buried everything. . . . We ourselves are already dead. . . . Oy, Mamochka my own, where are your bones? Oy, children, my own little dears, my own little darlings, I didn't cry over your little graves. . . . I handed you over to a stranger to bury without any coffins."

Another, and still another, began to scream, to lament.

The singers bunched together. And several of the young women in garlands began crying out loud.

The director rushed to the brigade leader, who was standing to the side with the drivers who had brought the guests. The men were smoking roll-your-owns, looking off to the side. The cook sat down on the ground, covered her face with her bandanna. Her shoulders shook.

The brigade leader, a broad, almost square man with a reddish tan and a rusty stubble of many days growing up to his cheekbones, waved off the director irritably: "Just take it easy, dear comrade. . . . Let the women have their cry. . . . Their tears have welled up. . . . They're crying for everyone now. Don't interfere. They'll cry it out, then things'll be better."

Lev Kopelev, *The Education of a True Believer,* trans. Gary Kern (New York: Harper & Row, 1978), pp. 226–235, 280–281, 283–286.

I. V. Stalin, "New Conditions—New Tasks in Economic Construction," Stalin's Speech to a Conference of Economic Managers
June 23, 1931

This speech, which at first must seem a relatively anodyne presentation to a conference of khoziaistvenniki *(which I have translated here as "economic managers"), in fact was a major policy statement from the very top of the political hierarchy about a profound shift in economic and social policy. The period of the First Five-Year Plan (1928–1931) was also, in Sheila Fitzpatrick's suggestive phrase, a time of "cultural revolution," "a political confrontation of 'proletarian' Communists and the 'bourgeois' intelligentsia, in which the Communists sought to overthrow the cultural authorities inherited from the old regime."[1] Those years were marked by vigorous campaigns to promote workers, from the bench into positions of authority, into educational institutions and new jobs as engineers, and into the party, which became more effectively "proletarian" than it had ever been before. Radical egalitarianism was practiced by workers, and all things "bourgeois" were suspect. Particularly hard hit were the so-called "specialists," engineers and technicians, professionals who brought rare knowledge to their tasks.*

> *[T]he old Russian intelligentsia was buffeted by a military movement in which Communist youth were particularly prominent. Students challenged their professors, forcing them to undergo 'reelection' to their positions. In the professions, established authorities were overthrown by younger, more militant, Marxist groups, and scholars were urged to focus their research on topics that were of practical relevance to society and the economy. Along with a drive to link the whole educational process with the 'real life' of industry, kolkhoz agriculture, and the political campaigns of the day, Communist and working-class students were recruited to higher education in unprecedented numbers.[2]*

By all accounts, Stalin was an enthusiastic supporter of these policies. In February 1931, he proclaimed. "It is time that Bolsheviks became specialists. There are no fortresses which Bol-

---

1. Sheila Fitzpatrick, "Cultural Revolution as Class War," from her edited volume, *Cultural Revolution in Russia, 1928–1931* (Bloomington and London: Indiana University Press, 1978), p. 8.
2. Sheila Fitzpatrick, "Introduction," ibid., p. 1.

sheviks cannot storm."[3] But the failures in industry could not be solved by terrorizing the specialists, and the People's Commissar of Heavy Industry, Sergo Orjonikidze, became a mouthpiece for the complaints of the industrial managers and specialists. The Central Committee met in early June 1931 and sharply shifted industrial policy. Police interference in the economy was curbed.[4] In this speech, Stalin publicly announced that attacks on the old intelligentsia would no longer be tolerated. At the same time, Soviet wage policy gave up its pursuit of equality and promoted instead differentiation between skilled and unskilled labor. While the old specialists, no longer perceived as a threat to the regime, were welcomed back, the party continued to promote the new "red specialists," people from the party and the working class who were now trained to take over many of the technical positions in industry. These people, pushed ahead by the regime (the term for them in Russian is vydvizhentsy*), became its most loyal supporters and the core of the post-Stalin ruling elite in the Soviet Union—the "Brezhnev Generation."[5]*

WAGES

I have just spoken about the organised recruiting of workers for our factories. But recruiting workers is not all that has to be done. In order to ensure manpower for our enterprises we must see to it that the workers remain connected with their factories and make the composition of the labour force in the factories more or less constant. It scarcely needs proof that without a constant labour force who have more or less mastered the technique of production and have become accustomed to the new machinery it will be impossible to make any headway, impossible to fulfil the production plans. Unless this is achieved, we shall have to keep on training new workers and to spend half the time on training them instead of making use of this time for production. But what is actually happening now? Can it be said that the composition of the labour force at our factories is more or less constant? Unfortunately, this cannot be said. On the contrary, we still have a so-called *fluidity* of manpower at our factories. More than that, in a number of factories the fluidity of manpower, far from disappearing, is increasing and becoming more marked. At any rate, you will find few factories where the personnel does not change at least to the extent of 30 to 40 per cent of the total in the course of a half year, or even in one quarter. . . .

To "tolerate" the fluidity of manpower now would mean disintegrating our industry, destroying the possibility of fulfilling production plans and ruining any chance of improving the quality of the output.

What is the cause of the fluidity of manpower?

The cause is the wrong structure of wages, the wrong wage scales, the "Leftist" practice of wage equalisation. In a number of factories wage scales are drawn up in such a way as to practically wipe out the difference between skilled and unskilled labour, between heavy and light work. The consequence of wage equalisation is that the unskilled worker lacks the incentive to become a skilled worker and is thus de-

---

3. *Za industrializatsiiu*, February 5, 1931; Kendall Bailes, *Technology and Society under Lenin and Stalin: Origins of the Soviet Technical Intelligentsia, 1917–1941* (Princeton: Princeton University Press, 1978), p. 148.

4. Bailes, *Technology and Society*, p. 152.

5. Sheila Fitzpatrick, "Stalin and the Making of a New Elite," in her *The Cultural Front: Power and Culture in Revolutionary Russia* (Ithaca, New York: Cornell University Press, 1992), pp. 177–182.

prived of the prospect of advancement; as a result he feels himself a "visitor" in the factory, working only temporarily so as to "earn a little money" and then go off to "try his luck" in some other place. The consequence of wage equalisation is that the skilled worker is obliged to go from factory to factory until he finds one where his skill is properly appreciated.

Hence, the "general" drift from factory to factory; hence, the fluidity of man-power.

In order to put an end to this evil we must abolish wage equalisation and discard the old wage scales. In order to put an end to this evil we must draw up wage scales that will take into account the difference between skilled and unskilled labour, be-tween heavy and light work. We cannot tolerate a situation where a rolling-mill worker in the iron and steel industry earns no more than a sweeper. We cannot tol-erate a situation where a locomotive driver earns only as much as a copying clerk. Marx and Lenin said that the difference between skilled and unskilled labour would exist even under socialism, even after classes had been abolished; that only under communism would this difference disappear and that, consequently, even under so-cialism "wages" must be paid according to work performed and not according to needs. But the equalitarians among our economic executives and trade-union offi-cials do not agree with this and believe that under our Soviet system this difference has already disappeared. Who is right, Marx and Lenin or the equalitarians? It must be supposed that it is Marx and Lenin who are right. But it follows from this that whoever draws up wage scales on the "principle" of wage equalisation, without tak-ing into account the difference between skilled and unskilled labour, breaks with Marxism, breaks with Leninism.

In every branch of industry, in every factory, in every shop, there is a leading group of more or less skilled workers who first and foremost must be retained if we really want to ensure a constant labour force in the factories. These leading groups of workers are the principal link in production. By retaining them in the factory, in the shop, we can retain the whole labour force and radically prevent the fluidity of man-power. But how can we retain them in the factories? We can retain them only by pro-moting them to higher positions, by raising the level of their wages, by introducing a system of wages that will give the worker his due according to qualification.

And what does promoting them to higher positions and raising their wage level mean, what can it lead to as far as unskilled workers are concerned? It means, apart from everything else, opening up prospects for the unskilled worker and giving him an incentive to rise higher, to rise to the category of a skilled worker. You know your-selves that we now need hundreds of thousands and even millions of skilled workers. But in order to build up cadres of skilled workers, we must provide an incentive for the unskilled workers, provide for them a prospect of advancement, of rising to a higher position. And the more boldly we adopt this course the better, for this is the principal means of putting an end to the fluidity of manpower. To economise in this matter would be criminal, it would be going against the interests of our socialist industry.

But that is not all. . . .

We must realise that the conditions of life of the workers have radically changed in our country. The worker today is not what he was previously. The worker today, our Soviet worker, wants to have all his material and cultural needs satisfied: in respect of food, housing conditions, cultural and all sorts of other requirements. He has a right to this, and it is our duty to secure these conditions for him. True, our worker does not suffer from unemployment; he is free from the yoke of capitalism; he is no longer a slave, but the master of his job. But this is not enough. He demands that all his material and cultural requirements be met, and it is our duty to fulfil this demand of his. Do not forget that we ourselves are now making certain demands on the worker— we demand from him labour discipline, intense effort, emulation, shock-brigade work. Do not forget that the vast majority of workers have accepted these demands of the Soviet Government with great enthusiasm and are fulfilling them heroically. Do not be surprised, therefore, if, while fulfilling the demands of the Soviet Government, the workers in their turn demand that the Soviet Government should fulfil its obligations in regard to further improving their material and cultural condition.

Hence, the task is *to put an end to the fluidity of manpower, to do away with wage equalisation, to organise wages properly and to improve the living conditions of the workers.*

. . . we can no longer make do with the very small engineering, technical and administrative forces of industry with which we managed formerly. It follows that the old centres for training engineering and technical forces are no longer adequate, that we must create a whole network of new centres—in the Urals, in Siberia and in Central Asia. We must now ensure the supply of three times, five times the number of engineering, technical and administrative forces for industry if we really intend to carry out the programme of the socialist industrialisation of the U.S.S.R.

But we do not need just *any kind* of administrative, engineering and technical forces. We need *such* administrative, engineering and technical forces as are capable of understanding the policy of the working class of our country, capable of assimilating that policy and ready to carry it out conscientiously. And what does this mean? It means that our country has entered a phase of development in which the *working class must create its own industrial and technical intelligentsia,* one that is capable of upholding the interests of the working class in production as the interests of the ruling class.

No ruling class has managed without its own intelligentsia. There are no grounds for believing that the working class of the U.S.S.R. can manage without its own industrial and technical intelligentsia.

The Soviet Government has taken this circumstance into account and has opened wide the doors of all the higher educational institutions in every branch of national economy to members of the working class and labouring peasantry. You know that tens of thousands of working class and peasant youths are now studying in higher educational institutions. Whereas formerly, under capitalism, the higher educational institutions were the monopoly of the scions of the rich—today, under the Soviet system, the working class and peasant youth predominate there. There is no doubt that our educational institutions will soon be turning out thousands of new technicians and engineers, new leaders for our industries.

But that is only one aspect of the matter. The other aspect is that the industrial and technical intelligentsia of the working class will be recruited not only from those who have had higher education, but also from practical workers in our factories, from the skilled workers, from the working-class cultural forces in the mills, factories and mines. The initiators of emulation, the leaders of shock brigades, those who in practice inspire labour enthusiasm, the organisers of operations in the various sectors of our work of construction—such is the new stratum of the working class that, together with the comrades who have had higher education, must form the core of the intelligentsia of the working class, the core of the administrative staff of our industry. The task is to see that these "rank-and-file" comrades who show initiative are not pushed aside, to promote them boldly to responsible positions, to give them the opportunity to display their organising abilities and the opportunity to supplement their knowledge, to create suitable conditions for their work, not stinting money for this purpose.

Among these comrades there are not a few non-Party people. But that should not prevent us from boldly promoting them to leading positions. On the contrary, it is particularly these non-Party comrades who must receive our special attention, who must be promoted to responsible positions so that they may see for themselves that the Party appreciates capable and gifted workers.

Some comrades think that only Party members may be placed in leading positions in the mills and factories. That is the reason why they not infrequently push aside non-Party comrades who possess ability and initiative and put Party members at the top instead, although they may be less capable and show no initiative. Needless to say, there is nothing more stupid and reactionary than such a "policy," if one may call it such. It scarcely needs proof that such a "policy" can only discredit the Party and repel non-Party workers from it. Our policy does not by any means lie in converting the Party into an exclusive caste. Our policy is to ensure that there is an atmosphere of "mutual confidence," of "mutual control" (*Lenin*), among Party and non-Party workers. One of the reasons why our Party is strong among the working class is that it pursues this policy.

Hence, the task is *to see to it that the working class of the U.S.S.R. has its own industrial and technical intelligentsia.* . . .

SIGNS OF A CHANGE OF ATTITUDE AMONG THE OLD INDUSTRIAL AND TECHNICAL INTELLIGENTSIA

The question of our attitude towards the old, bourgeois industrial and technical intelligentsia is also presented in a new light.

About two years ago the situation was that the more highly skilled section of the old technical intelligentsia was infected with the disease of wrecking. More than that, at that time wrecking was a sort of fashionable activity. Some engaged in wrecking, others shielded the wreckers, others again washed their hands of what was going on and remained neutral, while still others vacillated between the Soviet regime and the wreckers. Of course, the majority of the old technical intelligentsia continued to work more or less loyally. But we are not speaking here of the majority, but of the most highly skilled section of the technical intelligentsia.

What gave rise to the wrecking movement? What fostered it? The intensification of the class struggle in the U.S.S.R., the Soviet Government's policy of offensive against the capitalist elements in town and country, the resistance of these elements to the policy of the Soviet Government, the complexity of the international situation and the difficulties of collective-farm and state-farm development. While the activities of the militant section of the wreckers were augmented by the interventionist intrigues of the imperialists in the capitalist countries and by the grain difficulties within our country, the vacillations of the other section of the old technical intelligentsia towards the active wreckers were encouraged by utterances that were in fashion among the Trotskyist-Menshevik windbags to the effect that "nothing will come of the collective farms and state farms anyway," that "the Soviet power is degenerating anyway and is bound to collapse very soon," that "the Bolsheviks by their policy are themselves facilitating intervention," etc., etc. Besides, if even certain old Bolsheviks among the Right deviators could not resist the "epidemic" and swung away from the Party at that time, it is not surprising that a certain section of the old technical intelligentsia who had never had any inkling of Bolshevism should, with the help of God, also vacillate.

Naturally, under such circumstances, the Soviet Government could pursue only one policy towards the old technical intelligentsia—the policy of *smashing* the active wreckers, *differentiating* the neutrals and *enlisting* those who were loyal.

That was a year or two ago.

Can we say that the situation is exactly the same now? No, we cannot. On the contrary, an entirely new situation has arisen. To begin with, there is the fact that we have routed and are successfully overcoming the capitalist elements in town and country. Of course, this cannot evoke joy among the old intelligentsia. Very probably they still express sympathy for their defeated friends. But sympathisers, still less those who are neutral or vacillating, are not in the habit of voluntarily agreeing to share the fate of their more active friends when the latter have suffered severe and irreparable defeat.

Consequently, the chief weapon in the "arsenal" of the old intelligentsia has gone by the board. As for the bourgeois intelligentsia's hopes of intervention, it must be admitted that, for the time being at least, they have proved to be a house built on sand. Indeed, for six years intervention has been promised, but not a single attempt at intervention has been made. The time has come to recognise that our sapient bourgeois intelligentsia has simply been led by the nose. That is apart from the fact that the conduct of the active wreckers at the famous trial in Moscow was bound to discredit, and actually did discredit, the idea of wrecking.

Naturally, these new circumstances could not but influence our old technical intelligentsia. The new situation was bound to give rise, and did actually give rise, to new sentiments among the old technical intelligentsia. This, in fact, explains why there are definite signs of a change of attitude in favour of the Soviet regime on the part of a certain section of this intelligentsia that formerly sympathised with the wreckers. The fact that not only this stratum of the old intelligentsia, but even definite wreckers of yesterday, a considerable number of them, are beginning in many factories and mills to work hand in hand with the working class—this fact shows without a doubt that a change of attitude among the old technical intelligentsia has already begun. This, of course, does not mean that there are no longer any wreckers in the country. No, it does not mean that. Wreckers exist and will continue to exist as long as we have classes and as long as capitalist encirclement exists. But it does mean that, since a large section of the old technical intelligentsia who formerly sympathised, in one way or another, with the wreckers have now made a turn to the side of the Soviet regime, the active wreckers have become few in number, are isolated and will have to go deeply underground for the time being.

But it follows from this that we must change our policy towards the old technical intelligentsia accordingly. Whereas during the height of the wrecking activities our attitude towards the old technical intelligentsia was mainly expressed by the policy of routing them, now, when these intellectuals are turning to the side of the Soviet regime, our attitude towards them must be expressed mainly by the policy of enlisting them and showing solicitude for them. It would be wrong and undialectical to continue our former policy under the new, changed conditions. It would be stupid and unwise to regard practically every expert and engineer of the old school as an undetected criminal and wrecker. We have always regarded and still regard "expert-baiting" as a harmful and disgraceful phenomenon.

Hence, the task is *to change our attitude towards the engineers and technicians of the old school, to show them greater attention and solicitude, to enlist their cooperation more boldly.* . . .

Pravda, No. 183, July 5, 1931; translated in J. V. Stalin, *Works* (Moscow: Foreign Languages Publishing House, 1955), xiii, pp. 57–62, 68–75.

Decree of the Council of People's Commissars of the USSR and of the Central Committee of the All-Union Communist Party (Bolsheviks), "On the Teaching of Civic History in the Schools of the USSR"
May 16, 1934

In the 1930s, the study of history became a battlefield strewn with the wounded bodies of historians. The past was too politically sensitive a subject to be left out of Stalin's grasp, and in October 1931, he intervened in a discussion about the history of the Bolshevik party. Instead of dealing with the real issues or producing evidence for his point of view, Stalin launched a furious attack on an author who had the temerity to suggest that Lenin had been mistaken in his judgments two decades earlier. Stalin accused the hapless historian of "rotten liberalism" and "a form of bungling that borders on crime, treason to the working class." The stakes had been raised—that historian later was arrested and spent years in a labor camp. No longer would the party tolerate a plurality of views on the party's past. Stalin now elevated himself to be the arbiter of "correct history."

Disciplining historians, however, required more than the threat of state reprisals. There also had to be a clearer view of what kind of history the party wanted. Marxist historiography in the 1920s and through the Cultural Revolution was dominated by the "Old Bolshevik" historian, Mikhail Pokrovskii. Hailed at the time of his death in April 1932 as the "Supreme Commander of the Army of Red Historians," Pokrovskii had fought hard against "bourgeois" historians of the so-called State School, which held that the Russian state had been the fountainhead of history, progress, and reform in Russia. Instead, he proposed a radical class interpretation that emphasized broad social forces rather than personalities or political authorities. Economic forces, reflected in the class struggle, were the principal causes of historical change. Ideas were "nothing more than reflections of the economy in the human brain."

Pokrovskii's history may have had impeccable Marxist credentials, but it hardly satisfied Stalin's requirements for building a great and powerful state. A history without heroes, with no glorious past to which a patriot might turn with pride, with nothing more than a succession of social structures, one more advanced than the former, failed to inspire readers with a deep patriotism. Pokrovskii treated tsarist Russia's expansion as imperial plundering, while Stalin appreciated the tsar's forging of a state that spanned continents. He wanted histories more in line with traditional narratives of nationmaking, although incorporating the liberating role of the working class and its vanguard, the Communist party.

The Council of People's Commissaries of the USSR and the Central Committee of the All-Union Communist Party (Bolsheviki) state that the teaching of history in schools of the USSR is unsatisfactory. The textbooks and oral instruction are of an abstract schematic character. Instead of the teaching of civic history in an animated and entertaining form with an exposition of the most important events and facts in their chronological sequence and with sketches of historical personages, the pupils are given abstract definitions of social and economic formations, which thus replace the consecutive exposition of civic history by abstract sociological schemes.

The decisive condition of a permanent mastery of history is the observance of historical and chronological sequence in the exposition of historical events, with a due emphasis in the memory of the pupils of important historical facts, the names of historical persons and chronological dates. Only such a course of historical teaching can ensure the necessary understanding, fidelity of presentation and a real use of historical material; correct analysis and correct explanation of historical events leading pupils to the Marxist conception of history, are possible only on this basis.

In accordance with this, the Council of People's Commissaries of the USSR and the Central Committee of the All-Union Communist Party (Bolsheviki) decree:—

1. To prepare by June, 1935, the following new historical textbooks: (*a*) history of the ancient world; (*b*) history of the Middle Ages; (*c*) modern history; (*d*) history of the USSR; (*e*) modern history of dependent and colonial countries.

2. To approve the following list of members of groups entrusted with compiling the new historical textbooks: *History of the Ancient World*—Prof. S. I. Kovalev (principal), academician N. M. Nikolsky, A. S. Svanidze and Prof. A. V. Minulin; *History of the Middle Ages*—Prof. E. A. Kosminsky (principal), Prof. A. I. Gukovsky, O. V. Trachtenberg and A. I. Malyshev; *Modern History*—academician N. M. Lukin (principal), Prof. G. S. Friedland, Prof. V. M. Dalin, Prof. G. S. Zaidel and Docent A. V. Efimov; *History of the USSR*—Prof. N. N. Vanag (principal), Prof. B. D. Grekov, Prof. A. M. Pankratova and Prof. S. A. Piontkovsky; *Modern History of Dependent and Colonial Countries*—K. B. Radek (principal), K. Z. Gabidulin, Prof. N. I. Konrad, A. S. Mukhadzhi, M. S. Godes, M. D. Kokin, L. I. Madyar, P. A. Mif and F. A. Rothstein.

3. In order to train qualified specialists in history, to reopen as from 1 September, 1934, faculties of history in the Moscow and Leningrad Universities, with the contingent of students to be admitted in the autumn at 150 for each faculty, and to fix the course of training at five years.

Chairman of the Council of People's Commissaries of the USSR, V. Molotov.
Secretary of the Central Committee of the All-Union Communist Party (Bolsheviki),
J. Stalin.

Izvestiia, no. 113 (5361), May 16, 1934; translation in *The Slavonic Review*, XIII, 37 (July 1934), pp. 204–205.

"For the Fatherland!" Editorial in Pravda

June 9, 1934

The new Soviet patriotism touted by the state received a boost in 1934 when aviators carried out a daring rescue of 104 Arctic explorers and crew stranded in the ice of the Northeast Pas-

sage. At their head was the intrepid Otto Schmidt, a genuine Soviet celebrity and a favorite of Stalin's. The survivors of the Cheliuskin (referred here as "Cheliuskints") were feted throughout the USSR and abroad, and their "epic" became part of a new Soviet mythology linking conquest of forbidding nature with the practical achievements of socialist construction.[1] At the same time, this new patriotism displayed a dark side. As a new supranational community in the Soviet Union was defined, as borders were hardened between who belonged to that community and who should be excluded, harsh punishments were enacted against those whom the state considered to be traitors.

At present the whole Soviet Union, even the remote corners of our unembraceable country, is excited by the news of the arrival of the glorious Cheliuskints, the heroes of the Soviet Union the courageous fliers. Tens of thousands of workers and Kolkhozniks greeted with admiration the great leader of the expedition, Comrade Schmidt.

Why is everybody so excited about the herioc exploits of the Soviet fliers, their life and their struggle on the drifting iceberg?

There is only one answer to this question. A small group of men laboring under unusually difficult conditions, lead by our Party and reared by Stalin, demonstrated unlimited love and devotion to their fatherland. This love for their fatherland, this devotion to the cause of the working class inspired them in their struggle against the elements. Consciousness of the fact that they are children of the Sovietland, of the country of socialism which united them, armed them and made them invincible in the struggle against such enemies as polar icebergs, fog, and blizzards.

Yesterday's issue of *Pravda* published a letter from the seven fliers, the heroes of the Soviet Union, Comrades Sleptsev, Liapidenskii, Doronin, Kamanin, Molokov, Levanevskii, and Vodop'ianov in which they write the following: "The Red fliers know what they fight for—in this is their pledge for victory. At the first call of the Party and the government, our planes are ready to fly at any moment to defend the inviolability of our borders. To defend our fatherland, thousands of mighty planes will fly over the Sovietland. Each plane will perform a great feat and each flier will become a hero."

Each plane will perform a feat and each flier will become a hero! These words express the strong conviction of these best people of our country, who are loved and whose example will be followed by millions of workers, kolkhozniks, engineers, and scientists.

Millions and tens of millions of people greet in the persons of the Cheliuskints, great patriots of our country, for whom honor and glory, might and the well-being of the Soviet Union represent the supreme law in life. Millions and tens of millions of people in the ardent greeting of the Cheliuskints, the heroic fliers, express their own willingness to do anything for the defence of their fatherland and for the honor and glory of the Soviet country.

The country of the October Revolution is endlessly dear to the workers, the kolkhozniks and the Soviet intelligentsia. The working people are bound to their factories, sovkhoze's and kolkhoze's, to their soil and to their culture by the indissoluble links of blood, heroism and love. For proletarians and kolkhozniks, for honest soviet

---

1. See, McCannon, *Red Arctic*, pp. 61–68.

specialists, there is nothing more beautiful and more clear than their own country liberated from the yoke of landowners and capitalists.

The best traditions of the Civil War and of the struggle with the interventionists, when the workers and peasants were armed to defend their right to a new life, are now being multiplied in the progress of techniques and Socialistic culture. That is why the Soviet Union has become an impregnable fortress and is capable of crushing all those who would dare to attempt to violate the sanctity of its boundaries.

For our fatherland! This call fans the flame of heroism, the flame of creative initiative in pursuits and all fields of our rich life. For our fatherland! This call arouses millions of workers and alerts them in the defence of their great country.

The defence of the fatherland is the supreme law of life. And he who raises his hand against his country, he who betrays his country should be destroyed.

Today we publish the decree of the Central Executive Committee of the U. S. S. R. regarding the supplementing of the statutes of the state criminal code with articles on treason. The Soviet country is very dear to the workers and kolkhozniks. They have paid for it dearly in blood and suffering in their struggle with exploiters and interventionists and they will not allow anyone to betray their country and will not allow anyone to bargain with her interests.

For high treason, for acts detrimental to the country's military might, or state independence, or inviolability of her territories, for espionage, for divulging military or state secrets, for deserting to the enemy, or escaping across the border, the Soviet court will punish the guilty by shooting or by confiscating all his property. In the case of a civilian, some leniency will be shown according to circumstances, and for the death penalty will be substituted the confiscation of his property or imprisonment for ten years. For a person in military service, however, for treason there will be only one measure of punishment—execution by shooting with confiscation of all his property. Individual members of his family are also responsible for the acts of traitors. "In the case of the escape or flight across the border of a person in military service, all mature members of his family, if they are implicated in aiding the criminal, or knew of his intentions and did not report them to the authorities the punishment is imprisonment from 5 to 10 years with confiscation of all their property.

The other members of the family of the traitor and all his dependents at the time he committed treason are subject to disfranchisement and exile to some remote region in Siberia for 5 years.

Traitors should be punished unmercifully. On the other hand, if a person in military service was aware of a plot to betray the government or of an act of betrayal and did not report this to the authorities, he is subject to imprisonment for 10 years. One cannot be a neutral observer where the interests of the country of the workers and peasants are concerned. This is a terrible crime; this is complicity in the crime.

This decree of the Central Executive Committee gives the workers of the great Soviet Union a new weapon in their hands in the struggle against the enemies of the proletarian dictatorship. The one hundred and seventy million working people who regard the Soviet land as their own mother who has nursed them to a happy and joyous life will deal with the traitors of their fatherland with all their force.

For the fatherland, for its honor and glory, might and well-being!

"For the Fatherland!" editorial in *Pravda,* June 9, 1934; translation in *The Communist Conspiracy, Part I: Communism Outside the U. S., Section B: the USSR: U. S. House of Representatives Report no. 2241, 84th Congress, 2nd Session* [Washington, Government Printing Office, 1956], pp. 286–288.

====== **Stalin's Letter to Kosior and Chubar in Kharkov** ======
January 2, 1930

The question of Stalin's initiating role in violence against the population is answered in letters like this one to two leading Ukrainian Communists. The targets here, at the height of the Cultural Revolution, were the "bourgeois specialists," in this case medical workers.

Kharkov, to Kosior, Chubar.

When are you going to hold the trial of Erfremov and the others? We here think that you should expose at the trial not only the insurrectionary and terrorist activities of the indicted but the medical tricks that aimed at the murder of important workers. We have no need to hide from the workers the sins of their enemies. Besides that, let so-called "Europe" know that repressions against the counter-revolutionary part of the *spetsy* who have attempted to poison and kill Communist patients are completely "justified" and essentially pale before the criminal activity of these counter-revolutionary bastards. We request that you submit the plan for carrying out the trial to Moscow.

I. Stalin.

2.1.30

RTsKhIDNI, f. 89, op. 48, d. 1, 1. 1; translated by the editor.

====== **Nadezhda Mandelstam, "A May Night,"** ======
(excerpts from *Hope Against Hope: A Memoir*)

Nadezhda Mandelstam, the widow of the great poet Osip Mandelstam (1891–1938), wrote a compelling memoir of her years with her husband. The poet's great misfortune was to have written a bitterly satirical poem about Stalin. Protected for a time by Bukharin, the poet fell victim to the dictator after his protector lost all authority. This excerpt relates the arrest of Mandelstam.

. . . . Whenever she came to see us, [Anna] Akhmatova stayed in our small kitchen. The gas had not yet been installed and I cooked our semblance of a dinner on a kerosene stove in the corridor. In honor of our guest we covered the gas cooker with oilcloth to disguise it as a table. We called the kitchen "the sanctuary" after Narbut had once looked in there to see Akhmatova and said: "What are you doing here, like a pagan idol in a sanctuary? Why don't you go to some meeting or other where you can sit down properly?" Akhmatova and I had now taken refuge there, leaving M. to the mercy of the poetry-loving Brodski. Suddenly, at about one o'clock in the morning, there was a sharp, unbearably explicit knock on the door. "They've come for Osip," I said, and went to open the door.

Some men in civilian overcoats were standing outside—there seemed to be a lot of them. For a split second I had a tiny flicker of hope that this still wasn't it—my eye had not made out the uniforms under the covert-cloth topcoats. In fact, topcoats of this kind were also a sort of uniform—though they were intended as a disguise, like the old pea-green coats of the Czarist okhrana. But this I did not know then. All hope vanished as soon as the uninvited guests stepped inside.

I had expected them to say "How do you do?" or "Is this Mandelstam's apartment?" or something else of the kind that any visitor says in order to be let in by the person who opens the door. But the night visitors of our times do not stand on such ceremony—like secret-police agents the world over, I suppose.

Without a word or a moment's hesitation, but with consummate skill and speed, they came in past me (not pushing, however) and the apartment was suddenly full of people already checking our identity papers, running their hands over our hips with a precise, well-practiced movement, and feeling our pockets to make sure we had no concealed weapons.

M. came out of the large room. "Have you come for me?" he asked. One of the agents, a short man, looked at him with what could have been a faint smile and said: "Your papers." M. took them out of his pocket, and after checking them, the agent handed him a warrant. M. read it and nodded.

In the language of the secret police this was what was known as a "night operation." As I learned later, they all firmly believed that they were always liable to meet with opposition on such occasions, and to keep their spirits up they regaled each other with romantic tales about the dangers involved in these night raids. I myself once heard the daughter of an important Chekist,[1] who had come to prominence in 1937, telling a story about how Isaac Babel had "seriously wounded one of our men" while resisting arrest. She told such stories as an expression of concern for her kindly, loving father whenever he went out on "night operations." He was fond of children and animals—at home he always had the cat on his knees—and he told his daughter never to admit that she had done anything wrong, and always to say "no." This homely man with the cat could never forgive the people he interrogated for admitting everything they were accused of. "Why did they do it?" the daughter asked, echoing her father. "Think of the trouble they made for themselves and for us as well!" By "us," she meant all those who had come at night with warrants, interrogated and passed sentence on the accused, and whiled away their spare time telling stories of the risks they ran. Whenever I hear such tales I think of the tiny hole in the skull of Isaac Babel, a cautious, clever man with a high forehead, who probably never once in his life held a pistol in his hands.

And so they burst into our poor, hushed apartments as though raiding bandits' lairs or secret laboratories in which masked carbonari were making dynamite and preparing armed resistance. They visited us on the night of May 13, 1934. After checking our papers, presenting their warrants and making sure there would be no resistance, they began to search the apartment. Brodski slumped into his chair and sat there motionless, like a huge wooden sculpture of some savage tribe. He puffed and wheezed with an angry, hurt expression on his face. When I chanced at one point to speak to him—asking him, I think, to get some books from the shelves for M. to take with him—he answered rudely: "Let M. get them himself," and again began to wheeze. Toward morning, when we were at last permitted to walk freely around the

---

1. Member of the Cheka, the secret police. At later periods the Cheka was known successively as the OGPU, GPU, NKVD, MVD, MGB, and KGB. In Russia today it is the FSB.

apartment and the tired Chekists no longer even looked searchingly at us as we did so, Brodski suddenly roused himself, held up his hand like a schoolboy and asked permission to go to the toilet. The agent directing the search looked at him with contempt. "You can go home," he said. "What?" Brodski said in astonishment. "Home," the man repeated and turned his back. The secret police despised their civilian helpers. Brodski had no doubt been ordered to sit with us that evening in case we tried to destroy any manuscripts when we heard the knock on the door. . . .

M. often repeated Khlebnikov's lines: "What a great thing is a police station! The place where I have my rendezvous with the State." But Khlebnikov was thinking of something more innocent—just a routine check on the papers of a suspicious vagrant, the almost traditional form of meeting between State and poet. Our rendezvous with the State took place on a different, and much higher, level. Our uninvited guests, in strict accordance with their ritual, had immediately divided their roles between them, without exchanging a word. There were five people altogether—three agents and two witnesses. The two witnesses had flopped down on chairs in the hall and gone to sleep. Three years later, in 1937, they would no doubt have snored from sheer fatigue. Who knows by what charter we are granted the right to be arrested and searched in the presence of members of the public, so that no arrest should take place without due process of law, and it could never be said that anyone had just disappeared at dead of night without benefit of warrant or witnesses? This is the tribute we pay to the legal concepts of a bygone age.

To be present as a witness at arrests had almost become a profession. In every large apartment building the same previously designated pair would regularly be roused from their beds, and in the provinces the same two witnesses would be used for a whole street or district. They led a double life, serving by day as repairmen, janitors or plumbers (is this why our faucets are always dripping?) and by night as "witnesses," prepared if need be to sit up till morning in somebody's apartment. The money to pay them came out of our rent as part of the expense of maintaining the building. At what rate they were paid for their night work I do not know.

The oldest of the three agents got busy on the trunk in which we kept our papers, while the two younger ones carried on the search elsewhere. The clumsiness with which they went about it was very striking. Following their instructions, they looked in all the places cunning people are traditionally supposed to hide their secret documents: they shook out every book, squinting down the spine and cutting open the binding, inspected desks and tables for hidden drawers, and peered into pockets and under beds. A manuscript stuck into a saucepan would never have been found. Best of all would have been to put it on the dining table.

I particularly remember one of them, a young puffy-cheeked man with a smirk. As he went through the books he admired the old bindings and kept telling us we should not smoke so much. Instead, he offered us hard candy from a box which he produced from the pocket of his uniform trousers. I now have a good acquaintance, a writer and official of the Union of Soviet Writers, who collects old books, showing off his finds in the secondhand book stores—first editions of Sasha Chorny and Severianin—and offering me hard candy from a tin box he keeps in the pocket of his smart stovepipe trousers which he has custom-made in a tailor shop exclusive to members of the Union of Writers. In the thirties he had a modest job in the secret police, and then fixed himself up safely as a writer. These two images blur into one:

the elderly writer of the end of the fifties and the young police agent of the middle thirties. It's as though the young man who was so fond of hard candy had changed his profession and come up in the world: now dressed in civilian clothes, he lays down the law on moral problems, as a writer is supposed to, and continues to offer me candy from the same box.

This gesture of offering hard candy was repeated in many other apartments during searches. Was this, too, part of the ritual, like the technique of entering the room, checking identity papers, frisking people for weapons and looking for secret drawers? The procedure was worked out to the last detail and it was all quite different from the hectic manner in which it was done in the first days of the Revolution and during the Civil War. Which was worse I find it difficult to say.

The oldest of the agents, a short, lean and silent man with fair hair, was squatting down to look through the papers in the trunk. He worked slowly, deliberately and thoroughly. They had probably sent us well-qualified people from the section in charge of literature—this was supposedly part of the third department, though my acquaintance in the stovepipe trousers who offers me hard candy swears that the department responsible for people like us is either the second or the fourth. This is only a minor detail, but the preservation of certain administrative distinctions from Czarist days was very much in the spirit of the Stalin era.★

After carefully examining it, he put every piece of paper either on a chair in the growing pile of those to be confiscated, or threw it on the floor. Since one can generally tell from the selection of papers what the nature of the accusation will be, I offered to help the agent read M.'s difficult writing and date the various items; I also tried to rescue what I could—for example, a long poem by Piast that we were keeping, and the drafts of M.'s translations of Petrarch. We all noticed that the agent was interested in the manuscripts of M.'s verse of recent years. He showed M. the draft of "The Wolf" and, frowning, read it out in a low voice from beginning to end. Then he picked up a humorous poem about the manager of an apartment house who had smashed a harmonium that one of the tenants was playing against the rules. "What's this about?" asked the agent with a baffled look, throwing the manuscript on the chair. "What indeed?" said M. "What is it about?"

The whole difference between the periods before and after 1937 could be seen in the nature of the two house searches we went through. In 1938 they wasted no time looking for papers and examining them—indeed, the police agents didn't even seem to know the occupation of the man they had come to arrest. When M. was arrested again in 1938, they simply turned over all the mattresses, swept his papers into a sack, poked around for a while and then disappeared, taking M. with them. The whole operation lasted no more than twenty minutes. But in 1934 they stayed all night until the early hours.

On both occasions, seeing me get M.'s things together, they made the same joking remark (also in accordance with instruction?): "Why so much stuff? What's the point? You don't think he's going to stay with us all that long? They'll just have a chat and let him go." This was the only relic from the era of "high humanism" in the twenties and beginning of the thirties. In the winter of 1937, reading a newspaper attack on Yagoda for allegedly turning the forced-labor camps into rest homes, M. said: "I didn't know we were in the paws of such humanists."

★ Under Nicholas I, the secret police was called "The Third Section."

The egg brought for Akhmatova lay untouched on the table. Everybody—M.'s brother Evgeni, who had recently arrived from Leningrad, was also there—walked around the rooms talking and trying not to pay attention to the people rummaging in our things. Suddenly Akhmatova said that M. should eat something before he left, and she held out the egg to him. M. took it, sat down at the table, put some salt on it and ate it.

The two piles of papers on the chair and on the floor continued to grow. We tried not to walk on them, but our visitors took no such care. I very much regret that among the other papers stolen by Rudakov's widow we have lost some drafts of M.'s early poems—since they were not to be confiscated, they were just thrown on the floor and were marked with excellent impressions of military boots. I valued these pages very much and gave them for safekeeping into hands I thought would be safest of all: those of the young Rudakov, who in his devotion to us spent a year and a half in exile with us in Voronezh, where we shared every scrap of bread with him because he had no way of earning a living there. When he returned to Leningrad he also took with him for safekeeping the papers of Gumilev, which Akhmatova had trustingly delivered to him on a sleigh. Neither she nor I ever saw our papers again. Akhmatova occasionally hears rumors about people buying letters which she knows to have been among them.

"Osip, I envy you," Gumilev used to say to M., "you will die in a garret." Both had written their prophetic lines by this time, but neither wished to believe his own forecast, and they took consolation in the French idea of what happens to ill-starred poets. But a poet, after all, is just a human being like any other, and he is bound to end up in the most ordinary way, in the way most typical for his age and his times, meeting the fate that lies in wait for everyone else. None of the glamour and thrill of a special destiny, but the simple path along which all were "herded in a herd." Death in a garret was not for us.

At the time of the campaign in defense of Sacco and Vanzetti—we were then living in Tsarkoye Selo—M. sent a message to the hierarchy of the Russian Orthodox Church (through a certain churchman) proposing that the Church should also organize a protest against the execution. The answer came back at once: the Church would be willing to speak out in defense of the two men on condition that M. undertook to organize a similar protest if anything similar should happen to Russian priests. M. was quite taken aback and confessed himself defeated. This was one of the first lessons he learned in those days when he was trying to come to terms with the existing state of affairs.

When the morning of the fourteenth came, all the guests, invited and uninvited, went away and I was left alone with Akhmatova in the empty apartment, which bore all the marks of the night's ravages. I think we just sat opposite each other in silence. At any rate we didn't go to bed, and it never occurred to us to make tea. We were waiting for the hour when we could leave the building without attracting attention. Why? Where could we go, or to whom? Life went on. I suppose we looked a little like the "drowned maidens," if I may be forgiven this literary allusion—God knows, at that moment nothing was further from our minds than literature. . . .

We never asked, on hearing about the latest arrest, "What was he arrested for?" but we were exceptional. Most people, crazed by fear, asked this question just to give themselves a little hope: if others were arrested for some reason, then they wouldn't be arrested, because they hadn't done anything wrong. They vied with each other in thinking up ingenious reasons to justify each arrest: "Well, she really is a smuggler, you know," "He really did go rather far," "I myself heard him say . . ." Or: "It was only to be expected—he's a terrible man," "I always thought there was something fishy about him," "He isn't one of us at all." This was enough for anyone to be arrested and destroyed: "not one of us," "talks too much," "a bad character" . . . These were just variations on a theme we had first heard in 1917. Both public opinion and the police kept inventing new and more graphic ones, adding fuel to the fire without which there is no smoke. This was why we had outlawed the question "What was he arrested for?" "*What for?*" Akhmatova would cry indignantly whenever, infected by the prevailing climate, anyone of our circle asked this question. "What do you mean, *what for?* It's time you understood that people are arrested *for nothing!*"

But even so, when M. was taken away, Akhmatova and I could not help asking the forbidden question "What for?" There were any number of possible reasons—by the standards of our laws, of course. It could have been for his verse in general, for what he had written about literature, or, more specifically, for the poem about Stalin. It could have been for slapping Alexei Tolstoi in the face. When this happened, Tolstoi had shouted at the top of his voice, in front of witnesses, that he would make sure M. was never published again, and that he would have him expelled from Moscow. . . . The same day, so we were told, he went to Moscow to complain to the boss of Soviet literature, Maxim Gorki. Before long we heard that Gorki had said—or at least the phrase was firmly attributed to him—"We'll teach him to strike Russian writers." People now tell me just as firmly that Gorki could not have said any such thing, and that he was really quite different from what we imagined him to be at the time. There is a widespread tendency to make Gorki out as a victim of the Stalinist regime, as a champion of free thought and a protector of the intelligentsia. I cannot judge, though I am sure Gorki had major disagreements with his master and was very hard-pressed by him. But from this it does not follow that he would have refused to support Tolstoi against a writer as deeply uncongenial to him as M. As regards Gorki's attitude to freedom of opinion, one only has to read his articles, speeches and books.

All things considered, our main hope was that M.'s arrest was indeed an act of vengeance for the slap in the face given to Alexei Tolstoi. However the charge was formulated, it could lead to nothing worse than banishment—and of this we were not afraid. Expulsion and exile had become a standard feature of our everyday life. In the years of the "breathing-space," before the terror began in earnest, there were always fairly widespread arrests, particularly among the intelligentsia, in the spring (mostly in May) and in the fall. They were meant to distract attention from our perennial economic failures. At that time there were scarcely any cases of people disappearing into thin air: they always wrote from exile, and returned at the end of their sentences—to be deported again. Andrei Bely, when we met him at Koktebel in the summer of 1933, said he could scarcely keep up with the business of sending telegrams and writing letters to all his friends who had just "returned"—there had evidently been a clean sweep of theosophists, who were then released all at the same time in 1933. Similarly, in the spring before M.'s arrest, Piast had returned. After three or five years' absence all such exiles came back and were allowed to settle in small towns beyond a hundred kilometers from Moscow. If it happened to everybody else, why shouldn't it happen

to us? Not long before his arrest, hearing M. talk rather carelessly with some people
we did not know, I said to him: "You'd better watch out—it's almost May!" M. just
waved his hand: "So what? Let them send us away. Others may be frightened, but what
do we care?" And it was true: for some reason we really weren't worried about exile.

But it would be quite another matter if they had found the poem about Stalin.
This was what had been in M.'s mind as he kissed Akhmatova goodbye before they
took him away. We none of us doubted that for verse like this he would pay with his
life. That was why we had watched the Chekists so closely, trying to see what they
were after. The "Wolf" poems were not so bad—they would mean being sent to a
camp, at the worst.

Mandelstam's poem on Stalin *(November 1933)*

We live, deaf to the land beneath us,
Ten steps away no one hears our speeches,

But where there's so much as half a conversation
The Kremlin's mountaineer will get his mention.[1]

His fingers are fat as grubs
And the words, final as lead weights, fall from his lips,

His cockroach whiskers leer
And his boot tops gleam.

Around him a rabble of thin-necked leaders—
fawning half-men for him to play with.

They whinny, purr or whine
As he prates and points a finger,

One by one forging his laws, to be flung
Like horseshoes at the head, the eye or the groin.

And every killing is a treat
For the broad-chested Ossete[2]

How might these potential charges be formulated? It was really all one! It is absurd to apply the standards of Roman law, the Napoleonic Code or any other legal
system, to our times. The secret police always knew exactly what they were doing and
they went about it systematically. Among their many aims were the destruction of
witnesses who might remember certain things, and the creation of the unanimity
needed to prepare the way for the millennium. People were picked up wholesale according to category (and sometimes age group)—churchmen, mystics, idealist
philosophers, humorists, people who talked too much, people who talked too little,
people with their own ideas about law, government and economics; and—once the
concept of "sabotage" had been introduced to explain all failures or blunders—engineers, technicians and agricultural specialists. "Don't wear that hat," M. once said to

---

1. In the first version, which came into the hands of the secret police, these two lines read:
    All we hear is the Kremlin mountaineer,
    The murderer and peasant-slayer.
2. "Ossete." There were persistent stories that Stalin had Ossetian blood. Ossetia is to the north of Georgia in the Caucasus. The people, of Iranian stock, are quite different from the Georgians.

Boris Kuzin, "you mustn't attract attention—or you'll have trouble." And he did have trouble. But fortunately the attitude toward hats changed when it was decreed that Soviet scholars must dress even better than their foppish Western counterparts, and after serving his sentence Boris was appointed to a very good academic post. M.'s remark about the hat may have been a joke, but the nature of the head under it certainly determined its owner's fate.

The members of the exterminating profession had a little saying: "Give us a man, and we'll make a case." We had first heard it in Yalta in 1928 from Furmanov, the brother of the writer. A former official of the Cheka who had switched to film-making, he was still connected with the secret police through his wife, and knew what he was talking about. In the small boardinghouse where we were staying most of the people were TB patients, but Furmanov had come to restore his shattered nerves in the sea air. There was also a good-natured Nepman with a sense of humor who quickly got on friendly terms with Furmanov. Together they invented a game of "interrogation" which was so realistic that it gave them both quite a thrill. Furmanov, to illustrate the saying about it being possible to find a case against any man, "interrogated" the trembling Nepman, who always became entangled in the web of ingenious constructions that could be put on his every single word. At that time relatively few people had experienced at first hand the peculiarities of our legal system. The only ones who had so far really been through the mill were those belonging to the categories mentioned above, as well as people who had had their valuables confiscated, and Nepmen—that is, entrepreneurs who took the New Economic Policy at its face value. That was why nobody, except for M., paid any attention to the cat-and-mouse game being enacted for their own amusement by the former Cheka interrogator and the Nepman. I wouldn't have noticed it either if M. hadn't told me to listen. I believe that M. was always intent on showing me things he wanted me to remember. Furmanov's game gave us a first glimpse of the legal process as it was while the new system was still only taking shape. The new justice was based on the dialectic and the great unchanging principle that "he who is not with us is against us."

Akhmatova, who had carefully watched events from the first, was wiser than I. Sitting together in the ransacked apartment, we went over all the possibilities in our minds and speculated about the future, but we put very little of it into words. "You must keep your strength up," Akhmatova said. By this she meant that I must prepare for a long wait: people were often held for many weeks or months, or even for more than a year, before they were banished or done away with. This was because of the length of time needed to "process" a case. Procedure meant a great deal to our rulers, and the whole farrago of nonsense was always meticulously committed to paper. Did they really think that posterity, going through these records, would believe them just as blindly as their crazed contemporaries? Or perhaps it was just the bureaucratic mind at work, the demon from the ink pot, feeding on legal formalities and consuming tons of paper in the process? If the formalities in question could be called "legal" . . .

For the family of an arrested man the period of waiting was taken up by routine steps (what M. in his "Fourth Prose" calls "imponderable, integral moves") such as obtaining money and standing in line with packages. (From the length of the lines we could see how things stood in our world: in 1934 they were still quite short.) I had to find the strength to tread the path already trodden by other wives. But on that May night I became aware of yet another task, the one for which I have lived ever since. There was nothing I could do to alter M.'s fate, but some of his manuscripts had survived and much more was preserved in my memory. Only I could save it all, and this was why I had to keep up my strength. . . .

Nadezhda Mandelstam, *Hope Against Hope: A Memoir,* trans. Max Hayward (New York: Atheneum, 1970), pp. 4–15.

_____   ## Stalin to All Members of the Central Committee _____
of the All-Russian Communist Party
March 31, 1937

Even the chief policemen were not safe from Stalin's purges. Genrikh Iagoda (1891–1938) was a career Chekist, who had served from 1924 as deputy chairman of the Cheka's successor (OGPU, Unified State Political Administration) and from 1934–1936 as head of the People's Commissariat of Internal Affairs (NKVD). Stalin was dissatisfied with Iagoda's performance at the time of Kirov's assassination and sent his special agent, Nikolai Ezhov, to Leningrad to carry on the investigation. Ezhov supplied Stalin with stories of Trotskyist conspiracies, while Iagoda believed that there was little evidence of danger from Trotsky or his sympathizers. Stalin phoned Iagoda and told him that he would punch him in the face if he did not change his ways. Meanwhile a bureaucratic record, accumulated through forced confessions, linked Zinoviev, Kamenev, Trotsky, and others to Kirov's murder and other imaginary crimes. Iagoda was considered too lenient in the new circumstances. Stalin and Zhdanov, vacationing together in Sochi, sent a telegram to Kaganovich, Molotov, and other members of the Politburo demanding Iagoda's immediate removal and replacement by Ezhov. "Iagoda has definitely proved himself to be incapable of unmasking the Trotskyite-Zinovievite bloc. The OGPU is four years behind in this matter." Demoted to People's Commissar of Communications, Iagoda served a few months before he was arrested, then tried in a great show trial along with Bukharin, and executed in March 1938. Just under two years later, Ezhov was shot without a public trial.

In view of the uncovered anti-state and criminal acts of People's Commissar of Communications Iagoda that were committed during his tenure as People's Commissar of Internal Affairs, and likewise after his transfer to the People's Commissar of Communications, the Politburo of the TsK VKP [Central Committee of the All-Russian Communist Party] considers essential his expulsion from the party and the TsK and his immediate arrest. The Politburo of the TsK VKP informs the members of the TsK VKP that in view of the danger of leaving Iagoda free even for one day, it is necessary to order the immediate arrest of Iagoda. The Politburo of the TsK VKP asks the members of the TsK VKP to sanction the expulsion of Iagoda from the party and the TsK and his arrest.

By assignment of the Politburo of the TsK VKP
Secretary of the TsK VKP   I. Stalin.

18:30
31/III/37

RTsKhIDNI, f. 89, op. 48, d. 2, 1. 1; translated by the editor.

Stalin on the Arrests and Executions of
Tukhachevskii, Iakir, Uborevich, and Others
June 11, 1937

*The purge of the officer corps of the Red Army was one of the gravest wounds that Stalin de-
livered to the security of the Soviet Union. With no warning on June 11, 1937, the Soviet
people learned that eight of their most respected military commanders had been arrested and
charged with treason; within a day the newspapers announced that they had been tried and
executed. Mikhail Tukhachevskii (1893–1937), hero of the civil war and of campaigns in
Poland and the Far East; Iona Iakir (1896–1937), the commander of the Kiev military district and a member of the Central Committee of the party; and Ieronim Uborevich (1896–
1937), who had fought against the Poles and participated in the final assault against the
Whites in Crimea were among the victims. Stalin and Molotov apparently suspected that the
military was plotting against Stalin, and their suspicions were alerted by disinformation fabricated in Europe and passed on by the Germans. By crushing the army, the dictator and his
henchmen eliminated the last force in the country that might have challenged Stalin's rule. Altogether it is estimated that 20,000 officers were arrested, many of them perished, others
wasted away in prison camps not to be released until the war. In this document, Stalin cynically manipulates public opinion by ordering the organization of mass meetings to condemn
the arrested officers to death.*

Absolutely Secret

Encoded

To National Central Committees, Territorial Committees, Regional Committees

In connection with the ongoing trial of spies and wreckers Tukhachevskii Iakir,
Uborevich, and others, the TsK proposes that you organize meetings of workers, and
where possible peasants as well, and also meetings of Red Army units, to pass resolutions on the necessity to carry out the highest measures of repression. The court ought
to be finished this evening. The communique about the sentence will be published
tomorrow, i.e., June 12th.

Secretary of the TsK   Stalin

11/VI/1937
16:50

RTsKhIDNI, f. 89, op. 48, d. 3, l. 1; translated by the editor.

Beria to Stalin on Counter-revolutionary
Organization in Ajaria
July 17, 1937

*Though much of the agenda for the purges was set at the top, in the Kremlin, local officials
showed their zealotry by "discovering" plots and conspiracies in their own regions. Lavrenti
Beria (1899–1953), who had made his early career in the secret police, was handpicked by*

Stalin to head the Georgian Communist party in 1931, against the wishes of many of the Old Bolsheviks who had ruled Georgia for much of the previous decade. From 1932 until its abolition in 1937, Beria also chaired the highest party committee of the Transcaucasian Federation (Armenia, Azerbaijan, and Georgia). He grew close to Stalin, who frequently vacationed in the Caucasus, and flattered him with a long speech, later a book, on Stalin's youthful leadership of the Transcaucasian Bolshevik organizations. A complex and sinister figure, Beria tried for a time to protect his party organization from the demands for blood from the center, but when Moscow warned that Transcaucasian Communists were not adequately self-critical, he carried out wide-ranging purges of party members, intellectuals, and Chekists. The party leaders of the autonomous regions of Ajaria and Abkhazia were liquidated. For his "Bolshevik vigilence," Stalin promoted Beria to head the NKVD after the fall of Ezhov. Paradoxically, this ruthless and unscrupulous man oversaw the police as the purges wound down, the harsh regime in prisons and camps was somewhat ameliorated, and many imprisoned victims were rehabilitated. Shortly after Stalin's death, several of the highest party officials, led by Nikita Khrushchev, who feared that the secret police chief would try to reproduce Stalin's autocratic power, had Beria arrested, secretly tried, and shot.

Ajaria was located on the border of Turkey and was populated by Muslim Georgians. Beria's police fabricated a conspiracy to indict local officials, had them removed, and replaced them with an Ajarian (rather than Georgian) official.

Strictly Secret   Must be returned in 48 hours
No Copying Permitted   (order of the Politburo, from May 5, 1927, no. 100, p. 5)
Sent to Ezhov
                                                  Cipher
From Tbilisi   Sent 16:25   July 17, 1937   Reached the TsK VKP
For deciphering   July 17, 1937 17:35   Vkh.
No. 1286/sh
          Moscow TsK VKP (b) to Comrade *Stalin*.
          A counter-revolutionary organization has been uncovered in Ajaria, connected with Turkish intelligence and aimed at annexing Ajaria to Turkey. The organization recruited adherents and followers in the villages of Ajaria, linking its work with emigrant elements located in Turkey. By the testimonies of almost all those arrested the chairman of the TsIK (Central Executive Committee [of Soviets] of Ajaria, Zekerii Lordkipanidze has been exposed as the leader of this counter-revolutionary organization and [found] to be connected with the Turkish consul in Batumi and [with] Turkish intelligence. I request that you sanction his arrest. At the present time Lordkipanidze is under observation in order to prevent his possible escape across the border. In the next few days I will present an Ajarian candidate for the post of chairman of the TsIK of Ajaria.
                              Secretary of the TsK KP(b) of Georgia
                                                  Beria

[scrawled across the document in pencil:]
                                          Comrade Beria
                    The TsK sanctions the arrest of Lordkipanidze.
                                          St(alin)
18/VII/37

RTsKhIDNI, f. 89, op. 48, d. 5, l. 1; translated by the editor.

Stalin to the Secretaries of Obkoms, Kraikoms, and Central Committees of the National Communist Parties
August 3, 1937

It was not enough to have the police or the political apparatus carry out the purges—for Stalin did not trust his own officers and officials. Ordinary people were mobilized to turn on officialdom to find "wreckers" (vrediteli) and "enemies of the people" (vragi naroda). Though local grievances certainly fed into denunciations and testimony at these local show trials, the initiative from the top played a key role in stimulating and legitimizing the terror in the localities. The trials often followed formulaic scripts, with virtuous peasants pitted against evil bosses. In her fascinating treatment of these trials, Sheila Fitzpatrick concludes:

> *The trials may be seen as a Soviet version of carnival—a people's festival (licensed, admittedly, by the state) where, for a day, the world is turned upside down, revelers celebrate in gaudy costumes, distinctions of rank are forgotten, mockery and humiliation of the proud are permitted. But the point about carnival is that it lasts only for a day or a week. After that, the proprieties and distinctions are restored, perhaps even reaffirmed. Real power relations are untouched. Carnival is not revolution.[1]*

But, as she goes on to note, "carnivals sometimes get out of hand."[2] Though the local trials appear to have been halted by December 1937—the curtain rung down by the stagemasters in Moscow—thousands of people suffered and agriculture itself remained in disarray.

In the last few years in the territories, regions, and republics, the destructive work of enemies of the people has been uncovered in the areas of agriculture, aimed at the undermining of the economy of the collective farms and toward stimulating the collective farmers' dissatisfaction with Soviet power by way of a whole system of insults and mockery against it.

The TsK considers it a major failure of the leadership in the matter of crushing the wreckers in agriculture that the liquidation of wreckers is dealt with only in a secret manner by the organs of the NKVD, but the collective farmers are not mobilized for the struggle with the wrecking and its carriers.

Considering absolutely essential the political mobilization of collective farmers in the work being carried out to destroy the enemies of the people in agriculture, the TsK VKP (b) requires the obkoms, kraikoms, and the central committees of the national Communist parties to organize in each district (*raion*) of each region (*oblast'*) two to three show trials against enemies of the people—against the wreckers in agriculture who have penetrated the district party, soviet, and land organs (workers of the MTS [machine-tractor stations] and district ZO [land departments], chairmen of the RIKs [district executive committees], secretaries of the RK [district committees], etc.), widely publicizing the progress of these trials in the local press. No. 11/s, no. 1178/sh

---

1. Fitzpatrick, *Stalin's Peasants*, p. 311.
2. Ibid.

Secretary of the TsK VKP   Stalin

> 3.VIII.37
> 20:40

RTsKhIDNI, f. 89, op. 48, d. 12, l. 1; translated by the editor.

================= **Iu. L'vova, "Is Pashchitskii Present?"** =================

With Gorbachev's policy of glasnost' in the mid-1980s, revelations about the horrors of Stalinism filled the pages of newspapers and magazines and television screens. Soviet citizens learned, often for the first time, of the extent of the killings and suffering of ordinary people, as well as high officials. In this short memoir, a teacher of Russian language and literature, Iu. L'vova, tells of an instance of great heroism at the height of the purges. She remembers back fifty years how a popular instructor, with unadorned courage, saved a student from arrest, and how she and her fellow students silently conspired to protect each other. Here human decency spontaneously understood that something had gone terribly wrong.

The tragic events connected with arrests and repression in the 1930s disrupted our school life in unexpected ways. Largely disinterested in political events and deeply involved in our student activities—lessons, sports, books, happy parties, and falling in love—we were far removed from serious consideration of the political trials, accounts of which filled the newspapers and the radio, alternating with cheerful songs and statements about the construction of new factories, mines, dams, and cities.

We sought enjoyment from the theater, ski trips, and meetings of a poetry and literature society organized by our favorite teacher, Nikolai Viktorovich. He embodied all our ideas of what it meant to be a truly good person. But one day we learned that to be a good person it was also necessary to be fearless.

Suddenly there was a rumor in the school that a ninth grade student, Igor Magai, whose father had been arrested, had been removed from a chemistry lesson and taken away somewhere, either to a special boarding school, or to prison, or directly to a concentration camp for convicted prisoners.

We were stunned and frightened. Before we could get over this news, we saw the very white face of Shura Pashchitskii in our class. He said that his father had also been arrested the night before.

The father of Shurkina, our Shurka the clever, so promising in mathematics, a harmless bumpkin who endured our mocking in physical education classes as good naturedly as when he dazzled us with original solutions to complex geometry problems.

Shurka, the son of an arrested person! This was how life touched us! An enemy of the people, an enemy of the nation, not somewhere far away, but right here, so close to us. The father of our comrade—that was how close to us.

The physics lesson continued as in a fog. We were nervous, and the teacher was nervous. Shura sat at his desk, sitting strangely upright, as if turned to stone.

Our next lesson was Russian literature. Nikolai Viktorovich began efficiently, almost sternly. Suddenly the door to the classroom was thrown open. With heavy tread, two men in civilian clothes approached the teacher's desk. Military-style boots and blue breeches were visible from under their short dark blue coats. We stood up.

"Is this the eighth grade?" asked one of the men. "Is Pashchitskii present? Come to the front."

"Pashchitskii?" repeated Nikolai Viktorovich. "But he is not here. Children, was Pashchitskii in the first lesson?" Our teacher looked over the entire class with attentive gaze, not omitting Shura.

And we, as if wondering whether Pashchitskii was in the classroom, followed our teacher in looking around and then began to speak at once. "No, he was not here! He was not here!"

"There is nothing to do, Aleksandr Pashchitskii is not here," Nikolai Viktorovich declared firmly, turning to the soldiers.

Frowning, they left the room.

"Sit down, comrades," said our teacher, more thoughtfully and a little more softly than usual, as he returned to the lesson.

Shura sat, without moving, and just stared, stared, and stared, at the face of Nikolai Viktorovich. We also stared, not listening to what he said or understanding what it meant. We stared with all our beings, because for the first time in our lives we were witnesses to human fearlessness.

On the same day Nikolai Viktorovich sent Shura to a distant Siberian village, where he had neither family nor friends . . .

In the same way, Lida Nikulina and Valia Plaskin, whose parents had also been repressed, also were sent to some other place.

None of us even whispered among ourselves about this, even in secret we never told anyone.

We were silent for so long . . .

But even then we had begun to think about a great deal.

By Iu. L'vova, teacher of Russian language and literature, candidate of pedagogical science

---

Iu. L'vova, "Kto zdes'—Pashchitskii?" *Narodnoe obrazovanie*, no. 3 (1990), p. 138; translated by Tom Ewing.

Nikolai Bukharin's Letter to Stalin
December 10, 1937

Nikolai Bukharin (1888–1938) was one of the most popular of the close comrades of Lenin, referred to as "the darling of the party." After his alliance with Stalin fell apart at the end of the 1920s, he continued to serve the party as editor of Izvestiia, *the government newspaper, and as one of the principal authors of the Soviet constitution of 1936. But many of his young followers, among them V. V. Kuzmin and A. Iu. Aikhenvald, met occasionally and discussed possible opposition to Stalin. Several "Young Bukharinists" were involved in discussions around the "Riutin Platform" of 1932, which called for the removal of Stalin, and at one meeting Kuzmin impetuously declared that he wanted to kill Stalin. The Bukharinists were arrested, and the confessions beaten out of them, as well as statements at the show trial of Kamenev and Zinoviev (August 1936), implicated Bukharin. One of those who accused Bukharin falsely was the Old Bolshevik Karl Radek (1885–1939), who later was killed in prison. Bukharin was arrested in February 1937, and hauled before a lengthy plenary meet-*

ing of the Central Committee, where Ezhov and others hurled accusations at him. Lan-
guishing in prison before his public trial in March 1938, Bukharin managed to write an au-
tobiographical novel, some philosophical essays, and a series of letters, several of them to his for-
mer comrade, Stalin, whom he addressed by his revolutionary nom-de-guerre, Koba.

Very Secret

Personal

I ask that no other read this without the permission of I.V. Stalin.

To I.V. Stalin

7 pages + 7 pages of memorandum

Iosif Vissarionovich!

I write this letter, as perhaps my last letter before my death. For this reason I ask
that you allow me to write it, despite the fact that I have been arrested, free of any
kind of official style; moreover, that I write it only to you, and the actual fact of its
existence or non-existence lies completely in your hands. . . .

At this moment the last page of my drama and, perhaps, my physical life, is turning over. I thought with torment, should I take up the pen or not,—I am shaking now
from anxiety and a thousand emotions and can hardly control myself. But precisely
because we are talking about the end, I want to *ask forgiveness* from you first, while it
is still not too late, and while my hand still writes, and while my eyes are still open,
and while my brain functions in some way or other.

So that there will be no misunderstandings, I say to you at the very beginning
that *for the peace* (of society) (1) do not intend to take anything back from what I have
written down: (2) in *this* sense (and in connection with this) I do not intend to ask
anything from you nor do I wish to plead that this matter be removed from the rails
down which it rolls. But it is for your *personal* information that I write. I cannot leave
life without having written to you these last lines, for I am possessed by torments
about which you ought to know.

1. Standing on the edge of an abyss, from which there is no return. I give you
my honest, last words before death, that I am not guilty of those crimes that I affirmed
at the investigation.

2. Turning over everything in my mind, as well as I am able, I can, in addition to
what I said at the plenum [of the Central Committee, February 23–March 5, 1937],
only note:

> a. that one time I heard from someone about the cry, it seems, of
> Kuz'min, but never gave it any kind of serious significance. This never en-
> tered my head;
>
> b. that *I knew nothing* about the conference (or about the Riutin plat-
> form), except when quickly on the street *post factum* Aikhenval'd told me
> ("the guys have met, made a report"),—or something to that effect, and I hid
> this at that time, feeling pity for "the guys".
>
> c. that in 1932 I acted as a double-dealer in relation to my "pupils," sin-
> cerely thinking that I *would bring them wholly to the party,* or otherwise I would

break with them. That is all. With this I cleanse my conscience *down to the smallest trifles. Everything else either never happened or, if it happened, then I had no knowledge of it.*

Thus, I spoke at the plenum *the exact truth,* only they did not believe me. And here I speak the absolute truth: All these last years I honestly and sincerely carried out the party line and learned wisely to value and love you.

3. I had no other "way out" except to confirm the accusations and testimonies of others and to develop them: or otherwise it would have come out that I had "not disarmed."

4. Except for the external moments and arguments of (3) (above), I, thinking about what is happening, constructed approximately such a conception:

There is some kind of *big and bold political idea* of a general purge (a) in connection with preparation for war, (b) in connection with the transition to democracy. This purge captures (a) the guilty, (b) the suspicious, and (c) the potentially suspicious. Here there is no way to do this without me. They render some harmless like this, others in another way, and still others in still another way. The moment of insurance is when people are forced to speak one about the other and *forever* sow doubt about one another (I judge by my own example: how I resented Radek, who spoke such nonsense about me! But then he himself went down this same path . . .). Thus, the leadership creates a *full guarantee.*

For God's sake, do not think that I am secretly reproaching you, even in my ruminations with myself. I have grown so much from children's swaddling clothes that I understand that *big* plans, *big* ideas, and *big* interests trump everything, and it would be petty to put forth a question about one's own person on the same level as the *world-historical* tasks that lie first and foremost on your shoulders.

And here is my *main* torture, and the principal tormenting paradox.

5. *If* I were absolutely sure that you thought in this way, then my soul would be much more peaceful. Well, what do you think! It must be so, that's the way it has to be. But believe me, my heart bleeds with hot streams of blood, when I think that you might *believe* in my crimes and that *you yourself* think in the depth of soul that I am actually guilty of all these horrors. *Then* what will come of this? That I *myself* caused a number of people to be destroyed (beginning with myself!), that is, I wittingly did *evil! Then* nothing justifies this. And everything is confused in my head, and one wants to scream and beat one's head against the wall: I became the cause of the destruction of others, you see. What can be done? What is to be done?

6. I do not bear an iota of malice and am not embittered. I am not a Christian. But I have my own eccentricities. I consider that I must atone for those years when I actually carried on a struggle [against you]. And if you want to know, more than anything, one fact depresses me, one that you, perhaps, have forgotten: once, probably in the summer of 1928, I was with you, and you said to me: You know why I am friends with you? You are incapable of intrigue, you see. I said: Yes. And at that very moment I ran to Kamenev ("the first meeting"). Believe it or not, but it is *this* fact that stands in my head like some original sin for an Israelite. God, how I was a child and a fool! And now I will pay for this with my honor and entire life. *For this,* forgive me, Koba. I write and I cry. I no longer need anything; you yourself know that it's more likely

that I make my situation worse by allowing myself to write this. But I am unable, I cannot simply keep silent, not having said to you my last "forgive me." Here is why I have no malice toward anyone, beginning with the leadership and ending with the interrogators, and I ask you for forgiveness, although I have already been punished so that everything has grown dim, and darkness has fallen on my eyes.

7. When I had hallucinations, I saw you a few times and Nadezhda Sergeevna.[1] She approached me and said: "What have they done to you?, N. I.? I will tell Iosif so that he takes you under his protection." This was so real that I nearly jumped and wrote to you, so that . . . you would protect me. This is how delirium carried away reality. I know that N. S. would never believe that I had malevolent intentions toward you, and it was not for nothing that my unconscious, unhappy ego called forth this delirium. And with you I talked for hours . . . Lord, if only there was such an instrument that you could see my whole unglued and tormented soul! If you could only see how I am tied to you inside, completely different from those Stetskiis and Tals.[2] Well, this is "psychology"—forgive me. Now there is no angel who pushed aside the sword of Abraham, and fatal fates are realized!

8. Allow me, finally, to go on to my last few requests:

> a. It is a thousand times easier for me *to die* than to live through the forthcoming trial: I simply do not know how I will control myself—you know my nature: I am no enemy either of the party or the USSR, and I will do everything in my power, but my powers in such a circumstance are minimal, and painful feelings rise in my soul; forgetting shame and pride, I would plead on my knees that this would not be so. But this, apparently, is no longer possible; I would ask, if it were possible, to allow me to die before the trial, even though I know how severely you look upon such questions.

> b. If[3] a death sentence awaits me, then I ask you beforehand, invoking all that is dear to you, not to shoot me but allow me to drink poison in my cell (give me morphine so that I fall asleep and never wake up). This point is extremely important to me. I do not know which words I ought to find to plead for this, for mercy: this will not hinder anything politically, will it, and no one will know about this. But allow me to live out the last seconds as I want. Have pity! You, knowing me well, will understand. I sometimes look death in the face with clear eyes, precisely because I know that I am capable of courageous acts. But sometimes I am so upset that nothing is left in me. Thus, if death is the judgment, I ask for a cup of morphine. I *pray* for this
> . . .

> c. I ask to be allowed to say farewell to my wife and son. It isn't necessary to do so with my daughter: I grieve for her, this will be much too heavy

---

1. Nadezhda Sergeevna Allilueva (1901–1932) was Stalin's second wife, the daughter of an Old Bolshevik, and a dedicated Communist who had once worked in Lenin's office. She became disillusioned and depressed in the early 1930s and, after a quarrel with Stalin at a Kremlin celebration of the October Revolution, she shot herself.

2. A. I. Stetskii was the director of a department of the Central Committee and the principal editor of the journal *Bolshevik*. B. M. Tal was the director of the department of the press and publishing of the Central Committee and had worked with Bukharin at *Izvestiia*.

3. After "if," the words "you have already decided" were written, then crossed out by Bukharin.

for her, as for Nadia and her father. But Aniuta[4] is young, she is suffering, and I want to say some last words to her. I request a meeting with her *before* the trial. The arguments go like this: if those in my home see what I *acknowledge* [to be true at the trial], they could commit suicide from the unexpected. I must somehow prepare them for this. It seems to me that this is in the interest of the case and in its official interpretation.

d. If my life is to be preserved, contrary to expectations, then I would ask (although it is still necessary that I speak with my wife):

*. either send me to America for *n* years. The arguments for this: I would carry on a campaign for the trials, would carry on a struggle to the death against Trotskii, would win over large parts of the wavering intellectuals, would be in fact an Anti-Trotskii, and would carry on this matter with all my might and enthusiasm; you can send with me qualified Chekists and, for an additional guarantee, keep my wife here for half a year until I show how I slug the face of Trotskii and company.

**. But if there is an atom of doubt, then send me, let's say, for twenty-five years to Pechora or Kolyma [in Siberia], to a camp. I would establish there: a university, a regional museum, a technical station, and so forth, institutions, picture galleries, an ethnographic museum, a zoological and botanical museum, a camp journal, a newspaper.

In a word, I would carry out pioneering, trail-blazing cultural work, settling there with my family until the end of my days.

In any case, I declare that I would work wherever required like a powerful machine.

However, to speak the truth, I do not place any hope in this, since the very fact of changing the directives of the February plenum speaks for itself (and I see that the case proceeds to a trial, if not today, then tomorrow).

Here, it seems, are all my last requests (also: *philosophical work,* having been left to me, I have done much that is useful).

Iosif Vissarionovich! In me you have lost one of your most able generals, someone really dedicated to you. But this is already in the past. I remember what Marx wrote about Barclay de Tolly [a general at the time of the Napoleonic wars], who had been found guilty of treason, that Alexander I lost such an aide to no purpose. It is bitter to think about all this. But I am preparing emotionally to leave the vale of life, and there is nothing in my attitude toward all of you and toward the party and toward the whole cause, nothing except a great, boundless love. I do everything that is humanly possible and impossible. I have written about everything to you. I have placed all the dots on the "i." I did this *beforehand* because I have no way of knowing in what state I will be tomorrow or the day after, etc.

Maybe I will have, like a neurasthenic, universal apathy so that I will be unable to move a finger.

But now, with my head aching and tears in my eyes, I write everything. My inner conscience is clear before you now, Koba. I ask of you a final forgiveness (a sincere

---

4. Aniuta, Anna Larina (1914–1996), the daughter of a prominent revolutionary, Iurii Larin, was Bukharin's second wife. She was arrested in June 1937, and remained in prison and camps until 1959. See her memoirs, *This I Cannot Forget: The Memoirs of Nikolai Bukharin's Widow,* trans. Gary Kern (New York: W. W. Norton, 1993).

one and no other). For this I mentally embrace you. Goodbye forever, and think kindly of your unfortunate one.

N. Bukharin

10.XII.37

[a seven-page appendix followed, but it was not deposited in the archive with the letter]

Arkhiv Prezidenta Rossiiskoi Federatsii, f. 3, op. 24, d. 427, 1. 13–18; published in *Istochnik,* no. 0 (1993), pp. 23–25; translation by the editor.

Mekhlis to Stalin and Ezhov
October 28, 1938

A long-time party and state apparatchik, L. Z. Mekhlis (1889–1953) reported back to Stalin on his fact-finding trip out to the Soviet East. The NKVD (People's Commissariat of Internal Affairs) had set quotas for the number of people to be arrested and executed, but local officials had exceeded these limits and requested that the limits be raised. By 1938, the terror was expanding beyond the Moscow's expectations, and the central authorities had to restrain the very local enthusiasts whose activities they had set in motion. That year Ezhov, the head of the NKVD, was arrested, and Lavrenti Beria, Stalin's Georgian client, was brought to Moscow to succeed him and wind down the terror.

I left Chita for Moscow on October 27. In Ulan-Ude [capital of the Buriat-Mongol Autonomous Soviet Socialist Republic] the secretary of the regional committee of the VKP (b), Ignat'ev, and the NKVD of the Buriat-Mongol ASSR, Tkachev, came to see me. In our conversation they communicated that they had exceeded the NKVD's limit of 447, and in the prisons were over 2,000 arrested people, whose terms of detention have long since run out, among them participants in the bourgeois nationalist and Lamist [Buddhist] counter-revolution—kulaks, lamas, and White Guardists. The cases have all been worked up long ago; the prisons are filled to overflowing, but the troiki[1] have not received permission to examine them. I am reporting that they request that the limit be raised to 2,500 persons.

28/X No. 672 Mekhlis.

RTsKhIDNI, f. 89, op. 73; d. 157, 1. 1; translation by the editor

1. Set up during the collectivization campaigns, troiki were three-person panels that principally judged political cases. They became the major tribunal during the purges. Peter Solomon writes that "the failure of judges on the special collegia and the military tribunals to cooperate fully with the security police may have led Stalin to rely on alternatives to the courts for the conduct of the Terror. Most of the 800,000 political persecutions of 1937 were handled not by courts but directly by the NKVD, including its revived *troiki.*" [Peter H. Solomon, Jr., *Soviet Criminal Justice Under Stalin* (Cambridge: Cambridge University Press, 1996), p. 234] In December 1937, Andrei Vyshinskii, the Procurator-General of the USSR, ordered that local procurators use the troiki instead of regular courts "'when the evidence of guilt will not allow its use at trial,' that is when it featured denunciations or false testimony from provocateurs." [Ibid., p. 238] The troiki were abolished by the decree of November 17, 1938 that essentially brought the Great Terror to an end.

Conference of Musicians at the Central Committee of the All-Union Communist Party, Moscow

January 1948

At the end of the war, many Soviet people experienced a sense that life would not only ease but become freer. The self-reliance of citizens and soldiers during the fighting in the early years of the war, when the party, state, and police structures could not enforce old rules and behaviors, has been characterized—by Soviet historian Mikhail Gefter—as an "elemental de-Stalinization".[1] It was accompanied by the development of a patriotic civic spirit—a "civic romanticism" in the words of Elena Zubkova. The sense of freedom combined with a feeling of personal responsibility for the fate of the fatherland. Stalin was revered, the embodiment of the hard-won victory, and both memories and practices of surveillance remained embedded in social life, tempering social relations with suspicion and wariness.[2] Everyone had suffered great personal losses, and the profound experience of war and victory linked people in a shared community of aspirations, attitudes, and material problems.[3]

The hopes that there would be a turn toward freedom was bitterly dashed, and in the postwar years the party reinforced the cultural conformity and political restrictions, though without the fury of the Great Purges, that had become the Stalinist norm of Soviet life. Andrei Zhdanov (1896–1948), a powerful Central Committee secretary, gave his name to the policy of cultural repression of the late 1940s—the Zhdanovshchina—which began with the Central Committee's decree of August 14, 1946 attacking the literary journals Zvezda *and* Leningrad. *In his speeches in September, Zhdanov denounced the poet Anna Akhmatova (1889–1966) as a "half-nun, half-harlot" and the satirical writer Mikhail Zoshchenko (1895–1958) for his cheap "heehawing" at Soviet life. In turn, philosophers and cinematographers felt the wrath of the party, and with the conference of musicians in January 1948, the axe fell on composers, most notably the internationally recognized Aram Khachaturian, Sergei Prokoviev, and Dmitrii Shostakovich. It began, however, with a glancing but devastating blow at a minor Georgian opera composer, Vano Muradeli (1908–1970), whose opera,* The Great Friendship, *had displeased the members of the Politburo at its premiere.*

FIRST DAY

A. A. ZHDANOV (Introductory speech): Comrades, the Central Committee decided to ask you to come here for the following reason. Recently the C.C. attended a pre-view of Muradeli's new opera, *The Great Fellowship.* You realise how keenly interested we all were in this new Soviet opera, after an interval of more than ten years, in the course of which no new Soviet operas were produced. . . . Unfortunately our hopes were not fulfilled. The new opera did not prove a success. Why was that? . . .

First, as regards its music. It has not a single melody one can remember. The music

---

1. M. Gefter, "'Stalin umer vchera . . .'," in Iu. Afanas'eva (ed.), *Inogo ne dano: Sud'by perestroiki; Vgliady-vasias' v proshloe; Vozvrashchenie k budushchemu,* p. 305

2. See the chapter "The Social Psychology of the War," in Elena Zubkova, *Russia After the War: Hopes, Illusions, and Disappointments, 1945–1957,* trans. Hugh Ragsdale (Armonk, N.Y.: M. E. Sharpe, 1998), pp. 11–19.

3. Ibid., p. 23.

does not "register" with the listener. The rather large and rather well-qualified audience of about 500 people did not react to a single passage in the opera. . . . What one found depressing was the lack of harmony, the inadequacy of the musical expression of the characters' emotions, the frequent cacophonous passages. . . . The orchestra is poorly used. Most of the time, only a few instruments are used, and then, at unexpected moments, the whole orchestra suddenly starts blaring. During lyrical moments the drums suddenly burst in, while the heroic moments are accompanied by sad, elegiac music. And, although the opera deals with the peoples of the Northern Caucasus, during an interesting period of their history, when the Soviet régime was being established there, the music is alien to the folk music of these peoples. . . .

We must try to assess the reasons for the failure of Muradeli's opera. If opera is the highest synthesis of musical art . . . then the failure of this opera is, after all these years, a great failure for Soviet music. It is not an isolated case, and we should like to establish the reasons for this failure.

The Art Committee and its leader, Comrade Khrapchenko, are chiefly responsible for this. He advertised Muradeli's opera all over the place. Without having been seen and approved by authoritative public opinion, it was put on the stage in Leningrad, Riga, Sverdlovsk, and other cities. At the Bolshoi Theatre in Moscow alone 600,000 roubles were spent on the production. . . . The fact that this is the second conference to be held by the C.C. in connection with Muradeli's opera—the first one was, chiefly, with the responsible leaders of the Bolshoi Theatre—shows how much importance we attach to this. . . .

I should like to recall some of the things Muradeli said during the first meeting. Muradeli claimed that he understood what the Party and the People expected from Soviet opera, that he also understood what melody meant, that he had a good knowledge of classical music, but that from his schooldays at the Conservatory he was taught not to respect the classical heritage. The students of the Conservatory were being constantly told, he said, that this heritage was out of date, that it was important to write new music, which was unlike classical music, and that it was important to be original and not to stick to "traditionalism". Also, that it was important to model oneself, not on the classics, but on the leading composers of to-day.

After he had graduated, he said, the same ideas continued to be drummed into him by our critics. . . . He also talked about the wrong education of our musical cadres, and about the way in which any opposition to modern canons was denounced as conservative and retrograde. . . .

Let us try to find out whether all this is true or not. . . . This is all the more important as the faults of Muradeli's opera are very like the mistakes which, in the past, marked Comrade Shostakovich's opera, *Lady Macbeth of Mtsensk.* I would not recall this, but for the great similarity of the two cases.

You will probably remember the article *Pravda* published in January, 1936, and called "Chaos instead of Music". This article was published on the instructions of the C.C. and expressed the C.C.'s view of Shostakovich's opera.

I shall recall a few passages from that article:

> From the first moment, the listener is knocked over the head by an incoherent, chaotic stream of sounds. The fragments of melody, the germs of musical phrases, are drowned in a sea of bangs, rasping noises and squeals. It is difficult to follow

such "music"; it is impossible to remember it. . . . And so it goes on, almost right through the opera. Screams take the place of singing. If, once in a while, the composer find his way on to a clear melodic path, he immediately dashes aside into the jungle of musical chaos, which sometimes becomes pure cacophony. . . . Expressiveness . . . is replaced by a crazy rhythm. Musical noise is supposed to express passion.

All this is not because the composer lacks talent, or because he is incapable of expressing "strong and simple emotions" in musical terms. This music is just deliberately written "inside-out", so that nothing should remind the listener of classical opera . . . and simple, easily-accessible musical speech. . . . The danger of this "Leftism" in music comes from the same source as all "Leftist" ugliness in painting, poetry, education, and science. Petit-bourgeois "innovation" produces divorce from real art, from real literature. . . . The author of *Lady Macbeth of Mtsensk* had to borrow from jazz its nervous, cramp-like fitful music, to give "passion" to his heroes. . . .

While there is all this talk of "Socialist realism", Shostakovich, in reality, produces nothing but the crudest naturalism. . . . It is crude, primitive and vulgar. . . . The music puffs and pants, groans and chokes, in order to present the love scenes in the most naturalistic way. . . . Such music can only appeal to esthetes and formalists who have lost all healthy tastes. . . .

That is what *Pravda* wrote twelve years ago. It is a long time ago; yet it is clear that the tendency that was then condemned is now alive, and not only alive, but setting the tone to Soviet music. The appearance of an opera of the same kind is a sign of atavism, and shows that what was condemned by the Party in 1936 is still going strong.

If the C.C. is wrong in defending realism and our classical heritage, then please say so openly. But let us not have any smuggling of anti-People formalism under the banner of devotion to our classics and loyalty to the ideas of Socialist realism. It is not quite honest. . . . It would be dangerous and disastrous if this renunciation of the heritage of the past, this degraded music, were to masquerade as Soviet music. We must call a spade a spade.

We do not know yet to what extent the well-known decisions of the C.C. on ideological questions have met with a response amongst our musicians, though we have been told of an alleged breaking of the ice in this direction. . . . Did you have any serious discussions on the subject? . . . We have serious doubts about it. Nor is it clear what form of government exists in the Composers' Union, and in its Organisational Committee. Is this form of government democratic, based on creative discussion, criticism, and self-criticism, or is it all more like an oligarchy, where everything is run by a small group of composers, and their faithful retainers—I mean music critics of the boot-licking kind—and where everything is millions of miles away from real creative discussion, criticism, and self-criticism?

Allow me now to open this conference . . . and to request the comrades to state their views on the questions I have raised and on other questions which, though not touched upon in my introductory remarks, have a bearing on the development of Soviet musical art.

SHAPORIN (Composer): I have listened to Andrei Alexandrovich [Zhdanov] with deep emotion and attention, and heartily support his analysis, and those very sharp conclusions which he drew. . . . Although Soviet music has many indis-

putable achievements to its credit, indeed some great achievements, we cannot be satisfied with the result. We still owe the Soviet people much, because we have not yet
reached that high ideological and artistic level the Party and Government require
from us.

Andrei Alexandrovich asked us whether the Composers' Union had dealt with the
C.C.'s ideological instructions of last year; and, if so, whether only formally. The answer is "Yes and No". We had a plenary meeting, where a long discussion took place;
but if in literature and painting the question of æsthetics has been more or less clari-
fied, in music we are still rather in the dark. Therefore, our plenary meeting really
came to no conclusions on many questions of musical æsthetics. Andrei Alexandrovich stressed that the departure from tradition had a pernicious effect on new output. Yet a large part of our critics identify tradition with epigonism.

ZHDANOV: What do you musicians mean by that term?

SHAPORIN: Epigonism is the worst form of traditionalism. Tradition means the
development of your predecessors' ideas.

ZHDANOV: I should like to get this straight. Who is branded an epigone? Is it
those who learn from the classics?

SHAPORIN: Epigonism is not, in fact, a development of ideas but . . .

A VOICE: Blind imitation!

SHAPORIN: Yes. Opera is, of course, the most democratic musical form. And we
are faced with the problem of creating a Soviet style of opera. In the last thirty years
300 operas have been written.

A VOICE: Six hundred.

SHAPORIN: Yet the number of operas that have established themselves is very
small indeed. Many operas never got as far as the stage. The fault there lies with the
theatres. . . . Tchaikovsky, however, succeeded only with *his* fifth opera—*Eugene
Onègin.* Rimsky-Korsakov succeeded only with *his* third opera—*The Snow Maiden.* I
consider that any opera of some artistic value should be put on the stage. Of course,
the Bolshoi Theatre should put on only the best, those that have passed the test elsewhere. . . .

MURADELI (Composer): Comrades, in the name of the Party and the Government, Andrei Alexandrovich rightly and sharply criticised my opera, *The Great Fellowship.* He first spoke about it some days ago. I thought it over very deeply. As a man,
as a citizen, and as a Communist, I must say that I agree with what he said. . . .

In 1936, while I was a student in Moscow, a Russian colleague at a meeting said:
"What I like about you young composers from the Caucasus and Central Asia is that
you do not lose touch with the creative genius of your own people." In reply to this
I said: "Thank you . . . but why is it that here, at the Moscow Conservatory, you
don't teach young Russians to follow in the traditions of the Russian people and of
the Russian classics? Why do young Russian composers follow in the footsteps of the
West?" . . .

Why do we find the same tendencies still alive to-day, both in Moscow and
Leningrad? All this is not due to accidental mistakes, but is directed by certain
forces. . . . Who could maintain that in thirty years we have produced a single So-

viet opera, accepted and beloved by the People? Or a symphonic work which has become a real favourite with the People? Some songs, it is true, have been picked up by the people, but not any of our major works. . . .

My First Symphony was well received both in Moscow and Leningrad. It was dedicated to the memory of Kirov, and was played at a Leningrad factory, where the workers liked it. But the critics thought it unoriginal and written in a poor musical language. To whom was I to listen? Naturally, I had to listen to the press. . . .

[When the young composer Weinberg came to Russia from the West,] we saw he was a gifted young man. But instead of saying to him "You have come to our Soviet country, and you must learn to reflect its life and its ideas", our critics went all crazy about him. They proclaimed him to be an outstanding composer, a star which would rise after Shaporin, Shostakovich, Miaskovsky, and so on.

Comrades, why are we ruining this young man? Is it not kowtowing to the West when we get excited about this music, and forget about the work done by our classics, and also by our own Soviet composers?

Once I also asked a comrade why, in Prague, they were playing Shostakovich's Eighth Symphony. I am sorry to put the question so brutally. . . .

ZHDANOV: That is what we have come here for.

MURADELI: I consider Shostakovich one of the most remarkable of modern composers—a man whom I love and respect, who is my friend, and whose friend I shall be for ever, if he does not become too offended by what I say to-day. . . . It was decided to stage an outstanding Soviet composer in Prague. It was quite right to send him there. But the Eighth Symphony had received very contradictory reviews in the Soviet press; it had not been awarded a Stalin Prize; the musical public were sharply divided; there was no unanimity as there is in the case of our best compositions. There was such unanimity in the case of the Fifth, but not in the case of the Eighth Symphony. Why did they not perform the Fifth instead? The reply I got from one comrade was: "But the Eighth is just the sort of music they like in the West."

So are we to export to the West the things that *they* like? Why should we not rather send to the West those works which clearly reflect our democratic Soviet features: Must we be guided by Western tastes? I consider that the policy of V.O.K.S. in distributing our musical works abroad should be re-examined. As a Soviet musician, I don't want our faults to be treated as achievements abroad. Let them "pan" our achievements if they like; it is our achievements which we ought to show them.

Comrades, to-day is a very important day in my life. . . . I must say that it hurts me very much to have made such a grave error. I worked sincerely; I wanted to do my best for the Thirtieth Anniversary of the Revolution, and I wanted to live so that I should not be ashamed on by deathbed. . . . I assure Andrei Alexandrovich, the C.C., and all my friends that I shall try to understand my mistakes, and shall try to do what the C.C. requires of us. . . .

SHOSTAKOVICH (Composer, and member of the Organisational Committee of Composers' Union): At this meeting many interesting ideas have been expressed; they will be fruitful in our reflections about the state of things in the world of music, which we all love. I cannot express my thoughts very well or in detail, but I should like to say just a few things. Shaporin said that, if Muradeli had gone to him for advice, the latter's opera would have been better. This remark caused some commotion here. . . . I don't suppose he meant this literally. What I think he meant to say was that we lack a creative atmosphere; composers write their works in a cell, as it were, without consulting anyone. What we need is creative friendship and not just "palliness" and mutual admiration.

Our musical criticism has not a good record. I do not mean critics only, I also mean the composers themselves. The composer must also be a critic. We must criticise each other. The composer, as one of the leaders of the musical world, must not be offended when he is criticised; he should be offended when there is no criticism, because criticism helps him to progress, while lack of criticism does not help, but, on the contrary, acts as an impediment.

The composer must be much more critical towards his own work. And maybe, before publishing his work, or having it performed, he should think hard whether he has the right to do so, and whether he has really worked on it to the best of his ability. Also, there is too much specialisation; some write symphonies, others write chamber music only, or opera only, or songs only. It seems to me that the composer should strive not to limit himself to one *genre*. It is said that Dzerjinsky has not progressed since his *Quiet Don*. Is it not because he wrote six operas since then? Should he not try his hand at something else, and not concentrate on opera only?

Comrade Zakharov was not very thoughtful in what he said about Soviet symphonies. It seems to me that he was not right, because there are, in our symphonic music, many great achievements; though there are also faults and failures, which should be pointed out.

The C.C. has brought us together so as to see what kind of air we breathe, and what our ailments are; to listen and talk to us; and to find out what should be done to raise our musical movement to a higher level, so that there should be no unsuccessful works, and so that Soviet music should advance. The C.C. has often pointed out what the "negative" sides were in the field of art and criticism; and now, I suppose, instructions will be given. From to-day's conference, and from the coming Congress, we should derive many highly valuable decisions, so that our art should advance, and should be even better than it is now. . . .

ZHDANOV: Comrades, allow me first of all to make a few remarks on the character of our discussion. The general conclusion was that the state of affairs was not up to much. Some complained of organisational flaws, of the lack of criticism and self-criticism; others added their dissatisfaction with the ideological tendencies of Soviet music. Finally, some tried to tone down the acuteness of the situation, and to pass over in silence some of the more unpleasant questions. . . . But, on the whole, the general conclusion was that things were not too good.

I don't want to bring any dissonnance or "atonalism" into this conclusion—even though atonalism is fashionable nowadays. (*Laughter.*) Things are really bad. It seems to me that the position is worse than was made out here. I am not denying that Soviet music has achievements to its credit. But if we think of what we might have, and what we actually have, or if we compare this with what we have in other ideological fields, then the achievements must be called very insignificant.

Take literature; our monthly magazines have so many new works in their files which are fit to be published, that it is becoming quite a problem. There is also progress in the cinema and the theatre. But music is lagging behind. There is an abnormal state of affairs at the Composers' Union and on the Art Committee. The latter was not sufficiently criticised here. Yet this Committee has played a most unenviable part. Posing as a champion of realism in music it was, in fact, exalting the formalists. Being, moreover, ignorant and incompetent, the Committee allowed itself to be led on by the formalists. The fate of Russian music was in the hands of a "monastery"—a closed circle of composers, and of a bunch of toadying critics. . . .

But the organisational question is not the main thing, though it is important. The fundamental question is the *direction* of Soviet music. This question got rather blurred in the course of the present discussion. We must get this question of *direction* straight. Are there two different directions in music? That at least became clear from this discussion, even though some comrades tended to play on muted strings, as it were. Yet it is clear that there is a striving to replace one direction by another direction. . . .

True, some comrades argued that there was really no need to make a fuss; there had been no qualitative departure from the traditions of Russian classical music, and what we were seeing now was merely a further development of that classical heritage—in Soviet conditions. . . . They preferred to talk about certain excesses of "technicism", occasional lapses into naturalism, etc. All this is camouflage.

It is not a question of occasional lapses, nor a question of the leaking roof of the Conservatory. This can be easily repaired. But there is a great big hole in the very foundations of Soviet music. The truth of the matter is that the leading part in the creative work of the Composers' Union is played by Comrades Shostakovich, Prokofiev, Miaskovsky, Khachaturian, Popov, Kabalevsky, Shebalin. Any more names that you would suggest?

A VOICE: Shaporin.

ZHDANOV: Let us consider these comrades as the principal figures of the formalist school. This school is radically wrong.

The comrades I have named have also complained that there was no proper atmosphere of criticism at the Composers' Union, that they were praised too much, that they hadn't enough contact with the other composers and with musical audiences. But, surely, they might have said so, without waiting for the performance of a not altogether successful opera. The truth of the matter is that they did not mind the past state of affairs. (*Cheers.*) . . . The time has come when a radical change must take place. Insofar as any sharp criticism of these would, as Comrade Zakharov said, have led to an explosion, it is apparent that the intolerable hothouse atmosphere . . . was, in fact, created by themselves, even though they now claim not to have liked it.

I do not think, however, that they clung to these posts simply for the fun of it, like Vladimir Galitzky, in *Prince Igor,* who wanted "to be prince for a bit". (*Laughter.*) Was not this domination exercised in order to give Soviet music a certain direction? . . . One couldn't accuse say, Comrade Shostakovich of mere administrative ambition.

There is a struggle going on, though an outwardly hidden struggle, between two schools. One stands for the healthy and progressive things in Soviet music, for the full recognition of the importance of our classical heritage, particularly of the Russian classical school; it stands for a high ideological level, truthfulness and realism, and a deep organic connection with the People and its folk songs—the whole combined with a high degree of craftsmanship. The other school stands for formalism, which is alien to Soviet art, a renunciation of classical traditions. It is anti-People, and prefers to cater for the individualistic experiences of a clique of æsthetes.

Here the beautiful, natural, human intonations of music are replaced by false, vulgar, and sometimes pathological music. Yet the revisionist activities of this school are camouflaged; for these people continue to pay lip service to Socialist realism. Such "smuggling" tactics are not new, of course. . . .

Yet any listeners will realise the vast difference between classical Russian music and the false, ugly, idealistic music of the formalists. . . .

Some Soviet composers also have a theory that they will be appreciated in fifty or a hundred years. That is a terrible attitude. It means a complete divorce from the People.

If I am a writer, painter, or Party worker and do not expect my contemporaries to understand me, then what am I living for? It leads to an emptiness of the soul. Yet such "consolations" are now being whispered to the composers by some critics of the boot-licking variety. . . . Think how different this attitude is from Glinka's or Mussorgsky's. . . . They also loved folk themes. Think of Glinka *Kamarinskaya* or Mussorgsky's *Gopak*. One must conclude that landowner Glinka, government official Serov, and nobleman Stasov were more democratically minded than you. . . .

Stasov advocated the close study of Western classical music, but was against any slavish kow-towing to the West. . . . But in modern Western music there is really nothing whatsoever worth imitating. It is in a state of decay. . . .

It is not true that the "over-emphasis" on the national features of Soviet music would detract from its internationalism. International music is born from national music; otherwise you become a mere cosmopolitan without any background. . . .

In renouncing the traditions of our classical heritage, our formalist composers have also departed from the sound principle of programme music. Nowadays it has become a trade to "interpret" the meaning of music, after it has already been composed. Yet classical Russian music was, in the main, programme music.

We also often hear the word "innovation". Is not this word used as propaganda of bad music? Stunts and contortions are not innovation. Innovation does not always mean progress, yet young composers are taught that if they don't "innovate" they will not be original. Moreover, the "innovation" of our formalists isn't particularly new in any case; for it smells of the decadent, bourgeois music of Europe and America. Now here's a case when one can talk of epigones!

Let me take a parallel. Painting is your sister—one of the Muses. Bourgeois influences were strong in our painting at one time, and these influences used to fly all kinds of "Left" banners—futurism, cubism, modernism: "Down with the rotten academic canons!" they cried. It was a madhouse. They would paint a girl with one hand and forty legs. . . . It all ended in a complete fiasco. The Party fully restored the importance of our classical heritage in painting as represented by such masters as Repin, Surikov, Vasnetsov, Brullov, Vereshchagin. . . . Were we not right to rescue this treasure house of classical painting, and to smash the liquidators of painting? The C.C. was then accused of being "traditionalist" and "conservative". What rubbish!

There is a lot of talk of "epigonism", and the young are taught not to learn from the classics. "The classics must be surpassed", they are told. That's all very well, but it is first necessary to reach their level. And to be quite candid, and to express what the

Soviet listener really feels, it would not be bad at all if we produced a lot of works which *were* like the work of the Russian classics, in content, form, elegance, and musical beauty. If that is "epigonism", well, then, "Good for the epigones", I say.

Now for naturalism. . . . Is it not true that drums and timpani must be an exception and not the rule in music? I must say that a whole number of works by modern composers are so full of naturalistic noises that they remind one—if you'll forgive this inelegant simile—of either a dentist's drill or a musical gas-wagon, the kind the Gestapo used. One just can't take it. (*Laughter and cheers.*)

Here we go beyond all the limits of the rational, beyond the limits of normal human emotions, beyond the limits of human reason. There are, it is true, some modern theories, according to which the pathological state of a man is a higher form of existence; and, in their delirium, schizophrenics and paranoics, we are told, can rise to spiritual heights inaccessible to normal people. This is typical of the rotting state of bourgeois culture. But let us leave these theories to lunatics and let us demand from our composers that they produce normal human music. . . .

It may surprise you that the C.C. of the Bolsheviks should demand beautiful and elegant music from you. But we mean it; we want music that would satisfy the æsthetic requirements and the artistic tastes of the Soviet People, and these requirements have grown immensely. Our People appreciate musical works if they deeply reflect the spirit of our time, and if they are accessible to the wide masses.

A work of genius in music is not a work that can be appreciated by only a handful of æsthetic gourmets. Genius is measured by its depth, and content, by its craftsmanship, by the number of people it can inspire, and by the number of people who accept it. Not all that is accessible is a work of genius, but a real work of genius is one that is accessible, and the more accessible it is to the widest masses of the people, the more clearly is it a work of genius. . . .

As you sow, so you shall reap. Composers who hope that future generations will appreciate them, or that the people will "grow up in time to appreciate them", are utterly wrong. Music that is unintelligible to the people is unwanted by the people. Let them not blame the people. Let them blame themselves. They've got to understand why they do not appeal to the people, and they've got to reform their work accordingly. Isn't that the right way? (*A voice:* "That's right!")

As for craftsmanship, you need not be afraid of following in the footsteps of the classics. To write as they did requires more craftsmanship than the formalist music that is now written. . . . It is also true that the people want different *genres*. Why are you so unlike the great masters of the past? You are much meaner to the people than they were. They wrote vocal music, choral music, orchestral music, and did not confine themselves to any one style. . . . Also, you neglect the requirements and the possibilities of the human voice in writing allegedly vocal music. And then there are stunts like using the piano as a percussion instrument. All this is not good enough.

All these are violations of the rules of musical art, of the functions of musical sound. They are also violations of the rules of normal human hearing. Unfortunately our science has not taught us enough about the physiological effect of music on the human organism. Yet one must bear in mind that bad, disharmonious music undoubtedly has a bad effect on the psycho-physiological activity of man. . . .

Comrades, if you value the high name of Soviet composer, you must prove that you can serve your people better than you have done so far. A severe test lies before you.

Formalist tendencies were severely condemned by the Party twelve years ago. In the interval the Government has conferred Stalin Prizes on many of you, including those who sinned in the formalist direction. . . . We did not consider, when we gave you these prizes, that your works were free of faults, but we were patient, and waited for you to choose the right road. Now, clearly, the Party has had to intervene. If you continue on the road you have hitherto followed, our music will win no glory. . . .

You must develop and perfect Soviet music. You must also be vigilant in not allowing any decadent Western influences to penetrate into it. The U.S.S.R. is not only the champion of humanity's musical culture, it is in all other respects the bulwark of human civilisation against bourgeois cultural decay. Your political hearing must become as acute as your musical hearing. . . . We fervently hope that like the "Mighty Kuchka" i.e. Rimsky-Korsakov, Borodin, Mussorgsky, Balakirev, and Cui, who amazed the world in the past, so we shall have an even mightier "Soviet Kuchka" now. We want you to be the mighty cohort of Soviet Music, of whom the Soviet people would be proud. (*Long, stormy applause.*)

Alexander Werth, *Musical Uproar in Moscow* (London: Turnstile Press, 1949), pp. 47–53, 61–62, 78–83.

Report to Stalin on Dissolving Jewish Writers' Associations; and Stalin's Decision
February 8, 1949

Before the Second World War, the Soviet Union enjoyed a reputation as a country hospitable to Jews and, at least in official rhetoric, dedicated to fighting anti-Semitism. The government passed laws, and Stalin spoke publicly, against anti-Semitic acts and expression. In the late 1930s, massive demonstrations were held protesting Hitler's policies against the Jews. During the war, the Jewish Anti-Fascist Committee was formed, headed by the star of the Yiddish theater, Shlomo Mikhoels, and in 1948, the USSR became the second country in the world to recognize the new state of Israel. But popular anti-Semitism continued to fester, and Stalin himself held strong prejudices about Jews. The outpouring of public affection for the first Israeli ambassador to Moscow, Golda Meir, appalled the Soviet leadership, and official policy turned swiftly against Jews in 1948. Mikhoels was mysteriously killed, most probably by the secret police; Jewish theaters and publications were closed down; and prominent Jews were accused of nationalism or Zionist conspiracy in a massive campaign against "cosmopolitanism." Many of the leaders of the Jewish Anti-Fascist Committee were tried and shot in 1952, a month before the Soviet public learned of the infamous "Doctors' Plot." The police arrested the doctors who had treated the most important political figures in the country, many of whom were Jewish, claiming that they had caused the death of Zhdanov and were attempting to poison other Soviet leaders. Stalin's personal physician was arrested; the doctors were tortured to obtain confessions; and only Stalin's death saved most of them from execution.

To Comrade J. V. STALIN

The general secretary of the USSR Union of Soviet Writers, Comrade Fadeev, raised the question of dissolving the associations of Jewish writers in Moscow, Kiev, and Minsk and also of closing the literary-artistic Yiddish-language miscellanies *Heymland* (Moscow) and *Der Shtern* (Kiev).

The Moscow Association of Jewish Writers has 45 writers, the one in Kiev has 26 writers, and the one in Minsk has six writers. The basic organizational principle of these associations—that of national homogeneity—seems to be mistaken. Other literary associations, created on the basis of such a principle, do not exist within the Union of Soviet Writers. Recently, the activity of these associations has acquired a nationalistic character. These associations have no prospects for increasing their cadre of writers. The works of the writers, the participants in these associations, do not have a wide readership.

The literary-artistic Yiddish-language miscellanies are a place for works of a nationalistic character.

The writer Stel'makh, in her story "Grandfather's Children," tells about the old Jewish intelligentsia, evacuated to the Urals from Ukraine. The writer gives significantly more attention to illustrating remnants of the past in the consciousness and behavior of the people described than to the sprouting of something new in their experiences and deeds. Traits of provincial narrow-mindedness stand out sharply in the story. The writer Der Nister, in his sketch "With the Immigrants to Birobidzhan," develops Zionist ideas; he talks about Birobidzhan: "Let the house of Israel be built anew"; and further: "How good that in the USSR there have already appeared small, daring Davids, who must even more actively be armed with the pride and worthiness of David, with love for his people . . . in order that no Goliaths frighten them anymore." At the basis of the stories printed in the publications *Heymland* and *Der Shtern* lies the mistaken idea that the task of Jewish literature consists of describing only Jews; these materials are mainly devoted to Jewish activists: Hero of Socialist Labor Baranbaum, engineer Dymshits, woman pilot Gel'man, the boxer Mekhanik, the director Rakhlin.

Nationalist tendencies also are manifested in poetic works printed in the publications *Heymland* and *Der Shtern*. In the verses of Markish, "The Caucasus," the joyful radiance of Caucasian nature is contrasted with the bitter experiences of the author: "At the foot of a mountain, in stony torpidness, I, brought there by my grief, had to sit in mourning for that which had been destroyed, obliterated in the suffering of millennia." In the verses of Gofshtein, "Golden Autumn," the author delights in the "dear square inscriptions at the railway station" (that is, signs in the Jewish language). In the poem of Vloshstein, "Letter to a Friend Abroad," the prophet Ezekial appears as the bearer of comfort for the Jewish population terrorized by the fascists and is the conveyer of a new life; the author writes, "I hear this voice and am comforted deep in my soul." The poet Velednitskii in the poem "By Mount Ararat," declares that this mountain is dear to him because it is mentioned in the Bible.

The publication of the miscellanies *Heymland* and *Der Shtern* is unprofitable.

The Central Committee of the Communist Party (of Bolsheviks) of Ukraine [*TSK KP(b)U*] (Comrade Khrushchev) agrees with the proposal to dissolve the Association of Jewish Writers in Kiev and to close the miscellany *Der Shtern*.

The Secretary of the Central Committee of the Communist Party (of Bolsheviks) of Belorussia [*TSK KP(b)B*], Comrade Gusarov, supports the proposal to dissolve the Association of Jewish Writers in Minsk.

It seems expedient to support the proposal of the USSR Union of Soviet Writers (Comrade Fadeev), of the *TSK KP(b)U* and the *TSK KP(b)B* to dissolve the associations of Jewish writers in Moscow, Kiev, and Minsk and also to close the publications *Heymland* and *Der Shtern*.

Decision by the Central Committee, February 8, 1949.

Statute, no. 415, para. 5s, session XVIII. *STRICTLY SECRET*

All-Union Communist Party (Bolshevik). [*VKP(b)*] CENTRAL COMMITTEE [*TSK*]

P 67/109	To Comrades	Malenkov, Shepilov; Fadeev,
February 1949		Khrushchev; the Organizational
		Bureau—everyone; Central Committee
		of the Communist Party (Bolshevik)
		of Belorussia-"a"

Excerpt from the minutes of meeting 67 of the Politburo of the *TSK VKP(b)*

Decision of February 8, 1949

109. *Concerning the dissolution of organizations of Jewish writers and the suppression of Yiddish-language literary miscellanies*

(Statute of February 2, 1949, order no. 415, para. 5-s)

To accept the proposal of the board of the Union of Soviet Writers of the USSR (Comrade Fadeev) to:

a) dissolve organizations of Jewish writers in Moscow, Kiev and Minsk;

b) suppress the Yiddish-language literary miscellanies *Heimland* (Moscow) and *Der Stern* (Kiev).

Secretary of the Central Committee
J. Stalin

[Stamp at bottom of document:] All-Union Communist Party (Bolshevik)

RTSKhIDNI, fond 17, op. 118, d. 305, ll. 20–22; translated in Diane P. Koenker and Ronald D. Bochman (eds.), *Revelations from the Russian Archives: Documents in English Translation* (Washington, D.C.: Library of Congress, 1997), pp. 222–223.

═══════════ **Nikita Khrushchev's Apology to Stalin** ═══════════
March 6, 1951

Even the most powerful men in the Soviet Union were completely at the mercy of Stalin, and they knew it. As the dictator's health declined, his arbitrariness and suspicions grew. In his turn, Nikita Khrushchev (1894–1971) fell victim to Stalin's steely gaze when he proposed consolidating collective farms and creating "agricultural cities." When Stalin disapproved, Khrushchev immediately wrote an obsequious letter of self-criticism asking, in effect, for a chance to redeem himself. Khrushchev survived and went on the following year to praise Stalin effusively at the Nineteenth Party Congress for his last major publication, Economic Problems of Socialism in the USSR. *Most observers at the time would have thought that Khrushchev was the least likely of the Soviet leaders to succeed Stalin, and yet with his populist talents and shrewd political maneuverings he outplayed his rivals, and five years after this apology he delivered the coup de grace to the cult of Stalin in his famous "Secret Speech."*

Dear Comrade Stalin

You completely correctly pointed out the mistakes I made in the article "On the Building and Improvement of Collective Farms," published on March 4 of this year.

After your corrections I tried to think deeply about these questions. Having thought things through, I understood that my entire publication was basically incorrect. Having published an incorrect statement, I have committed a grave error and thus have done great harm to the party. I would not have caused such harm to the party if I had consulted with the Central Committee. I did not do this, although it was possible to exchange opinions in the Central Committee. This I also consider my serious mistake.

Deeply suffering from the error I committed, I think how best to correct it. I decided to ask you to allow me to correct this mistake. I am prepared to appear in the press and criticize my article published on March 4, to tear to pieces its mistaken propositions. If this is permitted to me, I will try to think through these questions carefully and to prepare an article with a critique of my errors. I request that the article be looked over in the Central Committee before publication.

I ask you, Comrade Stalin, to help me correct the grave mistakes that I committed and by doing so to reduce the harm, as far as this is possible, that I caused the party by my incorrect actions.

N. Khrushchev

March 6, 1951

[handwritten note at the top of the page: ". . . Archive of the TsK," St[alin]"]

RTsKhIDNI, f. 89, op. 57, d. 10, 1. 1; translation by the editor.

CHAPTER FIVE

DANGERS AND OPPORTUNITIES: THE COMINTERN, WORLD WAR, AND COLD WAR

THE LUKEWARM WAR

Despite all its original revolutionary ambitions, the Soviet Union in the interwar period (1918–1939) was an isolated and weak state. The Left in the Communist party, and in the international Communist movement, constantly raised the red banner of revolution, but the Soviet People's Commissariat of Foreign Affairs just as consistently practiced a foreign policy based on peaceful coexistence with the imperialist countries. Communists had few successes before the Second World War; not a single country outside the USSR, with the exception of the Soviet satellite, Mongolia, came under Communist rule. For the first few years of Soviet power, the Communists expected that their example of revolution would inspire workers in Europe and anti-imperialists in the Middle and Far East to overthrow the "bourgeois" governments that had led their nations into the world war. The Communist International (Comintern) was founded in 1919 as a radical alternative to the old Socialist International, which was considered reformist rather than revolutionary. The Communists were ready to employ violence and terror to establish a new form of proletarian democracy, while the Social Democrats defended a gradualist, democratic, and nonviolent road to socialism. But by the early 1920s the tide of revolution receded; the capitalist powers restored their hegemony over Europe; and new states with parliamentary systems were created in East Central Europe. At the same time, the fear of communism and revolution encouraged an ominous new danger from the radical Right. First in Italy, then in several small states in Eastern Europe, and finally in Germany and Spain, varieties of fascism presented militant challenges to Soviet communism.

When the Great Powers redrew the map of Europe at Versailles in 1919, a series of new states—Finland, the Baltic republics, Poland, Czechoslovakia, Hungary, Austria, and Yugoslavia—stood between the Soviet Union and the rest of Europe. This "Cordon Sanitaire" kept the USSR isolated in the east, cut off from its one major ally, Germany. The Soviet Union and Germany were "revisionist" states, unhappy with the post-war settlement and the dominance of Britain, France, and the United States. Both were relatively weak until the coming to power of the Nazis in 1933 and the Stalinist industrialization. Just on the eve of the Great Depression, in 1928, the Comintern took a fiercely militant line. Communists predicted a new age of revolution precipitated by the contradictions inherent in capitalism and declared that not only fascists but social democrats (called "social fascists") were enemies of the working class. The Stalinists turned the Comintern from a union of affiliated Communist parties into an instrument of Soviet state policy. But the new militancy of international communism only further divided the Left and, consequently, facilitated the coming to power of Hitler.

THE ROAD TO HOT WAR

The worldwide depression of the 1930s brought down many of the liberal parliamentary regimes in Europe and increased the influence of fascism. Communist predictions that the economic collapse of capitalism would lead to socialist revolution proved to be mistaken, and the USSR faced the menace of a hostile, rapidly rearming Germany. Stalin's foreign policy shifted to a strategy of collective security, moderating its anti-imperialism and searching out allies among the democracies. The USSR joined the League of Nations; Foreign Commissar Maxim Litvinov secured American recognition of the Soviet Union in 1933; and the Soviet government signed non-aggression pacts with France and Czechoslovakia in 1935. The Comintern adopted a new "Popular Front" strategy inviting social democratic and liberal forces to join in a broad anti-fascist movement to protect democratic governments. As Hitler moved from victory to victory, and the Western powers attempted to appease his territorial appetites, Stalin feared that the democracies would join with Germany against the USSR. France and Britain acquiesced in Munich to Germany taking the Sudetenland from Czechoslovakia. When in 1939 Great Britain and France refused to join the Soviet Union to protect what was left of Czechoslovakia, Stalin began secret negotiations with the Germans. To gain time and break up what he believed was a potential anti-Soviet alliance, he agreed to a pact with the Nazis.

That strange marriage, between the two great anti-liberal movements of the twentieth century, lasted less than two years, but in that time the Soviet army fought a short, embarrassing war with Finland and marched into the Baltic republics of Estonia, Latvia, and Lithuania. When Hitler's forces invaded Poland on September 1, 1939, beginning the Second World War, Stalin's troops occupied the eastern part of the country and annexed the Belorussian- and Ukrainian-populated regions to their respective Soviet republics. But the breathing space offered by the Nazi-Soviet Pact was not effectively used by the Soviets to increase their defenses. Stalin trusted Hitler and expected that Germany would not open a second front in Europe before he had won the Battle of Britain. But on June 22, 1941, without a declaration of war, the Germans crossed the Soviet border and began what would become the most massive military confrontation between two states in history.

THE GREAT FATHERLAND WAR

Americans are justly proud of the "greatest generation," the men who fought in World War II and the women who "manned" the home front. But that pride has generally obscured the contribution of the Soviet army and people to the victory over Nazism. After initially suffering immense losses and being driven back to the gates of Moscow,

Leningrad, Stalingrad, and the Caucasus Mountains, the Soviet armed forces rallied to stop the Nazi *blitzkrieg*. As John Barber, an historian at Cambridge University, shows in his essay, in the early days of the war, patriotism mixed with outright hostility to the Soviet regime in the attitudes of ordinary Soviet citizens. Rumors filled the space left empty by managed news. The tide began to turn, both for the Red Army and the people's commitment to victory, with the great Battle of Moscow of the fall of 1941, but it was only after the colossal battles of Stalingrad and Kursk that the Red Army was able to reverse the advance of the Germans and push westward. The Soviet Union faced three-quarters of the German forces. Their casualties were enormous. When it was over and the Soviet Union was victorious, over twenty-five million Soviet citizens were dead, another twenty-five million homeless. They had broken the back of the Nazi war machine, destroying or disabling more than 600 enemy divisions. Ten million Germans perished on the Eastern Front. Though his country was battered and desperately in need of aid, Stalin saw the victory over Nazism as the ultimate vindication of his policies. His reward, he felt, should be a secure zone of friendly states along the western border of the USSR and large grants of assistance from his allies and the defeated states.

THE COLD WAR

The historiography on the Cold War is rich and controversial. Orthodox accounts place the blame for the near half-century of East-West hostility and division of Europe almost exclusively on the Soviet Union, while revisionists either level charges against the United States and Britain or attempt to see both sides as contributing to the breakdown of the wartime alliance. Most of the scholarship up to the 1990s was necessarily based on research in Western archives, and the intricacies of Soviet decision-making could only be conjectured. David Holloway, an expert on Soviet foreign policy at Stanford University, was among the first to use Soviet archives and extensive interviews in the USSR and post-Soviet Russia to flesh out the complexities of Stalin's aims in the last years of his rule.

Stalin used his limited resources ruthlessly to realize traditional Russian foreign policy goals. He established his hegemony over the countries of East Central Europe—Poland, Czechoslovakia, Hungary, Romania, and Bulgaria. After a few years (1944–1947) of tolerating coalition governments and even relatively free elections in the Soviet occupied part of Europe, Stalin clamped down hard and established Communist-dominated regimes in what became the Soviet Bloc. Though the Soviet Union opposed the division of Germany, it occupied the eastern quarter of the country and eventually established a satellite state with its capital in East Berlin. Independently of much Soviet support, Communists came to power in China, North Korea, and North Vietnam, and the United States feared that Western Europe would soon fall to the Soviets. The Western powers viewed the Soviet sphere of influence in Eastern Europe and the Communist victories in Asia as proof of a Soviet will to dominate the world. American food aid, and later the Marshall Plan, shored up the weakened states of Western Europe, and in 1949, the North Atlantic Treaty Organization (NATO) was formed to stand as a powerful bulwark against Soviet expansion. By the time of his death, Stalin's USSR was more powerful than any Russian state in history, but the country he ruled was faced by an even more powerful coalition of forces, armed with atomic weapons and determined to frustrate its ambitions.

POPULAR REACTIONS IN MOSCOW TO THE GERMAN INVASION OF JUNE 22, 1941

John Barber

. . . The German invasion on June 22, 1941 caught the Soviet government both strategically and psychologically ill-prepared. But it had at least had ample warning of the possibility of war, even if Stalin had chosen to ignore the evidence of German plans to attack. The Soviet population, however, had been given virtually no opportunity to prepare for what lay ahead. It had little if any knowledge of the growth of tension or the movement of military forces in the spring and summer of 1941. It had no sense of impending danger. On the contrary, the Soviet government had gone out of its way to deny reports of a German threat, while repeatedly assuring the population that its security was guaranteed by the might of the Red Army.

One consequence of the surprise attack, therefore, was that initial reactions to the outbreak of the Soviet-German war were probably more spontaneous than popular responses to any other major turning point in Soviet history. And with the authorities immersed in the massive task of rapidly mobilising the country's resources, their ability to exercise control over the population's behaviour was for a time significantly reduced. As a result, people's actions and statements in the first days and weeks of the war were far more than usually revealing of their attitudes towards their country, their rulers and the enemy.

For much of Moscow's population, the first news of the German attack came with Molotov's broadcast at noon on June 22. Since it was a Sunday, most people were not at work. None the less many went to their factory or office, some to work, others simply to get more information. Despite the confusion at the highest political level, lower down the apparatus lost no time in doing what came naturally to it. Everywhere it organised meetings. Resolutions were passed denouncing the German attack, loyalty was pledged to the motherland, the Soviet Union and Stalin, votes were carried to work an extra shift immediately.

Expressions of outrage and indignation abounded at these meetings. "Hatred of the enemy is exceptionally great," a secretary of the Kalininskii *raikom* reported on June 22. Given the shock of the invasion, this was probably a fair reflection of the general mood. So also were the many optimistic statements about the outcome of the war. In view of people's total ignorance of the catastrophe taking place far away at the front, it was natural for most to believe what they had for so long been told about the Red Army's invincibility. (Even Stalin at first seems to have thought that in invading the USSR Hitler had made a disastrous miscalculation.) "The wrath of the Soviet people is terrible," workers at plant no. 44 in Dzerzhinskii *raion* declared on June 22; "there is no force capable of resisting the Red Army." "What does Hitler think he's doing?," a worker at the Ordzhonikidze machine-tool plant asked. "If we beat them before with our bare hands, with pitchforks, then now that we have plenty of machinery, he's done for." The influence of years of propaganda was also reflected in the expectation of international support for the USSR. Workers at a brakes plant in Sverdlovskii *raion* on June 22 expressed confidence that the "proletariat of the whole world will come to the defense of the fatherland of the world proletariat."

Initially the question for many people was not whether the USSR would be victorious, but how soon; not how far the Red Army might have to retreat, but how far it would carry the war into enemy territory: "Who do they think they're attacking? Have they gone out of their minds?" . . . "Of course, the German workers will support us, and all other peoples will rise up" . . . "Our men will hit them so hard, it will all be over in a week" . . . "Well, it won't necessarily be finished in a week; they've got to get to Berlin. . . . It will take three or four weeks."

Confidence in a quick and easy victory, combined with patriotic anger at German treachery, was probably largely responsible for the remarkable surge of volunteers to help the war effort in late June and early July. Men who were exempt from conscription by virtue of age or profession still volunteered to serve at the front; so too did many women, as nurses. Both men and women enrolled in huge numbers in the people's militia. (At the time they could have had no idea that within a few months, thousands upon thousands of the *opol'chentsy* would have been slaughtered to little or no military advantage.) Workers and employees petitioned the government to increase the working day by two hours, and agreed to work extra overtime, or to simply continue working until the task in hand was completed. Housewives and pensioners volunteered to return to work. Everywhere people began to subscribe to defense bonds or to collect clothes for the Red Army or to give blood.

Obviously this was not a purely spontaneous movement. Party and *Komsomol* activists organised campaigns to mobilise the population, and they undoubtedly exerted pressure on people to volunteer. The often grandiloquent statements of men and women departing for the front or performing heroic acts on the shop floor cannot simply be taken at face value. Nevertheless, many of the reports of popular enthusiasm to contribute to the patriotic cause ring true. As in other wars at other times, some people were genuinely impatient to fight, to get to the front before the war was over. . . . A touching scene was reported on June 28 from Dzerzhinskii *raion,* where a one-armed pensioner, Saakian, implored the *raikom* secretary to send him to the front. He received the secretary's refusal with tears in his eyes, unable to come to terms with the thought that he could not go to the front.

But this was far from the whole picture. From the very beginning of the war, Muscovites expressed criticisms and doubts about past government policies, present conditions, and future prospects. And their actions reflected an independence of mind which not even years of Stalinist socialization had eradicated.

One of the most visible reactions to the outbreak of war was the rush on banks and food shops. "Colossal queues in all savings banks for withdrawing deposits and selling the 1938 state bonds" were reported from Sverdlovskii *raion* on June 22. Within thirty to forty minutes all the money available for a normal day had gone. Customers were withdrawing large amounts, up to fifteen thousand rubles. There were exceptions. One man at savings bank no. 5285 in Pervomaiskii *raion* demonstratively deposited 500 rubles until the war ended in a Soviet victory, and he was said to have persuaded others to leave the queue. But such patriots were in the minority; and by June 23 withdrawals were having to be limited to small amounts, causing considerable indignation. There were also large queues for food and paraffin. People from the suburbs were blamed for buying up everything available. Panic buying and withdrawals were not, however, confined to the lower orders. In the Sverdlovskii *raion* those withdrawing money on the first day of the war were said to be "for the most part from the intelligentsia". From Leninskii *raion,* the head of *gastronom* no. 21 reported on June 22 that "the initiative in panic buying was being taken by residents of the *dom pravitel'stva*", who were also withdrawing their bank deposits.

Vigorous action by the police, including numerous arrests, soon brought the situation under control; and eventually greater fairness in food distribution was achieved through rationing, which was introduced in Moscow and surrounding towns on July 18. It is interesting, however, that people were calling from the outset. On the very first day of the war, according to a report from Krasnogvardeiskii *raion* on people's attitudes following Molotov's broadcast, "housewives expressed the desire for the government to introduce rationing of basic necessities in order to eliminate queues." And residents of Gor'kii Street told agitators the following day that rationing would be the best means of getting rid of the queues "created by irresponsible elements."

In the first days of the war apprehension about the physical effects of enemy action gripped many people's minds. With the fighting far away, there was nothing resembling the desperate scenes of panic reported from the frontline areas. But fear of bombing was acute among Moscow's inhabitants. The authorities' decision to test the air-raid warning system early on the morning of June 23 had an unfortunate effect on morale. "Elements of panic" were reported as people rushed to bomb-shelters, often finding them locked or full or filthy. Although Moscow would not in fact be bombed until late July, it was widely assumed that enemy planes really had attacked the city, which only confirmed people's worst fears. "This alarm nearly killed me," a woman printer was quoted as saying. "If the Red Army is already letting German bombers get through to Moscow in the first days of the war, then we are in real danger." Fright literally killed one unfortunate Party member in Kievskii *raion*. Sleeping on a seventh floor balcony, he was woken by the siren, and in terror jumped to his death. Fear was not confined to ordinary citizens. "In the first days and weeks of the war," the secretary of the Sokolniki *raikom* told a meeting of the Moscow Party *aktiv* on September 29, "some secretaries of Party organizations literally ran away."

Awareness of the personal dangers and costs involved also tempered the public's response to mobilization. Despite considerable political and social pressure to volunteer, some individuals declined, pleading ill-health, family responsibilities or simply fear. "I don't want to be cannon fodder," an employee of the Carburetor plant in Leninskii *raion* said on June 30. "I won't serve in the army and I won't join the reserve." On the very day of Stalin's broadcast to the nation, July 3, the deputy head of a building enterprise in Sovetskii *raion* declared that "social organizations don't have the right to participate in mobilization," and refused to join the people's militia. So also did a worker at a textile factory in Kirovskii *raion;* "Hitler, Soviet power, they're all the same to me." Others took evasive action. Immediately after Molotov's broadcast on June 22, one Averechkina went to the chairman of her factory's Red Cross Society and demanded that her documents be destroyed, so that she would not be sent to the front as a nurse. In Kievskii *raion* even Communists were said to be giving excuses for not volunteering. "What about my dependent sister and mother—I must talk about it with mummy." One was said to have thrown her candidate's Party card in the lavatory on the first day of the war. Many *komsomol'tsy* at the beginning of the war, according to the secretary of the Moscow *Komsomol* later, tore up their cards and started wearing crosses so as to distance themselves from the regime in case the Germans should arrive. . . .

For conscripts there was little possibility of avoiding mobilization, and only a small percentage of men were reported to have not answered the call-up. But many adopted the time-honored means of cushioning the shock of leaving family and friends for an unknown and dangerous fate. In the first days of the war, conscription points were scenes of considerable disorder. At point no. 1 in Krasnogvardeiskii *raion* on June 24, one hundred out of six hundred conscripts were drunk, twenty of them "to the point of indecency." Some had turned up drunk, some had brought bottles in their rucksacks, others had them passed through the windows by their relatives. . . . At the Belorusskii station point on June 26, a "significant number" of drunken conscripts had to remain behind when their echelons left for the front.

Conscripts faced other problems. The sudden beginning of the war had resulted in considerable disorganization of transport, resulting in long delays for mobilized soldiers. Delays of three or four days at conscription points, often in rudimentary premises and with meagre supplies, were common. Patience wore thin and anxiety mounted. Conscripts besieged agitators with questions: what would become of their children in their absence, with their wives at work or also leaving Moscow. . . .

For the authorities, these were at any rate temporary problems. Of greater concern were the many expressions of hostility towards the government, from criticisms of particular aspects of official policy to completely anti-Soviet statements. The inadequacies of bombshelters and the lack of gas masks were subjects of frequent complaints; so too was the lack of food. "What concern of ours is it who wins?," asked a woman tram driver in Sovetskii *raion*. "Once I was full for thirty kopecks, now a thousand rubles isn't enough." There were also pointed questions about the country's lack of preparedness for war. "Why has it been possible for our towns to be bombed?," asked metal worker Zotov at the Ordzhonikidze Machine Tool plant on June 22. "Wasn't it possible to know beforehand that the Germans would start this?" To Medvedeva, a cleaner at Raznoimport, the situation was clear. "Earlier we made a treaty with the Germans, fed them with our bread, and thus helped them to fight." Dubasov, a fireman at the same plant, put the same point to some Party members more bluntly. "You've got what you deserved. First you fed him, now he'll shoot you."

Party agitators in Moscow, according to A. S. Shcherbakov, first secretary of the Moscow Party Committee, speaking at a meeting of activists on September 29, were continually being asked one fundamental question: "We had planned to fight on foreign soil, but we are fighting on our own, and on top of this we are surrendering our towns. . . . the Party supposedly promised an easy war . . . but will have to wait for victory. They said there will be little blood spilt, but the war is bringing many casualties."

Every speaker, wherever he or she was, observed the veteran propagandist Emelian Iaroslavskii, was asked the same question: "why are we retreating?" To which one agitator could only reply lamely that the answer was a military secret.

Once again attacks on government policy were not confined to ordinary citizens. One notorious case involved the Moscow Party Committee apparatus itself. A propagandist, Lependin, sent a letter to the Central Committee sometime in August or September saying that for a long time he had disagreed with the Party's foreign policy. "Soviet patriots warned about this policy a long time ago. . . . Why did we allow fascism to grow strong? We should not have entered Poland, we should have declared war when they seized Czechoslovakia." At meetings, he added, people often asked him questions on this subject. Not surprisingly, he was denounced by Shcherbakov for his "clearly counter-revolutionary words."

From the outset, there were reports of defeatist attitudes. "The Germans will win," tram driver Iurkin was quoted as saying on June 28; "they have technology and we haven't, they've got abundance, we've got a pittance." For some people, the crisis faced by the regime and its supporters was welcome. The satisfaction expressed by one Iratovna, whose husband had been sentenced to ten years imprisonment in 1938 for political crimes, was unmistakable. "Previously I wept, now you will weep." Prokof 'ev, a doorman at a brakes factory, drunkenly told his boss on June 25: "you're a Communist, but just wait, soon the time will come when it will be the end for all you Communists." Barmashenko, a worker at the Svoboda factory in Oktiabrskii *raion,* declared that the Germans were very strong; "they will take you apart and shoot the Bolsheviks."

Hostility to the Soviet government was not infrequently accompanied by admiration for the enemy. "We've got nothing to fear from the war," one Guseva told her neighbors on June 28; "the Germans will come and put Communists on the left and us on the right. They'll shoot the Communists, and we'll be left to live again." On the same day an engineer at the Stalin Automobile Plant (ZIS), Fomichev, was quoted as saying: "Hitler will get rid of you Communists: long live Hitlerism, down with Communism!" Kholodov, a metal worker at the Zaria factory was said to gather other workers in the entrance hall after each radio bulletin about the course of the war, and talk about the Germans' victories, showing that their army was powerful and would triumph.

Attractive though the anticipated massacre of Communists was to some, the most commonly mentioned reason for pro-German sentiment was anti-Semitism. This aspect of Nazism was clearly familiar to the Soviet public from the very beginning of the war—presumably a legacy of anti-fascist propaganda before August 1939, possibly the result of hearing German broadcasts or reading Nazi literature. "Good, the war's begun—they'll kill the Jews," some workers at ZIS were reported as saying on June 23. All Jews were to be expelled from Moscow, Guseva told her fellow workers she had heard on the radio on June 25.

Soon the rumor was circulating that only Russians were fighting, while Jews were exempt from being sent to the front. (This may have been reinforced by the presence of many Jews among the refugees arriving in Moscow from the western regions of the country.) Over the following weeks, anti-Semitism appears to have grown. In mid-August the Norwegian consul reported open signs of it in the capital. According to the secretary of Stalinskii *raion* speaking at the meeting of the Moscow Party *aktiv* on September 29, some Party members were spreading the story that Jews were fleeing from Moscow. Anti-Semitism, Shcherbakov told the same meeting, was a "shameful phenomenon" to which activists could not shut their eyes.

If people were aware of the Germans' intentions regarding Jews, they seem to have had little or no idea of Nazi attitudes towards Slavs. A policeman on duty at the Academy of Sciences library on July 1 was quoted as telling people "You've got nothing to fear, first and foremost they'll slaughter the Jews and Communists." At the meeting of Moscow Party activists on September 29, Shcherbakov denounced as "provocative fantasies" rumors that "the fascists kill Jews and Communists, but don't touch Russians."

Such beliefs were symptomatic of the general atmosphere of alarm and uncertainty. Given the lack of news about events at the front and the total unreliability of official communiques, rumors were inevitably a major influence on public opinion. Stories of all kinds abounded. Some were not far from the truth, if at all; the result of intelligent guesses or distorted reports. On June 30, for example, Riga was said to be in flames, with its own inhabitants acting as arsonists. Pioneers were reportedly being hung from lamp posts. (The city actually fell the following day.) According to a *komsomolets*, Ezhakov, on July 2, the Red Army was in retreat on all fronts. On the same day, a worker, Batuzov, was arrested for spreading "slanderous rumors" to the effect that the Red Army at the front was without arms and ammunition, and that "German planes fly over our territory as though they are at home."

But the great majority of rumors simply expressed people's optimistic hopes or worst fears. On June 23 there were reports that the Red Army had captured Warsaw. The unfortunate director of the 8th of May plant in Proletarskii *raion* who announced this to his employees was immediately arrested by the NKVD. The following day the rumor spread throughout Moscow.

Rumors of new dangers and disasters soon became more common. On June 30, a woman at printing house no. 18 in Kievskii *raion* said that Hitler would reach Moscow in three days time. . . . On June 27 officials at Narkomugol were said to be spreading the rumor that Japan had declared war on the USSR. A typist at Gosbank (who turned out to be the wife of an "enemy of the people") was reported on July 1 as "systematically spreading panic" with rumors such as that Leningrad had been captured by the Germans.

In Leninskii *raion* on June 30 there was said to be much talk about disguised fascist agents operating in the capital. The evacuation of children from Moscow was also a subject which gave rise to great anxiety and many rumors. A Moscow *gorkom* enquiry into mass work in enterprises dated August 8 spoke of women inundating agitators with questions about the plight of evacuees in Riazan oblast', who were said to be starving. The scope of rumors was virtually unlimited; a direct result of severe restrictions on information. As a worker at ZIS told the *gorkom* enquiry, "discussions with agitators stopped here the moment fascist air raids on Moscow began. There's no radio here . . . in practice we live only on rumors."

From all this, it is clear that the Soviet government faced real problems of motivating and controlling the population. While there was a significant degree of patriotism, faith in the country's leadership and confidence in the Red Army, discontent, pessimism and fear were also widespread. The collective psychology displayed complex and sometimes conflicting characteristics. It certainly provided no guarantee of unwavering support for the government. On the contrary, it had the potential, under extreme pressure, for producing a collapse of legitimacy, resistance to the authorities, failure of social control, breakdown of law and order, and even collaboration with the enemy. The panic of mid-October 1941 when the advance of the enemy to within a few kilometers of Moscow and the highly visible withdrawal of much of the state and Party apparatus from the capital led to widespread looting and chaotic mass evacuation—showed how close and how quickly society could come to the brink of anarchy.

The authorities were well aware of this danger, which is why they paid much attention to public opinion. . . . And the government did more than simply study popular attitudes. It made strenuous attempts to influence them, guide them, and where necessary repress them. . . . The decision taken at the very beginning of the war to concentrate on the patriotic theme of defending the motherland was crucial. It enabled the government to tap huge reserves of loyalty and commitment to the common cause. . . .

Other means were employed to ensure that popular attitudes should assist and not jeopardize the war effort. In his broadcast of July 3, Stalin called for a ruthless fight against "all disorganizers of the rear, deserters, panic-mongers, rumor-mongers." Those who hindered the work of defense, he said, "must be immediately hauled before a military tribunal." On July 6 the Supreme Soviet issued a decree "On responsibility for spreading false rumors which arouse alarm among the masses in wartime." False rumors were defined so as to include reports which did not correspond with Sovinformburo communiques; and punishment could mean execution. It is a sign of the importance attached to this measure that Party organizations immediately organised meetings to publicise this decree. While it did not stop rumors circulating, it at least checked the process.

Through a combination of persuasion and coercion, the government thus attempted to harness those elements in public opinion which contributed positively to its goals, and to contain the negative ones; and with some success. Fortunately for the authorities, popular attitudes. . . . were most influenced by the war itself. . . . In the first few weeks and months of the war, it had been possible to have illusions about German intentions, while belief in the Red Army's capacity to achieve victory had been seriously undermined by a succession of disasters. With the battle of Moscow in October–December 1941, involving the first defeat inflicted by any country on the Wehrmacht, the recapture of territory occupied by the Germans, and revelations of the attrocities suffered by its inhabitants, this situation changed; and with it so also did the social psychology of the population.

John Barber, "Popular Reactions in Moscow to the German Invasion of June 22, 1941," *Soviet Union/Union Soviétique,* XVIII, 1–3 (1991), pp. 5–18.

"The Premises of Policy,"
from *Stalin and the Bomb*

David Holloway

I

In his speech in the Bolshoi Theater on February 9, 1946 Stalin claimed that World War II had not been an accident, or the result of mistakes by political leaders. The war had happened, said Stalin, "as the inevitable result of the development of world economic and political forces on the basis of modern monopoly capitalism." Lenin had argued in 1916 that World War I was an imperialist war, which had its origins in the rivalry between capitalist states for raw materials and markets. Stalin paraphrased Lenin's theory of imperialism. "Marxists have more than once declared," he said,

> that the capitalist system of world economy is fraught with the elements of a general crisis and military clashes, that in view of this the development of world capitalism in our times proceeds not in a smooth and balanced forward movement, but through crises and military catastrophes.

The uneven development of capitalist countries, he continued, leads to situations in which some countries think that they are ill-provided with raw materials and markets, and take up arms to redress the situation. A periodic redistribution of raw mate-

rial supplies and markets in line with the shifting economic weight of different countries might make it possible to avoid war. But that was impossible in the capitalist
world economy. World War II, like World War I, had resulted from a crisis of the capitalist system of world economy. Yet World War II had been different, because it was
also an anti-Fascist war of liberation, one of the aims of which had been the restoration of democratic freedoms. This aspect had been greatly strengthened, Stalin
claimed, by the Soviet Union's entry into the war.

By opening his speech with Lenin's theory of imperialism, Stalin indicated that
this was still the relevant framework for analyzing international relations. He implied
that because capitalist states still existed, war could be expected in the future. He
claimed that his prewar policies had prepared the Soviet Union for war, and he made
it clear that those policies would have to be continued in order to prepare the country for a future war. Nikolai Voznesenskii, the head of Gosplan, made the same point
when he outlined the new Five-Year Plan to the Supreme Soviet on March 16. "We
should not forget," he said, "that monopoly capitalism is capable of giving rise to new
aggressors." "The Soviet people," Voznesenskii said at another point in his speech,
"wishes to see its armed forces even stronger and more powerful, in order to guarantee the country against all contingencies and stand on guard over peace."

Stalin's image of postwar international politics was rooted in Lenin's theory of
imperialism, but it was strongly influenced also by international relations between the
two world wars. He made several comments at the end of the war indicating that he
thought the postwar period would resemble the interwar years. In Teheran in November 1943 he warned Roosevelt and Churchill several times that Germany might
rise again in fifteen or twenty years. In October 1944 he told Churchill that Germany
should be deprived of the possibility of revenge: "otherwise every twenty-five or
thirty years there would be a new world war." In April 1945, during a dinner in his
dacha, he told the Yugoslav communist, Milovan Djilas that Germany would be on its
feet in another twelve or fifteen years. At one point during the dinner "he got up,
hitched up his trousers as though he was about to wrestle or to box, and cried out
emotionally, 'The War will soon be over. We shall recover in fifteen or twenty years,
and then we'll have another go at it.' "

Stalin drew a direct analogy between the interwar years and the postwar period
when he told T.V. Soong in July 1945 that Germany had recovered within fifteen to
twenty years of the Treaty of Versailles; Germany and Japan, he said, would rise again.
In his February 1946 speech he said that it would take at least three five-year plans to
prepare for "all contingencies." All of this suggests that he anticipated a new world war
after an interval similar to that between the two world wars. Moreover, a new world
war would originate, in Stalin's conception, in the rivalry between the imperialist
powers, including Germany and Japan, which would by that time have risen from defeat. He did not foresee the hegemonic position that the United States would come
to occupy in the capitalist world.

But Stalin did not expect war in the short term. This is clear from his policies of
industrial conversion and demobilization, which began in May and June 1945 and
continued steadily during 1946 and 1947. On May 26, 1945, little more than two
weeks after Victory Day, the State Defense Committee ordered the gradual conversion of industry to civilian production. Conversion was not easy, however, and military production declined much more rapidly than civilian production grew: defense
output fell 68 per cent from the first to the fourth quarter of 1945, while civilian pro-

duction rose only 21 per cent. Total industrial production in 1945 was 12 per cent lower than in 1944, and in 1946 it fell by almost 17 per cent compared with 1945.

In June 1945 the Supreme Soviet adopted a law on demobilization, and by the end of the year the Red Army, which numbered 11.365 million in May, had been cut by over 3 million men. Demobilization continued during 1946 and by the end of 1947 the armed forces had been reduced to 2.874 million troops. The shift to a peace-time footing was at least partially reflected in the defense budget, which fell from 137.8 billion roubles in 1944 to 128.2 billion in 1945, 73.6 billion in 1946 and 66.3 billion in 1947 (at 1946 prices it would have been 55.2 billion).

Stalin's confidence that a major war was not imminent rested upon three considerations. The first was that the Soviet Union had emerged from the war a more secure and more powerful state. Stalin and the other leaders argued in their speeches in late 1945 and early 1946 that the Soviet Union's victory over Germany and Japan had greatly strengthened its international position. Its "historic borders" had been restored. No longer would southern Sakhalin and the Kurile islands constitute a barrier to Soviet access to the Pacific Ocean, or serve as a base for Japanese aggression. A "free and independent" Poland would ensure that Germany did not have a spring-board for attacking Soviet Union. Germany, Italy, and Japan had been removed "for a period" from the list of great powers. Soviet leaders asserted, moreover, that by defeating Germany and liberating half of Europe from Nazism, their country had strengthened its international authority. "Important problems of international relations," declared Molotov on February 6, 1946, "cannot nowadays be settled without the participation of the Soviet Union or without heeding the voice of the country. The participation of Comrade Stalin is regarded as the best guarantee of a successful solution of complicated international problems."

Stalin reportedly expressed the same view in private. Shortly after the war a map showing the Soviet Union's new borders was brought to his *dacha*. Stalin pinned it to the wall. "'Let's see what the result is for us,'" he said.

> "In the North everything is in order, fine. Finland committed a great offense against us, and we have moved the border back from Leningrad. The Baltic coast—an age-old Russian territory!—is ours again, the Belorussians are all now living together with us, the Ukrainians are together, the Moldavians are together. In the West everything is fine." And at once he went to the Eastern borders. "What have we here? . . . The Kurile islands are ours now, all of Sakhalin is ours, see how good it is! And Port Arthur is ours, and Dairen is ours"—Stalin drew his pipe across China—"and the KVZhD [Chinese Eastern Railway] is ours. China, Mongolia—everything is in order. But here I don't like our border," said Stalin pointing south of the Caucasus."

Whatever the accuracy of this story, it merely repeats in more colorful terms what Soviet leaders were saying in public. Their concept of power and security was very largely a territorial one. "I saw it as my task as Minister of Foreign Affairs to extend as much as possible the bounds of our Fatherland," Molotov told an interviewer many years later. Stalin and Molotov had used the pact with Germany to expand Soviet territory in 1939 and 1940, and those acquisitions had now been consolidated. Seen in that light, Soviet security had been greatly enhanced.

The second consideration was that popular war-weariness would restrain bellicose leaders in Britain and the United States. This was the argument that Stalin used to dismiss war as "very unlikely" in March 1946, when he criticized Churchill for his "Iron Curtain" speech. Speaking in Fulton, Missouri, Churchill had warned of Moscow's increasing control over Eastern and Central Europe, and had called for an Anglo-American "fraternal association" to resist Soviet expansion. Stalin denounced Churchill's speech as "a dangerous act, calculated to sow discord between the allied states and hamper their cooperation." He accused Churchill of calling for war against the Soviet Union, and recalled that after World War I Churchill had helped to organize intervention by capitalist powers to suppress the Bolshevik regime. "I do not know," said Stalin, "whether Mr Churchill and his friends will succeed in organizing after the second world war a new campaign against 'Eastern Europe'. But if they do succeed—which is very unlikely because millions of 'simple people' are standing guard over peace—then one can say with certainty that they will be beaten, just as they were in the past, 26 years ago." A week later Stalin made his position on the likelihood of war even clearer: "I am convinced that neither nations nor their armies are seeking a new war—they want peace and are striving to ensure peace. . . . I think that 'the present fear of war' is caused by the actions of some political groups, who have taken up propaganda for a new war and are thus sowing seeds of discord and uncertainty."

The third factor affecting Stalin's assessment of the likelihood of war was his knowledge that the United States had few atomic bombs in 1945. Molotov later recalled that at Potsdam he and Stalin "understood that [the Americans] were not in a position to unleash war, they had only one or two bombs." Marshal Zhukov said in an interview in 1955 that the United States had had only five or six atomic bombs in the immediate postwar period, and that these did not have decisive significance. Klaus Fuchs informed the Soviet Union in September 1945 that the United States had very few bombs. One of the reasons for the urgency of the Soviet project is that Stalin wanted to acquire a Soviet bomb before American atomic forces grew large enough to pose an overwhelming threat to the Soviet Union. Fuchs was asked several times, after his return to Britain in the summer of 1946, about the United States rate of production, and the stockpile of atomic bombs. It is apparent, however, that Stalin did not regard the nuclear threat as immediate in 1945–6.

II

On November 27, 1945 Harriman cabled to Washington an assessment of the effect of the atomic bomb on Soviet policy. The Soviet Union, he wrote, had been able to obtain defense in depth at the end of the war by disregarding the interests and desires of other people. But

> suddenly the atomic bomb appeared and they recognized that it was an offset to the power of the Red Army. This must have revived their old feeling of insecurity. They could no longer be absolutely sure that they could obtain their objectives without interference.

Harriman based this assessment not only on his own impressions, but also on a conversation with George Andreychin, an old Comintern agent, who had paid him a visit at Spaso House, the ambassador's residence. The Kremlin leaders had been shocked by the bomb, Andreychin said, because it exposed the Soviet Union's comparative weakness, and it was to conceal that weakness that they were now being so aggressive.

On December 3 the British ambassador, Sir Archibald Clark Kerr, wrote to the Foreign Secretary with a similar analysis. The victory over Germany had made the Soviet leaders confident that national security was at last within their reach. "Then plumb came the Atomic Bomb," he wrote. "At a blow the balance which had now seemed set and steady was rudely shaken. Russia was balked by the west when everything seemed to be within her grasp. The three hundred divisions were shorn of much of their value."

This assessment echoed Stalin's remark to Vannikov and Kurchatov that Hiroshima had destroyed the balance of power, but it exaggerated the sense of immediate military insecurity that the bomb aroused in the Soviet leadership. Stalin did not believe that war was likely in the short term; nor . . . did he believe that Soviet divisions had lost their value. The immediate threat he saw was not military, but the threat of atomic diplomacy. He was afraid, as he had explained to Gromyko and Gusev, that the United States would try to use its atomic monopoly to impose a postwar settlement.

This raises an interesting analytical question. How could the atomic bomb affect the balance of power when the United States, as Stalin knew, did not possess a real atomic capability? The United States had a very small number of bombs—the stockpile was nine in mid-1946—and no desire to go to war. Yet the bomb was a political reality for Stalin. How is the difference between military capability and political effect to be explained? In an essay on the symbolic nature of nuclear politics Robert Jervis has argued that in the 1970s and 1980s the United States acquired nuclear weapons that were militarily useless in order to demonstrate resolve and political will. The same kind of argument can be made about the effect of the atomic bomb in the early postwar years. The disjunction between military capability and political effect can be explained in terms of the bomb's symbolic meaning. It symbolized the immense power—not only the military, but also the economic and technological power—of the United States. It was the "scepter of state power," as the novelist Vasilii Grossman aptly put it.

The symbolism of the atomic bomb had a pervasive effect on international politics in 1945–6, even though the bomb did not pose a real military threat to the Soviet Union at the time. Stalin tried to counter this symbolic power by treating the bomb as unimportant, and by showing that the Soviet Union would not be intimidated. The danger of the bomb, from Stalin's point of view, was that the United States would adopt a more confident and aggressive policy towards the Soviet Union, in the hope of extracting concessions. The Soviet response, in the months after Hiroshima, was to try to disabuse the United States of the idea that this would be an effective policy.

The Truman administration certainly expected that the bomb could be used to influence Soviet policy, but it did not know exactly how that could be done. Troubled by Soviet behavior at Potsdam, Stimson had written a memorandum to Truman during the conference, arguing that international control of atomic energy would be impossible as long as a police state like the Soviet Union was a major force in the international control agency; the Soviet desire to participate in atomic development should therefore be used to bring about democratic change in that country. By September 11, however, Stimson had been convinced by Harriman that the atomic bomb could not be used to induce internal change in the Soviet Union, and he now argued, in another memorandum to the President, that the United States and Britain should tell the Soviet Union that they wanted an agreement to control and limit the use of the atomic bomb as an instrument of war, and to direct atomic energy towards peaceful purposes. To do otherwise—to negotiate with "this weapon ostentatiously on our hip"—would, he warned, only increase Soviet suspicion and distrust.

Truman's new Secretary of State, James Byrnes, did not share Stimson's doubts. Byrnes went to the London meeting of the Council of Foreign Ministers, which opened on September 11, 1945, confident that the bomb would strengthen his hand. The council had been established at Potsdam to prepare peace treaties with Germany and its allies. There were many issues in dispute between the three great powers, and Byrnes believed that the atomic bomb would help him in the negotiations. "His mind," wrote Stimson in his diary on September 4, "is full of his problems with the coming meeting of foreign ministers and he looks to have the presence of the bomb in his hip pocket, so to speak, as a great weapon to get through the thing." Byrnes did not want to use the bomb overtly. He instructed his delegation to avoid any mention of it, in the belief that the reality of the bomb would by itself make the Soviet Union more tractable.

Soviet policy at the end of August had been conciliatory in Eastern Europe, agreeing to the postponement of elections in Hungary and Bulgaria. It was at the London meeting in September 1945 that the new Soviet tactic was unveiled. Molotov came to the London meeting with the bomb on his mind. Atomic energy was not on the formal agenda, but Molotov raised the issue himself, at a reception on the third day of the conference. When Byrnes approached him and asked when he was going to stop sightseeing and get down to business, Molotov enquired whether Byrnes had "an atomic bomb in his side pocket." "You don't know southerners," Byrnes replied, "we carry our artillery in our pocket. If you don't cut out all this stalling and let us get down to work, I'm going to pull an atomic bomb out of my hip pocket and let you have it." Molotov and his interpreter laughed at this remark which, though offered as banter, put into words the threat that Stalin and Molotov feared. Molotov evidently wished to laugh off the American bomb. Later that evening, at the embassy, Molotov proposed a toast, "Here's to the Atom Bomb! We've got it."

If the bomb made Byrnes stand firm, it made Molotov stubborn. Molotov found Byrnes unyielding when he pushed for a control commission for Japan, with Soviet participation, and pressed the Soviet claim to trusteeship over Libya. Molotov, in turn, resisted Western attempts to influence the complexion of the governments in Romania and Bulgaria. Moreover, although he accepted a British suggestion that the French and Chinese foreign ministers be allowed to take part in the discussions, he changed his mind ten days later and asked for them to be excluded. Appeals from Truman and Attlee to Stalin failed to change the Soviet position, and the conference ended on October 2 without agreement.

At a formal dinner during the conference Molotov said that "of course we all have to pay great attention to what Mr Byrnes says, because the United States are the only people making the atomic bomb." But pay attention to Byrnes was what Molotov conspicuously and pointedly declined to do. He behaved as though his overriding concern was to show that the Soviet Union would not be intimidated, or forced into concessions, by the American atomic monopoly. If this was indeed his goal, he succeeded brilliantly. Byrnes now realized that the Russians were, in his own words, "stubborn, obstinate, and they don't scare." Truman too was impressed by the bomb's failure to influence Molotov, and worried about the rapid rate of US demobilization. When his budget director, Harold Smith, told him that "you have an atomic bomb up your sleeve" he replied: "Yes, but I am not sure it can ever be used." . . .

In the Soviet Union too warnings were sounded about the breakdown of collaboration. An editorial in *Izvestiia* on October 5 declared that collaboration would be shaken unless the United States and Britain changed their attitude to existing agreements. Later in the same month Stalin told Harriman that the Soviet Union might pursue a "policy of isolation." Harriman thought that the element of unilateralism in Soviet policy had already increased since the London conference. Frank Roberts, Minister at the British embassy in Moscow, reported in the same month that the atomic bomb had "probably increased already existing Soviet suspicions of the outside world."

On November 6 Molotov, in the speech in which he announced that the Soviet Union would have "atomic energy, and much else," warned against the attempt to use the bomb as an instrument of power politics:

> It is necessary to speak about the discovery of atomic energy and about the atomic bomb, whose use in the war with Japan showed its huge destructive force. . . . *At the present time there can be no large-scale technological secrets that can remain the property of any one country or any one narrow group of countries. Therefore the discovery of atomic energy must not encourage . . . enthusiasm for using this discovery in a foreign-policy power game.* [Emphasis added]

These last two sentences point to the two major goals of Soviet atomic policy at the time: to break the American monopoly, and in the meantime to ensure that the United States did not derive political benefit from that monopoly. . . .

At dinner in the Kremlin on Christmas Eve Molotov returned to the tactics he had employed in London. James Conant had been brought to Moscow by Byrnes as adviser on atomic energy; Conant hoped to meet some of the Soviet nuclear scientists, but the Soviet authorities did not permit this. Molotov proposed a toast to Conant, saying (according to Conant's diary) "that after a few drinks perhaps we could explore the secrets I had and if I had a bit of the atomic bomb in my pocket to bring it out." As all stood up to drink the toast, Stalin broke in, apparently in anger. "Here's to science and American scientists and what they have accomplished. This is too serious a matter to joke about," he said. "We must now work together to see that this great invention is used for peaceful ends."

Charles Bohlen, who was a member of the American delegation, wrote later that "we saw Stalin abruptly change Soviet policy, without consulting his number-two man. The humiliated Molotov never altered his expression. From that moment on, the Soviet Union gave the atomic bomb the serious consideration it deserved." But Stalin had taken the atomic bomb seriously since Hiroshima, and must certainly have approved Molotov's tactics for dealing with atomic diplomacy. Stalin's rebuke may indicate that he took the threat of atomic diplomacy less seriously than Molotov did, or—more probably—that he thought that Molotov, whose stubbornness he sometimes found infuriating, was being too dogged in his pursuit of the "bomb in the pocket" line. If this was a humiliation for Molotov, as Bohlen suggests, then Stalin doubtless took pleasure in that too.

The Soviet government was pleased with the Moscow meeting. In his memoirs Novikov writes that the "principled and firm position of the Soviet government," demonstrated at the London meeting, had "forced the Western powers to reject the tactic of head-on pressure and to seek mutually acceptable solutions on the most important questions of the postwar period." This new approach, he believed, was apparent at the Moscow meeting. Byrnes agreed to recognize the Bulgarian and Romanian governments in return for token changes in their cabinets; he also agreed to set up a toothless Allied Council for Japan, in which the Soviet Union would be represented. Byrnes failed to obtain assurances from the Soviet Union that it would withdraw its troops from northern Iran, which it had occupied during the war, or to clarify Soviet intentions toward Turkey. Stalin wrote to Truman to say that he was pleased with the results of the meeting.

Truman did not share Stalin's satisfaction. He was irritated by Byrnes's failure to keep him informed about the course of the negotiations, and unhappy with the results of the meeting. Byrnes, he wrote in his memoirs, "had taken it upon himself to move the foreign policy of the United States in a direction to which I could not, and would not, agree." On January 5, 1946 he wrote a stiff letter reprimanding Byrnes and complaining about Soviet policy. He insisted that the governments in Romania and Bulgaria should not be recognized until radically changed; he regarded it as an outrage that the Soviet Union was keeping troops in Iran and stirring up rebellion there; and he was convinced that the Soviet Union intended to invade Turkey and seize the Black Sea straits. "Unless Russia is faced with an iron fist and strong language another war is in the making," he wrote. "I'm tired," he concluded, "of babying the Russians."

Truman's hardening attitude reflected a shift in official American opinion. Washington was increasingly frustrated by its dealings with the Soviet Union, and puzzled by Soviet unwillingness to cooperate on American terms, especially in view of the American atomic monopoly. In February 1946, after Stalin's speech in the Bolshoi Theater, a long telegram arrived from George Kennan. The Soviet Union, by its very nature, wrote Kennan, was "committed fanatically" to the belief that it could have no permanent *modus vivendi* with the United States, and that Soviet power could be secure only if the internal harmony of American society was disrupted and the international authority of the United States broken. This telegram answered the question that preoccupied the Truman administration: why was the Soviet Union so difficult to deal with? Besides, the answer it gave explained the difficulty in terms of the nature of the Soviet Union, and not of American policy. It expressed very eloquently the view that was taking shape in Washington.

Novikov noticed that the political atmosphere in Washington had worsened when he returned from Moscow in February 1946. It became even tenser, in his view, after Churchill's "Iron Curtain" speech on March 5. At just this time a serious crisis arose in United States-Soviet relations. In 1942 the Soviet Union and Britain had deployed troops in Iran to prevent that country from falling into German hands. At the end of 1945 Washington and London began to worry that the Soviet Union might not withdraw its forces from northern Iran, as it had agreed to do at Teheran in 1943 and at the London meeting of foreign ministers in September 1945.

The deadline for withdrawal of Soviet forces was March 2, 1946. On that date Soviet troops were still in Iran, and Washington feared that Stalin intended to annex the Iranian province of Azerbaijan. The United States had already made clear its concern to the Soviet government, and had supported a firm Iranian position in the negotiations with Moscow. Now Byrnes sent a stiff note to Moscow and, when no reply was received, made the note public. Moscow quickly promised to pull its forces out of Iran by early May. Truman later recollected that he had issued an atomic ultimatum, and claimed that it was this that had forced the Soviet Union to withdraw its forces. This was not so, however. The Truman administration issued no ultimatum, much less an atomic one. It did, however, engage in firm and skillful diplomacy, which resolved the crisis.

February and March 1946 marked a turning point in United States policy toward the Soviet Union. American attitudes had hardened to the point where cooperation and agreement were now much more difficult. The atomic bomb did not cause the deterioration in relations. There were serious issues in dispute between the Soviet Union and the Western Allies before Hiroshima. Nevertheless, the failure of the London conference, which took place under the shadow of the bomb, marked an important stage in the breakdown of cooperation. Byrnes felt that the bomb allowed him to adopt a tough and demanding position in London; Molotov evidently felt that the bomb required a tough and demanding Soviet position in return. Atomic diplomacy—the hope on the one side, the fear on the other, that the bomb would prove to be a powerful political instrument—contributed to the failure of the London conference, and to the deterioration of US-Soviet relations. . . .

IV

In the latter years of World War II Stalin had a choice between three basic policies for the postwar period. He could pursue an insurrectionist policy by encouraging the communist parties in Western Europe and in Asia to seize power, and by helping them where possible with the Red Army. There was some sentiment in support of this policy in Moscow, and some discussion of its feasibility. This is not surprising, since it had obvious appeal for anyone interested in socialist revolution. No prominent figure in the leadership advocated it, however, and Stalin chose not to encourage revolution in Europe or Asia. To have done so would have created a risk of war with the Western allies.

A second option was to pursue a policy of cooperation with the West. This was advocated by Maksim Litvinov, the People's Commissar of Foreign Affairs in the 1930s, who had been replaced by Molotov in May 1939, three months before the Nazi-Soviet pact. Litvinov was ambassador in Washington from December 1941 to the spring of 1943, when he was brought back to Moscow to a relatively unimportant post. Litvinov wanted collaboration between the Soviet Union and the United States after the war, because he saw this as the only sound basis for peace. In October 1944, however, he told the American journalist Edgar Snow that Britain was adopting its traditional balance-of-power policy in Europe and was unwilling to collaborate with the Soviet Union, which was now the strong power on the continent; and "we," he said, "are drifting more and more in the same direction," away from collaboration. In June 1946 he told Richard Hottelet, the CBS correspondent in Moscow, that there had been "a return in Russia to the outmoded concept of security in terms of territory—the more you've got the safer you are." If the West acceded to Soviet demands, he said, "it would lead to the West being faced, after a more or less short time, with the next series of demands." In February 1947 he told Alexander Werth that Russia could have cashed in on the goodwill it had accumulated during the war, but that Stalin and Molotov did not believe that goodwill provided a lasting basis for policy; "they had therefore grabbed all they could while the going was good."

The transcript of at least one of these conversations was given to Stalin and Molotov by the Soviet police. Litvinov remained alive only by accident, Molotov later remarked. It is possible, however, that Stalin left Litvinov alone not only to irritate Molotov, who detested him, but also to keep him in reserve in case he wanted to change Soviet policy; he could then produce Litvinov as a token of his desire for cooperation. Litvinov was dismissed from his position in the Ministry of Foreign Affairs on his seventieth birthday in July 1946, a month after his interview with Hottelet; he died at the end of 1951.

Stalin rejected the policy advocated by Litvinov. He did not make collaboration with the United States the overriding goal of policy. That would have involved concessions in Germany and Eastern Europe that he was unwilling to make. He may have rejected it also on the grounds that a foreign policy of cooperation with the United States would not fit well with a domestic policy of reasserting the regime's control over Soviet society. According to the writer Konstantin Simonov, who met Stalin several times after the war to discuss cultural policy, Stalin feared a repeat of the Decembrist revolt of 1825: "he had shown Ivan to Europe and Europe to Ivan, as Alexander I had done in 1813–1814." A policy of alliance with the Western powers might make it more difficult to tighten the regime's grip on Soviet life. Whatever the causal connection may have been, international tension went hand in hand with repression at home in Stalin's last years.

The policy Stalin pursued was one of *realpolitik,* within the framework outlined at the beginning of this chapter. Left-wing critics would later characterize it, correctly, as statist, because it treated states, rather than classes, as the primary actors in international relations, and because it put the interests of the Soviet state above those of international revolution. Stalin foresaw a difficult period in which capitalism would be wracked by crisis and war. He wanted to ensure that the postwar settlement enhanced Soviet power and security for the turbulent period that lay ahead. He rejected the analysis of Eugen Varga, the Hungarian director of the Academy of Sciences' Institute of World Economy and World Politics, who argued that the role of the state in capitalism had changed, and that as a result capitalism would develop in a more stable fashion than it had done in the interwar years. Stalin lamented to Molotov that Russia "wins wars but does not know how to exploit the fruits of victory"; he was determined not to make the same mistake. The defeat of Germany and Japan had created the basis for a redistribution of power in the international system. Stalin wanted to consolidate Soviet territorial gains, establish a Soviet sphere of influence in Eastern Europe, and have a voice in the political fate of Germany and—if possible—of Japan. He sought unilateral guarantees of Soviet security, rather than security through cooperation.

Stalin and Molotov were prepared to be tough in pressing Soviet claims and stubborn in resisting Western pressure. But they did not want war with the West, and they understood that there were limits beyond which they should not go. Stalin's decisions not to land troops on Hokkaido and to withdraw Soviet forces from northern Iran show that he was unwilling to press Soviet claims beyond a certain point. This was evident too in Soviet policy toward Turkey. At the end of the war the Soviet Union sought to regain from Turkey territory that had been ceded by a weak Russia in 1921. It also asked for a revision of the 1936 Montreux Convention governing the passage of ships through the Turkish Straits between the Black Sea and the Mediterranean, and for a naval and military base in the Straits.

The Soviet Union put pressure on Turkey in the summer of 1945 by moving Soviet troops in Romania and Bulgaria close to the Turkish border. At Potsdam the Western allies refused to grant Soviet claims, although they did accept that the Montreux Convention needed revision. The Soviet Union kept up the campaign of pressure against Turkey in 1945. In his letter of reprimand to Byrnes in January 1946 Truman expressed the fear that the Soviet Union intended to invade Turkey and seize the Straits. On August 7, 1946 the Soviet Union formally requested a share in the defense of the Dardanelles, and argued that the Black Sea powers alone should determine a new regime for the Straits. This was interpreted in Washington as a move to obtain control of Turkey, and to open the way to a Soviet advance into the Persian Gulf and Suez Canal area. On August 19 Acheson, as Acting Secretary of State, informed the Soviet government that the Turkish Straits regime was of concern to the United States as a signatory of the Montreux Convention, and that Turkey should continue to be responsible for the defense of the Straits. US naval units were dispatched to the eastern Mediterranean. The Soviet Union dropped its claims.

Many years later Molotov described the attempt to obtain joint Soviet—Turkish control of the Straits as a mistake. "Go on, apply pressure! For joint control," Stalin had told Molotov. When Molotov replied that they would not be given joint control, Stalin said to him, "You try." "It is good that we retreated in good time," Molotov later commented, "or that would have led to a joint aggression against us."

Stalin's choice of the postwar foreign policy line was not affected by the atomic bomb. The basic choice to pursue a realist, rather than a revolutionary or "liberal", foreign policy was made before the end of the war, and therefore before the atomic bomb had entered Stalin's strategic calculations. The bomb did not lead to a reevaluation of the foreign policy line. Stalin and Molotov interpreted the significance of the bomb in terms of its effect on the balance of power and on the postwar settlement. The tactic they devised for dealing with it was to show that the Soviet Union would not be intimidated. This tactic, however, appears to have led to a quicker breakdown of cooperation than Stalin might have envisaged before August 1945. In that sense the bomb contributed to the collapse of the wartime alliance and the origins of the Cold War.

In September 1946 Nikolai Novikov, now the ambassador in Washington, wrote a memorandum that provides an interesting insight into the Soviet view of the role of the atomic bomb in US foreign policy. Since Molotov instructed Novikov what to write, the result was, according to Novikov, a "report which could only conditionally be considered mine." The United States, wrote Novikov, had emerged from the war more powerful than before, and was now intent upon world domination. Two of its main imperialist rivals, Germany and Japan, had been defeated, while the British Empire faced great economic and political difficulties. The Soviet Union was the main obstacle to American expansion. The Soviet Union, for its part, now enjoyed a much more solid international position than before the war. Soviet forces in Germany and other former enemy states were a guarantee "that those countries will not be used again for an attack on the USSR." The Soviet Union carried great weight in international affairs, especially in Europe, and its growing political influence in Eastern and south-eastern Europe was inevitably regarded by American imperialists as an obstacle to their expansionist foreign policy.

Truman—"a politically unstable man with certain conservative tendencies"—had turned away from the search for cooperation among the wartime allies. He had

not yet responded to Churchill's call at Fulton for an Anglo-American military alliance, although he was clearly sympathetic to that idea, and maintained close military
ties with Britain. Nevertheless, concluded Novikov, present-day relations between the
United States and Britain could not last long, because they contained extreme contradictions. The most likely focus for this rivalry was the Middle East, where existing
agreements between the United States and Britain might come unstuck.

The United States was trying to impose its will on the Soviet Union, and to limit
or end Soviet influence in neighboring countries. Germany was a key element in this
policy. The United States was not doing enough to democratize and demilitarize its
zone of Germany, and might try to end the Allied occupation before these tasks had
been carried out. This would open the way to a revival of imperialist Germany, which,
Novikov asserted, the United States counted on using as an ally in a future war against
the Soviet Union.

Speculation about war was rife in the United States, wrote Novikov. At public
meetings and in the press, reactionaries were talking about war against the Soviet
Union, and even calling for such a war "with the threat of using the atomic bomb."
This campaign was intended to put pressure on the Soviet Union and force it to make
concessions, and also to create a war psychosis so that the government would be able
to maintain a high level of military preparedness. These measures were not an end in
themselves, argued Novikov. They were designed to create the conditions in which
the United States could win the new war that the most bellicose circles of American
imperialism were contemplating. No one, of course, could now determine when that
war would take place. But the United States was building up its armed forces for a
war against the Soviet Union, the main obstacle on the American path to world domination. Novikov did not present war as imminent, and implied that the immediate
aim of American military power, including the atomic bomb, was to force the Soviet
Union to accept the United States' plans for the postwar world.

Novikov's memorandum is rooted in the Leninist analysis of imperialism. He assumed that the United States was bent on world domination. Because Germany and
Japan had been weakened by their defeat, and Britain was in decline, the Soviet Union
was the main impediment to the expansion of American imperialism. It was inevitable, therefore, that the United States would try to undermine the Soviet Union
and put pressure on it. Yet Novikov still expected inter-imperialist contradictions to
come to the fore, and the Anglo-American alliance to break down as a result.

Novikov did not portray the atomic bomb as in any way shaping or transforming international relations, or as a preponderant element in the balance of power.
Rather he presented it—as most commentators did—as a political instrument that the
United States wanted to use to intimidate the Soviet Union. Stalin made the same
point on September 17, 1946, in one of his most important statements about the
atomic bomb. There was no real danger of a "new war," he said. He did not think that
Britain and the United States were trying to organize a "capitalist encirclement" of
the Soviet Union, and he doubted that they could do so, even if they wanted to.
"Atomic bombs are meant to frighten those with weak nerves," he said, in reply to a
question from Alexander Werth,

> but they cannot decide the outcome of a war, since atomic bombs are quite in-
> sufficient for that. Of course, monopoly ownership of the secret of the atomic
> bomb creates a threat, but against it there exist at least two means: a) monopoly

ownership of the atomic bomb cannot last for long; b) the use of the atomic bomb will be prohibited.

Since the prospects for banning the use of the bomb were not good, Stalin was indicating that the Soviet Union intended to end the American atomic monopoly before long. His reference to weak nerves suggested that the Soviet Union did not have weak nerves, and that it would not be intimidated.

David Holloway, "The Premises of Policy," *Stalin and the Bomb: The Soviet Union and Atomic Energy, 1939–1956* (New Haven and London: Yale University Press, 1994), pp. 150–161, 166–171.

"Theses on the National and Colonial Question"
1920

In the euphoria of the revolution, Communists expected that history's logic would carry their cause to victory in the colonized world. A declaration of alliance of the Comintern with the national liberation struggles of the colonial world, the "Theses on the National and Colonial Question" represented the results of an intense debate between Lenin and the young Indian Communist M. N. Roy (1887?–1954). In the Middle East, Central Asia, and the Far East, the only significant radical movements were often nationalist, rather than socialist, and were supported by the "bourgeoisie" and perhaps the peasantry, rather than the working class, which hardly existed in these agrarian countries. Lenin had originally been willing to concede the need to ally with the "bourgeois nationalists," but he was opposed by some militants who could not stomach working with them and agreed only to ally with truly proletarian movements. Roy, for example, believed that anti-colonial activists like Mohandas Gandhi in India only appeared to be revolutionary but were in fact politically reactionary. In the final draft of the "Theses," the Comintern declared its willingness to go part of the way with the anti-colonialist movements, to "arrive at temporary agreements and, yes, even establish an alliance," but not to merge with this movement.

1. An abstract or formal conception of the question of equality in general and of national equality in particular is in the very nature of bourgeois democracy. Under the guise of the equality of individuals in general, bourgeois democracy proclaims the formal, legal equality of the property owner and the proletarian, the exploiter and the exploited, thereby grossly deceiving the oppressed classes. Claiming to uphold the supposed absolute equality of individuals, the bourgeoisie transforms the idea of equality, which itself reflects the relations of commodity production, into a tool in the struggle against the abolition of classes. The real meaning of the demand for equality consists in its being a demand for the abolition of classes.

2. As the conscious expression of the proletarian class struggle to shake off the yoke of the bourgeoisie, the Communist Party, in line with its basic task of struggling against bourgeois democracy and exposing its lies and duplicity, should not base its policy on the national question on abstract and formal principles. Instead, it should first be based on an exact appraisal of specific historical and above all economic conditions. Second, it should clearly differentiate between the interests of the oppressed classes, the toilers, the exploited, and the general concept of the so-called interests of

the people, which means the interests of the ruling class. Third, it should with equal precision distinguish between the oppressed, dependent nations that do not have equal rights and the oppressor, exploiting nations that do, in order to counter the bourgeois-democratic lies that conceal the colonial and financial enslavement of the immense majority of the entire world population by a narrow minority of the richest, most advanced capitalist countries—a characteristic feature of the epoch of finance capital and imperialism.

3. The imperialist war of 1914 revealed with particular clarity to all enslaved nations and oppressed classes around the world the deceitfulness of bourgeois-democratic rhetoric. The war was justified by both sides with platitudes about national liberation and self-determination. Nonetheless, both the treaties of Brest-Litovsk and Bucharest and those of Versailles and St. Germain showed that the victorious bourgeoisie ruthlessly sets even "national" borders according to its economic interests. For the bourgeoisie even "national" borders are objects of trade. The so-called League of Nations is nothing but the insurance policy with which this war's victors mutually guarantee their loot. The attempts to reestablish national unity, to "reunify with detached portions of land," are for the bourgeoisie nothing but attempts by the vanquished to assemble forces for new wars. The reunification of nations artificially torn apart is also in the interests of the proletariat. However, the proletariat can achieve genuine national liberation and unity only through revolutionary struggle and by overpowering the bourgeoisie.

The League of Nations and the entire postwar policy of the imperialist states expose this truth ever more clearly and sharply, strengthening everywhere the revolutionary struggle of the proletariat of the advanced countries, as well as of all toiling masses of the colonies and dependent countries, and hastening the collapse of petty-bourgeois illusions about the possibility of peaceful coexistence and the equality of nations under capitalism.

4. It follows from these principles that the entire policy of the Communist International on the national and colonial questions must be based primarily upon uniting the proletarians and toiling masses of all nations and countries in common revolutionary struggle to overthrow the landowners and the bourgeoisie. Only such a unification will guarantee victory over capitalism, without which it is impossible to abolish national oppression and inequality.

5. The international political situation has now put the dictatorship of the proletariat on the order of the day. All events in world politics necessarily focus on one single central issue: the struggle of the world bourgeoisie against the Russian Soviet Republic, which rallies around itself both the soviet movement of the advanced workers of all countries and all national liberation movements of the colonies and oppressed peoples. These peoples are learning through bitter experience that their only salvation lies with the revolutionary proletariat and in the victory of soviet power over world imperialism.

6. Consequently, we cannot limit ourselves at this time merely to recognizing or proclaiming the friendship of the toilers of various nations. Rather we must pursue a policy of implementing the closest possible alliance of all national and colonial liberation movements with Soviet Russia. The forms of this alliance will be determined by the level of development of the Communist movement within the proletariat of each country or of the revolutionary liberation movement in the backward countries and among the backward nationalities.

7. Federation is a transitional form toward full unity of the toilers of all nations. Federation has already shown its usefulness in practice—in the Russian Soviet Federated Socialist Republic's relations to the other soviet republics (the Hungarian, Finnish, and Latvian in the past, the Azerbaijani and Ukrainian at present), and also within the Russian Soviet Federated Socialist Republic itself toward the nationalities that formerly had neither a state nor self-government (for example, the autonomous Bashkir and Tatar republics in the Russian Soviet Federated Socialist Republic created in 1919 and 1920).

8. The task of the Communist International in this respect consists not only in further perfecting these developing federations based on the soviet order and the soviet movement but also in studying and testing their experiences. Recognizing the federation as a transitional form toward complete unification, we must strive for an ever closer federal association. We must take into consideration first, that the soviet republics, surrounded by imperialist states of the whole world that are considerably stronger militarily, cannot possibly exist without close association with each other. Second, a close economic alliance of the soviet republics is necessary, without which it is impossible to restore the productive forces destroyed by imperialism and ensure the well-being of the toilers. Third, that there is a tendency to create a world economy unified according to a common plan, controlled by proletarians of all countries. This tendency has already begun to appear quite openly under capitalism and is bound to develop further and be completed under socialism.

9. In the field of relations between states, the national policy of the Communist International cannot stop at the bare, formal recognition of the equality of nations. Such lip service, carrying no obligation to act, is the limit to which the bourgeois democrats confine themselves—both those who frankly admit to being such and those who call themselves "Socialists."

Both within parliament as well as outside it, the Communist parties must incessantly expose in their entire propaganda and agitation the continually repeated violations of the equality of nations and guaranteed rights of national minorities in all capitalist countries despite their "democratic" constitutions. In addition, it must be explained persistently that only the soviet order can ensure true national equality by uniting first the proletariat and then the whole mass of the toilers in struggle against the bourgeoisie. Moreover, all Communist parties must directly support the revolutionary movement among the nations that are dependent and do not have equal rights (for example Ireland, the Negroes in America, and so forth), and in the colonies.

Without this last, especially important condition, the struggle against oppression of the dependent nations and colonies and recognition of their right to a separate state remains a dishonest facade, such as we see in the parties of the Second International.

10. Recognizing internationalism in word only, while diluting it in deed with petty-bourgeois nationalism and pacifism in all propaganda, agitation, and practical work, is a common practice not only among the centrist parties of the Second International but also among those that have left that International, and often even among parties that now call themselves Communist.

The fight against this evil, against the most deeply rooted petty-bourgeois, nationalist prejudices (which are expressed in all possible forms, such as racism, national chauvinism, and anti-Semitism) must be given all the more priority as the question becomes more pressing of transforming the dictatorship of the proletariat from a national framework (that is, a dictatorship that exists only in one country and is incapable of carrying out an independent international policy) into an international one (that is, a dictatorship of the proletariat in at least several advanced countries, capable of exercising a decisive influence on all of world politics).

Petty-bourgeois nationalism declares that internationalism consists of the mere recognition of the equality of nations (although this recognition is strictly verbal) and considers national egoism to be sacrosanct. Proletarian internationalism, on the contrary, requires subordinating the interests of the proletarian struggle in one country to the interests of this struggle on a world scale. It also requires that the nation that has overthrown its bourgeoisie has the ability and willingness to make the greatest national sacrifices in order to overthrow international capitalism.

Therefore, in the already fully capitalist countries that have workers' parties truly constituting a vanguard of the proletariat, the first and most important task is the fight against the opportunist and petty-bourgeois pacifist distortions of the concept and policies of internationalism.

11. With respect to the states and nations that have a more backward, predominantly feudal, patriarchal, or patriarchal-peasant character, the following points in particular must be kept in mind:

a. All Communist parties must support with deeds the revolutionary liberation movement in these countries. The form the support should take must be discussed with the Communist Party of the country in question, if there is such a party. This responsibility of most energetic assistance applies above all to the workers of the country upon which the backward country is colonially or financially dependent.

b. A struggle absolutely must be waged against the reactionary and medieval influence of the clergy, the Christian missions, and similar elements.

c. It is necessary to struggle against the Pan-Islamic and Pan-Asian movements and similar currents that try to link the liberation struggle against European and American imperialism with strengthening the power of Turkish and Japanese imperialism and of the nobles, large landowners, clergy, and so forth.

d. It is especially necessary to support the peasant movement in the backward countries against the landowners and all forms and vestiges of feudalism. We must particularly strive to give the peasant movement the most revolutionary character possible, organizing the peasants and all the exploited into soviets where feasible, and thereby establishing the closest connection between the western European Communist proletariat and the revolutionary peasant movement in the East, in the colonies, and in the backward countries in general.

e. A resolute struggle is necessary against the attempt to portray as communist the revolutionary liberation movements in the backward countries that are not truly communist. The Communist International has the duty to support the revolutionary movement in the colonies and the backward countries only on condition that the components are gathered in all backward countries for future proletarian parties—communist in fact and not only in name—and that they are educated to be conscious of their particular tasks, that is, the tasks of struggling against the bourgeois-democratic movement in their own nation. The Communist International should arrive at temporary agreements and, yes, even establish an alliance with the revolutionary movement in the colonies and backward countries. But it cannot merge with this movement. Instead it absolutely must maintain the independent character of the proletarian movement, even in its embryonic stage.

f. It is necessary continually to expose and explain to the broadest masses of toilers of all countries and nations, and especially the backward ones, that the imperialist powers, with the help of the privileged classes in the oppressed countries, are perpetrating a fraud. They are creating state structures that pose as politically independent states but are economically, financially, and militarily totally dependent upon the imperialist powers. The Palestine affair is a crass example of Entente imperialism and the bourgeoisie of the relevant country working together to swindle the working classes of an oppressed nation. Under the cover of creating a Jewish state in Palestine, Zionism actually delivers the Arab working population of Palestine, where the toiling Jews constitute only a small minority, to exploitation by Britain. In the present international situation, there is no salvation for the dependent and weak nations other than in alliance with soviet republics.

12. The age-old, ongoing enslavement of the colonies and weak peoples by the imperialist great powers left the toiling masses of the enslaved countries with feelings not just of bitterness but of mistrust toward the oppressor nations in general, including against the proletariat of these nations. Socialism was despicably betrayed during the years 1914–19 by the majority of the official leaders of this proletariat, when the social patriots used "defense of the fatherland" to conceal the "right" of "their" bourgeoisie to enslave the colonies and plunder financially dependent countries. Such a betrayal could only reinforce this completely justified mistrust. Abolishing such mistrust and national prejudices can proceed only very slowly. They can be eradicated only after imperialism is destroyed in the advanced countries and after the entire basis of economic life of the backward countries is radically transformed. The class-conscious Communist proletariat of all countries therefore has a responsibility to give particular care and attention to the survivals of national feelings in the long-enslaved countries and peoples, while making concessions to overcome more rapidly this mistrust and these prejudices. The victory over capitalism cannot be successfully accomplished without the proletariat and with it all working people of all countries and the nations of the entire world coming together in a unified alliance.

"Theses on the National and Colonial Questions," translated in John Riddell (ed.), *Workers of the World and Oppressed Peoples, Unite! Proceedings and Documents of the Second Congress, 1920,* vol. I (New York: Pathfinder Press, 1991), pp. 283–290.

"Theses on the Conditions for Admission" to the Communist International
1920

Better known as the "Twenty-One Conditions," these "Theses" adopted by the Second Comintern Congress laid down the rules for socialist parties to become Communist parties and enter the Communist International. Communists felt deep hostility to those Social Democrats who had supported their governments during the world war and who promoted reformist rather than revolutionary policies. Parties that wished to join the new "Third International" had to

*split with the "reformists and centrists" and be willing to carry out illegal, underground work
as well as legal activity. These "conditions" made it clear that the Communists were founding
a new form of international organization, more centralized and disciplined than the socialist
Second International. Within a few years, Communist parties had to conform to the general
policy directives of the Executive Committee of the Communist International (IKKI), and
when there were factional disputes within individual parties, the Comintern usually determined who represented the correct position and reprimanded or even expelled the "deviationists." The factional struggles within the Russian Communist Party bled over into the Comintern, but once the Stalin faction came out on top all Communist parties had to conform to
the program laid down in Moscow. Increasingly the policies of the Comintern and individual
Communist parties reflected the state interests of the USSR. Communists held that their first
duty was to protect the country where socialism was being established, and where the interests
of their home country conflicted with the international Communist movement, their loyalty
had to be to the International, which meant in fact to the Soviet Union.*

The Communist International is now frequently approached by parties and groups
that only recently belonged to the Second International and now want to join the
Communist International, although they have not in fact become communist. The
Second International has been definitively smashed. The intermediate parties and
the groups of the Center, seeing that the Second International has no prospects at all,
try to lean on the Communist International, which is becoming ever stronger. However, they hope to preserve enough "autonomy" to continue their former opportunist
or "centrist" policies. The Communist International is becoming rather fashionable.

The desire of some leading Center groups to join the Communist International
indirectly confirms that it has won the sympathy of the overwhelming majority of the
class-conscious workers of the whole world and is becoming a more powerful force
every day. It is in danger of being diluted by vacillating and irresolute groups that have
not yet broken with the ideology of the Second International.

Moreover, in some large parties in countries such as Italy, Sweden, Norway, and
Yugoslavia, where a majority takes a communist position, there remains to this day a
significant reformist and social-pacifist wing. This wing is just waiting for the moment
when it can raise its head again and begin actively sabotaging the proletarian revolution, thereby helping the bourgeoisie and the Second International.

No Communist may forget the lessons of the Hungarian soviet republic. The
Hungarian proletariat paid dearly for the unification of the Hungarian Communists
and the so-called left Social Democrats.

Accordingly, the Second Congress of the Communist International considers it
necessary to define very precisely the conditions for admission for new parties and to
call to the attention of parties accepted into membership the duties that are incumbent upon them.

The Second Congress of the Communist International establishes the following
conditions of membership in the Communist International:

1. *All propaganda* and *agitation* must have a truly communist character and correspond to the program and resolutions of the Communist International. All of the
party's publications must be directed by reliable Communists who have demonstrated
their dedication to the proletariat's cause. The dictatorship of the proletariat may not

be spoken of simply as if it were a stock phrase to be learned by rote. Instead, it must be popularized so that every ordinary working man and woman, every soldier and peasant, can understand the need for it from the facts of everyday life, facts that our press must systematically follow and utilize every single day.

Periodical and nonperiodical publications as well as all party publishing houses must be completely subordinate to the party executive committee, regardless of whether the party as a whole is legal or illegal at any given time. It is impermissible for the publishing houses to misuse their autonomy to pursue policies that do not correspond entirely to those of the party.

In the columns of the newspapers, at public meetings, in the trade unions, in consumer cooperative societies—anywhere that supporters of the Communist International can gain admission—it is necessary to denounce systematically and unmercifully not only the bourgeoisie but also its accomplices: the reformists of every shade.

2. Every organization wishing to join the Communist International must consistently and systematically remove reformists and centrists from all positions of any responsibility in the workers' movement (party organizations, editorial staffs, trade unions, parliamentary fractions, cooperative societies, local governments) and replace them with reliable Communists without being deterred by the prospect that, especially at first, ordinary workers from the masses will replace "experienced" opportunists.

3. In almost every country of Europe and America the class struggle is entering the phase of civil war. Under such conditions the Communists can place no faith in bourgeois legality. It is their duty to create everywhere a parallel organizational apparatus that in the crucial hour can help the party discharge its duty to the revolution. In all countries where a state of siege or emergency laws make it impossible for Communists to carry out all their work legally, it is absolutely necessary that legal and illegal activity be combined.

4. The duty to disseminate communist ideas carries with it a special obligation to conduct vigorous and systematic propaganda in the army. Where emergency laws hinder such agitation, it is to be conducted illegally. Refusal to carry out such work would be tantamount to a betrayal of revolutionary duty and incompatible with membership in the Communist International.

5. Systematic and consistent agitation is necessary in the countryside. The working class cannot be victorious unless it has the support of the rural proletariat and at least a part of the poorest peasants and has, through its policies, neutralized part of the remaining rural population. At the present time, communist work in the countryside is gaining exceptional importance. It must be carried out principally by revolutionary Communist *workers* of town and country who have ties with the countryside. To renounce this work or to leave it in unreliable, semireformist hands is tantamount to renouncing the proletarian revolution.

6. Every party that wishes to belong to the Communist International is duty-bound to expose not only overt social patriotism but also the duplicity and hypocrisy of social pacifism; to explain systematically to the workers that without the revolutionary overthrow of capitalism, no international courts of arbitration, no treaties of any kind curtailing arms production, no manner of "democratic" renovation of the League of Nations will be able to prevent new imperialist wars.

7. Parties wishing to belong to the Communist International are duty-bound to recognize the need for a complete break with reformism and the policies of the Cen-

ter and must conduct propaganda for this among the broadest layers of the party membership. Without this, no consistent communist policy is possible.

The Communist International demands unconditionally and as an ultimatum that this break be carried out at the earliest possible date. The Communist International cannot accept that notorious opportunists as, for example, Turati, Modigliam Kautsky, Hilferding, Hillquit, Longuet, and MacDonald should have the right to consider themselves members of the Communist International. That could lead only to the Communist International coming to resemble in large measure the ruined Second International.

8. In countries whose bourgeoisies possess colonies and oppress other nations, it is necessary that the parties have an especially clear and well-defined position on the question of colonies and oppressed nations. Every party wishing to belong to the Communist International is obligated to expose the tricks of "its own" imperialists in the colonies, to support every liberation movement in the colonies not only in words but in deeds to demand that the imperialists of its country be driven out of these colonies, to instill in the hearts of the workers of its country a truly fraternal attitude toward the laboring people in the colonies and toward the oppressed nations, and to conduct systematic agitation among its country's troops against all oppression of colonial peoples.

9. Every party wishing to belong to the Communist International must carry out systematic and persistent activity in the trade unions, the workers' and factory committees, the cooperatives, and other mass workers' organizations. In these organizations it is necessary to organize Communist cells that win the unions and other organizations to the cause of communism through persistent and unremitting work. In their daily work everywhere the cells are duty-bound to expose the betrayal by the social patriots and the fickleness of the Center. The Communist cells must be completely subordinate to the party as a whole.

10. Every party that belongs to the Communist International has the obligation to wage a tenacious struggle against the Amsterdam "International" of Yellow trade unions. It must conduct forceful propaganda among workers organized in unions on the need to break with the Yellow Amsterdam International. It must use all available means to support the emerging international association of Red trade unions affiliated to the Communist International.

11. Parties that wish to belong to the Communist International have the duty to review the individual composition of their parliamentary fractions, removing all unreliable elements from them, and to subordinate these fractions to the parties' executive committees not just in words but in deeds, demanding that each Communist member of parliament subordinate all of his activity to the interests of truly revolutionary propaganda and agitation.

12. Parties belonging to the Communist International must be organized on the basis of the principle of democratic *centralism*. In the present epoch of intensified civil war, the Communist Party will be able to fulfill its duty only if it is organized in the most centralized way possible and governed by iron discipline, and if its central leadership, sustained by the confidence of the party membership, is strong, authoritative, and endowed with the fullest powers.

13. Communist parties of countries in which Communists pursue their work legally must from time to time carry out purges (reregistrations) of the party membership in order to systematically cleanse the party of the petty-bourgeois elements that worm their way into it.

14. Every party that wishes to belong to the Communist International is obligated to render unconditional assistance to every soviet republic struggling against the forces of counterrevolution. Communist parties must conduct unambiguous propaganda aimed at preventing the shipment of war matériel to enemies of the soviet republics. In addition, they must use every possible means to carry out propaganda, etc.—legally or illegally—among troops sent to strangle workers' republics.

15. Parties that still have their old Social Democratic programs are required to change them as rapidly as possible and to formulate a new, communist program that corresponds to the specific conditions in their country and is in keeping with the resolutions of the Communist International. As a rule, the program of each party belonging to the Communist International must be approved by a regular congress of the Communist International or by the Executive Committee. If the Executive Committee of the Communist International does not approve a party's program, that party has the right to appeal to the congress of the Communist International.

16. All decisions by congresses of the Communist International as well as by its Executive Committee are binding on all parties that belong to the Communist International. The Communist International, working under conditions of most acute civil war, must be organized in a far more centralized way than was the Second International. At the same time, of course, in all their activity the Communist International and its Executive Committee must take into account the diverse conditions under which each party has to struggle and work, adopting universally binding decisions only on questions in which such decisions are possible.

17. Taking all this into consideration, all parties that wish to belong to the Communist International must change their name. Every party that wants to belong to the Communist International must bear the name: *Communist* Party of such and such country (Section of the Communist International). The question of name is not just a formality but a matter of great political importance. The Communist International has declared war on the whole bourgeois world and all Yellow, Social Democratic parties. It is necessary that the difference between the Communist parties and the old, official "Social Democratic" or "Socialist" parties, which have betrayed the banner of the working class, be clear to every ordinary toiler.

18. The leading publications of parties in all countries are required to print all important official documents of the Executive Committee of the Communist International.

19. All parties that belong to the Communist International or have applied to join it are required to call a special congress as soon as possible but no later than four months after the Second Congress of the Communist International to consider all these conditions. In doing so, the central leaderships must see to it that all local organizations become acquainted with the resolutions of the Second Congress of the Communist International.

20. Parties that want to join the Communist International now but have not radically changed their previous policies must, before joining, make certain that not less than two-thirds of the members of their central committees and of all their most important central bodies consist of comrades who even before the Second Congress of the Communist International publicly and unambiguously advocated that the party join it. Exceptions are permissible with the consent of the Executive Committee of the Communist International. The Executive Committee also has the right to make exceptions for representatives of the Center tendency mentioned in thesis 7.

21. Party members who reject on principle the conditions and theses laid down

by the Communist International must be expelled from the party. This applies in particular to delegates to the special congress.

"Theses on the Conditions for Admission," translated in John Riddell (ed.), *Workers of the World and Oppressed Peoples, Unite! Proceedings and Documents of the Second Congress, 1920,* vol. II (New York: Pathfinder Press, 1991), pp. 765–771.

Stalin, "On the Tasks of Workers in the Economy," excerpts from his speech to the First All-Union Conference of Workers of Socialist Industry
February 4, 1931

During what was called the "Third Period" (1928–1935) in Comintern and foreign policy, the USSR adopted a hostile attitude toward compromise with capitalist powers or Social Democrats. These were the same years as the launching of the First Five-Year Plan (1928–1931), the ferocious collectivization of peasant agriculture, and the "proletarian" phase in cultural life. Stalin made specific connections between foreign policy and the domestic program of rapid industrialization in his speech to the workers in 1931. Revealing his own thinking on the vulnerability of the Soviet Union in the refrain about being "beaten" and "backward," he appealed to a sense of patriotism in his listeners. He referred to "old Russia" and "Mother Russia," and turned the Marxist adage that the workers have no fatherland around to apply only to the past. Now there was a socialist fatherland that had to be defended by building up its socialist economy as rapidly as possible. By implication those who did not maintain "a genuine Bolshevik tempo" were unpatriotic, or worse, traitors.

It is sometimes asked whether it is not possible to slow down the tempo somewhat, to put a check on the movement. No, comrades, it is not possible! The tempo must not be reduced! On the contrary, we must increase it as much as is within our powers and possibilities. This is dictated to us by our obligations to the workers and peasants of the U.S.S.R. This is dictated to us by our obligations to the working class of the whole world.

To slacken the tempo would mean falling behind. And those who fall behind get beaten. But we do not want to be beaten. No, we refuse to be beaten! One feature of the history of old Russia was the continual beatings she suffered because of her backwardness. She was beaten by the Mongol khans. She was beaten by the Turkish beys. She was beaten by the Swedish feudal lords. She was beaten by the Polish and Lithuanian gentry. She was beaten by the British and French capitalists. She was beaten by the Japanese barons. All beat her—because of her backwardness, because of her military backwardness, cultural backwardness, political backwardness, industrial backwardness, agricultural backwardness. They beat her because to do so was profitable and could be done with impunity. You remember the words of the pre-revolutionary poet: "You are poor and abundant, mighty and impotent, Mother Russia." Those gentlemen were quite familiar with the verses of the old poet. They beat her, saying: "You are abundant," so one can enrich oneself at your expense. They beat her, saying: "You are poor and impotent," so you can be beaten and plundered with impunity. Such is the law of the exploiters—to beat the backward and the weak. It is the jungle law of capitalism. You are backward, you are weak—therefore you are wrong; hence you can be beaten and enslaved. You are mighty—therefore you are right; hence we must be wary of you.

That is why we must no longer lag behind.

In the past we had no fatherland, nor could we have had one. But now that we have overthrown capitalism and power is in our hands, in the hands of the people, we have a fatherland, and we will uphold its independence. Do you want our socialist fatherland to be beaten and to lose its independence? If you do not want this, you must put an end to its backwardness in the shortest possible time and develop a genuine Bolshevik tempo in building up its socialist economy. There is no other way. That is why Lenin said on the eve of the October Revolution: "Either perish, or overtake and outstrip the advanced capitalist countries."

We are fifty or a hundred years behind the advanced countries. We must make good this distance in ten years. Either we do it, or we shall go under.

That is what our obligations to the workers and peasants of the U.S.S.R. dictate to us.

Pravda, No. 35, February 5, 1931; translated in J.V. Stalin, *Works,* XIII (Moscow: Foreign Languages Publishing House, 1955), pp. 40–41.

Stalin's Interview with Roy Howard of the Scripps-Howard Publications

1936

In this interview with an American journalist, Stalin attempted to reconcile the Soviet policy of collective security, of cooperation and compromise with Western capitalist states, with the USSR's revolutionary legacy and the activity of foreign Communist parties. He distinguished between the capitalism of the Western democracies and capitalism's "imperialist stage," represented by the fascist states, which presented a danger of war. He also tried to allay the fears of the democracies by rejecting the idea of exporting revolution from the USSR. The rather benign face that Stalin presents here was one of the many different personas he could affect. Like most skilled politicians, Stalin was a consummate performer, alternately tough, cruel, wise, playful, angry, but always in control. He impressed those who met him, even Franklin Delano Roosevelt and Winston Churchill, as a shrewd and talented leader. But in his public acts he revealed only what he needed to reveal, and in that economy of expression he maintained an advantage over his interlocutors, who were left guessing.

HOWARD: What situation or condition, in your opinion, furnishes the chief war menace today?

STALIN: Capitalism.

HOWARD: In which specific manifestations of capitalism?

STALIN: In its imperialistic, annexationist manifestations.

You remember how the first world war broke out. It broke out as a result of the desire to divide the world. Today the background is the same. There are capitalist states which consider themselves cheated, during previous redivisions of spheres of influence, territories, sources of raw materials, markets, etc., and which would again desire to redivide them to their own advantage. Capitalism in its imperialistic stage is a system which regards war as a legitimate method for solution of international disputes—a method which is legitimate in fact if not legally so.

HOWARD: May there not be genuine fear in capitalistic countries of intent on the part of the Soviet Union to force its political theories on other nations?

STALIN: There is no justification for such fears. If you think that the people of the Soviet Union have any desire themselves, and, moreover, by force, to alter the face of surrounding states, then you are badly mistaken.

The people of the Soviet Union naturally desire that the face of surrounding states should change, but this is the business of surrounding states themselves. I fail to see what dangers surrounding states can see in the ideas of the Soviet people if these states are really firmly seated in their saddles.

HOWARD: You appreciate, no doubt, Mr. Stalin, that much of the world had long entertained a different impression.

STALIN: This is a product of misunderstanding.

HOWARD: A tragic misunderstanding?

STALIN: No, comic. Or perhaps tragic-comic.
You see, we Marxists believe that revolution will occur in other countries, as well. But it will occur at a time when it will be considered possible or necessary by revolutionaries of those countries. Exported revolution is nonsense. Each country, if it so desires, will make its own revolution. And if no such desire exists, no revolution will occur.

For instance, our country wanted to effect a revolution, and did effect it, and now we are building a new classless society. But to assert that we desire to bring about revolution in other countries, by interfering with their lives, is to speak of something which does not exist and which we never preach. . . .

HOWARD: You admit that communism has not been achieved in Russia. State socialism has been built. Fascism in Italy and National Socialism in Germany have claimed that they have attained similar results. Have not both been achieved at the price of privation and personal liberty sacrificed for the good of the state?

STALIN: The term "state socialism" is not precise. Under this term many understand an order under which a certain part of the wealth, sometimes a quite considerable part, passes into state ownership or under its control while in the great majority of cases the ownership of plants, factories, and land remains in private hands.

Many understand "state socialism" in this way. Sometimes a system is concealed behind this term in which the capitalist state, in the interests of preparation for the conduct of war, takes upon itself the maintenance of a certain number of private enterprises.

The society which we have built can in no way be termed "state socialism."

Our Soviet society is socialist because private ownership of factories, plants, land, banks, and means of transportation has been abolished in our country and replaced by public ownership. The social organization which we have created can be termed a Soviet, socialist organization which has not yet been quite completed, but is in its root a socialist organization of society. The foundation of this society is public ownership: state ownership, namely, ownership by the entire people as well as cooperative-collective farm property.

Neither Italian fascism nor German national "socialism" have anything in common with such a society, primarily because private ownership of factories, plants, lands, banks, means of transportation, etc., remain untouched there, and, therefore, capitalism in Germany and Italy remains in full force.

Yes, you are right that we have not yet built a communist society. It is not so easy to build such a society.

The difference between a socialist and communist society is probably known to you. A certain inequality in regard to property still exists in a socialist society. But in a socialist society there is no unemployment, no exploitation, no oppression of nationalities. In a socialist society, everybody is obliged to work even though he is remunerated for his labor and not yet according to his needs, but according to the quantity and quality of the labor expended.

Therefore, wages still exist, and unequally differentiated wages at that. Only when we succeed in creating such an order under which people receive for their labor from the society not according to the quantity and quality of labor, but according to their needs, will it be possible to say that we have built up a communist society.

You say that in order to build our socialist society we sacrifice personal liberty and suffer privations. In your question appears the notion that socialist society negates personal liberty.

This is incorrect. Of course, in order to build something new, one has to economize, accumulate means, temporarily limit one's requirements, borrow from others. If you want to build a new house, you save money temporarily and limit your requirements, otherwise you might not build your house.

This is all the more when the upbuilding of a whole new human society is concerned. It was necessary, temporarily, to limit certain requirements, accumulate necessary means, strain forces. We acted precisely in this way and built a socialist society.

But we built this society not for the curbing of personal liberty, but in order that human personalities should really feel free. We built it for the sake of real personal liberty, liberty without quotation marks.

It is difficult for me to imagine what "personal liberty" the unemployed can have who go hungry and cannot find utilization of their labor.

Real liberty exists only there where exploitation has been annihilated, where no oppression of some peoples by others exists, where there is no unemployment and pauperism, where a person does not tremble because tomorrow he may lose his job, home, and bread. Only in such a society is real, and not illusory, personal and every other liberty possible.

"Beseda s predsedatelem amerikanskogo gazetnogo ob" edineniia 'Skripps-Govard Niuspeipers' g-nom Roi Govardom" (Conversation with Roy Howard of the Scripps-Howard Publications), *Pravda,* March 5, 1936;" translated in Alfred Erich Senn (ed.), *Readings in Russian Political and Diplomatic History: Volume II: The Soviet Period* (Homewood, IL: The Dorsey Press, 1966), pp. 197–202.

The Nazi-Soviet Pact

August 23, 1939

The Soviet government tried to interest Britain and France in rejecting the German pressure on Czechoslovakia in 1938. Stalin declared his willingness to go to war to defend the threatened state, but instead Prime Minister Chamberlain and Premier Daladier went to Munich and capitulated to Hitler. Within months, both Britain and France signed declarations of non-aggression with Germany, and Stalin reasoned, mistakenly, that an anti-Soviet alliance was forming. A low-level Anglo-French military delegation came to Moscow, but nothing came of the negotiations. Stalin then decided to respond positively to German overtures for an agreement. Hitler pressed for an early meeting, for his plans called for an invasion of Poland in the coming weeks. On August 23, 1939, German Foreign Minister Ribbentrop flew to Moscow, narrowly missing being shot down by Soviet artillery uninformed about the visit. That same day, Molotov and Ribbentrop signed the pact. During the ceremony Stalin remarked, "Of course, we are not forgetting that your ultimate aim is to attack us."[1] Once the formalities had been completed, he lifted his champagne glass and toasted, "Let's drink to the new anti-Comintern Stalin! Let's drink to the health of the leader of the German people, Hitler!"[2]

The Nazi-Soviet Pact was a revolution in European diplomacy. Hitler was now free to attack Poland without considering Soviet opposition. When Britain and France responded by declaring war on Germany, the Nazis were able to turn westward without worrying about a two-front war. Stalin gained time and territory, but once Hitler defeated France and drove the British from the continent, the USSR faced an immensely powerful and determined Germany without any other significant opponents in Europe.

In the "secret protocol" to the Pact, Germany and the USSR divided Eastern Europe into spheres of influence. Stalin received the Baltic republics, eastern Poland, and Bessarabia. This part of the Pact remained a state secret in the Soviet Union, and its existence was denied well into the Gorbachev years, for it demonstrated the treachery through which Estonia, Latvia, and Lithuania were turned into Soviet states. Eventually Germany and the Soviet Union quibbled about the spoils in Eastern Europe, but such minor matters of real estate were not the principal cause for the collapse of the Pact. As Stalin suspected, Hitler intended to invade the Soviet Union all along, part of his imperial design for Lebensraum (living space) for Germans and the eradication of communism. But when German troops massed on the Soviet border, Stalin refused to believe the warnings that he received from his intelligence services.

Memorandum of a Conversation Held on the Night of August 23d to 24th, Between the Reich Foreign Minister, on the One Hand, and Herr Stalin and the Chairman of the Council of People's Commissars Molotov, on the Other Hand

VERY SECRET!

STATE SECRET

The following problems were discussed:

---

1. Dmitri Vokogonov, *Stalin, Triumph and Tragedy*, ed. and trans. by Harold Shukman (London: Weidenfel and Nicolson, 1991), p. 385.

2. Ibid., p. 386.

1) Japan:

The Reich Foreign Minister stated that the German-Japanese friendship was in no wise directed against the Soviet Union. We were, rather, in a position, owing to our good relations with Japan, to make an effective contribution to an adjustment of the differences between the Soviet Union and Japan. Should Herr Stalin and the Soviet Government desire it, the Reich Foreign Minister was prepared to work in this direction. He would use his influence with the Japanese Government accordingly and keep in touch with the Soviet representative in Berlin in this matter.

Herr Stalin replied that the Soviet Union indeed desired an improvement in its relations with Japan, but that there were limits to its patience with regard to Japanese provocations. If Japan desired war, it could have it. The Soviet Union was not afraid of it and was prepared for it. If Japan desired peace—so much the better! Herr Stalin considered the assistance of Germany in bringing about an improvement in Soviet-Japanese relations as useful, but he did not want the Japanese to get the impression that the initiative in this direction had been taken by the Soviet Union.

The Reich Foreign Minister assented to this and stressed the fact that his cooperation would mean merely the continuation of talks that he had for months been holding with the Japanese Ambassador in Berlin in the sense of an improvement in Soviet-Japanese relations. Accordingly, there would be no new initiative on the German side in this matter.

2) Italy:

Herr Stalin inquired of the Reich Foreign Minister as to Italian aims. Did not Italy have aspirations beyond the annexation of Albania—perhaps for Greek territory? Small, mountainous, and thinly populated Albania was, in his estimation, of no particular use to Italy.

The Reich Foreign Minister replied that Albania was important to Italy for strategic reasons. Moreover, Mussolini was a strong man who could not be intimidated.

This he had demonstrated in the Abyssinian conflict, in which Italy had asserted its aims by its own strength against a hostile coalition. Even Germany was not yet in a position at that time to give Italy appreciable support.

Mussolini welcomed warmly the restoration of friendly relations between Germany and the Soviet Union. He had expressed himself as gratified with the conclusion of the Nonaggression Pact.

3) Turkey:

Herr Stalin asked the Reich Foreign Minister what Germany thought about Turkey.

The Reich Foreign Minister expressed himself as follows in this matter: he had months ago declared to the Turkish Government that Germany desired friendly relations with Turkey. The Reich Foreign Minister had himself done everything to achieve this goal. The answer had been that Turkey became one of the first countries to join the encirclement pact against Germany and had not even considered it necessary to notify the Reich Government of the fact.

Herren Stalin and Molotov hereupon observed that the Soviet Union had also had a similar experience with the vacillating policy of the Turks.

The Reich Foreign Minister mentioned further that England had spent five million pounds in Turkey in order to disseminate propaganda against Germany.

Herr Stalin said that according to his information the amount which England had spent in buying Turkish politicians was considerably more than five million pounds.

4) England:

Herren Stalin and Molotov commented adversely on the British Military Mission in Moscow, which had never told the Soviet Government what it really wanted.

The Reich Foreign Minister stated in this connection that England had always been trying and was still trying to disrupt the development of good relations between Germany and the Soviet Union. England was weak and wanted to let others fight for its presumptuous claim to world domination.

Herr Stalin eagerly concurred and observed as follows: the British Army was weak; the British Navy no longer deserved its previous reputation. England's air arm was being increased, to be sure, but there was a lack of pilots. If England dominates the world in spite of this, this was due to the stupidity of the other countries that always let themselves be bluffed. It was ridiculous, for example, that a few hundred British should dominate India.

The Reich Foreign Minister concurred and informed Herr Stalin confidentially that England had recently put out a new feeler which was connected with certain allusions to 1914. It was a matter of a typically English, stupid maneuver. The Reich Foreign Minister had proposed to the Führer to inform the British that every hostile British act, in case of a German-Polish conflict, would be answered by a bombing attack on London.

Herr Stalin remarked that the feeler was evidently Chamberlain's letter to the Führer, which Ambassador Henderson delivered on August 23 at the Obersalzberg. Stalin further expressed the opinion that England, despite its weakness, would wage war craftily and stubbornly.

5) France:

Herr Stalin expressed the opinion that France, nevertheless, had an army worthy of consideration.

The Reich Foreign Minister, on his part, pointed out to Herren Stalin and Molotov the numerical inferiority of France. While Germany had available an annual class of more than 300,000 soldiers, France could muster only 150,000 recruits annually. The West Wall was five times as strong as the Maginot Line. If France attempted to wage war with Germany, she would certainly be conquered.

6) Anti-Comintern Pact:

The Reich Foreign Minister observed that the Anti-Comintern Pact was basically directed not against the Soviet Union but against the Western democracies. He knew, and was able to infer from the tone of the Russian press, that the Soviet Government fully recognized this fact.

Herr Stalin interposed that the Anti-Comintern Pact had in fact frightened principally the City of London and the small British merchants.

The Reich Foreign Minister concurred and remarked jokingly that Herr Stalin was surely less frightened by the Anti-Comintern Pact than the City of London and the small British merchants. What the German people thought of this matter is evident from a joke which had originated with the Berliners, well known for their wit and humor, and which had been going the rounds for several months, namely, "Stalin will yet join the Anti-Comintern Pact."

7) *Attitude of the German people to the German-Russian Nonaggression Pact:*

The Reich Foreign Minister stated that he had been able to determine that all strata of the German people, and especially the simple people, most warmly welcomed the understanding with the Soviet Union. The people felt instinctively that between Germany and the Soviet Union no natural conflicts of interests existed, and that the development of good relations had hitherto been disturbed only by foreign intrigue, in particular on the part of England.

Herr Stalin replied that he readily believed this. The Germans desired peace and therefore welcomed friendly relations between the Reich and the Soviet Union.

The Reich Foreign Minister interrupted here to say that it was certainly true that the German people desired peace, but, on the other hand, indignation against Poland was so great that every single man was ready to fight. The German people would no longer put up with Polish provocation.

8) *Toasts:*

In the course of the conversation, Herr Stalin spontaneously proposed a toast to the Führer, as follows:

"I know how much the German nation loves its Führer; I should therefore like to drink to his health."

Herr Molotov drank to the health of the Reich Foreign Minister and of the Ambassador, Count von der Schulenburg.

Herr Molotov raised his glass to Stalin, remarking that it had been Stalin who— through his speech of March of this year, which had been well understood in Germany—had brought about the reversal in political relations.

Herren Molotov and Stalin drank repeatedly to the Nonaggression Pact, the new era of German-Russian relations, and to the German nation.

The Reich Foreign Minister in turn proposed a toast to Herr Stalin, toasts to the Soviet Government, and to a favorable development of relations between Germany and the Soviet Union.

9) *When they took their leave, Herr Stalin addressed to the Reich Foreign Minister words to this effect:*

The Soviet Government takes the new Pact very seriously. He could guarantee on his word of honor that the Soviet Union would not betray its partner.

Hencke

Moscow, August 24, 1939.

August 23, 1939.

TREATY OF NONAGGRESSION BETWEEN GERMANY AND THE UNION OF SOVIET SOCIALIST REPUBLICS

The Government of the German Reich and the Government of the Union of Soviet Socialist Republics desirous of strengthening the cause of peace between Germany and the U.S.S.R., and proceeding from the fundamental provisions of the Neutrality Agreement concluded in April 1926 between Germany and the U.S.S.R., have reached the following agreement:

Article I

Both High Contracting Parties obligate themselves to desist from any act of violence, any aggressive action, and any attack on each other, either individually or jointly with other powers.

Article II

Should one of the High Contracting Parties become the object of belligerent action by a third power, the other High Contracting Party shall in no manner lend its support to this third power.

Article III

The Governments of the two High Contracting Parties shall in the future maintain continual contact with one another for the purpose of consultation in order to exchange information on problems affecting their common interests.

Article IV

Neither of the two High Contracting Parties shall participate in any grouping of powers whatsoever that is directly or indirectly aimed at the other party.

Article V

Should disputes or conflicts arise between the High Contracting Parties over problems of one kind or another, both parties shall settle these disputes or conflicts exclusively through friendly exchange of opinion or, if necessary, through the establishment of arbitration commissions.

Article VI

The present treaty is concluded for a period of ten years, with the proviso that, in so far as one of the High Contracting Parties does not denounce it one year prior to the expiration of this period, the validity of this treaty shall automatically be extended for another five years.

Article VII

The present treaty shall be ratified within the shortest possible time. The ratifications shall be exchanged in Berlin. The agreement shall enter into force as soon as it is signed.

Done in duplicate, in the German and Russian languages.

Moscow, August 23, 1939.

For the Government	With full power of the
of the German Reich:	Government of the U.S.S.R.:
v. Ribbentrop	V. Molotov

SECRET ADDITIONAL PROTOCOL

On the occasion of the signature of the Nonaggression Pact between the German Reich and the Union of Socialist Soviet Republics the undersigned plenipotentiaries of each of the two parties discussed in strictly confidential conversations the question of the boundary of their respective spheres of influence in Eastern Europe. These conversations led to the following conclusions:

1. In the event of a territorial and political rearrangement in the areas belonging to the Baltic States (Finland, Estonia, Latvia, Lithuania), the northern boundary of Lithuania shall represent the boundary of the spheres of influence of Germany and the U.S.S.R. In this connection the interest of Lithuania in the Vilna area is recognized by each party.

2. In the event of a territorial and political rearrangement of the areas belonging to the Polish state the spheres of influence of Germany and the U.S.S.R. shall be bounded approximately by the line of the rivers Narew, Vistula, and San.

The question of whether the interests of both parties make desirable the maintenance of an independent Polish state and how such a state should be bounded can only be definitely determined in the course of further political developments.

In any event both Governments will resolve this question by means of a friendly agreement.

3. With regard to Southeastern Europe attention is called by the Soviet side to its interest in Bessarabia. The German side declares its complete political disinterestedness in these areas.

4. This protocol shall be treated by both parties as strictly secret.

Moscow, August 23, 1939.

For the Government	Plenipotentiary of the
of the German Reich:	Government of the U.S.S.R.:
v. Ribbentrop	V. Molotov

Raymond James Sontag and James Stuart Beddie (eds.), *Nazi-Soviet Relations, 1939–1941: Documents from the Archives of the German Foreign Office* (Washington, D.C.: Department of State, 1948), pp. 72–78.

══════ Memorandum from Lavrenti Beria to Stalin ══════
March 5, 1940

With the dismemberment of Poland in 1939, tens of thousands of Polish military officers, political figures, and ordinary people ended up on the Soviet side of the German-Soviet parti-

tion line. The Soviets arrested and imprisoned anyone considered a potential enemy, and on March 5, 1940, Stalin and his associates signed their death warrants. When the invading German forces discovered the mass grave of Polish officers in the Katyn forest and exposed the killings to the world (April 13, 1943), the Polish government-in-exile, in London, called for an investigation. Stalin was furious and broke off relations with the London Poles. A Soviet investigation accused the Germans of killing the Poles, and for fifty years the USSR repeatedly denied massacring the imprisoned Poles. Only in the Gorbachev years was the truth admitted.

Point 13/144 Special File
Top Secret
USSR   March 5, 1940
People's Commissariat of Internal affairs [*NKVD*]
March 1940   Central Committee, All-Union Communist Party (of Bolsheviks)
[*TSK VKP (b)*]   No. 794/5
Moscow

To Comrade STALIN

NKVD USSR prisoner-of-war camps and prisons in western parts of Ukraine and Belorussia hold a large number of former Polish Army officers, former employees of Polish police and intelligence agencies, members of Polish nationalist counterrevolutionary parties, participants in exposed counterrevolutionary insurgent organizations, deserters, i.a. They are all sworn enemies of Soviet authority, filled with hatred for the Soviet system.

The prisoner of war officers and policemen held in the camps are trying to continue c-r work and are conducting anti-Soviet agitation. Each of them is just waiting to be freed so that he can have the chance to actively engage in the struggle against Soviet authority.

NKVD organs in western Ukraine and Belorussia have exposed a number of counterrevolutionary insurgent organizations. In all of these counterrevolutionary organizations an active leadership role was played by former officers of the former Polish Army, former policemen, and gendarmes.

Many persons participating in counterrevolutionary spy and insurgent organizations also have been discovered among the arrested deserters and violators of the national border.

Excluding enlisted personnel and noncommissioned officers, the prisoner-of-war camps hold a total of 14,736 former officers, civil servants, landowners, policemen, gendarmes, prison guards, settlers, and intelligence agents—more than 97% are of Polish nationality. Among them are:

Generals, colonels, and lieutenant colonels	296
Majors and captains	2,080
Lieutenants, second lieutenants, and ensigns	6,049
Officers and junior commanders of the police, border guards, and gendarmerie	1,030

Rank and file policemen, gendarmes, prison guards,
and intelligence officers   5,138

Civil servants, landowners, priests, and settlers   144

The prisons in the western parts of Ukraine and Belorussia hold a total of 18,632 internees (of which 10,685 are Poles), including:

Former officers	1,207
Former police intelligence agents and gendarmes	5,141
Spies and saboteurs	347
Former landowners, factory owners, civil servants	465
Members of various counterrevolutionary and insurgent organizations and various counterrevolutionary elements	5,345
Deserters	6,127

Because they all are inveterate, incorrigible enemies of Soviet authority, the *NKVD* USSR considers it essential to:

I. Order the *NKVD* USSR to give priority consideration (applying the supreme punishment of execution by shooting) to:

    1) the cases of 14,700 persons held in prisoner-of-war camps, namely former Polish officers, civil servants, landowners, policemen, intelligence agents, gendarmes, settlers, and prison guards,

    2) as well as the cases of 11,000 persons arrested and held in prisons in the western parts of Ukraine and Belorussia, namely members of various counterrevolutionary espionage and sabotage organizations, former landowners, factory owners, former Polish officers, civil servants, and deserters.

II. Conduct the examination of cases without summoning the prisoners and without presenting the accusation, the investigation finding, or the conviction, as follows:

    a) persons held in prisoner-of-war camps—according to information presented by the *NKVD* USSR Directorate of Prisoner of War Affairs,

    b) arrested persons—according to information presented by the *NKVD* of the Ukrainian SSR and the *NKVD* of the Belorussian SSR.

III. Assign responsibility for examining these matters and executing the decision to the trio of Comrades MERKULOV, KABULOV [handwritten], and BAShTAKOV (Chief of the First Special Division of the *NKVD* USSR).

PEOPLE'S COMMISSAR OF INTERNAL AFFAIRS OF THE USSR
[signed] L. Beria

[handwritten on first page]	SCRAWLED ACROSS FIRST page in handwriting]
Kalinin—for	For
Kaganovich—for	I. Stalin

[handwritten:]   K. Voroshilov
   Excerpt.   V. Molotov
   Beria   A. Mikoyan
      point 13/144
      March 5, 1940

RTsKhIDNI, F. 89, op. 14, d. 1-20, 11. 9–12; translated in Diane P. Koenker and Ronald D. Bachman (eds.),
Revelations from the Russian Archives: Documents in English Translation (Washington, D.C.: Library of Congress, 1997), pp. 165–167; some additions from the original document by the editor.

Letter to Nikita Khrushchev from Aleksandr Shelepin and Draft Resolution to Destroy the Documents Concerning the Katyn Massacre
March 3, 1959

This extraordinary memo from the head of KGB (Committee for State Security) nineteen years after the Polish officers were shot and buried at Katyn and in other mass graves requested that the personal files of those killed be destroyed in order to continue the cover-up of this crime.

To Comrade N. S. Khrushchev

There are preserved in the Committee of State Security [KGB] of the Council of Ministers of the USSR recorded files and other materials from 1940 on the imprisoned and interned officers, gendarmes, police, *osadniki,* landlords, and other people from the former bourgeoisie of Poland, who were executed in that year. By the orders of special *troiki* of the NKVD of the USSR altogether *21,857* people were shot—of which: *4,421* in the Katyn forest (Smolensk region), *3,820* in the Starobel'skii Camp near Kharkov, *6,311* in the Ostashkovskii camp (Kalinin region), and *7,305* were shot in other camps and prisons of western Ukraine and western Belorussia.

The whole operation of liquidating the said persons was carried out on the basis of the Resolution of the TsK KPSS [Central Committee of the Communist Party of the Soviet Union] of March 5, 1940. All were condemned to the highest measure of punishment according to the recorded files created for them as prisoners of war and interned persons in 1939.

From the moment of the carrying out of the operation in question, i.e., from 1940, no information on these files has been given to anyone, and all *21,857* files have been kept in a sealed building.

All these files have neither operational interest nor historical value for Soviet organs. It is unlikely that they would have any real interest for our Polish friends. On the contrary, it might be that an unexpected accident would lead to the uncovering [*raskanspiratsiia*] of the effected operation, with all kinds of undesirable consequences for our state. Moreover, in regard to those executed in the Katyn forest there exists an official version, confirmed by the production on the initiative of the Soviet organs of power in 1944 of an investigation of a Commission called: "The Special Commission to Establish and Investigate the Execution by the German Fascist Aggressors of Polish Officer Prisoners of War in the Katyn Forest."

According to the conclusions of this commission, all the Poles liquidated there were annihilated by the German occupiers. The materials of the investigations of that period were widely publicized in the Soviet and foreign press. The conclusions of the commission have been firmly established in international public opinion.

Following from this, it is considered expedient to destroy all the recorded files on those shot in 1940 in the above-mentioned operations.

For the use of possible inquiries by the TsK KPSS or the Soviet government the protocols of the *troiki* of the NKVD USSR that condemned the stated persons to death might be left, as well as the acts on carrying out the decisions of the *troiki*. These documents are insignificant in volume and may be kept in a special file.

A draft of a resolution of the TsK KPSS is attached.

Chairman of the Committee of State Security of the Council of Ministers of the USSR
A. Shelepin

March 3, 1959

Draft

Absolutely Secret

Resolution of the Presidium of the TsK KPSS.

_____ 1959

Allow the Committee of State Security of the Council of Ministers of the USSR to liquidate all the files on the operation carried out in connection with the Resolution of the TsK KPSS of March 5, 1940, except the protocols of the sessions of the *troiki* of the NKVD of the USSR.

RTsKhIDNI, f. 89, op. 14, d. 1–20, ll. 13–15; translation by the editor.

===== **Admiral N. G. Kuznetsov, "At Naval Headquarters"** =====

Stalin certainly expected that war with Germany would eventually break out, but he estimated that Hitler would wait until he had won the Battle of Britain. The Red Army was in a disastrous state as a result of the purge of more than 20,000 officers in 1937–1938. In the run-up to the German invasion a number of measures were taken to strengthen the armed forces: Voroshilov was replaced as People's Commissar of Defense by the able Marshall Semen Timoshenko; new officers were recruited, and others who had survived the Terror were reinstated (but by the summer of 1941, some 75 percent had been in their posts less than a year); General Georgii Zhukov was appointed Chief of the General Staff; and the size and quality of the army was improved, but it was too little too late. The Soviet leadership was convinced that Hitler would honor the Pact and that they from their side had to avoid being provoked into a war. To their shock, the German army crossed the Soviet borders on June 22, 1941, beginning the most colossal military struggle between two countries in modern times. In his memoirs, Admiral N. G. Kuznetsov, the People's Commissar of the Navy, recalls the confusion of that first night of the Russo-German war.

By early 1941 information began to seep through to us on Hitler's far from peaceful intentions. This information was at first very vague but then became much more definite and varied. Despite its efforts, the German command was unable to conceal its preparations for a major offensive on the far-flung front from the Barents Sea to the Bosporus. . . .

Indeed, what should have been done at the beginning of 1941 was to collate and analyze all these facts and to weigh them against Nazi promises and the nonaggression pact. There was the nonaggression pact with Germany, but there was also Hitler's *Mein Kampf*, in which he elaborated his plans for seizing "Lebensraum" in the East. He never renounced either the book or his plans. . . .

That same February I had a conversation with Zhdanov, who, as a member of the Supreme Naval Council, often came to the People's Commissariat. One day he stayed behind in my office after a meeting, and we discussed various topics. I then asked him whether he thought Germany's actions near our borders were preparations for war. He said he thought that Germany was incapable of fighting on two fronts. He believed the violations of our air space and the concentration of German forces on our borders were nothing more than precautionary measures on Hitler's part or a means of psychological pressure.

I expressed my doubts:

"If they are only precautionary measures, why should Hitler build up his forces in Finland and Rumania? Why do German reconnaissance planes fly over Hanko and Poliarnyi? After all, these places present no threat to them."

A few months before this talk, I heard Zhdanov make the rather categorical statement that both sides were bogged down in the war in the West and that this gave us the chance to go about our business in peace. On this occasion he did not say as much, but he still believed that a clash with Germany was improbable. He cited the experience of World War I, which showed that Germany was not equal to fighting on two fronts, and he also recalled Bismarck's well-known warning on this score.

Zhdanov may have had doubts in his own mind, or he may have had inside knowledge of some of Stalin's plans which I knew nothing about, and he must have been informed of the vast amount of work that was then being done at great speed to fortify our western frontiers. These efforts made sense mainly in the event of a war with Germany, so it seemed that the possibility of such a war was being taken into account. But it is still a mystery to me why Zhdanov answered as he did and what Stalin was planning. . . .

The last time that I saw Stalin on the eve of the war was June 13 or 14. I reported to him at that time on the latest intelligence from the fleets, on the training exercises conducted in the Black Sea, and on the *de facto* stoppage of deliveries by the Germans for the cruiser *Luetzow*. He did not raise any questions about the readiness of the fleets or issue any instructions in connection with a possible attack by Germany. "Is that all?" he asked me. Everyone present looked in my direction as if to say: Don't hold things up. I left the conference room quickly. I still wanted very much to report that German transports were leaving our ports and to ask whether the traffic of Soviet merchant ships in German waters shouldn't be restricted. But it seemed to me that my continued presence there was obviously unwelcome. The next day I was received by V. M. Molotov. He made decisions concerning several current questions. At the end of the conversation I offered my own unsolicited opinion concerning the suspicious behavior of the Germans, and as the weightiest argument I offered the graph of German merchant ship traffic. He expressed the same point of view on the possibility of war that A. A. Zhdanov had expressed earlier: "Only a fool would attack us."

Today, in pondering the behavior of Stalin and his closest aides, I am inclined to draw the conclusion that right up to the last moment they did not believe in the possibility of an attack by Hitler. Stalin was unnerved and irritated by persistent reports (oral and written) about the deterioration of relations with Germany. He brushed facts and arguments aside more and more abruptly. . . .

Saturday, June 21, passed much the same as the preceding days, full of alarm signals from the fleets. . . .

Silence reigned in the offices of the capital. On normal days it would be dinner time after 6:00 p.m., and the chiefs would go to their homes for about three hours or so, afterward working until late at night. But on Saturday many of them left town. The pressure of business abated.

That evening it was especially quiet somehow. The telephone did not ring at all, as if it had been disconnected. Even such "restless" People's Commissars as V. A. Malyshev and I. I. Nosenko, with whom I was in especially close contact, did not make their presence known with the question that had become habitual of late: "How are things going?"

I sat in my office. The usual city noises could be heard from the street—the rumble of vehicles and occasional loud, carefree youthful laughter. Absent-mindedly I went through my papers, unable to concentrate on them. A very short time before, I had chanced to see a survey of the foreign press and TASS reports. The most diverse newspapers were writing about the approaching war between Russians and Germans. They couldn't all be in collusion!

I recalled how wars had begun in the past, in particular, the Russo-Japanese War in 1904. We had frequently been reminded of it at officers' school and at the Naval Academy—perhaps because the first act of this war was played at sea. It began with a surprise torpedo attack which the Japanese destroyers launched against the Russian squadron anchored at the outer roadstead of Port Arthur.

While talking about Port Arthur, Gall', the instructor in tactics at the naval school, . . . emphasized that there was no point in being surprised that the enemy had attacked without a declaration of war; after all, he was the enemy. It would be naive to complain of his perfidy. Rather, one should wonder about our command, which had carelessly placed the fleet in a position where it could be attacked.

School recollections were followed by memories of what I had experienced in Cartagena, where bombs sometimes began exploding before the air raid signal sounded. I recalled the tension that gripped us during the days of the Khasan events when we were expecting Japanese aircraft to strike Vladivostok. . . .

The time passed slowly. . . .

About 11:00 p.m. the telephone rang, and I heard the voice of Marshal S. K. Timoshenko:

"There is very important news. Come to my office."

Quickly putting into a folder the latest data on the situation in the fleets and calling V. A. Alafuzov, I went with him. Vladimir Antonovich took maps. We were expecting to report about the situation on the seas. . . .

The Marshal was pacing about the room and dictating. It was still very warm. General of the Army Zhukov was writing at a desk, his tunic unbuttoned. Before him lay several sheets from a large pad of radiogram forms covered with writing. It was apparent that the People's Commissar of Defense and the Chief of the General Staff had been working for quite a long time.

Semen Konstantinovich noticed us and stopped. Briefly, without mentioning any sources, he said that an attack by Germany on our country was considered possible.

"The fleets must be ordered to be in combat readiness."

"In the event of attack, are they allowed to open fire?" I asked.

"They are."

Turning to Rear Admiral Alafuzov, he said:

"Run to headquarters and send a telegram to the fleets immediately concerning complete combat readiness. Run!"

There was no time to discuss whether it was dignified for an admiral to run down the street. Vladimir Antonovich started running, and I remained for a minute to verify whether I had understood correctly that an attack could be anticipated that very night. Yes, it was true. After midnight on June 22. And it was already past midnight!

As I returned to the People's Commissariat [of the Navy], I was beset by disturbing thoughts: when did the People's Commissar of Defense learn of the possible attack by the Hitlerites? At what hour did he receive the order to bring the forces to a state of full combat readiness? Why was it the People's Commissar of Defense and not the government itself that had given me the order to bring the fleet to a state of combat readiness? And moreover, why was this done in such a semi-official way and so late?

One thing was clear: several hours had already elapsed since the People's Commissar of Defense learned about a possible attack by Hitler. The sheets of paper covered with writing that I had seen on his desk were a confirmation of this. Later I learned that the leaders of the People's Commissariat of Defense—the People's Commissar and the Chief of the General Staff—had been called to Stalin on June 21 at about 5:00 p.m. Consequently, the decision was already made then, under the weight of incontestable proof, to bring the forces to a state of complete combat readiness and, in the event of attack, to repulse it. That means that all this happened approximately ten to eleven hours before the enemy actually invaded our land. . . . It confirms the fact that on the afternoon of June 21, Stalin considered a clash with Germany, if not inevitable, at least highly likely. It is very regrettable that the remaining hours were not used with maximal effectiveness. . . .

We were still thinking: "Can it really be war?" Somewhere inside us the weak hope continued to glimmer: perhaps it'll all pass? . . .

But it did not pass. This was about to be confirmed. In the meantime, a period of anguished waiting began for me. There was nothing to do. The fleets knew what had to be done. Emergency measures had been carefully defined and worked out. People were working according to plan, and it was better not to disturb them. . . .

In Moscow, dawn broke somewhat earlier than usual. At three o'clock it was already light. I lay down on the couch and tried to imagine what was happening in the fleets. The muffled ring of the telephone brought me to my feet.

"This is the Commander of the Black Sea Fleet reporting."

From the unusually excited voice of Vice Admiral F. S. Oktiabr'skii, I understood that something extraordinary had happened.

"An air raid has been carried out against Sevastopol'. Anti-aircraft artillery is fighting off the attack. Several bombs have fallen on the city—"

I looked at my watch. 3:15 a.m. This is when it started—I no longer had any doubts; this was war!

I immediately picked up the receiver and dialed the number of Stalin's office. The duty officer [Loginev] answered:

"Comrade Stalin is not here, and I don't know where he is."

"I have an exceedingly important message which I must immediately relay to Comrade Stalin personally," I said, attempting to convince the duty officer.

"I can't help you in any way," he answered calmly and hung up.

I did not put the phone down. I called Marshal S. K. Timoshenko. I repeated word for word what Vice Admiral Oktiabr'skii had reported about the air raid that was now in progress over Sevastopol'.

"Do you hear me?"

"Yes, I hear you."

It was no time to brief the People's Commissar on the situation in the fleets and on the state of their preparedness. He had enough of his own business to attend to.

I didn't leave the telephone for several more minutes. I tried again to reach Stalin at various numbers, to talk with him personally, all to no avail. I again telephoned the duty officer:

"I request that you inform Comrade Stalin that German planes are bombing Sevastopol'. This is war!"

"I shall report it to the proper person," the duty officer answered.

A few minutes later the telephone rang, and I heard a dissatisfied, somewhat irritated voice:

"Do you understand what you are reporting?" This was G. M. Malenkov.

"I understand and I report, taking full responsibility, that war has begun—"

G. M. Malenkov hung up. Later I learned that he did not believe me. He called Sevastopol' to verify my report. The talk with Malenkov showed that the hope of avoiding war was alive even at a time when the attack had begun and blood was being spilled over enormous areas of our land. Apparently the orders given to the People's Commissar of Defense the night before, on June 21, had not been very decisive and categorical. Therefore, they had been transmitted without particular haste, and the districts did not receive them before the Hitlerite attack.

Nonetheless, after Malenkov's call, I still hoped that any minute would bring government orders on the initial operation to be carried out now that war had begun. But no orders whatsoever were forthcoming. Then, on my own responsibility, I ordered that the fleets be sent an official message about the outbreak of war and the repulsion of enemy strikes by all means. On the basis of this, the military council of the Baltic Fleet, for example, announced throughout the fleet as early as 5:17 a.m. on June 22: "Germany has begun an attack on our bases and ports. Repulse all enemy attempts to attack by force of arms."

At that time, of course, the thing to do would have been not only to "repulse attempts to attack" but to inflict counterstrikes against the enemy. But the fleet could not do this alone. Coordinated plans and unified leadership of all the armed forces were required.

It was not difficult to imagine Stalin's state of mind in the face of the dreadful events which, according to his calculations, should have happened much later. He stubbornly denied the possibility of these events happening now, in 1941, right up to the very last days.

His condition communicated itself to those surrounding him, and they were unable to take the reins of command into their hands. They were not accustomed to independent action and could only carry out the will of Stalin, who stood above them. That was the tragedy of those hours. . . .

At about 10:00 a.m. on June 22 I went to the Kremlin. I decided to report on the situation personally. Moscow was resting peacefully. As always on holidays there were few people in the center, and the occasional passers-by looked festive. Only a few cars rushed along, frightening pedestrians with their honking. The capital still did not know that a fire was blazing on the frontiers and that our advance units were engaged in heavy fighting in an attempt to hold back the enemy.

In the Kremlin, everything looked as it did on a normal day off. The sentry at the Borovitskie Gates saluted smartly and, as always, looked into the car. Slowing down slightly, we drove into the Kremlin. I looked around carefully—there was no evidence of anxiety. An oncoming car stopped, as was the custom, and yielded the right of way to us. Everything was silent and deserted.

"Probably the leadership has assembled in some other place," I decided. "But why has there yet been no official announcement of war?"

Finding no one at the Kremlin, I returned to the People's Commissariat.

"Has anyone called?" was my first question.

"No, no one has called."

Main Naval Headquarters had already received more precise data from the fleets. . . . At the end of June 22 the overall picture did not seem gloomy to me, even though the first reports that the Germans were pushing toward Libava had arrived. The enemy did not dare attack the base by sea, and on land I hoped that he would be repulsed by ground units of the Baltic Military District, whose mission it was to defend the city and the base.

It was important that on the first day of war, the enemy did not sink a single ship of ours and that he caused the fleet only insignificant damage.

To be sure, in the future, I would see my errors with my own eyes and would convince myself that in many ways the enemy had forestalled us all the same. This was first apparent in the Baltic Sea. When the war started, the Germans had already succeeded in mining our shores. Their submarines had taken up positions in advance along the probable routes over which our ships would move. . . .

One thing is apparent to me beyond any doubt: Stalin not only did not exclude the possibility of war with Hitler's Germany; on the contrary, he considered such a war quite probable and even inevitable. He regarded the agreement of 1939 as only a breathing spell, but the breathing spell turned out to be much shorter than he had anticipated. I think his mistake was in miscalculating the date of the conflict. Stalin directed war preparations—extensive and many-sided preparations—on the basis of very distant dates. Hitler disrupted his calculations.

Stalin's suspicions of England and America aggravated the matter. Naturally there was basis enough for thinking that England and America were trying to bring us into conflict with Germany. It was no secret that this was the policy of the Western powers, and Stalin's distrust and hostility toward them was based on it. He received with suspicion or even rejected outright all information about Hitler's actions that came from the English or the Americans. This was his reaction not only to information from casual sources, but even to reports of our official representatives in those countries and to statements made by English and American government officials.

Our embassy people in England reported the transfer of German troops to the Soviet border, naming dates and numbers of divisions. These facts were considered dubious only because they came from English government circles, from Churchill and Cadogan. When such information came from other sources, even from Germany itself, unfortunately it was not taken into account either.

Distrust of Western European political leaders, although well-founded, grew to such proportions that it overshadowed everything. The English were interested in having us fight Germany; therefore everything said about the possibility of war in the near future had been fabricated by them—that is my estimate of Stalin's train of thought.

But despite that, why did he fail to take the simplest precautionary measures? As a man of vast experience, a great statesman, he naturally understood that the only way to sober an aggressor is to be prepared to give him a fitting reply—a blow for a blow. An aggressor can understand a fist; that means you have to show him one. The fist Hitler put up was the divisions he had concentrated on our border. Our fist, therefore, could have been Soviet divisions. But the mere availability of divisions, tanks, planes, and ships was not enough in those circumstances. What was also necessary was a high level of combat preparedness, the full readiness of every military organization and even of the entire country. Everyone—from the People's Commissar of Defense to the common soldier—ought to have known what he was to do immediately in case of war.

I feel that under the weight of irrefutable facts, Stalin began to realize in early 1941 that Hitler might attack. Convinced that his calculations for a war in the more distant future had been wrong and aware that the armed forces and the country as a whole were not ready for war in the coming months, he tried to exploit everything he thought might postpone the conflict. He acted so as to avoid giving Hitler the slightest pretext for an attack in order not to provoke a war. Out of a desire to show that we had no intention of going to war with Germany, he was neurotically sensitive to every retaliation on the part of our armed forces. As a result, when German planes photographed our bases, we were told: Hold your fire! When German air intelligence agents were caught over Soviet fortifications and made to land at our airports, the order was: Release them at once! When the English warned of the possibility of German attack, a declaration was published in answer: We don't believe any rumors; we're keeping faith with the agreement!

N. G. Kuznetsov, "Voenno-Morskoi Flot nakanune Velikoi Otechestvennoi voiny," *Voenno-istoricheskii zhurnal*, no. 9 (1965), pp. 73–74; N. G. Kuznetsov, "Pered voinoi," *Oktiabr'*, no. 11 (1965), pp. 146–171; translated in Seweryn Bialer (ed.), *Stalin and His Generals: Soviet Military Memoirs of World War II* (New York: Pegasus, 1969), pp. 189–200.

Report from Beria to Stalin
July 4, 1944

World War II was a time of great mobility for the Soviet peoples. Millions were driven eastward by the invading Germans; hundreds of thousands moved west to fight the enemy. Stalin ordered the deportation of various peoples from the borders of the USSR—Poles in the west, Koreans in the east—and in 1943–1944, he commanded that selected peoples whom he deemed to be collaborators and traitors be uprooted from their homelands and sent to Siberia or Central Asia. Along with Volga Germans, Chechens, Ingushi, Karachai, Balkars, Kalmyks, and Meshketian Turks, most of them from the Caucasus, he exiled the Crimean Tatars and other peoples from Crimea. The bland prose of this report disguises the horror of the transports, the loss of lives, and the psychological costs of a whole people being damned as treasonous. While most of the other peoples were eventually restored to their homelands after Stalin's death, the Crimean Tatars, Volga Germans, and Meskhetian Turks were not. Only in the last years of Soviet power did the Crimean Tatars organize a dissident movement demanding repatriation, but they never received official recognition of their right to return.

———————————————

copy

top secret

copy No. 2

No. 693/b

STATE DEFENSE COMMITTEE

July 4, 1994

to Comrade J. V. STALIN

The USSR People's Commissariat of Internal Affairs [*NKVD SSSR*] reports that the resettlement of special settlers from the Crimea—Tatars, Bulgarians, Greeks, and Armenians—has been completed.

In total, 225,009 people have been resettled, including:

Tatars	183,155 persons
Bulgarians	12,422 persons
Greeks	15,040 persons
Armenians	9,621 persons
Germans	1,119 persons
and other foreigners	3,652 persons

All the Tatars reached their places of settlement and have been resettled:

in the *oblast*'s of the Uzbek Soviet Socialist Republic (SSR)—151,604 persons

in the *oblast*'s of the Russian Soviet Federated Socialist Republic (RSFSR), in accordance with the decision of the State Defense Committee [*GOKO*] of May 21, 1944—31,551 persons

Bulgarians, Greeks, Armenians, and Germans, numbering 38,202 persons, are en route to the Bashkir Autonomous Soviet Socialist Republic [ASSR], the Mari ASSR, the Kemerovo, Molotov, Sverdlovsk, and Kirov *oblast*'s of the RSFSR and Gur'ev *oblast*' of the Kazakh SSR.

The 3,652 persons of other nationalities are destined for resettlement in Fergana *oblast*' of the Uzbek SSR.

All of the special settlers who have reached their destination have found satisfactory living conditions.

A significant number of the resettled, able-bodied Tatar special settlers have been engaged in agricultural work on collective and state farms, in logging, in industry, and in construction.

There were no incidents during the resettlement operation on site or during transit.

PEOPLE'S COMMISSAR OF INTERNAL AFFAIRS
of the Soviet Union
(L. Beria)

s-ta *NKVD*
Chernigov
One copy made for the special Crimea file.
July 3, 1944
True copy [signed] V. Popova
[Stamp at top of page:] No. 1-1 p. no. 198, SPECIAL FILE

TSGAOR [Tsentral'nyi Gosudarstvennyi Arkhiv Oktiabr'skoi Revoliutsii]; translated in Koenker and
Bachman (eds.), *Revelations*, p. 211.

Record of Conversations between Comrade I. V. Stalin and Chairman of the Central People's Government of the People's Republic of China, Mao Zedong
December 16, 1949; January 22, 1950.

*At the same time as the Soviet Union was installing Communist regimes in the countries of
East Central Europe, the Chinese Communists swept to power on their own, driving the nationalist Guomindang off the mainland and onto the island of Formosa (Taiwan), and Korean Communists took control of the north of the Korean peninsula. Stalin's relations with
the Chinese Communists had never been smooth. His advice to them to the 1920s to stay
allied to Chiang Kai-shek and the nationalists had proven disastrous, and his last-ditch suggestions to Mao Zedong in early 1949 that he negotiate with the nationalists were brusquely
rejected by Mao. A few months after the Communists entered Beijing, Mao traveled to Moscow
for Stalin's seventieth birthday, to attend the Nineteenth Congress of the Soviet Communist
party, and to negotiate treaties with the USSR. Stalin was both accommodating but firm in
establishing his superior role as "godfather" of the international Communist movement. Early
in the negotiations he made it clear that the USSR did not want a confrontation with the
United States and Britain, but in his second long meeting with Mao, Stalin indicated he was
willing to revise the Yalta agreements on China and take up "a struggle against the Americans" on these issues. At the same time, the Soviets were not willing to give the Chinese a
more prominent role in the administration of the railroad through Manchuria (KChZhD [Ki-
taiskaia Changchunskaia Zheleznaia Doroga]) or in the joint Soviet-Chinese enterprises
then being set up. The Chinese desperately needed Soviet assistance, but at the same time the
proud victors of the long struggle to win China were unhappy with the condescension of their
Soviet comrades. Stalin, on the other hand, was not above keeping Mao cooling his heals in
Moscow for months before seriously discussing the outstanding issues between the two "fraternal" states.*

[Classification level blacked out: "NOT SECRET" Stamped]

16 DECEMBER 1949

After an exchange of greetings and a discussion of general topics, the following conversation took place.

COMRADE MAO ZEDONG: The most important question at the present time is the question of establishing peace. China needs a period of 3–5 years of peace, which would be used to bring the economy back to prewar levels and to stabilize the country in general. Decisions on the most important questions in China hinge on the prospects for a peaceful future. With this in mind the CC CPC [Central Committee of the Communist Party of China] entrusted me to ascertain from you, comr[ade]. Stalin, in what way and for how long will international peace be preserved.

COMRADE STALIN: In China a war for peace, as it were, is taking place. The question of peace greatly preoccupies the Soviet Union as well, though we have already had peace for the past four years. With regards to China, there is no immediate threat at the present time: Japan has yet to stand up on its feet and is thus not ready for war; America, though it screams war, is actually afraid of war more than anything; Europe is afraid of war; in essence, there is no one to fight with China, not unless Kim Il Sung decides to invade China?

Peace will depend on our efforts. If we continue to be friendly, peace can last not only 5–10 years, but 20–25 years and perhaps even longer.

COMRADE MAO ZEDONG: Since *Liu Shaoqi's* return to China, CC CPC has been discussing the treaty of friendship, alliance and mutual assistance between China and the USSR.

COMRADE STALIN: This question we can discuss and decide. We must ascertain whether to declare the continuation of the current 1945 treaty of alliance and friendship between the USSR and China, to announce impending changes in the future, or to make these changes right now.

As you know, this treaty was concluded between the USSR and China as a result of the Yalta Agreement, which provided for the main points of the treaty (the question of the Kurile Islands, South Sakhalin, Port Arthur, etc.). That is, the given treaty was concluded, so to speak, with the consent of America and England. Keeping in mind this circumstance, we, within our inner circle, have decided not to modify any of the points of this treaty for now, since a change in even one point could give America and England the legal grounds to raise questions about modifying also the treaty's provisions concerning the Kurile Islands, South Sakhalin, etc. This is why we searched to find a way to modify the current treaty in effect while formally maintaining its provisions, in this case by formally maintaining the Soviet Union's right to station its troops at Port Arthur while, at the request of the Chinese government, actually withdrawing the Soviet Armed forces currently stationed there. Such an operation could be carried out upon China's request.

One could do the same with KChZhD [Chinese Changchun Railroad, which traverses Manchuria], that is, to effectively modify the corresponding points of the agreement while formally maintaining its provisions, upon China's request.

If, on the other hand, the Chinese comrades are not satisfied with this strategy, they can present their own proposals.

COMRADE MAO ZEDONG: The present situation with regard to KChZhD and Port Arthur corresponds well with Chinese interests, as the Chinese forces are inadequate to effectively fight against imperialist aggression. In addition, KChZhD is a training school for the preparation of Chinese cadres in railroad and industry.

COMRADE STALIN: The withdrawal of troops does not mean that Soviet Union refuses to assist China, if such assistance is needed. The fact is that we, as communists, are not altogether comfortable with stationing our forces on foreign soil, especially on the soil of a friendly nation. Given this situation anyone could say that if Soviet forces can be stationed on Chinese territory, then why could not the British, for example, station their forces in Hong Kong, or the Americans in Tokyo?

We would gain much in the arena of international relations if, with mutual agreement, the Soviet forces were to be withdrawn from Port Arthur. In addition, the withdrawal of Soviet forces would provide a serious boost to Chinese communists in their relations with the national bourgeoisie. Everyone would see that the communists have managed to achieve what [Nationalist Chinese leader] Jiang Jieshi [Chiang Kai-shek] could not. The Chinese communists must take the national bourgeoisie into consideration.

The treaty ensures the USSR's right to station its troops in Port Arthur. But the USSR is not obligated to exercise this right and can withdraw its troops upon Chinese request. However, if this is unsuitable, the troops in Port Arthur can remain there for 2, 5, or 10 years, whatever suits China best. Let them not misunderstand that we want to run away from China. We can stay there for 20 years even.

COMRADE MAO ZEDONG: In discussing the treaty in China we had not taken into account the American and English positions regarding the Yalta agreement. We must act in a way that is best for the common cause. This question merits further consideration. However, it is already becoming clear that the treaty should not be modified at the present time, nor should one rush to withdraw troops from Port Arthur.

Should not Zhou Enlai visit Moscow in order to decide the treaty question?

COMRADE STALIN: No, this question you must decide for yourselves. Zhou may be needed in regard to other matters.

COMRADE MAO ZEDONG: We would like to decide on the question of Soviet credit to China, that is to draw up a credit agreement for 300.000.000 dollars between the governments of the USSR and China.

COMRADE STALIN: This can be done. If you would like to formalize this agreement now, we can.

COMRADE MAO ZEDONG: Yes, exactly now, as this would resonate well in China. At the same time it is necessary to resolve the question of trade, especially between the USSR and Xinjiang [Sinkiang], though at present we cannot present a specific trade operations plan for this region.

COMRADE STALIN: We must know right now what kind of equipment China will need, especially now, since we do not have equipment in reserve and the request for industrial goods must be submitted ahead of time.

COMRADE MAO ZEDONG: We are having difficulties in putting together a request for equipment, as the industrial picture is as yet unclear.

COMRADE STALIN: It is desirable to expedite the preparation of this request, as requests for equipment are submitted to our industry at least a year in advance.

COMRADE MAO ZEDONG: We would very much like to receive assistance from the USSR in creating air transportation routes.

COMRADE STALIN: We are ready to render such assistance. Air routes can be established over Xinjiang and the MPR [Mongolian People's Republic]. We have specialists. We will give you assistance.

COMRADE MAO ZEDONG: We would also like to receive your assistance in creating a naval force.

COMRADE STALIN: Cadres for Chinese navy could be prepared at Port Arthur. You give us people, and we will give you ships. Trained cadres of the Chinese navy could then return to China on these ships.

COMRADE MAO ZEDONG: Guomindang [Kuomintang] supporters have built a naval and air base on the island of Formosa [Taiwan]. Our lack of naval forces and aviation makes the occupation of the island by the People's Liberation Army [PLA] more difficult. With regard to this, some of our generals have been voicing opinions that we should request assistance from the Soviet Union, which could send volunteer pilots or secret military detachments to speed up the conquest of Formosa.

COMRADE STALIN: Assistance has not been ruled out, though one ought to consider the form of such assistance. What is most important here is not to give Americans a pretext to intervene. With regard to headquarters staff and instructors we can give them to you anytime. The rest we will have to think about.

Do you have any assault landing units?

COMRADE MAO ZEDONG: We have one former Guomindang assault landing regiment unit which came over to join our side.

COMRADE STALIN: One could select a company of landing forces, train them in propaganda, send them over to Formosa, and through them organize an uprising on the isle.

COMRADE MAO ZEDONG: Our troops have approached the borders of Burma and Indo-China. As a result, the Americans and the British are alarmed, not knowing whether we will cross the border or whether our troops will halt their movement.

COMRADE STALIN: One could create a rumor that you are preparing to cross the border and in this way frighten the imperialists a bit.

COMRADE MAO ZEDONG: Several countries, especially Britain, are actively campaigning to recognize the People's Republic of China. However, we believe that we should not rush to be recognized. We must first bring about order to the country, strengthen our position, and then we can talk to foreign imperialists.

COMRADE STALIN: That is a good policy. In addition, there is no need for you to create conflicts with the British and the Americans. If, for example, there will be a need to put pressure on the British, this can be done by resorting to a conflict between the Guangdong province and Hong Kong. And to resolve this conflict, Mao Zedong could come forward as the mediator. The main point is not to rush and to avoid conflicts.

Are there foreign banks operating in Shanghai?

COMRADE MAO ZEDONG: Yes.

COMRADE STALIN: And whom are they serving?

COMRADE MAO ZEDONG: The Chinese national bourgeoisie and foreign enterprises which so far we have not touched. As for the foreigners' spheres of influence, the British predominate in investments in the economic and commercial sectors, while the Americans lead in the sector of cultural-educational organizations.

COMRADE STALIN: What is the situation regarding Japanese enterprises?

COMRADE MAO ZEDONG: They have been nationalized.

COMRADE STALIN: In whose hands is the customs agency?

COMRADE MAO ZEDONG: In the hands of the government.

COMRADE STALIN: It is important to focus attention on the customs agency as it is usually a good source of government revenue.

COMRADE MAO ZEDONG: In the military and political sectors we have already achieved complete success; as for cultural and economic sectors, we have as yet not freed ourselves from foreign influence there.

COMRADE STALIN: Do you have inspectors and agents overseeing foreign enterprises, banks, etc.?

COMRADE MAO ZEDONG: Yes, we have. We are carrying out such work in the study and oversight of foreign enterprises (the Kailan [?] mines, electric power plants and aqueducts in Shanghai, etc.).

COMRADE STALIN: One should have government inspectors who must operate legally. The foreigners should also be taxed at higher levels than the Chinese.

Who owns the enterprises mining wolfram [tungsten], molybdenum, and petroleum?

COMRADE MAO ZEDONG: The government.

COMRADE STALIN: It is important to increase the mining of minerals and especially of petroleum. You could build an oil pipeline from western Lanzhou to Chengdu [?], and then transport fuel by ship.

COMRADE MAO ZEDONG: So far we have not decided which districts of China we should strive to develop first—the coastal areas or those inland, since we were unsure of the prospects for peace.

COMRADE STALIN: Petroleum, coal, and metal are always needed, regardless of whether there be war or not.

COMRADE STALIN: Can rubber-bearing trees be grown in southern China?

COMRADE MAO ZEDONG: So far it has not been possible.

COMRADE STALIN: Is there a meteorological service in China?

COMRADE MAO ZEDONG: No, it has not been established yet.

COMRADE STALIN: It should be established.

COMRADE STALIN: We would like to receive from you a list of your works which could be translated into Russian.

COMRADE MAO ZEDONG: I am currently reviewing my works which were published in various local publishing houses and which contain a mass of errors and misrepresentations. I plan to complete this review by spring of 1950. However, I would like to receive help from Soviet comrades: first of all, to work on the texts with Russian translators and, secondly, to receive help in editing the Chinese original.

COMRADE STALIN: This can be done. However, do you need your works edited?

COMRADE MAO ZEDONG: Yes, and I ask you to select a comrade suitable for such a task, say, for example, someone from CC VKP/b/ [All-Union Communist Party of bolsheviks].

COMRADE STALIN: It can be arranged, if indeed there is such a need.

Also present at the meeting: comrs. Molotov, Malenkov, Bulganin, Vyshinskii, [Soviet translator N.T.] Fedorenko and [Chinese translator] Shi Zhe/Karskii/.

Recorded by comr. Fedorenko.

[signature illegible 31/XII]

22 JANUARY 1950

After an exchange of greetings, and a short discussion of general topics, the following conversation took place.

STALIN: There are two groups of questions which must be discussed: the first group of questions concerns the existing agreements between the USSR and China; the second group of questions concerns the current events in Manchuria, Xinjiang, etc.

I think that it would be better to begin not with the current events, but rather with a discussion of the existing agreements. We believe that these agreements need to be changed, though earlier we had thought that they could be left intact. The existing agreements, including the treaty, should be changed because war against Japan figures at the very heart of the treaty. Since the war is over and Japan has been crushed, the situation has been altered, and now the treaty has become an anachronism.

I ask to hear your opinion regarding the treaty of friendship and alliance.

MAO ZEDONG: So far we have not worked out a concrete draft of the treaty, only a few outlines.

STALIN: We can exchange opinions, and then prepare an appropriate draft.

MAO ZEDONG: Judging from the current situation, we believe that we should strengthen our existing friendship using the help of treaties and agreements. This would resonate well both in China and in the international arena. Everything that guarantees the future prosperity of our countries must be stated in the treaty of alliance and friendship, including the necessity of avoiding a repetition of Japanese aggression. So long as we show interest in the prosperity of our countries, one cannot rule out the possibility that the imperialist countries will attempt to hinder us.

STALIN: True. Japan still has cadres remaining, and it will certainly lift itself up again, especially if Americans continue their current policy.

MAO ZEDONG: Two points that I made earlier are cardinal in changing our future treaty from the existing one. Previously, the Guomindang spoke of friendship in words only. Now the situation has changed, with all the conditions for real friendship and cooperation in place.

In addition, whereas before there was talk of cooperation in the war against Japan, now attention must turn to preventing Japanese aggression. The new treaty must include the questions of political, economic, cultural and military cooperation. Of most importance will be the question of economic cooperation.

STALIN: Is it necessary to keep the provision, stated in article 3 of the current Treaty of friendship: ". . . This article shall remain in force up until that time when, by request of both High Participants in the Treaty, the United Nations is given the responsibility of preventing any future aggression on the part of Japan"?

MAO ZEDONG: I don't believe it is necessary to keep this provision.

STALIN: We also believe that it is unnecessary. What provisions do we need to specify in the new treaty?

MAO ZEDONG: We believe that the new treaty should include a paragraph on consultation regarding international concerns. The addition of this paragraph would strengthen our position, since among the Chinese national bourgeoisie there are objections to the policy of rapprochement with the Soviet Union on questions of international concern.

STALIN: Good. When signing a treaty of friendship and cooperation, the inclusion of such a paragraph goes without saying.

MAO ZEDONG: That's right.

STALIN: To whom shall we entrust the preparation of the draft? I believe that we should entrust it to [Soviet Foreign Minister Andrei] Vyshinskii and [Chinese Foreign Minister] Zhou Enlai.

MAO ZEDONG: Agreed.

STALIN: Let us move over to the agreement on KChZhD. What proposals do you have on this question?

MAO ZEDONG: Perhaps we should accept as the guiding principle the idea of making practical changes concerning the KChZhD and the Port Arthur agreements, while legally continuing them in their present state?

STALIN: That is, you agree to declare the legal continuation of the current agreement, while, in effect, allowing appropriate changes to take place.

MAO ZEDONG: We must act so as to take into account the interests of both sides, China and the Soviet Union.

STALIN: True. We believe that the agreement concerning Port Arthur is not equitable.

MAO ZEDONG: But changing this agreement goes against the decisions of the Yalta Conference?!

STALIN: True, it does—and to hell with it! Once we have taken up the position that the treaties must be changed, we must go all the way. It is true that for us this entails certain inconveniences, and we will have to struggle against the Americans. But we are already reconciled to that.

MAO ZEDONG: This question worries us only because it may have undesirable consequences for the USSR.

STALIN: As you know, we made the current agreement during the war with Japan. We did not know that Jiang Jieshi would be toppled. We acted under the premise that the presence of our troops in Port Arthur would be in the interests of Soviet Union and democracy in China.

MAO ZEDONG: The matter is clear.

STALIN: In that case, would you deem the following scenario acceptable: declare that the agreement on Port Arthur shall remain in force until a peace treaty with Japan is signed, after which the Russian troops would be withdrawn from Port Arthur. Or perhaps one could propose another scenario: declare that the current agreement shall remain in place, while in effect withdrawing troops from Port Arthur. We will accept whichever of these scenarios is more suitable. We agree with both scenarios.

MAO ZEDONG: This question should be thought through. We agree with the opinion of comrade Stalin and believe that the agreement on Port Arthur must remain in force until a peace treaty is signed with Japan, after which the treaty shall become invalid and the Soviet soldiers will leave. However, we would like for Port Arthur to be a place for military collaboration, where we could train our military naval forces.

STALIN: The question of Dalny [Dairen; Dalian]. We have no intention of securing any Soviet rights in Dalny.

MAO ZEDONG: Will Dalny remain a free port?

STALIN: Since we are giving up our rights there, China must decide on its own the question of Dalny: will it remain a free port or not. During his time Roosevelt insisted that Dairen remain a free port.

MAO ZEDONG: So the preservation of the free port would be in the interests of America and Britain?

STALIN: Of course. It's a house with open gates.

MAO ZEDONG: We believe that Port Arthur could serve as a base for our military collaboration, while Dalny could serve as a base for Sino-Soviet economic collaboration. In Dalny there is a whole array of enterprises that we are in no position to exploit without Soviet assistance. We should develop a closer economic collaboration there.

STALIN: In other words, the agreement on Port Arthur will remain in force until a peace treaty is signed with Japan. After the signing of the peace treaty the existing agreement shall become invalid and the Russians shall withdraw their troops. Did I sum up your thoughts correctly?

MAO ZEDONG: Yes, basically so, and it is exactly this which we would like to set forth in the new treaty.

STALIN: Let us continue the discussion of the KChZhD question. Tell us, as an honest communist, what doubts do you have here?

MAO ZEDONG: The principal point is that the new treaty should note that joint exploitation and administration will continue in the future. However, in the case of administration, China should take the lead role here. Furthermore, it is necessary to examine the question of shortening the duration of the agreement and to determine the amount of investment by each side.

MOLOTOV: The conditions governing the cooperation and joint administration of an enterprise by two interested countries usually provide for equal participation by both sides, as well as for alternation in the appointment of replacements for management positions. In the old agreement the administration of the railroad belonged to the Soviets; however, in the future we think it necessary to alternate in the creation of management functions. Let's say that such an alternation could take place every two-three years.

ZHOU ENLAI: Our comrades believe that the existing management of KChZhD and the office of the director ought to be abolished and a railroad administration commission be set up in their place; and that the offices of the commission chairman and of the director should be replaced by Chinese cadres. However, given comrade Molotov's proposals, this question requires more thought.

STALIN: If we are talking about joint administration, then it is important that the replacements for the managing position be alternated. That would be more logical. As for the duration of the agreement, we would not be against shortening it.

ZHOU ENLAI: Should we not change the ratio of capital investment by each side, by increasing the level of Chinese investment to 51%, instead of the current requirement for parity?

MOLOTOV: This would go against the existing provision for parity.

STALIN: We do indeed have agreements with the Czechs and the Bulgarians which provide for parity and equal-footing for both sides. Since we already have joint administration, then we might as well have equal participation.

MAO ZEDONG: The question needs to be further examined, keeping in mind the interests of both sides.

STALIN: Let us discuss the credit agreement. We need to officially formalize that which has already been agreed to earlier. Do you have any observations to make?

MAO ZEDONG: Is the shipment of military arms considered a part of the monetary loan?

STALIN: This you can decide yourself: we can bill that towards the loan, or we can formalize it through trade agreements.

MAO ZEDONG: If the military shipments are billed towards the loan, then we will have little means left for industry. It appears that part of the military shipments will have to be billed towards the loan, while the other part will have to be paid with Chinese goods. Can't the period of delivery of industrial equipment and military arms be shortened from 5 to 3-4 years?

STALIN: We must examine our options. The matter rests in the requisition list for our industry. Nevertheless, we can move the date that the credit agreement goes into effect to 1 January 1950, since the shipments should begin just about now. If the agreement specified July 1949 as the time for the commencement of the loan, the international community would not be able to understand how an agreement could have been reached between the Soviet Union and China, which at the time did not even have its own government. It seems that you should hasten somewhat to present the requisition list for industrial equipment. It should be kept in mind that the sooner such a list is presented, the better for the matter at hand.

MAO ZEDONG: We believe that the conditions of the credit agreement are generally favorable to China. Under its terms we pay only one percent interest.

STALIN: Our credit agreements with people's democracies provide for two percent interest. We could, says comr. Stalin jokingly, increase this interest for you as well, if you would like. Of course, we acted under the premise that the Chinese economy was practically in ruin.

As is clear from the telegrams that we have received, the Chinese government intends to use its army in the reconstruction of its economy. That is very good. In our time we also made use of the army in our economic development and had very good results.

MAO ZEDONG: That's right. We are drawing on the experience of our Soviet comrades.

STALIN: You raised the question of China receiving a certain amount of grain for Xinjiang?

MAO ZEDONG: Wheat and textile.

STALIN: For this you need to come up with the necessary requests that include numbers.

MAO ZEDONG: Very well, we shall prepare these.
How shall we proceed with the trade agreement?

STALIN: What is your opinion? Up until now we have only had a trade agreement with Manchuria. We would like to know what sort of a situation we should look forward to in the future: will we be signing separate agreements with Xinjiang, Manchuria and other provinces, or a single agreement with the central government?

MAO ZEDONG: We would like to have a single, central agreement. But in time Xinjiang may have a separate agreement.

STALIN: Just Xinjiang; what about Manchuria?

ZHOU ENLAI: A separate agreement with Manchuria can be ruled out, since in the agreement with the central government China's obligations would in essence be fulfilled by shipments made from Manchuria.

STALIN: We would like the central government to sanction and take the responsibility for the agreements with Xinjiang or Manchuria.

MAO ZEDONG: The agreement with Xinjiang must be signed in the name of the central government.

STALIN: Right, since [a] provincial government might not take many things into account, whereas things are always clearer to the central government.

What other questions do you have?

MAO ZEDONG: At the present time the main question is economic cooperation—the reconstruction and development of the Manchurian economy.

STALIN: I think that we will entrust the preparation of this question to comrs. Mikoyan, Vyshinskii, Zhou Enlai, and [CCP CC member and Vice Chairman of Finance and Economics Commission] Li Fuchun.

Any other questions?

MAO ZEDONG: I would like to note that the air regiment that you sent to China was very helpful. They transported 10 thousand people. Let me thank you, comrade Stalin, for the help and ask you to allow it to stay a little longer, so it could help transport provisions to [CCP CC member and commander of the PLA's Second Field Army] Liu Bocheng's troops, currently preparing for an attack on Tibet.

STALIN: It's good that you are preparing to attack. The Tibetans need to be subdued. As for the air regiment, we shall talk this over with the military personnel and give you an answer.

The meeting took two hours.

Present at the meeting were comrs. Molotov, Malenkov, Mikoyan, Vyshinskii, Roshchin, Fedorenko and Mao Zedong, Zhou Enlai, Li Fuchun, [PRC Ambassador to the USSR] Wang Jiaxiang, [CCP CC member] Chen Boda, and Shi Zhe/Karskii/.

Arkhiv prezidenta Rossiiskoi Federatsii, f. 45, op. 1, d. 329, ll. 9–17, 29–38; translation by Danny Rozas, in *Cold War International History Project Bulletin,* nos. 6–7 (Winter 1995–1996), pp. 5–9.

4

REFORM AND STAGNATION

CHAPTER SIX

FROM AUTOCRACY TO OLIGARCHY

When Stalin died, people in the Soviet Union looked anxiously to the future, fearful about what might happen next. An infallible deity had shown himself to be mortal, and he had left behind underlings who appeared all the more fallible. Almost immediately the new leadership dismantled much of the apparatus of terror, releasing over a million prisoners (including common criminals), rehabilitating those convicted in the Doctors' Plot, and emphasizing the need for "socialist legality." Without the authority of Stalin, and hesitant to use the police in the arbitrary way he had, the new governors of the USSR needed to find new sources of legitimacy for their continuance in power. They proposed revised social and economic policies that emphasized consumer goods, the improvement of material comfort for Soviet citizens, greater opening to the West, and more freedom of expression—at least outside public spaces. Writers and artists seized the new opportunities to call for a "struggle with bureaucratism" and the need for truthfulness in literature and art. A public social conscience and a somewhat broader arena for public opinion became possible.

Yet for all their reforms, Stalin's successors did not touch the foundations of the system that Stalin built. They maintained the "command economy" entirely controlled by the state and run by bureaucrats. The monopoly of political decision-making remained within the Communist party. Censorship, if not as strict as before, continued, and periodically the regime cracked down on the bolder intellectuals, forcing the most courageous into the so-called dissident movement. In 1956 Khrushchev, now the most powerful leader in the USSR, gave his famous "secret speech" on the crimes of Stalin, but within months his government sent tanks into Hungary to crush a popular revolution that took the end of Stalinism too seriously. The years 1953–1964, the so-called "Khrushchev era" (as if an era covers only eleven years), can be seen as a period of gradual, hesitant reform within the contours of an authoritarian regime, with short lurches forward and long, slow retrenchments. After Khrushchev was overthrown and Leonid Brezhnev emerged as paramount leader (1964–1982), reform slowed down even more, and the party limped into the future holding tightly to the reins of power.

Until recently, scholarship on the Khrushchev period was largely the prerogative of contemporary political scientists. Like archaeologists, they read the shards of evidence from the press or the positioning of leaders in photographs. In time, this Kremlinological approach broadened to include studies of policy and its effects, the social transformations taking place in the new urban USSR, and the fluctuations in post-

Stalinist culture. George Breslauer, author of a major study of Khrushchev and Brezhnev, explored how the post-Stalinist regimes sought to build authority, that is, how they legitimized power. Both leaders and their comrades, he argued, were convinced that the extremes of Stalinism were to be avoided—no more mass terror—and that government had to make greater efforts to provide material satisfaction to the Soviet people. The social openings offered by post-Stalinism form the context of historian Deborah Field's investigation of the gap between private interests and official morality in the Khrushchev years, a time when greater individualism and a developing sense of private life challenged the older norms of public service and collective life. The Khrushchev years were their own kind of "sixties," a time of limited experimentation and hope for change.

While he ameliorated life in the Soviet Union, Khrushchev ultimately left much of the Stalinist economic and political structure in place. When he threatened his colleagues with greater uncertainty about their positions in the power elite, they turned on him. In October 1964, a group of his closest associates, led by Brezhnev, forced him from office. They blamed him for "harebrained scheming." For the next seventeen years, the new leader of the party kept most of his cronies in power, slowed down any significant reform, and made it clear to other countries of the Soviet Bloc that deviation from policies approved by the Kremlin would not be tolerated.

Irreconcilable Differences: Divorce and Conceptions of Private Life in the Khrushchev Era

Deborah A. Field

A short story published in *Sem 'ia i shkola* [*Family and School*] in 1962 described a marriage that had fallen apart because the wife was in love with another man. The seven-year-old daughter of the family was desperately unhappy and made various futile efforts to get her parents back together. The husband was willing to reconcile for the child's sake, but the wife refused, explaining that people "must not violate . . . [their] nature in the name of some principles. Humankind is made for happiness, like a bird for flight." Such an attitude, the narrative made evident, was not an acceptable one. The husband got the last word, expressing what obviously was supposed to be the moral of the story: "The heart must be not only happy in love, but also good and . . . egotistical happiness is not full happiness." This story exemplifies some of the key features of official discourse on marriage and divorce during the Khrushchev era. Moralists and party propagandists emphasized that divorce was selfish, and they urged married people to control their passions for the sake of their children, and by extension, the country's future.

Despite demands for marital stability, in the early 1950s journalists, judges, lawyers, and reform-minded legal scholars began to propose legislative changes that would make divorce easier to obtain. Judges became increasingly lenient over the course of the subsequent decade, and more couples applied for divorces. As a result, between 1955 and 1965 the divorce rate rose by 270 percent. Clearly, judges and unhappily married couples resisted moralistic dictates in making decisions about divorce, and this conflict between official prescriptions and actual practices grew out of fundamentally different notions about private life. While theorists and propagandists insisted that Soviet citizens could willingly and easily subordinate private interests to public needs, master their emotions and coordinate duty and desire, divorce court judges and unhappy spouses acted upon different assumptions about personal life. For the most part, they took for granted that will, reason, and conscience could not always govern emotion, that relations between men and women were complicated and their feelings for one another mutable, and that love could not be regulated by law. In a few divorce cases, spouses did invoke official rhetoric; however, the way in which they did so modified its meaning and subverted its goals. . . .

Khrushchev believed that the achievement of his political and economic policies required the diligent labor and social activism of Soviet citizens and he tried to inspire such mass initiative and enthusiasm. In order to work hard and to commit themselves whole-heartedly to the fulfillment of government priorities, Soviet people could not be distracted by family discord, unruly passions, and narrow personal interests. Thus an orderly, tranquil private life was a fundamental requirement for the ideal citizen, who in turn was responsible for the realization of Khrushchev's goals. Wide-spread rejection of official prescriptions about personal conduct thus had dire implications for his success.

COMMUNIST MORALITY AND
OFFICIAL DEFINITIONS OF PRIVATE LIFE

Khrushchev had to establish new sources of legitimacy and methods of government in the wake of his repudiation of Stalinism, made public at the Twentieth Party Congress in 1956. The solutions he adopted included abolishing wide-scale state terror, curtailing bureaucratic privilege, and encouraging mass participation in economic development and the maintenance of social order. This populist approach, George Breslauer has argued, was not solely a strategic maneuver in Khrushchev's struggle for power, but came out of his sincere conviction that economic progress required reducing officials' immunity from criticism and unleashing popular initiative. Khrushchev's ideal, he adds, depended upon "the creation of an active, self-regulating society of like-minded individuals." Scholars have described how Khrushchev's populist vision in part motivated his attempts to reorganize state and party structures, reform Soviet law, transfer power to trade unions and voluntary groups, and devise such ideological innovations as the concept of the all-people's state. But a society based on activism, rather than coercion, also requires the proper personnel. In addition to political and economic reform, the achievement of Khrushchev's aspirations entailed the reshaping of individual Soviet people, who had to become capable of assuming the new responsibilities entrusted to them.

The reconstruction of the Soviet citizenry envisioned in the 1950s was much less radical than some of the transformative projects formulated in the 1920s. Its blueprint was Communist morality, a code of ethics governing both public and private life that combined in a milder form the activism valorized in the 1920s with the domestic virtues endorsed in the Stalin years. Formulations of Communist morality included familiar Soviet values: devotion to communism, collectivism, diligent work for the good of society, patriotism, honesty, modesty, as well as a conscientious attitude toward family responsibilities, especially child rearing. Theorists emphasized the social and political importance of "correct" personal conduct, and in numerous books, articles, lectures, and radio programs, various experts detailed the ethical, Communist way to fall in love, marry, rear children, and establish a home. They stressed that every personal decision, from sexual and reproductive choices to taste in interior decorating, had ramifications for society as a whole.

Such ideas and instructions had been a feature of Stalin-era discourse; what changed during the Khrushchev period was not the content of Communist morality but the greater importance ascribed to it. Given his government's limited use of coercion, persuading people to live according to Communist morality was essential for the realization of Khrushchev's ideal society. Citizens who willingly complied with Communist morality's demand for hard work would provide the labor force needed for economic development. Those who internalized prescriptions about personal conduct would help to ensure social stability by establishing secure families and leading orderly personal lives, and making sure that their coworkers and neighbors did the same.

Official concern with instilling Communist morality intensified throughout the 1950s and early 1960s, especially after Khrushchev's announcement in the late fifties that the Soviet Union had now embarked on the road to communism. "It is necessary to develop Communist morality in Soviet people," Khrushchev declared at the Twenty-first Communist Party congress in 1959. Two years later, the Twenty-second Party Congress distilled the tenets of Communist morality into twelve principles, dubbed the Moral Code of the Builder of Communism, and included it in the party program. In addition to its role in stimulating labor and maintaining order, theorists envisioned another, more grandiose purpose for morality in the now imminent Communist epoch: its principles would eventually replace law and force in governing all interactions between individuals. One text asserted that "moral norms in socialist society gain greater and greater meaning," and predicted that "in developed Communist society they will be the only form of regulation of the relations between people." The Twenty-second Party Congress Program described the same process: during the "transition to communism, the role of moral principles in social life grows, the sphere of activity of moral factors widens, and correspondingly the importance of the administrative regulation of the relations between people decreases."

The government's emphasis on Communist morality sparked additional educational and propagandistic efforts. For example, publishing houses produced an increasing number of manuals on family and everyday life, and in 1959 education officials designed a required class for institutions of higher learning entitled "The Foundations of Marxist Ethics."

Moreover, there were new methods of enforcing prescriptions about personal conduct. The taming of the secret police meant that, for the most part, state terror no longer disrupted intimate and family relationships as it had under Stalin; instead, opportunities for less drastic forms of intervention had appeared. Moralists made clear that in cases where people refused to follow officially sanctioned standards, the community was supposed to scold or punish the erring individuals. While party and Komsomol groups were thus empowered under Stalin, the Khrushchev government's expansion of social welfare programs, together with the revival of volunteer groups such as house committees and comrade's courts, meant that this privilege was extended to more people. Teachers, social workers, local bureaucrats, and neighbors, as well as party, Komsomol, and trade union officials, were now all authorized to monitor and intervene in individuals' private lives.

Two basic assumptions about the nature of private life were embedded in texts on Communist morality and in didactic materials about family and domestic life. First, theorists and moralists assumed psychological simplicity and harmony, taking for granted that personal relationships were straightforward and that once people understood how to conduct their private lives correctly, they would be willing and able to do so. Reason and will, in this formulation, invariably governed emotion, thus eliminating the possibility of internal conflict and ambivalence. For example, a manual for propagandists on how to discuss love and marriage with young people included the following recommendation. The commonly asked question, "How [can I] harmonize impulses of the heart with the voice of reason and feeling of duty?" should be answered, "For the Soviet person, for whom consciousness and social purposefulness have penetrated all of life, there cannot be an irreconcilable conflict between feelings and reason: impulses of the heart must be controlled by the demands of sense and duty."

The absence of self-interest was a second feature of Communist morality's delineation of the private. Many theorists insisted that public and private interests were identical. While others admitted that contradictions could arise during the contemporary transition period from socialism to communism, they stressed that in such circumstances, personal needs should always be subordinated because "the interests of society are higher than the interests of the family, the interests of the family are higher than the interests of the individual." Eventually, moralists explained, the repression of individual interests and desires would become second nature. "In Communist society, there will be such harmony of personal and social interests, such high consciousness, that when 'conflicts' arise between the personal and the social, people, without special difficulty, by habit will subordinate their desires to social interests."

Only people who had mastered their feelings and desires could make the kind of sacrifices for the public good that Soviet moralists required. In an imagined world governed by Communist morality, individual interests were identical with or subordinate to public goals, and personal relations were uncomplicated. Citizens' emotional harmony, and the resolution of all their personal conflicts, were the prerequisites for economic development, social order, and progress toward communism.

Texts on marriage and divorce were written in accordance with Communist morality. Writers therefore emphasized social obligation, community intervention, and emotional restraint, stressing that spouses should sacrifice any potentially disruptive personal desires for the greater social benefit of preserving their marriages. A harmonious two-parent family, they explained, provided the best atmosphere for raising the next generation of Soviet citizens. One moralist explained that since divorce had a bad effect on children, "for the sake of future citizens of our country, for the sake of their correct upbringing, for the sake of fulfilling their duty, husband and wife are obligated to do everything to save the family."

Because intact marriages were so important to the stability and future of the nation, social interference in marital relations and sexual behavior was justified, even necessary in some instances. As one expert explained, "The public (*obshchestvennost'*) can do much, using all forms and methods, to influence spouses so that the matter does not go as far as the dissolution of the marriage." Party and Komsomol organizations, and volunteer groups such as apartment house committees and comrades' courts, were all supposed to take an active role in settling disputes and teaching peo-

ple to become better spouses. A manual for propagandists describes how, after a Komsomol agitator's lecture, a woman approached him to discuss her problems. She
claimed she needed a divorce, but after a long conversation, it became evident that
her marital difficulties grew out of her family's extremely cramped living conditions.
The lecturer described the new apartments that were to be built as part of the seven-
year plan, assured her that her problems were temporary, and eventually convinced her
not to file for a divorce.

Married people who found themselves attracted to acquaintances were supposed
to subdue their illicit desires by force of will. In the words of one physician/sex edu-
cator, "the interests of society as a whole, and also the interests of people involved in
the conflict (the children first of all and the other spouse), demand that in these circumstances love is subordinated to social obligations." Behind such statements lay the
belief that people could and should be able to control their passions and emotions. As
one moralist intoned, "We must not regard love as a force of nature, which can not be
subordinated to any discipline and forces reason to be silent."

In addition to subduing adulterous attraction in order to preserve their marriages,
conscientious spouses also had to rein in the annoyance and aggravation caused by
close living quarters, cohabitation with in-laws, and material hardship. Will power and
a good attitude were supposed to enable people to transcend these problems. For example, a pamphlet for young people provided a description of one couple who lived
in a two-room apartment, earned good salaries, and had a TV, a radio, a washing machine, and no children, but nonetheless fought frequently. Another pair, by contrast,
lived with their child and another family of three in a sixteen-square-meter room divided by a curtain. They all managed to get along together and preserve their marriages because "everything is shared, they all help one another."

Propagandists and experts writing about marriage and divorce, adopting Communist morality's basic premises, denied the validity of private interests and demanded
that individuals regulate emotions and suppress inconvenient desires, both sexual and
material. However, court records reveal that judges and unhappily married couples
usually ignored Communist morality in making decisions about divorce. Instead, they
acted upon a conception of private life that encompassed individual interests and a
sense of the power and complexity of emotion.

JUDGES AND THE INEVITABILITY
OF EMOTIONAL COMPLEXITY

From 1944 to 1965, obtaining a divorce was an arduous process. Plaintiffs first had to
pay a fee in order to present a divorce petition to the local raion people's court, and
then place an advertisement in a local newspaper announcing intent to divorce. Next,
both parties had to appear at a raion level people's court hearing, where the judge
tried to reconcile them. If this was unsuccessful, the plaintiff could appeal to the city
or oblast court, where the case was decided and the fee, ranging from fifty to two
hundred (new) rubles, was assigned to one or another party or divided between them.

There were no specific legal grounds for divorce; a Supreme Court Plenum decree "On Court Practice in Cases of the Dissolution of Marriage," which was in force
from September 1949 to 1965, instructed judges to grant a divorce only when the
plaintiff had "well grounded motives," and when the preservation of the marriage

would "contradict the principles of Communist morality" and prevent the spouses from successfully raising their children. In making decisions about divorce, it was the responsibility of judges to implement the law in such a way as to fulfill its educational and propagandistic potential. The 1949 decree cautioned that judicial rulings on divorce cases "must contribute to the correct understanding of the meaning of family and marriage in the Soviet state and teach the population respect for family and marriage, based on the highest principles of Communist morality."

This meant that judges were supposed to reconcile couples whenever possible and to deny divorces in cases in which the plaintiff's motivation was not appropriately serious. . . .

In the atmosphere of relative openness following Stalin's death, jurists once more began to debate various aspects of the Soviet legal system. One aspect of this controversy was the lively campaign carried out in the press and among legal experts to reform family law and simplify divorce procedures. In 1965 the government issued a new edict that simplified the divorce procedure, although a new comprehensive family code did not appear until 1968. Even well before the new laws had taken effect, however, higher court judges became less and less likely to insist that couples stay together despite their problems, and they granted divorces with increasing frequency. . . .

The 1949 Supreme court decree specified that a divorce should be granted only when continuation of the marriage posed a threat to Communist morality. Moscow city court judges, however, seldom even referred to Communist morality in their verdicts. Instead, they usually cited at least several of the following reasons in their decisions granting divorces: bad relations between the spouses, the existence of children from another relationship, the fact that spouses had been living separately, the couple's failure to make any discernible attempts to reconcile, or simply that the couple had no desire to live together. A typical decision granting divorce read, "The family has in fact disintegrated. Hostile, sharp relations have arisen between the spouses, under which there is no basis for supposing that the their family could be revived." Such reasoning indicates an acceptance of the changeable nature of relationships and love. . . .

DIVORCING SPOUSES AND THE ASSERTION OF SELF-INTEREST

Communist morality demanded the subjugation of individual needs and desires to public requirements. Because intact marriages were deemed socially beneficial, couples were in theory, permitted to divorce only if they could demonstrate that the continuation of their marriages would have a negative impact on society as whole; for example, by damaging their children. However, most plaintiffs and defendants in the divorce cases I examined eschewed the rhetoric of social responsibility, focusing instead on the specific relationship between spouses.

Many divorcing couples seem to have shared the assumptions that deteriorating relations between spouses constituted adequate cause for divorce and that judges should accommodate the inevitable contingencies of domestic life. In their applications for divorce to the Moscow city court many plaintiffs simply stated that husband and wife had become estranged, could not live together, or had found new partners. In 1957, for example, a woman applied for divorce because "we have already been actually separated for the last two years because of complete disparity of characters and ways of life." After four years of marriage, another plaintiff sought a divorce in 1959, explaining that "the feelings which bound us earlier have left. . . . We live in one room like people who are strangers to one another."

Defendants, by contrast, sometimes contested their spouses' applications for divorce on the grounds that true love remained. In 1956 a woman protested the decision granting her husband a divorce because, she argued, she still loved him, his current relationship with a woman twenty-six years his junior would not last, and he would eventually return to his family. She pointed to the correspondence between herself and husband and criticized the court's refusal to consider it, although it "testifies to our deep sincere feelings, our great respect for one another." It is not clear how sincere declarations of loyal devotion or disregard actually were. What is more important for my argument, however, is that plaintiffs and defendants thought that their professions of love or indifference should be the basis for judge's decisions. . . .

None of the plaintiffs in these cases referred to the 1949 Supreme Court decree on divorce, or to Communist morality. They believed that abuse, neglect, and the loss of love were valid reasons for divorce, that judges should take into account the relations between spouses, and that emotions and personal behavior were the critical questions in divorce suits. By ignoring Communist morality's concern over whether the dissolution of their marriages was good or bad for society as a whole, such individuals denied the invariable primacy of public goals and implied that, in some circumstances, individual interests and needs were paramount.

APPROPRIATING COMMUNIST MORALITY

Occasionally, however, plaintiffs and defendants in divorce cases stepped outside of this purely personal discourse. They invoked Communist morality either explicitly or less directly by trying to compel party and societal groups to correct their spouses' behavior. Such appeals for outside intervention and appropriations of official rhetoric did not occur in the majority of cases, but they are significant because they illuminate the contradictions that arose as Communist morality was put into practice.

Some divorcing spouses made specific references to Communist morality. In 1954, for example, a woman denied her husband's assertion that she had been unfaithful, and instead cited her mother-in-law's interference as the source of marital conflict. She concluded that "such a wish of the mother of the plaintiff is a direct contradiction of the foundations of Communist morality aimed at strengthening the Soviet family." In a 1958 case a woman who had been married for nineteen years accused her husband of having an affair with a woman twenty years his junior and, in doing so, disregarding "the high principles of Communist morality." And in an usually thorough statement, a defendant responded to her husband's 1961 application for divorce with a fourteen-page typed rebuttal. She cited the Moral Code of the Builder of Communism and its demand for good family relations, attention to child rearing, and "harmonious coordination of family and social upbringing." But, she continued, though her husband was a member of the party, he "did not understand the directives and demands of our party, the government, and the historic decisions of the Twenty-second Party Congress." He had failed to show concern and affection for his wife and family by reforming, so that rather than "striding with all the Soviet people toward communism, being an example in the struggle to strengthen the principles of Communist morality," he had "used great quantities of alcoholic drinks and . . . begun a battle against his family."

It is impossible to ascertain whether these dissatisfied spouses referred to official principles because they sincerely believed in them or because they thought such allusions would add credibility to their cases. Regardless of their true motivations, it seems clear that they regarded Communist morality not just as a guide to behavior or as the ethical basis for the Communist future but also as a powerful language that could be invoked to help them with more immediate personal concerns, such as reining in wayward spouses or subduing officious in-laws. In other words, they used Communist morality for their own ends. . . .

The fundamental gender inequality that persisted in Soviet society, despite claims to the contrary, perhaps made women more anxious to preserve their marriages. Women made less money than men did, and so were more likely to depend financially on their husbands, especially if they had children. Furthermore, as a result of war causalities, women far outnumbered men throughout the Soviet Union during this period. According to census data from 1959, there were 81.9 men per 100 women, but this ratio was much higher in certain age groups; in the 45–49-year-old cohort, for example, there were only 62.3 men per 100 women. It was thus much harder for women to find new spouses. . . .

Malice, revenge, neediness, despair, or some combination thereof, lay behind many complaints to party and societal organizations. Communist morality required these groups to intervene in order to insure that people led their personal lives correctly. In the cases I have described, however, it was individuals rather than collectives who took initiative. This shift had the effect of undermining Communist morality. Collective and party intervention was meant to help create the kind of people who could build communism; in other words, the proper family life was an essential tool for the construction of communism. The people who sought outside help, however, were appropriating the language of Communist morality and involving the institutions that were supposed to support it to pursue their own goals of preserving their marriages, punishing their spouses, or securing a satisfactory private life. Ironically, they were using Communist morality as a means of advancing the individual interests that official moralists demanded they suppress.

According to the Soviet leadership, the order of citizens' internal lives ensured the social and political order of the country. Personal relations were consistent and straightforward, reason and morality governed passion and impulse, and individuals' interests and needs never conflicted with public requirements nor superseded them in importance. In divorce cases, however, judicial decisions were based on an assumption of the uncontrollability of love and the fragility of marriage. The actions and explanations of plaintiffs and defendants reveal, furthermore, a determined pursuit of personal, rather than social, goals. The resilience of these unofficial notions about private life had an important effect on the success of Khrushchev's campaign to reform Soviet society. In Khrushchev's vision, developing the economy, keeping order, and progressing from socialism to communism required active, enthusiastic, self-sacrificing workers, people untroubled by family problems, conflicting emotions, and illicit desires. The philosophers who developed Communist morality and the agitators and experts who publicized it were supposed to produce these exemplary citizens; their attempts to inculcate official prescriptions about private life were thus vital for the achievement of government priorities. However, these endeavors did not always meet with success. As we have seen in divorce cases, judges often ignored the principles they were supposed to enforce. In some cases, efforts to instill the Communist version of private life even strengthened opposing ideas: the courts and party organizations charged with putting

Communist morality into practice afforded people new means by which they could pursue their supposedly obsolete personal interests. This suggests that in addition to the structural weaknesses of the planned economy, the intractable problems of agriculture, and the disaffection of military, industrial, and government elites, another reason for the Khrushchev government's inefficacy was the determination of Soviet citizens to define and defend private life.

Deborah A. Field, "Irreconcilable Differences: Divorce and Conceptions of Private Life in the Khrushchev Era," *The Russian Review,* LVII, 4 (October 1998), pp. 599–613.

Evgenii Evtushensko, from *A Precocious Autobiography*

Tall, thin, and dramatic in his self-presentation, the poet Evgenii Evtushenko exploded on the Moscow literary scene in the first years after Stalin's death. Part of a group of young poets that included his wife Bella Akhmadulina, Andrei Voznesenskii, and Robert Rozhdestvenskii, he pushed the edge of what was permissible stylistically and politically. Poetry readings became popular gatherings for young people, and poets enjoyed celebrity. Evtushenko wanted to revive the civic role of Russian literature and thought of Russian poets as "the spiritual government of their country." Like many of his contemporaries, he was inspired by the example of the poet Boris Pasternak, whom he saw as "a man of complete integrity." Never a dissident but always a loyalist and Russian patriot, Evtushenko hoped to return the original revolutionary inspiration to Soviet society. His poems "Babyi Yar," which lamented the lack of a monument at the site where Kiev's Jews were massacred by the Nazis, and "Stalin's Heirs," which expressed the fear that Stalinism lurked behind the public faces of officials, were bold interventions into the constricted public debates of the Khrushchev years. Dogmatic critics within the USSR constantly criticized him, while in the West some enthusiasts celebrated his courage, and skeptics were suspicious of his commitment to a reformed Soviet socialism.

I

On the 5th March, 1953, an event took place which shattered Russia—the death of Stalin. I found it almost impossible to imagine him dead, so much had he been an indispensable part of life.

A sort of general paralysis came over the country. Trained to believe that Stalin was taking care of everyone, people were lost and bewildered without him. The whole of Russia wept. So did I. We wept sincerely with grief and perhaps also with fear for the future.

At a writers' meeting, poets read out their poems in Stalin's honour, their voices broken by sobs. Tvardovsky, a big and powerful man, recited in a trembling voice.

I'll never forget going to see Stalin's coffin.

I was in the crowd in Trubnaya Square. The breath of the tens of thousands of people pressed against one another rose up in a white cloud so thick that on it could be seen the swaying shadows of the leafless March trees. It was a fantastic and a fearful sight. New streams poured into the human torrent from behind, increasing the pressure. The crowd turned into a monstrous whirlpool. I realised that I was being carried straight towards a traffic light. The post was coming relentlessly closer. Suddenly

I saw that a young girl was being pushed against the post. Her face was distorted by a despairing scream which was inaudible among all the other screams and groans. A movement of the crowd drove me against the girl; I did not hear but felt with my body the cracking of her brittle bones as they were broken on the traffic light. I closed my eyes in horror, I could not bear the sight of her insanely bulging, childish blue eyes, and I was swept past. When I looked again the girl was no longer to be seen. The crowd must have sucked her under. Wedged against the traffic light was someone else, his body twisted and his arms outflung as on a cross. At that moment I felt I was treading on something soft. It was a human body. I picked my feet up and was borne along by the crowd. For a long time I was afraid to put my feet down again. The crowd closed tighter and tighter. I was saved by my height. Short people were smothered alive. We were caught between the walls of houses on one side and a row of army trucks on the other.

'Get the trucks out of the way!' people howled. 'Get them away!'

'I can't. I've got no instructions,' a very young, fair, bewildered police officer shouted back from one of the trucks, almost crying with desperation. And people were being hurtled against the trucks by the crowd, and their heads smashed. The sides of the trucks were running with blood. All at once I felt a savage hatred for everything that had given birth to that 'No instructions' shouted at a moment when people were dying of someone's stupidity. For the first time in my life I thought with hatred of the man we were burying. He could not be innocent of the disaster. It was the 'No instructions' that had caused the chaos and bloodshed at his funeral. Now I saw once and for all that it's no good waiting for instructions if human lives are at stake—you must act. I don't know how I did it, but working energetically with my elbows and fists, I found myself thrusting people aside and shouting:

'Form chains! Form chains!'

They didn't understand, so I began to join neighbouring hands together by force, all the while spitting out the foulest swear words of my geological days. Some hefty young men were now helping me. And now people understood. They joined hands and formed chains. The strong men and I continued to work at it. The whirlpool was slowing down. The crowd was ceasing to be a savage beast. 'Women and children into the trucks!' yelled one of the young men. And women and children, passed from hand to hand, sailed over our heads into the trucks. One of the women who were being handed on was struggling hysterically and whimpering. The young police officer who received her at his end stroked her hair, clumsily trying to calm her down. She shuddered a few times and suddenly became still. The officer took the cap off his tow-coloured head, covered her face with it and burst out crying.

There was another whirlpool farther ahead. We worked our way over, the tough boys and I, and again with the help of curses and fists made people form chains in order to save them.

The police too finally began to help us.

Everything quietened down.

'You ought to join the police, Comrade, we could use fellows like you,' a police sergeant said to me, wiping his face with his handkerchief after a bout of hard work.

'Right. I'll think it over,' I said grimly.

Somehow, I no longer felt like going to see Stalin's remains. Instead, I left with one of the boys who had been organising chains; we bought a bottle of vodka and he walked home with me.

'Did you see Stalin?' my mother asked me.

'Yes,' I said discouragingly, as I clinked glasses with the boy.
I hadn't lied to my mother. Stalin was really what I had seen.

Yevgeny Yevtushenko, *A Precocious Autobiography,* trans. by Andrew R. MacAndrew (London: Collins and
Harvill Press, 1963), pp. 89–92.

Nikita Khrushchev's "Secret Speech" to the Twentieth Congress of the Communist Party of the Soviet Union
February 25, 1956

*The Twentieth Congress of the Soviet Communist party in February 1956 was a momen-
tous event that shook both the Soviet Bloc and the international Communist movement.
Khrushchev spoke for hours to a stunned audience about the crimes of Stalin, both the repression of Communists in the Great Purges and his lack of preparedness for the Second World
War. He revealed Lenin's "testament," which for decades Communists had denied was genuine. Although he aimed to re-legitimize Marxism-Leninism by his call for a "return to
Lenin, by dethroning Stalin," Khrushchev opened a Pandora's Box of different interpretations
of the Soviet past, the "socialist" present, and the Communist future.*

*When Poland and Hungary exploded in strikes and revolution, and Soviet tanks rolled
into Budapest, hundreds of thousands of foreign Communists left their national parties. The
international movement headed by the Soviet Union began to splinter, with the Chinese Communists marching off to the Left. The views of Soviet Communists were no longer sacrosanct.
Within the Soviet Union there were scattered manifestations of support for the Hungarians,
and in Tbilisi, Georgia, students marched in the streets to show their affection for their native
son, Stalin. The Soviet authorities responded with gunfire. Khrushchev was forced to restrain
his liberalizing tendencies, and the party came down hard on intellectuals and students at the
end of the year. For all his reforming zeal, Khrushchev was prepared to use his police and army
to enforce the party's power. When workers in the southern Russian city of Novocherkassk went
on strike in June 1962, tanks were sent in and twenty-four people killed.[1]*

Comrades! In the Party Central Committee report to the 20th Congress, in a number of speeches by delegates to the Congress, and earlier at plenary sessions of the
Party Central Committee, quite a lot has been said about the cult of the individual
leader and its harmful consequences.

After Stalin's death the Party Central Committee began to implement a policy of
explaining concisely and consistently that it is impermissible and foreign to the spirit
of Marxism–Leninism to elevate one person, to transform him into a superman pos-
sessing supernatural characteristics akin to those of a god. Such a man supposedly
knows everything, sees everything, thinks for everyone, can do anything, is infallible
in his behavior.

Such a belief about a man—specifically about Stalin—was cultivated among us
for many years.

---

1. Samuel H. Baron, *Bloody Saturday in the Soviet Union: Novocherkassk 1962* (Stanford: Stanford University Press, 2001).

The objective of the present report is not a thorough evaluation of Stalin's life and work. Concerning Stalin's merits, an entirely sufficient number of books, pamphlets and studies had already been written in his lifetime. Stalin's role in the preparation and execution of the socialist revolution, in the Civil War, and in the fight for the construction of socialism in our country is universally known. Everyone knows this well. At present we are concerned with a question which has immense importance for the Party now and in the future—[we are concerned] with how the Stalin cult gradually grew, the cult which became at a certain specific stage the source of a whole series of exceedingly serious and grave perversions of Party principles, of Party democracy, of revolutionary legality.

Because not all as yet realize fully the practical consequences resulting from the cult of the individual leader, the great harm caused by the violation of the principle of collective direction of the Party, and because immense and limitless power was gathered in the hands of one person, the Party Central Committee considers it absolutely necessary to make the material pertaining to this matter available to the 20th Congress of the Communist Party of the Soviet Union. . . .

We have to consider this matter seriously and analyze it correctly in order that we may preclude any possibility of a repetition, in any form whatever, of what took place during the life of Stalin, who absolutely did not tolerate collegiality in leadership and in work and who practiced brutal violence not only toward everything which opposed him, but also toward what seemed, to his capricious and despotic character, contrary to his concepts.

Stalin acted not through persuasion, explanation and patient cooperation with people, but by imposing his concepts and demanding absolute submission to his opinion. Whoever opposed this concept or tried to prove his viewpoint and the correctness of his position was doomed to removal from the leading collective and to subsequent moral and physical annihilation. This was especially true during the period following the 17th Party Congress, when many prominent Party leaders and rank-and-file Party workers, honest and dedicated to the cause of communism, fell victim to Stalin's despotism.

We must affirm that the Party fought a serious fight against the Trotskyites, rightists and bourgeois nationalists, and that it disarmed ideologically all the enemies of Leninism. This ideological fight was carried on successfully, and as a result the Party was strengthened and tempered. Here Stalin played a positive role.

The Party led a great political ideological struggle against those in its own ranks who proposed anti-Leninist theses, who represented a political line hostile to the Party and to the cause of socialism. This was a stubborn and a difficult fight but a necessary one, because the political line of both the Trotskyite-Zinovievite bloc and of the Bukharinites led actually toward the restoration of capitalism and capitulation to the world bourgeoisie. Let us consider for a moment what would have happened if in 1928–1929 the political line of right deviation had prevailed among us, or orientation toward "cotton-dress industrialization," or toward the kulak, etc. We would not now have a powerful heavy industry, we would not have the collective farms, we would find ourselves disarmed and weak in a capitalist encirclement.

It was for this reason that the Party led an inexorable ideological fight and explained to all Party members and to the non-Party masses the harm and the danger of the anti-Leninist proposals of the Trotskyite opposition and the rightist opportunists. And this great work of explaining the Party line bore fruit; both the Trotskyites and the rightist opportunists were politically isolated; the overwhelming Party majority supported the Leninist line and the Party was able to awaken and organize the working masses to apply the Leninist Party line and to build socialism.

Worth noting is the fact that even during the progress of the furious ideological fight against the Trotskyites, the Zinovievites, the Bukharinites and others, extreme repressive measures were not used against them. The fight was on ideological grounds. But some years later, when socialism in our country had been fundamentally established, when the exploiting classes had been generally liquidated, when the Soviet social structure had radically changed, when the social base for political movements and groups hostile to the Party had shrunk sharply, when the ideological opponents of the Party had long since been defeated politically, then the repression directed against them began.

It was precisely during this period (1935–1937–1938) that the practice of mass repression through the state apparatus was born, first against the enemies of Leninism—Trotskyites, Zinovievites, Bukharinites, long since politically defeated by the Party—and subsequently also against many honest Communists, against those Party cadres which had borne the heavy burden of the Civil War and the first and most difficult years of industrialization and collectivization, which had fought actively against the Trotskyites and the rightists for the Leninist party line.

Stalin originated the concept "enemy of the people." This term automatically rendered it unnecessary that the ideological errors of a man or men engaged in a controversy be proved; this term made possible the use of the most cruel repression, violating all norms of revolutionary legality, against anyone who in any way disagreed with Stalin, against those who were only suspected of hostile intent, against those who had bad reputations. This concept, "enemy of the people," actually eliminated the possibility of any kind of ideological fight or the making of one's views known on this or that issue, even issues of a practical nature. In the main, and in actuality, the only proof of guilt used, contrary to all norms of current law, was the "confession" of the accused himself; and, as subsequent investigation has proved, "confessions" were obtained through physical pressures against the accused.

This led to glaring violations of revolutionary legality, and to the fact that many entirely innocent persons, who in the past had defended the Party line, became victims.

We must assert that, in regard to those persons who in their time had opposed the Party line, there were often no sufficiently serious reasons for their physical annihilation. The formula "enemy of the people" was specifically introduced for the purpose of physically annihilating such individuals.

It is a fact that many persons who were later annihilated as enemies of the Party and people had worked with Lenin during his life. Some of these persons had made mistakes during Lenin's life, but, despite this, Lenin benefited by their work, he corrected them and he did everything possible to retain them in the ranks of the Party; he induced them to follow him. . . .

Everyone knows how irreconcilable Lenin was with the ideological enemies of Marxism, with those who deviated from the correct Party line. At the same time, however, Lenin, as is evident from the given document, in his practice of directing the Party demanded the most intimate Party contact with people who had shown indecision or temporary nonconformity with the Party line, but whom it was possible to return to the Party path. Lenin advised that such people should be patiently educated without the application of extreme methods.

Lenin's wisdom in dealing with people was evident in his work with cadres.

An entirely different relationship with people characterized Stalin. Lenin's traits—patient work with people; stubborn and painstaking education of them; the ability to induce people to follow him without using compulsion, but rather through the ideological influence on them of the whole collective—were entirely foreign to Stalin. He [Stalin] discarded the Leninist method of persuading and educating; he abandoned the method of ideological struggle for that of administrative violence, mass repressions and terror. He acted on an increasingly larger scale and more stubbornly through punitive organs, at the same time often violating all existing standards of morality and of Soviet law.

Arbitrary behavior by one person encouraged and permitted arbitrariness in others. Mass arrests and deportations of many thousands of people, execution without trial and without normal investigation created conditions of insecurity, fear and even desperation.

This, of course, did not contribute toward unity of the Party ranks and of all strata of the working people, but, on the contrary, brought about annihilation and the expulsion from the Party of workers who were loyal but inconvenient to Stalin. . . .

Lenin used severe methods only in the most necessary cases, when the exploiting classes were still in existence and were vigorously opposing the revolution, when the struggle for survival was decidedly assuming the sharpest forms, even including a civil war.

Stalin, on the other hand, used extreme methods and mass repressions at a time when the revolution was already victorious, when the Soviet state was strengthened, when the exploiting classes were already liquidated and socialist relations were rooted solidly in all phases of national economy, when our party was politically consolidated and had strengthened itself both numerically and ideologically. It is clear that here Stalin showed in a whole series of cases his intolerance, his brutality and his abuse of power. Instead of proving his political correctness and mobilizing the masses, he often chose the path of repression and physical annihilation, not only against actual enemies, but also against individuals who had not committed any crimes against the Party and the Soviet government. Here we see no wisdom but only a demonstration of the brutal force which had once so alarmed V. I. Lenin. . . .

In practice Stalin ignored the norms of Party life and trampled on the Leninist principle of collective Party leadership.

Stalin's willfulness vis-à-vis the Party and its Central Committee became fully evident after the 17th Party Congress, which took place in 1934.

Having numerous data showing brutal willfulness toward Party cadres, the Central Committee created a Party commission under the control of the Central Committee Presidium; it was charged with investigating what had made possible the mass repressions against the majority of the Central Committee's members and candidates elected at the 17th Congress of the All-Union Communist Party (Bolsheviks).

The commission has familiarized itself with a large amount of materials in the N.K.V.D. archives and with other documents and has established many facts pertaining to the fabrication of cases against Communists, to false accusations, to glaring abuses of socialist legality which resulted in the death of innocent people. It became apparent that many Party, Soviet and economic activists who were branded in 1937–1938 as "enemies" were actually never enemies, spies, wreckers, etc., but were always honest Communists; they were only so stigmatized, and often, no longer able to bear barbaric tortures, they charged themselves (at the order of the investigating judges—falsifiers) with all kinds of grave and unlikely crimes. The commission has presented to the Central Committee Presidium lengthy and documented materials pertaining to mass repressions against delegates to the 17th Party Congress and against members of the Central Committee elected at that Congress. These materials have been studied by the Central Committee Presidium.

It was determined that of the 139 members and candidates of the Party Central Committee who were elected at the 17th Congress, 98 persons, i.e., 70 per cent, were arrested and shot (mostly in 1937–1938). (*Indignation in the hall.*)

What was the composition of the delegates to the 17th Congress? It is known that 80 per cent of the voting participants in the 17th Congress joined the Party during the years of the [Bolshevist] underground before the revolution or during the Civil War; this means before 1921. By social origin the basic mass of the delegates to the Congress were workers (60 per cent of the voting members).

For this reason it was inconceivable that a Congress so composed would have elected a Central Committee, a majority of which would prove to be enemies of the Party. The only reason why 70 per cent of the Central Committee members and candidates elected at the 17th Congress were branded enemies of the Party and of the people was that honest Communists were slandered, accusations against them were fabricated, and revolutionary legality was gravely undermined.

The same fate befell not only the Central Committee members but also the majority of the delegates to the 17th Party Congress. Of 1966 delegates with either voting or advisory powers, 1108 persons were arrested on charges of counterrevolutionary crimes, i.e., decidedly more than a majority. This very fact shows how absurd, wild and contrary to common sense were the charges of counterrevolutionary crimes made, as we now see, against a majority of the participants in the 17th Party Congress. (*Indignation in the hall.*)

We should recall that the 17th Party Congress is historically known as the Congress of Victors. Delegates to the Congress were active participants in the building of our socialist state; many of them had suffered and fought for Party interests during the prerevolutionary years in the underground and at the Civil War fronts; they fought their enemies valiantly and often nervelessly looked into the face of death. How then can we believe that such people could prove to be "two-faced" and had joined the camp of the enemies of socialism during the era after the political liquidation of the Zinovievites, Trotskyites and rightists and after the great accomplishments of socialist construction?

This was the result of the abuse of power by Stalin, who began to use mass terror against the Party cadres.

What is the reason that mass repressions against activists increased more and more after the 17th Party Congress? It was because at that time Stalin had so elevated himself above the Party and above the nation that he ceased to consider either the Central Committee or the Party. While he still reckoned with the opinion of the collective before the 17th Congress, Stalin in even greater measure ceased to reckon with the views of the members of the Party's Central Committee and even the members of the Political Bureau after the complete political liquidation of the Trotskyites, Zinovievites and Bukharinites, when the Party had achieved unity as a result of that fight and socialist victories. Stalin thought that now he could decide all things alone and all he needed were statisticians; he treated all others in such a way that they could only listen to and praise him.

After the criminal murder of S. M. Kirov, mass repressions and brutal acts of violation of socialist legality began. On the evening of Dec. 1, 1934, on Stalin's initiative (without the approval of the Political Bureau—which was passed two days later, casually) the secretary of the Presidium of the Central Executive Committee, Yenukidze, signed the following directive:

1. Investigative agencies are directed to speed up the cases of those accused of the preparation or execution of acts of terror.

2. Judicial organs are directed not to hold up the execution of death sentences for crimes of this category in order to consider the possibility of pardon, because the Presidium of the U.S.S.R. Central Executive Committee does not consider it possible to accept petitions of this sort.

3. Agencies of the N.K.V.D. [Commissariat of Internal Affairs] are directed to carry out the death sentences against criminals of the above-mentioned category immediately after the passage of sentence.

This directive became the basis for mass abuses of socialist law observance. During many of the fabricated court cases the accused were charged with the "preparation" of terroristic acts; this deprived them of any possibility that their cases might be re-examined, even when they stated before the court that their "confessions" were secured by force, and when, in a convincing manner, they disproved the accusations against them.

It must be asserted that to this day the circumstances surrounding Kirov's murder hide many things which are inexplicable and mysterious and demand a most careful examination. There are reasons for the suspicion that the killer of Kirov [Leonid V.] Nikolayev, was assisted by someone from among the people whose duty it was to guard Kirov's person. A month and a half before the killing, Nikolayev was arrested on the ground of suspicious behavior, but he was released and not even searched. It is an unusually suspicious circumstance that when the Chekist assigned to protect Kirov was being brought in for interrogation, on Dec. 2, 1934, he was killed in an automobile "accident" in which no other occupants of the car were harmed. After the murder of Kirov, top functionaries of the Leningrad N.K.V.D. were given very light sentences, but in 1937 they were shot. We can assume that they were shot in order to cover the traces of the organizers of Kirov's killing. (*Stir in the hall.*)

Mass repressions grew tremendously from the end of 1936 after a telegram from Stalin and Zhdanov, dated from Sochi Sept. 25, 1936, was addressed to Kaganovich, Molotov and other members of the Political Bureau. The content of the telegram was as follows:

"We deem it absolutely necessary and urgent that Comrade Yezhov be nominated to the post of People's Commissar for Internal Affairs. Yagoda has definitely proved himself to be incapable of unmasking the Trotskyite-Zinovievite bloc. The O.G.P.U. is four years behind in this matter. This is noted by all Party workers and by the majority of the representatives of the N.K.V.D." Strictly speaking we should stress that Stalin did not meet with and therefore could not know the opinion of Party workers.

This Stalinist formulation that the "N.K.V.D. is four years behind" in applying mass repression and that there is a necessity for "catching up" with the neglected work directly pushed the N.K.V.D. workers onto the path of mass arrests and executions.

We should state that this formulation was also forced on the February–March plenary session of the Party Central Committee in 1937. The session resolution approved it on the basis of Yezhov's report, "Lessons Ensuing From the Harmful Activity, Diversion and Espionage of the Japanese-German-Trotskyite Agents," stating:

"The Plenum of the Party Central Committee considers that all facts revealed during the investigation into the matter of an anti-Soviet Trotskyite center and of its followers in the provinces show that the People's Commissariat of Internal Affairs had fallen behind at least four years in the attempt to unmask these most inexorable enemies of the people."

The mass repressions at this time were made under the slogan of a fight against the Trotskyites. Did the Trotskyites at this time actually constitute such a danger to our party and to the Soviet state? We should recall that on the eve of the 15th Party Congress in 1927 only about 4000 votes were cast for the Trotskyite-Zinovievite opposition, while there were 724,000 for the Party line. During the ten years that passed between the 15th Party Congress and the February–March Central Committee plenary session Trotskyism was completely disarmed; many former Trotskyites had changed their former views and worked in the various sectors building socialism. It is clear that there was no basis for mass terror in the country in this situation of socialist victory.

Stalin's report at the February–March Central Committee plenary session in 1937, "Deficiencies of Party Work and Methods for the Liquidation of the Trotskyites and Other Double-Dealers," contained an attempt at theoretical justification of the mass terror policy under the pretext that class war must allegedly sharpen as we march forward toward socialism. Stalin asserted that both history and Lenin taught him this.

Actually, Lenin taught that the application of revolutionary violence is necessitated by the resistance of the exploiting classes, and this referred to the era when the exploiting classes existed and were powerful. As soon as the nation's political situation had improved, when, in January 1920, the Red Army took Rostov and thus won a most important victory over Denikin, Lenin instructed Dzherzhinsky to stop mass terror and to abolish the death penalty. Lenin justified this important political move of the Soviet state in the following manner in his report at the session of the All-Union Central Executive Committee Feb. 2, 1920:

"We were forced to use terror because of the terror practiced by the Entente, when strong world powers threw their hordes against us, without scruples over any type of conduct. We would not have lasted two days had we not been ruthless in meeting these actions of the officers and White Guards; this meant the use of terror, but this was forced upon us by the terrorist methods of the Entente.

"But as soon as we attained a decisive victory, even before the end of the war, immediately after taking Rostov, we gave up the use of the death penalty and thus proved that we intend to carry out our program in the manner that we promised. We say that the application of violence stems from the decision to crush the exploiters, the big landowners and the capitalists; as soon as this was accomplished we gave up the use of all extraordinary methods. We have proved this in practice."

Stalin deviated from these clear and plain precepts of Lenin. Stalin put the Party and the N.K.V.D. to using mass terror when the exploiting classes had been liquidated in our country and when there were no serious reasons for the use of extraordinary mass terror. . . .

At the February–March Central Committee plenary session in 1937 many members actually questioned the rightness of the established course regarding mass repressions under the pretext of combating "double-dealing."

Comrade Postyshev most ably expressed these doubts. He said:

"I have philosophized that the severe years of the struggle have passed; Party members who lost their backbone broke down or joined the camp of the enemy, healthy elements fought for the Party. Those were the years of industrialization and collectivization. I never thought it possible that after this severe era had passed Karpov and people like him would find themselves in the camp of the enemy." (Karpov was a worker in the Ukrainian Central Committee whom Postyshev knew well.) "And now, according to the testimony, it appears that Karpov was recruited in 1934 by the Trotskyites. I personally do not believe that in 1934 an honest Party member who had trod the long road of unrelenting fight against enemies, for the Party and for socialism, would now be in the camp of the enemies. I do not believe it. . . . I cannot imagine how it would be possible to travel with the Party during the difficult years and then, in 1934, join the Trotskyites. It is an odd thing. . . ." (*Stir in the hall.*)

Using Stalin's formulation, namely, that the closer we are to socialism, the more enemies we will have, and using the resolution of the February–March Central Committee plenary session, adopted on the basis of Yezhov's report, the provocateurs who had infiltrated the state security agencies, together with unconscionable careerists, began to protect with the Party name the mass terror against Party cadres, cadres of the Soviet state and ordinary Soviet citizens. Suffice it to say that the number of arrests based on charges of counterrevolutionary crimes grew tenfold between 1936 and 1937. . . .

An example of vile provocation, of odious falsification and of criminal violation of revolutionary legality is the case of the former candidate member of the Central Committee Political Bureau, one of the most eminent workers of the Party and of the Soviet government, Comrade Robert I. Eikhe, who had been a Party member since 1905. (*Commotion in the hall.*)

Comrade Eikhe was arrested April 29, 1938, on the basis of slanderous materials, without the sanction of the Prosecutor of the U.S.S.R., which was finally received 15 months after the arrest.

Investigation of Eikhe's case was made in a manner which most brutally violated Soviet legality and was accompanied by willfulness and falsification.

Eikhe was forced under torture to sign ahead of time a protocol of his confession prepared by the investigative judges, in which he and several other eminent Party workers were accused of anti-Soviet activity.

On Oct. 1, 1939, Eikhe sent his declaration to Stalin in which he categorically denied his guilt and asked for an examination of his case. In the declaration he wrote: "There is no more bitter misery than to sit in the jail of a government for which I have always fought."

A second declaration of Eikhe has been preserved which he sent to Stalin Oct. 27, 1939; in it he cited facts very convincingly and countered the slanderous accusations made against him, arguing that this provocatory accusation was on the one hand the work of real Trotskyites whose arrests he had sanctioned as First Secretary of the West Siberian Territory Party Committee and who had conspired to take revenge on him, and, on the other hand, the result of base falsification of materials by the investigative judges. Eikhe wrote in his declaration:

". . . On Oct. 25 of this year I was informed that the investigation of my case has been concluded and I was given access to the materials of this investigation. Had I been guilty of only one-hundredth of the crimes with which I am charged, I would not have dared to send you this pre-execution declaration; however, I have not been guilty of even one of the things with which I am charged and my heart is clean of even the shadow of baseness. I have never in my life told you a word of falsehood and now, when I stand with both feet in the grave, I am also not lying. My whole case is a typical example of provocation, slander and violation of the elementary basis of revolutionary legality. . . .

"The confessions which were made part of my file are not only absurd but contain some slander of the Communist Party Central Committee and the Council of People's Commissars because correct resolutions of the Party Central Committee and of the Council of People's Commissars which were not made on my initiative or with my participation are presented as hostile acts of counterrevolutionary organizations performed at my suggestion. . . .

"I am now alluding to the most disgraceful part of my life and to my really grave guilt before the Party and you: that is, my confession of counterrevolutionary activity. . . . The case is as follows: not being able to suffer the tortures to which I was put by Ushakov and Nikolayev—and especially by the former—who utilized the knowledge that my broken ribs have not properly mended and have caused me great pain—I have been forced to accuse myself and others.

"The majority of my confession has been suggested or dictated by Ushakov, and the remainder is my reconstruction of N.K.V.D. materials from Western Siberia for which I assumed all responsibility. If some part of the story which Ushakov fabricated and which I signed did not properly hang together, I was forced to sign another variant. The same thing was done to Rukhimovich, who was at first designated as a member of the reserve network and whose name later was removed without telling me anything about it; the same was also done with the leader of the reserve network supposedly created by Bukharin in 1935. At first I wrote my name in, and then I was instructed to insert Mezhlauk. There were other similar incidents.

". . . I ask and beg you that you again examine my case and this not for the purpose of sparing me but in order to unmask the vile provocation which wound itself like a snake around many persons, in large measure through my meanness and criminal slander. I have never betrayed you or the Party. I know that I perish because of vile and mean work of the enemies of the Party and of the people, who fabricated the provocation against me."

It would appear that such an important declaration was worth an examination by the Central Committee. This, however, was not done, and the declaration was transmitted to Beria, while the terrible maltreatment of the Political Bureau Candidate, Comrade Eikhe, continued.

On Feb. 2, 1940, Eikhe was brought before the court. Here he did not confess any guilt and said as follows:

"In all the so-called confessions of mine there is not one letter written by me with the exception of my signatures under the protocols, which were forced from me. I have made my confession under pressure from the investigative judge, who from the time of my arrest tormented me. After that I began to write all this nonsense. . . . The most important thing for me is to tell the court, the Party and Stalin that I am not guilty. I have never been guilty of any conspiracy. I shall die believing in the truth of Party policy, as I have believed in it during my whole life."

Eikhe was shot Feb. 4. (*Indignation in the hall.*) It has been definitely established now that Eikhe's case was fabricated; he has been posthumously rehabilitated. . . .

Comrades! In order not to repeat errors of the past, the Central Committee has declared itself resolutely against the cult of the individual leader. We consider that Stalin was excessively extolled. However, in the past Stalin undoubtedly performed great services to the Party, to the working class and to the international workers' movement.

This question is complicated by the fact that all that we have just discussed was done during Stalin's life, under his leadership and with his concurrence; here Stalin was convinced that it was necessary for the defense of the interests of the working classes against the plotting of the enemies and against the attack of the imperialist camp. He saw this from the position of the interests of the working class, the interests of the working people, the interests of the victory of socialism and communism. We cannot say that these were the deeds of a giddy despot. He considered that this should be done in the interests of the Party, of the working masses, in the name of defense of the revolution's gains. In this lies the whole tragedy! . . .

Comrades! We must resolutely abolish the cult of the individual leader once and for all; we must draw the proper conclusions concerning both ideological-theoretical and practical work.

It is necessary for this purpose:

First, in a Bolshevist manner to condemn and to eradicate the cult of the individual leader as alien to Marxism-Leninism and not consonant with the principles of Party leadership and the norms of Party life, and to fight inexorably all attempts at bringing back this practice in one form or another.

To return to and actually practice in all our ideological work the very important Marxist-Leninist theses about the people as the maker of history and the creator of all mankind's material and spiritual benefits, about the decisive role of the Marxist party in the revolutionary struggle to change society, about the victory of communism.

In this connection we shall be obliged to do much to examine critically from the Marxist-Leninist viewpoint and to correct the widespread, erroneous views connected with the cult of the individual leader in the spheres of history, philosophy, economics and other sciences, as well as in literature and the fine arts. It is especially necessary that in the immediate future we compile a serious textbook of the history of our party, edited in accordance with scientific Marxist objectivism, a textbook of the history of Soviet society, a book pertaining to the events of the Civil War and the great patriotic war.

Secondly, to continue systematically and consistently the work done by the Party Central Committee during the past years, work characterized by scrupulous observance—in all Party organizations, from bottom to top—of the Leninist principles of Party leadership; characterized above all by the main principle, collective leadership; characterized by observance of the norms of Party life described in the Statutes of our party; and, finally, characterized by wide practice of criticism and self-criticism.

Thirdly, to restore completely the Leninist principles of Soviet, socialist democracy expressed in the Constitution of the Soviet Union; to fight willfulness of individuals abusing their power. The evil caused by acts violating revolutionary socialist legality which accumulated over a long period as a result of the negative influence of the cult of the individual leader must be completely corrected. . . .

We are absolutely certain that our party, armed with the historic resolutions of the 20th Congress, will lead the Soviet people along the Leninist path to new successes, to new victories. (*Stormy, prolonged applause.*)

Long live the victorious banner of our party—Leninism! (*Stormy, prolonged applause, culminating in an ovation. All rise.*)

Nikita Khrushchev's "Secret Speech" to the Twentieth Congress of the Communist Party of the Soviet Union, February 25, 1956 [Excerpts from Thomas P. Whitney (ed.), *Khrushchev Speaks: Selected Speeches, Articles, and Press Conferences, 1949–1961* (Ann Arbor: University of Michigan Press, 1963). pp. 207–265.

===== **Joseph Starobin, "1956—A Memoir"** =====

Joseph Starobin, a longtime American Communist and onetime foreign editor of the party's newspaper, The Daily Worker, recalled the shock with which Khrushchev's revelations about Stalin were met by Communists. What they had defended for decades against the accusations of liberals and conservatives as the best hope of humankind now was exposed as a record of political savagery. The American Communist party had never been a large organization and was marked by its unquestioned loyalty to the Soviet Union, even as the "party line" of the International twisted one way and another. In the late 1940s and early 1950s, American authorities persecuted communists for their affiliation with the United States' major enemy, and when some Communists were convicted of espionage, the party as a whole was tainted as a disloyal, treasonous organization. The revelations of 1956 dealt the party a severe blow, and its membership plummeted. The young radicals of the next decades thought of Communists as stodgy old Marxists with rigidly orthodox views, and the New Left that developed out of the civil rights movement and the anti–Vietnam War protests generally eschewed Marxism and, instead of forming a "vanguard party," opted for what they thought of as a particularly American form of radicalism— "participatory democracy."

That something was rotten in Moscow was not too astonishing an idea to someone who had visited there several times since 1950. In far-off Peking, where I finally landed for a year, a prominent French Communist, the late Pierre Courtade (then a member of the PCF Central Committee and foreign editor of *l'Humanité*) had once teased me an entire afternoon: It was September 1952, and Courtade, who had himself just passed through Moscow, exclaimed: "Who is Stalin, after all—a genial leader or a terrible old man?"

"*Dirigeant génial ou vieillard terrible?*"—the question had shaken me profoundly although it was of a piece with that cynical banter not uncommon among sophisticated Italian and French Communists of the time. In the summer of 1955, I had heard Russians make the same suggestion. This time no Gallic banter could leaven the harshness of the words. I remember a prominent correspondent of *Pravda* at some United Nations function who blurted out the thought: "Stalin was a dictator. Maybe this Khrushchev will do better. . . ." Later, a prominent Polish writer-diplomat, whom I had once seen celebrating the 1953 New Year in Moscow with his Soviet counterparts, was now plunged in fearsome despair. When I ventured the thought that the whole conception of the "dictatorship of the proletariat" would have to be re-examined, he became visibly excited. A new kind of international solidarity seemed to be arising, based on the mutual recognition of revisionist thinking which now could be safely expressed.

The year 1955 seemed then like a vast intellectual black market in which many of us traded, half in a daze, unable to voice everything on our minds, often misunderstood by those who were closest to us because our experiences had been different. We were all governed and inhibited by a common determination to see things through one way or another. I refused to resume activity in the American party in the conviction that somehow a protest had to be made against the way William Foster and his friends had run it into the ground, threatening to expel everyone who called their ideas into question. I remember telling those leaders returning from jail, but still on parole, what I thought had to be done, and urging them to do it *before* the 20th Congress, which the Soviets had just announced for the following February, lest the necessary re-orientation of the American movement again come as an aftermath of international changes. I published a most Aesopian book that autumn, full of allusions, with ghostly ideas between the lines: a poor book for its lack of courage, but immediately attacked in the Communist press. It was as much as a man could say to those whom he knew to be floating in the clouds of a lifelong honest commitment—and like himself troubled but immobilized by this very loyalty.

The year 1956 was, of course, a time of continual shock. But the greatest shock to the Communist believer was not so much the revelation of how Stalin had governed; it was the way his coworkers proceeded to admit some of the ugly truths, but dragged their feet in drawing fundamental conclusions from their own admissions.

It was, for example, a shock to learn that Lenin's "testament"—which voiced agonizing doubts about Stalin's suitability as party leader, even urging his removal in its famous postscript—was genuine. (Indeed, there were millions of rank-and-file party members who had never heard of it at all.) With how many young socialists and Trotskyists had we not argued, in far-off days, that Lenin could not possibly have held Stalin in such low esteem?

It was also a shock to read in Anastas Mikoyan's address to the 20th Congress that "we are lagging seriously in our study of the present phase of capitalism, do not engage in a profound study of facts and figures, and frequently, for agitational purposes, pick out isolated facts relating to the oncoming crisis, to the impoverishment of the working people, but fail to give an all-round and profound evaluation of the phenomena observed in the life of foreign countries." Indeed, Mikoyan disclosed that the institutes for the study of both the West and the East had been closed, and he expressed envy that, by contrast, the Soviet Union was being studied at numerous institutes in the United States. How little this squared with the firm conviction among believers that the Soviet Communists unquestionably knew what they were talking about!

The most searing shock, of course, was to learn that over half of the delegates to the Soviet party's 17th Congress in 1934, the "Congress of the Victors in Building Socialism," had never survived that decade; also, that two-thirds of the Central Committee elected by the Congress had been murdered on trumped-up charges originated by Stalin himself. For consider what the year 1934 signified for Communists of the West: it was a time when tens of thousands of new young militants flocked into the American, the French, the Spanish and even the Chinese Communist parties. The great anti-fascist upswing was at full tide. Yet two decades later we learned that the men and women identified with what seemed in retrospect the movement's finest hour were framed and murdered only a few years later, and by their own leaders at that.

Thus it was that millions of dedicated people who had stood up to attacks and persecution, whose boundless loyalty to the Soviet Union they had so proudly proclaimed, were suddenly confronted in 1956 with the admission of Stalin's coworkers that the Moscow Trials had no substance whatsoever. That *Verbatim Report* in the dull, gray binding, which reverently went into the libraries of countless millions of homes and formed the basis of popularizations of the supposed "great conspiracy against Soviet Russia," turned out to have been a monstrous concoction. Even while writing these lines, I look up to my bookshelf to verify the title, and the mingled emotions which the sight of this unclean volume arouses make it hard to continue writing.

It turned out that hundreds of thousands of Soviet Communists (some have said millions), the same ones who evaded the Tsarist police, languished in the Siberian camps, seized power from Kerensky, held the country together against famine and intervention and then built a new society with bare hands—the flower of a fabled revolutionary generation—had been shipped off to concentration camps, this time in "socialist Siberia," where they endured torture and death at the hands of the same party to which they had entrusted their deepest hopes and life itself. And all the while the charge that such was in fact happening had been denied all over the world on the grounds that it came from the enemies of socialism! It also turned out that Stalin was not the military genius the world had been led to believe. The Soviet people had paid for Stalin's comparative military unpreparedness with thousands of lives, and this unpreparedness was itself astonishing. Communists had argued that even such strange moves as the Soviet-German non-aggression pact of 1939 had been justified by the Soviet Union's need to gain time, to prepare itself better for the Nazi attack—and now it turned out that Stalin had indeed wasted that time!

Yet the trauma of 1956 rested on deeper ground. Not only the oversized statues and preposterous portraits of Stalin came crashing down, but the basic myths on which the structure of international communism rested—namely, that the Soviet party incarnated integrity, wisdom and knowledge, and hence deserved the admiration and obedience of all the other parties. Even today, a decade later, academic colleagues often ask me by what mechanisms Moscow maintained its hold on the "fraternal parties," as though the essence of the matter were to be found in secret orders, in Soviet gold, in the fealty of this or that leader, or even in the armies of liberation that stayed to occupy. All of these things played their part, of course. But to most Communists, the acceptance of the Soviet party's preeminence was at bottom voluntary, arising from something quite simple and on its own terms quite noble: millions of people believed in, and wanted, an *international* movement; and they thought they had it.

The Communist leaders from Europe, Asia and America deferred without question to the Russians because the Russians had supposedly upheld the ideal with honor. They had proven their mettle, their devotion, their foresight, and they were therefore entitled to a leadership commensurate with their hard-won power—a power intended as a bulwark and shield for others. Most Communists believed what they wanted to believe, and led themselves to disaster more than others misled them.

Hadn't the Second International become a "stinking corpse," as the martyred Rosa Luxemburg said, because its leaders had failed to honor their pledges of mutual aid at the "moment of truth" in 1914? Lenin borrowed and repeated that phrase, and the Third International was going to be different. There was no holier moment in the average party member's experience then to hear the strains of the *Internationale* soaring above a forest of clenched fists and radiant faces, proclaiming "a better world's in birth" and the final line's prediction that "The Internationale will be the human race. . . ."

But at the 20th Congress, Comrade Khrushchev spoke in secret, to Russian ears only, and only to a few of them at that. The 55 foreign delegations had been given special receptions, had been wined, dined and well-lodged, and their most important figures had addressed the Congress, to the accompaniment of "stormy applause." Yet the Soviet leaders had so little regard for those movements which had staked everything on the leading role of the CPSU that they never bothered to inform the revered international leaders about the revelations concerning Stalin or to discuss with them the new ideas which the Congress projected. Though the time was ripe and the occasion opportune, no debate seems to have taken place. Not even the proposition of diverse paths to socialism, nor the new prospects for coexistence and the maintenance of world peace (the strategic framework of global political evolution), were put forward for the consideration of fraternal parties, except as previously-adopted Soviet views, *ipso facto* binding on everyone.

Thus, upon returning from Moscow late that winter, the Western Communist leaders were making reports on the 20th Congress, still using the Aesopian phrase "cult of personality" but not mentioning the secret speech. The Communist audience outside the USSR was placed in the humiliating position of learning what had happened in Moscow from the "bourgeois press," although their leaders had been there, as honored guests, a few weeks earlier.

Was the speech a fabrication of the State Department, as some Communist papers suggested in a familiar reflex? Were Togliatti or Thorez concealing from their own followers what they had known all along? That would have been bad enough, indeed shocking. Or had these intimates of Stalin also been kept in the dark? That was worse, incredible and intolerable. But if the Khrushchev speech was genuine, why did the Russians not make it public, in keeping with their assurances that they were turning a new leaf? Ten years later, it is something to ponder that the Soviet people have not yet had a full and authoritative text of so historic and meaningful a contribution to their own history.

Having failed to make destalinization a common project, an uneven development then set in and took its fierce revenge. All the latent contradictions of the apparent monolith came to the surface, unevenly and explosively. The Russians could not control what they had themselves set in motion, for their own contradiction lay in continuing to cling to Stalinist methods even as they tried, by fits and starts, to destalinize. This spectacle placed the most basic tenets of the movement in question. Unable to lead, the "leading party" persisted in doing so, and its leadership—and much else with it—fell into discredit.

The famous interview of the Italian Communist leader, the late Palmiro Togliatti, published in *Nuovi Argomenti* in mid-June 1956, unwittingly accelerated this process. Togliatti, it will be remembered, enjoyed great prestige not only as the chief of a powerful movement arising from the ruins of two decades of Italian fascism, but as the former secretary of the Communist International—the famous "Ercoli" whom an entire generation of Communists the world over held in great regard. In the interview Togliatti voiced the question whether, in the discussion as led by the Russians, "the true problems are evaded." He asked "why and how Soviet society could reach and did reach certain forms alien to the democratic way and to the legality which it had set for itself, even to the point of degeneration." The difficulty was, he said, that "our Soviet comrades, having limited themselves substantially to denouncing the facts and undertaking the proper correction, have neglected up to now the still-unfulfilled task of dealing with the difficult subject of an overall political and historical judgment."

What was needed, everybody thought, was a "Marxist-Leninist analysis." The Soviet leaders were asked before the bar of history and the entire movement to supply it. If the transformation of Lenin's heir and disciple into a Byzantine tyrant was to be explained on grounds of personal psychology, of paranoia, or if the deformations of socialism were the product of a specifically Russian backwardness (few Communists abroad even imagined that such backwardness could survive the "building of socialism" and the "transition to communism"), then Marxism-Leninism was itself in danger. It ran counter to every ideological precept that one individual could have abased the principles of so trusted and true a revolutionary party. And if specifically national factors could outweigh the universal power and truth of scientific socialism, the impact was equally disastrous.

In Togliatti's tormenting queries, the red thread ran backwards from Stalin to Lenin, toward the methods and ideas by which the Bolshevik party had won power and maintained it. The Soviet leaders were confidently talking about a return to "Leninist norms," but history was unreeling, as though someone had lost control of the film and the projector, and the camera suddenly focussed on the "ten days that shook the world." People began to talk about Rosa Luxemburg (who had been revered by young Communists in the 1930's but whose works had not been read until 1956). The accusing questions which she had addressed to Lenin in 1918 rose up again, and every question mark became a ghost. Suddenly the skeletons in the closet of the Communist International began to rattle in every country.

In the same *Nuovi Argumenti* interview, Togliatti broached some other notions which could not possibly have occurred to us before. "The whole system," he said, "becomes polycentric, and even in the Communist movement itself we cannot speak of a single guide but rather of a progress which is achieved by following paths which are often different." In some countries, socialism might be built without the Communists as the leading party, and indeed, "in still other countries, the march toward socialism is an objective for which there is a concentration of efforts coming from various movements, which, however, have not yet reached either an agreement or a reciprocal understanding." Thus, perhaps a Communist party was not needed at all.

This was something quite intoxicating and novel. The concept of different roads to socialism, put forward at the Congress but advanced even earlier, in the declaration following Khrushchev's visit to Belgrade in May 1955, was not an entirely new one: it was part of the memory bank of communism from the 1944–47 period. But polycentrism was a more challenging concept, although elusive like so many of Togliatti's ideas. It suggested that West European, North American, Latin American and Far Eastern parties might in fact be better off if they divested themselves of their ties to Moscow. It suggested further that Communist parties in many countries should enter into *genuine* partnerships with socialist parties and, most important, that they should change their character, fashioned during their long tutelage to the CPSU. Only then would their aims be trusted, and their cooperation accepted. . . .

As for the Soviet Communists, they attempted to confine the discussion with their own declaration of June 30, 1956. Togliatti's projection of polycentrism, with all that it suggested, was sidestepped. At the same time, the Italian leader was rebuked for daring to suggest a "degeneration" of the Soviet system, as though he had touched an exposed nerve. To some Communists, the Soviet declaration went further than anything previously heard; to most, it was an apology, a refusal to undertake a systematic and probing analysis, a sign of resistance to the destalinization process.

At this point, events replaced discussion. In Poznan, Poland, a surprise protest of workers about rates of pay developed into a political demonstration against the regime. All those "dangerous thoughts" which had gripped the cadres of the Polish United Workers Party in 1955, and then spread through party ranks after the 20th Congress, now gripped the masses, and—to use a Marxist term—became a "material force." The first reactions of the Soviet leaders, and of their Polish counterparts, were typical: the events in Poznan were ascribed to "imperialist agents taking advantage of economic difficulties and grievances in certain factories in Poznan." Yet so swiftly was this proven untrue that Communist power in Poland was saved only because of the availability of a group of leaders, with Wladislaw Gomulka at their head, who took matters out of the hands of the Polish Stalinists, in defiance of the top Soviet leaders who rushed to Warsaw in panic. The damage of an entire decade—and in the Polish case, the damage had its macabre inception with Stalin's arbitrary dissolution of the Polish Communist movement in 1938—could now be repaired only as the Soviet Union accepted the monumental criticism implicit in Gomulka's rehabilitation and his dramatic return.

In Hungary similar events developed at the same time, but matured a week or ten days later. Here the blow was even more stunning. It would take us afield to review all the questions that wracked the Communist world at that time—whether the Imre Nagy government had in fact lost control of the uprising to counterrevolutionary elements, whether Hungary's withdrawal from the Warsaw Pact should have been posed at all. Naturally, most believers were appalled by the spectacle of troops and tanks of the leading socialist nation smashing a working class which had risen in arms against what it felt were the traducers of the dream. They were also appalled at the treachery with which the Russians behaved, flooding the country with military power while at the same time promising to withdraw in deference to Hungarian Communist wishes—all of which contradicted the important declaration of October 30, 1956, in which the Soviet Union admitted its own mistakes in dealing with Eastern Europe.

But beyond these reactions, what dismayed so many Communists throughout the world was the incapacity of the Soviet leaders to learn from the Polish experience, or to accept the advice of the Yugoslav leaders which they had gone to such lengths to solicit. What was destroyed in the flames over Budapest was the very conception of a Communist movement that, in so aping the Soviet model under Mátyas Rákosi, had painted itself into a corner. Despised and repudiated, the Stalinists had still not grasped the enormity of the debacle.

Paradoxically, however, the deepest blow was suffered by the Soviet leaders themselves. Having so long and so arrogantly treated their comrades-in-arms as flunkies,
and having tried so desperately to keep the destalinization process from assuming a
truly meaningful character, their mistakes could be rectified only by tanks and guns
and planes—in itself, the most tragic mistake of all. To paraphrase Marx, the Communists had resisted the weapons of criticism and been forced in the end to resort to
the criticism of weapons. After that, the line of division in the Communist world
came to rest between those who realized the tragedy of the era and drew the fullest
conclusions, and those who resisted the meaning of this tragedy, sinking into apologetics, and thus inhibiting the very process of change. . . .

Joseph Starobin, "1956—A Memoir," *Problems of Communism*, XV, (November-December 1966), pp. 1,
64–70.

Report of Vladimir Semichastnyi, chairman of the KGB
July 25, 1962

*During the Khrushchev years, the political police (KGB) were much more constrained in their
activities than the NKVD of Stalin's time had been. Innocent citizens were not arrested without cause as they had been during the Great Terror of the 1930s, and a degree of political discussion was permitted. But Semichastnyi's report to First Secretary Khrushchev testifies to the
ever-vigilant activity of the secret police. The authorities kept watch on dissident groups and
samizdat (self-published materials) and rounded up those who organized public demonstrations. Ironically, this illegal and semi-legal political activity was possible only because of the
greater degree of liberality of the Khrushchev regime. Nothing remotely approaching it would
have been possible under Stalin. What is striking is that dissent from officially sanctioned ideas
and practices affected educated people, urban dwellers, and certain non-Russian nationalities
and that members of the Communist party were involved in such activities.*

Completely Secret

USSR
State Security Committee of the
Council of Ministers of the USSR
July 25, 1962
No. [illegible]
City of Moscow

I report that recently there has been a significant growth in the number of hostile manifestations connected with the spread of anti-Soviet anonymous documents.
In the first six months of this year on the territory of the country were distributed
7,705 anti-Soviet leaflets and anonymous letters prepared by 3,522 authors, which is
twice as high as the number in the same period of 1961.

The greatest number of anti-Soviet documents were discovered in Ukraine, Azerbaijan, Georgia, Latvia, Stavropol', and Krasnoiarsk territories, Rostov, Leningrad, and Moscow regions.

In the leaflets and anonymous letters were contained calls for active struggle against the existing system in the USSR, malicious, slanderous fabrications concerning certain leaders of the Soviet state, nationalist attitudes, lack of faith in the building of a Communist society in our country, and slander against Soviet democracy. In a number of anonymous documents hatred toward the CPSU [Communist Party of the Soviet Union] and Communists is expressed, as well as threats toward local party and soviet activists.

After a long interval, once again anonymous documents are being circulated lauding the participants in the Anti-Party Group.[1] Significantly more letters containing terrorist intentions directed at leaders of the Communist party and the government have begun to appear.

After the publication of the decision of the CC CPSU and the Council of Ministers of the USSR on the raising of prices on livestock products, the flow of anonymous letters increased. Since the month of June alone, 83 incidents of distributing anti-Soviet leaflets and graffiti were registered. In that time, the organs of the KGB received from the editorial offices of newspapers and journals more than [illegible number] anti-Soviet anonymous letters in which dissatisfaction with the standard of living of the population of our country, calls for the organization of mass protests, strikes, demonstrations, meetings, boycotts with demands for lowering prices on food products and raising wages were expressed. The distribution of such documents has been observed principally in the industrial centers of our country.

Under the influence of the foreign radio stations, "Free Russia" and "Freedom," there have been more frequent incidences of anonymous documents with hostile contents signed with the name of the so-called "People's Laboring Union" (NTS) and prepared by Soviet citizens. Such incidents have taken place in many populated places in the European part of the Soviet Union.

We have observed the growth in the number of anonymous letters sent to foreign anti-Soviet radio stations and organs of the bourgeois press, in which the authors of these letters, along with offering slanderous fabrications about Soviet reality, offer their services in the carrying out of hostile activities.

As a result of measures taken by the organs of state security in the first half of this year, we have identified 1,039 authors, who have distributed 6,726 anti-Soviet documents (5,032 leaflets; 1,694 letters). Included among the distributors of anonymous documents are 364 workers, 192 salaried employees, 210 students and pupils, 108 persons without any identifiable occupation, 105 pensioners, and 60 collective farmers; 434 authors, that is more than 40 percent, have secondary or higher education; more than 47 percent of the discovered "anonymous" are younger than 30 years of age.

Among the identified authors of anti-Soviet anonymous documents, 89 are members and candidates for membership in the CPSU, 116 are Komsomols [members of the Young Communist League]. . . .

---

1. The so-called Anti-Party Group were those leading Communists—Molotov, Malenkov, Kaganovich, Voroshilov, and others—who tried to unseat Khrushchev in June 1957 but were defeated in a Central Committee vote and demoted from the Politburo.

As became clear during the interrogation, some of the identified authors had been convicted and served time for various crimes, including anti–Soviet activity.

The analysis of this material shows also that, along with the general increase in the quantity of distributed anonymous documents, there has been a significant rise in the number of attempts at carrying out organized anti-Soviet activity. As a result of searchs by agents in the first half of 1962, 60 local anti-Soviet groups were discovered, with 215 participants, mostly young people; in the same period in 1961, 47 groups with 186 participants were discovered.

In preparing hostile documents, copying mechanisms (print type, typewriters, homemade forms and stamps) are most often used.

For example, in Moscow an anti-Soviet group made up of students and young workers and called "Union of Free Reason" was liquidated. The members of this group put together the text of an anti-Soviet leaflet, and to distribute it they made 400 copies on the printing press of the military publishing house. . . .

On the territory of the Crimea an anti-Soviet group was identified under the name "Free Tavrida," and made up of 10 students in the 8–9 grades, who had prepared and distributed more than 100 anti-Soviet leaflets.

In the last half year, 38 authors have been discovered of anonymous documents that contain terrorist threats against leaders of the party and Soviet government. . . .

In the first half of 1962, the organs of state security have brought to justice 105 persons (in contrast to 52 in the first half of 1961), have interrogated 366, and have taken preventive measures against 568 persons for preparing and distributing anti-Soviet anonymous documents.

The State Security Committee has taken measures for the speediest investigation and unmasking of these criminals.

Chairman of the State Security Committee
V. Semichastnyi

RTsKhIDNI, f. 89, op. 51, d. 1, ll. 1–4; translation by the editor.

CHAPTER SEVEN

STAGNATION

Looking from the present back to the last decades of the Soviet Union, historians and political scientists view the Brezhnev years as the prelude to the fall of the Communist system. Gorbachev labeled the decades of the late sixties and seventies the "stagnation" (*zastoi*), a time when the Soviet economy and political structure appeared to be suffering from the same arteriosclerosis that its aging leaders endured. But if one steps back and observes the USSR from the vantage point of the mid-1970s, the internal decline was partly masked by a massive military buildup and the expansion of Soviet influence into new parts of the world—Africa, the Mediterranean, and Southeast Asia. For the first time, the USSR reached rough parity in military might with the United States, though its economy staggered at less than half the production of its principal rival. The USSR faced unrest in its Eastern European empire, "the Achilles heel of the Soviet system," where the local Communist regimes were rapidly loosing the last vestiges of legitimacy.[1] In Czechoslovakia in 1968, the Communist party itself, under Alexander Dubcek, attempted to reform and popularize a "socialism with a human face," only to be met with Soviet tanks. In Poland in the 1970s and 1980s, massive strikes by workers and an extraordinary alliance of trade unionists and intellectuals eventually made Communist party rule untenable. Most disastrously, Soviet power overextended itself into Afghanistan to prop up a leftist government in late 1979, only to find itself mired in a debilitating and costly war against Muslim guerrillas backed by the United States, Pakistan, and China.

Internally, the Soviet system reached the limits of the Stalinist model of industrialization based on expansion of the physical plant rather than intensification and improvement of production. The "command economy" could no longer command significant increases in either industrial or agricultural output or labor productivity. In the 1970s, both Western capitalist and Soviet-style economies suffered the end of the period of spectacular growth of the 1950s and 1960s, but the Soviet economy continued its decline into the next decade. The only bright spot was that oil-rich Russia benefited from high world oil prices and exported cheap energy to its "satellite" neighbors and to the rest of the world in exchange for industrial goods and grain. As Mark Mazower explains, "communist regimes could not for political reasons adjust the economy through deflation and through mass unemployment after the fashion of their Western counterparts. They therefore chose the opposite strategy to that followed in

---

1. Eric Hobsbawm, *The Age of Extremes. A History of the World, 1914–1991* (New York: Pantheon Books, 1995), p. 475.

the West, and kept consumers suffering through scarcity and shoddy goods in prefer-ence to throwing workers out of their jobs."[2] Some state socialist regimes, like Hun-gary and China, turned toward marketization with notable success, but in Brezhnev's Soviet Union conservative and entrenched bureaucrats relied on imports paid with gold and oil rather than fundamental economic reform. Yet European Communist regimes did not collapse because of economic decline or Cold War rivalry with the United States. Fundamentally, these conditions contributed to a more significant and dangerous phenomenon—the progressive erosion of the aging Communist leader-ship's claim to a right to rule. What Communists had done well in the past—industri-alize the country, turn peasants into workers, educate the illiterate, and improve the material life of the people—had created populations that no longer required the pa-ternalistic, tutelary government of a political elite out of touch with its own con-stituents. Communist parties and the socioeconomic and political systems they sought to preserve had not only become irrelevant, but obstacles to further development.

As an observer of Soviet life in the 1970s, historian John Bushnell of Northwest-ern University chronicled the downward shift in popular mood as the traces of ideal-ism faded and materialist appetites were frustrated. Though there was no social crisis in the country and the regime managed to "deliver the goods" that its people needed, the long years of mediocre leadership and slow economic improvement sapped the op-timism and faith in the Soviet system, first among intellectuals and then, gradually, among other segments of the population. Both his essay and that of economist James Millar of George Washington University mention Vera S. Dunham's conception of the "Big Deal"—the tacit compact that the regime made with the emerging middle strata in society. Millar adapts this idea to the Brezhnev period and speaks of a "Little Deal," an arrangement by which the regime, now aware that it cannot satisfy the material wants of its population, tacitly agrees to allow semi-legal and even illegal economic ac-tivity by private individuals in order to supply consumer goods and services. As eco-nomic growth slowed down in the 1970s and the country experienced food shortages, the Soviet Union was forced to import grain from the West and tolerate widespread private economic activity. Corruption spread throughout the country, reaching the highest levels of the state, into the family of the general secretary himself.

The evident degeneration of Soviet socialism and its evident loss of legitimacy was intolerable to men like KGB chief Yuri Andropov. A number of younger Soviet leaders, like the party secretary of Stavropol region in southern Russia, Mikhail Gor-bachev, and his friend, the party secretary of the republic of Georgia, Eduard She-vardnadze, also concluded that "things cannot go on the way they were." But the rigidities, hierarchies, and conventional practices of deference to those higher up in the apparatus prevented any reform until Brezhnev died in 1982.

THE "NEW SOVIET MAN" TURNS PESSIMIST

John Bushnell

If a Soviet George Gallup had polled his country's middle class in the 1950s, he would have discovered a resoundingly upbeat mood. The Soviet middle class would have re-

---

2. Mark Mazower, *Dark Continent: Europe's Twentieth Century* (New York: Alfred A. Knopf, 1998), p. 365.

sponded with enthusiastic optimism to questions such as, "Are you better or worse off than before?" "What is your outlook for the future?" "Do you think things are getting better or worse?" The results of the poll would have been published in *Pravda,* a spate of self-congratulatory articles would have followed, and opinion surveys would have become an established Soviet science. Had our Soviet Gallup taken a similar poll twenty years later, the results never would have seen the light of day: by then, the Soviet middle class was sliding into an abyss of pessimism. Gallup would have been under a cloud, and opinion surveys would have been disestablished. Something very much like the preceding scenario has in fact been the fate of Soviet opinion surveys. Of course, there have been no Soviet Gallup polls. Nevertheless, if we marshall the impressionistic evidence and fragmentary opinion samples, and if we attempt to do no more than establish roughly the levels of middle-class optimism and pessimism, it is possible to identify some important trends.*

The argument presented here is that during the 1950s the Soviet middle class became increasingly optimistic about the performance of the Soviet system and about its own prospects for material betterment, that this optimism persisted through the 1960s, but that in the 1970s it has given way to pessimism. The rise and decline of middle-class optimism can be linked in part to political developments, but the crucial determinant has been the changing perception of Soviet economic performance. The degree of the Soviet consumer's present and anticipated future satisfaction has been influenced by the real performance of the consumer sector. However, since at least the early 1960s the perception of Soviet economic performance has been affected as well by comparisons that the Soviet middle class has been able to make with consumer standards in other, primarily East European, countries. Such comparisons are not to the advantage of the Soviet Union, and the Soviet middle class does not anticipate any narrowing of the consumption gap in the foreseeable future. This pessimistic outlook on future consumption has contributed to mounting skepticism and cynicism about the values and performance of the regime in other areas as well.

"Middle class" is not a term often employed in discussions of Soviet society. It is used here to refer to what most Western studies have called, following Soviet practice, the intelligentsia. . . .

In terms of occupation and education, the Soviet "intelligentsia" approximates the white-collar middle class in the West. It includes middle-level office functionaries, doctors, dentists, engineers, agronomists, and so on, as well as members of the intellectual professions. It is a middle class, too, in that it occupies a position between the small socio-political elite and the very numerous workers, peasants, and unskilled white-collar employees. In the USSR even more than in the West, the defining trait of the middle class is status rather than income. A doctor earning 110 rubles a month is perceived to have a higher social status than a bus driver earning 180 rubles or more a month. Although members of the elite enjoy markedly higher incomes and other perquisites denied to the middle class, these are the consequences, rather than the cause, of elite status: as a rule, special privileges are granted to those chosen for the elite on political or other grounds. . . .

Between 1950 and 1974 this group expanded from 3.3 to 21.4 million employed persons (excluding military personnel as well as retirees and students), or from 5 to 18 percent of the Soviet work force. Besides providing access to middle-class jobs, the

---

* My own sense of the public mood derives from four years (1972–76) in the Soviet Union as exchange student and translator. Though I was based in Moscow, my contacts were not limited to middle-class Muscovites.

educational system lends intergenerational stability to the Soviet middle class. While there is considerable upward mobility into the white-collar middle class, middle-class children enjoy preferential access to the higher and special secondary education that ensures access to middle-class jobs; there is little downward mobility out of the middle class. The Soviet middle class has been expanding around a core that is by now as hereditary as any Western middle class.

THE DRIFT FROM OPTIMISM TO PESSIMISM

A survey of postwar refugees conducted by Harvard's Russian Research Center in 1950–51 found that in Stalin's last years there was a fairly broad acceptance of the Soviet social and economic systems. Soviet citizens—including those in white-collar middle-class occupations—identified with the Soviet Union's military and industrial achievements. They expected the state to provide a wide range of social benefits and services, as well as job security, and they approved of the regime's stated welfare objectives. While there was pronounced hostility to terror and to the methods of Communist Party rule, the regime was judged not so much by its formal and informal political arrangements as by its performance. A major source of low-level but persistent resentment was the regime's failure to deliver on its proclaimed welfare policies. The middle class was unhappy about its low standard of living. However, the leadership, or the regime, rather than the system, was faulted. Indeed, Soviet citizens did not see any acceptable alternative to the Soviet system, and they certainly did not believe that a capitalist system could provide the social benefits they had come to expect. Terror excepted, the existing system was taken for granted. The Harvard project found that acceptance of the institutional parameters of the Soviet system was stronger with each succeeding generation; there is no evidence that this perceived legitimacy of the system has lessened since then among any but the relatively small contingent of dissidents and critically minded intellectuals. Attitudes toward the performance of the system and toward the leadership have fluctuated, but the system has consistently been judged sound in its principles.

   Given the wide acceptance of the system found among the postwar refugees in the late 1940s and early 1950s, Alex Inkeles and Raymond Bauer predicted that if terror were reduced and if the system were perceived to be meeting welfare expectations, the regime would tap a large reservoir of popular support. This is precisely what happened. The 1950s saw a surge of confidence and optimism that stemmed from the virtual cessation of Stalinist terror, very real improvements in living standards, symbolic achievements—such as the Soviet space program—that reenforced patriotic pride, and to a certain extent the progress of national liberation in the Third World, which seemed to indicate that Soviet socialism was the high road to the future. During the late 1950s the Soviet leadership promised that the housing shortage would be eliminated within a decade, that by the mid-1960s Soviet citizens would have a standard of living surpassing the West European average, and that the younger generation would live to see true communism. Against the background of perceived (and quite real) gains, middle-class expectations for the future were fully in accord with official projections.

   Alexander Werth, who informally sampled the mood of the middle class in the late 1950s and was struck by its optimism, concluded that there was, indeed, a "New

Soviet Man." This New Soviet Man was proud of his country's accomplishments, confident that the Soviet Union was *the* rising power in the world, convinced that the Soviet Union's rapid economic advances were being translated into a rising level of personal well-being, and certain that the Soviet system provided unlimited personal opportunities, especially for the young. Not all observers detected the same degree of middle-class optimism as did Werth, himself an inveterate optimist about things Soviet. Nevertheless, almost all reported a widespread middle-class conviction that the system worked well, that economic development was yielding tangible personal benefits, and that the sense of well-being was enhanced by the marked relaxation of the political atmosphere. Soviet survey data, such as they are, are congruent with the observations of outsiders. Seventy-three percent of the respondents to a poll conducted in October 1960 by the Public Opinion Institute of *Komsomolskaia Pravda,* the newspaper of the Communist youth organization, reported that their standard of living had improved in recent years, while only seven percent reported a deterioration. . . .

The only deviations from this pervasive optimism occurred among intellectuals and university students (the children and future members of the middle class). Even among these groups, however, it is evident that the disaffection that followed Khrushchev's 1956 "Secret Speech" was limited largely to demands for the further reduction of intellectual regimentation. This kind of dissatisfaction was a minority phenomenon. Many intellectuals, for instance, viewed continued limitations on freedom as a necessary trade-off for economic development that would ultimately make greater freedom possible; in any case, an appreciable minority of intellectuals did not view political freedom as a desirable end. Even among students, who in 1956 and the years immediately following were more inclined than any other group to voice dissatisfaction, the majority were pleased with their own prospects and projected their own satisfaction onto society at large. If anything, in the late 1950s the average student was more optimistic than his middle-class elders. Asked about their chances for acquiring their own automobiles, fifty-two of eighty-five fifth-year students at Moscow University polled by Jerzy Kosinski said they expected to be able to purchase a car within two or three years, another twenty-eight estimated four to six years, while only five believed they would never own an automobile. Given the virtual nonexistence of a market in private automobiles at the time, these students' expectations were wildly unrealistic. Yet there does not seem to have been generational discontinuity in middle-class optimism, only a slight difference in degree—excessive optimism was characteristic of all members of the middle class.

Middle-class optimism apparently peaked by the early 1960s—it could scarcely have mounted higher—and then remained at a constantly high level into the second half of the decade. As before, confidence about future prospects was based on perceptions of present national achievement and personal betterment. Remarkably, this attitude persisted despite economic difficulties in the mid-1960s that led the post-Khrushchev leadership to back off publicly from unrealistic promises. Judging by the comments of most observers, even the return of food shortages in 1962 and 1963 barely dented middle-class optimism. Exchange students who spent those years in Moscow, for instance, do not mention that difficulties in food supply were a matter of concern to their informants. It may be that students continued to be more optimistic than the older generation, for whom the food shortages were unpleasantly reminiscent of the bad times of the past, and who consequently worried that the recovery of 1965 might not be permanent. But again, student attitudes differed from

those of their elders only in degree, not in kind. The middle class appreciated the sobriety of the Brezhnev-Kosygin team that came to power in the mid-1960s and became more convinced than ever that the system was in good hands and that the standard of living would continue to improve.

The few available opinion surveys suggest that the bulk of the middle class remained reasonably optimistic about the condition of the Soviet system until the beginning of the 1970s. . . . Jewish emigres surveyed in Israel (1972) and Detroit
(1976) reported relative satisfaction with the material side of life in the USSR. Of the
respondents in Israel, 90.2 percent claimed that there had been material improvements in Soviet society in the last twenty-five years (this figure is perhaps not very
meaningful given the time span). More significantly, 67.2 percent of the respondents
in Israel said that the Soviet regime had the interests of the people at heart. . . .

While the above describes what we know of the attitudes of the great majority of
the middle class, by the late 1960s the attitudes of middle-class intellectuals had begun
to diverge from those of nonintellectuals: the minority of intellectuals had become decidedly pessimistic. The changed mood of the intellectuals can be attributed in large
measure to shifts in the regime's stance on de-Stalinization, the not-so-secret trials of
dissident writers and demonstrators, and the invasion of Czechoslovakia. While the
tightening of domestic political and economic controls obviously had the greatest impact on intellectuals, we may hazard the supposition that symbolically prominent
events—trials, the Czechoslovak affair, and the concurrent resumption of jamming—
caused a quickening of unease in the middle class as a whole. However, for all but intellectuals this apprehension dissipated when it became clear that there was to be no
return to pervasive terror, and that there was no political threat to the well-being of
those who observed the written and unwritten rules of Soviet society. . . .

Even in the mid-1970s, when there could be no question about the regime's hard
line on open expression of dissent, the bulk of the middle class had no fear of political repression. The September 1974 exhibit of modernist art at Izmailovo Park in
Moscow illustrates how selective repression has left intact the sense of personal security of the average member of the middle class. Although an attempt to stage an exhibit two weeks earlier had been broken up by force, when the exhibit did open it
was attended—despite the highly visible police presence—by thousands of Muscovites from all (but primarily middle-class) walks of life. Even a sprinkling of army
officers put in an appearance. Most members of the middle class do not share the intellectuals' political and cultural distress. While the middle class has little expectation
of political liberalization, liberalization that goes beyond assurances of personal security—which they feel they already have—is for most simply irrelevant.

Yet after a brief lag the middle class as a whole did pick up the intellectuals' pessimism, not in association with political developments but in association with a perception of economic decline. Not surprisingly, intellectuals were the first to become
economic pessimists. By the late 1960s they were speaking of stagnation and even re-
gression not just as a short-term problem but as the long-term outlook for the Soviet
economy. For intellectuals, economic pessimism was bound up with the perception
of political rigidity: declining growth rates (the extent of the decline was greatly exaggerated) were pointed to as an example of overall systemic stagnation. Since the
early 1970s, economic (or consumer) pessimism has spread to the rest of the middle
class, and with gathering momentum. As of the middle of the decade, the Soviet middle class had lost its previous certainty that the economic gap with the West would
eventually be closed. Furthermore, the middle class no longer believed that even the

slower rate of economic growth was yielding any appreciable improvement in the standard of living. In fact, the middle class was beginning to deny that there had recently been any improvement at all in the standard of living.

It should be emphasized that the drift towards economic pessimism was under way before the agricultural disaster of 1975, which threw the Soviet middle class into a state of depression verging on despair. Neither Polish blue jeans nor Japanese umbrellas, then much in evidence, could offset that devastating blow to middle-class confidence in Soviet economic performance. Neither the uncertainties of the weather nor the fact that Soviet agriculture had been overextended by the drive to increase the proportion of meat in the Soviet diet provided solace: these were felt to be poor excuses indeed for a country that claimed to embody "highly developed socialism."

The shock caused by the 1975 crop failure—and the several years' disruption in the food supply that followed—has yet to wear off. Since 1976 pessimism over the state of the Soviet economy has taken on the blackest hues, and there is now near unanimity that "things are getting worse" and will continue to get worse for the foreseeable future. Exaggerated pessimism might seem a natural response to crop failure and so not particularly significant, but it is worth recalling that nothing similar occurred after the crop failures of the early 1960s. Clearly, the underpinnings of confidence in the performance of the Soviet economy had been eroded prior to 1975. In the early 1960s, consumer difficulties were considered deviations from the overall upward movement. In the 1970s, they have been viewed as the norm.

Apprehension about Soviet economic performance has done more than anything else to shape the present mood of the middle class, but the malaise extends considerably beyond that. Not only has Soviet economic performance been discredited, the very direction of economic policy is now suspect. Middle-class Soviets do not now believe that Soviet economic development benefits them; indeed, it is a middle-class commonplace that whatever economic growth may now be occurring is at the *expense* of the Soviet public. Skepticism about official economic policy is but one manifestation of middle-class disengagement from the regime's goals. Civic cynicism and alienation are so pervasive that by comparison post-Watergate America seems a hotbed of utopian optimism: few members of the Soviet middle class will admit that they do more than go through the motions of their professional and civic duties. Antipathy to Third World countries (not to mention Third World nationals in the Soviet Union) is universal. Even the space program, once the object of so much pride, is now met with apathy—perhaps because, as in the United States, it has been playing too long. What was most remarkable about the public reaction to the Apollo-Soyuz mission were not the smallish crowds that gathered in front of TV stores to watch launch, link-up, and landing, but the much larger crowds on the streets who paid no attention whatsoever to these much ballyhooed events. In almost every respect the mood of the middle class in the late 1970s was very nearly the mirror image of the mood twenty years earlier.

Many of the features of the Soviet system that now contribute to middle-class pessimism have been around for a long time, but of course it is the altered perception of them that is at issue. The changing middle-class attitude toward the black (or multicolored) market is of special interest. The black market and bribery to obtain privileged access to scarce goods are certainly not of recent origin, although the size of the black market has no doubt increased in proportion to Soviet economic growth: a larger economy provides a larger base for black-market operations. But again the crucial change is in perception, not scale. In the 1950s participation in the black market was viewed as an unavoidable necessity, but it was a matter of course, not something salient to the middle-class view of the system. In the new perceptual configuration, corruption is salient, while the formal rules of public life and good citizenship are subordinate and are observed only to the extent necessary for survival. At the least, the middle class is indifferent to rampant petty corruption and pilferage, and increasingly, these phenomena meet with approval. This attitude complements the middle-class view of official economic policy: "It's a crime not to steal from them, all they do is steal from us," is the watchword of the Soviet middle class in the 1970s.

Of course, middle-class pessimism and cynicism are not absolute. Neither attitude is easy to sustain, and the Soviet middle class is anyway not wholly preoccupied with economic and civil life. Furthermore, there are eddies of optimism even within the strong tide of pessimism. Far more significant is the fact that underneath the pervasive pessimism of the middle class there is a residue of systemic optimism: there is still a feeling that in the very long run things will turn out all right, because the Soviet socialist system is, after all, better than the Western capitalist system. The shifting attitudes sketched thus far have to do with the perceived performance of the Soviet system, not with the system in principle. Many intellectuals and most dissidents have bridged the gap by rejecting the system as well as the performance, but for most members of the middle class the implicit contradiction remains for the time being unresolved. . . .

Today, it is the older generation that is marginally the more optimistic, worldly experience again making the difference. Those over forty continue to fall back on the devastation of the war as the explanation of last resort for present deficiencies. This is a clutching at straws, but the war is more than a convenient rationale: to this day the older generation has vivid memories of the war, and measured against that low point, even the presently perceived stagnation marks a significant advance. On the other hand, the memories of young people do not extend back to the really bad times. Consequently, younger members of the middle class are less impressed by advances in the standard of living over the last twenty years—those whose civic memories go back no more than ten years perceive no improvement at all—and so they are more likely to project their present discontents into the future. Some degree of historical optimism is present in all generations, if only because almost all accept the present system in principle. Yet at the same time the distant, optimistic future is abstract; it is the universally perceived stagnation of the present and bleak short-term future that are operative.

SOURCES OF PESSIMISM

Real economic performance and regime policy. Thus far we have been considering the swing from optimism to pessimism without really coming to grips with its causes. Since middle-class pessimism is so firmly rooted in the perceived performance of the Soviet economy—the consumer sector above all—we should note first that there is much to be pessimistic about. Both the overall rate of economic growth and the rate of increase of consumption have been declining since the late 1960s. Furthermore, sudden and mysterious shortages of even the most basic consumer goods are endemic, the quality of goods available is low, and the assortment is limited. . . .

When per capita consumption increased by 5.3 percent annually between 1951 and 1955, and by 4.2 percent between 1956 and 1960, middle-class optimism waxed

strong; it was not shaken by the precipitous decline in the rate of increase in consumption to an annual rate of 2.5 percent between 1961 and 1965. The rate of increase in consumption rose to 4.7 percent per year between 1966 and 1970—yet it
was in the immediate aftermath of this rising prosperity that middle-class optimism
began to erode. The plunge itno pessimism in the early 1970s paralleled a real decline
in the rate of increase in consumption (3.2 percent per year, 1971–75), but there is no
basis for the middle-class view that the standard of living has not risen at all of late,
or that it has even declined. . . .

Khrushchev's "goulash communism" did indeed contribute to the optimism of
the 1950s, but his successors' proclaimed consumerist policies have not sustained it.
Failure to deliver on consumerist promises has without question contributed to middle-class cynicism, as has the collapse of all attempts at structural reform of the economy. Economic slogans are the butt of countless jokes, and over the years the regime's
broken promises have tended to produce an effect opposite to that intended. . . .

Middle-class materialism. The fact that consumer-goods shortages and policy failures are perceived differently now than they were twenty years ago is due in part—
not so paradoxically—to the fact that the middle class is now much better off than
before. All observers since the late 1950s have reported a decline in the Soviet citizen's ideological fervor and an ever-more-resolute determination to lead at least a
moderately comfortable life. Most commentators have located this development in
the student population. Since 1956 regime spokesmen have complained repeatedly
that students are ideologically flabby, preoccupied with creature comforts, and un-
conscionably indifferent to the past sacrifices that made such self-indulgence possible. . . . The late 1950s saw a sudden upsurge of materialism because it was then
that the bulk of the middle class had the first opportunity for material indulgence.
. . . But during the succeeding decades materialism has become a way of life and it
has become increasingly difficult for the regime to meet middle-class expectations.
Nothing fails like success: the regime's earlier success, its welcome promise to provide
the good life, generated ever greater expectations and contributed to the current perception of failure.

International comparisons: the semi-mythical West. . . . the rise in standard of living
and expectations has been accompanied by increasing familiarity with the rest of the
world.

The Voice of America, the BBC, and the presence of foreign nationals (tourists
and others) have been an important source of information about the West (as well as
about the Soviet Union itself). The Western information that has had the greatest impact on the USSR has been cultural rather than political. The penetration of the Soviet Union by Western fads and fashions is widely recognized. It is worth noting,
however, that the domestic political consequences of mini-skirts and chewing gum
have not been properly assessed. While the demand for chewing gum is entirely apolitical, it has produced a political response by the leadership in the diversion of resources to establish a Soviet chewing-gum industry. More generally, the demonstration effect of Western standards has helped to shape Soviet consumer expectations.

However, it is not the Western model by which the average member of the Soviet middle class judges Soviet economic performance. . . . Moreover, even those
most awestruck by what they have heard of the West are ambivalent about the Western system . . . the price the West pays for oppulent self-indulgence is thought,
somewhat inconsistently, to be exploitation, unemployment, and job insecurity. (Soviet white-collar professionals value their own secure inefficiency so highly that they

have grossly exaggerated notions of the difficulties of finding and retaining employment in the West.) Too, the West is commonly viewed as an intellectual and cultural
wasteland—exciting, perhaps, but spiritually empty. The "materialistic" West is a convenient object onto which the Soviet middle class can project and thereby exorcise
its own loss of larger purpose. In short, prosperity within the Western system is, to the
Soviet mind, the apple of temptation, succulent but fearful. If this description of the
Soviet middle-class view of the West seems metaphorically overwrought, it is because
for the ordinary Soviet citizen the West *is* largely a metaphor, a symbol to which potent but contradictory meanings have been attached.

International comparisons: the subversive influence of Eastern Europe. Of much more
immediate relevance to the Soviet experience is Eastern Europe. Overlooked in the
usual "Russia and the West" dichotomy, Eastern Europe is for Soviet citizens an external reference both more meaningful and more accessible than the West. It has often
been noted that East European goods are the standard of excellence for Soviet consumers, and that East European magazines (though not the broadcast media) have
served as the major source of information on fashion and modern culture. Furthermore, the volume of East European consumer "information"—i.e., goods—flowing
into the Soviet Union has been increasing. . . .

In the last two decades millions of Soviet citizens *have* traveled to Eastern Europe.

Between 1960 and 1976, approximately 11 million Soviet tourists made the jour-
ney. . . . To this we should add at least 2,500,000 Soviet soldiers who have been stationed in Eastern Europe. While the total number of Soviet citizens who have seen
Eastern Europe at first hand can only be approximated, it is likely to be on the order
of 12 to 15 million, of which half have been there more than once. . . .

Eastern Europe, then, is the principal standard against which the Soviet middle
class measures the performance of the Soviet system, and it is a standard with which
the middle class is quite familiar. It does not appear to be coincidental that increasing
familiarity with Eastern Europe—more broadly, the increasing openness of the Soviet
system—has been accompanied by a decline in middle-class optimism. . . .

The Soviet middle class is strongly predisposed to accept a centrally managed socialist economy as the norm. That being the case, it is more likely to draw comparisons invidious to the Soviet system from socialist Eastern Europe than from the less
acceptable, capitalist West. Since the Soviet middle class will not become less familiar
with Eastern Europe, and the Soviet consumer sector will not in the forseeable future
close the gap with Eastern Europe, the current pessimistic mood will almost certainly
continue.

IMPLICATIONS

. . . Whatever its origins, middle-class pessimism is the product of convictions arrived at autonomously, in opposition to the image of Soviet society projected by the
media, and evidently held quite tenaciously. And if pessimism has settled in for the duration, how long can it remain predominantly associated—as it is now—with the perception of poor economic performance?

There is presently no pronounced tendency among any but the intellectuals to
draw political conclusions from the differential performance of the East European and
Soviet economies. However, because of the perceived similarity of the two systems,
the logical conclusion to draw is that it is the management of the Soviet system—that

is, the leadership—that is at fault. Most members of the middle class believe that, in theory, the USSR's economic ills can be remedied—but not by the present regime. Because the legitimacy of the Soviet regime, in the eyes of the middle class, rests so heavily on the promise and expectation of material betterment, the perception that the economic system is being mismanaged must inevitably erode the regime's political legitimacy. Erosion of legitimacy is a far cry from de-legitimation, and the deep-rooted support for the system provides the regime with political capital on which to draw. But the regime today enjoys nothing like the middle-class support that Khrushchev enjoyed in the late 1950s. . . .

In what literary scholar Vera Dunham has recently called the "Big Deal," the middle class was then [in the 1930s] endowed with a system of rewards and privileges. In fact, it was the extension of privileges that produced a distinctively Soviet middle class, whose mission was to halt the social disintegration brought on by collectivization and the industrialization drive. Though of modest proportions for all but the elite, the privileges were nonetheless gratefully received as a modicum of relief from the austerity of the period. Moreover, as Dunham has demonstrated, by the 1940s materialistic aspirations were being given ideological sanction.

The price that the regime paid for buying the support of the middle class was the gradual alienation of the working class, which was cut out of the Big Deal. The rewards, privileges, and public esteem extended to the middle class caused workers to feel slighted in their own proletarian state. Judging by the scanty evidence available, the middle-class optimism of the 1950s and 1960s was not shared by the working class. Though the working class in fact benefited from the increasing prosperity, the rising standard of living may have further alienated the workers, who felt that the middle class was receiving a disproportionate share of the benefits. At any rate, all reliable observers have reported that the working class has, since the 1950s, been consistently suspicious of the middle class and antagonistic to the "bosses." Furthermore, working-class discontent is more volatile than middle-class discontent: strikes and other working-class disorders, if not massive or numerous by Western standards, have been endemic since the early 1960s.

In the last decade or so, then, the regime's base of support in the middle class has been eroding without offsetting gains in the working class. In the long run, the Big Deal has failed to achieve its purpose: those dealt out remain dissatisfied; the expectations of those dealt in have not been met. It should be reiterated that discontent is not now political in nature—we have not been examining the attitudes of dissidents—and that public opinion is not the most important factor in Soviet politics. Nevertheless, it is a factor. At a minimum, the leadership would like to retain public support. . . . The problem for the regime is that the middle-class perception of economic stagnation is fundamentally correct: in order to maintain overall growth rates, the promise made in the early 1970s that the consumer sector would henceforth have priority has been deferred, but even renewed emphasis on heavy industry has failed to stem the decline in the rate of growth. In neither the short nor the long run can middle-class expectations be met, and the pressure of public dissatisfaction will continue to mount. The pressure will probably not be vented violently, but neither is it likely to dissipate entirely without effect.

John Bushnell, "The 'New Soviet Man' Turns Pessimist," in Stephen F. Cohen, Alexander Rabinowitch, and Robert Sharlet (eds.), *The Soviet Union Since Stalin* (Bloomington and London: Indiana University Press, 1980), pp. 179–199.

THE LITTLE DEAL: BREZHNEV'S CONTRIBUTION TO ACQUISITIVE SOCIALISM

James R. Millar

Vera Dunham described the accommodation that emerged between regime and middle class in the Soviet Union under Stalin as the "Big Deal." It represented a dilution of the idealistic, egalitarian goals of Marxian socialism by means of a tacit accommodation in practice to the materialistic, self-regarding behavior of the new Soviet middle class. For technocrats and skilled workers in preferred sectors, material incentives increasingly displaced moral incentives. For the middle class, privilege and perquisite replaced egalitarianism and self-denial. The accumulation of private, personal property not only became acceptable, it was now protected against public encroachment, and acquisitive impulses gained relative to altruistic ones. The rhetoric of Bolshevism continued, of course, to glorify self-sacrifice, collectivism, and egalitarianism, but these goals, like a particular kind of optical illusion, retreated farther and farther into the future with each new official pronouncement. One day in the future collective farms would be elevated to full status as socialist enterprises. Private agricultural plots would disappear. Public distribution of consumer goods and services would be entirely socialized and thus depecuniarized. "Commodity production," the "law of value," and other relics of capitalism would eventually become otiose and disappear simultaneously with the appearance of the new Soviet man (and woman). Meanwhile, however, first the building of heavy industry, then prosecution of World War II, next reconstruction of the postwar economy took precedence. Thus private production, markets, differential wages, private wealth, and personal acquisitiveness had to be tolerated, and even encouraged, for the duration.

The economy under Stalin relied heavily upon powerful, noneconomic disincentives as well as upon material incentives. Success was rewarded materially *and* morally. Failure was unacceptable. Discipline and punishment provided a counterpoint to privilege and perquisite, and they insured that acquisitiveness would not jeopardize the aims of the state, however it might militate against the early appearance of the new socialist citizen.

High rates of growth and a general rise in the material standard of living of the majority of the Soviet population during the early years of Khrushchev's rule created a strong sense of optimism. Egalitarianism was taken seriously by Khrushchev and his advisers, or so it would appear. Wage differentials were reduced for managerial staff and skilled workers, and the urban-rural gap narrowed too. These changes were masked in the early years by the general rise in material well-being. Everyone, or almost everyone, was experiencing real income increases, and the reduction in differentials did not appear to be at anyone else's expense.

After increasing at an average annual rate of about 6 percent during the 1950s, the increase in GNP slowed to 5 percent in the 1960s and to 4 percent for 1970 to 1978. Since then growth has averaged less than 2 percent per year. This decline reflected the exhaustion of postwar slack, the diversion of investment to defense as well as to agriculture, where marginal capital productivity was low, and social policies and demographic trends that reduced the rate of growth of effective labor force.

Khrushchev had been inclined toward large-scale programs and reforms. The Virgin Lands Program, de-Stalinization, abolition of the Machine Tractor Stations and of the old four-channel agricultural procurement system, development of *sovnarkhozy*, creation of parallel rural and urban party organs are principal examples. Except for the Kosygin reforms of industrial management in 1965, which had been conceived and designed in the Khrushchev years, the Brezhnev years did not witness large-scale institutional reform or further de-Stalinization. It was instead a period of institutional stability at the macrolevel. Reform and change were confined to the microlevel, mainly in the forms of increased political and economic freedom within close kinship and friendship networks and greater tolerance of petty private enterprise and trade. These represented the main components of Brezhnev's "Little Deal."

The overthrow of Nikita Khrushchev ushered in a new era that was more conservative in at least three respects. The new regime elected to avoid the risks associated with further de-Stalinization. It decided to avoid system-wide institutional reform. And it initiated and sustained a substantial increase in military spending. The steep rise in defense spending, which became the hallmark of the Brezhnev years, jeopardized continued rapid improvement in living standards and progress toward Khrushchev's ambitious targets for production and consumption for 1980.

The consumerism of the Khrushchev period collided, therefore, with a new, ambitious defense policy, and the collision was all the more serious because of the general slowdown in growth rates. This slowdown was partly a consequence of demographic changes that reduced the rate of growth of the labor force. It was also caused by an inefficient managerial system. Poor weather conditions and the failure of agriculture to respond to large investments with substantial total factor productivity increases were also important. The success of Khrushchev's egalitarianism, the reduction in differentials within industry and between industry and agriculture, may also have had an unfavorable influence upon work incentives. Moreover, shortages of the most desirable consumer goods and the continued need for queuing reduced the effectiveness of material incentives. In the absence of illegal middleman activity or privileged access, chronic disequilibrium in consumer goods markets reduces the effectiveness of income differentials. Purchase requires queuing time as well as cash. Each household must, therefore, allocate some of its members' time to queuing as well as to remunerable work, and any individual with pent-up demand is wise to slight his job in favor of slipping off to stand in line.

The Brezhnev regime did not repudiate consumerism as a principal goal, as increasingly heavy agricultural imports during the period testify. It did halt and begin to reverse the egalitarian results of Khrushchev's wage reform. It also chose not to reverse the policy of retail price stability that had been established and repeatedly promised ever since Stalin's death. Hence the resource crunch could not but be reflected in lengthened queues for desirable consumer goods and in decreased incentives to work hard or to work at all.

The problem of "deficit commodities" could not be resolved by 1980, as Khrushchev had hoped, by increasing output to absorb excess demand. Raising prices to equilibrium levels was ruled out too, apparently for political reasons. Under these circumstances, the temptation to individuals who were favorably situated with respect to deficit commodities (and services) to profit themselves and their families would certainly be overwhelming in the absence of severe, swift and certain punishment for doing so. Ideological commitment to the collective, and to socialist goals in general, was no longer sufficient to avert favoritism, nepotism, or even outright corruption. Stalin's system of discipline and punishment apparently could not be reestablished. Consequently, the very structure and functioning of the Soviet socialist economy, and the policies the Soviet leadership believed could be invoked successfully, created the cracks and crevices in which private economic activity could flourish to redistribute, and in some cases to augment, Soviet national product.

As the Brezhnev regime matured, existing, but little-noted, private nonagricultural enterprise gained new significance and augmented the flow of private goods and services partly through the *rynok,* but mainly through direct, unlicensed, floating free markets. Stalin's compromise with the peasantry in the 1930s had been forced by violence and the threat of destabilization, and it had forced retention of at least one free market in the Soviet economy, the collective farm market. Despite several attempts to drive it out of existence, Khrushchev was forced to accept private plots and the collective farm market, too. His government accepted an increased flow of consumer goods through regulated state retail markets as well at the expense, proportionately speaking, of direct, nonmarket distribution.

The Brezhnev leadership struck a new but tacit bargain with the urban population: to tolerate the expansion of a wide range of petty private economic activities, some legal, some in the penumbra of the legal, and some clearly and obviously illegal, the primary aim of which was the reallocation by private means of a significant fraction of Soviet national income according to private preferences. A new institutional mix was tacitly approved at the microlevel, one that elevated the importance of private markets—of which the officially sanctioned *rynok* was only one—of private enterprise, and of kinship and friendship reciprocity networks relative to official state retail outlets. Ironically, the Little Deal afforded the individual increased freedom to wheel and deal at the microlevel of Soviet society, while at the macrolevel managerial discretion was restrained, overt political dissent was persecuted and generally repressed, and a gray, conservative pallor overspread the regime. Freedom of petty private economic transactions was accompanied by greater freedom of association and of private conversation (and criticism).

Western economists have long agreed that free exchange among marketeers who start out each with different initial resource endowments and with different preference functions can achieve an increase in total welfare of all marketeers taken together—without anyone losing in the process. There is little doubt that this was one outcome of the Little Deal, although we cannot know whether it was anticipated or an aim of the leadership. The advantages to potential participants, who would have included a very large proportion of the population, may have seemed so patent and so harmless to households that the regime elected not to stand in their way. Tolerance of petty marketeering and of petty private enterprise was the obverse side of the decision to set aside for the duration managerial and other reforms for state enterprises.

Gur Ofer described the Soviet consumer economy as a "cash and carry" system, in which the consumer is obliged to pay cash and to transport goods home from the point of sale. Expansion of petty marketing represents a means to offset to some degree the inefficiency and maldistributions caused by the cumbersome Soviet retail distribution system. In any event, the Little Deal included tolerance of an expansion of private enterprise, especially in service activities—hair dressing, auto and electrical appliance repair, and similar services—of illegal middleman activity, of nepotism, and of the conversion of public property for personal use or for private pecuniary gain.

The Little Deal tolerated an expansion of private nonmarket as well as private market activities. The second of these has been widely described as the "second," the "parallel," or the "underground" economy and represents straight-forward market transactions. The former is composed primarily of reciprocity exchanges, which have not been dealt with extensively thus far in the literature. Both kinds of exchange have existed legally in the Soviet Union at least from the beginning of the New Economic Policy. Both shade from the legal and overt into the illegal and covert, passing through a region in which legality is a matter of judicial discretion. . . .

Petty trade, petty middleman activities, petty private enterprise, even petty theft or personal (illegal) use of government property have, for the most part, been winked at by the regime. This represents a "deal" in the sense that these activities frequently take place in plain view of police, citizens, bureaucrats, and high officials. What is striking is not so much the total magnitude of petty enterprise and marketeering, which in any case would be difficult if not impossible to measure. It is the pervasiveness of these activities which proves that a deal, albeit tacit, was struck between the regime and an acquisitive population.

Anyone who has spent an extended period living and working in the USSR will have witnessed and perhaps participated in a wide variety of *nalevo*[1] transactions. . . . almost everyone, including party members, has obtained some goods *nalevo,* and discretion is usually exercised by those engaging in *nalevo* transactions, but it is not so great as to disguise their pervasive character from official eyes.

A few examples will be useful. Anyone seeking a taxi in Moscow will from time to time be offered a ride by a chauffeur in a state limousine. The driver will expect a gratuity for the transportation he provides. He is, of course, using the state's gasoline and time he would otherwise spend waiting for his boss or perhaps for a delegate to a congress in Moscow. Such experiences are so common as to cause no remark. Similarly, taxi drivers expect special gratuities for certain services, for instance, driving to an out-of-the-way hotel or residence after public transportation has shut down for the night. They frequently have vodka that they will sell to partying citizens after hours for a premium price. From any apartment overlooking garages for private automobiles one periodically witnesses the arrival of official cars and trucks from which petrol is siphoned into private vehicles. I witnessed such activities from my kitchen window in 1979, and, as the number of chauffeured limousines arriving each morning before my building clearly indicated, so could many high Soviet officials, including academics, party members, and high-ranking police and military officers who also lived in the building. It would, in fact, have been impossible to miss. These kinds of activities became so common and obvious during the last years of the Brezhnev era that one can only suppose that punishment for such infractions was too mild or improbable to make reporting them worthwhile.

The case appears to have been similar for the resale of one's own "special distributions," as for instance the special packages of cold cuts and other delicacies that

---

1. *Nalevo* means "on the left" literally, but also refers to illicit activities "on the side."

widows of former high-ranking officials and officers receive, or the occasional purchase and resale of items purchased through privileged access to special state stores or from foreign colleagues. Once again, scale appears to have determined risk. Large-scale middleman dealings are clearly illegal and severely punished. Not so petty, infrequent transactions conducted in modest volume with discretion. The degree of risk associated with most of these transactions appears to have been less during the later Brezhnev years than buying a marijuana cigarette or two at any urban high school or university campus in the United States today.

When one sees state retail clerks selling special cuts of meat, or chocolate, or other deficit commodities at hastily improvised outdoor stands, one cannot but wonder how far petty profit seeking has penetrated the state retail network itself. Willingness to pay a slightly higher price, or a rebate, allows the customer to jump the queue. The question is, however, who pockets the premium? Is the individual the profiteer, or is the state mimicking private trade as a way of charging a price more nearly at an equilibrium level?

It is certainly common for individuals who occupy state-owned apartments to barter them and to pocket, in the process, the "rent of location" that technically should accrue to the state. A three-room apartment, well located in Moscow, for example, can readily be traded for an apartment elsewhere, in Moscow or in another city, *plus* a consideration reflecting the locational or other desirable features. Dachas are also sold at prices that reflect the value of the location as well as of the structure, even though individuals do not have title to the land. And so it goes. As a general proposition, true for the Brezhnev years at least, Soviet citizens have been able to collect these kinds of economic "rents," attributable to scarcity of desirable properties, because the state does not. Only fear of swift, certain, and severe penalties could prevent them from doing so. This is an aspect of the Little Deal too. . . .

Contrary to the belief of many outside the USSR, private enterprise is not illegal there. It is illegal to put money out at interest or to rent out land or housing professionally. It is also illegal to hire others for profit or to engage in middleman activities. What you sell and profit from must be of your own (or your family's or your cooperative's) making; it cannot embody the labor of others. People rent out "corners," of course, and they legally hire typists, housekeepers, washerwomen, and the like. But it is the prohibition on hiring others for profit, on middleman activities, on putting out money at interest, and on the purchase or rental of land that insures that legal private enterprise will be small both in scale of production and in distribution.

Apart from the production and marketing of agricultural products from private plots of kolkhozes and sovkhozes, legal private enterprise in the USSR during the Brezhnev years has been composed primarily of individuals offering services in an economy starved for services. The repair of automobiles, of television, radio, and stereo systems, and of other consumer durables represents a large category of such activities. Hair dressing, tutoring, clerical help, housekeeping, and similar direct services to the individual, including private medical care, represent a second large category of petty private enterprise. The variety is endless. Some individuals, for example, make a substantial living queuing for others for profit. In an economy where the most desirable goods, and even some necessities at times, are in deficit supply, it can pay to shop for others.

The activities described above are characterized by being small scale, individual or family enterprises, and by a dubious legal standing. That they persist and are so pervasive is evidence that the Little Deal was a conscious, if tacit, contract between Brezhnev's leadership and the population of the USSR's urban centers.

An example will indicate some of the ambiguities that characterize the legal status of petty, private service enterprises. My typewriter broke down during a recent extended stay in Moscow, and I was anxious to have it repaired promptly. Friends put me onto a private repairman, who appeared a day later at 5:15 p.m. with an apprentice in tow. The master's coat liner was lined with tools and spare parts, and he soon "manufactured" a workable spare part for my German-made machine. The charge was high, but reasonable given my haste. The question is: was the transaction legal? In general, the answer is "yes." He was free to charge what the traffic would bear, and I paid in rubles. The repairman was off duty, working on his own time. What, however, about the apprentice? Is it legal to take someone other than a family member as an apprentice? What about the tools he used? It is unlikely that such tools are sold retail anywhere in the USSR. The spare part he adapted had probably the same dubious provenance. And this enterprising repairman also offered to buy my typewriter at the time of my departure. The probability is, therefore, considering all factors, that the transaction was illegal and that criminal sanctions could have been invoked against the repairman, and perhaps against his customer too. This kind of complex interdependency between private and public transactions is what makes most private transactions (outside the collective farm market) *nalevo* transactions, that is, transactions that are either illegal or in the penumbra of the legal only.

These questionably legal and illegal private enterprises and private marketeering in general have been studied in some detail by Western scholars. Gregory Grossman and Vlad Treml call them part of the "second economy." Others describe them as composing the "parallel" or "underground" economy of the USSR. These studies suggest that such activities comprise a significant fraction of total final product transactions in the Soviet economy, and they include large-scale, Mafia-type black market activities as well as petty private marketeering and enterprise. The term "second," or "parallel," economy implies a degree of separateness that is misleading, however, especially when the focus is upon the small-scale transactions covered by what I have called the Little Deal. These transactions do not necessarily operate outside the system, or parallel to it. They stand, instead, in a symbiotic relationship with state enterprise and marketing, serving to make the total system more flexible and more responsive to household demand. They also produce some products and services that would otherwise not be available. . . .

The symbiotic character of most *nalevo* transactions and enterprises is sufficient evidence that both state and marketeer stand to gain from the deal. The final distribution of consumer goods and services would be less satisfactory from a welfare standpoint should *nalevo* activity be halted by strict police action—unless the state is prepared to reform the systems by which consumer goods and services are produced, priced, and distributed by the state. This is the sense in which the Little Deal represents an alternative to serious, thorough-going, large-scale economic reform. The Brezhnev regime elected instead to temporize, and the Little Deal was thereby contracted.

Nalevo economic transactions in the USSR comprise more than market transactions. A large number of nonmarket transactions take place by means of reciprocity. This aspect of private economic activity in the USSR has hardly been examined at all by Western scholars. Reciprocity systems for the distribution and redistribution of goods and services were first discovered by anthropologists. The most systematic analysis of these systems was produced by Karl Polanyi.[2] All economies we know of have relied upon reciprocity to distribute certain valued goods and services. It represents a non-market distributional system. In Polanyi's words, the distributional function is "embedded in social relations" and driven by them, as, for example, by kinship or friendship relations.

As a principle for organizing economic activity, reciprocity is familiar to us all. Take, for example, the mutual dependence of parents and children. As is typical of many reciprocal systems, this relationship is temporal. Tradition calls for parents to care for children when they are young and helpless and, in turn, for them to be cared for by their children when old age, misfortune, or illness have undermined the parents' ability to support and care for themselves. Reciprocal economic obligations are still quite obvious even in highly industrial, pecuniary societies within the family and within friendship networks. Blood is thicker than water, as mutual obligation among siblings testifies even in today's atomized Western economies. But friendship reciprocity systems remain strong too.

The important point about reciprocity systems is that the initial contribution of a valued good or service does not establish a contractual or legally negotiable claim on the recipient. The obligation of parents to children may be codified in law, but the child is not required by any enforceable claim to render a quid pro quo. The claim is enforceable only by custom and tradition, by the shame attached to an ungrateful child. It is defined and socialized as a kinship obligation, not as an economic exchange of "equivalents." In many, if not most, reciprocal relationships, the initial contributor does not himself receive a quid pro quo even from those who benefited initially. For example, friends help one another move, or neighbors get together to harvest the crops of an ill or widowed acquaintance. Fraternity and sorority members benefit from alumni, and they will contribute themselves to a completely different membership generation.

Benefits that parents provide their children may appear to be comparable to an investment on which a return is expected, but this is misleading because the children's performance cannot be enforced as an economic contract or transferred to a third party. A reciprocal obligation is not comparable to a debt or other market transaction. It is an IOU enforceable only by custom and tradition, and it may be collected, if at all, from *any* member of the kinship or friendship circle when it falls due, whether or not he or she was a member at the time the obligation was undertaken. The result of failure to meet a reciprocal obligation is not bankruptcy but the destruction of that particular reciprocal relationship. Parents disown children. Siblings cease to communicate. Friendships end. Blood feuds begin.

Reciprocity relationships may permeate the economy, but they are confined to specific kinship and friendship networks. They are thus fragmented and necessarily small in scale. They cannot link all households in the economy the way open markets do, or the way nationwide taxation-benefit systems do. Reciprocity is distinctly personal and attached to the person or family. As a principle for organizing economic activity, reciprocity is nonmarket *and* nonstate, and it has flourished under all sorts of economic systems. It has represented for centuries the main way that families and friends have traditionally protected the individual against both the vagaries of economic fortune and the arbitrary exercise of economic power by the state.

---

2. See, for example, Karl Polanyi, *The Great Transformation* (Boston, Mass.: Beacon Press, 1957), especially chap. 4.

The Little Deal of the Brezhnev years extended to reciprocal economic relationships as well as to petty marketeering. The ever-present condition of excess demand in the Soviet economy not only creates opportunities for personal gain for individuals willing to act as middlemen or to intercept rents the state declines to gather from deficit goods and services. It also enhances the benefits that flow from membership in kinship and friendship networks. It pays to have a relative or friend located strategically with respect to deficit commodities: someone in Moscow to buy scarce goods when they appear and to store them for your arrival from Omsk; someone employed by a retail fur outlet to set aside a real fur coat from the next shipment before the store opens; someone in admissions at the university to shepherd your child's papers. The very structure and functioning of the Soviet economy, with its deficit commodities and services and its faltering, uneven retail distribution system, reinforces the benefits of reciprocity systems and therefore reinforces kinship and friendship ties.

Brezhnev's Little Deal included a tacit accommodation with private reciprocity systems as well as with petty private marketeering and enterprise. Soviet citizens have been openly allowed to obtain goods and services not merely *nalevo,* but also *po druzhbe, po znakomstvu, po sviazi,* and *po protektsii* (through friends, contacts, influence, or patronage). In its most attractive form, reciprocity reflects the concern of family and friends for one another. In its less attractive form it is nepotism, favoritism, and cronyism. Reciprocity has the advantage of not being a straight economic exchange, and thus the risk of a penalty for setting a deficit commodity aside, for using state enterprise tools or spare parts to private advantage, for allowing someone to jump the queue for tickets to the Bolshoi or Taganka theaters is much smaller.

Although participation in reciprocity networks is less risky in general than petty marketeering or enterprise, many reciprocity transactions violate either the letter or the spirit of the law. Every adult member of society is in a position to do some kind of favor for someone else. The main function of reciprocity systems in the USSR has been to allow individuals access to deficit commodities or services that would otherwise be unavailable or uncertain. A few examples will be sufficient to illustrate this point.

With reciprocity systems it is difficult to know where friendship or kinship feeling ends and pure economic calculation begins. A friend or relative on the admissions committee to Moscow State University is of incalculable value if one has university-age children. A friend or relative with access to tickets to the Bolshoi or the Taganka Theater is essential if an ordinary Muscovite wants to attend performances. Friendly relations with the neighborhood butcher pay dividends in an economy in which all cuts of any red meat are 2 rubles a kilo. Having relatives, or friends, who know one is "in the market" for a special type of boot, fur coat, or rare book will maximize one's chance of satisfying this desire. If one lives outside the main "cash and carry" supermarkets of the USSR, that is, outside Moscow, Leningrad, Kiev, and a few other major state retail markets, relatives or friends are essential to a reasonable style of life, regardless of income level. The payoff on reciprocal relationships is so great that young people find it difficult to survive independently of their families, for the family is the nexus of reciprocity networks. Relatives and friends are both more desirable and more burdensome in the USSR for this reason. As in the case of petty marketeering and private enterprise, any given reciprocal transaction may involve illegal or questionable elements. Repairing a friend's television set privately may involve company time, company tools, or illegally acquired spare parts. Setting aside a fur coat for a relative or friend to buy later, even without a private markup, could bring the law down upon one's head. Giving a regular customer better than average cuts of meat at no extra cost, but in return for a future possible gift of American-made cigarettes, or an occasional "single" to the Bolshoi, could mean trouble. And it is not difficult to imagine much more gross violations of law in the realm of nepotism, expensive durables, or contacts with foreigners from hard-currency countries.

I have argued that the Brezhnev regime contracted a "deal" with the Soviet population, especially with the urban population, tacitly agreeing to overlook and thus condone petty private marketeering and enterprise as well as instances of petty reciprocal advantage. The critical element has been the state's willingness to permit an expansion throughout Soviet society of the quest for the individual's, but especially of the individual household's, gain, as opposed to collectivist and traditionalist socialist aims. This implicit contract has tended not only to increase the rewards to petty materialism and self- or family-centered acquisitiveness, but it has also tended to strengthen the family as *the* fundamental societal unit of authority, employment, and distribution. . . .

Because time, especially queuing time, but even time to negotiate, plan, and scout, has been so important a requisite for the acquisition of deficit commodities in the USSR, the Little Deal has tended, in all likelihood, to produce a more equal distribution of real consumption than would otherwise have been the case, for time is distributed essentially equally on a per capita basis.

Ironically, the Brezhnev government was not prepared to accept fully this implication of the Little Deal. . . . Hence special access stores, "closed medical clinics," and similar special distribution systems multiplied during the later Brezhnev years, for party members, high officials, successful scientists, artists, workers in priority industries, and others of importance to the state.

The growth of special distribution and of limited-access outlets highlights a chronic dilemma for the Soviet leadership. The goal of Marxism is equity in the distribution of (real) income, regardless of "rents" of ability, location, special training, and so forth. But "equity" seems to fly in the face of the need to reward those who are prepared to make a special effort to become skilled, to accept extra responsibilities, to work efficiently, or to render a full day's work.

The tension, between the desire to ensure that each citizen has his or her needs met and the need to motivate each to contribute his or her best, is not new. The tension between "moral," or spiritual, incentives and material incentives antedates Marxism by many centuries, and no clear resolution has been achieved anywhere, whether sought by religious, secular, or revolutionary organization. Acceptance of the imperative of material incentives pushes the Soviet leadership toward increased use of markets, money, and other pecuniary institutions, that is, toward accepting operation of the "law of value" and of "commodity production" under socialism. Aspiration of the leaders to a society governed by "moral" incentives pushes them toward a completely different model, one in which a small but *pure* minority imposes its spiritual aims on the majority. The Soviet government is not the first institution in the history of Western civilization to be faced with this choice, nor is it the first to try first one and then the other, and then to reconsider. . . .

One way to eliminate petty marketeering and enterprise and the most blatant and undesirable forms of reciprocity is to initiate system-wide macroreforms designed to eliminate the rewards that the system now affords those activities. This would require increasing the prices of deficit commodities and services to equilibrium levels, thus eliminating the "scarcity rents" that so tempt individuals today. It would require increased powers by which enterprise managers could reward good, efficient workers and penalize poor, inefficient ones. Reform would be required also to ensure that goods and services produced in state enterprises are distributed solely according to ability to pay, regardless of the location of the customer. This would require a complete overhaul of the retail distribution system to reflect consumer preferences and to overcome geographical obstacles. In the end, reform would have to include improvements in product and service quality, and, in all likelihood, an increased share of resources flowing to the household sector. . . .

The establishment of equilibrium, or market-clearing, prices in state retail outlets would have to be accomplished in one fell swoop. Prices would have to be raised to or above equilibrium levels at once, or things would in fact get worse. A general popular expectation of a sequence of price increases would only make matters worse by encouraging spending now rather than later when prices will be higher. . . .

The reluctance of the state to revise prices periodically over the last twenty-five to thirty years has caused most food products, for example, to be underpriced relative to manufactured goods. But the problem is even more complex because the costs of producing various food products, consumer goods, and services have changed over time at different rates. And wholesale prices are similarly out of alignment. Merely setting "correct" prices would itself, therefore, be a horrendous task.

Assuming that the regime were successful in establishing market-clearing prices, the result on the day they became effective would be a massive redistribution of real income. . . .

It appears, therefore, that the privileged, the poor, and the gregarious would all stand to lose real purchasing power as a result of the establishment of market-clearing prices, and theirs is potentially a powerful alliance. Price reforms would of necessity, therefore, have to be accompanied by an incomes policy designed to cushion the impact of the reform, and, once again, piecemeal reforms would be worse than no reform at all.

The Soviet experience with socialism has produced several important lessons. Among the most important is that socialization of production and distribution politicizes even the pettiest economic problem. Hence the decision to change or not to change a given price must be taken on political rather than economic grounds.

Political wisdom would argue for gradual adjustments of prices toward equilibrium levels. Economic wisdom argues decisively for a once-and-for-all adjustment. The outcome is a deadlock that no regime since Stalin has been able to break. It will be interesting to see whether the new administration will be able to deal more effectively with the economy than Brezhnev's did. When all is said and done, there is much to be said for continuing the Little Deal.

James R. Millar, "The Little Deal: Brezhnev's Contribution to Acquisitive Socialism." *Slavic Review*, IV, 4 (Winter 1985), pp. 694–706.

Fedor Burlatskii, "Brezhnev and the End of the Thaw: Reflections on the Nature of Political Leadership"

One of the bright young men who made up the generation of the Soviet "Sixties," Fedor Burlatskii worked for the International Relations Department of the CPSU Central Committee during the Cuban Missile Crisis of October 1962. Closely associated with Yuri Andropov, he fell from grace during the Brezhnev years because of his liberal views but re-emerged in the Gorbachev years as a major spokesman for political reform. Elected as a deputy to the

Supreme Soviet of the Soviet Union, he briefly served as editor-in-chief of Literaturnaya
gazeta *(Literary Newspaper), an influential weekly widely read by the intelligentsia. He was
an advisor to Gorbachev at the US-USSR summit meetings in Geneva, Reykjavik, and
Washington. This article was published at the height of* glasnost', *when the years of "stagnation" were castigated as a time of waste and delay. His particular analysis focused on the
personality of the leader, implicitly contrasting the stolid, aging* apparatchik *Brezhnev with
the dynamic young Gorbachev, who represented the hope that the structural reforms so desperately needed by the Soviet Union might be implemented.*

. . . The abandonment of reforms (and in many respects the return to the com-
mand-and-administer system of the Stalinist era), the freeze of living standards, the
general delay of absolutely self-evident decisions and the substitution of trite political verbiage in their place, the corruption and degeneration of power in which whole
strata of the people became increasingly involved, the loss of moral values and the
universal decline in morality—if that is stagnation, what is a crisis? Foreign policy in
particular fully reflected the contradictory nature of Brezhnev's time, when every step
forward along the path of détente was followed by two steps back. Only a few years
separate two events of such disparate nature, the Final Act in Helsinki and the war in
Afghanistan.

Out of all the multifaceted aspects of stagnation, I would like to touch on just one:
How did it come about that in such a difficult period in the history of our motherland, and indeed in world history, the man at the helm of the country's government
was the weakest of all the leaders who had held that position in Soviet times, and perhaps even in prerevolutionary times? I am very anxious to avoid giving way to the
temptation to ridicule this man who set up with almost childlike simplicity the acces-
sories of his own cult: four times Hero of the Soviet Union, Hero of Socialist Labor,
Marshal of the Soviet Union, International Lenin Prize, a bronze bust in his birthplace,
the Lenin Prize for Literature, the Karl Marx Gold Medal. All that was lacking was the
title of generalissimo: His life was cut short too soon. Ridicule is too easy a way; it is
the way, moreover, that accords with what is probably the most persistent Russian tradition, alas. It was Vasily Klyuchevsky, I think, who observed that each new Russian
czar began his career by repudiating his predecessor. There is a saying in the West: Speak
no ill of the dead. With us, it is the other way round: Make immoderate litanies in praise
of the living and endless abuse of the dead. Clearly this is a sublimation to make up for
the lack of opportunity to criticize current leaders . . .

Power was thrust upon Brezhnev as a gift of fate. In order to turn the post of party
Central Committee general secretary, at that time a modest post, into the office of
"master" of our country, Stalin "had to" eliminate virtually every member of Lenin's
Politburo (except himself, naturally) as well as a huge portion of the party *aktiv.* After
Stalin's death Khrushchev was second in line and not first, as many people think, because Malenkov was regarded as first at the time. Khrushchev won the struggle against
mighty and influential rivals, including such people as Viacheslav Molotov, who had
formed the basis of the state practically since Lenin's time. Perhaps that was why the
Stalin and Khrushchev eras, each in its own way, were filled with dramatic changes,
major reformations, disturbance, and instability.

Nothing of the kind happened with Brezhnev. He assumed power as smoothly as if someone had tried the crown of Monomakh on various heads well in advance and settled on this one. And this crown fitted him so well that he wore it for eighteen years without fears, cataclysms, or conflicts of any kind. And the people closest to him longed for only one thing: for this man to live forever, it would be so good for them. Brezhnev himself, at a meeting with people from his regiment, showing off his new marshal's uniform, said, "You see? Service rewarded at last." This phrase is also very appropriate to describe the process by which he succeeded to the "office" of party and state leader: "service rewarded."

Brezhnev embodied the exact opposite of Khrushchev's boldness, willingness to take risks, adventurous spirit, and hunger for novelty and change. If we knew Nikita Sergeyevich less well, we might find it a mystery that Khrushchev so patronized a man of the opposite cast of mind and temperament. As an authoritarian personality not inclined to share power and influence with other people, he surrounded himself mainly with the kind of leaders who hung on his every word, said yes to everything, and willingly fulfilled his every instruction. He had no need for comrades in arms, and still less for captains [vozhdi]. He had had enough of them after Stalin's death, when Malenkov, Molotov, and [Lazar] Kaganovich tried to expel him from the political Olympus and perhaps let him rot in a faraway province.

It must be observed that Brezhnev did indeed owe his entire career to Khrushchev. He graduated from the land use surveyors' technical school in Kursk and only joined the party at the age of twenty-five. Then, after graduating from the institute, he began his political career. In May 1937 (!) Brezhnev became deputy chairman of Dneprodzerzhinsk municipality, and a year later he was working in the party *obkom* in Dnepropetrovsk. It is hard to say whether Khrushchev assisted Brezhnev in these first steps, but his entire subsequent career had the most active support of the then first secretary of the Ukrainian Communist Party Central Committee, later secretary of the All-Union Communist party (Bolsheviks). When Brezhnev was appointed to the post of first secretary of the Moldavian Communist Party Central Committee, he took along many of his friends from Dnepropetrovsk, and there he also acquired as a close colleague the then chief of the republic's Communist Party Central Committee's Propaganda and Agitation Department, Konstantin Chernenko.

After the 19th Party Congress (1952) Brezhnev became a candidate member of the Central Committee Presidium, and after Stalin's death he was at the Soviet Army and Navy Main Political Directorate. The stronger Khrushchev grew, the higher Brezhnev rose. By the October 1964 *plenum* he was second secretary of the Central Committee. Thus Khrushchev built his successor's pedestal with his own hands.

The most dramatic problem very soon became clear: Brezhnev was entirely unprepared for the role that unexpectedly fell upon him. He became first secretary of the party Central Committee as a result of a complex, multifaceted, and even bizarre symbiosis of forces. It involved a little of everything: dissatisfaction with Khrushchev's scornful attitude toward his colleagues; fear arising from the unrestrained extremes of his policy and the adventurist actions that played a part in the escalation of the Caribbean missile crisis; illusions about the "personality" basis of the conflict with China; and particularly the annoyance felt by the conservative section of the government *apparat* with the constant instability, jolts, changes, and reforms that were impossible to foresee. An important part was played by the struggle between different generations of leaders: the 1937 generation, to which Leonid Brezhnev, Mikhail Suslov, and Alexei Kosygin belonged, and the postwar generation, including Alexander Shelepin, Gennady Voronov, Dmitry Polyansky, and Yuri Andropov Brezhnev was in the center, at the intersection of all these roads. So in the initial stage he suited nearly everyone. Or, at any rate, no one protested. His very incompetence was a blessing: It offered the *apparat* workers plenty of opportunities. The only person made to look a fool was Shelepin, who thought he was the smartest. He did not advance a single step in his career, because not only Brezhnev but also Suslov and the other leaders detected his authoritarian ambitions.

Meanwhile, a fierce struggle broke out over the choice of the country's path of development. One person, as was mentioned above, unequivocally proposed a return to Stalinist methods. Another path was proposed to the leadership by Andropov, who submitted a detailed program based more consistently on the decisions of the anti-Stalinist 20th Party Congress than had been done in Khrushchev's time. It is not difficult to reconstruct these ideas today, because they were set forth in a more general form in an editorial article prepared at the time for *Pravda* ("State of the Entire Country," December 6, 1964). They are: (1) economic reform, (2) the transition to modern, scientific management, (3) the development of democracy and self-management, (4) the party's concentration on political leadership, (5) the ending of the nuclear missile race, which had become senseless, and (6) the USSR's entry into the world market with a goal of acquiring new technology.

Andropov expounded this program to Brezhnev and Kosygin during a trip to Poland in 1965. Some elements of it found support, but as a whole it did not meet with sympathy from either Brezhnev or Kosygin, although for different reasons. Kosygin supported economic transformations, but he insisted on the restoration of relations with China at the cost of conceding to China by renouncing the "extremes" of the 20th Party Congress.

As for Brezhnev, he was in no hurry to define his position, because he was keeping an eye on the correlation of forces inside the CPSU Central Committee Presidium and in the party Central Committee.

Thus Brezhnev's main feature as a political leader was immediately revealed. Being an extremely cautious man who had not taken a single rash step during his rise to power, being what is known as a "weathercock leader," Brezhnev adopted a centrist position from the beginning. He did not accept one extreme or the other, neither the program of reform in the spirit of the 20th Congress, nor neo-Stalinism. . . .

By his very nature, his type of education, and his career, he was a typical *oblast-level apparatchik:* not a bad executor of orders, but no leader [*vozhd*]. He therefore took a good deal from Stalin, but a little from Khrushchev, too.

At first after coming to power, Brezhnev began his working day in an unconventional way, devoting a minimum of two hours to telephone calls to other members of the top leadership and to many powerful secretaries of union republic Central Committees and *obkoms*. As a rule he always talked in the same way: "Look, Ivan Ivanovich, we are studying this matter. I wanted to consult you, to hear your opinion." You can imagine the sense of pride that filled Ivan Ivanovich's heart at that moment. That is how Brezhnev's prestige grew stronger. He created the impression of an impartial, calm, tactful leader who would not take a single step without consulting with other comrades and receiving the full approval of his colleagues.

When questions were discussed at sessions of the Central Committee Secretariat or the Presidium he almost never spoke first. He allowed everyone to have a say, listened attentively, and if there was no consensus he preferred to postpone the matter, do some more work, agree it with everyone, and submit it for examination again. It was under him that very complicated agreements flourished, requiring dozens of signatures on documents, bringing the decisions to be adopted to a standstill or entirely distorting their meaning.

As for the Brezhnevian style, this was perhaps precisely of what it consisted. People with that style are not very competent at resolving substantive questions of the economy, culture, or policy. But they do understand very well whom to appoint to what post, whom to reward, when, and how. Leonid Illyich worked hard to install in leadership posts (in the party organizations and in the economy, science, and culture) exponents of this style, "little Brezhnevs" who were not hasty, not incisive, not outstanding, and not particularly concerned about their jobs, but well able to handle valuables.

The people of the 20th Party Congress or those who were simply bold innovators were not shot, as they might have been in the 1930s. They were quietly pushed aside, pushed out, hampered, suppressed. More and more "mediocrities" triumphed everywhere, people who were not exactly stupid or entirely incompetent, but who were patently untalented, who lacked fighting qualities and principles. They gradually filled posts in the party and state *apparat,* in the leadership of the economy, and even in science and culture. Everything grew dull and went into a decline. The underlings increasingly resembled the boss.

Here is a curious fact. After Nikolai Yegorychev's removal from the post of secretary of the Moscow party organization, Leonid Illyich called him and said something like this: "Forgive me, these things happen. Do you have any problems at all, family problems or anything else?" Yegorychev, whose daughter had married not long before and was struggling with a husband and child without an apartment, was weak enough to tell Brezhnev about this. And guess what? A few days later the young family had an apartment. Brezhnev did not want anyone to bear a grudge. . . .

Brezhnev arrived without his own program for the country's development. This is a rare case in modern political history of a person taking power as such, with no specific plans. But it cannot be said, in Mao Tse-tung's expression, that he was a clean sheet of paper on which any characters could be written. A deeply traditional and conservative man by nature, he was most afraid of abrupt movements, sharp turns, major changes. Condemning Khrushchev for voluntarism and subjectivism, he was concerned most of all with erasing his radical initiatives and restoring what had been approved in Stalin's day. First of all, the regional economic councils and the division of party organs into industrial and agricultural bodies (a form of Khrushchevian pluralism?) which had so annoyed the government *apparat* were abolished. Major leaders who had been sent off against their will to the periphery, near and far, returned to their old places in Moscow. The idea of cadre rotation was quietly and almost unnoticeably nullified. As a counterweight to it, the slogan of stability—the cherished dream of every *apparatchik*—was put forward. Brezhnev did not return to the Stalinist repressions, but he dealt summarily with dissidents.

People in the *apparat* used to recount Brezhnev's words on the subject of Kosygin's report at the September *plenum:* "What is he thinking of? Reform, reform. Who needs it, and who can understand it? We need to work better, that is the only problem."

What I really cannot agree with is the concept of "two Brezhnevs" (before and after the mid-1970s), the assertion that at the beginning of his time in office he was a supporter of economic and other reforms. People cite a lengthy quotation from Brezhnev's speech at the September 1965 *plenum* that is supposedly particularly characteristic of his position. But even then it was known for sure that Brezhnev was an active opponent of the reform proposed by Kosygin and that it was first and foremost his fault that it had failed.

Brezhnev's rule was twenty years of wasted opportunities. The technological revolution that had begun in the rest of the world passed us by. We did not even notice it, but instead we continued to talk about the traditional sort of scientific and technical progress. During that time Japan became the world's second industrial power, South Korea was hot on the heels of Japan, Brazil joined the ranks of the new centers of industrial might. True, we achieved military parity with the biggest industrial power of the modern world. But at what cost? At the cost of an increasing technological laggardness in all other spheres of the economy, a further disruption of agriculture, a failure to create a modern service sphere, and a freezing of the people's living standard at a low level.

The situation was complicated by the fact that any endeavor to modernize the model of socialism itself was rejected. On the contrary, faith in organizational and bureaucratic decisions grew stronger. No sooner had a problem arisen than the country's leadership reacted with one voice: Whose responsibility is it? We must set up a new ministry or some analogous organ.

Agriculture and the food problem were still the Achilles' heel of our economy. But decisions were sought according to the traditional patterns, which had already demonstrated their ineffectiveness in the preceding era. The policy of converting collective farms into state farms, that is, further state control, continued.

The wide use of [agricultural] chemicals did not yield the expected results. Despite the fact that in the 1970s the USSR was ahead of the United States in fertilizer production, labor productivity in agriculture was several times lower. One fourth of the working population of the USSR was unable to feed the country, while 3 percent of the U.S. population, the farmers, produced so much that they sold a significant portion of it abroad.

There was only one reason for the economic and technological laggardness: incomprehension and fear in the face of urgently needed structural reforms; that is, the transition to economic accountability in industry, cooperativization of the service sphere, and team and family contracts in the countryside. And the most dreadful thing of all, for the regime of those years, would have been to agree to democratization and the restriction of the power of Brezhnev's main power base—the bureaucracy.

All attempts to progress along the path of reform and show economic independence or independence of thought were mercilessly clamped down.

The first lesson of the Brezhnev era is the collapse of the command-administrative system that grew up under Stalin. The state not only failed to ensure progress, it acted increasingly as a brake on society's economic, cultural, and moral development. Brezhnev and his entourage accumulated, in one respect, experience that is not entirely useless, although unfortunately it took nearly twenty years. There is no going back! Even if Brezhnev had decided to shore up the decaying edifice by regressing into Stalinist repressions, he would have been unable to make that system effective. Because the technological revolution demands free labor, personal initiative and commitment, creativity, continuous endeavor, rivalry. Structural reforms and restructuring were the essential, logical way out of stagnation.

The second lesson is that it is time to put an end forever to a system whereby people become the country's leaders not as a result of the normal democratic procedure and public activity in the party and state, but by means of backstage deals or, worse, conspiracies and bloody purges. Experience has already shown sufficiently that in this situation those who come to power are by no means the most capable leaders, the most committed Leninists, or those who are most devoted to the people; instead, they are the most cunning Ulysses types, the masters of infighting, intrigues, and even common corruption.

The most important guarantee against a recurrence of Brezhnevism is socialist pluralism, which the party has hit upon and is now implementing. It has its model in the Lenin period. At the same time we have the potential to go considerably further. Exaggerated fears about the extremes of *glasnost*—and such extremes undoubtedly do accompany the generally healthy flow—do not reflect concern for socialism, they are generated by an authoritarian political culture.

Here what we are up against most of all is the conservative tradition. Russian political culture has not tolerated pluralism of opinions or freedom to criticize government activity. It was only after the 1905 revolution that a small breach was made. But even then it was basically impossible to criticize the czar, czarism, or the existing system. . . .

And most recently, Brezhnev—surely he was not alone? The vast majority in the government *apparat* idolized him and received everything from him, titles, prizes, academy money, dacha buildings, bribes. He was also supported by those social strata that lived fearlessly, and still live now, on unearned income . . .

Doubtless all political leaders from all peoples like flattery. But in our own time Stalin and Brezhnev liked flattery of the most exaggerated variety, the cult variety. And not because they believed such praise, but because the humiliation of the flatterer, his trampled, flattened demeanor, pleased them. Some of our homegrown Fouchés and Talleyrands have gone through all the political regimes as easily as a knife through butter, and are now bustling feverishly in the struggle for self-preservation.

Fortunately people who have a clear program for the country's development and regard radical political reform as paramount have come and are coming to power in our country. Let us hope that the formation of a new school of political leadership and a new democratic culture of the whole people has begun. This will be a guarantee against a recurrence of Stalinist and Brezhnevian traditions.

Fedor Burlatskii, "Brezhnev and the End of the Thaw: Reflections on the Nature of Political Leadership." *Literaturnaia gazeta,* September 14, 1988 [translated in Isaac J. Taraulo (ed.). *Gorbachev and Glasnost: Viewpoints from the Soviet Press* (Wilmington. DE: SR Books. 1989). pp. 50–62.

Report of Vladimir Semichastnyi to the Central Committee on Armenian Nationalists
February 7, 1966

The Armenian Soviet Socialist Republic was the smallest in territory of the fifteen union republics. Formed in 1920, Soviet Armenia was a small corner of the historic lands inhabited by Armenians for millennia but largely denuded of Armenians after the Ottoman genocide of 1915. Young Armenian intellectuals agitated for the Soviet Union to pressure Turkey to "return" the Armenian lands and to revise the borders of the Armenian republic to include other irredenta in Georgia (Akhaltsikhe and Akhalkalaki) and Azerbaijan (Nagorno-Karabakh and Nakhichevan). The Soviet government had interest neither in conflict with Turkey, a NATO country with American bases, nor in stirring up interethnic confrontations among Armenians, Azerbaijanis, and Georgians. On April 24, 1965, Armenians marched through the streets of their capital city, Erevan, to mark the fiftieth anniversary of the Armenian Genocide. The failure of the Communist party chief in Armenia to contain this expression of nationalist sentiments led to his dismissal. Here KGB chief Vladimir Semichastnyi reported to his Moscow superiors on the extent of underground nationalist activities in the republic. Over the next decades, both illegal nationalist activity and officially approved "patriotic" expression increased, until in February 1988, a broad-based popular movement in support of merging Nagorno-Karabakh with Armenia mobilized masses of people in Karabakh and Armenia and stimulated violent reactions from Azerbaijanis. Gorbachev's refusal to agree to the merger turned Armenians from support of perestroika *into advocates of separation from the Soviet Union.*

Secret

CC CPSU

Beginning in 1962, nationalist groups of Armenians abroad have been carrying on a campaign for the "just" resolution of the "Armenian Question," for the tearing away from Turkey of the former territories of Armenia. Under the influence of this campaign, leaflets and anonymous letters have circulated in the Armenian SSR demanding not only the return of territories belonging to Turkey but the annexation [by Armenia] of the Nagorno-Karabakh Autonomous Region and the Nakhichevan ASSR, now parts of Azerbaijan.

In 1963–1964, the organs of the KGB uncovered anti-Soviet nationalist groups, whose participants aimed to create an "independent" Armenia and merge the abovementioned territories to it. Seven participants in the most active group have been convicted, and preventive measures have been taken against many others.

Despite measures taken by party organs together with the Committee for State Security to cut off these nationalistic phenomena on the territory of Armenia, at the present time various groups are being created among the intelligentsia and youth that are determined by means of instigation to arouse the Armenian population to massive demonstrations for the annexation to the republic, not only Nagorno-Karabakh and the Nakhichevan ASSR, but also the Akhaltsikhe and Akhalkalaki districts of Georgia.

To these ends, for example, a group of persons—notably Rafik Harutiunian, a candidate in philosophy who was expelled from the CPSU; Ashot Babakhanian, candidate in philosophy; member of the CPSU Manvel Asatrian, dean of the Section of Armenian Language of the Philological Department of [Erevan] State University; Varuzhan Mushkambarian, teacher of manual labor at Middle School No. 12; Eghishe Babakhanian, fifth-year student in the Polytechnical Institute; and Telunts, a third-year student of the Art-Theater Institute—are preparing and distributing leaflets.

Besides this, the members of this group have distributed a letter that purports to have been written by Turkish students studying in the United States and addressed to a committee memorializing the victims of the massacres of 1915, that justifies the policy of genocide. [They] also [have distributed] a letter, published in the Beirut Armenian newspapers, *Harach* and *Nairi,* in December 1965, from a Polish historian at Hamburg University to U Thant [Secretary General of the United Nations] in which he proposes to create a sovereign Armenian state on the territory of eastern Anatolia.

The letters mentioned, copied on a typewriter, are spreading through the creative intelligentsia, the students of the Institute of Oriental Studies, the principal library of the Academy of Sciences, the Matenadaran [Repository of Armenian Manuscripts], the Museum of Art and Literature, the Institute of Geology, and other scientific establishments.

Another group, which includes the engineer of the Ministry of Automobile Transport, Khachatrian; the commodity researcher of the consumer cooperative, Stepanian; the inspector at the same establishment, Hovannesian; the salesman of the village store of Ujan, Ashtarak district, Tovmasian; the worker at the watch factory, Avanesian; and others, carry on agitation for the annexation to Armenia of territories located in other republics. On January 9 of this year, Khachatrian, Stepanian, and Avanesian organized a meeting in the home of Babaian, who had been expelled from the CPSU (his son, P. Babaian, was convicted in 1964 as one of seven leaders of an anti-Soviet nationalist group), where they discussed the question of gathering signatures among the population for an appeal to the Twenty-third Congress of the CPSU for the annexation of Nagorno-Karabakh Autonomous District and the Nakhichevan ASSR to Armenia.

The Committees of State Security of the Armenian, Azerbaijan, and Georgian SSRs have established that on the territory of Armenia exists an organization with many branches named the "Union of Armenian Youth," which has a program and by-laws . . . The members of the organization work on individuals in order to attract them to politically harmful activity, give out membership cards, collect dues. They spread the appeals they have written to the population of Nagorno-Karabakh, Akhaltsikhe, and Akhalkalaki districts, calling people to gather on the eve of the Twenty-third Congress of the CPSU at a meeting in Erevan to discuss and adopt demands to the Congress on the annexation to Armenia of territories now in the Azerbaijan and Georgian SSRs.

In January of this year, the KGB of the Georgian SSR detained in the city of Akhalkalaki A. M. Kirakosian, born in 1940, member of the CPSU, third-year student in the Philological Department of Erevan State University. From him were taken: twenty-five copies of the appeal of the "Union of Armenian Youth," one copy of the oath of a member of the "Union" on fidelity to the struggle for the final resolution of the fate of Armenian territories; four handmade membership cards, one of which had been filled out in his name; an article entitled "The Cannibals are thirsty for blood," signed "Union of Armenian Youth," which appears to be an answer to the letter supposedly written by the Turkish students studying in the USA.

Kirakosian said that he had been recruited into the "Union of Armenian Youth" in December 1965 by P. P. Mikaelian, a fourth-year student in the Department of History at Erevan State University, born in 1939, non-party. Mikaelian charged him with distributing the appeal in the cities of Akhaltsikhe and Akhalkalaki and to explain the reaction to it. Besides that, Kirakosian was supposed to recruit new members into the "Union," give out membership cards, have them swear the oath, and receive dues in the amount of one ruble. Kirakosian managed to distribute twelve copies of the appeal but was unable to fulfill his assignment because he was detained.

Another student at Erevan State University, Igit Garibian, went to Nagorno-

Karabakh with a similar assignment and a companion whose identity has not been established. He tried to recruit a methodologist at the regional library of the city of Stepanakert, B. M. Sahakian, into the "Union," gave him four copies of the program and bylaws of the "Union," and about 200 copies of the appeal. Kirakosian and Sahakian explained that the "Union of Armenian Youth" is built on the principle of five-member groups for conspiratorial reasons, so that members ought not to know one another.

The Committee of State Security of the Council of Ministers of the Armenian SSR is taking measures to cut off nationalist and politically harmful phenomena in the republic.

The CC CP of Armenia has been informed about all these matters.

Appendix: Copies of the Program and By-Laws . . .

Deputy Chairman of the Committee of State Security

N. Zakharov

From the Program (the beginning):

"The Armenian Youth Union is created, operates, and will operate as long as it is needed for the just resolution of the question of Armenian lands. The Union is completely in solidarity with the CPSU; all its resolutions are considered obligatory; and in its activities [the Union] will never adopt an oppositional position. . . .

[We] absolutely, positively evaluate the Soviet period of the history of Armenia and the friendship of the Armenian, Georgian, and Azerbaijani peoples under Soviet Power.

The exception: the so-called Moscow treaty of March 16, 1920. It is comparable to the Brest Peace. And as such it ought to be annulled. The Nakhichevan AO [sic] ought to be returned. . . .

The AYU considers this act to be an outrage, and Karabakh should be united to the Armenian republic.

The AYU considers what is going on in Karabakh an act of violence."

TsKhSD (*Tsentr Khraneniia Sovremennoi Dokumentatsii*), f. 5, op. 30, d. 487; translated by the editor.

Was the 1968 Prague Invasion Justified?

Like the year 1956, the year 1968 began in hope and ended in disillusion. Another moment of significant reform in the Communist system seemed at hand when the leadership of the Czechoslovak Communist party began a series of radical transformations of one of the most rigid Stalinist political structures. Under Alexander Dubcek, the Czechoslovaks ended censorship, opened up the economy, and experimented with a more pluralistic politics. The phenomenon of a Communist regime reforming itself from the top down inspired intellectuals in the USSR, but frightened the Brezhnev leadership. Without warning, Soviet troops invaded Czechoslovakia on August 21 and crushed the "Prague Spring."

For a number of intellectuals and activists in the Soviet Union, the brutal suppression of a reformed and more democratic socialism turned them toward active opposition to the Soviet state. Some, like Alexander Solzhenitsyn, reverted to Russian traditionalism, others to nationalism, and still others to Western-style liberalism. The prominent physicist and "father of the Soviet hydrogen bomb," Andrei Sakharov (1921–1989), became the most eminent spokesman for a liberal agenda, stressing human rights, respect for the individual, and the rule of law. The government exiled him and his wife to the Volga city of Gorky (Nizhnu Novgorod), where he remained under house arrest until December 1986. It was not until two years later, in the third year of Gorbachev's rule, that the end of censorship allowed open discussion of the invasion of Czechoslovakia. This article from the Soviet press on the twenty-first anniversary of the events presents the contrasting views of a prominent leader at the time, K. T. Mazurov, of the military commander of the operation, General I. G. Pavlovsky, and of an ordinary soldier, Private First Class V. V. Nefyodov, on the turning point at which history did not turn.

Pages from History: IT HAPPENED IN PRAGUE.—An Izvestia Correspondent Interviews a Politician, a Military Commander and a Soldier About What Happened In the Czechoslovak Capital On August 21, 1968.

The newly awakened yearning for justice that extends across many pages of Soviet history is still skirting the morning of Aug. 21, 1968, when troops from five Warsaw Treaty member-states entered the territory of Czechoslovakia. Assessing their past is the right of the Czechs and Slovaks themselves. We, by contrast, want to look at what happened through the eyes of our compatriots who participated in the events. Never having had a chance to tell their stories, they have kept the vow of silence that the administrative system demanded of them. The time has come to end their silence. . . .

These interviews, it seems to me, also give some idea of the spectrum of views that exist in our society today.

★★★

In 1968, K. T. Mazurov was a member of the CPSU Central Committee Politburo and First Vice-Chairman of the USSR Council of Ministers.

QUESTION: Kirill Trofimovich, what specific aspects of the international situation in August 1968 forced the top political leadership, led by Brezhnev, to take the step of sending troops into the fraternal country?

ANSWER: It's hard to understand if we look at the past today without taking the trouble to delve into the circumstances of that different historical period. What was called the cold war was at its peak. Relations between the FRG and the GDR were strained, and the construction of the Berlin Wall triggered outright hysteria in the West. The Caribbean crisis had inflamed passions. We had high hopes for a meeting with the US President, but the Powers reconnaissance flight derailed it. We learned of plans by certain circles to provoke a nuclear attack on the Soviet Union. We had the wherewithal to respond and could have struck fear in them, but we hardly had it in the same quantities as they had.

The West was gambling on Czechoslovakia in its attempts to dismantle the socialist commonwealth. . . . Those who wanted to heighten tensions had something to work with. There was mounting public discontent with the way the country was imitating the Soviet model of development. The mechanical copying of our way of doing things aggravated economic imbalances. Again, discussions about the victims of the Stalinist repressions in the 1940s and 1950s hurt us in one way or another. Opponents of the new order attributed all the distortions to cooperation with our country. The opposition openly espoused anti-Soviet and antisocialist slogans.

The Soviet leadership watched with alarm as right-wing forces stepped up their activities in Czechoslovakia. The Czechoslovak Communist Party Central Committee lost control of the mass media. This was pointed out to Czechoslovakia's leaders at the time on more than one occasion. In the difficult international situation, we had but one desire—to close ranks, to prevent war and to keep everyone out of harm's way. The Czechoslovak Foreign Minister's clear hint of a Czechoslovak withdrawal from the Warsaw Treaty came as a total surprise to us. At the time, the border between Czechoslovakia, on one hand, and the FRG and Austria, on the other, was being opened. Sudeten Germans and their militant activists began slipping into the country. Kosygin, who observed their excesses in Karlovy Vary while he was vacationing there, cut short his stay and returned to Moscow. As an eyewitness, he confirmed the danger of what was taking place.

After the Czechoslovak leadership refused to travel to Warsaw for discussions with the leaders of the fraternal countries, an agreement was reached to hold a meeting between the Politburo of the CPSU Central Committee and the Presidium of the Czechoslovak Communist Party Central Committee in Cierna nad Tisou. The meeting was strained. We sat across from each other in a school building for several hours. The Czechoslovaks responded to all our arguments with assurances that we had nothing to worry about. We parted on cool terms. No one slept on the train back to Moscow; rather, we all tried to figure out what to do.

We drew up a memorandum based on the meeting's outcome for the leaders of the fraternal parties. They telephoned us constantly to propose solutions. It was Ulbricht and Gomulka who insisted on the harshest steps. Despite some nuances, the overall view shared by all was that intervention was essential. It was hard to imagine that a bourgeois parliamentary republic that would be flooded with Germans from the FRG and then by Americans could arise on our border. This was not at all in keeping with the interests of the Warsaw Treaty. The week before the troops went in, the Politburo members hardly slept or went home: There were reports of an imminent counterrevolutionary coup in Czechoslovakia. The Baltic and Belorussian Military Districts were put on alert status No. 1. On the night of Aug. 20 another meeting was held. Brezhnev said: "We're going to send in troops."

A general sigh of relief was heard: We finally knew what we were going to do. Brezhnev added: "One of us will have to be sent to Prague. The military could make a mess of things. Let's have Mazurov fly there." . . .

I went home, woke up my wife and told her I had to make an urgent trip to Kirgizia. At 3 a.m. my plane headed for Prague.

We circled over the Prague airport for a long time, waiting for the Soviet and Bulgarian assault troops who had just arrived to clear the landing strip.

When I drove through Prague that morning, at about 5 a.m., tanks were already in the city, and the air was thick with their exhaust fumes. I had been a member of a tank crew myself, and I had the feeling we were at war. I remembered the Politburo members' parting words: "Do everything in your power to prevent a civil war there."

Q: I have heard from our comrades who were in Prague at the time that all power was concentrated in the hands of Gen. Trofimov.

A: That was my new name. Wearing the uniform of a colonel (my military rank) and going by the name of Gen. Trofimov, I gave orders to our military and civilian personnel. . . . The main task was to protect our soldiers from gunfire. You know, I was astounded by our soldiers' restraint, by the way they managed to keep their composure when the young people rampaging in the squares insulted them and threw anything handy at them. . . .

Enterprises shut down, the stores closed, and people were left without food. We appointed the commander of the 20th Division as commandant of Prague. "Do whatever you want," I told him. "Drag the store managers out of their apartments, if you have to, but see to it that the stores are open for business and that people don't go hungry."

I returned to Moscow on Aug. 27. Brezhnev was in a state of euphoria: "Thank God it's all over." He meant that we had managed to prevent hostilities. But I knew that things were far from over. And when I got home, I said to my wife: "The main thing is not that I returned, but that I returned without having buried a single Czech."

You want to ask me whether I would agree to direct such an operation today. No! Under no circumstances. But in the concrete situation that existed in August 1968, I acted in accordance with my convictions. And if that situation were to recur today, I would do the same thing.

★★★

In 1968, I. G. Pavlovsky was an Army General, USSR Deputy Minister of Defense and commander of the allied troops that entered Czechoslovakia.

Q: Ivan Grigoryevich, it must have been difficult to take charge of an operation that was unusual for a general and carried out on the territory of a fraternal country.

A: I was given the appointment on Aug. 16 or 17, three or four days before the operation began. . . .

The operation was set to begin on Aug. 21 at 1 a.m. [Then Soviet Defense Minister] Grechko warned me: "Moscow will give the orders; it's your job to see that they are carried out."

The troops moved out at the appointed hour. Then came another call from Grechko: "I just talked to Dzur (the Czechoslovak Minister of National Defense) and warned him that if, God forbid, the Czechs open fire on our troops, it could end badly. I asked him to order Czechoslovak units to stay put, not to open fire, and not to put up any resistance to us." . . .

[After landing in Prague,] I went with Lt. Gen. Yamshchik, who had met me at the airport, to see Dzur at the General Staff. Dzur and I quickly agreed that there should be no fights between our soldiers and that no one should think we had come with the aim of occupying Czechoslovakia. We had sent in troops, and that was all. Let the political leadership sort things out beyond that. . . .

Q: How many tanks did we have in Czechoslovakia?

A: About 500. And to be honest, I wouldn't say that the public was friendly to us.

Despite the fact that our army had liberated Prague and that we and Czechoslovak troops had taken part in joint combat operations against Hitler's forces, every Czech had a right to resent us. Why had we come? We dropped leaflets from airplanes and tried to explain that we had come with peaceful intentions. But you yourself can understand: If I were to come into your home as an uninvited guest and start giving orders, you wouldn't like it very much.

Q: Has your view of the events of August 1968 changed over the past two decades?

A: You know, I am reminded of a play about Ivan the Terrible at the Maly Theater. A monk came to the tsar and tried to convince him that he was dealing with his enemies too harshly. The tsar stood up from his throne and said to the monk: "Sit in my place and rule, and I will watch how you do it." It has now become popular in our country to criticize everything, to say "we did everything wrong!" But let's examine the question in light of the politico-military situation that actually existed. Forgive me, but I am a man of convictions. My views do not change.

★★★

In 1968, V. V. Nefyodov was a Private First Class in the Seventh Guards Airborne Assault Division. He now works as an equipment foreman at the Vnukovo Refractory Materials Plant.

Q: Valery Vladimirovich, you were among the first troops to enter Prague on the morning of Aug. 21.

A: I was 19 years old. In my regiment were more than 20 fellows from my hometown of Odintsovo in Moscow Province. Our regiment was a model one, and our company even more so. . . .

In our political classes, we had been told about events in Czechoslovakia: Extremists were trying to seize power, to wrest the republic from the socialist commonwealth and to restore capitalism. At first we never suspected that we would end up being involved in this. But in early August we were suddenly put on alert, loaded into trucks and taken to an airfield. We were told that right-wing elements in Czechoslovakia had stepped up their activities. We would have to provide assistance to the fraternal people.

We did not fly out at that time but set up a tent camp not far from the airfield. Two weeks went by. About four days before we flew out, our commanders distributed ammunition to us; each soldier was given as much as he could carry. We were even given gas masks. We were told there was no way to know what to expect on landing. The border between Czechoslovakia and the FRG was now open, and we were to forestall a German invasion.

Aug. 20 arrived. Just before dinner the company commander (Lt. Dorokhin) gave us our orders: We would fly out at 4 a.m. We tried to settle down to get some rest, but the uncertainty gnawed at us. It wasn't terrifying, just a mild uneasiness, like before your first jump. We dozed off. Suddenly, at about 10 or 11 p.m., we were put on alert: We had to assemble in 30 minutes. We rushed [to get our gear together,] . . . and ran to the plane. The company commander said that intelligence had established that

FRG troops were preparing to cross the Czechoslovak border at 4 a.m. Our command had had to move up our departure time. . . .

[After we disembarked at the airport outside of Prague,] the company commander gave us our orders: to secure a line along the highway from the airport to downtown Prague. We were warned that a Czechoslovak tank army was passing through the area on the way to training exercises in the Tatra Mountains, and that if the army intercepted us, it might occur to some commander from the right-wing elements to turn the tanks on us. Meanwhile, Soviet tanks were coming in from the GDR. . . .

[Once in the city,] the company was assigned to guard the General Staff, and later the Soviet Embassy building. Attractive Czech girls in military uniforms clustered around us and said: "Everything is fine in our country, why did you fellows come?"

Q: Were there any times when you asked yourself that question?

A: Yes, there were. Not the first day, but later, after we had had a chance to look around. People in the towns and villages were well dressed. Apple and pear trees were growing alongside the roads, but no one would ever think of picking fruit from trees that didn't belong to them. The streets were clean and free of trash—not like in our town of Odinstovo. Apart from the Czech fellows who were provoking clashes, the people of the city remained calm and bore themselves with dignity. A lot of people came up to us, told us about themselves and asked in bewilderment: "Why did you come here? We can sort out our problems ourselves." I saw the pain with which they spoke to us about this and their sympathy for us. Some of these people were old enough to be our parents, others were Czechs our own age. My thoughts became confused, and I felt ashamed. Forgive us, Prague. . . .

★★★

We must assume that Czechoslovak and Soviet historians will fully sort out the considerable complexity and contradictory nature of the events of August 1968. Let us agree once again that assessing Czechoslovak history is the exclusive right of Czechoslovakia's peoples. The events touched on the interests of political parties, the principles of co-operation among fraternal countries, the problems of their collective security, and the right of peoples to choose their own path. The lessons of those days of crisis give us renewed strength to defend the gains of the new political thinking with even greater conviction. This thinking is revolting against the practice of solving the problems of world politics behind closed doors, a practice whereby the popular masses have been excluded from the discussion of such problems but left to pay dearly for all disasters. The past must not be repeated.

Leonid Shinkarev, "Pages from History: It Happened in Prague," *Izvestiia*, August 19, 1989, p. 5; abridged and translated as "Was 1968 Prague Invasion Justified?" *The Current Digest of the Soviet Press*, XL, 34 (1989), pp. 11–13.

The Case of Boris Kochubiyevsky

The story of Soviet Jews took another twist in the late 1960s after the victory of Israeli forces over Arab states in the Six Day War of 1967. Jews, like all Soviet nationalities, had their ethnicity recorded on their internal passports. In various republics advantages were given to some nationalities (e.g., the titular nation of the republic), while other peoples suffered discrimina-

tion. Although the worst persecutions of Jews ended with the death of Stalin, widespread anti-Semitism pervaded the population and official circles. Usually urban and well-educated, concentrated in the largest Russian cities, Jews faced unacknowledged quotas in admission to university, difficulty obtaining certain jobs or advancement, and quotidian experiences of petty harassment. Most Soviet Jews were not religious, did not know Hebrew or Yiddish, and were very assimilated, but beginning in the late 1960s, significant numbers began petitioning to emigrate to Israel or the West. Their cause was taken up in Europe and the United States, and diplomatic and economic pressure was applied to the USSR to open its borders. The illegal dissident publication, A Chronicle of Current Events, *published this account of a young engineer whose crime was simply to express his disagreement with official views on Israel and the position of Jews in the Soviet Union.*

THE CASE OF BORIS KOCHUBIYEVSKY

At the beginning of December 1968 a thirty-year-old radio engineer, Boris Kochubiyevsky was arrested in Kiev.

In 1967 he spoke at a lecture on the international situation given at the radio factory where he worked, argued with the lecturer, and expressed his disagreement with the description of Israel's actions in the Six-Day War as being aggression. Afterwards his case was discussed by the factory committee of the trade union and they proposed that he should leave 'of his own free will'. He refused, and it was only after nearly a year, in which they tried every means to 'persuade' him, that he left in May 1968. In June 1968 he married a student in her fourth year at a pedagogical institute and in August he applied for permission to leave for Israel. In September a similar application was submitted by his wife, who is of Russian nationality. His application was rejected because of 'the non-existence of diplomatic relations', and hers because she had 'ageing parents' in Kiev. Later Larissa Kochubiyevskaya was expelled from the Young Communist League for 'Zionism'. She was not immediately expelled from the institute: for a long time they tried to persuade her to get a divorce, using arguments that would have done the Black Hundreds [Russian chauvinists of the early 1900s] proud. For example, to the young woman's sole and sincere argument ('I love him'), the deputy dean, Groza, replied almost word for word as follows: 'I know a girl who's married to a Jew, and she says all Jews stink. You love him—that's nothing; where you're going, the whole country will stink.' Larissa's parents (her father is a K.G.B. official, her mother a respected teacher) have renounced her.

On September 29th an official meeting was held at Baby Yar near Kiev. The *Chronicle* has already reported the way in which the Kiev authorities replaced the traditional meeting by the Shevchenko monument with an official festival. In exactly the same way [in 1968] they replaced the traditional annual meeting at Baby Yar with an official one. The official speakers were principally concerned with condemning Israeli aggression, but they also used the usual stock phrases about the fascists who had killed Soviet people, without mentioning that the majority of those killed were Jews. An acquaintance came up to Boris Kochubiyevsky and told him about a conversation he had just overheard there:

MAN: What's going on here?

WOMAN: Here the Germans killed a hundred thousand Jews.

MAN: That wasn't enough.

Boris flared up, declaring that people talked like that because, on that very day and in that very place, Israeli aggression had been condemned from the official platform and no mention made of the facts that Jews had been killed here. Straight away a man came up to him, wishing to argue, and said that not only Jews had been killed here. Boris objected that Jews had been killed just because they were Jews. He began saying that he was not allowed to emigrate to Israel, and related the history of his family. One of his relatives had served in the Jewish Ministry under the Central Rada and had been shot as a follower of Petlyura. Another had been a commissar at the end of the 'thirties and had been shot 'as a Trotskyite'. A third, an admiral, had been shot at the same time, as a result of one of the military trials. Boris's grandparents were wiped out by a gang of nationalists in Zvenigorod after the withdrawal of Soviet troops and before the arrival of the Germans. His mother and father were killed by the Germans, perhaps even here in Baby Yar. 'In this country,' said Boris, 'I belong to no one. I want to go somewhere where I shall belong.'

In November Boris and Larissa Kochubiyevsky were given permission to leave for Israel. On November 28th they were due to go to the passport and visa office with their documents. That morning their flat was searched and they signed a statement that they would not leave. The report on the search stated that it had been carried out 'to remove documents, letters, etc.', without any reference to the content of the documents. In the search only copies of letters that Kochubiyevsky had written to official departments were removed. On or about December 7th Boris Kochubiyevsky was arrested on a charge of spreading by word of mouth deliberately misleading fabrications which defamed the Soviet political and social system, under Article 187-1 of the Ukrainian Criminal Code. Held against him are his address at the lecture on the international situation, his appearance before the radio factory committee, his statements at Baby Yar and the 'speeches' (?) he delivered at the passport and visa office.

On January 20th the investigation was completed and the case handed over to the court. But the court has returned the case for further investigation because of the lack of evidence of any intention to spread his views.

One of the principal witnesses in the case is that same unknown person who approached Kochubiyevsky at Baby Yar and provoked him into an argument. In addition evidence against Kochubiyevsky was given by a number of Jewish witnesses, including two victims of Baby Yar who figure in Anatoly Kuznetsov's book *Baby Yar*. Many of those who were present at Kochubiyevsky's 'addresses', and could appear as defence witnesses, are themselves applying for permission to emigrate to Israel and do not wish to prejudice their chances.

THE TRIAL OF BORIS KOCHUBIYEVSKY

On May 13th–16th, 1969, the Kiev Regional Court examined the case of Boris Kochubiyevsky, accused under article 187-1 of the Ukrainian Criminal Code, which corresponds to article 190-1 of the Russian. Kochubiyevsky was charged with making statements on the position of the Jews in the U.S.S.R. Of the charges described in *Chronicle* No. 6 the speech Kochubiyevsky made at the lecture on Israel's 'aggression' in the Six-Day War did not figure in the indictment. The court found him guilty, and Kochubiyevsky was sentenced to three years in ordinary-régime camps.

Kochubiyevsky pleaded not guilty. He denied that his statements had been untrue, and said that even if some of them might be found to be untrue, they were not deliberate untruth, since he had been convinced of the truth of his words when he spoke them. The Procurator objected on this point: 'You have received higher education, passed graduate examinations in philosophy, you are acquainted with the Constitution of the U.S.S.R., and therefore you could not fail to know that in our country none of the things you spoke about can exist.' This formula, in almost identical wording, was included in the verdict as proof of the deliberate untruth of Kochubiyevsky's statements.

On one of the main charges in the indictment, concerning Baby Yar, eight witnesses appeared, only three of whom reinforced the prosecution's case. Kochubiyevsky asked one of the three, Rabinovich, how he came to be in Baby Yar. Rabinovich replied that he had been looking for a shop and arrived there accidentally. The court rejected the evidence of the defence witnesses, stating that all five of them were friends of the accused and had without exception supported the accused's 'Zionist views' in court.

Both Judge and Procurator constantly used the clichés 'Zionist' and 'Zionist views', in spite of the fact that Kochubiyevsky categorically objected to this. To take a specific example, the Procurator asked: 'And have you thought what you've done to your wife? You've infected this sweet young Russian girl with your Zionist views.'

Here are two more examples of the logic of the prosecution:

PROCURATOR: You know what we were fighting against?

KOCHUBIYEVSKY: Fascism.

P: And what were we fighting for? Was it freedom?

K: Yes.

P: Did we win?

K: Yes.

P: Well, there you are, then, we have freedom.

JUDGE (or PROCURATOR): I know you will claim there is anti-semitism here, in view of the fact that there are 200,000 Jews in the Ukraine, but no Jewish schools, newspapers or theatres.

KOCHUBIYEVSKY: Yes, and that too.

J: But you know very well that here they don't all live together, they are scattered.

K: But in Canada there is a smaller Ukrainian population, yet they have their own papers, schools and theatres.

J: But what comparisons are you making? I mean, they live in a bourgeois state, they still have to win their freedom!

It is not an accident that no one could remember if it was the Judge or the Procurator who conducted this dialogue. The Judge on the whole behaved more like a spokesman for the prosecution; his manner was much more aggressive than that of the relatively mild Procurator. He kept interrupting the accused, and mocking him; he whipped up the unsympathetic elements among the public to make hostile remarks, and all the while he did not once call the public to order. All he did was to drop a gentle hint at one point to the effect that he disapproved of comments from the public benches.

Present in the courtroom were the relatives of the accused, and, after giving evidence, the witnesses. The remaining seats were occupied by the 'public', amongst whom several K.G.B. men were spotted. When people asked the policemen and the escorts why the public were not being admitted to the courtroom, they replied—besides giving the traditional answer 'full up'—that 'the K.G.B. won't allow it'. A policeman asked one of the K.G.B. men: 'Hey, Chief, which are your men here?' Without the permission of the 'Chief', the audience was not allowed out for a smoke during breaks. This 'Chief', who at one point gave his name to someone as Yury Pavlovich Nikiforov, stood behind Vitaly Kochubiyevsky, brother of the accused, and from time to time repeated quietly 'And you're a Yid, you're a Yid.'

Many members of the public were not allowed into the courtroom, although they had arrived long before the start of the proceedings and long before the appearance of the 'public' in the court. They sent a declaration to the Chairman of the Court, and later a protest to the Kiev City Procurator, but without result. The only thing that everyone managed to hear was the sentence. Among those who protested at not being allowed into the courtroom was the daughter of an active witness for the prosecution, Rudenko.

In the second half of June the appeal in the Kochubiyevsky case was examined by the Ukrainian Supreme Court, and the sentence passed by the Kiev Regional Court was confirmed.

"The Case of Boris Kochubiyevsky," from *Uncensored Russia: Protest and Dissent in the Soviet Union: The Unofficial Moscow Journal, A Chronicle of Current Events,* ed., trans., and commentary by Peter Reddaway (New York: American Heritage Press, 1972), pp. 301–305.

====== Letter from Vladimir Vysotskii to Petr Dimichev ======
April 17, 1973

The gravelly voice of Vladimir Vysotskii could be heard on homemade tapes passed from hand to hand in the 1970s and 1980s. A singer, poet, and actor at the Taganka Theater in Moscow, Vysotskii was a beloved figure whose music and words cut through the pompous official style of the mass songs and light vaudeville promoted by the state. Along with Bulat Okujava, he represented that part of popular culture that fell outside of what was acceptable to the political establishment." Vysotskii," writes Katerina Clark, "was the icon of alternative culture, alternative because it provided an account of 'the Russian people' that was the functional antonym of the kind of Folklorico being peddled on television and in the concert hall. Vysotskii, who abjured conventional musical form and expectations to render music, as it were, 'from the guts' in a harsh, unmelodic, highly stylized, 'authentic' voice, with minimal variation in the strident guitar accompaniment, became a cult figure with a wide following among disparate segments of the population who otherwise found little in common."[1] No longer considered dangerous

---

1. Katerina Clark, "Aural Hieroglyphics? Some Reflections on the Role of Sound in Recent Russian Films and Its Historical Context," in Nancy Condee (ed.), *Soviet Hieroglyphics: Visual Culture in Late Twentieth-Century Russia* (Bloomington: Indiana University Press, 1995), p. 14.

after he died, he was recognized, even by officialdom, as an important Russian folk poet—in the words of Michael Urban, "a veritable icon of authenticity for a mass public."[2] Today his statue stands in a central Moscow park.

To Candidate Member of the Politburo, Secretary of the TSK KPSS

Comrade P. N. Demichev

From Artist of the Moscow Drama and Comedy Theater at Taganka

V. S. Vysotskii

ESTEEMED PETR NILOVICh!

Lately, I have become the object of the hostile attention of the press and the Ministry of Culture of the RSFSR.

For nine years I have been unable to receive official permission to perform my songs before a live audience. All my efforts to go through concert organizations and ministries of culture have been fruitless. That is why I am addressing you; at issue is the fate of my creative work, which is my own fate.

You probably know that in this country it is easier to find a tape recorder playing my songs than one that is not. For nine years I have asked for one thing only: to be allowed to perform live in front of an audience, to select songs at my concerts, to control my program.

Why have I been put in a position where my responsible civic creativity is construed as independence? I will answer for my art before the nation that sings and listens to my songs, even though they are not advertised on the radio or television or by concert promoters. But I see how the short-sighted caution of the cultural officials who must resolve these problems directly is undermining all my efforts to work creatively within the traditional performance framework. This has involuntarily provoked the explosion of pirated tapes of my music; moreover, my songs in the final analysis are life-affirming, and I am placed in the role of the sufferer, the persecuted poet. I realize that my art is somewhat unorthodox, but in all seriousness, I understand that I can be a useful tool for promoting ideas, not only those that are acceptable but also vitally necessary to our society. There are millions of spectators and listeners whom I can reach with my genre of song poetry, which almost no other artist performs.

That is why when I received the first official invitation in years to perform to audiences of Kuzbas workers, I happily accepted, and I can say that I gave the performance everything I had. The concerts went well. At the end of the show, the workers gave me a special medal cast in steel as an expression of their appreciation; the *oblast'* party and government functionaries thanked me for these performances, invited me to come again. I returned to Moscow a happy man, for I had hoped of late that my performance would finally enter official channels.

Instead, [I got] an undeserved spit in the face, an insulting commentary on a journalist's letter by A. V. Romanov in the newspaper *Sovetskaia kul'tura,* which could be a signal of a campaign against me, just as has happened before.

---

2. Michael Urban, with Vyacheslav Igrunov and Sergei Mitrokhin, *The Rebirth of Politics in Russia* (Cambridge: Cambridge University Press, 1997), p. 26.

In the cosmonauts' village, in student dorms, in academic and almost any worker community in the Soviet Union, my songs are heard. Commanding such popularity, I want to place my talent in the service of spreading ideas about our society. It is strange that I am the only one concerned about this. This is not a simple problem, but can it really be solved by trying to shut me up or devising some way of publicly humiliating me?

I desire only one thing—to be the poet and the artist of the people, whom I love, of the people whose pain and happiness I seem to be able to express in tune with the ideas that shape our society.

And the fact that I am not like others is part of the problem that requires the attention and involvement of the leadership.

Your assistance will enable me to bring much greater benefit to our society.

V. Vysotskii

TsKhSD (no further cite); translated in Diane P. Koenker and Ronald D. Bachman (eds.), *Revelations from the Russian Archives: Documents in English Translation* (Washington, D.C.: Library of Congress, 1997), pp. 296–297.

5

REFORM AND REVOLUTION

CHAPTER EIGHT

THE ROAD TO REVOLUTION

In the first half of the 1980s, the succession of aging and infirm leaders who governed the Soviet Union—first Brezhnev (1964–1982), then Andropov (1982–1984), followed by Konstantin Chernenko (1984–1985)—came to an end with the succession of Mikhail Gorbachev (1985–1991). When a radio journalist called to ask an American scholar what he thought of the new, younger general secretary, he replied that it was "good that the Soviets finally have a leader that can think on his feet. Indeed, it is good that they have one that can stand on his feet!" Even enthusiastic supporters of Gorbachev, already known to harbor ideas of political and economic reforms, could not have predicted how radical, and simultaneously liberating and destructive, those reforms would be. In just over six years, Gorbachev eliminated censorship and allowed a free press, devolved power to elected legislatures, ended the Communist party's monopoly of power, brought the Cold War to an end, and presided over the disintegration of the state he had hoped to preserve. In fact he carried out a revolution that brought new, popular figures like his rival Boris Yeltsin to power and rendered himself superfluous.

Gorbachev began his reforms cautiously, attempting in the Andropov manner to make the system more efficient without fundamental changes. The watchwords were acceleration, discipline, and a fight against corruption and drunkenness. In his first year, he gathered around him men upon whom he thought he could depend: the moderate reformer Egor Ligachev, who became his second in command; the radical Aleksandr Iakovlev, put in charge of propaganda; the impetuous Boris Yeltsin, made head of the Moscow party committee; the able manager Nikolai Ryzhkov as prime minister, and his friend Eduard Shevardnadze as his new foreign minister. But much of the party and state apparatus dragged its feet, and even replacing thousands of officials could not make the lumbering economic machine move. By 1986, Gorbachev spoke of the "restructuring" of the system (*perestroika*) and "transparency" (*glasnost'*), allowing open criticism of faults and failings. In December, Gorbachev placed a famous phone call to Sakharov, then in exile in a Volga city, inviting him to return to Moscow. This was a signal to all intellectuals that they were free to think more boldly and write more critically. By this time, Gorbachev had concluded that the problem with reform was the system of power itself, the heavy-handed control from above and the lack of initiative from below. Jack Matlock, the American ambassador (1987–1991), remembers Gorbachev saying,

Throughout our history change has come from above. And it was always implemented by force. Now, I cannot use force or I will defeat the goal itself. You cannot *impose* democracy on people, you can only give them the possibility of exercising it. What we are trying to do is unprecedented. We have to turn Russian
history upside down. We have to teach our people to rule themselves, something
they have never been permitted to do throughout our history.[1]

Gorbachev's strategy for change within the Soviet Union depended on ending
the expensive military competition between the superpowers. The USSR simply did
not have the material resources to sustain both the nuclear arms race and restructure
internally. Its economy produced only about one-half the output of the US economy
but maintained approximately the same level of military spending. He and Shevardnadze advocated "new thinking" in foreign policy and began to soften the Soviets'
confrontational stance toward the West. The old thinking was expressed by Ligachev,
who insisted that foreign policy reflect class interests rather than a generalized human
interest. In answer to this call for continuation of Cold War conflict, Iakovlev stated
in a speech in Lithuania that Marxism was concerned with "common human interests" and "the development of all mankind, not only that of individual countries or
classes, peoples or social groups." Although the American president Ronald Reagan
(1981–1989) had referred to the Soviet Union as "an evil empire," by the time Gorbachev came to power he too was prepared to negotiate arms reductions and improve
relations. Step by step, the two leaders slashed the numbers of nuclear weapons and
missiles in their arsenals. Gorbachev began a withdrawal of Soviet troops from
Afghanistan and ceased interfering in the internal affairs and foreign policies of the
East European states. In 1989, the ruling Communist parties lost power in one after
the other of the "socialist" countries. The Soviet Bloc disappeared as an alliance, and
the two Germanys were united into a single state dominated by the more powerful
western part. Even as the Soviet Union progressively grew weaker and less influential
in international affairs, Gorbachev was awarded the Nobel Prize for Peace in 1990 for
his efforts to end the Cold War.

For all his successes abroad, Gorbachev was unable to reinvigorate the Soviet
economy and to hold together the broad political coalition he needed to carry out
fundamental reforms. Yeltsin and Ligachev pulled from opposite ends against Gorbachev, the former calling for more rapid and radical change, the latter digging in his
heals against too much change. To the "democrats," Gorbachev appeared to be too
hesitant, too cautious, insincere, and unwilling to give up his commitment to a more
democratic socialism. To the old-line Communists, he seemed too willing to tamper
with their sources of power, too conciliatory to critics of Soviet socialism, and much
too enamored of the West. Tacking first to the Left and then to the Right, Gorbachev
essentially weakened the structure of Communist party power while keeping his most
dangerous opponents at bay. The most extraordinary and ultimately subversive political reform was his suggestion to the Nineteenth Party Conference in June 1988 that
elections be held for representatives to a Congress of People's Deputies, a supreme
body that would essentially draft a new constitution for the USSR. The rules for the
elections were only partially democratic and favored the Communist party. Nevertheless, the televised sessions of the Congress, beginning in May 1989, were a virtual

---

1. Jack F. Matlock, Jr., *Autopsy on an Empire: The American Ambassador's Account of the Collapse of the Soviet Union* (New York: Random House, 1995), p. 66.

classroom in parliamentary democracy. The Soviet people watched with wonder as their leader tried to run an often unruly meeting and was occasionally rudely criticized. A torrent of legislation poured out in the next few years, which created new democratic institutions, locally elected soviets, a Soviet presidency (to which Gorbachev was elected), and rules for republics to secede from the Union. The infamous Article VI of the Soviet constitution, which gave the Communist party supreme power, was officially rescinded in February 1990. Politics moved out from the Kremlin into the Congress halls, the local soviets, the republics, and onto the streets.

There had already been warnings of problems in the non-Russian areas of the USSR, when in December 1986, Kazakh students in Alma-Ata, capital of the Central Asian republic of Kazakhstan, demonstrated against the replacement of a popular native leader by a Russian. In late February 1988, Armenians in Nagorno-Karabakh demonstrated to merge their region, which lay within the republic of Azerbaijan, with Armenia. The demonstrations spread to Armenia proper, only to be followed by vicious killing of Armenians in the Azerbaijani city of Sumgait. Soon protests in the Baltic republics and violence in Kyrgyzstan and Georgia made it imperative that Moscow deal with the problems of nationalism and ethnic conflict. But Gorbachev equivocated on this issue, unwilling to shift boundaries between republics or make concessions to those calling for sovereignty, and later independence, of the national republics. Yeltsin, who in July 1990 left the Communist party, emerged as the major leader of the Russian republic and used that platform to propel himself to a position rivaling Gorbachev's. Even as *perestroika* transformed Communist oligarchy into a more democratic, pluralistic political order, the weakening of the central power stimulated nationalists and local leaders to move steadily away from the center toward separation from the union.

The Soviet Union began to unravel at an extraordinarily rapid pace. *Glasnost'* had opened a society-wide discussion of all aspects of Soviet society and history, and influential people turned from reform socialists into fervent democratic capitalists. The example of East European states ridding themselves of Communist governments in 1989 encouraged thinking about the possibility of creating a Western-style capitalist democracy in the USSR. Lithuanians proclaimed their independence from the Soviet Union, and other republics—Armenia, Georgia, Moldova, Estonia, and Latvia—also declared their intention to secede. The Soviet army moved into Baku, the capital of Azerbaijan, to put down more killing of Armenians by Azerbaijanis in January 1990, and Moscow cracked down on "separatists" by firing into crowds in the Baltic republics. At a crucial moment in the fall of that year, Gorbachev wavered, fearful that the KGB or the army would turn on him. He broke an alliance with Yeltsin based on a radical economic program known as the "500-Day Program" and appointed conservatives to high state positions. Several of his closest colleagues, among them Iakovlev and Foreign Minister Shevardnadze, resigned their posts. Yeltsin increased his popularity, and republics like Russia now appeared to be leading the struggle for radical reform.

As the power of the center evaporated, the more orthodox Communists called on Gorbachev to assert the Kremlin's power over the rebellious Baltic republics. In January 1991, troops fired on demonstrators in Riga, Latvia. Yet Gorbachev recoiled before the use of force and refused to assert presidential rule in the republics. He tried to negotiate a new "union treaty" with the leaders of the republics, basically reconstituting the Soviet Union as a voluntary association of states. In March, three-quarters of the voters in nine republics (Russia, Ukraine, Belorus, Azerbaijan, Kazakhstan, Kyrgyzstan, Tajikistan, Turkmenistan, and Uzbekistan) overwhelmingly approved a referendum to preserve the union, but at the same time six republics (Armenia, Georgia, Moldova, Estonia, Latvia, and Lithuania) indicated their desire for separation.

The endgame for Gorbachev came in August 1991, when a small clique of conservative Communists, including the KGB chief, the head of the army, and the vice president launched a coup against the president, then vacationing in Crimea. Yeltsin sprang into action, defending democracy and reform from the embattled White House in the center of Moscow. With little support in the population, the coup folded within three days, but when Gorbachev returned to Moscow he came back to a new country. Yeltsin pressured him to disband the Communist party and the Congress of People's Deputies, and within a few months the Russian president conspired with the presidents of Belorus and Ukraine to dissolve the Soviet Union. A fragile, ineffectual Commonwealth of Independent States was established, but in fact the links between the fifteen new states that came out of the USSR proved to be quite weak. In his last, pathetic act, Gorbachev resigned as president of the Soviet Union, a country that had already ceased to exist.

The debate about why the Communist system collapsed and the USSR disintegrated—two discrete but related processes—began almost immediately after the demise of the Soviet Union. While some scholars see the collapse as deeply rooted in the economic and authoritarian structures of the Soviet system and consider reform impossible, others argue that the final failure was largely due to contingent factors, such as the rapidity and complexity of Gorbachev's reforms or his unwillingness to use state power against his opponents. Victoria E. Bonnell of the University of California, Berkeley, and Gregory Freidin of Stanford University, professors of sociology and Slavic literature respectively, present a unique analysis of the effects of television on the final crisis of the Soviet Union.

Televorot: The Role of Television Coverage in Russia's August 1991 Coup

Victoria E. Bonnell and Gregory Freidin

When the State Committee on the State of Emergency (henceforth the Emergency Committee) seized power in the early morning of 19 August 1991, it took steps immediately to assert control over Central Television, radio, and the press. At one o'clock in the morning on 19 August, Gennadii Shishkin, first deputy director of TASS, was awakened by a phone call from Leonid Kravchenko, the conservative director of Gosteleradio (the State Committee on Television and Radio) and asked to come to Central Committee headquarters. By 2:00 a.m., the chief editor of the nightly news program *Vremia* had been awakened. Then, at dawn, military vehicles and paratroopers surrounded the Gosteleradio building at Ostankino.

By 6:00 a.m., arrangements were complete. From that time until the flight of the putschists on Wednesday afternoon, 21 August, regular television programming was suspended, and the central channels became instead vehicles for the transmission of official announcements, news, and press conferences. A similar policy went into effect in radio broadcasting, although several local stations managed to elude official control. In Moscow, all but nine central and local newspapers were silenced by the Emergency Committee.

Since the actions of the plotters were concentrated in Moscow, Leningrad, and the Baltic Republics, most people in the Soviet Union (and even some who lived in these places) acquired information about the events, especially during the first two critical days, primarily through television and, to a much lesser extent, through newspapers and radio. Eventually, television brought into people's homes most of the dramatic moments occasioned by the coup: the tanks rolling into Moscow, the building of barricades, and Yeltsin mounting a tank on 19 August; mass prodemocracy rallies in Moscow and Leningrad on 20 August; the tank incident that led to the death of three civilians defending the White House in the early hours of 21 August; the return of Gorbachev to Moscow twenty-four hours later; the celebration of Freedom Day on 22 August; and the funeral on 24 August. Television provided people with a great deal of information during the coup and by no means all of it proved favorable to the plotters. Predictably, the plotters attempted to use television as a mouthpiece for the Emergency Committee and to suppress information that contradicted the image of a smooth transition to emergency rule. They operated on assumptions that dated from the era before glasnost, when television had been a dependable, cowed propaganda instrument of the regime, promoting the regime's glories and editing out the slurred speech and mispronunciations of its leaders.

Here, as in other respects, members of the Emergency Committee and their supporters underestimated the changes that had taken place in Soviet mass media since 1985. The previous six years had brought far-reaching changes to television, gradually transforming it into a genuine forum for a broad range of ideas. When Kravchenko was appointed the head of Gosteleradio in the autumn of 1990, he took steps to eliminate some of the more outspoken programs, such as the popular *Vzgliad* [*Viewpoint*] which featured controversial reporting and discussions of current affairs. Such repressive measures soon provoked a response from those more sympathetic to the aims of glasnost. The U.S.S.R. Journalists' Union expelled Kravchenko on 12 April 1991, citing his efforts to reintroduce censorship on television. A number of well-known commentators resigned from Central Television in "a dramatic protest" against Kravchenko's policies.

That the spirit of glasnost had made deep inroads into Gosteleradio despite Kravchenko's conservative leadership became evident on 19 August. Faced with an order to return to the pre-1985 style and content of journalism, some reporters, cameramen, editors, and supervisors at Gosteleradio did their best to circumvent the new rules. The situation at Leningrad television—for some years a maverick station in the production of controversial programs—was even more remarkable. Boris Petrov, the president of Leningrad television, cooperated fully with the democratic opposition, led by Mayor Anatolii Sobchak. With a viewing audience of about forty-five million people, extending to Moscow, the Baltic republics, and Belarus, the Leningrad station exerted considerable influence. On the first day of the coup, Petrov secured a satellite connection to facilitate broadcasting beyond the station's normal range.

From the inception of the crisis, Central and Leningrad television transmitted reports, images, and commentary that conveyed not just one version of the events—the official version promoted by the Emergency Committee—but several other views of what was happening and why. There were, in fact, three major "scripts" that dominated media coverage of the coup. By "script" or "scenario" we do not mean a prepared text that a director or an actor uses in a theatrical performance. Rather, we are suggesting that the leading individuals and groups during the coup had intellectual agendas and political outlooks already well formed before the curtain rose on the putsch (hence, our "script"), and that these, in turn, shaped their responses to the events that unfolded during the crucial three days and thereafter. Furthermore, "script" implies for us a set of symbols, images, and styles that, in accordance with a given situation, signal actors to act or improvise and signal "audiences" to interpret what they see in particular ways. The theatrical metaphor is, of course, an essential ingredient in politics in general and in mass politics in particular, a theme well researched and well documented in cultural and political scholarship. What makes "script" [*tsenarii*] even more apposite is that it was used by various public figures, along with such related theatrical notions as "plot" [*siuzhet*], "action" or "performance" [*igra*], "characters" [*personazhi*], and "to perform or act according to a script" [*razygryvat'*]. Gorbachev's recollections of the coup offer a telling passage:

> . . . during the preceding days, I had actually been working with my assistant Chernyayev on a major article. It dealt with the situation in the country and the possible ways it might evolve. And one of the *scenarios* considered was in fact the introduction of a state of emergency. And now the *characters* from it had turned up here. My reasoning about that *scenario* was that it would be a disaster for our society and a dead end, that it would turn the country back and ruin everything we now have [emphasis added].

The Emergency Committee's script was signalled, first of all, by its "Appeal to the Soviet People," and other decrees and resolutions issued on the morning of 19 August. But the Committee's views were already well known. In the months preceding the coup, conservative groups in the Communist Party of the Russian Republic (RSFSR) and leading members of the KGB, Ministry of Internal Affairs (MVD), and military forces had closed ranks with ultranationalist writers in opposition to perestroika and the impending Union Treaty. In mid-June, future putschists Valentin Pavlov, Dmitrii Yazov, Boris Pugo, and Vladimir Kriuchkov attempted to carry out a "constitutional coup d'état" by expanding the power of Prime Minister Pavlov, an outspoken critic of the Union Treaty that was then being negotiated. Their efforts failed. On 23 July, twelve Soviet leaders, including high-ranking army officers, published a dramatic appeal in a right-wing paper, *Sovetskaia Rossiia,* calling on Soviet citizens to resist the breakup of the union.

According to the conspirators, the crisis in the Soviet system—a situation they characterized as imminent chaos and anarchy—could only be resolved by revitalizing the country's links with the past, which for them meant the Soviet Union before perestroika. This desire to reconnect was encoded in the very designation of their committee, the GKChP, translating into the lumbering *Gosudarstvennyi komitet po chrezvychainomu polozheniiu* [State Committee on the State of Emergency]. These initials implied an association with the venerable ChK (Cheka), the progenitor of the KGB, with KP, the Russian initials for the Communist Party, and, of course, with ChP (an emergency situation), an overused colloquialism over the seventy-five years of incessant "emergency situations" in the economy, society, and politics. The continuity thus implied was that of the Communist Party, the military-industrial complex, the secret police, and, more generally, a unified state untroubled by the nationalist aspirations of its member republics.

The most important counterpoint to the Emergency Committee's scripting of events from 19 through 21 August came from the democratic resistance, led by Yeltsin. Yeltsin's response to the formation of the GKChP was swift. By 9:00 a.m., he had issued an appeal, "To the Citizens of Russia." This was followed by other statements and decrees in the course of the day. Shortly after noon, he held a press conference in the White House, and at 1:00 p.m. he mounted tank 110 of the Taman Division near the White House and appealed to Muscovites and all citizens of Russia to give a worthy response to those involved in the putsch and to demand the return of the nation to normal constitutional development.

When the crisis began, the position of Yeltsin and the Russian democrats was also already widely known. They advocated the creation of a new Russia—a country, a culture, and a polity—that would be, through a miraculous act of will and plenty of wishful thinking, discontinuous with Soviet and much of pre-Soviet history. Theirs was to be a democratic Russia, one that had no connection with either Communism or the empire. The barricades were not related to those of the Paris Commune or the 1905 "dress rehearsal of 1917." They hailed instead from the landmarks of struggle against Communism: the streets of Budapest in 1956 and Prague in 1968, the Gdansk shipyards, and, most recently, the streets of Vilnius in January 1991, where the old tried-and-true Bolshevik script of "national salvation" was applied on a smaller scale in preparation for the August counterrevolution.

A third script—the perestroika script—remained on the sidelines during the first two days of the crisis, only to emerge with Gorbachev's release from incarceration on 21 August. Unwilling to change his perspective even after the coup, Gorbachev persisted in reading from that script, which portrayed the country's democratic future as flowing out of her cruel and tyrannical Communist past. Socialism, and the Communist Party as the sole surviving pan-Union political institution, could not be omitted from his script. But, if before the putsch a drama revolving around the socialist idea and the Party was attracting fewer and fewer good actors, not to mention an increasingly sparse audience, it became a solo performance in a nearly empty theater after the coup had failed.

In an era of instant replay, major political players and commentators tend to swap rhetoric as much as they swap their primary functions: commentators are a real force in the political game, which in the era of nationalism and democracy revolves around symbols, whereas politicians use their authority and visibility to shape the public discourse in a way that automatically implies a framework of legitimacy for their policies. Having gone through the school of Bolshevism, with its treasury of experience in manipulating public discourse, having graduated from the academy of Gorbachev's glasnost, which introduced into public consciousness the necessity of logical reasoning, open-minded analysis, humanistic values, and, almost, public honesty, the players and commentators of the August days were offered an unprecedented opportunity to deploy their rhetorical and aesthetic skills. It was as if their lives depended on it, and in fact they did.

19 AUGUST, DAY ONE: TWO SCRIPTS

With the seizure of power in the early morning of 19 August, the eight plotters declared their actions to the world and put forward their claim to legitimacy. Even before the specific formulations in the GKChP's decrees, resolutions, and appeals could be grasped, the style of presentation by television announcers immediately gave a distinctive clue concerning their position: a vintage Soviet script, the absence of the word "Communism" notwithstanding. In fact, the tone of voice and intonations—ponderous and solemn, reminiscent of the days when the Party still had its sacred aura and its pronouncements resonated like the word of God—alerted people to a major change not just of government but of their entire style of life. After six years of glasnost and perestroika, the announcers of 19 August were, discursively and gesturally, herding people back to a time before 1985.

The Emergency Committee's major declaration, the "Appeal to the Soviet People," was read numerous times on television the first day. With its heavy emphasis on the vocabulary of Soviet patriotism and official Russian nationalism, it is reminiscent of the "developed socialism" of the Brezhnev era. The terms "Fatherland" [*Otechestvo*] and "Motherland" [*rodina*] appear numerous times. They are code words, loosely but unmistakably associated with the renascent right-wing Russian nationalism of the imperial variety [*otechestvo*] and traditional Soviet-style patriotism [*rodina*]. The proclamation concludes with a summons to manifest "patriotic readiness" and to restore "age-old friendship in the unified family of fraternal peoples and the revival of the Fatherland."

Apart from regular readings of the Emergency Committee's proclamations and decrees, Central Television broadcast no additional news or information until the late afternoon of 19 August. Ballet, opera, and classical music—all harking back to the good old days when Soviet mass media were dominated by edifying material—replaced the "aerobicized" fare found on Central Television in the twilight years of perestroika. Then a real TV news event took place: the Emergency Committee's press conference was broadcast live, in its entirety, on Central Television.

For their first—and as it turned out, only—press conference, the plotters adopted the format introduced by Gorbachev in 1985, which permitted spontaneous questioning by foreign and Soviet reporters. Considering the care with which the plotters attempted to seize control of the mass media—even to the point of forbidding employees of Gosteleradio to leave with film except by permission of the chief editor—it is certainly puzzling that they submitted to a press conference of that kind, with all its attendant risks. One can only surmise that they felt compelled to do so in an effort to establish their credibility with foreign powers and, perhaps, the Soviet population as well. The press conference cast in sharp relief the style of the conspiracy, leaving little to the imagination with regard to its master script and the ineptitude of its members. Five of the eight plotters participated: conspicuously missing were KGB head Kriuchkov, Defense Minister Yazov, and Prime Minister Pavlov. Since it was a matter of common sense that neither the KGB chief nor the chief officer of the armed forces could have played second fiddle in a conspiracy of this magnitude, their absence diminished the stature and seriousness of the Emergency Committee. Attention was focused on Gennadii Yanaev, the least respected and least powerful member of Gorbachev's entourage and, it turns out, the most reluctant participant in the conspiracy. Yanaev held center stage and answered nearly all the questions, with Interior Minister Pugo participating occasionally. Aleksandr Tiziakov and Oleg Baklanov made only one comment each, and Vasilii Starodubtsev spoke twice. The press conference was, for the most part, Yanaev's show.

In camera work, there are always choices, and the camera lens can be a merciless eye, if so directed. During the press conference, the choice was to focus on Yanaev in such a way that his hands were continuously visible—hands that trembled intermittently, conveying great agitation, in contrast to his authoritative booming voice. Remarkably, the camera returned again and again to that particular framing of Yanaev, though it would have been easy enough to direct the camera's eye elsewhere—perhaps to a close-up of Yanaev's face or a long shot in which the telltale tremors would have been invisible to the television audience. In the control room, a decision had been made to capture the image in a particular way. According to David Remnick, veteran *Vremia* director Elena Pozdniak, who had made a career splicing out Brezhnev's bloopers from videotape, "decided she would do what she could to preserve, at the very least, a marginal sense of honesty. She got a word from Kravchenko and his deputies that, if it was technically possible, she should edit out Yanayev's trembling hands at the press conference, the laughter in the hall, and the scoffing reactions of the correspondents. Although that was very easy to do, Pozdniak thought, 'Let them see it all!' She'd had enough of the lies." Thus, even the officially engineered coverage of the press conference turned out to be a visual humiliation for the plotters.

In the charged atmosphere of an unfolding conspiracy, the desire to understand and to interpret every detail pertaining to it is overwhelming. Yanaev's trembling hands and runny nose (like Nixon's legendary five-o'clock shadow) became for many people a symbol of the plotters' criminality, ineptitude, and inexperience. They evoked the common Russian saying, "trembling hands give away the chicken thief" [*ruki drozhat—kur voroval*], and the usage of *soplivyi*, literally meaning someone with a runny nose, and figuratively meaning a person who is inept, untutored, unskilled, and infantile. The journalist corps contributed to transforming what was planned as a show of political savvy and competence into a chillingly comic farce. One correspondent asked Yanaev about the state of his health, another whether Yanaev had consulted with General Pinochet concerning the plan for the takeover. These questions and others elicited occasional snickers from the assembled correspondents and, in the case of the health question, uproarious laughter at Yanaev's expense. The high point of the press conference came when Tatiana Malkina, a young reporter from *Nezavisimaia Gazeta,* pointedly asked Yanaev, "Could you please say whether or not you understand that last night you carried out a coup d'état [*gosudarstvennyi perevorot*]?" No other correspondent was quite so blunt. Yanaev responded to her question during a prolonged close-up of Malkina, whose face took on an expression of disdain. The camera work, the mocking attitude of the journalists, and the words and gestures of the plotters combined to deprive the Emergency Committee of the appearance of authority and legitimacy it sought to create.

The press conference had a profoundly discouraging effect on potential supporters, such as KGB Major General Aleksandr Korsak and his fellow officers. When Korsak first heard the announcement of the state of emergency at 6:00 a.m., he responded favorably: "The words were the right ones, and the people on the committee carried some weight." The support of KGB officers was indispensable if the coup was to succeed, but the press conference helped to turn them against the conspirators. According to Korsak, "after the press conference by the GKChP, the general impression was created that this was a simple adventure, and the perplexing questions multiplied." Many army and police officers shared Korsak's reservations and refused to cooperate with the Emergency Committee.

In Leningrad, not long after the live broadcast of the press conference, the Leningrad TV news program *Fakt* went on the air. The high point of the program came at 7:20 p.m., when Leningrad Mayor Sobchak made a dramatic live appearance, accompanied by Vice Mayor Viacheslav Shcherbakov, A. N. Beliaev, president of the Leningrad city soviet, and Iurii Iarov, the president of the regional soviet. The plotters had listed both Shcherbakov and Iarov in the local Emergency Committee, without consulting them. The three men repudiated the conspirators and made a moving appeal to the television audience, addressing them as "dear Leningraders," "dear countrymen" [*zemliaki*], and "fellow citizens" [*so-grazhdane*]. Their appearance had a profound effect on Leningraders. According to an interview with Sobchak conducted soon after the coup, the television appeals helped to dispel "the suffocating atmosphere and disorientation" that people were experiencing and to mobilize in Leningrad popular resistance to the putsch.

19 AUGUST, DAY ONE: *VREMIA*

At 9:00 p.m. on the nineteenth, millions of television viewers eagerly awaited Central Television's authoritative evening news program, *Vremia*. It began as an archetypal Soviet performance, with incredibly somber, stone-faced announcers—the sexless Adam and Eve of Soviet television—reading the Emergency Committee's first declarations. Time and again, the announcers stressed the dangers of "chaos" and "anarchy" in the country. Reading from the Emergency Committee's "Appeal to the Soviet People," the two announced that "The country is sinking into an abyss of violence and lawlessness." This alarmist language remained central to the plotters' scripting of the events. The tanks, after all, had ostensibly been sent to Moscow in response to the imminent threat of chaos and anarchy. These dangers provided justification for such a massive show of force in Moscow and, more generally, for placing troops on alert in other parts of the country.

But Monday's edition of *Vremia* presented a far more complex and contradictory picture of the situation than the plotters and their supporters at Gosteleradio had intended. Following the lengthy reading of appeals and decrees issued by the Emergency Committee, the announcers introduced reports from Moscow and Leningrad. The first of these is a five-minute segment by Sergei Medvedev, the reporter, and Vladimir Chechel'nitskii, the cameraman. They get off to a good start—visually. The tanks are rolling from across the river and onto Red Square, passing St. Basil's at high speed. As if to provide some link to the overwhelmingly Soviet ambiance of what had preceded this scene, the voice-over of the Soviet announcer comments cheerfully, as though welcoming a shipment of bananas, "Today, on the streets of Moscow, there appeared tanks and armored personnel carriers. They moved quickly toward the center of the city." With these words, the lifeline connecting this report to the Soviet universe is severed. Unlike the preceding voice-over, Medvedev speaks with urgency and animation, each phrase punctuated with a gasp. From the very first line, it is a report from a battlefield. The gasping in the reporter's voice conveys the immediacy of battle, the fright, and also the resolve, with great conviction and force. Held unsteadily, as if by a man elbowing his way through a crowd, the camera pans in all directions, pausing for a moment on the faces of the soldiers, looking confused and apprehensive, smoking, reading a protest leaflet, confronting civilians. The trolleybuses block the tank traffic, and a group of political activists stand atop a speakers' platform in Manège Square, one of them addressing the crowd through a megaphone: "An indefinite political strike has begun, a strike of political protest." More shots of tanks, with children and civilians in the background. Commenting on the shots of small crowds surrounding and haranguing the soldiers, Medvedev resorts to metaphors: "And the human waves kept rolling in, one after another. . . . They were forming eddies. . . ."

Finally, the camera cuts to Yeltsin mounting a tank near the White House to read his first declaration. In a clear and steady voice-over, Medvedev announces that the decree "defines the actions of the Emergency Committee as a coup d'état." With Yeltsin's voice in the background and his towering figure filling the entirety of the frame, Medvedev carefully summarizes the main points of the declaration, down to the very last one, the call for an indefinite political strike. The report concludes with footage of the barricades outside what had become the front line, the immediate surroundings of the White House. Long shots of people building barricades are followed by an interview with a few men who had come to defend the White House, including a worker, an engineer, a student, and an intellectual. Yes, they are planning to stay there all night if need be. "Do you have enough bread to last you?" "Yes, we do," answer some. "We don't need any bread," answers a younger man (a worker, judging by his appearance) with grim determination, "We'll do it without any bread at all." "What made you think that this was the place you should come to?" Medvedev asks them. "It's Vilnius; Vilnius taught us our lesson," answers the intense-looking intellectual with a carefully trimmed beard. One of them, a man in his fifties, most likely a worker, points to his chest and says that his heart told him to be there. He works at the ZIL factory, one of Moscow's biggest industrial employers, and his bosses gave him time off when he informed them of his plans. "We are here because we have something to defend—our legitimate elected representatives, our power," the intellectual cuts in.

Medvedev's interview not only conveyed a great deal of information about developments around the White House, it also presented a symbolic image of the support that Yeltsin enjoyed among a broad cross-section of Muscovites. None of this spectacular theater would have had significant impact had it not been for the framing by the cameramen and the later editing of segments, such as the one by Medvedev on *Vremia*. For example, the image of Yeltsin on the tank, an image reminiscent of Lenin's famous speech on top of an armored car in Petrograd in April 1917, almost immediately became emblematic of the democratic resistance. Yet the crowd around Yeltsin and the tank was quite small, virtually lost in the vast space of the White House driveway and the steps leading down to the embankment; many spectators held umbrellas to shield themselves from a light drizzle. One can easily imagine a long shot through a telephoto lens from atop the high banister. Such an angle and frame could easily have diminished Yeltsin's considerable physical stature to a visually unimpressive human figure flailing impotently on top of a mammoth piece of hardware, surrounded by a sparse crowd of onlookers who were melting away as the drizzle turned into a shower. This memorable symbol of opposition to the conspiracy was carefully scripted, cast, directed, shot, and produced. The team that was present on the spot improvised—it had no time to do anything else—but it improvised from a particular point of view. Thus filtered, most likely through the eye of a CNN cameraman, Yeltsin's rather awkward bulk makes him appear someone "larger than life," his unrefined speaking style the "voice of the people," his rather unkempt appearance a sign, not of the confusion of a politician caught by surprise but of a strong leader, right-eously indignant and full of selfless resolve.

Yeltsin's first statement on the morning of the nineteenth was addressed "To the Citizens of Russia," as Medvedev indicated in his report. The plotters' major appeal, by contrast, was directed to "Compatriots, Citizens of the Soviet Union." The language of propaganda encoded two very different ideas about national allegiances and political unity—one was based on a vision of an independent Russia, the other on the tradition of the all-powerful, unitary Soviet state. Visual symbols reinforced these differences: whereas the Soviet flag remained the national emblem of the Emergency Committee, the pro-Yeltsin forces were shown displaying the old Russian tricolor flag, which symbolized Russian national identity.

The circumstances surrounding the filming and the airing of Medvedev's segment disclose a great deal about the situation confronting the plotters at Gosteleradio. Medvedev did not get out into the streets until early in the afternoon. Until then, his main source of information was CNN. Officials at Gosteleradio had attempted to shut off CNN, but the staff had resisted. Medvedev's crew was the only one that applied for permission to film the first afternoon of the coup, and permission was granted. According to Medvedev, he returned to the studio from the White House around 8:00 p.m. The segment was prepared under great time pressure; about five minutes before *Vremia* went on the air at 9:00 p.m., it still had not been completed. Valentin Lazutkin, a deputy to Kravchenko responsible for overseeing the content of the program, looked at the first part of the report and asked what came next. "Well, we'll show the barricades and the people on them," Medvedev replied. The footage of Yeltsin on the tank originally ran for four minutes, but Lazutkin told Medvedev to shorten. "The rest of what [Yeltsin] said I will try to put in my script," said Medvedev. Lazutkin gave his approval. Lazutkin and Medvedev were just two of the Gosteleradio employees who cooperated spontaneously to undermine the plotters' effort to create an illusion of calm and unanimity in the country.

The conspirators and their supporters reacted swiftly to the airing of Medvedev's segment. As Medvedev said, "It was as though the ceiling crashed in on my head. All the telephones began to explode." Calls came from Yurii Prokof'ev, secretary of the Moscow party committee, and Aleksandr Dzasokhov, a member of the Politburo. Interior Minister Pugo phoned Lazutkin and angrily accused him: "The story on Moscow was treacherous! You have given instructions to the people on where to go and what to do. You will answer for this." By contrast, Yanaev, who had not seen *Vremia,* as Lazutkin suspected, congratulated him for a "good, balanced report." "It showed everything from different points of view," concluded the acting president of the U.S.S.R. Apparently, even the plotters could not agree about *Vremia.* Kravchenko subsequently ordered the chief editor to demote Medvedev from commentator to senior editor, with half the salary. Medvedev was also deprived of the right to appear on the air. The chief editor advised him to "go hide somewhere, because I don't know what will happen next. Go take a vacation immediately." Some among the *Vremia* staff were also appalled by Medvedev's uncompromising stance:

> I didn't wait around to see how everything would come out, although before I left, one of the deputy editors began to shout at me, "How could you deceive us? You gave an interview to people in the opposition." He blamed me for a

phrase at the end of the report: "If we have the chance, then we will give you additional information later about what is happening in Moscow." Everyone blamed me for this phrase.

But the next day, the obstinate Medvedev took a cameraman and again went to the White House to film. The footage he shot that day did not get on the air until Thursday, when Medvedev himself anchored the first uncensored *Vremia* since the coup began.

Medvedev's segment provided the high point for Monday's *Vremia*. It was followed by a brief report on the situation in Leningrad, showing an antiputsch gathering in Palace Square and many tricolor flags. Juxtaposed to the Moscow and Leningrad reports were a number of short segments designed to show that in provincial cities and other republics—Latvia, Moldova, Estonia, Alma-Ata—life was proceeding as usual, with no disturbances. The repetitive images in these short segments showed ordinary but mostly well-dressed people (especially women and children) walking down streets, standing in lines, or working at their jobs. Within the framework of the pre-Gorbachev Soviet-style reporting, it was, of course, impossible to present scenes of disorder or popular resistance to the government in any form. In these segments, *Vremia* reporters attempted to follow the old script: everything was peaceful, harmonious, and industrious in the country. The scenes of pedestrians moving smoothly along well-paved streets created precisely the desired imagery of Soviet citizens—imagery that prompted both Elena Bonner and Anatolii Sobchak to comment on Tuesday, "They think we are cattle [*bydlo*]."

By the end of the first day of the coup, the Emergency Committee had made its case to the Soviet people and had applied massive force to ensure its hegemony. Nevertheless, television coverage already revealed major weaknesses in these efforts. Despite strict censorship, the takeover of Gosteleradio and the closure of many newspapers, by Monday evening everyone in the Soviet Union who watched Central or Leningrad television knew that resistance to the Emergency Committee had begun to take form. Viewers saw images of barricades, prodemocracy demonstrations, and tricolor flags.

The Medvedev segment on *Vremia* had a profound impact. As Medvedev told *New York Times* correspondent Bill Keller a few days after the putsch, "Later, I learned that many who defended the White House found out where to go and what to do precisely from this report." His segment turned the image of Yeltsin on a tank into a symbol of resistance, and it brought into millions of homes Yeltsin's memorable words declaring the actions of the Emergency Committee a "right-wing, reactionary, anti-constitutional *perevorot*," spoken from the rostrum of a tank—in a symbolic appropriation of Lenin's famous armored-car speech at the Finland Station—as the minicams were rolling. *Perevorot*—commonly used by Soviet sources to describe the Bolshevik takeover of October 1917 and translated into English variously as "coup d'état, revolution, overturn, and cataclysm," was not the only term in the rhetoric of the democratic movement to describe the situation. In Yeltsin's appeal "To the Citizens of Russia," and on the streets of Moscow where chalk-scrawled slogans soon appeared on armored personnel carriers (APCs), tanks, and sidewalks, the events were quickly encapsulated in the word "putsch," the plotters were labeled the "junta." These words of foreign origin, reminiscent of the Nazi takeover and banana republics, made their way onto national television and from there into the national consciousness, before the takeover was even a day old.

20 AUGUST, DAY TWO:
THE STRUGGLE OF SCRIPTS, IMAGES, AND SYMBOLS

The second day of the coup brought an intensification of the struggle in the war of scripts, images, and symbols that had begun on Monday. Central Television remained under the control of the Emergency Committee. The same announcers as the preceding day presented news in the somber and officious Soviet style. But once again, the official news program *Vremia* was far from consistent in its presentation of events. Two very different interpretations could again be inferred from the reports. Tuesday's *Vremia* and its late-night version, *Novosti,* contained a good deal of information to suggest that things were not running smoothly for the Emergency Committee. Viewers learned, for example, that the Moscow Cadets refused to participate in the imposition of martial law; a rally against the coup had taken place in Kishinev; people in Volgograd supported Yeltsin; in Latvia, parliament called the Emergency Committee "illegal"; young soldiers were reading leaflets of Yeltsin's decrees and proclamations; and Estonians, dismayed by the arrival of tanks in Tallinn, appealed to all democratic forces to express solidarity.

Particularly telling were two reports on the situation in Moscow. Both contained similar images: civilians, especially children, sitting and climbing on tanks and APCs with no interference from soldiers or officers. The reports attempted to convey an atmosphere of calm by showing people eating ice cream on tanks, while others posed for pictures in front of them. A bouquet of roses in a gun barrel at the conclusion of the first Moscow report (though the report was obviously cut abruptly at this point) was probably intended to suggest cordial relations between soldiers and civilians, but it also indicated that the fraternization, reported on Monday by Medvedev, was continuing. The implication was that soldiers were refusing to use their guns. A "normalcy" shot focused on a line of people queuing up for vodka. The camera panned to a solitary bottle of Moskovskaya vodka placed on the pavement by an old lady. For several seconds, viewers were treated to a close-up of the bottle, transformed into a visual metaphor of Russia at the crossroads, with vodka as a symbol of the country's future.

The second report on Tuesday's *Vremia,* put together by B. Baryshnikov and A. Gromov, contains a striking visual image. A huge banner is stretched across a street above a tank. The banner announces the premiere of a play whose title is clearly etched in bold letters: *Tsar Ivan the Terrible.* Beneath are teenagers and children romping on the tanks and young soldiers reading Yeltsin leaflets. The juxtaposition between the tyrannical tsar and the Emergency Committee leaps out from the screen. The framing of this image for the television audience—and there can be no doubt that the sequence was deliberately shot and knowingly inserted into the report—sent a powerful message to viewers. The segment also includes an interview with an army major, disclosing that some Muscovites viewed the soldiers and their hardware as "the enemy" and not saviors, as the plotters would have had them believe. A youthful reporter wraps up the report with the statement, "Now everyone understands that the troops are a necessary guarantee of general safety."

Following the first report, *Vremia* abruptly brought to the screen the reporter Vladimir Stefanov. His appearance was pointedly informal: hair slightly ruffled, a casual sports shirt open at the collar. Stefanov reminded viewers that the Emergency Committee consisted of important people, "members of the Government," appointed by even more important people. Although he himself did not like the precise procedure involved in this transfer of power, he did not believe it was worthwhile to risk one's life over the quarrel among top-ranking politicians. "We may not like what has happened," he continued "but life willed it otherwise." With emotion welling in his voice, Stefanov implored his audience, "Anything, anything at all, but please no blood!" [*vse chto ugodno—tol'ko by ne krov'*]. Stefanov's appearance was strikingly different from other *Vremia* announcers and reporters on Monday and Tuesday, with the exception of Medvedev. And, like Medvedev, the camera showed Stefanov speaking with earnestness and informality directly to the television viewer. The decision to put him on the air during Tuesday's *Vremia* emphasizes the importance of style as a component in the battle of the competing scripts: precisely by appropriating the style of their democratic opposition, officials at Gosteleradio expected to make their message more palatable and plausible to the viewing audience or, at least, to some critical portion of it.

On Tuesday, Leningrad television continued its presentation of programs supporting the democratic resistance. The appearance and demeanor of the anchor on *Fakt* immediately suggested a deviation from the straight-laced, Soviet-style announcer favored by the conspirators, a style that dominated Central Television throughout the day. This anchor was a modern-looking, well-dressed young woman who looked straight at the camera and functioned more as a pleasant interlocutor than a mouthpiece for official decrees. *Fakt* included a report of the mass meeting in Palace Square earlier that day, attended, the reporter declared, by 120,000 people. Sobchak was shown addressing the crowd, and many tricolor flags appear in the film footage. Leningrad television also presented a lengthy interview with the Leningrad Party boss, who amiably chatted with the reporter about the impossibility of committing oneself one way or the other regarding the Emergency Committee. A special program on Leningrad television that evening featured Mayor Sobchak, flanked by Vice Mayor of Leningrad Shcherbakov and Rear Admiral E. D. Chernov, commander of the Atomic Flotilla of the Northern Fleet. Shcherbakov minced no words: the junta stands for totalitarianism, he said; they want to make us pay with our bodies for the Communist paradise. Chernov and Sobchak urged people to use their consciences and honor [*sovest'* and *chest'*] to defend the legal government, to assert their human individuality [*chelovecheskaia lichnost'*] in defense of the "great Motherland" [*velikaia rodina*] and "great city" [*velikii gorod*]. The alternative, Sobchak pointed out, was to submit to the junta and be transformed back into cattle [*bydlo*].

Both the Leningrad station and Central Television aired news programs on Tuesday that, in one way or another, alerted viewers to the mounting opposition to the Emergency Committee, not just in Moscow and Leningrad, but in Kishinev, Volgograd, Tallinn, and elsewhere. The mere presence of this information on *Vremia* implied a serious weakness in the Emergency Committee, which had obviously tried and failed to control the one and only news program on Central Television. On this second day of the crisis, the progress of the events could be measured and assessed in terms of television coverage: what began as a *perevorot* had turned into a *televorot,* with television occupying the front line for political struggle over legitimacy and authority.

21–23 AUGUST, DAYS THREE, FOUR, FIVE:
THE VICTORIOUS VERSION OF THE
RUSSIAN DEMOCRATIC SCRIPT

By Wednesday afternoon, it was clear to all who followed the news that the Emergency Committee was in a full-scale retreat from the democratic forces under Yeltsin's leadership. Seen in retrospect, the victory over the conspirators was, first and foremost, a symbolic one: the conspirators never achieved enough cooperation from the military and the KGB to overwhelm the opposition physically. As it turned out, the really critical struggle was fought not only in the streets but on millions of television screens, where competing scripts, images, and styles offered viewers starkly opposed versions of the past, present, and future. The Emergency Committee suffered defeat in this critical battle over hearts and minds when it failed—whether through oversight or inability—to control Central Television completely and to deploy rhetoric and symbols in a compelling and credible manner in support of its claim to rule.

While the coup was in progress, *Vremia* functioned as the authoritative news program on Soviet Central Television and also, to a considerable extent, the mouthpiece of those in power. When the conspirators' ship sank, so did their supporters in high places. On the afternoon of 21 August, Yeltsin issued Decree No. 69, "On the Means of Mass Communication in the RSFSR," abrogating the GKChP's measures to reinstate censorship, dismissing Kravchenko from his position as president of Gosteleradio, and placing Gosteleradio under control of the government of the Russian republic. At 5:00 p.m. Central Television began broadcasting live the session of the Russian parliament that was in progress. Gorbachev had not yet returned to Moscow, and what was left of his government was in disarray.

Wednesday's *Vremia* was produced in a power vacuum. The program aired that evening was a hybrid, combining elements from the Russian democratic narrative and some of the style and ambiance of the Soviet script. The announcers were the same dour figures who had presided during the previous two days, but the content of the program was radically different. In a voice that showed little emotion or deviation from the Soviet standard, the announcer began with the dramatic statement that the putsch had been overthrown by the democratic forces. Members of the Emergency Committee were labeled "adventurists" by the same announcers who only twenty-four hours earlier had reported on behalf of the Emergency Committee. Although the plotters had been repudiated, the scripting of Wednesday's *Vremia* did not disengage entirely from the rhetoric and format of the junta days. The key word was still *stabil'nost'*, and the format of the program duplicated that of the previous two evenings; only the political content had changed. After a summary of the major developments, the program showed segments from different parts of the country. As on previous evenings, pictures of urban serenity dominated the newscasts; only now, in such cities as Alma-Ata, Barnaul, and Kuzbass, the proverbial man or woman in the street was implacably opposed to the junta.

Vremia gave extensive coverage on Wednesday evening to public protest in Leningrad. The camera dwelled on the vast crowd that filled Palace Square, many people carrying tricolor flags. Here was the archetype for the victory script of the Russian democratic forces: the finale of the narrative that began with the putschists seizing power in order to reimpose totalitarian rule on the Soviet people. According to this version, ordinary citizens in great numbers and with great courage and conviction defeated the junta. They were inspired by their love of democracy and country, Russia, symbolized by the tricolor flag. A memorable image concluded the report: the Alexander Column archangel blessing the city, and above and around it, Russian tricolor flags. The struggle, according to this scenario, was between good and evil. As Khasbulatov put it to the Russian Supreme Soviet on Wednesday afternoon (in an ironic appropriation of Stalin's wartime slogan), "We won because our cause was right!" Live television and radio coverage of the Supreme Soviet meeting that day made it possible for millions of people to witness this remark and others praising Muscovites, and Russians more generally, for their resistance to the junta.

Only on Thursday did a dramatic change take place in *Vremia*. The day had been proclaimed a national holiday, Freedom Day, by the Russian parliament. Most members of the Emergency Committee had been arrested; one, Pugo, had committed suicide. Yeltsin was at the peak of his popularity. When *Vremia* came on the air, the anchors had been changed: now Sergei Medvedev, the reporter who had put together Monday's prodemocratic segment, presided over the news program. Not only was this a great vindication for Medvedev, but his appearance marked an important shift in the style as well as the content of reporting. Far more casual and direct than his predecessors, he functioned as an anchorman and commentator rather than a mere mouthpiece. Young, energetic and articulate, he spoke in a natural and unformulaic way, without the standard Soviet rhetoric.

The heart of Thursday's *Vremia* was film footage, apparently unedited, of an incident early Wednesday morning that had left three men dead. This clip, shot in semi-darkness and accompanied by somber music, had a moving, almost piercing effect: a Moscow street, the barricade of trolleybusses, unarmed people trying to prevent the APCs from passing through the barricades, shots, bodies falling and crushed by tank treads, Molotov cocktails going off, more shots, blood on the pavement, and, later that day, an improvised shrine and grief-stricken Muscovites mourning the "martyrs" who "perished as a result of an unsuccessful attempt to storm the White House." The report helped to create a national surge of feeling for the three young men who lost their lives "defending our freedom." The *Vremia* broadcast was a feast of symbols. The tricolor flag was now the official flag of the Russian Republic, adopted by the Russian parliament the preceding afternoon, and flags were prominently featured in footage shown on the program. The area behind the White House was renamed Freedom Square. And it was the Day of Freedom, a Russian version of the Fourth of July or Bastille Day, complete with fireworks in the evening. The celebratory events of the day, the speeches by Yeltsin and others, the gathering on Dzerzhinsky Square and the subsequent removal of Dzerzhinsky's statue (another highly symbolic moment), were all televised live. Television once again—this time with live uncensored coverage by reporters who had a style and demeanor much like Medvedev's—brought the events and the Russian democratic script to viewers throughout the country.

With the return to television of the feisty program of news and commentary, *Vzgliad,* 253 days after it had been banned by Kravchenko, the Russian democratic script was recast to correspond to the victorious but tragic culmination of events. The Thursday and Friday programs featured documentary films, both called *Perevorot,* that chronicled the preceding three days of political turmoil.

To appreciate the rescripting of the events that was under way, it is helpful to note what the documentary montage did not include in *Perevorot*. Excluded were scenes of the fraternization between Moscow civilians and soldiers, as was the footage of the animated exchanges alongside tanks and APCs, the instances of camaraderie. All of that remained on the cutting room floor. A similar fate befell numerous film clips of civilians who had climbed on tanks and APCs, eaten ice cream atop the tank turrets, scrawled slogans on the armor and used the heavy equipment as so many soapboxes from which to address assembled multitudes. (Yeltsin's was only the most famous among the numerous improvisations in the "Finland Station" style.) The children romping on the tanks—a familiar sight on the nineteenth and the twentieth—were likewise excluded from the documentary. In the version of *Perevorot* shown on Thursday, the ominously rumbling tanks and APCs in Moscow encountered unarmed civilians, who used their own bodies to prevent the tanks and APCs from moving forward (some remarkable footage of this resistance appears in the film). Soldiers, always very youthful, read Yeltsin's decrees. Yeltsin—in person and through his decrees and proclamations—was central to this version and, of course, *Perevorot* included the footage of his appearance on a tank. The democrats' most important symbol, the tricolor flag, found its way into many of the film's segments—a reminder that the resisters owed their primary allegiance to Russia. Brief interviews with such well-known figures as the cellist Mstislav Rostropovich (in the White House on Tuesday evening, sporting a rifle), the film director Sergei Mikhalkov, and the editor of *Moscow News* and newly appointed Gosteleradio president, Egor Iakovlev, were included in the film, juxtaposed to a short segment from the Emergency Committee's press conference, including the famous image of Yanaev's trembling hands.

In *Vzgliad*'s scripting of events, the junta and its military hardware now emerged as truly threatening and ominous—no more occasion for child's play! Ordinary citizens were shown as fantastically courageous, to the point of holding back tanks and defending the White House with their bodies; entreaties to soldiers and gifts of sausage and cigarettes did not do justice to this level of heroic resistance. The degree of peril faced by those on the barricades was now fully evident: three had died. But ordinary citizens were not the only heroes. They were helped by soldiers who crossed over to Yeltsin's side, such as Major Sergei Evdokimov's tank battalion from the Taman Division which was shown making the heroic move from one side of the barricade to the other on Monday evening.

Soldiers appeared in the narrative as extremely young and naive but receptive to Yeltsin's decrees. It was Yeltsin whose words and deeds won soldiers over to the Russian democratic cause, instead of middle-aged Russian matrons entreating soldiers not to shoot at their mothers. Yeltsin is the larger-than-life hero of the film, the inspiration and the leader of the democratic resistance. His appearance on the tank now had all the qualities of an iconographic image. The interviews with leading Russian cultural figures during the coup was a novelty; in these segments may be discerned a process of "heroization": tell me what you were doing during the August coup, the film implicitly argues, and I will tell you who you are.

22 AUGUST, DAY FOUR: THE PERESTROIKA SCRIPT

Gorbachev's first public statement following his release from confinement to his Crimean dacha was aired on *Vremia* on Thursday evening. Here Gorbachev spoke of the "attempted coup, foiled as a result of the decisive actions taken by the country's democratic forces. . . ." The term "attempted coup" [*popytka perevorota*] attested to a very different interpretation of the events from the one put forward by Yeltsin and his democratic supporters. Earlier that same day, television had carried a live broadcast of Yeltsin's speech before Russia's Supreme Soviet, where he offered a threefold narrative, reminiscent of Russian folk tales: thrice the right-wing forces tried to stage a coup d'état; twice they failed; the third time, they succeeded:

> [T]he first attempt took place at the beginning of the year, but at that time they were scared off by the statement made by the minister of foreign affairs, Eduard Shevardnadze, and the corresponding reaction of public opinion in Russia, the country, and the world. You all recall the session of the USSR Supreme Soviet, when the same people—Pavlov, Kriuchkov, Yazov—tried to extract for themselves some special powers at the expense of the authority of the president of the country, which virtually amounted to his removal from office, and so forth. But this second attempt also failed: the Supreme Soviet gave them no support. *And finally, the third, this time successful, attempt* came when the president was vacationing away from Moscow. . . . [emphasis added]

Yeltsin's message in his Thursday speech to parliament was that, while the coup might have failed miserably in Russia, it had succeeded in the U.S.S.R., since no major all-union institution had declared itself squarely against the conspiracy: not the army, nor the KGB, nor the MVD, nor the Supreme Soviet, nor the cabinet, nor the Communist Party. Indeed, the leaders of these institutions were the key conspirators and, now that they had been routed, the U.S.S.R. had only an ephemeral existence. Gorbachev swiftly countered this rhetoric of Russia's supremacy over the Union. Returning to Moscow in the early hours of 22 August, in his first statement before the television cameras, he offered praise, first and foremost, to the *Soviet* people:

> I congratulate the *Soviet* people, who have a sense of responsibility and a sense of dignity, who care, who respect all those whom they have entrusted with power. . . . Some pathetic bunch, using attractive slogans, speculating on the difficulties . . . , wished to divert our people to a road that would have led our entire society to a catastrophe. *It did not work.* This is the greatest achievement of perestroika. . . . I want to express my appreciation to the *Soviet* people, to the citizens of Russia, for their principled position, to Boris Nikolaevich Yeltsin, to the Supreme Soviet of the Russian Federation, to all the deputies, work collectives, which took a decisive stand against this caper. [Emphasis added.]

The scripts offered by the two presidents differed down to the very last detail. Whereas Gorbachev tried to diminish the whole affair by referring to the conspirators as a "pathetic bunch" of treacherous but incompetent men engaged in a "caper" [*avantiura*], Yeltsin portrayed the Emergency Committee as dangerous opponents of epic proportions—powerful men who had presided over the government as part of Gorbachev's latest perestroika team. The stature of the enemy, apparently, conferred stature also on the resisters: the men and women who stood up to tyranny.

In Gorbachev's further statements on Thursday, 22 August, including a press conference broadcast live on Central Television, he appeared chastised but unreformed, still insisting on the role of the Communist Party as a necessary bridge between Soviet totalitarianism and democracy. The scripting of events by the democratic opposition was by then triumphant in the mass media, and his appearance was framed by scenes from the mass rhetoric and ideas accorded poorly with the images of a courageous people celebrating a heroic victory over a formidable enemy.

24 AUGUST, DAY SIX: THE FUNERAL

On Saturday, 24 August, the live televised broadcast of the funeral for the three who had died on Wednesday morning gave the democratic Russia script its most moving, most fitting coda. The camera followed the progress of the funeral, which began in Manège Square where the mourners were addressed by several prominent political figures including Gorbachev. After the speeches, the funeral procession turned its back on the Kremlin and moved on to the White House. Here Yeltsin, somber, proud, fully in control, spoke the most memorable words of the day, if not of his entire career. Addressing the victims' parents and implicitly the entire nation, expressing traditional humility before the people and implicitly projecting the image of the nation's patriarch, he spoke slowly and clearly: "Forgive me, for I have failed to protect your sons." Now transformed by Yeltsin's speech into a symbol of the entire nation, the procession moved on to the Vagan'kovo Cemetery for the two religious services—Russian Orthodox and Jewish—and finally the interment.

The funeral rally and procession were carefully choreographed media events viewed by millions of people throughout the Soviet Union. The images and rituals served to crystallize some of the major themes developed by the democratic opposition over the preceding week. The main symbolic leitmotif was that of a nation— Russia—committed to common citizenship in civil society. That this commitment was now sealed by the martyrs' blood was of singular ritual importance, especially in view of the long-standing Russian tradition, both secular and religious, of defining the nation around a martyr's ultimate sacrifice. The phrase, "they gave their lives for our freedom," was repeated again and again throughout the broadcast of the funeral. Naturally, the leitmotif of this new social bond found its fullest expression in the television coverage of the two funeral services conducted concurrently for the victims: one in a Russian Orthodox church, the other, a Jewish service, held out-of-doors.

The television coverage moved back and forth between the Jewish and Russian Orthodox services, from the rabbi and cantor to the priests and Patriarch and back again, with an evenhandedness that bespoke deliberate staging for the television audience. In light of the many decades of Soviet antireligious and anti-Semitic policies, the lengthy coverage of both services provided a fascinating spectacle for millions of viewers. But equally remarkable and politically eloquent was the balanced treatment given to the two religions. That all three should be mourned together was critically important for the victorious democratic resistance. The coverage was scripted to emphasize not only the ecumenical, but also the multiethnic, multiclass citizenship in the new Russia (Dmitrii Komar', an Afghan veteran and a worker, was, judging by his name, Ukrainian; Il'ia Krichevskii, was a Moscow artist of Jewish origin; Vladimir Usov was Russian and an entrepreneur). This important *ecumenical* message was captured in the civic ritual of the heroes' interment. The coffins were covered with a Russian tricolor flag and then lowered into the grave to the accompaniment of the *Russian* national anthem. The TV cameras were positioned high above the graves, figuratively transporting the viewers high into the sky. The image of the flag-draped coffins, with the Russian anthem playing in the background, signalled the fact that this was, above all, a funeral for national heroes, "martyrs," whose deaths were inextricably linked to the forging of a new nation.

The week ended as it had begun: millions of television screens beaming the gripping, real political drama into people's living rooms, bringing the affairs of state and nation building into a close and intimate relationship with every viewer. The funeral served as the culmination of the television coverage of the *perevorot*—coverage that created the first true media event in the history of the Soviet Union. The crisis in high politics had been profoundly and decisively shaped by the electronic eye that transformed, instantly and continuously, elements of a political confrontation into meaningful scripts with their corresponding images, styles, and symbols. The 1991 *televorot* that began at 6:00 a.m. on 19 August with the televised announcement of the formation of the Emergency Committee received a fitting closure on Saturday afternoon, 24 August, with live coverage of a funeral that was as much a memorial to the three men as the consecration of a nation.

Victoria E. Bonnell and Gregory Freidin, "Televorot: The Role of Television Coverage in Russia's August 1991 Coup," in Nancy Condee (ed.), *Soviet Hieroglyphics: Visual Culture in Late Twentieth-Century Russia* (Bloomington and Indianapolis: Indiana University Press, 1995), pp. 22–44.

Mikhail Gorbachev, from *Memoirs*

Out of work after a lifetime spent in the party apparatus, Mikhail Gorbachev found himself a relatively young "elder statesman" in the post-Soviet Union. During the Yeltsin years (1991–1999), he was marginalized by the vindictive Russian president, and his particular brand of socialist democracy found little support. He set up a foundation, worked in the environmental movement, and wrote his memoirs. Gorbachev was always welcome abroad during his years of eclipse in Russia, but after the coming to power of Vladimir Putin, who attempted to reconcile market reformers with statist nationalists and Communists, Gorbachev became more visible in public arenas within Russia. In this excerpt, the former general secretary lifts the curtain on the intrigues at the very top of the Soviet political apparatus and reveals how he came to the conviction that reform was imperative.

[Yuri Vladimirovich] Andropov and I were drawn even closer together in our work during his early months as General Secretary. I sensed his trust in me and his support. At the very end of 1982 he suggested meaningfully: 'You know what, Mikhail, don't limit your work to the agrarian sector. Try to look at other aspects.'

He fell silent and then added: 'In general terms, act as if you had to shoulder all the responsibility one day. I mean it.'

The first question we had to grapple with after Andropov's election concerned a decision which had been taken by the Politburo when Brezhnev was still alive, to increase prices for bread and cotton fabrics. Andropov asked [Nikolai] Ryzhkov and me to examine the matter once more and to report our conclusions to him. Trying to understand the essence of the whole business, we asked for access to the budget, but Andropov simply laughed that off: 'Nothing doing! You're asking too much. The budget is off limits to you.'

I must say that many 'secrets' of the budget were so well kept that I found out about some of them only on the eve of my stepping down as President. Nonetheless, I knew the greatest 'secret', namely that our budget was full of holes. It was being continually replenished by the savings bank, in other words money was drawn from the savings of the citizens and by raising the internal debt. Meanwhile, it was officially proclaimed that the revenues always exceeded the expenditure and that all was very well balanced.

Ryzhkov and I arrived at the conclusion that an increase in bread and cotton prices, in and of itself, would not really work. Andropov's first reaction was to reject our arguments. He may have thought that such a step would demonstrate his courage and resolve. We nevertheless insisted on our opinion: a price increase of that kind was inappropriate for economic and political reasons. Having once more considered all the arguments for and against, the Politburo cancelled the decision it had earlier adopted.

The next priority was the question of purchasing grain from abroad. As usual, we were confronted with government opposition. The reasons were understandable: there was not enough money, yet there was no other visible solution. The General Secretary had to take a stance in that matter and, having listened to representatives of both sides, Andropov himself proposed the purchase.

The absence of 'quick' results led Yury Vladimirovich to take steps which struck me as, to say the least, of dubious value. I am referring to the manner in which the campaign for greater discipline and order was conducted, with people being 'caught loafing' during working hours in subways and shops, at hairdressers and in public baths and saunas. In waging this campaign, Andropov relied primarily on the state security and interior agencies, instead of engaging the help of civic organizations. To him this short-cut was easier.

I tried to argue to him that it was unseemly for people to be seized, in the name of Andropov, while they were taking turns to queue because they had no other time to do their shopping. I told him that these actions undermined his authority, and that jokes were already circulating.

Yury Vladimirovich sincerely believed that these measures would rally the ordinary people to his side. Brushing aside my objections, he would say: 'Just wait and see; when you get to my age, you'll understand.'

This 'understanding' of the people culminated in the sale of cheap vodka, which was immediately nicknamed 'Andropovka' or, according to the display of letters on the label, 'the crankshaft'. And, ironically, in some respects Yury Vladimirovich was right: as time has rushed by, much of what happened then has now fallen into oblivion or is scarcely remembered, but this episode of the struggle for discipline' still lingers on in the memory of many people. . . .

BIDDING FAREWELL TO ANDROPOV

In the summer of 1983, it became manifest that hopes for the better were jeopardized by Andropov's health, which suddenly took a sharp turn for the worse. His illness was caused by a malfunctioning of the kidneys. Very few people knew about it. But as his illness progressed, even his looks changed: his face came unnaturally pale and his voice grew hoarse. . . .

At first weekly, then twice weekly, and eventually even more frequently, he had to undergo agonizing kidney dialysis treatment, connected to a special apparatus that purified his blood. It was no longer possible to conceal the marks visible on his arms, and everybody could see the bandages that began at his wrists. The rumour spread that 'Andropov has had it'. All those for whom Andropov's illness was a gift from heaven became active. At first there was whispering in the corners and, subsequently, some people no longer disguised their joy. . . .

Yury Vladimirovich suffered terribly. We exchanged telephone calls, and whenever the doctors permitted it I went to the hospital. In fact, everybody had been visiting him—some less often, others more frequently; some to support him, others to check on his condition once more. October and November passed. The suffering induced by his illness was aggravated by another worry: he sensed the intrigue.

Because of the General Secretary's illness, Politburo and Secretariat meetings were chaired by Chernenko. Rarely did he entrust me with the Secretariat. I believe that Tikhonov made an abortive attempt at taking over the chairmanship of the Politburo. Meanwhile, Yury Vladimirovich, seriously ill as he was, had not lost his lucidity.

Meanwhile, the manoeuvrings and whisperings among some members of the Politburo were becoming unseemly. It looked almost as if a division of power was under way, and a man was being buried alive. Andropov's aides, obviously sensitive to this kind of talk, were perhaps even overstating this. All this triggered off Andropov's outburst.

One day in December I had hardly crossed the threshold of my office when Ryzhkov rushed in: 'Yury Vladimirovich has just telephoned. He is in a terrible state. He was asking whether we had decided to replace him. I tried to tell him that this was out of the question, but he was not reassured.'

I immediately contacted his doctors and they agreed to let me see Andropov the following day. When I entered his room he was sitting in an armchair and made a weak attempt to smile. We greeted each other and embraced. The change since my last meeting with him was striking. I saw a totally different person in front of me. He was puffy-faced and haggard; his skin was sallow. His eyes were dim, he barely looked up, and sitting was obviously difficult. I exerted every effort to glance away, to somehow disguise my shock. It was the last time I saw Yury Vladimirovich.

Andropov's aides visited him almost daily. I believe Laptev and Volsky were the most frequent visitors. Just before the plenum he received Ligachev, who was to be elected a Central Committee Secretary. Apparently, it was the aides' idea to draft Andropov's address and have it read out at the plenum. That is what happened. I learned about the background story of the text years later, after the publication of Volsky's memoirs. Earlier, only vague rumours were circulating. The essence of the matter was as follows: at the conclusion of the address there was to be a statement to the effect that in connection with his serious illness, considering state interests and with a view to safeguarding the continuity of the Party and national leadership, the General Secretary proposed that I should chair the Politburo meetings.

When Yury Vladimirovich's text was distributed to the Politburo members on the eve of the plenum, and subsequently, bound in a red cover, to the Central Committee members, that statement was missing. Rumour had it that something had been distorted or deleted. Personally I can neither corroborate nor disprove this version. Neither Andropov, nor Chernenko, nor Volsky himself ever talked to me about it. . . .

I was profoundly affected by Yury Vladimirovich's death. Among the leaders of the country, there was no-one else with whom I had such close and old ties, and to whom I owed so much. Over many years I had shared my thoughts and my doubts with him. I had always been aware of his unfailing good feelings towards me. He was never condescending. It was not that he fully opened up to me, sharing his innermost feelings. Some hidden recesses in his life remained inaccessible—maybe because he himself was not too happy about their existence. Or maybe it was because he did not want to burden anyone with this information.

Raisa Maksimovna was shocked by the funeral ceremony in the Hall of columns—genuine grief, tears and a show of respect by some people were in sharp contrast to the unconcealed joy, even triumph, you could see in other people's faces. A number of Central Committee secretaries were in high spirits and did not hide it, as if eager to tell her 'Your time is over.'

In trying to characterize Andropov's work, two aspects should be clearly distinguished: first, Andropov viewed as a practitioner of Realpolitik, and second, the Andropov phenomenon. Without such an approach, confusion, exaggerations and serious distortion could hardly be avoided. What was this Andropov phenomenon? There had been at first a general atmosphere of expectation and hope that the arrival of a new leader would generate beneficial changes. It was—if you like—a repudiation of all that was associated with Brezhnevism in the minds of the people, along with the conviction that reform was imperative and inevitable.

Andropov did not betray these hopes. First and foremost, he was a brilliant and large personality, generously endowed with gifts by nature, and a true intellectual. He resolutely denounced all the features commonly associated with Brezhnevism, that is, protectionism, in-fighting and intrigues, corruption, moral turpitude, bureaucracy, disorganization and laxity. Andropov's tough, and sometimes exaggerated, attitude to these problems instilled hope that an end would at last be put to all the outrageous practices, that those who had alienated themselves from the people would be held responsible. Consequently his actions, though they were sometimes excessive, created hope and were considered the harbingers of general and deeper changes. And here is the crux of the matter—would Andropov have gone any further and embarked upon the path of far-reaching transformations had his fate turned out differently? I do not believe so. Some of those who were not close to Yury Vladimirovich asserted that he had been nurturing ideas of reforming the system long before becoming General Secretary. I do not believe it. He realized the need for changes, yet Andropov always remained a man of his time, and was one of those who were unable to break through the barrier of old ideas and values.

The thought often occurs to me: he knew Stalin's crimes better than anyone else. Yet he never mentioned them. He witnessed Brezhnev's attempts to revive both Stalin's image and his model of organizing society. Nonetheless, he did not even attempt to counteract it. And what about his role in the events in Hungary and Czechoslovakia, in the Afghan War, and in the struggle against those who thought differently, the 'dissidents'?

Apparently the years spent in KGB work had left an imprint on his attitudes and perceptions, making him a suspicious man condemned to serve the system.

No. Just like Khrushchev, Andropov would not have initiated drastic changes. Who knows, maybe it was his fate that he died before he came face to face with the problems which would have inevitably frustrated him, dispelling people's illusions about him.

But such speculation will remain tentative and incomplete until the crucial fifteen-year period of his life as KGB chairman is studied. Much remained hidden behind the heavy walls of Lubyanka, even for me. Without such knowledge it is difficult to tell what would eventually have happened.

Andropov's stay at the peak of power was short-lived, but it instilled hope in people. All that bound us to each other with Yury Vladimirovich is indelibly engraved in my memory. How can I ever forget the southern night near Kislovodsk, the star-studded sky, the bright flame of the bonfire—and Yury Vladimirovich gazing at the fire in a dreamy serene mood? And the tape-recorder playing Yury Visbor's mischievous song, Andropov's favourite:

'Who needs it? No-one needs it.'

A SICK MAN AT THE HELM

I considered D. F. Ustinov, despite his seventy-five years, as Andropov's most suitable successor. Why? They had been close friends, and to me Ustinov would have been the only one capable of continuing Andropov's policies. Moreover, he enjoyed great prestige in the Party and the country.

I 'pressed' the claim of Dmitry Fedorovich, since I saw no other alternative. Some of the other candidates could no longer assume the responsible functions of a General Secretary, others were not up to it yet. Meanwhile Ustinov could have prepared the new generation of leaders.

Later, I learned that the possibility of my own nomination was not excluded. This information reached me from two sources. On the second or third day after Yury Vladimirovich's funeral, Raisa Maksimovna paid a visit to his wife in order to give her some moral support. Sick and agitated, Tatyana Filippovna got up from her bed, lamenting: 'Why did they elect Chernenko? Why did they do it? Yura wanted it to be Mikhail Sergeyevich . . .'

Raisa Maksimovna soothed her and tried to change the subject.

To some extent this story corroborates the rumours mentioned above, concerning amendments introduced by the General Department to Andropov's speech at the December plenum.

Moreover, one of my colleagues, with whom I have worked for many years, told me about his conversation with G. M. Kornienko, who was then First Deputy of the USSR Minister of Foreign Affairs. According to him, immediately after Andropov's death, Gromyko, Ustinov, Tikhonov and Chernenko met, but failed to reach an agreement on a new candidate for the post of General Secretary. Allegedly, Ustinov stated that it would be up to the Politburo to make the choice and, as far as he was concerned, he would nominate me.

These consultations took place in the office of the deputy head of the Central Committee General Department. After the conversation Chernenko stayed behind in the office while Gromyko, Ustinov and Tikhonov went into the corridor. There they were eagerly awaited by their aides and bodyguards, whose nostrils were virtually quivering with curiosity. Luckily for them, Tikhonov was somewhat hard of hearing and he spoke louder than the others. According to eye-witnesses, Nikolai Aleksandrovich suddenly burst out, loudly enough to make heads turn in the corridor: 'I think we did the right thing. Mikhail is still young. And who knows how he would have behaved? Kostya is what we need.'

Let me repeat that I cannot vouch for this story. But that both Andropov and Ustinov had put their stakes on me I learned later directly from Dmitry Fedorovich. Why it turned out differently, he did not explain. Of course I, in turn, never questioned him about it.

Whatever happened, the election of the new General Secretary was extremely simple and, I would say, even routine. It was decided by Tikhonov's aggressive tactics.

Chernenko had barely opened the proceedings when Nikolai Aleksandrovich asked for the floor to speak 'on a point of order'. To foil any possible surprises on Ustinov's part and skipping any niceties, he proposed to elect Konstantin Ustinovich as the next General Secretary. It may well be that Dmitry Fedorovich expected a refusal, a rejection of the nomination by Chernenko, who knew best the state of his health and ought to have admitted that the leadership of the country was, as we say, 'too big a piece of the pie to swallow'. But nothing happened. Raising one's voice 'against' was not in the tradition of that Politburo. Tikhonov's proposal was unanimously accepted by everyone, including myself. And the justification was ready: 'first and foremost to avoid a schism'. But for our society, the emergence of Chernenko as the leader of a great power was a shock.

After the Politburo meeting and in the day that followed, Ustinov, who had always been known for his cheerful disposition, appeared depressed, taciturn and withdrawn. But at the plenum I saw other faces: those cheered by the hope that their times were coming back, the tranquil, 'stable' times, in other words Brezhnevism.

Whom did we acquire in the post of General Secretary? Not merely a seriously sick and physically weak person but, in fact, an invalid. It was common knowledge, and immediately visible with the naked eye. It was impossible to disguise his infirmity and the shortness of breath caused by emphysema. The doctor who accompanied Margaret Thatcher to Andropov's funeral soon afterwards published a prognosis on Chernenko's life-span and erred by only a few weeks.

Chernenko had always been at Brezhnev's side, anticipating all his wishes, his confidant, that is to say, his shadow. A powerful weapon in his hands was the omnipotent Party apparatus. Still, it is difficult to understand how such ambitious plans were conceived in the mind of such a man, a quiet, withdrawn and typical red-tapist. I believe he was urged on by people who had their own ambitions. His first public address, at the commemorative meeting on the occasion of Andropov's funeral on 14 February 1984, left a sad and painful impression on all of us, on the country as a whole, and on our foreign guests. Chernenko was bound to evoke such feelings. . . .

The year 1984 finished with my visit to Great Britain. I arrived in London on 15 December as head of our parliamentary delegation. Fifteen years had passed since a similar delegation had visited England, although the relations between our countries had been rather strained in those years and such visits would have been helpful. Visits by parliamentary groups were then regarded as a formality, a matter of pure protocol. The Ministry of Foreign Affairs clearly did not attach much significance to our mission.

But this one turned out to be very different indeed . . .

On the second day of our stay in England we met the Prime Minister of Great Britain, Mrs Margaret Thatcher. Raisa Maksimovna and I went to Chequers, where the Prime Minister, in the company of her husband Denis and several ministers, welcomed us. Reporters were waiting for us at the entrance, and the famous photograph of the four of us, with Mrs Thatcher courteously pointing out where and how we should stand, was taken on that occasion. Funnily enough, many people later interpreted that photograph in a different way—Margaret Thatcher was supposed to have carefully scrutinized Raisa Maksimovna's clothes.

The meeting started with a lunch. Margaret Thatcher and I sat on one side of the table, Denis and Raisa Maksimovna on the other. Everything looked rather formal and proper. But even at luncheon our conversation took a rather polemic tone.

Mrs Thatcher is a confident and, I would say, a self-confident woman, the gentle charm and feminine façade disguising a rather tough and pragmatic politician. Her nickname the 'Iron Lady' is very apt. I told Mrs Thatcher: 'I know you are a person of staunch beliefs, someone who adheres to certain principles and values. This commands respect. But please consider that next to you is a person of your own ilk. And I can assure you that I am not under instructions from the Politburo to persuade you to join the Communist Party.'

After that statement she burst into a hearty laugh, and the stiff, polite and somewhat acerbic conversation flowed naturally into more interesting talk, which continued after lunch. The subject turned to disarmament problems. We started by using our prepared notes, but eventually I put mine aside while Mrs Thatcher stuffed hers into her handbag. I unfolded a large diagram representing all nuclear arsenals, grouped into a thousand little squares.

'Each of these squares,' I told Mrs Thatcher, 'suffices to eradicate all life on earth. Consequently, the available nuclear arsenals have a capacity to wipe out all life a thousand times.'

Her reaction was very eloquent and emotional. I believe she was quite sincere. Anyway, this conversation was a turning-point towards a major political dialogue between our countries. . . .

Sad news reached me while I was in London—Ustinov had died. I interrupted my stay and returned to Moscow. Ustinov's death was a grave loss, particularly painful in those troubled times. The leadership of the country was in a deplorable state. Problems arose even with the weekly Politburo meetings. Quite often Konstantin Ustinovich was unable to attend scheduled meetings—fifteen or thirty minutes before the beginning there would be a telephone call and I would be instructed to take the chair. The reaction of the Politburo members to my assumption of the chairman's role was equivocal. Some were unperturbed, considering that it was a natural development, but others showed bewilderment and even ill-disguised irritation. Tikhonov repeatedly asked rather tactlessly: 'Did he instruct you to preside over the Politburo?'

I answered: 'Nikolai Aleksandrovich, do you really think I would come and open the meeting just like that, on my own? You've got the wrong idea about me.'

By the end of the year the problem had acquired dramatic proportions, inasmuch as Chernenko had dropped out altogether. Yet no decision was made about mandating anyone, whether Gorbachev, Tikhonov or someone else, to chair the meetings on a regular basis.

I know for a fact that some comrades had suggested to Chernenko that I should be entrusted 'temporarily' with the chairmanship of the Politburo. Meanwhile the immediate entourage of the General Secretary recommended that he retain this function. And every time I was in a quandary. But it was not a question of me personally; the situation affected the work of the Politburo and the Central Committee apparatus. In these circumstances the schemers got a free hand, whereas it was a disaster so far as business was concerned.

Thinking it over I decided to follow some rules. First, to deal with the work calmly, to bring up problems firmly and make no concessions to the 'retainers', whatever their rank. Second, to be loyal to the General Secretary and consult him on all major issues. Third, to work for unity in the Politburo and prevent a collapse of central authority. And fourth, to keep the secretaries of the republic, oblast and krai committees of the Party informed of what was going on. They would have to be aware of

the gravity of the situation and understand the circumstances in which we had to
function.

I believe that, overall, this policy proved itself. Working closely with my colleagues, I tried to keep things under control, taking decisions on current affairs and
sometimes on more important issues. The renewal of cadres continued, despite the
difficulties involved. Two major plenums were held—in spring on school reform and
in October on a long-term land reclamation programme, with a report by Tikhonov.

Moreover, that winter was particularly severe. The centre was swamped with
telegrams from various areas soliciting help. In the Urals, blizzards caused such huge
snow-drifts that all traffic stopped. Hundreds, not dozens, of trains were abandoned.
The national economy was threatened with total standstill.

It was even more difficult to work when Konstantin Ustinovich was taken to
hospital. Everybody tried to argue his point by referring to a conversation with Chernenko. More often than not, one person would say one thing and the other quite the
contrary, though both had referred to the General Secretary. In the leadership and the
apparatus, factions were being formed. Some people tried to make my work more difficult, to confuse me. Others, and their number was growing, openly took the line of
backing Gorbachev.

Looking at Chernenko, who was not only unable to work but had difficulties in
speaking and breathing, I often wondered what had kept him from retiring and taking care of his health. What made him commit himself to the heavy burden of the
leadership of the country?

The answer is not easily found on the surface.

It goes without saying that anyone dismissed from power—and no-one ever retired willingly in our country—felt, to put it mildly, rather uncomfortable, like any
ousted person. But the main problem was that we had no normal democratic process
by which power could change hands. The system existed according to its own laws,
and a hopelessly sick, even senile person could sit at the top of the pyramid.

On 10 March 1985, I had barely returned home after work when the telephone
rang and Chazov informed me of Chernenko's death. After that call I immediately
contacted Gromyko, Tikhonov and Bogolyubov and convened a Politburo meeting
for eleven p.m. that night.

I arranged to meet Gromyko twenty minutes before the scheduled meeting. I
quote our conversation from memory:

'Andrei Andreyevich, we have to consolidate our effort, the moment is crucial.'

'I believe everything is clear.'

'I will proceed from the assumption that we now have to work together.'

Other Politburo and Central Committee Secretariat members began arriving.

At the start of the meeting I announced the news. We got up and there was a
moment of silence. We listened to Chazov, who had been invited to the meeting. He
briefed us on the circumstances of Chernenko's death. Having repeated my condo-
lences on Konstantin Ustinovich's demise, I stated that documents would have to be
prepared and a Central Committee plenum convened.

It was so decided. Ligachev, Bogolyubov and Sokolov were assigned the task of
organizing the speedy arrival of Central Committee members in Moscow, with the
assistance of the Ministry of Railways and the Air Force.

A funeral commission was set up, including all the Politburo members. When the
issue of the commission chairman arose there was a slight hitch. As a rule, the future
General Secretary was elected to head the commission on the funeral arrangements

for a late General Secretary. Suddenly Grishin spoke up: 'Why the hesitation about the chairman? Everything is clear. Let's appoint Mikhail Sergeyevich.'

I suggested not rushing and scheduled a plenum for five p.m. the following day, with a Politburo meeting beforehand at two p.m. There was enough time for everybody to consider the problems and reflect upon them—a whole night and half a day. The decision would be made at the Politburo, and subsequently submitted to the plenum. Soon the urgently summoned members of the Central Committee staff began assembling. Working groups were set up to draft documents. I discussed with Medvedev, Yakovlev and Boldin the main themes of the speech I was to deliver at the plenum next day.

WE CAN'T GO ON LIVING LIKE THIS

It was about four o'clock in the morning when I returned home. Raisa Maksimovna was waiting up for me. We went out in the garden. From the very beginning of our life in Moscow we never carried on serious conversations in the apartment or at the dacha, one never knew . . . We walked the garden paths for a long time discussing the events and their possible implications.

It is difficult now to reproduce the details of our talk. However, my last words that night stand out in my memory: 'You see, I have come here with hope and the belief that I shall be able to accomplish something, but so far there was not much I could have done. Therefore if I really want to change something I would have to accept the nomination—if it is made, of course. *We can't go on living like this.*'

It was almost morning. The dawn of a new and fateful day was descending upon us.

I had a telephone call from Ligachev in the morning who said that he was virtually assailed by the first secretaries, one after another, inquiring about the Politburo's stance on the choice of a new General Secretary. I went to the Central Committee. The Politburo meeting and the plenary were to be held that day.

Many different rumours are still buzzing concerning those meetings. They can be summed up as follows: allegedly, a regular fight broke out and several candidates were proposed for the post of General Secretary, so the Politburo proceeded to the plenum without reaching agreement. Nothing like that happened. And the participants in those events, many of whom are still in good health, know this well.

The problems of a successor had indeed been discussed, in view of the sharp decline in Chernenko's health. Central Committee officials talked about nothing else. There were some who did not want me. Shortly before the General Secretary's demise, Chebrikov, then head of the KGB, told me about a talk with Tikhonov, who had tried to convince him that my election to the post of General Secretary was inadmissible. Chebrikov was amazed that Tikhonov never mentioned any other name except mine.

'Did he really expect to get the job?' Chebrikov wondered.

Meanwhile, my ill-wishers must have known the mood among the people, and the feeling of the regional first secretaries, who were increasingly determined not to let the Politburo juggle another old, sick or weak person into the top position again.

Several groups of oblast Party first secretaries came to see me. They appealed to me to take a firm stand and assume the tasks of the General Secretary. One of these groups declared that they had created an organizational nucleus and had no intention of allowing the Politburo to decide this kind of problem without taking their views into account.

Ustinov, on whose support one could have counted, was no longer there. Gromyko's attitude towards me was now tinged with jealousy, particularly after my visit to Great Britain. . . .

On that day—10 March—I knew by intuition that throughout the night and half the day things would be developing in the right direction: it was corroborated by the information received by the Central Committee. Ligachev was in touch with the Party cadres and Ryzhkov with the ministers.

I should like to emphasize that I had not pronounced a definite 'yes' or 'no', not even to Ligachev and Ryzhkov. Why was that? I had to have a clear mandate. After all, I understood what was at stake. Should I get a mere 50 percent plus one vote or something like that, I would be unable to solve the current problems. Frankly speaking, had there been any opposition to my candidacy in the Politburo or the Central Committee I would have withdrawn.

At two p.m. I took over the chair—in recent times it had been my regular seat—and opened the proceedings, stating that on behalf of the Politburo we had to submit a proposal on the post of General Secretary to the Central Committee plenum. Gromyko rose immediately and proposed my nomination. The floor was then taken by Tikhonov, who supported Gromyko's proposal 'without reservation'. Grishin followed, then the others. There was unanimous backing.

The Central Committee plenum was to follow. My comrades, who had taken soundings among its members, argued that they were so much in favour of my candidacy that no debate was necessary there and no other candidacy conceivable.

The plenum opened at five p.m. I sensed from the beginning an atmosphere of full support, which was further solidified by Gromyko's speech proposing my candidacy for the post of General Secretary on behalf of the Politburo. He spoke without a written text, apparently extempore and therefore especially sincere, and charged with potent emotion. It was a well-prepared and well-thought-out address, its effect on the listeners all the greater because it echoed the mood of the audience.

I was stirred—never before did I have a chance to hear such words about myself and such great appreciation.

The atmosphere at the plenum and the thunderous applause after my name was mentioned, the unanimity of the Central Committee members in electing me General Secretary, all this showed that my closest associates and I had made the right choice when we decided that right there, in my speech at the plenum I should set forth our positions and goals. We were aware that everybody was waiting for the new Soviet leader to speak up.

Sensing this, I decided that I had to state my fundamental principles in my very first statements, even as I was bidding farewell to Chernenko. I stressed that the strategic policy developed at the XXVIth Congress and at subsequent Central Committee plenums would remain intact. It was a policy of accelerating the social and economic development of the country and seeking improvement in all aspects of the life of our society.

I must confess, however, that in this statement I deliberately ventured to stretch the point slightly. A reference to the XXVIth Congress was necessary insofar as the rules of the game had to be observed. Nevertheless, developed socialism was not mentioned, being replaced by a reference to accelerated social and economic progress in the light of new ideas. I emphasized that accelerating our progress was possible only if we shifted the national economy onto the path of intensive development, rapidly achieved leading positions in science and technology, and a world-class level of labour productivity. All this required perseverance in upgrading the economic mechanism and the system of management in its entirety.

In conjunction with the economic tasks, mention was made of the need to focus our attention on social policy, the improvement and development of democracy, and the formation of a social consciousness. Other issues concerned order, discipline, and legality. I emphasized the need for transparency (*glasnost*) in the work of Party, Soviet, state and public organizations.

With regard to foreign policy: continuity in the efforts to implement the policy of peace and progress. Our positions were expounded with utmost clarity: 'We want to stop and not to continue the arms race and, consequently, propose to freeze nuclear arsenals and stop further deployment of missiles; we want a genuine and large-scale reduction of accumulated armaments and not the creation of new arms systems.'

Referring to the CPSU I noted that the Party was a force capable of uniting society, thereby facilitating the enormous changes that were simply imperative. In conclusion, I expressed my firm conviction that we would be able to unfold the creative forces of socialism on a larger scale.

This was our declaration of intent. The ideas it contained had not crept up unexpectedly. Many of them were already present in earlier speeches. Now the emphasis was stronger, the problems raised more pointedly than before. The main objective was to reach the public consciousness and to stress the need for profound changes—and to show that our intentions were of the most resolute nature. . . .

There was a sense, an intuition, that an era was coming to a close. In less than three years, three General Secretaries, three leaders of the country, had died. So had many of the prominent Politburo leaders. Kosygin died at the end of 1980. In January 1982, it was Suslov's turn. In November, Brezhnev. In May 1983, Pelshe. In February 1984, Andropov. In December, Ustinov. In March 1985, Chernenko.

All this was fraught with symbolic meaning. The very system was dying away; its sluggish senile blood no longer contained any vital juices.

I realized the weight of responsibility I had to shoulder.

Mikhail Gorbachev, from *Memoirs* (New York: Doubleday, 1995), pp. 146–148, 150–156, 160–168.

Election of Mikhail Gorbachev as General Secretary of the Communist Party of the Soviet Union

The very evening of Chernenko's death, the Politburo of the Communist Party of the Soviet Union (CPSU) chose Mikhail Gorbachev as chair of the funeral commission. This symbolic election meant that he had been slated to succeed Chernenko as general secretary of the party. Earlier, at the time of his final illness in 1983–1984, Andropov had indicated that Gorbachev should succeed him, but the older members of the Politburo, fearful of a young reformer, conspired to elect the frail Chernenko instead. Yet during the year of Chernenko's ineffective rule, Gorbachev emerged as the clear heir apparent. The official stenographic report of the session of the Politburo that made the fateful decision to give the top job to Gorbachev is strikingly dry and formal; the discussions and intrigues had already led to the only possible decision. Here only unity, indeed unanimity, was displayed. The venerable Andrei Gromyko

(1909–1989), Minister of Foreign Affairs since 1957, then carried the resolution to the Central Committee (CC), where he spoke of Gorbachev's warm smile and iron teeth, his congenial personality and his "Bolshevik" toughness. There too the members unanimously placed their country's (and their own) fate in Gorbachev's hands.

Comp[letely] secret
Only Copy
(Working Notes)

SESSION OF THE POLITBURO OF THE CC OF THE CPSU

March 11, 1985

Chair: Comrade M. S. Gorbachev

Present: Comrades G. A. Aliev, V. I. Vorotnikov, V. V. Grishin, A. A. Gromyko, D. A. Kunaev, G. V. Romanov, M. S. Solmentsev, N. A. Tikhonov, P. N. Demichev, V. I. Dolgikh, V. V. Kuznetsov, B. N. Ponomarev, V. M. Chebrikov, E. A. Shevardnadze, M. V. Zimianin, I. V. Kapitonov, E. K. Ligachev, K. V. Rusakov, N. I. Ryzhkov.

GORBACHEV: Comrades, yesterday at 7:20 pm Konstantinov Ustinovich Chernenko died. His death followed a long and serious illness. We have lost our dear and respected friend, a leader, the General Secretary of the Central Committee of the CPSU, the Chairman of the Presidium of the Supreme Soviet of the USSR. I request that we honor the blessed memory of Konstantin Ustinovich Chernenko with a minute of silence.

(Everyone stands)

GORBACHEV: Comrade Chazov [the Kremlin doctor] is here. I give him the floor.

[Chazov reports on Chernenko's illness and death].

GORBACHEV: His sickness was in fact very serious. We all saw this ourselves. The doctors, of course, tried to help the patient, but the illness was so serious that therapeutic measures taken by the doctors were without positive result. It is very hard to imagine that Konstantin Ustinovich is no longer among us.

But life goes on, there is nothing you can do. We gathered today in order to decide questions connected with the funeral of Konstantin Ustinovich, with personnel matters, and with the convening of a special plenum of the CC of the CPSU.

TIKHONOV: Yes, all these questions must be decided by us immediately.

I. *On the matter of the General Secretary of the CC of the CPSU*

GORBACHEV: Considering that all members and candidates for membership of the Politburo of the CC CPSU are present, as well as all the secretaries of the CC CPSU, with the exception of Comrade Shcherbitskii, who is now on route here, it is essential before anything else to decide the question of the General Secretary of the CC CPSU. I request that the comrades express themselves on this question.

GROMYKO: Of course, all of us are depressed by Konstantin Ustinovich Chernenko's passing. But no matter what feelings grip us, we ought to look to the future and should not give up our historic optimism, our faith in the rightness of our theory and practice.

I will speak frankly. When you think about a candidate for the post of General Secretary of the CC CPSU, then, of course, you think of Mikhail Sergeevich Gorbachev. This would be, in my view, absolutely the right choice. You all know Mikhail Sergeevich well. We have worked together with him seven years. I remember how L. I. Brezhnev was interested in my opinions and in the opinions of other comrades when we spoke about the transfer of M. S. Gorbachev to work in Moscow. I do not doubt that we all correctly supported this proposition.

What qualities first impress you when you evaluate the considerations of Mikhail Sergeevich?

First, is his indomitable creative energy, the striving to do more and do it better.

Second. This is his attitude toward people. The higher a person stands, the greater the role his ability to get along with people, his principled and exacting relationships, plays. No one says about Mikhail Sergeevich that his personal views prevail. No, he always places the interests of the party, the interests of society, the interests of the people first.

Third. M. S. Gorbachev has enormous experience in party work. This experience includes work both in the provinces and in the center. He worked as a secretary of the CC, was a candidate member of the Politburo, and finally a full member of the Politburo. He led the meetings of the Secretariat, as well as the Politburo in the absence of Konstantin Ustinovich. For such work it is necessary to have not only knowledge but also endurance, party feeling [*partiinost'*]. This is a very valuable quality.

One more consideration. When we glance into the future, we ought to sense future developments. And this means that we do not have the right to allow any breaking of our unity. We have no right to allow the world to notice the slightest crack in our relationships, or to speculate about this abroad. And this means we must act together, united, with knowledge of our full responsibility for our great cause.

I do not pretend that I have noted all the qualities of Mikhail Sergeevich. But I think that, without hesitation, we can say that we make no mistake if we elect him General Secretary of the CC of the CPSU. I want once more to emphasize that he possesses great knowledge and significant experience, but this experience must be increased by our experience. And we promise to help and work in all possible ways with our new General Secretary. You, Mikhail Sergeevich, can rely fully on this collaboration and help.

TIKHONOV: We have recently worked a great deal with Mikhail Sergeevich Gorbachev. We got to know each other especially closely during the work of the Commission on the Perfection of the Economic Mechanism.

What can I say about Mikhail Sergeevich? This is a person who keeps in touch, with whom it is possible to discuss questions, discuss them on a very high level. This is the first of the secretaries of the CC who knows the economy well. You can imagine how important that is. Tomorrow we will bury Konstantin Ustinovich Chernenko, but we cannot postpone questions of the development of the economy; they will not wait. We must decide them and decide them together, just as we did in close contact between the Central Committee of the party and the government.

For this reason my unequivocal opinion is: the person who deserves to be General Secretary of the CC CPSU is Mikhail Sergeevich Gorbachev. Here is a person who possesses the knowledge, experience, and ability to work with people. For this reason I consider that we can put forth the candidacy of Mikhail Sergeevich Gorbachev to the plenum of the CC CPSU with full confidence.

GRISHIN: We are deciding today an exceptionally important question. I am speaking about the continuation of the cause of the party, about the succession of the leadership. The General Secretary of the CC is the person who organizes the work of the Central Committee. Therefore a person should occupy this post who meets the highest requirements. He ought to possess knowledge and principle and experience and, besides this, very great tolerance. When we learned yesterday about the death of Konstantin Ustinovich, we to some extent already decided this question, agreeing to confirm Mikhail Sergeevich the chairman of the funeral commission. In my view, he meets the requirements needed by the General Secretary of the CC to the highest degree. This is a very erudite man. He graduated from the law school of Moscow University and the economics department of the agricultural institute. He has much experience in party work. Therefore, I think that we have a proposal, and cannot have any other but the proposal to put forth M. S. Gorbachev for election to the post of General Secretary of the CC of the CPSU. As for us, each of us at his post will support him actively. . . .

[Similar speeches were given in turn by Solomentsev, Kunaev, Aliev, Romanov, Vorotnikov, Ponomarev, Chebrikov, Dolgikh, and Kuznetsov.]

SHEVARDNADZE: It is very good that each of us has the opportunity to speak at this historic meeting. This once more is characteristic of the genuinely Leninist collective style of the work of the Central Committee of the party, its Politburo. I knew Mikhail Sergeevich Gorbachev before he came to work as a secretary of the CC of the CPSU. I will say frankly that after his election to the Politburo of the CC, he remained the same simple, modest, and responsible person. We have a huge multinational country. And I know how sensitively and attentively Mikhail Sergeevich Gorbachev deals with the national question. This is a great, most important quality for the General Secretary of the CC of the CPSU, and I will say frankly that our whole country and our whole party awaits such a decision. I have no doubts whatsoever.

DEMICHEV: I will speak very briefly. I am sure that today we are making the completely correct choice. Mikhail Sergeevich Gorbachev is well known in our country. He is pretty well known abroad as well. He is able to work abroad, as is convincingly shown by his trips to England, Canada, and the People's Republic of Bulgaria.

GROMYKO: And Italy as well.

DOLGIKH: Mikhail Sergeevich Gorbachev has a feel for the new, a great erudition and organizational talent. This is a charming fellow. It is not a secret, is it, that after the death of Iu. V. Andropov, he was concerned with all aspects of the work of the Central Committee, but especially did much in the field of development of our agroindustrial complex. Without exaggeration one can say that our scholars, creative intelligentsia, and writers are attracted to him. All in all, this is a completely worthy person for such a high post.

[Similar speeches were given by Kapitonov, Ligachev, Ryzhkov, and Rusakov.]

GORBACHEV: First of all, I would like to say that the most important, the principal thing is that our meeting of the Politburo today occurred in the spirit of unity. We have gone through a very complicated period of change. Our economy needs great dynamism. Our democracy and the development of our foreign policy need this dynamism.

I understood very well that in the end the Politburo of the CC of the CPSU would always find the necessary resolution, would always have come up with the needed candidate. But since today the speeches are about me, then I take all your words with a feeling of great excitement and anxiety. With these feelings I listen to you, dear friends.

I understand extremely well that we are speaking about extraordinarily difficult work. To undertake it without support, without an atmosphere of mutual understanding in the Politburo, is practically impossible. That is why I, time and again, conclude to myself that collectivity and unity are the priceless qualities of our party, of our Central Committee, of our Politburo.

Nine years of my work in Stavropol Province and seven years working here have shown me with all clarity that our party contains enormous creative potential. It has this potential first of all because the people actively support the Communists. The latest elections to the Supreme Soviet and local soviets convincingly affirm this. These elections demonstrate the great confidence of the people in our party and at the same time show what great responsibility lies on our shoulders.

I see as my task first of all to search together with you for new resolutions, paths for further forward movement of our country, paths for elevating the economic and defensive power of the Motherland, improving of the lives of our people.

I am deeply devoted to the idea of collective work and think that this is a potential that we have far from completely used. We ought to use our collective potential even more actively to realize yet greater return.

We do not need to change our policy. It is a true, correct, genuinely Leninist policy. We must pick up the tempo, move forward, expose inadequacies and overcome them, see clearly our bright future.

I assure you that I will do everything to justify the great confidence of the party, your confidence, comrades. I will do everything to make our harmonious work go smoothly. And I have great hopes for our mutual support, for our unity.

All the members of the Politburo, candidate members of the Politburo, and secretaries of the CC have expressed themselves here. Thus, as I understand, your opinion is unanimous, and we can go to the Plenum of the CC of the CPSU, which opens in thirty minutes, with a united recommendation.

MEMBERS OF THE POLITBURO: Correct.

GORBCHEV: It is clear that it would be sensible, considering that A. A. Gromyko spoke first today, that we charge him with taking the resolution approved by the Politburo to be examined by the Plenum of the CC of the CPSU.

MEMBERS OF THE POLITBURO: Correct, A. A. Gromyko may be so charged.

The resolution is adopted. . . .

RTsKhIDNI, f. 89, op. 36, d. 16, ll. 1–14; translated by the editor.

===== Nina Andreeva, "I Cannot Give Up My Principles" =====

At home, Gorbachev's coalition of reformers began to fracture in 1987. Ligachev was resistant to any changes that weakened the grip of the Communist party on society, and he particularly opposed the greater freedom of expression in the country. Yeltsin, on the other hand, considered the pace of reform to be too slow and the direction not radical enough. In October, he spoke out at a Central Committee plenum, stirring up a storm of debate that led to his dismissal. Though he briefly went into decline, Yeltsin soon emerged as a martyr of the Communist conservatives and the champion of the "democratic" forces. Early the next year, the conservatives found a voice in an obscure Leningrad schoolteacher, Nina Andreeva, who published an open letter to the country's leaders defending the old Soviet traditions. To many it appeared as if Ligachev had had a hand in publishing the letter at a time when Gorbachev and Iakovlev were out of the country. The Politburo spent two days discussing the letter, and there was much sentiment in favor of her views. But Gorbachev insisted that the letter was an attack on perestroika, and the highest party body authorized Iakovlev to write a refutation. Ligachev and the conservatives suffered a major defeat. But Nina Andreeva's letter remained a manifesto of the conservative Communist opposition to perestroika.

"I CANNOT GIVE UP MY PRINCIPLES"

Letter to the Editors From an Instructor at a Leningrad Higher School. By Nina Andreyeva

I decided to write this letter after a great deal of thought. I am a chemist, and I teach at the Leningrad Soviet Technological Institute in Leningrad. Like many others, I am an adviser for a group of students. In our days, after a period of social apathy and intellectual dependence, students are gradually beginning to be charged with the energy of revolutionary changes. Naturally, debates arise—about the paths of restructuring and its economic and ideological aspects. Openness, candor and the disappearance of zones closed to criticism, as well as emotional fervor in the mass consciousness, especially among young people, are frequently manifested in the posing of problems that, to one extent or another, have been "prompted" by Western radio voices or by those of our compatriots who are not firm in their notions about the essence of socialism. What a wide range of topics is being discussed! A multiparty system, freedom of religious propaganda, leaving the country to live abroad, the right to a broad discussion of sexual problems in the press, the need for the decentralization of the management of culture, the abolition of compulsory military service—Among students, a particularly large number of arguments are about the country's past. . . .

So much has been written and said about the Great Patriotic War and the heroism of those who took part in it. But recently a meeting took place in one of our

Technological Institute's student dormitories with Hero of the Soviet Union V. F. Molozev, a retired colonel. One of the things he was asked about was political repressions in the Army. The veteran replied that he had not encountered any repressions, and that many of those who had started off the war with him and seen it through to the end had become major military commanders. Some of the students were disappointed with his answer. The now commonplace subject of repression has become excessively magnified in the perception of some young people, pushing an objective comprehension of the past into the background. Examples of this sort are not rare.

It's very gratifying, of course, that even "technos" [*tekhnari*] have a lively interest in theoretical problems of the social sciences. But too many things have turned up that I cannot accept, that I cannot agree with. The constant harping on "terrorism," "the people's political servility," "uninspired social vegetating," "our spiritual slavery," "universal fear," "the entrenched rule of louts"—It is from these mere threads that the history of the period of the transition to socialism in our country is often woven. Therefore, it comes as no surprise, for example, that in some students nihilistic views are intensifying, and ideological confusion, a dislocation of political reference points and even ideological omnivorousness are appearing. Sometimes one hears assertions that it is time to call to account the Communists who supposedly "dehumanized" the country's life after 1917.

At the February plenary session of the Central Committee, it was emphasized once again that it is urgently necessary for "young people to learn the class vision of the world and gain an understanding of the connection between common human and class interests. This includes an understanding of the class essence of the changes taking place in our country."[1] This vision of history and the present day is incompatible with political anecdotes, base gossip and the highly dramatic fantasies that one can frequently encounter today.

I read and reread the much-talked-about articles. What, for example, can they give young people except disorientation and revelations "about the counterrevolution in the USSR at the beginning of the 1930s" and about Stalin's "guilt" for the coming to power of fascism and Hitler in Germany? Or a public "counting" of the number of "Stalinists" in various generations and social groups?

We are Leningraders, so it was with special interest that we recently viewed the excellent documentary film about S. M. Kirov. But the text accompanying the shots at some points not only diverged from the film-document but also gave it a certain ambiguity. For example, shots in the film show an explosion of enthusiasm and joie de vivre and the elan of people who were building socialism, while the narrator's text speaks of repression and lack of information.

Probably I am not the only one who has been struck by the fact that the calls of Party leaders to turn the attention of the "unmaskers" back to the facts of real achievements at various stages of socialist construction are drawing, as if on command, more and more flare-ups of "exposes." A noteworthy phenomenon in this, alas, unfruitful field is the plays of M. Shatrov. . . . In "The Peace of Brest" [*Brestsky mir*], Lenin, at the will of the playwright and the director, kowtows to Trotsky. What a symbolic embodiment of the author's conception. It is developed further in the play "Onward, Onward, Onward!" [*Dalshe, dalshe, dalshe!*]. A play is not a historical treatise, of course.

---

1. The quotation is from Ye. K. Ligachev's report on education at the plenary session.

But after all, in a work of art the truth is ensured by nothing so much as the author's position. Especially if what we're talking about is political theater.

The playwright Shatrov's position has been analyzed in a detailed and well-reasoned way in reviews by historians that were published in *Pravda* and *Sovetskaya Rossia*. I would like to express my opinion as well. In particular, I can't help agreeing with the contention that Shatrov deviates substantially from the accepted principles of socialist realism. In elucidating an extremely crucial period in the history of our country, he elevates the subjective factor of the development of society to the status of an absolute and clearly ignores the objective laws of history that are manifested in the activity of classes and of the masses. The role of the proletarian masses and the Party of Bolsheviks is reduced here to the "background" against which the actions of irresponsible politicians unfold.

Guided by the Marxist-Leninist methodology for studying concrete historical processes, the reviewers convincingly showed that Shatrov distorts the history of socialism in our country. . . .

Unfortunately, the reviewers did not succeed in showing that, for all his authorial pretensions, the playwright is not original. It seems to me that, in the logic of his evaluations and arguments, he is very close to the themes of B. Souvarine's book ["Stalin: A Critical Survey of Bolshevism"—Trans.], which was published in Paris in 1935. In his play, Shatrov puts into his characters' mouths what was asserted by opponents of Leninism concerning the course of the Revolution, Lenin's role in it, relations among members of the Central Committee at different stages of the inner-Party struggle—That is the essence of Shatrov's "new reading" of Lenin. I will add that even A. Rybakov, the author of "Children of the Arbat" [*Deti Arbata*], has frankly admitted that he borrowed certain plot elements from emigre publications.

While I have not yet read the play "Onward, Onward, Onward!" (it has not been published), I have read laudatory reviews of it in some publications. What could such haste mean? Then I learned that a stage production is being hurriedly prepared.

Shortly after the February plenary session, Pravda published a letter headed "A New Round?," signed by eight of our leading theater people. They warn against what, in their opinion, are possible delays in the staging of M. Shatrov's latest play. This conclusion is drawn from critical assessments of the play that have appeared in the newspapers. For some reason, the letter writers exclude the authors of critical reviews from the ranks of those "to whom the fatherland is dear." Just how does this harmonize with their desire to have a "stormy and impassioned" discussion of the problems of our history, some of it recent and some rather old? What does it come down to—are they the only ones who are allowed to have an opinion of their own? . . .

In talking with students and pondering crucial problems with them, I automatically come to the conclusion that a good many distortions and one-sided views have piled up in our country, notions that obviously need to be corrected. I want to devote special attention to some of these things.

Take the question of the place of J.V. Stalin in our country's history. It is with his name that the entire obsession with critical attacks is associated, an obsession that, in my opinion, has to do not so much with the historical personality itself as with the whole extremely complex transitional era—an era linked with the unparalleled exploit of an entire generation of Soviet people who today are gradually retiring from active labor, political and public activity. Industrialization, collectivization and the cultural revolution, which brought our country into the ranks of the great world powers, are being forcibly squeezed into the "personality cult" formula. All these things are being questioned. Things have reached a point at which insistent demands for "repentance" are being made on "Stalinists" (and one can assign to their number whomever one wishes). Praise is being lavished on novels and films that lynch the era of tempestuous changes, which is presented as a "tragedy of peoples."

Let me note at the outset that neither I nor the members of my family have any relationship to Stalin or his entourage, retainers or extollers. My father was a worker in the Leningrad port, and my mother was a mechanic at the Kirov Plant. My older brother worked there, too. He, my father and my sister were killed in battles against the Hitlerites. One of my relatives was repressed and was rehabilitated after the 20th Party Congress. Together with all Soviet people, I share the anger and indignation over the large-scale repressions that took place in the 1930s and 1940s through the fault of the Party and state leadership of that time. But common sense resolutely protests the monochromatic coloring of contradictory events that has now begun to prevail in certain press organs.

I support the Party's call to uphold the honor and dignity of the trailblazers of socialism. I think that it is from these Party and class positions that we should assess the historical role of all Party and state leaders, including Stalin. In this case, one must not reduce the matter to the "court" aspect or to abstract moralizing by people far removed from that stormy time and from the people who lived and worked then. Indeed, they worked in such a way that what they did is an inspirational example for us even today.

For me and for many other people, the decisive role in assessing Stalin is played by the firsthand testimony of contemporaries who came into direct contact with him, on both our side of the barricades and the other side. Those in the latter group are not without interest. For example, take Churchill, who in 1919 was proud of his personal contribution to organizing the military intervention of 14 foreign states against the young Soviet Republic but who, exactly 40 years later, was forced to use the following words to characterize Stalin—one of his most formidable political opponents:

"He was a man of outstanding personality who left an impression on our harsh times, the period in which his life ran its course. Stalin was a man of extraordinary energy, erudition and inflexible will, blunt, tough and merciless in both action and conversation, whom even I, reared in the British Parliament, was at a loss to counter. His works resounded with gigantic strength. This strength was so great in Stalin that he seemed unique among leaders of all times and peoples. . . . This was a man who used his enemies' hands to destroy his enemy, who made us, whom he openly called imperialists, do battle against imperialists. He found Russia with a wooden plow, but he left it equipped with atomic weapons" [retranslated from the Russian—Trans.]. This assessment and admission on the part of a faithful guardian of the British Empire cannot be attributed to dissimulation or political expediency.

The basic elements of this characterization can also be found in the memoirs of De Gaulle and in the reminiscences and correspondence of other European and American political figures who dealt with Stalin, both as a wartime ally and as a class adversary. . . .

From long and frank discussions with young people, we draw the conclusion that the attacks on the state of the dictatorship of the proletariat and on the leaders of our country at that time have not only political, ideological and moral causes but also their own social substratum. There are quite a few people who have a stake in broadening the staging area of these attacks, and not just on the other side of our borders. Along with the professional anticommunists in the West, who long ago chose the supposedly democratic slogan of "anti-Stalinism," there live and thrive the descendants of the classes overthrown by the October Revolution, by no means all of whom have been able to forget the material and social losses of their forebears. One must include here the spiritual heirs of Dan, Martov and others in the category of Russian Social Democratism, the spiritual followers of Trotsky or Yagoda, and the descendants of the NEPmen, the Basmachi [participants in armed resistance to Soviet rule in Central Asia in 1918–1924—Trans.] and the kulaks, who bear a grudge against socialism.

As is known, any historical figure is shaped by specific social, economic, ideological and political conditions, which have a determining influence on the subjective and objective selection of aspirants who are called upon to solve various social problems. Having come to the forefront of history, such an aspirant, in order to "remain afloat," must satisfy the requirements of the era and of the leading social and political structures and must realize an objective pattern in his activity, inevitably leaving the "imprint" of his personality on historical events. In the final analysis, for example, few people today are disturbed by the personal qualities of Peter the Great, but everyone remembers that the country rose to the level of a great European power during this rule. Time has condensed the result that is now contained in our assessment of the historical personality of the Emperor Peter. And the ever-present flowers on his sarcophagus in the cathedral of the Peter and Paul Fortress embody the respect and gratitude of our contemporaries, who are far removed from the autocracy.

I think that, no matter how contradictory and complex a given figure in Soviet history may be, his true role in the construction and defense of socialism will, sooner or later, receive an objective and unambiguous assessment. Needless to say, it will be unambiguous not in the sense of being one-sided, of whitewashing or eclectically summing up contradictory phenomena, of an assessment that makes it possible, with qualifications, to create any kind of subjectivism, to "forgive or not forgive," to "discard or keep" elements of history. An unambiguous assessment means above all a historically concrete, nonopportunistic assessment that manifests—in terms of historical result!—the dialectics of the conformity of a given individual's activity to the basic laws of the development of society. In our country, these laws were also connected with the resolution of the question "Who will win?," in its domestic and international aspects. If we are to follow the Marxist-Leninist methodology of historical research, then we must first of all, in M. S. Gorbachev's words, vividly show how millions of people lived, how they worked and what they believed in, and how victories and setbacks, discoveries and mistakes, the radiant and the tragic, the revolutionary enthusiasm of the masses and violations of socialist legality, and sometimes even crimes, were combined.

For me, there is no doubt that, in the question of assessing Stalin's activity, the Party Central Committee's resolution on overcoming the personality cult and its effects, adopted in 1956, and the report of the General Secretary of the CPSU Central Committee devoted to the 70th anniversary of the Great October Socialist Revolution remain the scientific guidelines to this day.

Recently, one of my students startled me with the revelation that the class struggle is supposedly an obsolete concept, as is the leading role of the proletariat. It would be all right if she were the only one maintaining such a thing. But, for example, a furious argument broke out recently over a respected academician's assertion that the present relations between states of the two different social and economic systems are devoid of class content. I admit that the academician did not deem it necessary to explain why for several decades he had written the exact opposite—that peaceful coexistence is nothing other than a form of class struggle in the international arena. It turns out that the philosopher has now repudiated that notion. Well, views do change. However, it seems to me that the duty of a leading philosopher does enjoin him to explain, at least to those who have learned and are learning from his books: What—does the international working class today, in the form of its state and political organs, really no longer act as a countervailing force to world capital?

It seems to me that the same question—which class or stratum of society is the guiding and mobilizing force of restructuring?—is at the center of many current debates. This was talked about, among other things, in an interview with the writer A. Prokhanov in our city newspaper *Leningradsky rabochy* [Leningrad Worker]. Prokhanov proceeds from the premise that the special nature of the present state of social consciousness is characterized by the existence of two ideological currents or, as he says, "alternative towers" that are trying, from different directions, to overcome the "socialism that has been built in battle" in our country. While he exaggerates the significance and acuteness of the mutual confrontation between these "towers," the writer nevertheless rightly emphasizes that "they agree only on exterminating socialist values." But both, their ideologists assure us, are "in favor of restructuring."

The first, and deepest, ideological current that has already revealed itself in the course of restructuring claims to be a model of some kind of left-liberal dilettantish socialism, to be the exponent of a humanism that is very true and "clean" from class incrustations. Against proletarian collectivism, the adherents of this current put up "the intrinsic worth of the individual"—with modernistic quests in the field of culture, God-seeking tendencies, technocratic idols, the preaching of the "democratic" charms of present-day capitalism and fawning over its achievements, real and imagined. Its representatives assert that we have built the wrong kind of socialism and that only today, "for the first time in history, has an alliance come about between the political leadership and the progressive intelligentsia." At a time when millions of people on our planet are dying from hunger, epidemics and imperialism's military adventures, they demand the immediate drafting of a "legal code for the protection of animal rights," ascribe a singular, supernatural intelligence to nature, and claim that cultivation is not a social but a biological quality, transmitted genetically from parents to children. Tell me: What does all this mean?

It is the champions of "left-liberal socialism" who are shaping the tendency to falsify the history of socialism. They suggest to us that in the country's past only the mistakes and crimes are real, in doing so keeping quiet about the supreme achievements of the past and the present. Laying claim to complete historical truth, they substitute scholastic ethical categories for social and political criteria of the development of society. I would very much like to understand: Who needs, and why, to have every prominent leader of the Party Central Committee and the Soviet government compromised after he leaves office and discredited in connection with his actual or supposed mistakes and miscalculations, made while solving some very complex problems on roads uncharted by history? Where did we get this passion for squandering the prestige and dignity of the leaders of the world's first socialist country?

Another special feature of the views of the "left-liberals" is an obvious or camouflaged cosmopolitan tendency, a sort of nationality-less "internationalism." I have read somewhere that when, after the Revolution, a delegation of merchants and factory owners came to the Petrograd Soviet to see Trotsky "as a Jew," complaining of oppression by Red Guards, he declared that he was "not a Jew but an internationalist," which thoroughly bewildered the supplicants.

For Trotsky, the concept of the "national" meant a kind of inferiority and narrowness in comparison to the "international." That's why he emphasized the "national tradition" of October, wrote about "the national element in Lenin," maintained that the Russian people "had received no cultural legacy," etc. For some reason, we are ashamed to say that it was the Russian proletariat, which the Trotskyists slighted as "backward and uncultured," that carried out, in Lenin's words, "the three Russian Revolutions," or that the Slavic peoples were in the vanguard of mankind's battle against fascism.

Of course, what I have said does not signify any disparagement of the historical contribution of other nations and nationalities. It only, as the current saying goes, ensures a full measure of historical truth. When students ask me how it could have happened that thousands of villages in the Non-Black-Earth Zone and Siberia have become deserted, I reply that this, too, is the high price paid for victory [in World War II] and the postwar rehabilitation of the national economy, as is the irretrievable loss of large numbers of monuments of Russian national culture. I am also convinced that the pacifist erosion of defense and patriotic consciousness, as well as the desire to list the slightest manifestation of national pride by Great Russians under the heading of great-power chauvinism, stem from disparagement of the significance of historical consciousness.

Here is something else that alarms me: Militant cosmopolitanism is now linked with the practice of "refusenikism"—of "refusing" socialism. Unfortunately, we suddenly think of this only when its neophytes plague us with their outrages in front of Smolny or under the Kremlin's walls. Moreover, we are somehow gradually being trained to see this phenomenon as an almost inoffensive change of "place of residence," not as class and nationality betrayal by persons most of whom have been graduated from higher schools and graduate schools at public expense. In general, some people are inclined to look at "refusenikism" as some kind of manifestation of "democracy" and "human rights," feeling that the talents of those involved have been prevented from blossoming by "stagnant socialism." Well, if over there, in the "free world," their tireless enterprise and "genius" aren't appreciated and selling their conscience doesn't interest the special services, they can come back— . . .

Whereas the "neoliberals" are oriented toward the West, the other "alternative tower" (to use Prokhanov's expression), the "guardians and traditionalists," seeks to "overcome socialism by moving backward"—in other words, to return to the social forms of presocialist Russia. The spokesmen for this unique "peasant socialism" are fascinated with this image. In their opinion, a loss of the moral values that the peasant community had accumulated through the dim haze of centuries took place 100 years ago. The "traditionalists" have rendered undoubted services in exposing corruption, in fairly solving ecological problems, in combating alcoholism, in protecting historical monuments and in countering the dominance of mass culture, which they rightly assess as a psychosis of consumerism.

At the same time, the views of the ideologists of "peasant socialism" contain a misunderstanding of the historical significance of October for the fatherland's fate, a one-sided appraisal of collectivization as "frightful arbitrary treatment of the peasantry," uncritical views on religious-mystical Russian philosophy, old tsarist concepts in scholarship relating to our country's history, and an unwillingness to see the postrevolutionary stratification of the peasantry and the revolutionary role of the working class.

In the class struggle in the countryside, for example, there is frequently an overemphasis on "village" commissars who "shot middle peasants in the back." There were, of course, all kinds of commissars in our enormous country, which had been stirred to new life by the Revolution. But the basic tenor of our life was determined by those commissars who were themselves shot. It was they who had stars cut into their backs or were burned alive. The "attacking class" had to pay not only with the lives of commissars, Chekists [state security personnel], village Bolsheviks, members of poor peasants' committees and "twenty-thousanders" [industrial workers who helped in the collectivization of agriculture in the early 1930s—Trans.], but also those of the first tractor drivers, rural correspondents, girl-teachers and rural Young Communists, with the lives of tens of thousands of other unknown fighters for socialism.

The difficulties in the upbringing of young people are deepened still more by the fact that unofficial [neformalny] organizations and associations are being created in the pattern of the ideas of the "neoliberals" and "neo-Slavophiles." In some cases, extremist elements capable of provocations are gaining the upper hand in the leadership of these groups. Recently, the politicization of these grass-roots [samodeyatelny] organizations on the basis of a pluralism that is far from socialist has been noted. Frequently the leaders of these organizations talk about "power-sharing" on the basis of a "parliamentary regime," "free trade unions," "autonomous publishing houses," etc. In my opinion, all this makes it possible to draw the conclusion that the main and cardinal question in the debates now under way in the country is the question of recognizing or not recognizing the leading role of the Party and the working class in socialist construction, and hence in restructuring—needless to say, with all the theoretical and practical conclusions for politics, the economy and ideology that stem therefrom. . . .

Today, the question of the role and place of socialist ideology has taken on a very acute form. Under the aegis of a moral and spiritual "cleansing," the authors of opportunistic constructs are eroding the boundaries and criteria of scientific ideology, manipulating openness, and propagating an extrasocialist pluralism, which objectively impedes restructuring in social consciousness. This is having an especially detrimental effect on young people, something that, I repeat, we higher-school instructors, schoolteachers and all those who deal with young people's problems are distinctly aware of. As M. S. Gorbachev said at the February plenary session of the CPSU Central Committee: "In the spiritual sphere as well, and perhaps in this sphere first of all, we must be guided by our Marxist-Leninist principles. Comrades, we must not forgo these principles under any pretexts."

We stand on this, and we will continue to do so. We have not received these principles as a gift: We have gained them through suffering at decisive turning points in the history of the fatherland.

Sovetskaia Rossiia, March 13, 1988, p. 3; condensed and translated in *The Current Digest of the Soviet Press*, XL, 13 (1990), pp. 1–6.

The Rehabilitation of Bukharin

Part of the glasnost' campaign, according to Gorbachev, was filling in the "blank pages" of Soviet history. A stream of historical texts, documentary films, novels, and memoirs appeared, avidly devoured by the public's seemingly insatiable appetite for revelations about the Soviet past. At first the rehabilitations of repressed Communists and innocent victims of Stalinism suggested that an improved, purified form of Soviet socialism would be constructed. This was certainly Gorbachev's intention. Bukharin was an iconic figure, a "soft" Bolshevik, close to Lenin, opposed to Stalin, and favoring a gradualist, less violent road to socialism. The New Economic Policy that he had promoted in the 1920s seemed to provide an alternative to the command economy that had an impeccably Leninist pedigree. The biography of Bukharin by the American historian Stephen F. Cohen was translated and published in Russian, and Gorbachev read it, though he told Cohen that he had some disagreements with it.[1] But this "Leninist" moment passed quickly, and as darker revelations about the pre-Stalinist years of Soviet power and of Lenin's role in repression during the civil war appeared, the erosion of faith in any form of socialism tore at the very foundations of the Soviet system.

IN THE COMMISSION OF THE POLITBURO
OF THE CPSU CENTRAL COMMITTEE

On the Additional Study of Materials Connected With the Repressions That Took Place During the 1930s and 1940s and the Early 1950s

At its session on Feb. 5, 1988, the commission heard a report from the Chairman of the USSR Supreme Court on the results of its examination of the protest lodged by the USSR Prosecutor General in the case of N. I. Bukharin, A. I. Rykov, A. P. Rozengolts, M. A. Chernov, P. P. Bulanov, L. G. Levin, I. N. Kazakov, V. A. Maksimov-Dikovsky, P. P. Kryuchkov and Kh. G. Rakovsky, who had been held criminally responsible in the case of the so-called "anti-Soviet right-Trotskyist bloc."

These persons were convicted by the Military Collegium of the USSR Supreme Court in March 1938 on charges that, on assignment from the intelligence services of foreign states hostile to the USSR, they had organized a conspiratorial group with the aim of overthrowing the socialist, social and state system existing in the USSR and had conducted sabotage, wrecking, terrorist and other hostile activity.

It has been established that the preliminary investigation in this case was conducted with flagrant violations of socialist legality, that facts were falsified, and that confessions were extracted from the accused by unlawful methods.

The commission took note of the announcement by the Chairman of the USSR Supreme Court to the effect that a plenary session of the Supreme Court, by a resolution dated Feb. 4, 1988, has rescinded the sentence of the Military Collegium against the convicted persons N. I. Bukharin, A. I. Rykov, A. P. Rozengolts, M. A. Chernov, P. P. Bulanov, L. G. Levin, I. N. Kazakov, V. A. Maksimov-Dikovsky, P. P. Kryuchkov and Kh. G. Rakovsky and has dismissed the case, owing to the absence of a corpus delicti in their actions.

Earlier, the USSR Supreme Court, in the same case and for the same reasons, had fully rehabilitated N. N. Krestinsky, G. F. Grinko, I. A. Zelensky, V. I. Ivanov, S. A. Bessonov, A. Ikramov, F. Khodzhayev, V. F. Sharangovich, P. T. Zubarev and D. D. Pletnev.

---

1. Stephen F. Cohen, *Bukharin and the Bolshevik Revolution: A Political Biography, 1888–1938* (New York: Alfred A. Knopf, 1973; Oxford University Press, 1980).

The USSR Prosecutor's Office did not lodge a protest with respect to G. G. Yagoda, who was tried in this case.

The commission of the Politburo of the CPSU Central Committee is continuing its work. . . .

HE WANTED TO REMAKE LIFE BECAUSE HE LOVED IT

An Ogonyok Correspondent Interviews Anna Mikhailovna, the Widow of Nikolai Ivanovich Bukharin, on Bukharin's Fate

(Prepared by Feliks Medvedev)

"To Comrade Mikhail Sergeyevich Gorbachev, General Secretary of the CPSU Central Committee. Despite the tense international situation, I put before you the question of the posthumous Party rehabilitation of my husband and the father of my son—Nikolai Ivanovich Bukharin. I submit this petition not only on my own behalf but also on behalf of Bukharin himself. As he left me for the last time for the February–March plenary session in 1937 (the plenary session lasted several days), Nikolai Ivanovich, having a presentiment that he would never return, asked me, in view of my youth at the time, to fight for his posthumous vindication. That unbearably painful moment will never die in my memory. Tormented by the investigation and by dreadful confrontations that he found inexplicable, and weakened by the hunger strike he had undertaken as a sign of protest against the monstrous accusations, Bukharin fell to his knees before me and, with tears in his eyes, asked that I not forget a single word of his letter addressed 'To a Future Generation of Party Leaders,' asked that I fight for his vindication: 'Swear that you will do this. Swear! Swear!' And I swore. To violate that oath would go against my conscience."

Anna Mikhailovna Larina grew up in a family of professional revolutionaries. The name of Yu. Larin (Mikhail Aleksandrovich Lurye, 1882–1932), her father, is now forgotten, although he is buried at the Kremlin wall. Anna Mikhailovna has tender memories of her father, a man so popular in the first years after the Revolution that at a demonstration Anya once heard his name coupled with that of Bukharin in a song. Before the Revolution Larin led the life of a professional revolutionary, organizing Party cells, moving about from city to city and country to country, enduring police surveillance, arrests and exile, staging escapes. At the time of the Revolution, he was a member of the Petrograd Soviet Executive Committee and played an active role in the revolutionary events. He later wrote about economic problems and undertook various assignments for Lenin.

Of all my father's many friends, Bukharin was my favorite. As a child, I was drawn by his irrepressible joie de vivre, his mischievousness and love of nature. I used to call him Nikolasha and addressed him using the familiar "*ty*," eschewing the more formal first name and patronymic with which I addressed father's other comrades.

I once heard Lenin, in my father's office, refer to Nikolai Ivanovich as the "darling of the Revolution," a tribute that subsequently became widely known in Party circles.

I by no means want to oversimplify or idealize the relations among the leaders of the Revolution. They did argue among themselves, but Vladimir Ilyich was always principled in relations with his comrades-in-arms. He did not approve of all of Nikolai Ivanovich's views. But I will always remember the Communists' openness, friendliness, devotion to principle, honesty and determination.

Lenin died on Jan. 21, 1924—the funeral was on Jan. 27, my 10th birthday. Father told me: "Henceforth, this day will be a day of mourning. From now on, we will celebrate your birthday on May 27—when nature is reawakening and everything is in bloom."

I'll never forget Lenin's funeral. From the windows of our apartment in the Metropol Hotel, I could see the round-the-clock, unending procession of mourners filing into the Hall of Columns.

Bukharin first met my father in 1913, when both were in Italy. From the summer of 1915 to the summer of 1916, they lived in Sweden. And from 1918 to mid-1927 both Bukharin and my family lived in the Metropol. Father and Nikolai Ivanovich didn't always hold the same views, but this did not affect their friendship. They spoke to each other with the utmost candor. Many years later, at Nikolai Ivanovich's wish, we named our son Yury in memory of my father.

I encountered Stalin at Nikolai Ivanovich's apartment many times. One time in 1925, in a burst of childish affection, I wrote a love letter to Nikolasha. As I walked down the stairs to his second-floor apartment to deliver it, I met Stalin, who was on his way to see Bukharin. On the spur of the moment, I asked Stalin to deliver the letter for me, and he agreed. And so it was through Stalin—what a sinister irony!—that I conveyed my first declaration of love to Bukharin.

In the autumn and winter of 1930 and in early 1931, Nikolai and I sought to spend our free time together, going to the theater, to art exhibits, or talking in his Kremlin office. One evening he proposed to me. I didn't give him an answer then but gave way to tears, out of a combination of joy, shock and indecision. Only some time later did I accept.

We had grown accustomed to my father's progressively worsening health, but no one expected the end would come so soon. The diagnosis was double pneumonia. He died an agonizing death, sitting in a chair; he could no longer breathe lying down. The torture went on for two weeks; he died on Jan. 14, 1932. Near the end, mother summoned his closest friends—Rykov, Milyutin, Kritsman. (Nikolai was vacationing in Nalchik; he was unable to return in time for the funeral.) At that critical moment of leave-taking, Stalin telephoned and asked to speak to Larin. But father was too weak to hold the receiver. "What a pity," Stalin said. "I wanted to offer him a high position." All those in the room were shocked by Stalin's call, most of all Milyutin, who only a few days before had told Stalin that Larin was dying. "Could he possibly have forgotten?" Milyutin asked in bewilderment.

Anna Mikhailovna spent the entire day of Nov. 2, 1987, in front of her television set, devouring every word of the report by the General Secretary of the CPSU Central Committee on the 70th anniversary of the Revolution. When she heard Lenin's words to the effect that "Bukharin is legitimately considered the whole Party's favorite," she sighed with satisfaction. For the first time in 50 years, Bukharin's name had been spoken in a positive context.

Nikolai Ivanovich was a complicated person, Anna Mikhailovna continued. One could never know how he would react to something, nor did he himself always know what he might do. He was capable of rash deeds. Political calculation was alien to him, and this hindered him as a politician. He tolerated emotional stress very poorly, with the result that he was not always able to win an argument, even when he was right. He also tended to give in on more trivial matters. He apologized to the poets who were stung by his criticisms at the First Congress of Soviet Writers. At the February-March (1937) plenary session, he apologized—on Stalin's advice—for the hunger strike he had undertaken to protest the unheard-of accusations against him. This amounted to showing weakness.

His emotional nature often left him in a hysterical state. He wept easily, though always over something serious. When Lenin died, I saw tears in the eyes of many of his comrades-in-arms, but only Bukharin sobbed like a woman. In the Ukraine during collectivization, Bukharin saw throngs of begging children, their stomachs swollen with hunger. He gave them all the money he had with him, and later sobbed hysterically over what he had seen. When he learned that about 1,000 people were killed during the October uprising in Moscow, he burst into tears. Emotional stress took a physical toll on Bukharin, and he regularly fell ill.

This is not to say that Nikolai Ivanovich was some sort of "whining old woman." On the contrary, overflowing emotions were just one facet of his rich and complex character. He was also a revolutionary of enormous potential, obsessed with the idea of bringing about a more humane society.

Two months after her husband's arrest, Anna Mikhailovna, her son and Bukharin's father were moved out of the Kremlin and into Government House, which the writer Yury Trifonov later dubbed "the house on the embankment." When the rent bill arrived, Anna Mikhailovna had no money to pay it. Instead, she wrote a terse note to M. I. Kalinin: "Mikhail Ivanovich! Fascist intelligence has failed to make material provision for its hireling Nikolai Ivanovich Bukharin. I have no way of paying for the apartment, so I'm sending you the unpaid bill."

A. M. Larina said that Bukharin never amassed any wealth. He donated the royalties from his writings to the Party. He refused to take a salary as editor of Izvestia, living instead off his pay as a member of the Academy of Sciences. Sometimes he borrowed money from his chauffeur.

We talked about Bukharin and Pasternak. Anna Mikhailovna recalled that in the days before Bukharin's arrest, the newspapers suddenly reported that the case against Bukharin had been dropped (this was another one of Stalin's tricks). Bukharin received a congratulatory letter from Pasternak, which caused him to worry greatly for the poet. When Bukharin was removed as editor of Izvestia in late January 1937 and it became clear that things were going very badly for him, Pasternak sent him another short letter in which the poet affirmed his faith in Bukharin's innocence and expressed his bewilderment at what was happening in the country. Bukharin was struck by the poet's courage but was deeply concerned about his fate.

At my request, Anna Mikhailovna talked about the final months and days of her life with N. I. Bukharin. It was a tragic and complex time, when Stalin was displaying the despotic essence of his nature in full force, especially with respect to Bukharin. Anna Mikhailovna believes that preparations for Bukharin's physical destruction began with the trial of Zinovyev and Kamenev in August 1936.

Anna Mikhailovna had recently given birth to a son, and the 47-year-old father was happy. He was off on a hunting trip in the Pamir Mountains on Aug. 19, when Anna Mikhailovna read the terrifying news in the papers. The trial of the so-called Trotskyist United Center had begun, and many of the defendants had implicated

Bukharin. Shortly thereafter, it was announced that the Prosecutor's Office was investigating her husband. The news of Tomsky's suicide was published.

On learning of the investigation, Bukharin flew back to Moscow and returned to his Kremlin apartment. Repeated attempts to contact Stalin by telephone were unsuccessful. In early September, Bukharin was summoned to a meeting in the Central Committee, at which a confrontation had been arranged with his longtime friend Sokolnikov, who gave false evidence against him. Then, on Sept. 10, 1936, the newspapers announced that the USSR Prosecutor's Office had dropped its investigation of Bukharin and Rykov. In fact, this was a tactical move by Stalin, intended to show that the investigation had been "objective." Stalin sought to capitalize on public affection for Bukharin while simultaneously preparing his destruction.

On Nov. 7, at the Red Square ceremonies marking the 19th anniversary of the Revolution, Stalin, atop the Lenin Mausoleum, spotted Bukharin in the crowd. A guard was sent to summon Bukharin to a place of honor on the mausoleum. Bukharin went, but Stalin left the ceremony before Bukharin got a chance to talk to him.

The next month passed in relative calm. Nikolai Ivanovich worked on a long article about the ideology of fascism. But by late November the stress was so great that he could work no more. He looked in the issues of Izvestia to see if he was still listed as editor. He was. In early December, he was summoned to a plenary session of the Central Committee. At the meeting, Yezhov, the new People's Commissar of Internal Affairs, furiously denounced Bukharin as a conspirator and an accomplice in the assassination of Kirov. Bukharin protested the accusations to Stalin, who told him that his past services were not in doubt but declined to discuss the matter further.

Bukharin spent most of the next three months in his cramped apartment office. Although it was increasingly obvious that Stalin was orchestrating the investigation, Bukharin sent him several letters protesting his innocence. Anna Mikhailovna was at her husband's side almost continuously during this period. Shut up in his apartment, Bukharin grew thin and aged; his red beard turned gray. Then came another confrontation, this time with Radek. Another plea to Stalin proved futile. Finally, Bukharin was summoned to the February-March plenary session, with himself and Rykov an item on the agenda. He refused to attend, and on Feb. 16 began a hunger strike in protest. His health deteriorated further. When the plenary session reconvened after Ordzhonikidze's funeral [held Feb. 20, 1937—Trans.], Bukharin's "anti-Party behavior" was on the agenda. Stalin asked him: "Against whom have you declared this hunger strike, Nikolai? The Party Central Committee? Ask the plenary session's forgiveness." "Why, if you intend to expel me from the Party?" Bukharin countered. "No one is going to expel you from the Party," Stalin replied. And a trusting Bukharin asked the plenary session's forgiveness.

I remember, as if it were yesterday, the fateful day of Feb. 27, 1937, when Stalin's secretary, Poskrebyshev, telephoned to order Bukharin to attend that plenary session. I will never forget our tragic and terrible farewell. Nikolai Ivanovich fell to his knees before me and, with tears in his eyes, asked me to forgive him for having ruined my life. He asked me to raise our son as a Bolshevik. He asked me to fight for his vindication and never to forget a single line of his letter and testament.

"The situation will change, it's bound to change," he kept saying. "You're young, you'll live to see it happen. Swear that you will preserve my letter in your memory!" I swore. He rose from the floor, embraced me, kissed me, and said in a trembling voice:

"Look, don't be bitter, Anyutka, there are annoying misprints in history, but the truth will prevail!"

We knew we were parting forever.

Bukharin believed in the ideals of the Revolution and wanted me to regard that dark period of history as temporary. That was why he addressed his letter "To a Future Generation of Party Leaders." He wrote it a few days before his arrest. He was already psychologically prepared for the fact that he would be arrested and would lose his life. Having given up hope that he would be spared, he had decided to tell posterity that he was innocent and to ask for posthumous reinstatement in the Party. I was 23 at the time, and Nikolai was convinced I would live to see a time when I could convey his letter to the Central Committee. Certain that the letter would be confiscated in a search and fearing that I would be subjected to repression if it were found, he asked me to commit it to memory. He read the letter to me over and over, and then I would repeat it back to him. How irritated he would get when I made an error! Finally, convinced that I had it firmly fixed in my memory, he destroyed the handwritten text.

He wrote his final appeal on a small table on which lay Lenin's letters to him— he spent those final days reading the letters over and over.

KNOW, COMRADES—

(By Lev Voskresensky)

On the eve of the February–March 1937 plenary session of the Central Committee, he [Bukharin] knew that his days of freedom were numbered.

"Despairing of winning vindication in his lifetime," A. Larina [Bukharin's widow] recalls, "Nikolai Ivanovich wrote a letter two or three days before his arrest. A search was expected. Fearing that the letter would be discovered, he charged me with committing it to memory. When he was convinced that I had learned the letter by heart, he destroyed the handwritten text. All through the years of imprisonment and exile, I repeated these words like a prayer:

"I am leaving life. I do not hang my head before the proletarian ax, which must be merciless but also chaste. I feel my helplessness before an infernal machine that, probably by using medieval methods, possesses gigantic power, fabricates organized slander, and acts boldly and confidently. Dzerzhinsky is no more. The remarkable traditions of the Cheka [Extraordinary Commission for Combating Counterrevolution and Sabotage, 1918–1922—Trans.], when the revolutionary idea guided all its actions, justified cruelty to enemies and guarded the state against any counterrevolution, have gradually receded into the past. It was for these traditions that the Cheka agencies deserved special trust, special honor, prestige and respect. . . .

"Any member of the Central Committee, any member of the Party can be ground into dust, turned into a traitor, a terrorist, a saboteur or a spy. If Stalin were to doubt himself, confirmation would instantly follow.

"Storm clouds loom over the Party. My totally guiltless head alone will drag down thousands more innocent heads. For an organization has to be created, a Bukharin organization, which in actuality not only does not exist now, when for more than six years there has been not a shadow of disagreement between me and the Party, but did not exist then, in the years of the right opposition. I knew nothing about the secret organizations of Ryutin and Uglanov. Together with Rykov and Tomsky, I expounded my ideas openly.

"I have been in the Party since I was 18, and the goal of my life has always been the struggle for the interests of the working class, for the victory of socialism. These days, the newspaper bearing the sacred name *Pravda* [Truth] is printing the most vile lie that I, Nikolai Bukharin, wanted to destroy the gains of October and to restore capitalism. This is unheard-of insolence; it is a lie which could be equaled in impudence, in irresponsibility to the people, only by such a lie as this: 'It has been discovered that Nikolai Romanov devoted his entire life to the struggle against capitalism and monarchy, to the struggle to bring about a proletarian revolution.'

"If I was mistaken more than once about the methods of building socialism, let posterity judge me no more harshly than Vladimir Ilyich did. We were moving toward a single goal for the first time, along an as yet untrodden path. Other times, other customs. *Pravda* carried a 'discussion page'; everyone argued, sought ways of doing things, quarreled and made up, and advanced together.

"I appeal to you, a future generation of Party leaders, whose historical mission will include the duty of unraveling the monstrous tangle of crimes that is growing more and more immense in these terrible days, is flaming up and suffocating the Party. I appeal to all members of the Party. In these, perhaps the last days of my life, I am confident that, sooner or later, the filter of history will inevitably wash the filth from my head. I have never been a traitor. I would have paid for Lenin's life with my own without hesitation. I loved Kirov, and I have undertaken nothing against Stalin."

And the last lines, stamped in her memory:

"Know, comrades, that the banner you will carry in the victorious procession to communism also bears a drop of my blood.—N. BUKHARIN."

He left for the plenary session, but he didn't come home; he never returned. That was on Feb. 27. Soon after, Anna Mikhailovna was arrested. Yura, who was less than a year old, found himself in a children's home.

Sentence was pronounced on March 13, 1938. . . .

Pravda, February 1, 1988, p. 1; *Izvestiia*, February 7, 1988; translated in *The Current Digest of the Soviet Press*, XL, 5 (March 2, 1988), p. 1; *Ogonek*, no. 48 (November 1987, pp. 26–31; *Current Digest*, XL, 5 (March 2, 1988), pp. 6–8; *Moskovskie novosti*, December 6, 1987, p. 12; *Current Digest*, XL, 5 (March 2, 1988), p. 8.

Boris Yeltsin Resigns from the Communist Party at the Twenty-Eighth Congress of the CPSU

July 1990

By the summer of 1990, the Communist party was losing its authority throughout the country. Shocked by the defeat of Communists in the East Central European countries the year before, Soviet Communists divided between conservatives who wished to halt or reverse Gorbachev's reforms and the "democrats" who wanted to accelerate them and create a democratic, multiparty polity with a market economy. Boris Yeltsin came out of political eclipse after two years and became the most visible and popular leader of the democratic forces. At the Congress, which proved to be the last of the Soviet Communist party, he argued against the notion of renewal of the party (Gorbachev's strategy) because the conservative forces were too numerous and entrenched in the apparatus. He proposed a radical program of transforming the party into an organization that could compete in parliamentary elections, but once the new composition

of the Central Committee was announced, Yeltsin dramatically broke ranks, announced his res-
ignation from the party, and walked out of the Congress. As some in the hall whistled and
clapped derisively, it was apparent that Gorbachev's plans had suffered a blow and that the
Communist party now had a formidable opponent in Yeltsin. As chairman of the Russian re-
public's Supreme Soviet, Yeltsin had a platform from which to express the mood of frustration
and expectation of the growing opposition to gradual top-down reform.

SPEECH BY B. N. YELTSIN,
CHAIRMAN OF THE RUSSIAN SFSR SUPREME SOVIET

Comrades, the Party approached its Congress with a load of grave problems. They are numerous, but some are especially important. After taking the defensive in the initial stage of restructuring, the conservative forces later shifted to the offensive. They have begun a struggle against the economic reform, a struggle that, although timid and halfhearted, creates a real threat to the Party's full power. . . . As the past few years have shown, it has not been possible to neutralize the effect of the conservative forces in the Party. On the contrary, too much has been said to the effect that we are all in the same boat, on the same side of the barricades, in the same ranks, and have common thinking. This position has discredited those Communists who are sincere and consistent supporters of changes. This position has created safe conditions for the conservative forces in the CPSU and has strengthened their confidence that they can take revenge. This was demonstrated by the Founding Congress of the Russian SFSR Communist Party.

In order to understand what our Congress can and should decide, first it is necessary to see clearly what it represents. The Politburo could not bring itself to adopt the only correct procedure for electing delegates under restructuring: democratically, from all platforms and groups, regardless of the Party's former structures. If any united group of 6,000 Communists had been allowed to elect its own delegate directly, we wouldn't have wound up with a Congress made up as this one is.

Therefore, during the discussion at the Congress, the main question is not that of restructuring in the country and the paths of its development. That question is being decided by the people, beyond the walls of this building; it is being decided in the Soviets of People's Deputies. This Congress is faced first of all with the question of the fate of the CPSU itself. To be more precise, only the question of the fate of the apparatus of the Party's upper echelons is being decided here. This question is extremely critical. Will the CPSU apparatus find the strength to decide on changes? Will it take advantage of this last chance that is being offered to it by the Congress? Either it will or it won't. Either the Party apparatus, under the pressure of political reality, will decide on a fundamental restructuring of the Party, or it will cling to doomed forms and end up in opposition to the people, in opposition to restructuring.

In the latter case, representatives of the apparatus will inevitably be ousted from all bodies of legitimate power. Such a Party will not hold up, either in the role of a vanguard or even in the role of a Party with representation in the Soviets.

Those who think that, after all the differently-minded people who do not want to be drive belts or cogs in the Party apparatus leave the Party, the apparatus will be left with all the CPSU's property and the associated power are suffering from utopian illusions. That will not happen. In this scenario, which, incidentally, the conservatives are pushing for, a nationwide struggle will begin for complete nationalization of the property of the CPSU, as a Party that has gone bankrupt and is obliged to repay its debts to the people with its property, if nothing else. The only legacy that will be left for the Party apparatus will be a signboard reading "CPSU."

One can surmise that a struggle will begin to put on trial Party leaders at all levels for the damage they have personally done to the country and the people. I can name at least one of these cases—on the damage resulting from the antialcohol campaign. The people will hold someone to account for all the rest, too: for the failures in foreign trade and agriculture, for nationalities policy, the policy with respect to the Army, and so forth and so on. The country should know what kind of legacy the CPSU has left it.

That is the possible future for an apparatus-based Party. Those who think there are some kind of other options, let them look at the fate of the Communist Parties in the countries of Eastern Europe. They lost touch with the people, they didn't understand their role—and they ended up on the wayside.

Is everything so gloomy? Is there another way out? There is. True, there is little chance for it to win out at this Congress. That is perfectly clear. But all of us who have given the Party decades of our life considered it our duty to come here to try to say that there is still a way out for the CPSU. It is hard and difficult, but it is a way out.

In a democratic state, a changeover to a multiparty system is inevitable.

Various political parties are gradually being formed in our country. At the same time, a fundamental renewal of the CPSU is inevitable. What is the most civilized process of modernizing the Party, the one least painful for the people?

First. It is necessary to organizationally codify all the platforms that exist in the CPSU and to give every Communist time for political self-determination. I am sure that most rank-and-file Communists link the Party's future with the democratic wing.

Second. To change the name of the Party. It should be a party of democratic socialism.

Third. This Congress is too early to discuss platforms and the Statutes. Only a general declaration on the transformation of the CPSU should be adopted. Then a new leadership should be elected, one capable of making preparations for a new Congress sometime six months to a year from now.

Fourth. The Party should divest itself of all state functions. Primary Party organizations should be abolished in the Army, in the state security system and in state institutions. In production facilities, the fate of the primary Party organizations should be determined by the labor collectives themselves and the Party members themselves. In the new Party or alliance, members should pay minimal dues. In this way, a parliamentary-type Party will emerge. Only this kind of Party, provided that there is a mighty renewal of society, will be able to be a leading Party and to win elections for one or another of its factions.

Any socialist-oriented factions of other parties may join the alliance of the country's democratic forces. The people will recognize this alliance and follow it, especially if it offers an economic program for getting out of the crisis that does not involve deceiving the people or putting an additional burden on them. The alliance will act as a federation of national alliances. It will have a form that corresponds to the meaning and spirit of the new Union Treaty between the country's sovereign states.

With the development of democratic movements in the country and the further radicalization of restructuring, it will be possible for this alliance to become the vanguard of society in actual fact. This will provide a broad social base for the renewal of society, erect a barrier against attacks by the conservatives, and guarantee the irreversibility of restructuring. That is the second alternative. Thus, there is either the option of an apparatus-based CPSU, then a split and, sooner or later, its departure from the ranks of the country's real political forces, or a renewed Party with a changeover to an alliance of democratic forces and the prospect of preserving its role as an active participant in restructuring. . . .

The country cannot be given orders any longer. It cannot be lulled to sleep with demagoguery, and it cannot be intimidated with threats. The people can send any political force into retirement, no matter how influential it was in the past. It will support only a political organization that does not summon them to a distant prospect of communism beyond the clouds but that, through its daily deeds, defends the interests of everyone and helps make them and our country advanced, rich and happy.

On July 12, Delegate B. Yeltsin asked for the floor. He said that, after thinking the matter over for a long time, he had come to a conclusion and had wanted to announce his decision after the 28th Party Congress. But in view of his nomination as a candidate for the Party Central Committee, he had decided to make the announcement that day. Citing his election as Chairman of the Russian SFSR Supreme Soviet and his "enormous responsibility to the people and to Russia," and taking into account society's transition to a multiparty system, he said that he cannot carry out only the decisions of the CPSU. As head of the republic's supreme legislative authority, he went on, I must submit to the will of the people and their authorized representatives. Therefore, in accordance with the commitments I made in the preelection period, I announce my withdrawal from the CPSU, so as to have a greater opportunity to exert an effective influence on the Soviets' activity. I am prepared to cooperate with all parties and public-political organizations in the republic.

The Congress took note of B. Yeltsin's statement and instructed the Credentials Commission to submit a proposal to invalidate the credentials of the delegate from the Sverdlovsk Province Party organization.

Pravda, July 8, 1990, p. 4; July 13, 1990; translated in *Current Digest of the Soviet Press*, XLII, 32 (September 12, 1990), pp. 11–12; 35 (October 3, 1990), p. 20.

══════ Boris Yeltsin Calls for Gorbachev's Resignation ══════
February 1991

Toward the end of 1990, Gorbachev tacked to the Right and brought into his administration many of the leading conservative leaders in the country—his Prime Minister Valentin Pavlov, Vice President Gennadii Yanaev, the Minister of the Interior Boris Pugo, and Defense Minister Dmitrii Yazov. Foreign Minister Shevardnadze resigned, and talk of a dictatorship by conservatives was in the air. Early in 1991, the police cracked down on separatist demonstrators in Lithuania and Latvia, killing over a dozen people. The democrats and non-Russian nationalists saw Gorbachev as an obstacle to greater freedom, while the conservative Communists saw the Soviet Union unraveling and the state withering away in a way never intended by Marx. Yeltsin impetuously called for Gorbachev's resignation. The speech was widely criticized. A month later, after a referendum supported preservation of the Soviet federation, Gorbachev and Yeltsin began negotiating on the form of the new union. The future of the USSR and the fate of democracy was now deeply intertwined with the personal political rivalry of Yeltsin and Gorbachev.

I HAVE MADE MY CHOICE

In the first two years after 1985, Gorbachev inspired some hope in many of us. In making promises, one has to think, he didn't have a very good idea about how to fulfill those promises. Having inspired hope in people, he began acting according to different laws. This has been shown especially well recently, when it has become perfectly obvious that what he wants is, while retaining the word "perestroika" [restructuring], not to do any essential restructuring but to preserve the system, preserve rigid centralized power, and not to give independence to the republics, especially not to Russia. His antipopular policy has manifested itself here. This includes the monetary manipulations, the unprecedented price increase that Pavlov is preparing, the sharp list to the right, the use of the Army against the civilian population, the bloodshed in relations between nationalities, the collapse of the economy, people's low standard of living, and so forth. There you have it, the result of six years of perestroika—and that's the most important thing.

Today there is a recoil in the reverse direction; an attempt is under way to revive command-administrative methods and to strengthen the command-administrative center. At the same time, no desire is being shown to acknowledge the processes taking place in the republic. After I was elected Chairman of the [Russian SFSR] Supreme Soviet, the voters voiced insistent demands that I move toward co-operation with the central leadership. I will say frankly, and God is my witness, that I made many attempts to really cooperate.

Since that cooperation, I consider the excessive trust I put in the President to be my personal mistake. From all indications, the center is not going to allow the republics to take independent steps. Carefully analyzing the events of recent months, I can say that I warned in 1987 that Gorbachev had in his character a desire to make his personal power absolute. He has done all of this and has led the country to a dictatorship, prettifying it with the name "presidential rule." I dissociate myself from the position and policy of the President, and I call for his immediate resignation and the transfer of power to a collective body—the Council of the Federation. I have faith in Russia, and I urge you, esteemed fellow citizens and esteemed residents of the Russian Republic, to have faith in our Russia. I have made my choice. Everyone must make his choice and define his position. I want you to hear and understand me. This is the choice I have made, and I will not turn off this road.

(From B. Yeltsin's speech on Central Television on Feb. 19, 1991.)

Komsomolskaia pravda, February 22, 1991, p. 1; translated in *Current Digest of the Soviet Press.* XLIII, 7 (March 20, 1991), p. 1.

The August Coup

Just days before the scheduled signing of the new Union Treaty that would have refashioned the Soviet federation, Gorbachev flew to Crimea for a brief vacation. On August 18, 1991, his chief lieutenants in Moscow, fearing the effects of the Treaty, announced that Gorbachev

was being replaced by a State Committee of Emergency (GKChP). The conspirators at-
tempted to have Gorbachev agree to the new authority, but he refused. Troops occupied
Moscow, but the newly self-proclaimed leaders failed to act resolutely. Yeltsin managed to es-
cape to the parliament building, the White House, and standing on a tank he proclaimed his
resistance to the coup. The conspiracy was poorly planned; Yeltsin's phone lines were not even
cut off, and he was able to order lunch from Pizza Hut. Muscovites flocked to the White
House, erected barricades, and prepared to defend the fledgling Russian democracy. Soldiers de-
fected to Yeltsin. The standoff turned violent on August 20, when three young men were killed.
The tanks soon turned back; soldiers refused to shoot at the crowds; and on the third day, the
coup leaders surrendered, and Gorbachev, weary and shaken, returned to Moscow.

The world of Soviet politics, however, had made a revolutionary turn. Yeltsin emerged as
the most popular and powerful leader in Russia. He humiliated Gorbachev publicly and
steadily stripped him of his institutional powers. He abolished the Communist party and
seized its property. Various Soviet republics declared themselves independent states, and the
president of the Soviet Union became an impotent figurehead.

DECREE OF THE VICE-PRESIDENT OF THE USSR

In connection with the inability of Mikhail Sergeyevich Gorbachev to perform his duties as President of the USSR due to the state of his health, I have, on the basis of Art. 127.7 of the USSR Constitution, assumed the duties of acting President of the USSR as of Aug. 19, 1991.

G. I. YANAYEV,
Vice-President of the USSR.

Aug. 18, 1991.

STATEMENT BY THE SOVIET LEADERSHIP

In connection with the inability of Mikhail Sergeyevich Gorbachev to perform the duties of President of the USSR due to the state of his health, and the transfer of the powers of President of the USSR to Gennady Ivanovich Yanayev, Vice-President of the USSR, in accordance with Art. 127.7 of the USSR Constitution;

with the aim of overcoming the profound and comprehensive crisis, the political and civil confrontation, the confrontation between nationalities, and the chaos and anarchy that are threatening the lives and security of the citizens of the Soviet Union and the sovereignty, territorial integrity, freedom and independence of our fatherland;

proceeding from the results of the nationwide referendum on the preservation of the Union of Soviet Socialist Republics;

guided by the vitally important interests of the peoples of our homeland and of all Soviet people,

WE STATE:

1. That, in accordance with Art. 127.3 of the USSR Constitution and Art. 2 of the USSR law "On the Legal Conditions Applying in a State of Emergency," and moving to accommodate the demands of broad strata of the population concerning

the need to take very decisive measures to prevent society from sliding toward a nationwide catastrophe and to safeguard legality and order, a state of emergency is introduced in certain localities of the USSR for a period of six months, beginning at 4 a.m. Moscow time on Aug. 19, 1991.

2. That it is established that the USSR Constitution and USSR laws have unconditional supremacy throughout the USSR.

3. That, to administer the country and provide effective implementation of the conditions applying in a state of emergency, a State Committee for the State of Emergency in the USSR (USSR SCSE) is formed, with the following members: O. D. Baklanov, First Vice-Chairman of the USSR Defense Council; V. A. Kryuchkov, Chairman of the USSR State Security Committee (KGB); V. S. Pavlov, Prime Minister of the USSR; B. K. Pugo, USSR Minister of Internal Affairs; V. A. Starodubtsev, Chairman of the USSR Peasants' Union; A. I. Tizyakov, President of the Association of State Enterprises and Industrial, Construction, Transportation and Communications Facilities; D. T. Yazov, USSR Minister of Defense; and G. I. Yanayev, acting President of the USSR.

4. That unswerving fulfillment of the decisions of the USSR State Committee for the State of Emergency is mandatory for all bodies of power and administration, officials and citizens throughout the USSR.

[signed] G. YANAYEV, V. PAVLOV and O. BAKLANOV.

Aug. 18, 1991.

RESOLUTION NO. 1 OF THE STATE COMMITTEE FOR THE STATE OF EMERGENCY IN THE USSR

For the purpose of protecting the vitally important interests of the peoples and citizens of the USSR and the independence and territorial integrity of the country, restoring legality and law and order, stabilizing the situation, overcoming the grave crisis and preventing chaos, anarchy and a fratricidal civil war, the State Committee for the State of Emergency in the USSR resolves that:

1. All bodies of power and administration of the USSR, the Union and autonomous republics, territories, provinces, cities, districts, settlements and villages are to ensure unswerving observance of the conditions applying in a state of emergency, in accordance with the USSR law "On the Legal Conditions Applying in a State of Emergency" and the resolutions of the USSR State Committee for the State of Emergency. In cases of inability to ensure fulfillment of these conditions, the powers of the relevant bodies of power and administration are to be suspended, and the performance of their functions is to be assigned to individuals specially empowered by the USSR State Committee for the State of Emergency.

2. Structures of power and administration and paramilitary formations acting in defiance of the USSR Constitution and USSR laws are to be immediately disbanded.

3. Laws and decisions of bodies of power and administration that are at variance with the USSR Constitution and USSR laws are henceforth to be considered invalid.

4. Activity by political parties, public organizations and mass movements that impedes the normalization of the situation is to be suspended.

5. In connection with the fact that the State Committee for the State of Emergency in the USSR is temporarily assuming the functions of the USSR Security Council, the activity of the latter is suspended.

6. Citizens, institutions and organizations are to immediately surrender all types of firearms, ammunition, explosives and military equipment that are in their possession illegally. The USSR Ministry of Internal Affairs, the State Security Committee and the Ministry of Defense are to ensure the strict fulfillment of this requirement. In cases of refusal, the firearms, etc., are to be taken by force and strict criminal and administrative charges are to be brought against the violators.

7. The USSR Prosecutor's Office, the Ministry of Internal Affairs, the State Security Committee and the Ministry of Defense are to organize effective interaction among law-enforcement agencies and the Armed Forces to ensure the safeguarding of public order and the security of the state, society and citizens in accordance with the USSR law "On the Legal Conditions Applying in a State of Emergency" and the resolutions of the USSR State Committee for the State of Emergency.

The holding of rallies, street processions and demonstrations, as well as strikes, is not permitted.

When necessary, a curfew may be introduced, patrolling may be instituted, inspections may be conducted, and measures may be taken to reinforce border and customs regulations.

The most important state and economic facilities, as well as systems providing vital services, are to be taken under control, and, when necessary, put under guard.

The dissemination of inflammatory rumors, actions that provoke violations of law and order and the stirring up of discord between nationalities, and failure to obey officials who are ensuring the observance of the conditions applying in the state of emergency are to be resolutely curbed.

8. Control is to be established over the news media, with the implementation of this control assigned to a specially created agency under the USSR State Committee for the State of Emergency.

9. Bodies of power and administration and executives of institutions and enterprises are to take measures to enhance the level of organization and to establish order and discipline in all spheres of the life of society. The normal functioning of enterprises in all branches of the national economy, the strict fulfillment of measures to preserve and restore—during a period of stabilization—vertical and horizontal ties among economic—management entities throughout the USSR, and the unswerving fulfillment of established volumes of production and of deliveries of raw and other materials and components are to be ensured.

A policy of strict economizing with respect to materials, equipment and currency is to be established and maintained, and concrete measures are to be worked out and implemented to combat the mismanagement and squandering of public property.

A decisive struggle is to be waged against the shadow economy, and inescapable measures of criminal and administrative liability are to be applied in instances of corruption, embezzlement, speculation, the concealment of goods from sale, mismanagement and other law violations in the sphere of the economy.

Favorable conditions are to be created for increasing the real contribution of all types of entrepreneurial activity, carried out in accordance with USSR laws, to the country's economic potential and for providing for the urgent requirements of the population.

10. The holding of a permanent position in the structures of power and administration is to be considered incompatible with participation in entrepreneurial activity.

11. Within one week, the USSR Cabinet of Ministers is to conduct an inventory of all available resources of prime-necessity foodstuffs and industrial commodities, report to the people on what the country has at its disposal, and put the safekeeping and distribution of these resources under the strictest possible control.

All restrictions impeding the shifting of food and consumer goods from one place to another in the USSR, as well as of material resources for their production, are to be lifted, and observance of this directive is to be strictly monitored.

Special attention is to be given to the top-priority supplying of children's preschool institutions, children's homes, schools, specialized secondary and higher educational institutions and hospitals, as well as of pensioners and disabled persons.

Within one week, proposals are to be submitted on putting in order, freezing and reducing prices for certain types of manufactured goods and foodstuffs, first of all goods for children, services to the population and public catering, and also on increasing wages, pensions, allowances and compensation payments for various categories of citizens.

Within two weeks, measures are to be worked out to put in order the size of salaries for executives at all levels of state, public, cooperative and other institutions, organizations and enterprises.

12. In view of the critical situation regarding harvest operations and the threat of hunger, emergency measures are to be taken to organize the procurement, storage and processing of agricultural output. Rural toilers are to be provided with the greatest possible assistance in the form of equipment, spare parts, fuel and lubricants, etc. The sending of workers and office employees from enterprises and organizations, students and servicemen to the countryside in the numbers needed to save the harvest is to be organized immediately.

13. Within one week, the USSR Cabinet of Ministers is to work out a resolution stipulating the provision, in 1991–1992, of plots of land up to 0.15 hectares in size to all urban residents who wish to use this land to grow fruit and vegetables.

14. Within two weeks, the USSR Cabinet of Ministers is to complete the planning of urgent measures to bring the country's fuel and energy complex out of crisis and to prepare for winter.

15. Within one month, real measures for 1992 aimed at fundamentally improving housing construction and providing housing to the population are to be prepared and reported to the people.

During a six-month period, a concrete five-year program for the accelerated development of state, cooperative and individual housing construction is to be worked out.

16. Central and local bodies of power and administration must devote top-priority attention to the social needs of the population. Possibilities for a substantial improvement in free medical services and public education are to be sought out.

APPEAL TO THE SOVIET PEOPLE

Fellow countrymen! Citizens of the Soviet Union! At this grave, critical hour for the fate of the fatherland and of our peoples, we appeal to you! A mortal danger threatens our great homeland! For a number of reasons, the policy of reforms begun at the initiative of M. S. Gorbachev and conceived of as a means of ensuring the dynamic development of the country and the democratization of the life of society has reached an impasse. The initial enthusiasm and hopes have given way to unbelief, apathy and despair. The authorities at all levels have lost the trust of the population. In the life of society, political intrigue has supplanted concern for the fate of the fatherland and the citizen. Malicious mocking of all state institutions is being propagated. In essence, the country has become ungovernable.

Taking advantage of the liberties that have been granted and trampling the shoots of democracy, which have just emerged, extremist forces have come into being and embarked on a course aimed at the liquidation of the Soviet Union, the breakup of the state and the seizure of power at any cost. The results of the nationwide referendum on the unity of the fatherland have been trampled. The cynical exploitation of national feelings is only a screen for satisfying ambitions. These political adventurists are troubled neither by the current misfortunes of their peoples nor by their future troubles. In creating an atmosphere of psychological and political terror and trying to hide behind the shield of the people's trust, they forget that the ties they are condemning and breaking were established on a basis of far broader popular support—support that, moreover, has undergone the test of history for many centuries. Today those who are essentially working toward the overthrow of the constitutional system should have to answer to mothers and fathers for the deaths of the many hundreds of victims in conflicts between nationalities. The crippled lives of more than half a million refugees are on their conscience. Because of them, tens of millions of Soviet people who only yesterday were living in a united family but today find themselves outcasts in their own homes have lost tranquillity and the joy of life.

The people should decide what the social system should be like, but they are being deprived of this right.

Instead of showing concern for the security and well-being of every citizen and of society as a whole, the people who have acquired power frequently use it for interests that are alien to the people, as a means of unscrupulous self-assertion. The streams of words and mountains of statements and promises only underscore the scanty and wretched nature of their practical deeds. The inflation of power, more frightening than any other kind of inflation, is destroying our state and society. Every citizen feels growing uncertainty about tomorrow and deep concern for the future of his or her children.

The crisis of power has had a catastrophic effect on the economy. The chaotic, ungoverned slide toward a market has caused an explosion of selfishness—regional, departmental, group and personal. The war of laws and the encouragement of centrifugal tendencies have brought the destruction of the unified national-economic mechanism that took shape over decades. The result is a sharp falloff in the standard of living for the overwhelming majority of Soviet people and the flourishing of speculation and the shadow economy. It is high time to tell the people the truth: Unless urgent and resolute measures are taken to stabilize the economy, hunger and a new round of impoverishment are inevitable in the very near future, from which it is only one step to large-scale manifestations of spontaneous discontent, with destructive consequences. Only irresponsible people can set their hopes on some kind of help from abroad. No hand-outs are going to solve our problems; salvation is in our own hands. The time has come to measure the authority of every person or organization in terms of actual contributions to the restoration and development of the national economy.

For many years, we have heard from all sides incantations about commitment to the interests of the individual, to concern for his rights and social safeguards. But in fact people have been humiliated, their real rights and possibilities have been infringed, and they have been driven to despair. All the democratic institutions created through the expression of the people's will are losing their authority and effectiveness before our very eyes. This is the result of purposeful actions by those who, blatantly flouting the USSR Basic Law, are staging an unconstitutional coup, to all intents and purposes, and longing for an unbridled personal dictatorship. Prefectures, mayoralties and other unlawful structures are increasingly supplanting, in an unauthorized way, the Soviets that have been elected by the people.

An offensive against the rights of the working people is under way. The rights to work, education, health care, housing and recreation have been called in question.

Even people's basic personal safety is increasingly under threat. Crime is growing at a rapid rate and is becoming organized and politicized. The country is sinking into an abyss of violence and lawlessness. Never before in the country's history has the propaganda of sex and violence gained such wide scope, jeopardizing the health and lives of future generations. Millions of people are demanding that measures be taken against the octopus of crime and glaring immorality.

The deepening destabilization of the political and economic situation in the Soviet Union is undermining our positions in the world. Revanchist notes have been heard in some places, and demands for the revision of our borders are being put forward. Voices are even being heard calling for the dismemberment of the Soviet Union and for the possible establishment of international trusteeship over certain facilities in and regions of the country. Such is the bitter reality. Only yesterday, a Soviet person who found himself abroad felt that he was a worthy citizen of an influential and respected state. Now he is often a second-class foreigner whose treatment bears the imprint of scorn or sympathy.

The pride and honor of Soviet people must be restored in full.

The State Committee for the State of Emergency in the USSR is fully aware of the depth of the crisis that has struck our country; it is assuming responsibility for the fate of the homeland, and it is fully resolved to take very serious measures to bring the state and society out of crisis as quickly as possible.

We promise to conduct a wide-ranging, nationwide discussion of the draft of a new Union Treaty. Everyone will have the right and opportunity to think about this highly important act in a calm atmosphere and to make up his mind about it, for the fate of the numerous peoples of our great homeland will depend on what the Union will be like.

We intend to immediately restore legality and law and order, to put an end to bloodshed, to declare a merciless war against the criminal world, and to eradicate shameful phenomena that discredit our society and degrade Soviet citizens. We will clean the criminal elements from the streets of our cities and put an end to the high-handedness of the plunderers of public property.

We favor truly democratic processes and a consistent policy of reforms leading to the renewal of our homeland and to its economic and social prosperity, which will enable it to take a worthy place in the world community of nations.

The country's development should not be built on a fall-off in the population's living standard. In a healthy society, continual improvement in the well-being of all citizens will become the norm.

Without relaxing concern for the strengthening and protection of the rights of the individual, we will focus attention on protecting the interests of the broadest strata of the population, of those who have been hit the hardest by inflation, the disorganization of production, corruption and crime.

In the process of developing a mixed national economy, we will support private enterprise, providing it with the necessary possibilities for developing production and the service sphere.

Our top-priority concern will be solving the food and housing problems. All available forces will be mobilized for the satisfaction of these very urgent requirements of the people.

We call on workers, peasants, the working intelligentsia and all Soviet people to restore labor discipline and order in the shortest possible time and to raise the level of production, so as then to move resolutely forward. Our life, the future of our children and grandchildren and the fate of the fatherland will depend on this.

We are a peace-loving country and will unswervingly observe all the commitments we have made. We have no claims against anyone. We want to live in peace and friendship with everyone, but we firmly state that no one will ever be allowed to encroach on our sovereignty, independence and territorial integrity. Any attempts to talk to our country in the language of diktat, no matter where they come from, will be resolutely curbed.

For centuries, our multinational people have been filled with pride in their homeland; we have not been ashamed of our patriotic feelings, and we consider it natural and legitimate to raise present and future generations of citizens of our great power in this spirit.

To do nothing in this critical hour for the fate of the fatherland is to assume a grave responsibility for the tragic, truly unpredictable consequences. Everyone who cherishes our homeland, who wants to live and work in an atmosphere of tranquillity and confidence, who does not accept a continuation of bloody conflicts between nationalities and who sees his fatherland as independent and prosperous in the future must make the only correct choice. We call on all true patriots and people of goodwill to put an end to this time of troubles.

We call on all citizens of the Soviet Union to recognize their duty to the homeland and provide every kind of support to the State Committee for the State of Emergency in the USSR and to efforts to bring the country out of crisis.

Constructive proposals from public-political organizations, labor collectives and citizens will be gratefully accepted as a manifestation of their patriotic readiness to participate actively in the restoration of centuries-old friendship in the single family of fraternal peoples and in the revival of the fatherland.

—[signed] THE STATE COMMITTEE
FOR THE STATE OF EMERGENCY IN THE USSR.

Aug. 18, 1991.

STATEMENT BY THE CHAIRMAN
OF THE USSR SUPREME SOVIET

In connection with numerous requests I have received from working people asking
that I state my attitude toward the draft of the published Treaty on the Union of Sovereign States, I consider it necessary to note the following:

As is known, the draft treaty was supported, in the main, by the USSR Supreme
Soviet on July 12, 1991. At that time, the Supreme Soviet formed a fully empowered
Union delegation and directed it, in the process of doing further work on the draft
treaty and reaching agreement on it, to proceed from a number of propositions formulated by the country's supreme body of power.

Above all, the need was indicated to have the treaty's name and basic principles
reflect the results of the all-Union referendum, in which an absolute majority of the
country's citizens supported the preservation of the Union of Soviet Socialist Republics as a renewed federation of equal and sovereign republics. A similar approach
to the name and nature of our Union state was formulated by the Congress of USSR
People's Deputies. At the meeting of leaders of authorized delegations in Novo-
Ogarevo, detailed arguments were presented in support of this position of the USSR
Supreme Soviet. However, it was not reflected in the treaty's final text. Of course, this
question will no doubt require additional discussion by the Congress of USSR People's Deputies, and perhaps also in the form of an all-Union referendum connected
with the adoption of a new Constitution.

The USSR Supreme Soviet considered it advisable to provide in the draft Union
Treaty for the existence in the USSR of a single economic space, a single banking system and the allotment to the Union of property necessary for its normal functioning
as a federal state. Special stipulation was made for a requirement that independent tax
receipts for the Union budget be established. Unfortunately, the published text of the
treaty does not reflect these highly important propositions in a sufficiently explicit
fashion. This is also borne out by recent statements of the USSR Cabinet of Ministers, the Board of the USSR State Bank and a number of other Union agencies. Apparently, considerable adjustments are required in the treaty's text in this regard as
well.

The USSR Supreme Soviet devoted some extremely serious attention to terminating the so-called "war of laws," which in effect amounts to flagrant lawlessness. In
this connection, it was proposed that the treaty include a norm that would not allow
the USSR to suspend republic laws or the republics to suspend Union laws, and that
would require that possible disputes be resolved through conciliation procedures or
decisions by the USSR Constitutional Court. Despite the fact that this proposal was
supported by some very prominent Soviet legal experts, it too is not properly reflected
in the text of the treaty drawn up at Novo-Ogarevo. There is no special need to prove
how dangerous this is for the formation of a stable legal system in our country.

A procedure for the treaty's implementation during the transitional period that
ensures continuity in the operation of the bodies of state power and administration
also must be spelled out in the treaty's text with considerably greater precision. Without this, it will be impossible to maintain, to even a minimal extent, the functioning
of the national economy in the extremely grave crisis atmosphere that has developed
in the country.

In my opinion, all these problems require additional discussion at a session of the USSR Supreme Soviet and later, evidently, at a Congress of the country's People's Deputies.

Without this, such a supremely important document for the future of our state as the Union Treaty will not be able to fully express the Soviet people's will with respect to the preservation of the USSR—a great power that is called upon to serve the interests of citizens of all nationalities and that exerts a very important influence on the international situation the world over.

A. LUKYANOV,
Chairman of the USSR Supreme Soviet.

Aug. 16, 1991.

YELTSIN ACTS AGAINST THE COUP

To the Citizens of Russia

On the night of Aug. 18–19, 1991, the legally elected President of the country was removed from power.

Whatever reasons are used to justify this removal, what we are dealing with is a right-wing, reactionary, unconstitutional coup.

Despite all the difficulties and very grave trials that the people are experiencing, the democratic process in the country is assuming ever deeper dimensions and is becoming irreversible. The peoples of Russia are becoming the masters of their fate. The uncontrolled rights of unconstitutional bodies, including Party bodies, have been substantially restricted. The leadership of Russia has taken a resolute position on the Union Treaty, striving for the unity of the Soviet Union and the unity of Russia. Our position on this question made it possible to significantly accelerate the drafting of this treaty, clear it with all the republics, and set a date for signing it—Aug. 20, 1991.

This development of events aroused the animosity of reactionary forces and drove them into irresponsible, adventurist attempts to solve very complicated political and economic problems by methods of force. There were earlier attempts to stage a coup.

We have believed and continue to believe that these methods of force are unacceptable. They discredit the USSR before the whole world, undermine our prestige in the world community, and return us to the era of the cold war and the Soviet Union's isolation from the world community.

All this compels us to declare the so-called committee that has come to power illegal. Accordingly, we declare all the decisions and orders of this committee illegal.

We are confident that bodies of local power will unswervingly follow constitutional laws and the decrees of the President of the Russian SFSR. We call on the citizens of Russia to give the putschists the response they deserve and to demand that the country be returned to normal constitutional development.

Certainly **Gorbachev,** the country's President, must be given an opportunity to speak to the people. We demand the immediate convening of an Extraordinary Congress of USSR People's Deputies.

We are absolutely certain that our fellow countrymen will not allow the high-handedness and lawlessness of the putschists, who have lost all shame and conscience, to become firmly established. We appeal to servicemen to display lofty civic spirit and not to take part in the reactionary coup.

Until these demands are fulfilled, we call for a general strike of unlimited duration. We have no doubt that the world community will make an objective assessment of this cynical attempt at a right-wing coup.

—[signed] Yeltsin, President of Russia; Silayev, Chairman of the RSFSR Council of Ministers; and Khasbulatov, acting Chairman of the RSFSR Supreme Soviet.

Aug. 19, 1991, 9 a.m.

BORIS YELTSIN'S PRESS CONFERENCE

A rehearsal was held on March 28, 1991. Now the political play is being performed according to a set script. Once again armored personnel carriers, tanks, troops and special police units are in Moscow. This morning 50 tanks of the Taman Division surrounded the "White House" [the Russian SFSR Supreme Soviet's building—Trans.] on Krasnaya Presnya Embankment. In this situation, Russian President Boris Yeltsin and the Russian government held a press conference for Soviet and foreign journalists. Before the press conference began, the priest Gleb Yakunin, a Russian SFSR People's Deputy, reported that Col. Vitaly Urazhtsev, RSFSR People's Deputy and cochairman of the Shield [*Shchit*] union, had been arrested last night. The arrests of many democratic leaders may follow. At any rate, State Security Committee personnel have already tried to arrest Gleb Yakunin and RSFSR People's Deputy Bella Denisenko. Bella Denisenko reported that, beginning at 12 noon today, miners are declaring a political strike.

After reading out the appeal to the people that had been signed by the Russian President, Prime Minister Ivan Silayev and Ruslan Khasbulatov, acting Chairman of the RSFSR Supreme Soviet, Yeltsin said that, unfortunately, he could not convey it to the people, since all the news media are under the putschists' control. The Echo of Moscow radio station has been shut down, and broadcasting by Radio Russia and Russian Television has been stopped. Boris Yeltsin has issued a decree in which he emphasizes that this event is a military coup and that neither the President of Russia nor the Russian government can recognize the group of putschists who have seized power as the country's legitimate government. He urged the citizens of Russia to go on a political strike of unlimited duration. This is the only chance to defend freedom and democracy, since the legitimate government elected by the people has neither tanks nor bullets, unfortunately. Yeltsin reported that he had been unable to make contact with Mikhail Gorbachev, the country's President, but that he would use every means open to him to try to see to it that the President of the USSR is given an opportunity to speak to the country's citizens. It is not known what has happened to Gorbachev or what his condition is. The putschists' lie about the poor state of Gorbachev's health can be disproved by reading the Western news agencies' reports that he has been arrested.

At present, how to convey accurate information to the people is a very crucial question. Yeltsin expressed the hope that at least the Western news media will be able to report the true state of affairs through their channels. But this morning, in violation of international accords, all Western broadcasting was jammed again.

One last thing. This morning, in the center of Moscow, leaflets appeared urging people to go to Manege Square. Yeltsin said that someone is simply using his name to bring people out into the streets. Right now, this is very dangerous. After all, the "black colonels" are always thirsting for blood.

DECREE OF THE PRESIDENT OF THE RUSSIAN SOVIET FEDERATED SOCIALIST REPUBLIC

In connection with the actions of a group of individuals who have declared themselves the State Committee for the State of Emergency, I decree that:

1. The declaration forming the committee is unconstitutional, and the actions of its organizers constitute a coup d'état, which is nothing less than a crime against the state.

2. All decisions made in the name of the so-called Committee for the State of Emergency are to be considered illegal and invalid on the territory of the RSFSR. A legally elected government is in operation in the Russian Federation, consisting of the President, the Supreme Soviet and the Chairman of the Council of Ministers, and all state and local bodies of power and administration of the RSFSR.

3. Actions by officials to carry out the decisions of the aforesaid committee fall under the purview of the RSFSR Criminal Code and are subject to prosecution under the law.

This decree takes effect as of the moment it is signed.

B. YELTSIN,
President of the RSFSR.

Pravda and *Izvestiia,* no. 197, August 20, 1991, p. 1; *Megapolis-Express,* special edition, August 19, 1991, p. 1; *Kuranty,* special edition, no. 1, August 19, 1991; translated in *Current Digest of the Soviet Press,* XLIII, 33 (September 18, 1991), pp. 1–7.

End of the USSR: Formation of the Commonwealth of Independent States

Meeting secretly outside Minsk, the capital of Belorus, the leaders of the three Slavic republics—Yeltsin of Russia, Leonid Kravchuk of Ukraine, and Stanislav Shushkevich of Belorus—decided to dissolve the Soviet Union. On December 8, 1991, they signed the "Agreement Establishing the Commonwealth of Independent States," which noted that "the talks on the drafting of a new Soviet Treaty have become deadlocked and that the de facto process of withdrawal of republics from the Union of Soviet Socialist Republics and the formation of independent States has become a reality." It declared that the USSR no longer existed as a subject of international law and a geopolitical reality and invited former Soviet republics, as well as other states, to join the new Commonwealth. The meeting and agreement had been hastily arranged, and Gorbachev was shocked to discover that his beloved federation had been so summarily abolished. Several of the non-Slavic republics were also dismayed about the end of the

USSR, and a summit conference was held in the Kazakh capital, Alma-Ata, to confirm the decisions taken in Belorus. On December 21, 1991, almost exactly sixty-nine years after the official proclamation of the Soviet Union, eleven leaders of the former Soviet republics (Georgia absented itself) agreed that "with the establishment of the Commonwealth of Independent States, the Union of Soviet Socialist Republics ceases to exist." A decision taken by leaders, not by referendum, it was soon confirmed by international recognition. Opposition to the dissolution of the USSR would become a hallmark of the Communist parties of the post-Soviet republics, but, as political scientist Gail Lapidus has pointed out, these preemptory decisions probably prevented much conflict in a process of "decolonization" that potentially could have led to bloodshed.

STATEMENT BY THE HEADS OF STATE OF THE REPUBLIC OF BELARUS, THE RUSSIAN SFSR AND UKRAINE

(Izvestia, Dec. 9, p. 1. Complete text:) We, the leaders of the Republic of Belarus, the RSFSR and Ukraine,

—noting that the talks on the drafting of a new Union Treaty have reached an impasse and that the objective process of the secession of republics from the USSR and the formation of independent states has become a real fact;

—stating that the shortsighted policy of the center has led to a profound economic and political crisis, the collapse of production and a catastrophic decline in the living standard for virtually all strata of society;

—taking into consideration the increase in social tension in many regions of the former USSR, which has led to conflicts between nationalities with numerous human casualties;

—aware of our responsibility to our peoples and the world community and of the urgent need for the practical implementation of political and economic reforms, hereby declare the formation of a Commonwealth of Independent States, on which the parties signed an Agreement on Dec. 8, 1991.

The Commonwealth of Independent States, consisting of the Republic of Belarus, the RSFSR and Ukraine, is open for accession by all member-states of the former USSR, as well as for other states that share the goals and principles of this Agreement.

The member-states of the Commonwealth intend to pursue a course aimed at strengthening international peace and security. They guarantee the fulfillment of international obligations stemming from the treaties and agreements of the former USSR and ensure unified control over nuclear weapons and their nonproliferation.

S. SHUSHKEVICH,
Chairman of the Supreme Soviet
of the Republic of Belarus.

B. YELTSIN,
President of the RSFSR.

L. KRAVCHUK,
President of Ukraine.

Minsk, Dec. 8, 1991.

LEADERS EXPLAIN RATIONALE FOR MINSK PACT

Ukraine: 'WE WILL DO EVERYTHING WE CAN SO THAT THERE WILL NEVER BE A CENTER.'

President Leonid Kravchuk Said, Summing Up. (By Vladimir Skachko.) At the airport on their return from Minsk late on the evening of Dec. 8, President Leonid Kravchuk and Prime Minister Vitold Fokin, the leaders of the Ukraine delegation, answered journalists' questions about what had taken place in the Belorussian capital.

Leonid Kravchuk said: "The most important event of the meeting was the signing of the agreement on the Commonwealth of Independent States. . . .

"Immediately after this agreement was signed, a conversation with Mikhail Gorbachev took place. Stanislav Shushkevich, Chairman of the Belorussian Supreme Soviet, told him on our behalf that the agreement had been signed in accordance with the Constitutions of Russia, Ukraine and Belorussia.

"Minsk was designated as the city in which our commonwealth's coordinating agencies will be located. Everything was honest, open and lawful. USSR President Mikhail Gorbachev was informed of our meeting in advance. We will try to take in hand the uncontrolled collapse of the USSR. Don't try to shift the blame to us, saying that we have gone and ruined the Union. The Union started to collapse in 1985, and the authors of this destructive process are known. We have pooled the efforts of three great states so that enterprises will not shut down and people's situation will not worsen to the point of no return. We acted in the fundamental interests of the peoples."

Commenting on Gorbachev's efforts to preserve a common Center, Leonid Kravchuk said: "We have done everything we could so that there will never again be a Center in our lives and so that no Center will ever again be in charge of our states."

On M. Gorbachev's Future and the Muscovites' New Year's Table

Leonid Kravchuk's Press Conference. (By Staff Correspondent S. Tsikora.) [At the Dec. 8 press conference] L. Kravchuk was asked about the possibility of the USSR President's using forcible methods to reconstitute the former Union. In reply, the President of Ukraine said that forcible methods are not M. Gorbachev's element. "I have known Mikhail Sergeyevich for a long time: He will act within the framework of the Constitution and democratic norms. I don't think that at the end of his career he will want to tarnish his reputation as a democrat."

A fundamentally new approach to the nuclear weapons on the territory of Belarus, the Russian SFSR and Ukraine was announced at the press conference. The heads of the three states have agreed that, with the creation of the commonwealth, control over nuclear potential should be tightened. The leadership of the three countries reached an accord in principle that henceforth the use of nuclear might will be possible only with the agreement of the three states and the simultaneous pushing of three launch buttons by the leaders of these republics. In other words, the degree of control over nuclear weapons will be tightened threefold.

Special emphasis was put on the point that, in forming the commonwealth, the heads of the three states acted in strict accordance with the laws of their republics. "We want to stop the process of breakdown that is taking place today under the leadership of the 'glorious' center," [Kravchuk said]. . . .

The Creation of the New Commonwealth Should Avert Tragedy

Stanislav Shushkevich's Press Conference. (By Staff Correspondent N. Matukovsky.) Minsk—S. Shushkevich, Chairman of the Supreme Soviet of the Republic of Belarus, met with journalists from the central and republic press for the first time since returning from Belovezhskaya Pushcha.

"Realizing that the collapse of the Union threatens the country's peoples with many calamities, we decided to avert a tragedy by creating an improved form of Union—a Commonwealth of Independent States. . . . It was impossible to keep sitting with arms folded and watching as dangerous processes built up rapidly. At State Council meetings, which we are often invited to attend, we only sit and listen to what the President says, but he barely listens to what we say. At first, the idea of a 'troika' went no further than economic problems," S. Shushkevich said, "but when we started discussing them, we realized that it was impossible to ignore the resolution of political questions. I would like to warn right now against an incorrect understanding of the nature of the Commonwealth. It is not based on national or ethnic hallmarks. . . . We proceeded primarily from economic considerations. Belarus, Ukraine and Russia border on one another, and any economic action in one republic is immediately reflected in another. . . .

"We took an extremely careful and deliberate approach to each point in the agreement. Every article went through four or five versions. . . ."

Answering a question as to what his attitude is toward Gorbachev's idea of holding a Congress of People's Deputies, Stanislav Stanislavovich replied:

"I personally am in favor of holding a Congress that would dot all the i's and cross all the t's. But I'm afraid it is already impossible to convene one—the Deputies from Ukraine and Belarus wouldn't go to a Congress, and some Deputies from Russia wouldn't go either. And let's be frank. The President himself buried the idea of a Congress in the recent past. There is hardly any point in assembling a Congress in order to preserve presidential power."

QUESTION: Why will the coordinating center be located in Minsk, not in Moscow?

ANSWER: For two reasons. First—in Moscow, the unnecessary structures that are eliminated are reborn right away under various new signboards. We were afraid that these structures would crush us. The second reason. We were looking for a quieter, calmer city, and a relatively small one. Everyone agreed on Minsk. . . .

Q: What did you talk about with M. Gorbachev when you telephoned him from Belovezhskaya Pushcha?

A: It was a difficult conversation. It was my understanding that the President's inner circle had given him incorrect information on many points and that he was not well-versed on some important questions. Otherwise, it is impossible to explain his position and his prediction regarding Ukraine's future. . . .

Kazakhstan Interprets the New Realities

Nursultan Nazarbayev's Press Conference. (By G. Alimov.) On Dec. 9, [Kazakhstan] President Nursultan Nazarbayev was in Moscow for a meeting in the Kremlin with Presidents Mikhail Gorbachev and Boris Yeltsin. During a 90-minute conversation, they discussed the documents signed in Minsk by the leaders of Belarus, Russia and Ukraine. Immediately after the conversation in the Kremlin, N. Nazarbayev held a press conference at Kazakhstan's permanent mission. He answered numerous questions from Soviet and foreign journalists.

QUESTION: Three republics have announced their denunciation of the 1922 treaty. Does this mean that as of yesterday there is no longer a Union, or does it mean something else?

ANSWER: Both Yeltsin and Shushkevich (I have not yet had a chance to talk with Kravchuk) have stated that there is no Slavic union; there was a meeting, and these documents came out of it in the course of the discussion. At the meeting with M. Gorbachev, Boris Nikolayevich reaffirmed that there was no question of any kind of Slavic union. The Minsk documents can be perceived as an initiative of the three republics.

Now about whether the Soviet Union does or does not exist. What you are talking about raises a question for me, too. The Minsk documents emphasize that the laws of third countries are inoperative on the signatories' territory, and that Union bodies are also eliminated. But we are talking about bodies that were created by the fifth Congress of USSR People's Deputies. They are constitutional, they are legal, and hence these questions, I believe, can be decided only by a Congress. In general, such questions should be resolved in a coordinated way, not without consulting the other republics. They didn't even know about them. I can only regret that it happened this way. . . .

Q: If you believe that this is an initiative, but the leaders of the three states consider it a fait accompli, where does that leave Kazakhstan and President Gorbachev?

A: Today, when I went in to see Gorbachev, and Yeltsin arrived a minute later, we agreed that the agreement signed by the three republics would be sent to the republic parliaments as an initiative and would be discussed along with the draft treaty on a Union of Sovereign States. . . . After the Supreme Soviets have discussed these documents and decided in favor of one document or the other, the question of convening a Congress of People's Deputies will probably arise.

The treaty on the USS provides a place for both a President and a Union government. The Minsk document contains nothing of the sort. You know, I have a mixed attitude toward President Gorbachev and have criticized him more than once for mistakes he has made and for conservative and inhibitory features in his policies, for lagging behind events. But I believe that at the present difficult moment, Gorbachev has not yet exhausted all his possibilities. That is my personal opinion. At this extremely difficult time of transition, I think he is needed. . . .

Q: What was the atmosphere like at the meeting with President Gorbachev in the Kremlin?

A: Gorbachev, like me, did not know that such a document was going to be signed. In talking with me before-hand, Yeltsin, Shushkevich and Kravchuk all said that they were going to discuss how to jointly change over to a market economy, co-ordinate their positions, and discuss what to do next about the draft treaty on the USS. As far as Mikhail Sergeyevich's reaction is concerned, I think he was distressed. But I didn't see anything so terribly extraordinary in this document, except for maybe two or three points. . . .

Q: You say that you still hold to the idea of a confederation. At the same time, you have declared that you are a pragmatist. If the option of a commonwealth turns out to be more progressive, will you change your viewpoint?

A: Yes, I always act as a pragmatist, and I will proceed on the basis of reality. . . .

Q: Do you admit the possibility that there could be another initiative—from the Central Asian republics, for example?

A: I am categorically opposed to treaties being concluded on a national, ethnic basis. I think that is medieval. I would caution my neighbors against doing that. . . .

Q: What will happen if the parliaments of the three republics that signed the document vote for the commonwealth option, while the others vote for the USS treaty?

A: That will be bad. I hope very much that people in all the republics will be reasonable, that the people will show wisdom.

Izvestiia, December 9, 1991, p. 1; *Nezavisimaia gazeta,* December 10, 1991, p. 3; *Izvestiia,* December 10, 1991, p. 2; translated in *Current Digest of the Soviet Press,* XLIII, 49 (January 8, 1992), pp. 10, 5–6, 4–5.

===== **Mikhail Gorbachev, "Speech of Resignation"** =====
December 25, 1991

Mikhail Sergeevich Gorbachev is arguably the person who brought more freedom to more people than anyone else in the twentieth century. His achievements were enormous: the end of the Communist monopoly of power in the USSR and the devolution of political decision-making from the center to republics and localities; the initiation of economic reforms that led to a market economy; the end of state censorship; the opening of Soviet borders; the end of the Soviet empire in East Central Europe and the withdrawal of Soviet troops from Afghanistan; and the end of the Cold War and the nuclear arms race. At the same time, his failures were also great: the decline and near collapse of the Soviet economy; the progressive weakening of the state and its legitimacy; his inability to ameliorate the interethnic and nationality problems of the federation; the fall of Soviet influence abroad and its steady retreat from superpower status; the failure to achieve a more democratic form of socialism; and finally the disintegration and disappearance of the very state and system that he hoped so desperately to preserve. His legacy is undeniable but deeply contradictory. As one Russian commentator, who lived through the seven years of Gorbachev's rule, remembered, "Fear departed. The valves of our self-respect were opened. . . . So, what has Gorbachev left us? From his adversaries' viewpoint—a broken power that used to be called the Soviet Union; unchecked inflation, beggars on the streets;

millionaires and, it is said, up to 80 percent of the people at the poverty line. But on the other
hand, we have the name of Andrei Dmitrievich Sakharov and the recovery of our sight. We
have the books of Aleksandr Isaevich Solzhenitsyn and the comprehension of a great truth—
the words "human being" really can sound proud. Is this all that little?" [1]

MIKHAIL GORBACHEV'S SPEECH
ON CENTRAL TELEVISION [DECEMBER 25]

Dear compatriots! Fellow citizens! Due to the situation that has taken shape as a result of the formation of the Commonwealth of Independent States, I am ceasing my
activity in the post of President of the USSR. I am making this decision out of considerations of principle.

I have firmly advocated the independence of peoples and the sovereignty of republics. But at the same time I have favored the preservation of the Union state and
the integrity of the country.

Events have taken a different path. A policy line aimed at dismembering the
country and disuniting the state has prevailed, something that I cannot agree with.

Even after the Alma-Ata meeting and the decisions adopted there, my position
on this score has not changed.

Moreover, I am convinced that decisions of such scope should have been adopted
on the basis of the free expression of the people's will.

Nevertheless, I will do everything in my power to ensure that the agreements
signed there lead to real concord in society, make it easier to get out of the crisis and
facilitate the process of reform.

Speaking to you for the last time as President of the USSR, I consider it necessary to express my assessment of the path traversed since 1985. Especially since there
are a good many contradictory, superficial and unobjective opinions on this score.

Fate ordained that when I became head of state it was already clear that things
were not going well in the country. We have a great deal of everything—land, petroleum, gas and other natural resources—and God has endowed us with intelligence
and talent, too, but we live much worse than people in the developed countries do,
and we are lagging further and further behind them.

The reason was evident—society was suffocating in the grip of the command-
bureaucratic system. Doomed to serve ideology and to bear the terrible burden of the
arms race, it had been pushed to the limit of what was possible.

All attempts at partial reforms—and there were a good many of them—failed,
one after the other. The country had lost direction. It was impossible to go on living
that way. Everything had to be changed fundamentally.

That is why I have never once regretted that I did not take advantage of the position of General Secretary just to "reign" for a few years. I would have considered
that irresponsible and immoral.

I realized that to begin reforms on such a scale and in such a society as ours was
an extremely difficult and even risky endeavor. But even today I am convinced of the

---

1. Inna Muravova, "It Was, It Was," *Rossiiskaia gazeta,* December 27, 1991, p. 1; translated in *Current Digest
of the Soviet Press,* XLIII, 52 (January 29, 1992), p. 3.

historical correctness of the democratic reforms that were begun in the spring of 1985.

The process of renewing the country and of fundamental changes in the world community proved to be much more complex than could have been surmised. However, what has been accomplished should be appraised on its merits.

Society has received freedom and has been emancipated politically and spiritually. This is the most important gain, one that we have not yet become fully aware of, and for this reason we have not yet learned to make use of freedom.

Nevertheless, work of historic significance has been done:

—The totalitarian system, which for a long time deprived the country of the opportunity to become prosperous and flourishing, has been eliminated.

—A breakthrough has been achieved in the area of democratic transformations. Free elections, freedom of the press, religious freedoms, representative bodies of power and a multiparty system have become a reality. Human rights have been recognized as the highest principle.

—Movement toward a mixed economy has begun, and the equality of all forms of ownership is being established. Within the framework of a land reform, the peasantry has begun to revive, private farming has appeared, and millions of hectares of land are being given to rural and urban people. The economic freedom of the producer has been legalized, and entrepreneurship, the formation of joint-stock companies and privatization have begun to gather momentum.

—In turning the economy toward a market, it is important to remember that this is being done for the sake of human beings. In this difficult time, everything possible must be done for their social protection, and this applies especially to old people and children.

We are living in a new world:

—An end has been put to the cold war, and the arms race and the insane militarization of the country, which disfigured our economy and the public consciousness and morals, have been halted. The threat of a world war has been removed.

I want to emphasize once again that, for my part, during the transitional period I did everything I could to preserve reliable control over nuclear weapons.

—We opened up to the world and renounced interference in the affairs of others and the use of troops outside the country's borders. And in response we received trust, solidarity and respect.

—We have become one of the main bulwarks in the reorganization of present-day civilization on peaceful, democratic principles.

—Peoples and nations have received real freedom in choosing the path of their self-determination. Searches for democratic reforms in the multinational state led us to the threshold of concluding a new Union Treaty.

All these changes required enormous effort and took place in an acute struggle, with mounting resistance from old, obsolete and reactionary forces—both the former Party-state structures and the economic apparatus—and also from our habits, ideological prejudices, and a leveling and parasitic mentality. The changes ran up against our intolerance, low level of political sophistication and fear of change.

For this reason, we lost a great deal of time. The old system collapsed before a new one had time to start working. And the crisis in society became even more exacerbated.

I know about the dissatisfaction with the present grave situation and about the sharp criticism that is being made of the authorities at all levels, and of my personal activity. But I would like to emphasize once again: Fundamental changes in such an enormous country, and one with such a legacy, could not proceed painlessly or without difficulties and upheavals.

The August putsch brought the general crisis to the breaking point. The most disastrous aspect of this crisis was the disintegration of the state system. Today I am alarmed by our people's losing their citizenship in a great country—the consequences may prove to be very grave for everyone.

It seems vitally important to me to preserve the democratic gains of the past few years. They were achieved through suffering throughout our history and our tragic experience. Under no circumstances and on no pretext can they be given up. Otherwise, all hopes for something better will be buried.

I am saying all this honestly and straightforwardly. This is my moral duty.

Today I want to express my gratitude to all citizens who supported the policy of renewing the country and joined in the implementation of democratic reforms.

I am grateful to the state, political and public figures and the millions of people abroad who understood our plans, supported them, met us halfway, and embarked on sincere cooperation with us.

I am leaving my post with a feeling of anxiety. But also with hope and with faith in you, in your wisdom and strength of spirit. We are the heirs to a great civilization, and its rebirth into a new, up-to-date and fitting life now depends on each and every one of us.

I want to thank from the bottom of my heart those who during these years stood with me for a right and good cause. Certainly some mistakes could have been avoided, and many things could have been done better. But I am sure that sooner or later our common efforts will bear fruit and our peoples will live in a prosperous and democratic society.

I wish all of you the very best.

Rossiiskaia gazeta, December 26, 1991, pp. 1–2; translated in *Current Digest of the Soviet Press,* XLIII, 52 (January 29, 1992), pp. 1, 3.

CHAPTER NINE

THE SECOND RUSSIAN REPUBLIC AND THE "NEAR ABROAD"

The end of the "Soviet experiment" was followed by another experiment, this time in building a democratic, capitalist society as quickly as possible. The central figure in this radical "transition to democracy" was the charismatic Boris Yeltsin, the courageous defender of democracy against the coup plotters in August 1991. But a mere two years later, Yeltsin deeply tarnished his image when he suppressed the parliament and sent troops to evict them from the White House. The bloody suppression of his political opponents in October 1993 marked a turning point in Russia's evolution. Although a more stable political structure was built around a powerful presidency, in the second half of the 1990s, Yeltsin himself appeared more and more to be a weak and confused leader, capricious and often indecisive, the victim of too much alcohol and poor health, and too tolerant of the widespread, metastasizing corruption in the country. The Russian invasions of the breakaway republic of Chechnya in December 1994, and again in the summer of 1999, confirmed the doubts of many that Yeltsin was incapable of dealing with the colossal problems facing a divided and dispirited Russia.

The twenty-five month period between the August 1991 coup and the September 1993 coup was marked by a vigorous, even vicious struggle for power within the ruling elites. That struggle was all the more intense because it would determine the future shape of Russia's political system and the distribution of property and wealth, as the old command economy was transformed into a capitalist system. A lesson some would draw from that period was that it was impossible in Russia both to impose shock therapy and maintain the existing constitutional order. With the breakup of the Soviet Union, the generally pro-Yeltsin parliament agreed that emergency powers should be given to the president, who could then guide the ship of state to a more tranquil harbor. But the first year of Yeltsin's rule was marked, not by compromise and consensus, but by the launching of a radical economic program—Yegor Gaidar's policy of "shock therapy"—which further divided opinion and the leadership. Lurching toward a free market in 1992 only increased the misery of the population and threatened the positions of many industrial and political leaders. Russia was faced by a deepening crisis of political legitimation, with the population growing increasingly disillusioned by politics and its leaders. The parliament sought to become the dominant branch of government and resisted Yeltsin's efforts to create a stronger presidency.

The crisis came to a head in September–October 1993, when Yeltsin dissolved the parliament, and the parliamentarians refused to budge. The army launched an attack on the White House, which soon was aflame, and Russia witnessed fighting in the streets of its capital and the arrest of the leading members of its legislature. While Yeltsin's seizure of power and the subsequent violence damaged the president's democratic reputation, it also ended the division of central power and paved the way for a new, presidential system of government. Yeltsin's first two years in power had been a failure—in economic policy and in building the broad political coalitions needed to move Russia toward capitalism. But he managed both to create a new political structure and keep the country from disintegrating.

The liberal reformers around Yeltsin lost the next two parliamentary elections, and Communists and nationalist oppositionists held the majority in the new state Duma. Though Yeltsin was nearly counted out in the run-up to the 1996 presidential elections, his forces rallied. They monopolized the media, spent lavishly, demonized their Communist opponents, and pulled off a stunning victory by allying with General Aleksandr Lebed, a popular candidate. But in his second term, Yeltsin proved to be even more erratic. Just after Lebed negotiated an end to the first Chechen war, the president fired him as secretary of the Security Council. In 1998, Yeltsin rid himself of Prime Minister Viktor Chernomyrdin (1992–1998) and rapidly went through a succession of heads of government—Sergei Kirienko (March–August 1998), Chernomyrdin again (August–September, 1998; rejected by the Duma), Evgenii Primakov (1998–1999), Sergei Stepashin (May–August 1999), ending up with Vladimir Putin, an obscure veteran of the KGB. Parliament watched and fumed as real decisions were made in the court of the president, where people intrigued to reach the ear of the president. Within the circles of court politics, the most powerful person was Yeltsin's daughter, Tatiana Diachenko, who was implicated in complex financial dealings that further blackened her father's reputation. Unpredictably, on December 31, 1999, Yeltsin suddenly announced his retirement, elevating Putin to acting president. The young heir apparent had gained popularity by ruthlessly pursuing a second war against the Chechens, and he easily glided through the elections of March 2000.

As the millennium ended, Yeltsin's peculiar road to democracy and capitalism had left Russia with a crippled state and a battered society. Huge amounts of property and wealth had passed into the hands of a "new bourgeoisie," which rather than developing the country, squandered its resources and siphoned off billions into foreign banks. Criminal and political mafias competed for control of the economic pie, while about 40 percent of the population watched its incomes fall. In the 1990s, only a quarter of workers received their wages on time; average life expectancy for men fell from 65 to 58 years, for women from 75 to 71; and the suicide rate rose 43 percent. The state could neither collect taxes nor control crime. The Russian government was fighting a new war in Chechnya, provoked by Chechen militants into breaking its earlier agreement to wait five years before deciding the final status of the region. Isolated internationally and repeatedly humiliated by the Western powers, Putin's Russia set out to regain its lost status in its neighborhood and the world.

Although Russia had not yet become a fully democratic state, its evolution over the 1990s involved the internal generation among many elite politicians, as well as younger members of society, of an identification with democratic values, a grudging acceptance of its current state boundaries, and a formal respect for the sovereignty and territorial integrity of its neighbors. Russian leaders and intellectuals continued to identify their country as a great power and shared the view that the state had to be stronger and more unified. The government negotiated a series of agreements with the various republics and regions of the Russian Federation, granting special powers to many of them in a system known as "assymetrical federalism."

Weaker and more decentralized than before, Russia's status as a great power became a purely symbolic issue. Yet the Russian government continued to see the "Near Abroad," the countries of the former Soviet Union, as its sphere of interest and resented intrusions by other powers. Like the United States in the Western Hemisphere, Russia sought to police its own neighborhood and reserve the right to guard frontiers that impinge on its security. But Russia's self-proclaimed status was a highly imaginative one that no longer corresponded to its actual power. Even if Russia wanted to reconstruct an empire, it was no longer capable of doing so. The debilitating wars in Chechnya were a potent demonstration of the heavy costs of imperialism. Yet because of its own internal confusion and corruption and its occasional pretensions to empire, Russia engendered fear and insecurity among its neighbors. The other post-Soviet states learned to live with a large, unpredictable Russia that had neither a clear sense of its own national identity and interests nor a consistent idea of what its policies toward the former Soviet states should be. The hope that at least some of the newly independent states, perhaps Armenia or Kyrgyzstan, would become consolidated democracies dissipated as those in charge restricted the media, arrested opponents, and manipulated elections.

Lilia Shevtsova, a researcher at the Moscow office of the Carnegie Endowment, is one of the most acute and unbiased Russian analysts of the current political scene. Sympathetic to the aims and goals of the democratic transition, she has become ever more critical of the political and economic consequences of the way in which democratization and marketization have been carried out. The essay by Ronald Grigor Suny looks beyond Russia proper to the new states of the South Caucasus (Transcaucasia) to understand why the collapse of communism led to civil war in Georgia, a restoration of the old Communist elite in Azerbaijan, and the triumph of the nationalists in Armenia.

RUSSIA'S POST-COMMUNIST POLITICS: REVOLUTION OR CONTINUITY?

Lilia Shevtsova

BORIS YELTSIN'S "REVOLUTIONARY LIBERALISM"

The first stage of Russia's post-communist development began in December 1991 with the abolition of the USSR and ended in September 1993 with Yeltsin's dissolution of the Russian parliament. The period witnessed a transfer of power from traditional Soviet institutions to a new Russian center headed by Yeltsin and his advisors . . . Hoping to transform Russia's state-run economy into a market-based system "in a single bound," Yeltsin launched a program designed to transform Russian society radically. At the same time, he adopted a foreign policy aimed at preserving

Russia's status as a superpower and securing Moscow's position as an ally, not simply a partner, of the United States.

It soon became clear, however, that Yeltsin's program was deeply flawed. Economic reforms were launched without adequate knowledge of how marketization was to be accomplished and without the benefit of a stable political order. Moreover, the attempt to preserve Russia's superpower status interfered with the demands of democratization and complicated Moscow's efforts to establish good relations with the outside world, particularly with the other Soviet successor states. The new elite, like the old, continued to approach politics as a Manichean struggle that could lead only to the unconditional victory of one side over the other.

Russia's post-communist transformation was uniquely difficult. In most of the post-communist countries of Central Europe, the collapse of communism did not bring with it the total collapse of the state. Russia, on the other hand, was forced not only to build a new economy and a new regime but to reconstruct at the same time the state structures needed to carry out these tasks. Moreover, the USSR's superpower status, Russia's military-oriented economy, the multinational character of its federation, and the deeply-rooted hegemonic and messianic sentiments of both elite and society further complicated the transformation process in Russia.

The lack of elite consensus about the principal agenda of reform also differentiates Russia's transition from that in other countries. In most post-communist states in Central Europe, political elites agreed upon basic priorities and developed mechanisms for peacefully negotiating the early stages of the transition. The economic and political pragmatism of former communists also contributed to stability and support for reform from below. In Poland and Hungary, for example, old and new ruling elites succeeded in working out "roundtable" agreements on powersharing and reform priorities that were backed by a coalition of the most powerful political forces in each country. As a result, responsibility for the consequences of reform was shared by all signatories to the agreement.

Russian political society, in contrast, was far more divided from the very outset. In the aftermath of the failed August 1991 coup, the Russian Communist Party was banned, and its activists became completely disoriented. Conservative statist and national-patriotic forces, on the other hand, had yet to consolidate or even articulate their programs. The only political movement with significant influence at the time was Democratic Russia, the mass-based movement that had helped bring Yeltsin to power in 1990 and 1991. Although it represented liberals and democrats among the intelligentsia as well as the new entrepreneurial class, Democratic Russia's support was mainly limited to large cities. As a result, Yeltsin was forced to launch his reforms without a coherent opposition with which to negotiate.

To be sure, a segment of the anti-communist opposition and pragmatists among the traditional *nomenklatura* managed to conclude a shaky, informal pact in the wake of the failed coup. This "August Pact" provided for the devolution of power from USSR institutions to those of the RSFSR (soon to be renamed the Russian Federation). The pact was worked out, however, by a small group of people and without public discussion. Moreover, it left few of the participants with a role, and hence a stake, in the future order. Lacking unified political support, clear obligations for participants, and incentives to fulfill the agreement, the pact quickly collapsed. Russia's political elite was therefore unable to reach a consensus on the character of the new Russian state or the model of postcommunist transformation.

Of equal importance, Yeltsin failed to build broad social support for reform. Instead of using Democratic Russia to build support at the grass roots, Yeltsin chose to rely on a narrow circle of close advisors, most of whom were pragmatic members of the old *nomenklatura*. At a critical moment in late 1991, Yeltsin refused to hold preterm elections to legislative and executive bodies, both in Moscow and in the provinces. He also missed the opportunity to create a new, more coherent institutional order with clearly defined spheres of responsibility for different branches of power. Finally, he gave no attention to establishing a well-functioning party system. In the absence of mass-based parties or social movements, corporatist groups rooted in the old ruling class proved better at articulating their interests and influencing policy. Instead, Yeltsin concentrated on building a vertical system of presidential power through the appointment of loyalists as "presidential representatives" (*predstaviteli prezidenta*) and "heads of administration" (*glavy administratsii* or *gubernatory*) in the provinces. The end result was a collection of ill-designed institutions with few social roots, which immediately became a source of constant conflict.

In short, Yeltsin embarked on a course of "revolutionary liberalism" from above in a style characteristic of many authoritarian rulers. He relied not on society but on the administrative apparatus of the *ancien régime* to implement his program. Ironically, his "revolution from above" was reminiscent of Soviet-era "campaigns," while his strategy of reform resembled Gorbachev's—the use of charisma to personalize the political process; reliance on a vertical system of presidential power to implement his policies; and improved relations with the West in the hope that a new "Marshall Plan" would rescue the country. Also like Gorbachev, Yeltsin chose many policies at random, "winging it" rather than operating from a well-chosen, carefully considered plan.

Despite these similarities, there were also important differences between Yeltsin and Gorbachev. Gorbachev attempted to transform the communist system, not destroy it. Yeltsin's primary political goal, in contrast, was the obliteration of the old power structures and the state that supported them, while attempting at the same time to build entirely new political institutions. This simultaneous attempt to destroy and create accounts for the revolutionary nature of Yeltsin's policies and distinguishes him from Gorbachev.

In retrospect, however, it is clear that Yeltsin failed to break with the style of governance and the mentality he had acquired as a Communist Party *apparatchik*. His tendency was to purge supporters when doing so served his political interests. This flexibility helped him maneuver on the highly polarized Russian political scene. But it also made it impossible to elaborate a stable and viable policy, to strike stable alliances, or to secure a power base. Yeltsin's reform government was therefore doomed to be a cabinet of loners—of "kamikazes," as former Prime Minister Yegor Gaidar once described himself. Yeltsin's revolutionary style was thus contradictory and inconsistent. He would attempt to make a radical breakthrough on one issue and ignore the price this breakthrough would exact on his program in general. He also allowed himself to become involved in haggling over details and would make sudden and unjustified concessions.

In the final analysis, Yeltsin proved unable to meet the new challenges he had himself helped create. His decision in late 1991 to forego political reform, his failure to force his allies in the democratic movement to be more accommodating, and his unwillingness or inability to present society with a clear vision of reform, all contributed to the political crises that deepened over the course of 1992 and 1993.

CONFLICT AT THE TOP:
ELITE OPPOSITION TO "SHOCK THERAPY"

Almost immediately after the August coup, groups that had previously supported Yeltsin began to splinter. The "democrats" crystallized into two competing factions: "functionaries"—those at the upper strata of power whose loyalties lay wholly with Yeltsin—and "ideologues"—representatives of the liberal intelligentsia who remained outside the inner sanctum of power and became some of its most vocal critics. In turn, the president's inner circle also splintered. An increasingly visible struggle for power and the ear of the president was waged by a "second echelon" of political leaders—Vice President Aleksandr Rutskoi, State Secretary Gennadii Burbulis, and Chairman of the Supreme Soviet Ruslan Khasbulatov. By early 1992, Rutskoi and Khasbulatov, key allies of Yeltsin during the events of August 1991, had become his most vocal critics and powerful rivals.

At the same time, other groups with a specifically anti-democratic orientation and an even deeper antipathy to Yeltsin's reform program began to coalesce. In contrast to Central Europe, where opposition forces formed to the left or the right on the basis of socio-economic issues, Russia's opposition united around the theme of Russia's lost great-power status. A loose alliance formed between three somewhat dissimilar groups—"national-patriots," former communists, and advocates of a strong Russian state (*gosudarstvenniki*), who demanded above all that the state vigorously defend Russia's national interests.

This coalition made its presence felt for the first time during a vociferous public demonstration in February 1992. Although neither side of this "right-left bloc" succeeded in galvanizing public opinion, the event constituted a turning point in Russian political life. It dramatized the growing popular disappointment with Yeltsin's radical reform program and an increasing popular apathy that threatened to make politics the exclusive province of back-room deals and secret "sweetheart" agreements.

Sensing the popular disillusionment with his program, Yeltsin appeared to agree to ameliorate the harsh consequences of the January 1992 price liberalization—the first element of Economic Minister Yegor Gaidar's program of IMF-approved "shock therapy." Nevertheless, a previously muted struggle for power between the executive and legislative powers in Moscow began to intensify and quickly became the decisive factor in Russian political life.

The roots of this confrontation were complicated. It was only partly the result of the lack of a clear division of powers and the incompatibility of the institutions of the new Russian presidency and the remnants of the old political system represented by the Supreme Soviet and the Congress of People's Deputies. More important was the fact that every faction in this struggle felt compelled to monopolize power. Moreover, the impasse was made even more dangerous by the zealotry of its main actors—President Yeltsin, Supreme Soviet Chairman Khasbulatov, and those around them.

Accompanying this executive-legislative conflict in Moscow in early 1992 was a deepening struggle between the federal "center" and local officials and institutions in the provinces. A chain reaction began as one after another of Russia's ethnic republics declared "sovereignty," a process that met with growing dissatisfaction from Russia's non-ethnic regions. Increasingly, edicts passed in Moscow were ignored in both the republics and the regions. Tuva, Sakha-Yakutia, and Checheno-Ingushetia passed laws asserting that their constitutions legally superseded the federal constitution. Russian regional elites, unhappy at the perceived privileges being afforded the ethnic republics in the Federation Treaty signed in March 1992, also tried to "extort" greater financial benefits from the central government. Again, these center-periphery tensions were driven only in part by the lack of a well-established division of powers between Moscow and the provinces—equally important was the unwillingness of elites both in the capital and in the localities to compromise.

Lacking a clear vision of a new federal structure, the Yeltsin team chose the worst possible strategy for dealing with the challenge from the provinces: individual ar-rangements, conducted in secret, negotiated alternately with republics and regions, that promised inordinate financial advantages to some and temporary compromises to others. Federal-republic and federal-regional relations were thereby transformed into a process of endless haggling. This only weakened the embryonic structures of the new Russian state and distracted attention from the critical issues of economic re-form and the cleavages that lay behind Moscow's problems with the provinces.

The president's vertical system of power was designed to serve as a yardstick by which Yeltsin and his lieutenants could judge provincial leaders. Nevertheless, Yeltsin soon found that his edicts were being contradicted or ignored by local leaders who were angered by what they perceived to be Yeltsin's usurpation of their power. A dual system of power (*dvoevlastie*), already established in Moscow, began to find its way to the provinces. Indeed, an openly anti-Yeltsin orientation emerged in some regions with both branches of power united in opposition to Moscow.

Controversy also developed in early 1992 about where the reforms should be carried out—in the Russian Federation only, or throughout the Commonwealth of Independent States (CIS). For a period, Yeltsin wavered between an isolationist, Russia-only policy on the one hand, and one geared to the CIS on the other. As a re-sult, the adoption of a reform program specifically tailored to Russia was postponed. Ukraine's open rivalry with Russia eventually forced policy makers in Moscow to focus on Russia's national interests. Nevertheless, opposition from "old believers" committed to Soviet-style hegemony delayed the emergence of a consensus in Moscow about Russia's national interests as distinct from those of the other post-Soviet states. Only in 1993, under the influence of deepening economic crises in most of Russia's new neighbors, did a painful and contradictory process of economic rein-tegration begin in the former Soviet Union.

THE EMERGENCE OF THE ANTI-DEMOCRATIC OPPOSITION

In April 1992, the deepening polarization of Russian politics, and particularly the in-tensifying struggle between the president and the legislature, came to a head. There-after, the great demarcation in Russian political life became whether to support Yeltsin and the executive or Khasbulatov and the legislature.

The precipitating event of the confrontation was the Sixth Congress of People's Deputies, which convened in April 1992. The Congress itself, with its over 1000 members, was more a political rally than a civilized parliament. . . .

Despite strong opposition to Gaidarnomics at the Congress, Gaidar's government was preserved. But Yeltsin's victory was not followed by an acceleration of reform. On the contrary, Yeltsin seemed to lose the political initiative. It was seized instead by con-servatives—representatives of the "directors' lobby," regional elites, and representatives of agrarian interests, all of whom favored a more moderate and controlled approach to reform. As a result, Yeltsin was forced to bring three members of the directors' lobby into the cabinet: Vladimir Shumeiko, Georgii Khizha, and future Prime Minister Viktor Chernomyrdin. Shortly thereafter, Viktor Gerashchenko, former director of the USSR State Bank, was appointed head of the Russian Central Bank. Gerashchenko's appointment in effect marked the end of "shock therapy" in Russia, as the government soon adopted a more moderate policy on economic reform.

Yeltsin reacted to the growing opposition he faced from the legislature by creating a new presidential structure—the Security Council—headed by conservative Yurii Skokov, to monitor the activities of all other executive organs, particularly the military services, the Ministry of Security (the former KGB), and the Ministry of Internal Affairs (MVD). The decision reflected Yeltsin's style—inconsistent in details, but consistent in his stubborn efforts to concentrate control of key administrative and political instruments in his own hands. In practice, however, the new structure only increased the growing chaos within the government and weakened Yeltsin by making him hostage to his powerful administration.

Indeed, Yeltsin continued to rely on top-down "campaign" methods, thereby alienating the democrats. Their unhappiness with Yeltsin, as well as their general disarray, in turn helped the political fortunes of the antidemocratic opposition. At the same time, it became evident that the majority of political and social groups in Russia were opposed to the way Yeltsin was pursuing the goals of marketization and democratization. . . .

As the summer of 1992 progressed, the anti-democrats began to warn of an imminent disaster with predictable vitriol and frequency. Gaidarism, they argued, was leading the country to ruin, and something dramatic would have to be done to stop it. Fears arose of another coup, this time directed against Boris Yeltsin. Even the Chairman of the Constitutional Court, Valerii Zorkin, warned that the threat of armed conflict should not be taken lightly. . . .

From that time on, Russian society lived in a state of permanent anxiety amidst predictions of a military solution to the political crisis. The two branches of power in Moscow had, it seemed, become substitutes for traditional parties. Each represented different, antagonistic interests: the executive power representing liberals and technocrats, and the legislature representing nationalists and populists. With every new failure of Yeltsin's liberal revolutionary program, the confrontation intensified, forcing a split in society at large. Moreover, the standoff soon brought reforms to a halt. By the end of the summer, then, the president found himself facing a host of profound political challenges: the growing strength of the opposition; the increasing assertiveness of provincial elites; and an accelerating decline in social and political support for his policies.

RUSSIA CHANGES COURSE

. . . Aware that his political support was shrinking, Yeltsin made a sudden change of course in September. Throughout 1992, he had attempted to avoid needless fights with the Supreme Soviet and the Congress. He had tried, albeit with limited success, to court political groups within the legislature to prevent a unified opposition from forming. In September, however, he threw down the gauntlet, demanding that the deputies "desist from pointless activity." However, he offered them and also the administrative heads in the regions a two-and-one-half-year extension to their terms of office. To further sweeten the deal, he reshuffled some of his key advisors, pointedly dismissing Burbulis, who had always been a lightning rod for the opposition, and elevating several of his more conservative and uncompromising advisors—Yurii Skokov, Yurii Petrov, and Oleg Lobov. His hope was that by doing so he would neutralize some of the conservative opposition to his policies.

In October, however, Yeltsin again appeared to yield to growing demands for a softening of shock therapy. For the first time, he criticized Gaidar publicly. . . .

When the Congress finally convened in November, Yeltsin's camp was divided but not without its strengths. Radicals around him favored a decisive showdown between the executive and the legislature, and advised Yeltsin to play his final trump card of a plebiscite—the "appeal to the people." Yeltsin's moderate advisors, on the other hand, favored a continuation of the uneasy armistice between the two branches, though they clearly understood that executive-legislative relations were rapidly deteriorating. . . .

But the Congress was in no mood for compromise. It staked everything—even its very existence—on the attempt to dethrone Gaidar and prevent the president from having any influence over government policy or cabinet portfolio.

Yeltsin responded by announcing a national referendum on a new constitution. The deputies in turn declared that any attempt to hold a referendum would be anticonstitutional. Attempting to play the role of arbiter, the Chairman of the Constitutional Court, Valerii Zorkin, came up with a way for both parties to overcome their deadlock—the "December Compromise." The agreement called on the Congress to permit a national referendum in April 1993. In turn, Yeltsin was persuaded to sacrifice his two most trusted advisors—Burbulis and Gaidar. Gaidar was replaced as Prime Minister, with Yeltsin's consent, by a man who appeared to be an archetypical Soviet industrialist and a former minister in Gorbachev's government—Viktor Chernomyrdin. . . .

Unlike the compromise reached earlier in April, however, Yeltsin suffered a genuine defeat on this occasion. For the first time, the president was widely seen as weak and frustrated, struggling unsuccessfully to break a vicious cycle of events that were spinning out of control. Not only did he suffer the indignity of having his democratic advisors whittled away one by one, but he also appeared to have lost the support of the heads of his security services—the Ministers of Defense, Internal Affairs, and State Security.

The departure of Burbulis and Gaidar also convinced the public that a change of course was taking place—"revolutionary liberalism," it seemed, was being abandoned. It turned out, however, that the December Compromise was only one in a long series of temporary armistices. . . .

THE EXECUTIVE-LEGISLATIVE IMPASSE

. . . By February, all major political actors—the Supreme Soviet, the Constitutional Court, and a majority of republican and regional leaders—had publicly rejected the

December Compromise. Yeltsin suggested another option—a provisional agreement to regulate the responsibilities of the various branches of government and provide for sanctions in the case of violations by any of the signatories. Yeltsin would in turn pledge not to push for a referendum or force the adoption of a new constitution. However, he also let it be known that should the Supreme Soviet *not* sign the accord, he might have resort to a "third path"—i.e., a resort to force.

YELTSIN'S SLEIGHT OF HAND

. . . When the Eighth Congress adjourned, Yeltsin faced a dilemma: either continue the struggle or resign himself to losing his battle with the legislature. Again influenced by radicals in his entourage, he chose the former. On Saturday, March 20, 1993, Yeltsin announced a "special regime" in a television broadcast to the nation. Only the most radical segment of the democrats reacted favorably, while most political forces, including most democrats, expressed embarrassment, even shock: the vice president, the chairman of the Constitutional Court, the state prosecutor, and, naturally, the speaker of the Supreme Soviet, and provincial leaders immediately and predictably denounced the president.

Yeltsin's move did not catch the leaders of the Western democracies unaware; they were informed in advance by German Chancellor Helmut Kohl, who was meeting with Yeltsin in Moscow. The West reacted favorably, no doubt spurring him on. The major surprise came from Yurii Skokov, Yeltsin's close advisor and the powerful secretary of the Security Council, who joined in denouncing the move. The Constitutional Court immediately began hearings on the legality of the president's decree, despite the fact that the text of the decree had not yet been circulated. The Supreme Soviet, after the briefest of deliberations, called for a special session of the Congress of People's Deputies to impeach Yeltsin.

Faced with a threat of being unseated, and lacking the support of either the "power ministries" or the regional elite, Yeltsin retreated. In the version of his announcement that appeared on Monday (newspapers in Russia are not published on Sunday), no written mention was made of any "special regime." Some observers speculated that the television address may have been a bluff, while others felt it had been a serious attempt to institute a presidential dictatorship. Although Yeltsin claimed at the time that his television address had been misunderstood, it would later become clear that he had been serious indeed, for he would soon try again.

As both sides prepared yet again for a decisive confrontation, Yeltsin and Khasbulatov unexpectedly announced that they had reached an agreement. Yeltsin would retreat from his plans to hold a referendum, and would agree to the zero-sum option of holding simultaneous elections for both the executive an the legislature. Khasbulatov in turn announced his willingness to disband the Congress and replace it (and presumably the Supreme Soviet) with a newly-elected bicameral legislature.

The agreement would have meant political suicide for the deputies of the Congress and Supreme Soviet. Outraged at a back-room deal made without their consent or knowledge, the deputies tried to remove both Yeltsin and Khasbulatov. Yet another session of the Congress convened, at which a motion to impeach Yeltsin failed by only 72 votes, just short of the required 689. Khasbulatov fared better, winning 558 votes against impeachment, with only 339 for. Despite their open dissatisfaction with the speaker, then, the deputies had decided that no one was better qualified to advance their interests.

The Congress marked the beginning of an even more complicated stage in Russia's post-communist political development. Both sides understood that the existing institutional order was unworkable, but neither side could offer a solution. Having painted themselves into a corner, the deputies at the Congress were compelled to agree to Yeltsin's proposal to hold a nationwide referendum in April 1993. They did, however, manage to reword the questions in the referendum significantly, to the disadvantage of the president.

The four questions Yeltsin had wished to put to the electorate were: Do you agree that the Russian Federation should be a presidential republic? Do you agree that the Russian Federation's supreme legislative organ should be a bicameral parliament? Do you agree that the new Constitution of the Russian Federation should be adopted by a Constituent Assembly? And, finally, Do you agree that every citizen is entitled to possess, use, and dispose of land as an owner? The Congress, however, insisted on the following: Do you trust the president, Boris Yeltsin? Do you support the socioeconomic policies of the government? Do you favor early elections for the presidency? And, Do you favor early elections for parliament?

The conventional wisdom in Moscow and elsewhere was that Yeltsin would suffer a significant defeat in the referendum. The results therefore came as a great surprise. Out of a total electorate of 107.3 million, 69.2 million (64.5%) went to the polls, with 58.7% of those voting supporting the president, and 53.0% supporting the government's controversial socioeconomic policies. At the same time, less than half (49.5%) of those voting expressed approval for early presidential elections, while 67.2% favored early elections for the legislature.

Yeltsin had clearly won a moral and a political victory. Nevertheless, 38 million had not voted in the referendum, and in two republics it was not even held. Yeltsin failed to win a majority in 12 out of the other 19 republics, as well as in a score of Russian regions. Most voters, it seemed, had not voted *for* Yeltsin as much as they had voted *against* the extreme opposition. Thus many moderate political observers, taking into account not only those who voted against the president and reform but also those who did not turn out for the referendum, interpreted the results as a vote against a dramatic change of course and for the retention of both branches of power. In any case, the referendum was a purely plebiscitarian act of opinion sampling; its results were not legally binding.

In the aftermath of the referendum, Yeltsin's team submitted a new draft constitution that greatly expanded the powers of the president and subordinated the other branches of government to the executive. After much discussion, Yeltsin agreed on a forum to debate the text of the draft—a constitutional convention (*konstitutsionnoe soveshchanie*). . . .

By the middle of August, Yeltsin realized that he had failed to neutralize the legislature with the help of a new constitution. The regions and republics were not responding positively to his draft. Moreover, it had become clear that there was no legal way to adopt a new constitution. Yeltsin therefore decided to seek another way to rid himself of the parliament. On August 13, 1993, he organized a meeting of regional and republic representatives in Petrozavodsk to create yet another organ of state power—the Council of the Federation. In doing so, he was going over the heads of the Supreme Soviet and the Congress of People's Deputies. Nevertheless, the move seemed risky: in principle, the regions and republics could use their new-found power to oust Yeltsin himself. . . .

THE "SECOND OCTOBER REVOLUTION": THE SOVIET ERA COMES TO AN END

. . . [T]he president took a fateful step. On September 21, 1993, Yeltsin issued Decree 1400, dissolving the Supreme Soviet and calling for new legislative elections on December 12, at which time the electorate would also decide the fate of Yeltsin's draft constitution. Direct presidential rule had finally come to pass.

Whether Yeltsin clearly understood the reaction his decree would provoke remains a subject of bitter controversy. In any case, the Supreme Soviet chose not to leave the political stage gracefully, as the USSR Supreme Soviet had done two years earlier. For two weeks, supporters of the parliament, including many deputies, occupied the White House, refusing to leave despite being isolated by the militia and despite having their electricity and water cut off. Finally, on October 3, supporters of parliament, catching the Moscow militia and MVD off guard, broke through police barricades, reaching the White House and then, at the urging of Rutskoi, moving on to storm the Moscow mayor's office and the Ostankino radio tower. These acts began the bloodshed.

Yeltsin reacted swiftly and brutally the next day. After a period of apparent indecision and disorder, the president managed to convince the military to storm the Supreme Soviet building. After firing on the White House with tanks, the military forced the few hundred deputies and their supporters left inside to surrender. The White House was charred black with fire, and over one hundred people were killed. Both the vice president and the speaker were led to prison in handcuffs, although neither was charged with treason—a crime which would have necessitated the death penalty.

Thus ended the period of peaceful political development in Russia. In the final analysis, both sides shared responsibility for the tragedy, though to what extent remains debatable. The upshot was undeniable, however: "soviet power" had come to a decisive end in Russian history even as the taboo on violence in Moscow had been breached. Having adopted the principle that "the end justifies the means," Yeltsin had opened the door for an even more ruthless and cynical round of politics in Moscow. But the ideological contradictions between his goals and the use of means drawn from the traditional arsenal of communist politics were too great to bridge. As a result, Russia entered a new, even more turbulent period of political development.

In the wake of the October tragedy, the presidential team drafted a revised constitution that greatly increased the executive's already considerable powers. The draft created the basis for an authoritarian regime with little counterbalance to presidential power.

A pro-presidential political movement, Russia's Choice, was quickly created. Led by Gaidar, the party was given preferential treatment by the state-controlled media in a two-month, orchestrated election campaign designed to deny other political groups time to consolidate and campaign on an equal footing. The idea was to organize elections as rapidly as possible, making use of the time bought by the devastation of the extreme opposition. A significant part of the governmental apparatus put itself up for elections to the legislature, thus guaranteeing the fusion of the two branches and preventing the legislative branch from embarking on another confrontation with the executive—a practice taken from the pre-*perestroika* period when such appointments were routine.

Having gone to such lengths to secure their positions, the democrats expected that their problems would be over. But the confidence of Yeltsin and his staff proved excessive, and the results of the December 12, 1993 elections came as a profound shock. According to official (and still controversial) results, the constitution was approved by 58% of those voting. However, only 54.8% of the electorate took part in the referendum. In the party list elections for the State Duma (the new lower house of the parliament), Russia's Choice won only 15% of the vote. Shockingly, Vladimir Zhirinovsky's Liberal-Democratic Party—with its openly fascist tendencies—won 24% of the party list vote. The Russian Communist Party, together with its allies in the Agrarian Union, won a combined 19% of the party list vote. The elections clearly showed that what the electorate wanted, more than anything, was order.

Once again, then, Russian politics showed an uncanny disposition toward ironic paradoxes. Not only were the majority of its seats won by an anti-presidential bloc, but it was now a new, post-communist legislature with even greater legitimacy than the president, who had been elected in June 1991 during the communist era. Moreover, Yeltsin found himself facing a serious political challenge not only from Aleksandr Rutskoi, who had often been a reckless and clumsy politician, but also from Vladimir Zhirinovsky, a demagogue whose behavior was completely unpredictable. Compounding Yeltsin's political difficulties was a split within Yeltsin's entourage, as a result of which some of his former lieutenants, such as Sergei Shakhrai, entered the race to replace Yeltsin in the next presidential elections.

Democratic groups seem not to have understood that by resorting to force to crush the opposition in October, they had dug their own graves in December. Relieved of most of their responsibilities, the liberals and radicals were left with a single task—to form a minority opposition in the lower chamber of the new parliament. At the same time, the election allowed regional elites to reconsolidate on a sharply antireformist platform.

Sensing the growing populist and statist sentiments of both the elite and the electorate, Yeltsin formed a government in January 1994 headed by a new centrist Prime Minister, Viktor Chernomyrdin. Neither Gaidar nor another key representative of radical economic reform, Boris Fedorov, was included. The generally conservative character of the new government was reflected in the large representation of members of the Agrarian Lobby and the military-industrial complex, the real winners of the "September Revolution." . . .

By 1994, then, the period of "great leaps forward," revolutionary phraseology, reformist utopianism, and irrational expectations of financial assistance from the West had come to an end in Russia. Left-center and extreme right-wing groups, whose sole political orientation was an unremitting hostility toward the pro-Western orientation of the radical-liberals, now dominated the new politics, and their views shaped not only elite behavior but also the discourse of society at large.

As for Yeltsin, he had become entirely distant from society, obsessed not so much with finding a "kinder and gentler" social contract as with reconcentrating political power in his own hands. Under the new constitution, the broad range of powers granted the president enabled him to interfere constantly in the business of other institutions. This not only prevented mid-course policy adjustments, but narrowed the possibility of dissent within the government. Most importantly, it undermined the executive branch by making it appear responsible for every political blunder regardless of whether it had occurred in Moscow or in the provinces.

At the same time, the executive branch had divided into two functioning governments. The first, the "political government" of Yeltsin, controlled the activities of the Ministries for Security, Defense and Internal Affairs, and Communication, as well as the press, radio, and television. The second, the "economic government" of Prime Minister Viktor Chernomyrdin, managed financial and budgetary affairs. The division created new conflicts between a powerful presidential apparatus and a weak cabinet deprived of real control over the machinery of state. As a result, state and society continued to lack an effective communications link, despite the new constitution. . . .

THE MIXED LEGACY OF "REVOLUTIONARY LIBERALISM"

. . . Without doubt, Yeltsin can take credit for the final collapse of communism. He was also responsible for overcoming the heady romanticism of the early post-coup period. During his tenure, Russia's statehood was consolidated and the first steps toward marketization were taken. The force of his personality not only kept extremist elements from triumphing, but also was the overriding—and occasionally the only—stabilizing element in a fragile new society.

Nevertheless, there have also been many failures for the president. When the need for genuine radical change in both the economic and political spheres was most acute, neither the president nor his inner circle had a clear notion of how to proceed—although in all fairness, neither had anyone else. Instead of working out a clear strategic plan, they chose to govern by intuition, reacting to events and finding themselves always one step behind. Yeltsin also proved a master of confrontation—he clearly reveled in a charged political atmosphere and performed best in crises. Indeed he often seemed to provoke conflict deliberately. He thus lost the opportunity to become a leader of national unity, as Lech Walesa and Vaclav Havel had during the first stage of the post-communist transitions in Poland and Czechoslovakia, and as Alfredo Suarez had during the democratic transition in Spain.

Perhaps Yeltsin's greatest failing was his poor sense of timing. Unwilling to construct a new political system immediately after the August 1991 coup, he helped create the political standoff that would eventually force him to take the violent measures of October 1993. And like Gorbachev, Yeltsin too chose many policies at random, in effect "winging it" rather than operating from a well-chosen, carefully considered plan. . . .

The liberal-revolutionary period was thus a time when myths that took root during the excessively optimistic Gorbachev era, as well as immediately after the August coup, were overcome by force. The greatest myth of all was the notion that the August 1991 coup failed because of a popular uprising "from below." In reality, bureaucrats "from above" played at least as important a role, and their "coming of age" did not easily translate into a victory for democracy. A second myth was that Russia could somehow transcend the vast space between a socialist authoritarianism and a capitalist democracy in a single leap. Yet another was that the West—particularly the United States—would come to Russia's economic rescue. . . .

The name [revolutionary liberalism] captures the ideological intent of the reformers, but the careful reader has no doubt observed that Yeltsin's policies have been subject to constant compromise. How, then, can we characterize them as truly revolutionary?

The answer is in the content of those policies, not the rhetoric. The vast majority of Yeltsin's promises to soften his economic program, replace key personnel, or compromise with the legislature, were tactical in nature. At no time did he depart from the radical orientation of his reforms. And tactical compromise, as Lenin had understood, is not necessarily a departure from ideology.

A second objection to the description of Yeltsin's program as "revolutionary" is that his reforms achieved little of substance. Russia's precipitous economic decline continued, and Russia's superpower status was not restored. To some extent, this was due to individual incompetence and inexperience. But to a greater extent, it resulted from the inability of revolutionary liberalism to solve Russia's problems. Revolutionary liberalism did not offer a method by which any of the goals of the new state—whether economic recovery, the restoration of global prestige, or the consolidation of new political structures—might be met.

It was where politics intersect with economics, however, that the deficiencies of revolutionary liberalism were most glaring. Gaidar's economic policies were a giant laboratory experiment carried out in Russia in order to fulfill the grand designs of someone else. As a result, the experiment was undertaken without regard for the sociological, psychological, and political conditions of the laboratory itself—in short, without regard for the welfare of the "animals" being experimented upon. Indeed, the IMF-approved economic reform program ignored the fact that the government had an obligation to meet its responsibilities under Russia's post-communist social contract, however, informal that contract may have been.

THE DILEMMAS OF RUSSIAN STATECRAFT:
REFORM AND CONTINUITY

By the end of 1993, then, revolutionary liberalism had been abandoned and the pragmatic wing of the old Party *nomenklatura* had reasserted control of the government and governmental policy. At the same time, privatization was turning other elements of the traditional *nomenklatura* into property owners. Yesterday's *apparatchiks* had thus become today's entrepreneurs, and these new entrepreneurs were making every effort to use their economic muscle to achieve political ends.

It is the extent of this elite continuity that distinguishes Russia's political transformation from those of Central Europe. In the latter case, the non-communist opposition and leaders such as Lech Walesa and Vaclav Havel arose from outside the established political order. In Russia, by contrast, the opposition emerged from *within* the ranks of the existing elite, indeed in many cases from within the Central Committee itself. Members of this traditional elite, including both Gorbachev and Yeltsin, led the transformation effort, and were predictably reluctant, and in some respects unable, to carry out a broad-based purge of the elite to which they belonged.

This staying power of the *nomenklatura,* along with other continuities between the Gorbachev and Yeltsin eras, have led some Russian radicals to conclude that Russia has not been transformed at all—rather it has been "modified," and only partially at that. Yurii Burtin, the well-known correspondent, has concluded that out of two possible scenarios—the "popular" and the "bureaucratic"—the Russian apparat was able to secure the latter, the essence of which was the preservation of traditional positions and relationships in the guise of a new political-ideological framework. As Burtin put it,

> For the time being it seemed to us that the stagnation and economic ineffectiveness of the state-party system went hand in hand with its precarious instability. Whether the reverse is now true—that our seeming inability to get on with the business of progressive development is connected with a highly developed skill on the part of our ruling class to ever change its outward appearance—remains to be seen. This system is like a werewolf—it changes its external hide whenever it pleases, but its essence remains the same.

Have the modifications to the old communist system meant the retention of the essential qualities of the old regime, or have reforms changed the system's essence? If the latter, then a *nomenklatura* "renaissance" may be indispensable to post-Soviet transformation, particularly for a regime that never experienced its own Prague Spring or Hungarian version of reform.

Indeed, many observers claim that the scenario that unfolded in Russia after August 1991 was a classic case of counter-revolution—the victorious "democrats," they argue, in fact adopted a program little different from the agenda of the coup leaders. As one analyst put it, "Who can play dumb to the fact that had the notorious State Committee for the State of Emergency emerged the victor, it would have done exactly what the victorious democrats have?"

A different interpretation has been offered by Gavriil Popov, the former mayor of Moscow and one of the leaders in the democratic movement, who has argued that the bureaucracy has triumphed, but only in part. "We [democrats] did not have the strength needed to steer the transition," he has admitted. The *apparat* was therefore not destroyed, but "its power was instead redistributed among its various factions." Moreover, the democrats wasted an opportunity to share power in a coalition with more moderate, reform-oriented members of the apparat. Thus, even though the pragmatists in the *nomenklatura* have yet to exhaust their capacity to carry out reforms, the democrats must constantly push them down the reform path. . . .

FUTURE PROSPECTS:
LIBERAL AUTHORITARIANISM AND REGIME STABILITY

In post-communist Russia, as well as in the other Soviet successor states and the post-communist states of Central Europe, the transformation of the old regimes was initiated by the Communist Party from the top down. On the one hand, this has limited the threat of widespread social turbulence that has accompanied revolutions elsewhere. But on the other, it has steered the transformations in a highly bureaucratic, "administered" direction.

The administrative tendencies of Russia's new ruling elite indicate just how strongly traditional beliefs that democracy and marketization must somehow be "constructed" are embedded in Russian political culture. One of the most serious obstacles to Russia's normal development is the assumption that one can "liberate" a country from communism by communist methods. Nevertheless, it is difficult to deny that without a shove, society will be unable to build its own self-regulating mechanisms.

As a result, it seems clear that the transition period requires a strong state—not only to set up new procedural rules, but to guarantee the stability those rules require if they are to be implemented. Russian experience has already demonstrated that a weak state will itself contribute to new instability. But can a strong state voluntarily limit its power after having created new rules? Will the first "shove" mean another round of authoritarianism? If so, it may turn out that a liberal authoritarian state is no better than a communist one at safeguarding social and individual freedoms. . . .

Lilia Shevtsova, "Russia's Post-Communist Politics: Revolution or Continuity?" in Gail W. Lapidus (ed.), *The New Russia: Troubled Transformation* ((Boulder, CO: Westview Press, 1995), pp. 5–31.

ELITE TRANSFORMATION IN LATE-SOVIET AND POST-SOVIET TRANSCAUCASIA, OR WHAT HAPPENS WHEN THE RULING CLASS CAN'T RULE?

Ronald Grigor Suny

. . . In each of the three Transcaucasian republics, old elites were at one time replaced at the top of the political structure by nationalist, anti-Communist counter-elites. But, as in much of the former Soviet Union, the older political players managed to preserve considerable influence in the political structure and economy and even to return to power in some cases. The transformation of elites in the region was accompanied by more violence than in most of the former USSR, particularly in Georgia, where political disintegration and interethnic conflict resulted in civil war. Armenia experienced the most peaceful transfer of power and for a long time enjoyed the most stable democratic government, but in Azerbaijan transfers of power from the old elite to the nationalists and back again came only after brief armed struggles.

THE END OF SOVIET POWER

Soviet oligarchic rule effaced alternative political elites. Only the academic and literary intelligentsia remained somewhat autonomous in some republics. Once the Communist elite lost its ideological conviction, once its political will was weakened (from the top) during the Gorbachev revolution, the alternative elites that emerged proved to be extraordinarily weak and in most republics without broad social bases. One considerable source of strength was the ability of some intelligentsias to express their aspirations in the language of national revival or survival, but in many republics the old elites quickly attempted to appropriate the now-hegemonic discourse of nationalism. . . .

However artificial some of the fifteen newly independent states might have been at their creation in the first decades of the twentieth century, they had become, through the years of Soviet power, something like nation-states. Almost all had majorities of the titular nationality (Kazakhstan was the single exception), and national

Communist political elites remained in power in most of them, in one form or another.

Second, in all three South Caucasian republics a deep and persistent substructure of regional and clan loyalties continues to be the touchstone of political identification and affiliation. Political, regional, familial, and even criminal mafias offer powerful resistance to sovereign law-based states. Displaced Communists remain the most coherent and unified presence, often well established in the governing structure of certain regions or institutions. One of the most powerful threats to the local nationalist government in Azerbaijan was the former chief of the Communist Party, Heidar Aliev, who had his own power base in the semiindependent Nakhichevan region and used his network of associates to return to power in June 1993.

Third, the Transcaucasian nationalist counterelites come from the same social background: academic and literary intellectuals (relatively cosmopolitan) outside the old power elite. They fit the stereotypic picture of a revolutionary elite—"overeducated outgroups" "whose capital is [their] knowledge." They came to power against the old ways of doing business, but once in power they accommodated the existing structures of power.

Finally, the project of state building and the building of authority (legitimated power) for the new elites in all three republics goes on in conditions of extreme physical difficulty, economic collapse, interrepublic and civil war, and blockade.

The similarities belie enormous differences among the three republics. To explain the winding paths into and out of power by the nationalists and former Communists. I consider the varying character, coherence, and content of the nationalist discourses in the three republics, their inclusive or exclusive rhetorics; the ability of nationalist counterelites to constitute themselves as an effective leadership and control their mass following; and the flexibility (or intransigence) of the local Communist elites. I argue that among the factors that lead to the successful reconstitution of a stable political elite are the availability of a political discourse that binds the elite and a significant part of the population around shared cultural and political goals and to which the elite can easily refer; the absence of interethnic cleavages that have the potential of initiating and maintaining among the population a habit of violence; and the relative willingness of the old political elite to surrender power and accept the new rules of the political game.

ARMENIA

When perestroika provided an opening for pent-up political frustrations, the Armenian intelligentsia mobilized around three major issues: environmental pollution and the danger posed by the nuclear plant at Metsamor, near Erevan; the perennial issue of Karabakh; and the corruption and stagnation connected with the long reign (1974–1988) of party chief Karen Demirchian. At the same time, the political leadership in Armenia was being undermined both from within and from above. After the accession of Gorbachev, the central party press attacked the Armenian Communist Party (ACP) for corruption and favoritism. Yet the ACP elite, unified around Demirchian, managed to forestall reform of the party and the removal of Demirchian until the outbreak of the Karabakh movement in February 1988. Only then did the ACP, discredited in the eyes of much of the population, rapidly lose authority to the growing movement in the streets.

After Demirchian fell in May, his successor, Suren Harutiunian (Arutiunian), attempted to find common language with the national movement. But the Karabakh Committee, made up of nationalist intellectuals, many of them members of the Communist Party, became more radical, calling for full democratization and national sovereignty. Moscow's refusal to agree to the merger of Karabakh with Armenia and its failure to deal firmly with the perpetrators of the Sumgait pogrom by Azerbaijanis against Armenians contributed to the intransigence of the opposition.

Shortly after the earthquake of December 7, 1988, Soviet officials decided to restore their authority by arresting the members of the Karabakh Committee. This attempt to rule, in a sense, "without the nation" led to voters boycotting the general elections called by Gorbachev in March 1989 and to massive demonstrations in early May. Harutiunian's gestures to win over popular sentiment—recognizing a holiday on May 28, the day the nationalists had proclaimed Armenian independence in 1918, and accepting the tricolor flag of the independent republic—culminated in the release of the Karabakh Committee to the joyful greetings of demonstrators in Erevan.

The next five months (June–October 1989) were marked by a kind of condominium of the Communists and the Karabakh Committee. As uncomfortable allies, much like the popular fronts and communists in the Baltic republics, the competing Armenian elites actually made it possible for the popular nationalist movement to grow in a relatively free environment and for an eventual, peaceful transfer of power to ensue. In June the mushrooming unofficial organizations joined together to form the Pan-Armenian National Movement (Haiots Hamazgayin Sharzhum, HHSh), and the government gave them official recognition. The effective leader of the opposition, Levon Ter Petrosian, praised Harutiunian's defense of Armenian national interests at the Congress of People's Deputies and stated his belief that the interests of the ACP and the HHSh were converging.

But by late fall 1989 the cooperative relationship had broken down. The benefits of moderation had been exhausted, as Moscow not only refused to cede Karabakh to Armenia but decided to return control of the region to Baku. The Karabakh movement accelerated its efforts toward democratization and independence. Under HHSh pressure, the Armenian Supreme Soviet revised the republic's constitution and gave itself the power to invalidate USSR laws.

Torn between the Kremlin's refusal to allow the merger of Karabakh with Armenia and the growing popular movement that would be satisfied with nothing less, Harutiunian resigned as first secretary of the ACP on April 6, 1990. The Communists, identified with the by then unpopular Gorbachev, with the refusal to allow Karabakh to join Armenia, and with a legacy of corruption and repression, had accumulated too many liabilities to govern effectively in Armenia. They fared poorly in the elections of spring and summer 1990, and the new Armenian parliament chose Ter Petrosian instead of the new Communist chief, Vladimir Movsesian, as its chairman.

As it moved step by cautious step toward independence through 1990 and 1991, the Armenian national leadership loosened political and ideological ties with Moscow, all the while assiduously avoiding direct confrontation. Its leading theorists rejected the traditional Russian orientation of the Armenian intelligentsia. In place of the long-held view that Armenia required Russian or Soviet protection against the danger of Pan-Turkism, the HHSh argued that Armenians must abandon their reliance on a "third force," rethink their traditional hostility toward and fear of the Turks, and create their own independent state now that the opportunity had arisen. These views echoed those long expressed by the leading diaspora party, the Dashnaktsutiun, though with significant differences. Exhibiting caution and pragmatism, the HHSh noted that it was prepared to defer the question of Armenian lands in Turkey until the issue of full sovereignty and independence was resolved.

When the anti-Gorbachev plotters in August 1991 delivered the final blow to Soviet unity, Armenian voters struck out on their own political path. On September 20 they affirmed the commitment to independence in a referendum; on October 16 they elected Ter Petrosian president of the republic with an overwhelming 83 percent of the vote. The Karabakh Committee had by fall 1991 been transformed into the popular government of an independent state with only a weak and divided opposition. Ideologically forged in the struggle for Karabakh, the movement had quickly developed into a successful movement against the mafialike party in Armenia.

The leaders of the post-Communist government in Armenia were the small circle of friends and colleagues who had graduated from the informal Karabakh Committee in 1988 and 1989 to become the core of a broad-based nationalist movement. Emblematic of their social origins in the academic intelligentsia was the newly elected president of Armenia, Levon Ter Petrosian, formerly a philologist who worked in the Matenadaran, the repository of medieval Armenian manuscripts in Erevan. . . . His greatest political quality seems to be balance and moderation—his ability to steer a course first away from Russia toward Turkey and back again while fending off advocates of a more militant stance toward the Karabakh problem. . . .

The national movement, which from its inception has employed a repertoire of symbols and cultural constructions immediately recognizable to large numbers of Armenians, was able both to mobilize large numbers of people in a single cause and to remain relatively united around its leadership. The leaders' strategy of gradualism and steady pressure rather than confrontation contributed to the peaceful and relatively violence-free transfer of power, though the absence of enduring interethnic conflicts within the republic was the most important factor freeing Armenians from a cycle of violence at home. The perceived danger of the Azerbaijanis worked also to unify much of the population around the emerging nationalist leadership. When the Karabakh conflict escalated into the killings at Sumgait and then into a blockade and open warfare, Armenians forcibly deported Azerbaijanis from the republic but with relatively little bloodshed.

In some ways the Armenian case parallels those in the Baltic regions, but in other ways it is quite different. As in Lithuania, so in Armenia the majority of the Communist Party chose the nation rather than the Soviet Union. Unlike in Latvia and Estonia, there were no so-called internationalist factions of Communists in Armenia to appeal to the forces of order in Moscow. The Armenian Communist Party, which worked with the nationalist movement for a time, resisted pressure from Moscow to take a harder line toward the Karabakh movement and eventually rejected the option of a coup against the elected majority in parliament, a choice that further contributed to the low level of internal violence. Even though Armenia was the first of the Transcaucasian republics to form a non-Communist government, the nationalists deliberately adopted a strategy of working within the limits of the Soviet law of secession and thereby avoided much of the violence from the center that ensued in response to the more uncompromising push for independence, particularly in Lithuania and in Georgia.

In the first three and a half years after independence, the Ter Petrosian government displayed an enviable stability, despite the ongoing war in Karabakh and the growing opposition in parliament and society. The unity of the original band of nationalists who had led the Karabakh movement in Erevan splintered within the first year when key members broke with the government and formed opposition parties. Banditry and armed militias in the streets of the cities, along with the growth of independent centers of economic power, threatened the almost nonexistent state apparatus. Yet a series of victories in the Karabakh war, beginning in early 1993, and the expansion and stabilization of the front with a cease-fire in the spring of 1994, gave the Armenian government the breathing space it needed to bring civil order to its towns, lay the basis for a restoration of the economy, and win over foreign friends and aid. At the end of 1994, Ter Petrosian responded to the assassination of one of his former associates, Hambartsum Galstian, by cracking down hard on the Dashnaktsutiun, arresting its leaders and closing its newspapers. Though this breach of democratic practice shocked the diaspora and led to mild protests from the American government, the political crisis within the counterelite did not derail the most stable government in Transcaucasia from its steady consolidation of state authority. Ter Petrosian remained in power until early 1998 when his efforts to compromise on the Karabakh issue led to his downfall. His successor, Robert Kocharian, soon became the most powerful man in the country when his two principal rivals were assassinated in October 1999. The road to democracy wandered into a wilderness of political disunity, popular apathy, and the debilitating effects of the unresolved Karabakh conflict and the chronic economic problems stemming from blockade.

AZERBAIJAN

The story of the emergence of the Azerbaijani nationalist elite differs from the Armenian experience, not least because the two nations were formed before and during the Soviet period in significantly different ways. Armenians in Transcaucasia were the most urban of the three major ethnic groups; they occupied positions of economic and political power in Tbilisi (Tiflis) and Baku, from which they would be largely displaced during the Soviet period. Yet even as Azerbaijanis and Georgians became the hegemonic nationality in political and intellectual life in their respective republics, they retained resentments against the Armenians. Armenians were disproportionately represented in the technical and other subelites, particularly in Azerbaijan. As Azerbaijanis moved into towns, suffering from the highest levels of unemployment in the Soviet Union and encountering a corrupt political elite of their own nationality, they directed much of their social and ethnic resentment toward the Armenian population of their own republic.

Whereas Armenians both in Karabakh and Armenia proper could refer to a clear sense of nationhood with a textual tradition of continuous existence and past statehood, the Azerbaijanis were more immediately a nation in the making. Specifically national traditions, as distinct from traditions shared by the larger Shia Muslim world, the Persian cultural milieu, or the Turkic-language community, were largely built during the Soviet period, as were a sense of shared history, a national (rather than regional or religious) identity, and a rootedness in a specific territory. Construction of a national tradition occurred in all the Soviet republics, and in each the titular nationality of the republic was privileged to the near exclusion of minority peoples. Only with the outbreak of the Karabakh movement did the underlying sense of threat from Armenians coalesce with myriad other threats and anxieties to propel, first, small numbers of Azerbaijanis to take revenge on the Armenians of Sumgait for imagined injuries and, later, tens of thousands of others to join in massive demonstrations.

The ruling Communist elite in Azerbaijan has been the subject of several studies of the powerful interweaving of political and economic patron-client networks, or what is referred to in the vernacular as the "mafia." After the ten-year reign of the incompetent and venal party first secretary, Veli, Akhundov, Moscow decided in 1969 to appoint Heidar Aliev, the republic's KGB chairman, in order to revive the Azerbaijani economy and uproot the pervasive corruption within the ruling elite. New officials personally loyal to Aliev, drawn from his native region of Nakhichevan and from his associates in the security apparatus, were rapidly introduced into positions of power. But instead of fighting mafia rule in general, Aliev ended up replacing the old clientelistic network with one of his own. Ethnically homogeneous and ruthless, the Aliev elite was able to convince Moscow that it was competent in maintaining both political stability and a modicum of economic growth. In fact, the regime was falsifying results, repressing (sometimes killing) its critics, and lavishly enriching its favored members.

Aliev left for Moscow in 1982, replaced by a loyal client, Kiamran Baghirov. Only with the ascent of Gorbachev and Aliev's dismissal from the Politburo in October 1987 was any serious attempt made to break up the Aliev machine. In May 1988, Baghirov was replaced by Abdulrahman Vazirov, who, like Harutiunian in Armenia, was from outside the republic (from the diplomatic corps). Like other Gorbachev appointments in national republics, Vazirov set out to purge the party apparatus of corrupt and time-serving officials, removing over forty district and city committee secretaries, cutting the number of central committee departments and secretaries, and reorganizing the party structure. But Vazirov, who like all other post–Aliev Azerbaijani leaders had earlier been associated with Aliev, only superficially pushed the program of perestroika and the fight against the deep infrastructure of Azerbaijani politics. As in Armenia, the party entered the period of growing nationalism unsure of its mandate and its future role. Its traditional vanguard role was being undermined from both above and below; and with the erosion of a single, authoritative center as a source of authority and legitimation, the ruling elite faced a bitter choice between accommodation of the popular mood or harsh repression.

Vazirov did not so much face an aroused counterelite, as did Harutiunian in Armenia, as a restless population torn by social strains and agitated by fears of Armenian nationalism. Nearly a year of Armenian protests and demands for Karabakh mobilized nonelite Azerbaijanis to defend what they considered the territorial integrity of their republic. Crowds gathered outside Government House, 20,000 during the night, 500,000 during the day. This disparate movement was led, at first, by workers and was peopled by Azerbaijani refugees from Armenia and migrants from the Azerbaijani countryside. A lathe operator, Neimat Panakhov, emerged as the major spokesman at mass rallies, expressing social as well as ethnic discontents and complaining that Azerbaijani workers were not given apartments when they relocated in the towns and were forced to live in dormitories. The targets of these resentments were the relatively privileged, the people of Baku—one slogan heard was "Baku bez bakintsev" (Baku without the Bakinians)—and Armenians.

In June 1988, seven intellectuals, who earlier had formed a group within the research section of the Azerbaijani Academy of Sciences to support the goals of perestroika, wrote up a manifesto and created the Azerbaijan Popular Front (Azarbayjan

Khalg Jabhasi. AKhJ). These cosmopolitan Baku intellectuals, said by some to speak better Russian than Azeri, were of a social democratic orientation, but they soon joined with other unofficial associations, broadening their base and program. The AKhJ promoted the political and economic sovereignty of the republic of Azerbaijan within a democratic Soviet Union but was unable to reach the popular masses or control the opposition in the streets that exploded in November.

The Communist authorities refused to register the AKhJ as a legal organization and broke up its first congress by force. Meeting secretly, the AKhJ leaders organized a series of crippling strikes and a rail blockade of Armenia. Only in September did the Communist leaders reluctantly open negotiations with the front, eventually capitulating to the evident strength of the popular movement. On September 23, 1989, the Supreme Soviet of Azerbaijan recognized the sovereignty of the republic, and a few weeks later, the AKhJ was officially registered. In November, Moscow ended its direct control over Karabakh and ceded authority to Azerbaijan.

As in Armenia, the brief period of condominium lasted only a few months. Though there was regular consultation between the government and the AKhJ on the Karabakh issue, the question of democratic elections led to a split. The greater resistance by the Communists in Azerbaijan to power sharing with, let alone transfer of power to, the national movement contributed both to an escalation of internal violence and radicalization of the nationalist leadership. By mid-November 1989, protesters were tearing down the border posts separating Soviet Azerbaijan from Iranian Azerbaijan. Independent militants attacked party and police offices in the name of the AKhJ. Unable to follow the Armenian course by combining the goals of perestroika and national self-association, the Azerbaijani intelligentsia divided into more nationalistic and more democratic factions. Paralyzed and divided, the AKhJ neither controlled its own membership nor had much influence on the crowds in the streets.

Suddenly, on January 13, 1990, as a quarter of a million Azerbaijanis listened to speeches in the central square in Baku, groups of young people broke away and began running through the city beating and killing ethnic Armenians. Two days later the Soviet government declared a state of emergency in Azerbaijan and launched a series of military maneuvers, first in Karabakh and then toward Baku. On January 20, as the AKhJ (loosely connected to an ad hoc National Defense Council) organized a haphazard defense of the city, the Soviet army stormed Baku, killing hundreds. Most Armenians had already been evacuated, and the military's objective was clearly to restore the power of the Communist Party of Azerbaijan and remove the nationalist threat. Some 800 members of the AKhJ were arrested, and twelve regional organizations were closed.

"Reborn like a phoenix from the ashes of burnt party membership cards," the old Communist elite was able to restore its rule, if not its authority, thanks to the Soviet military. Vazirov was replaced by Ayaz Niyaz Oghlu Mutalibov, the chairman of the Council of Ministers, who in May was selected president by the Supreme Soviet. For much of 1990 and 1991, a de facto alliance of convenience between Mutalibov and Gorbachev tilted Soviet policy in Transcaucasia toward Azerbaijan. Whereas Armenia was already committed to leaving the Soviet Union, rejecting Gorbachev's referendum, Mutalibov's government agreed to participate. In March 1991, 92 percent of those voting in Azerbaijan (75 percent of the electorate participated) endorsed preservation of the USSR. . . .

When the Azerbaijani president failed to condemn the August 1991 coup, demonstrations organized by the AKhJ called for his resignation. Mutalibov reacted quickly, resigning not as president but from his post as head of the local Communist Party. The next day he engineered a unanimous vote in the Supreme Soviet to "restore" the independence of Azerbaijan, and on September 8, he was elected president of the republic by popular vote. The AKhJ boycotted the election.

The fragility of political power in Azerbaijan and its contingent relationship with the war in Karabakh were vividly demonstrated in the six months from the coup in August to Mutalibov's resignation in early March 1992. In that half year, Mutalibov acted as if he were still a Communist first secretary, though now presenting himself as first representative of the nation. . . . When news came of "massacres" by Armenians at Khodjaly, Mutalibov was forced to resign, but the new government was unable to bring stability to the country. The war in Karabakh went badly, as the Armenians took advantage of the political confusion in Baku. In rural districts armed men acting in the name of the AKhJ attempted to overthrow local authorities.

Early in May, as violence nearing civil war engulfed the country, Mutalibov returned to the presidency, backed by his supporters in the streets and by a cowed parliament. The AKhJ reacted quickly, mobilizing tens of thousands of its own armed supporters around the parliament. Mutalibov fled to Moscow, and on May 16, the National Council formed a coalition government including members of the AKhJ in the powerful posts controlling police and security. New elections on June 6 confirmed Abulfaz Elchibey as president.

The new leader of Azerbaijan was a historian of the Orient, widely respected as a man of integrity and principle. His personal authority stemmed from his past as an implacable enemy of Moscow and his arrest in 1975 for "slandering" the Soviet state. Like other post-Mutalibov nationalist politicians in Baku, Elchibey was opposed to joining the CIS. His party was hostile to both Russia and Iran and oriented toward Kemalist Turkey, which he saw as the model democratic secular republic in the Muslim world. . . .

The AKhJ government proved unable to demonstrate that it could effectively prosecute the war in Karabakh. By April 1993, Armenians had expanded the war from Karabakh to neighboring regions of Azerbaijan proper, and the crisis of a nation still in formation became even more acute. In June a military revolt led by Suret Huseinov drove Elchibey from Baku and brought Aliev to power. . . . Bolstered by yet another presidential election in October, in which he won the customary 90-plus percent of the vote, Aliev set out to stabilize his regime by removing the principal factor, the Karabakh conflict, that had undermined Azerbaijan's three previous governments. . . . A cease-fire in the summer of 1994 raised fragile hopes of a negotiated settlement in the Karabakh war. . . .

After the "turn toward Turkey" under Elchibey, Aliev distanced his government somewhat from Ankara and drew closer to Moscow. But, sensitive to public opinion, he has steadfastly opposed the stationing of Russian troops in the republic. . . . Though it was far from a democratic government, Aliev's Azerbaijan had become a more stable state, riding the surface of a fragmented and dispirited society. Even though he suffered from ill health, Aliev remained the strong man of Azerbaijan, grooming his son for succession. But the promised plenty from Caspian oil riches remained elusive, as did a final settlement of the conflict over Karabakh.

GEORGIA

The cases of Armenia and Azerbaijan illustrate the differential effects of the flexibility or intransigence of the old ruling elite and the importance of the counterelite's ability to lead a mass movement. Georgia adds to these elements the salience of particular kinds of leaders and the specific appeals they use to secure influence and power. Although the Georgian story can be told in many different ways, the complex, intersecting, but divergent careers of two principal figures Eduard Shevardnadze and Zviad Gamsakhurdia, reflect the contrasting rhetorical approaches to political struggle. In the multinational context of the Georgian republic, where ethnic Georgians made up a little over two-thirds of the population and where severe strains had alienated ethnic minorities from the dominant nationality throughout the Soviet period, leaders' rhetoric and symbolic choices could work to ameliorate these divisions in a unified struggle for independence and democracy or to reinforce and exacerbate the interethnic cleavages within the republic. . . .

Shevardnadze's career reveals a man complexly formed by integrity and stubbornness, shrewd calculation of risk, and the ability to please his superiors. He knew the limits of what was possible within the system and yet often pushed right up against those limits without transgressing them. His campaigns against corruption were only partly successful, so deeply ingrained were the practices of the "second economy" in Georgian life. And for, all his expressed humanism, Shevardnadze tolerated some of the worst police practices, including torture, in the Soviet Union. As a post-Stalinist leader operating after the elimination of the worst excesses of the terror system, Shevardnadze both negotiated with representatives of dissident views in society and repressed the most intransigent in the extralegal dissident movement.

Shortly after Shevardnadze became first secretary of the Georgian Communist Party in 1972, a small group of intellectuals formed the Initiative Group for the Defense of Human Rights in Tbilisi. Among the founders of this embryonic dissident movement were Merab Kostava and Zviad Gamsakhurdia. The son of the most famous Georgian novelist of the twentieth century, Konstantine Gamsakhurdia, Zviad grew up a child of privilege and became a teacher of American literature at Tbilisi State University. . . .

The government cracked down in 1977, arresting Gamsakhurdia and Kostava and charging them with disseminating anti-Soviet propaganda. Sentenced to three years in prison and two in exile, Gamsakhurdia decided to recant his views on television in order to receive a pardon. Kostava refused to capitulate, and Gamsakhurdia's authority as a dissident suffered for a time, although he reemerged briefly in 1981 during a campaign to protest restrictions on the Georgian language.

The Georgian Communist elite, both before, during, and after Shevardnadze's rule, was ethnically and personally cohesive and was able to withstand penetration by outside authorities. The solidarity of the elite had a complex ethnic coloration to it directed upward against Russians and downward against minority nationalities living in the republic—Armenians, Abkhaz, Ajars, Azerbaijanis, Osetins, and others. An "official" nationalism favoring Georgians over other peoples was tolerated, indeed encouraged by the Georgian leadership; even Shevardnadze, who periodically attacked "half-baked nationalism," accommodated himself to it. The illegal economic activities found in other parts of the Soviet Union took on a specifically ethnic tone and a systemic quality in Georgia. The center's policy of "indirect rule" permitted

the local elite a degree of tolerance of deviant behavior. Close friendship and kinship ties within the elite reinforced the exclusionary character of politics in the republic—the sense of superiority of the titular nationality and inferiority of the
non-Georgians.

During the early years of perestroika (1985–1988), Georgia was relatively quiet.
Shevardnadze's successor, Jumber Patiashvili, was a somewhat conservative party
leader who maintained a tight rein on dissent, attacked the church, and refused to engage in dialogue with the informal associations springing up in the republic. But the
Communist elite was caught between the policies of Gorbachev, who in 1986 and
1987 encouraged open critical expression by the nonparty intelligentsia, and Georgia's own literary intelligentsia, which had long before become fervently nationalistic. Not only were Georgian intellectuals dedicated to the preservation and dissemination of the Georgian language, but they also expressed a chauvinistic sense of
Georgian superiority over non-Georgians in the republic. The discourse of the nation, with its inherently anti-Communist and anti-Russian overtones, was appropriated so completely by the extraparty intellectuals that Communists and communism
were easily constructed as alien to Georgianness. . . .

Events in neighboring Armenia and Azerbaijan stimulated the explosion of a new
politics of ethnic conflict in Georgia. In June 1988, fifty-eight Abkhaz Communists
sent a letter to the Nineteenth Party Conference in Moscow demanding the secession of Abkhazia from Georgia. The growing fear on the part of Georgians of an Abkhaz "Karabakh" in Georgia, combined with threatened changes in the USSR constitution that seemed to deny union republics the right to secession, led to massive
demonstrations in Tbilisi in November.

Approximately 100,000 people defied the government's restrictions on demonstrations and marched through the streets carrying the red-black-and-white Georgian
national flag and demanding an end to discrimination against Georgians by Abkhaz,
Azerbaijanis, Ajars, and Osetins. . . .

The problem of the non-Georgians, more than any other, resounded outside the
Tbilisi intelligentsia and provided the dissident intellectual leaders with a mass following. Georgians made up 70 percent of the population of the republic as a whole,
but non-Georgians were strategically located around the periphery. Although Abkhaz
were a minority in Abkhazia (17 percent with 46 percent of the population Georgians), Osetins had a clear majority (66 percent) in the South Osetin Autonomous
District. In each of the autonomous regions, the titular nationality had a dominant,
though contested, political weight that was increasingly becoming intolerable to nationalist Georgians. To the non-Georgians, the republic fit the image drawn by Andrei Sakharov and others of Georgia as a "miniature empire." The Georgians' alarm
was deepened not only by fears that nearly one-third of the republic's population
could have potentially separatist agendas but also by anxiety about the chronically low
birthrate for ethnic Georgians and the higher rates for non-Georgians.

Gaining a sense of its own power, the Georgian nationalist movement maintained
its pressure after November through demonstrations and hunger strikes against the
perceived Abkhaz threat. After a mass meeting of Abkhaz on March 18, 1989, called
for separation of Abkhazia from Georgia, the protests escalated. Faced by growing
crowds in the center of the capital and fearing for its survival, the Patiashvili government asked Moscow for permission to repress the demonstrators. Early in the morning of April 9, 1989, Soviet troops wielding sharpened shovels and using toxic gas

waded into the peaceful crowds in central Tbilisi. Nineteen people were killed, mostly women, and hundreds injured.

The Georgian national movement was further radicalized by the Tbilisi massacre. When Merab Kostava was killed in October 1989 in an automobile accident. Gamsakhurdia was left as the major figure in the movement. His rhetoric included calls for "national wholeness" but left little room for compromise with or tolerance of alternative views. The more moderate groups—such as the Popular Front, the Rustaveli Society, and the Social Democratic Party—sought to lay the foundations for a multiparty system and agreed to participate in the parliamentary elections. . . . But it was the radicals, wanting no association with the "illegitimate" Communist regime, who determined the pace and shape of the movement. . . .

Gamsakhurdia both reflected the militance of many of the nationalists and inflamed it by his inflexible response to the non-Georgians, whom he accused of being stooges of Moscow. The national movement failed to develop a discourse of civil or human rights that expressed an unconditional right of national self-determination for its minorities. Instead, the non-Georgians were depicted as "foreigners," recent arrivals living on authentically Georgian land, and as more loyal to the imperial Russian power than to Georgia.

Six nationalist blocs competed against the Communists in the parliamentary elections of October 28, 1990. Gamsakhurdia's Round Table coalition swept the elections with the Communists a distant second. Elected chairman of the Supreme Soviet, Gamsakhurdia formed a non-Communist government headed by Tengiz Sigua. As the Communists retired from power, the new government made clear its intention to lead Georgia toward full independence from the Soviet Union. . . .

The euphoria of political renaissance was darkened by ominous shadows of not only interethnic warfare but also rival centers of power within the Georgian national movement and the growing authoritarianism and arbitrariness of the new leader of the republic. Gamsakhurdia took control of the mass media and arrested both the leader of the Osetin resistance and his principal Georgian opponents, most notably Jaba Ioseliani, the commander of the paramilitary force *mkhedrioni*. Instead of local power being devolved to elected councils, Gamsakhurdia appointed regional prefects to carry out his policies. When the regional soviet of south Osetia decided to proclaim itself an autonomous republic, Gamsakhurdia declared publicly that "if [the Osetins] do not wish to live peacefully with us, then let them leave Georgia."Within two weeks, 200 buses from Tbilisi drove toward Tskhinval to rally against the soviet's decision, and for twenty-four hours Osetins and Georgians faced each other with Ministry of Internal Affairs troops between them.

After a referendum in which almost 90 percent of the voters endorsed a "restoration of the state independence of Georgia," the formal declaration took place on the second anniversary of the Tbilisi killings, April 9, 1991. A few days later, the parliament unanimously selected Gamsakhurdia president of the republic. And on the seventy-fourth anniversary of the first declaration of Georgian independence, May 26, 1991, voters overwhelmingly (86.5 percent of the ballots cast) chose Gamsakhurdia as Georgia's first popularly elected president.

Fearful of Communist designs on his republic, surrounded by armed men, his house guarded by vicious dogs, Gamsakhurdia saw enemies everywhere. A particular target of his wrath was Shevardnadze, whom, he said, had been falsely portrayed as a martyr to democracy. . . .

As the president moved steadily toward a more dictatorial posture, the opposition took advantage of Gamsakhurdia's failure to condemn resolutely the August 1991 coup against Gorbachev. Battle lines formed through the autumn, and compromise between two opposing coalitions within the nationalist movement proved impossible. On December 22, the president's opponents launched armed attacks on the parliament building in central Tbilisi, where Gamsakhurdia was holed up in a basement bunker. The "Soviet" army did not intervene—Georgia had rejected membership in the Commonwealth of Independent States—and dozens of people were killed as tanks roamed the streets. By January 2, 1992, the opposition had gained the upper hand, freed political prisoners, and set up a military council to replace the Gamsakhurdia government. When pro-president demonstrators rallied the next day, gunmen fired into the crowd killing two and wounding twenty-five On January 6, Gamsakhurdia escaped from the parliament building and fled the country.

In late February 1992, the Tbilisi nationalists invited Shevardnadze to return to Georgia, and within days of his arrival in early March, the former party chief was appointed chairman of the State Council. With no real power base of his own within Georgia, Shevardnadze had to form an alliance of convenience with the politicians—Ioseliani, Kitovani, and Sigua—who had invited him back to Georgia. His role was one of mediation and reconciliation, and his enormous international prestige contributed to the growing sense, both within the country and abroad, that he alone could bring peace to Georgia.

Though the painful fractures in the Georgian political elite in Tbilisi were not overcome by Shevardnadze's arrival, the principal source of political instability through 1992 and 1993 came from the Gamsakhurdia forces, mostly in western Georgia, and the renewed conflict in Abkhazia.

The anti-Gamsakhurdia coalition was as disunited as the nationalist movement from which it emerged. Kitovani and Ioseliani both had their own armed retinues, and yet neither of them could control their followers completely. The State Council sought to broaden its base and legitimize its rule by mounting a campaign to discredit Gamsakhurdia, who was depicted as a madman and a force of disintegration within Georgia, and by easing pressure on non-Georgians, freeing the press, registering political parties, and organizing elections to a new parliament. On October 11, 1992, the voters gave Shevardnadze the kind of mandate that a year and a half earlier they had given Gamsakhurdia: Of those voting (about 60 percent of the electorate participated), 89 percent voted for Shevardnadze as speaker. . . .

The elections accomplished the first goal of Shevardnadze—to create a legitimate, inclusive organ of power in order to create a strong executive for Georgia. But, as in Azerbaijan, political stability was hostage to the internal ethnic war. In September 1993, Abkhaz nationalists abandoned a Russian-brokered cease-fire and took Sukhumi. At the same time, Gamsakhurdia's followers revived the war in western Georgia, driving back Shevardnadze's forces. Shevardnadze was forced to invite in Russian troops and agree to have Georgia enter the Commonwealth of Independent States, by then increasingly dominated by Yeltsin's Russia.

Although the ethnic, regional, ideological, and political divisions remained deep in Georgia, most of the Georgian political and intellectual elite recognized that Shevardnadze was the man most likely to bring about reconciliation of hitherto irreconcilable elements. Zviad Gamsakhurdia's mysterious death in December 1993 removed the main alternative to Shevardnadze for the moment, and the reentry of Russia into Transcaucasian politics also contributed to stabilization of the former party secretary's powers. Though the Georgian state remained weak and the country disunited,

Shevardnadze managed to install a democratic framework and a degree of internal peace. . . .

CONCLUSION

To explain the collapse of the Communist elites and the rocky roads to power of the new elites in Transcaucasia, I have emphasized several factors: the degree of unity and consensus achieved within the nationalist movements; the intransigence or flexibility of the ruling Communist elites; the nature of leadership in the nationalist movements; the nature of the various, competing nationalist discourses (inclusive, tolerant, and democratic or exclusivist, intolerant, and authoritarian); and the divisive factor of interethnic strife (largely absent in Armenia; thrust upon the Azerbaijanis by the Karabakh resistance; and fomented and encouraged by nationalist leaders in Georgia).

The relatively peaceful and democratic victory of the nationalists in Armenia was facilitated by the moderately flexible Communist elite, which by mid-1989 was already working with the nationalists. The homogeneous ethnic composition of the republic, which precluded internal ethnic problems (Azerbaijanis were quickly deported from the republic in late 1988 and early 1989), and the displacement of armed conflict outside the republic, to Karabakh, allowed Armenians to experience a relatively violence-free transition to democracy. The transformation of elites, finally, was lubricated by the ability of the nationalists to generate leadership and language that emphasized measured, pragmatic policies.

The delayed ascension to power of the Azerbaijani nationalists can be explained by the successful resistance of the Communist elite; its relative coherence and determination to hold on to its power; and the late formation, weak social base, and internal divisions of the nationalist elite. The inability of the nationalists to control effectively the autonomous mass movement, which expressed social as much as ethnic discontents, combined with the unpredictable and radicalizing factor of the Karabakh war to undermine the legitimacy of the old elite and open the way for the return of representative figures from the old regime. Azerbaijan's nationalist intellectuals suffered from the relative weakness of a widely accepted discourse of the nation and the absence of an overwhelming commitment to the nation-state of Azerbaijan that might have superseded local and clan loyalties.

The road to civil war in Georgia lay through the extremism of the nationalist leadership that emerged in the conflict with the Communists. The April killings radicalized the opposition and made accommodation with the Communists almost impossible, even as the latter attempted to find common ground. The multinationality of the Georgian republic became a source of conflict, in part because of the legacy of Georgian hegemonic and privileged rule, in part because so little effort was made to find an inclusivist rhetoric and program. Conflicts with the Abkhaz and Osetins created a cycle of violence that eventually enveloped the Georgian factions as well. When the divisiveness of Gamsakhurdia's policies and rhetoric reached into the very heart of the nationalist counterelite, leading politicians coalesced to overthrow the elected president and invite Shevardnadze, seen as a more conciliatory and prestigious figure, to reunify and pacify the fractured nation.

With the collapse of the Soviet Union and the simultaneous erasure of the "socialist choice," the new political game in town was nationalism. Only nation-based claims could compete in the new discursive and political environment for the available political and economic resources—for legitimacy and recognition by the great capitalist democracies and the multinational sources of funding, the International Monetary Fund and the World Bank. But in order for the claims of nationality to self-determination, sovereignty, and independent statehood to be fully acceptable to the international community, they had to be combined with the rhetoric and practice of democracy and a commitment to build a market system and to reject what was thought to be socialism. The difficulties in the short run in creating stable democratic states based on a dominant nationality were compounded by the deep and continuing weakening of state power, which was well under way under Gorbachev and only accelerated after him. Just as a rule of law seemed within reach, a new and pervasive lawlessness overwhelmed the means of enforcement. The successor states, particularly the least repressive ones, lost their monopoly over violence, as semiindependent militias (like *mkhedrioni* in Georgia), nationalist guerrillas (*fedayee* in Armenia), and remobilized Afghan veterans and mercenaries (in Azerbaijan) turned into independent, armed political actors. Over the whole process of state and market building hung the ever present threat of civil and interethnic war.

All of these elite transformations occurred in the broader Soviet, post-Soviet, and international contexts in which communism rapidly experienced an erosion of legitimacy, and national self-determination, democracy, and market capitalism gained powerful, universal resonance.

Ronald Grigor Suny, "Elite Transformation in Late-Soviet and Post-Soviet Transcaucasia, or What Happens When the Ruling Class Can't Rule?" in Timothy J. Colton and Robert C. Tucker (eds.), *Patterns in Post-Soviet Leadership* (Boulder, CO: Westview Press, 1995), pp. 141–162, 167.

⹀ Valentin Rasputin, "After Events, On the Eve of Events" ⹀
January 1992

Born in 1937 in Siberia, Valentin Rasputin was a journalist before turning to short fiction in the 1960s. His work was sensitive to his native environment, the beauties of rural Russia and the strength of its people, and the need for humans to forgive, care for one another, and accept responsibility for their acts. Like other writers of the "village prose" school, who sought to depict rural life honestly and without embellishment, Rasputin pushed his work past the limits of Socialist Realism. He took up the cause of environmental preservation (as in his famous story "Farewell to Matera" [1976]) and decried the assault of Soviet programs on the Siberian way of life. His celebration of traditional Russia led to his being labeled a "nationalist," a term of abuse in the Soviet lexicon. His love of Russia and its traditions was combined with an antipathy to the influx into Russia of Western culture, an attitude he shared with conservatives like Ligachev. During perestroika, he spoke at the Congress of People's Deputies against the spread of Russophobia among non-Russians. "Perhaps it is Russia which should leave the Union," he said prophetically, "since you accuse her of all your misfortunes. . . . Without fear of being called nationalists we could then pronounce the word Russian and speak openly about national self-awareness."[1]

1. Quoted in John B. Dunlop, *The Rise of Russia and the Fall of the Soviet Empire* (Princeton: Princeton University Press, 1993), p. 17.

. . . Every people must have a national and state idea. For Russians, it is to free themselves from the inferiority complex that has been thrust upon them, recognize their worth and uniqueness, and interpret that worth not as national arrogance but as qualitative spiritual development. For Russia, it is the preservation of its statehood and the return of its former glory and honor.

Grandfathers, often by the most direct kinship, adopted communism, and their grandsons cursed it—it got into the hands of the wrong people, they said. But that is not the point. As long as communism played the role of destroyer of the state, as long as it ground the people underfoot in the name of a common internationalist spirit, it was to the liking of both Western democracy and the "vanguard" intelligentsia at home. Everything was fine. We are unwilling to acknowledge one very important thing that has totally changed the intelligentsia's attitude toward its own doctrine. It was like digesting a nuclear bomb, but at the price of enormous sacrifice and suffering, Russia digested communism and placed it in the service of Russian statehood. Intended to destroy the country, it gradually became a supporter of a strong state— in its own thick-skulled and categorical manner, of course, which does not come very close to the desired good.

Still, something had happened that was not expected of communism, and it could not be forgiven for that degeneration, that betrayal. . . .

[Now there has been] a change in the ideological baggage. The "idea," in general, has remained the same—to stop Russia—but the means of implementing it have changed. . . .

Really, what kind of intelligentsia is this, if it harbors malice toward its own country, is aggressive and unscrupulous in instilling the tastes and views that it preaches, and takes a free-and-easy attitude toward morals, conscience and other "superfluities" of human character? If it does not feel a kinship with its people and seeks the latter's well-being in other lands?

But that is in fact the nature of the revolutionary radical intelligentsia, rootless, not knowing the salt of its native earth, drawing its nourishment from the atmosphere of "civilizing influences." It is brought up on that, and probably sincerely believes that Russia, in its historical and spiritual aspect, is bad, uneducated and mistaken and that its salvation lies in complete reconstruction according to the models that exist in the lands of plenty. . . . But since Russia evinced no desire for this, these people first had to dismember it, rob it of its strength, slander it and use any means possible to compromise their opponents from the national intelligentsia and destroy their resistance—and then, off with our country to the dominion of world democracy, which is truly taking the whole world in hand and has long been hankering after Russia, after its wealth and vast expanses, so as to keep moving onward. . . .

If there is a people, if it hasn't let itself be reduced entirely to ruin, there must also be a national intelligentsia. This intelligentsia is not indifferent to where, under whose yoke the neck of its long-suffering motherland is bowed; it wants that neck to be free of any economic or political collar and to hold up its own head.

Hence our differences with the cosmopolitan intelligentsia, and all the rest. For it, home is where life is easier; for us, it is only here among our native sights and sounds, no matter how those sights may grieve us. Mikhail Antonov was right when he commented recently that our society today is divided not into rightists and leftists, but into those who are selling Russia and those who are protecting her. . . .

I have the impression that our policy has become a component part of the big, overall policy that is being made somewhere else. The current state of our country and its too rapid decline are proof of that. Even our enemies did not expect such stunning success. If our policy had been independent and just a little firmer, this would not have happened. . . . To surrender such a mighty country in just the slightly more than two years in which the major events unfolded—such a thing has never happened before. I mean surrender in the literal sense: The victors now have to rack their brains over how to feed us, as prisoners, and whether to feed us at all.

What did the former President of the USSR receive the Nobel Prize for? . . .

The plans for dismembering our country were laid quite a bit earlier. For example, back in 1959 the US Senate passed a resolution proclaiming the last week of July the week of enslaved nations and giving its blessing to efforts by the government to free those enslaved nations from the yoke of Communist Russia. Which has indeed happened, in exact accordance not with the will of the peoples, but with the will of the politicians who control the world's destiny.

I consider the CIS, where the former members of the Soviet Union have now cast anchor, to be only a temporary, transitional phenomenon before further national quarreling and separation. If they haven't exercised common sense up to now, where will they find any when they have to deal with territorial, property, ethnic and many other problems? . . .

And worst of all—just as Russia suffered as part of the fraternity, so it is suffering now and losing more than anyone else in the breakup. Once again, it is paying all the costs; once again it is being torn to pieces, and claims are being made on its property.

At the beginning of this conversation, I said that the right thing for Russia is a Russian idea. What kind of idea? There is the idea of Russians as a people, but what about Russia as a country? What sort of idea might that be? I think it is the idea of coexistence on an equal footing, the Russian people's cohabitation with the other peoples who are part of Russia. The Russian is unusually easy to get along with; this is what Dostoyevsky called his universal humaness. Both myths, one malicious—that the Russian is intolerant of his neighbor—and the other pitiful—that he is ready, to his own detriment, to serve and oblige everyone else—are equally far from the truth. His tolerance and friendliness are what every people should have in order to live in peace and harmony. Then there would be no reason to try to inculcate and implement ideas of taking away everyone's national identity and creating a single, universal conglomeration of peoples, and no one would ever succeed in doing so. . . .

Cries of "nationalist," won't send me running into the bushes in fear, and I won't hide there and excuse myself by saying: No, no, I'm one of you, I'm a thoroughgoing internationalist. . . . I favor the kind of internationalism in which there would be a palette of all nations, not interfering with but only complementing one another. The concept of "nationalism" has been deliberately slandered. It should be judged not by the extremes and foolishness that go along with any healthy idea, but by its true core and its moral and spiritual principles. Enlightened, civilized nationalism is the work of qualitatively transforming one's people, liberating their moral strength, and pointing out everything that is worthy of their name. Who could be the worse for that? . . .

The conspiracy against Russia existed long before perestroika. It wasn't we who made perestroika, but we participated in it. Without Russia's wealth of raw materials, flourishing capitalism faced hard times; it was flourishing beyond its means. But the tsar has the power of authority, and the people have the power of opinion. Now no one has any authority, but the power of opinion remains. And the people will make use of that power.

I don't want to talk about the ways in which public opinion might be expressed; that has nothing to do with the forecasts that I would venture to make. God forbid that things reach the point of a revolt. But if no other means are left, the people won't be asking for anyone's advice. Their patience is not endless. . . .

Valentin Rasputin "After Events, On the Eve of Events," *Sovetskaia Rossiia,* January 23, 1992; translated in *Current Digest of the Soviet Press,* XLIV, 8 (March 25, 1992), pp. 16, 27.

Gavriil Popov, "August 1991"

The economist Gavriil Popov was a leading democrat and early supporter of Yeltsin. A founding member of the democratic Interregional Group at the Congress of People's Deputies, Popov was elected mayor of Moscow in 1990 when the Democratic Russia movement won the majority of seats in the city council. He was a key organizer of DemRossiia, the first independent political party in Soviet Russia and the principal political vehicle that brought Yeltsin to power. In this essay Popov tells how the Russian democrats failed to consolidate their position after the August 1991 coup and in essence surrendered power to the better-positioned former Communist nomenklatura. Popov himself left politics for business and did very well.

[I.]   "USING A VICTORY WELL IS MORE IMPORTANT THAN WINNING"[1]

. . . In a political sense, the range of assessments of both the coup and the way events developed after it is exceptionally broad. In one view, it was "a great revolution equal in significance to October 1917." In another, it was "a revolution of missed opportunities." According to a third view, it was "a revolution betrayed." And according to a fourth, "there was no revolution at all."

My overall assessment is that the democrats' victory over the coup plotters did not bring to power the democrats, who were totally unprepared to be in that position, but finally forced the reformist apparatchiks and nomenklatura to do what they had not done in 1985, 1989 or 1990—to organize themselves, unite, cleanse themselves of ideological garbage, remove the conservatives and start making reforms. To start slowly, but to start.

A Clash Involving Force Became Inevitable

. . . I am inclined to think that, for the most part, the organizers of the coup were people faithful to an idea, loyal servants of the pyramid that had raised them to great heights. They were thinking about the interests of the country—according to their own, communist understanding. . . .

The country was falling apart. Either there had to be a break with the center and each republic had to follow its own path, or the center had to strengthen its authority and try to do something itself. A clash became inevitable. Both the democrats and

1. Plutarch, *Selected Lives,* Vol. 2, p. 193.

the conservatives realized this. The conservatives decided to anticipate events, and they acted first.

In a recent interview, Mikhail Sergeyevich [Gorbachev] said again that a normal process was under way that was interrupted by the coup. Over the course of six years Mikhail Sergeyevich tried to convince us dozens of times that a normal process was under way. But in actuality the noose was tightening. Therefore, the signing of the Union Treaty that was coming up on Aug. 20, 1991, was only a new stage in the process of tightening the knot. Or else Gorbachev intended to finally begin destroying the center and its backbone—the CPSU structure—after the treaty was signed, or was prepared to give the republics the opportunity to do this. Possibly. But judging from his speeches during the first hours after he returned to Moscow and from his actions, he wasn't ready to do such things. Consequently, there was no foreseeable prospect of anything "normal" appearing. So one can agree with the coup plotters on one thing: The "process" required radical, surgical intervention.

Therefore, the coup was not something unexpected. The coup plotters had previously had a chance to stage a legal coup in favor of the center—when Pavlov demanded extraordinary powers five days after Yeltsin was elected President of Russia, when Yeltsin was in the US. I was among those who contributed to the collapse of that plan. I will talk about this . . . sometime. The question of extraordinary powers was dropped at the time.

The conservatives realized that we [the democrats] would give battle in the fall—because, like them, we couldn't wait any longer either. The people were demanding reforms from us, and we would have had to begin them by taking away the center's right to interfere in Russia's affairs. The conservatives tried to forestall us.

In light of what I have said, I have my own attitude toward the idea of putting the State Committee for the State of Emergency on trial. The CPSU, yes. But as for the SCSE, that's debatable. The SCSE was a violation of legality, of course. But we, too, would have had to violate legality (as happened, incidentally, in the dissolution of the USSR). Great turning points cannot be judged by the articles of former laws, since they involve a changeover to a system of new laws. . . .

The Success of the Democratic President.—Only the leaders of the republics could act against the SCSE. And Boris Yeltsin became the key figure. In the hour of trial he proved—as an individual, a citizen and a leader—that millions of voters had not made a mistake in voting for him.

In Russia the importance of the top man is immeasurably higher than his formal functions would indicate, and than that of his counterparts in other countries. The fact that there was a legitimate President in Russia, that his orders had to be obeyed and that opposition to the SCSE was not a rebellion but only compliance with the instructions of the Russian President enabled thousands of administrators who were against the SCSE in their hearts but felt very uncomfortable in the role of "resisters" to "rest assured." The orientation toward the will of the authorities that had been fostered during the era of totalitarianism now worked against the coup.

Did the SCSE members know the significance of this factor? Yes. Without a doubt. . . .

[But] they clearly underestimated the special significance to Russia of the emergence of an official center of resistance as a mobilizing and consolidating principle.

Furthermore, they believed that Yeltsin's personal resentment against Gorbachev (for which there were more than ample grounds; they knew what had been done against Yeltsin with Gorbachev's consent or without his opposition) was so great that

Yeltsin would rejoice over the fall of "the enemy." The fact that Yeltsin would turn out to be a relentlessly clear-headed politician capable of suppressing his emotions and oriented toward political goals came as a surprise to them. . . . In the hour of trial, Yeltsin did not allow personal resentments to overshadow the interests of the cause. . . .

The leaders of the other republics were an important consideration. Former or current leaders of the Central Committees of the republic Communist Parties, they yielded, for the most part, to the persuasion of the SCSE members. Evidently the latter promised to give the other republics—not Russia—more than Gorbachev promised them. But the destruction of the chief republic leader would have meant that the SCSE had the right—just as in the good old days—to change the leadership in the republics. Neither Kravchuk nor Nazarbayev could consent to that. And it is not impossible that Yeltsin's freedom was a condition for their reacting calmly to the SCSE: Changes in your own circle, in the center, are one thing. But you can't touch the leaders of the republics. If Russia is treated that way, what can the others expect?

But it seems to me that the most important thing was the following. I call it the Beria syndrome. Some member of the SCSE would have personally had to give the order to destroy Yeltsin. The person who gave such an order, or even failed to prevent it, would have been doomed. He—like Beria in his time—would have been made the scapegoat for all the blood that this option would have involved (and it would have been the blood of thousands of people). . . . All the members of the SCSE realized this. It is symptomatic that each of them demanded that the others issue an order concerning Yeltsin, but no one wanted to issue it himself. There were no kamikazes to be found among the SCSE members, even for the sake of the Communists' cause.

This unwillingness was immediately conveyed to the second echelon of leaders, especially in the Army and the State Security Committee [KGB], who then had even less desire to be responsible for an attack and, moreover, seeing the hesitation of the SCSE leaders, began to seek an agreement with Yeltsin.

As a result, Yeltsin remained free and immediately began to act. He chose the following tactic. . . .

As his first and chief demand, Boris Nikolayevich called for the restoration of power to the legitimate President. He did precisely what the SCSE least expected. Why would Yeltsin fight for Gorbachev's return? After all, anyone taking Gorbachev's place would certainly be a weaker opponent for Yeltsin. Wouldn't it be better for him to face someone like Lukyanov in the ring and untie his hands for a fight and a victory?

But the removal of Gorbachev was the SCSE's weakest spot, and that is precisely where Yeltsin struck. In so doing, he immediately gained several advantages.

First of all, he knocked the Gorbachev card out of the SCSE's hand. People had doubts: Was the SCSE really against Gorbachev, or was there some sort of plot between them? By demanding Mikhail Sergeyevich's return, Yeltsin immediately, on the one hand, deprived the SCSE of the possibility of reaching an agreement with Gorbachev, and, on the other hand, put Gorbachev himself in a position in which an agreement with the SCSE would have been a betrayal of a Russia that had remained loyal to him. If the SCSE didn't return Gorbachev, that would mean the SCSE was against the Constitution. If it did return him, that would be a point for Yeltsin and a failure for the SCSE. On the whole, the return of Gorbachev became the symbol of the SCSE's failure.

In sticking up for Gorbachev, Yeltsin immediately turned all the West's sympathy toward himself. Now everyone in the West who cared about Gorbachev would have to help Yeltsin.

And finally, Gorbachev's own supporters in the USSR, who at first tried to wait (Primakov, Volsky and others), sooner or later had to show solidarity with Yeltsin. . . .

Now to address Yeltsin's strategy. It was to use the coup to turn the SCSE leaders into violators of legality and destroy the CPSU elite.

And, along with the elite, to destroy the structure of the CPSU. . . .

And to seize from the CPSU control of the Army, state security, the Ministry of Internal Affairs and the press, and to eliminate the very foundation of totalitarianism.

In sum, to destroy the very center that had proven to be the chief obstacle to reforms.

Behind these strategic objectives, one overriding objective arose—how to govern Russia afterwards.

The chief thing for which Yeltsin deserves credit as a politician is that he completely rejected the idea of turning the victory over the SCSE into an all-out purge of the previous system, into a Leninist-type revolution.

It is to Boris Yeltsin's credit that the storming of the Central Committee buildings in Moscow, unlike the storming of the Winter Palace in Petrograd, did not become the beginning of a wave of riots and anarchy throughout Russia. I can say now that after Aug. 22, groups of democrats from various cities poured into Moscow. There had been no sound out of them during the days of the coup, but now they were bursting to prove their readiness to fight for democracy. There was an influx of groups of curiosity-seekers and outright bandits who expected that there would be something to make a profit off of. A crowd of informers besieged the KGB in a fierce effort to be the first to break into the building and burn all traces of the deeds they had done over many years. Without the support of the Russian President, I, as mayor, would never have been able to avert the masses' "revolutionary" wrath.

That the victory over the bureaucratic center did not touch off internethnic slaughter and did not turn the USSR into a Yugoslavia is also to the credit of the Russian President.

Whereas the CPSU leadership deserves the "credit" for the fact that a clash involving force became inevitable, it is to the credit of the first President democratically elected by the people of Russia that—in contrast to 1917—this clash involving force was not the beginning of riots, anarchy and rebellion. The President preserved Russia and opened the way to the possibility of peaceful transformations. That is his contribution to Russia's experience.

And he achieved all these successes alone—he advanced the idea of transferring power from the CPSU to a coalition of democrats and reformist apparatchiks. . . .

In the coup situation, why didn't Yeltsin follow Lenin's path? There is nothing accidental about this. Yeltsin's course of making an alliance with part of the overthrown apparatus was the result of many factors.

Boris Yeltsin had left the ranks of CPSU leaders. Like many of us, he had started out with confidence that working actively and honestly within the CPSU system was the main way to improve the situation of the people and the state. Later, after seeing the ineffectiveness of his efforts, he called for a reform of the CPSU. Finally he broke with the CPSU over the reluctance of its leadership and the apparatus that controlled the Party to embark on any kind of significant reforms.

But, after breaking with the CPSU, Yeltsin could see very well how many reformers there were among the apparatchiks. They expressed both overt and, especially, covert support for him. They did not have his inherent courage to break with the CPSU, but in everything else they were very close to him. . . . Unlike the leaders of the 1917 Russian Revolution, who personally were totally alien to the class that had ruled Russia before them, Yeltsin could view the reform-minded part of the Party apparatus and other apparatuses of the USSR as a potential reserve. . . .

On the other hand, Yeltsin succeeded in arranging his cooperation with the democratic forces in such a way that he could be both declared and elected leader without binding himself by any formal commitments to democratic organizations. He did not commit himself to propose and to secure the approval of personnel or draft laws in any democratic structures. . . .

Therefore, when I was besieged by representatives of Democratic Russia who were indignant over certain appointments or decrees, I always answered: Your complaints have no basis; Boris Nikolayevich isn't deceiving anyone. Show me his commitments! I think that Yeltsin would have refused cooperation outright if the democrats had made such demands on him. In this regard, Yeltsin confirmed once again that he is a high-class politician. . . .

The democrats, rejoicing during the days after the coup, never even dreamed that the idea of a coalition with the reformist apparatchiks had also triumphed during those days. In the most critical hours, while waiting for the expected attack, I saw Yury Petrov at Yeltsin's side, standing his ground just as firmly as all the democrats. I thought, "It is during these days that the reformist apparatchiks have made their final break with the CPSU leadership and made the most important choice of their lives. Now their future will be linked with Yeltsin, and it isn't hard to foresee how actively they will begin to work beside him." . . .

[Yeltsin] did not deceive the democrats: He offered them a place in the coalition and every opportunity to become the chief figures in that coalition. What's more, the President himself was prepared for this to happen. Nothing more could be demanded of him. Who would prevail in the new coalition? It seemed as though after the coup, all the circumstances gave the better chance to the democrats. But the democrats were unable to take advantage of the opportunity offered to them by the President. . . .

[II.]   . . . COULD THE DEMOCRATS HAVE TAKEN POWER?

. . . [The democrats'] main mistake [was] that they imagined they had taken power in Russia after the coup. Unfortunately, the people believed this, too. . . .

But the democrats were thinking only about posts. . . .

The idea had become firmly rooted in the minds of the people, the CPSU and its leaders that obtaining power meant obtaining an appointment to a post.

It wasn't even realized that power is a complex mechanism that binds together in tightly knit interaction the rank-and-file functionary who fills out the most trivial form at the borough building-maintenance office, the journalist at a newspaper, the door guard at a ministry, the sales clerk in a state store, old-age pensioners living on state pensions and assistance from sons who are officers in the service of the state, and hundreds of instructions and laws that are comprehensible only to a bureaucrat. The democrats didn't even have a concept of what "taking power" means. . . .

If we are going to talk seriously about power, then, besides the problem of taking control of its entire mechanism, there was also the problem of what the democrats actually were before and after the coup. . . .

When the coup occurred, the democrats were split by numerous schisms and were characterized by organizational weakness within individual blocs and the movement as a whole. Organizationally, the democrats were not ready to take power.

Added to the organizational weakness was weakness in terms of programs. After all, for a long time we had acted on the assumption that we would be only an opposition. We waited for various government actions and then saw it as our role to form a democratic attitude toward them.

In all the main areas—nationalities policy, the state system, privatization, structural reorganization of the economy, microeconomic policy, agrarian reform, a social program for the USSR, foreign relations—we lacked concrete programs in versions that were suitable for practical application. We had documents on objectives—for an opposition, that was sufficient.

The actual programs—the 500 Days, the law on privatization, etc.—were not programs developed by the democrats but programs developed by reformist apparatchiks, drawn up with a view toward democratic approaches and ideas.

Yeltsin was reproached for the fact that for an entire month after the coup there was no new program from the Russian government, but what could he do if the movement as a whole, though it possessed the country's best minds, had not come up with a program that could become the starting point for the development of a government plan? . . .

Even then—though not as clearly as now—I saw in general outlines that we had not taken any sort of power, that we had only entered a coalition, but that we would not be able to be the leaders in it, either. . . .

I had an obligation to insist that Yeltsin agree to become President of the USSR as well as of Russia. . . .

I was well enough acquainted with Gorbachev that he would have listened without bias to a suggestion from me that he hand over his post to Yeltsin on the very first day after the coup. On his own he couldn't bring himself to do this; his associates were putting pressure on him. But after all, Mikhail Sergeyevich himself had once let drop the phrase, "Should I perhaps turn everything over to Boris?" . . .

I am certain that it would not have been possible to change the course of events in any fundamental way. Power was bound to be transferred to the reformist apparatchiks. But within the framework of that historically inevitable process, it would have been possible to create more conditions conducive to democratic versions of reform, if instead of the two birds in the bush we had thought about the one in our hand. . . .

III.   THE NOMENKLATURA WITHOUT THE CPSU

. . . In contrast to the democratic movement, the apparatus acted with exceptional skill. Someday historians will write a lot of works on this subject. Here I would like to note what has already become clear during the first year since the coup.

First of all, the apparatus supported the general illusion that the democrats had taken power. This gave it many advantages. It was able to "transfer to the democrats' account" a lot of the past sins of totalitarianism. Whenever anything bad came to light, no matter what and where it was, it was immediately linked with the democrats' being in power. . . .

The apparatus had to learn to live without the CPSU. Without running to the Central Committee, province committees or district committees with complaints against someone. Without its own members' being called "on the carpet" there. It needed time to figure out in practical terms how to live: without the CPSU, but still retaining power for itself.

It also needed time to restructure itself. It was necessary to ascertain which people were willing to become reformist apparatchiks; to get acquainted with each other, reach agreements and unite. Simply put, to "sniff each other out." While the democrats were arguing about posts, the apparatus was feverishly reorganizing its ranks.

The apparatus judiciously singled out a minimum that it could not let go of under any circumstances—administration and personnel. . . .

Its wisest decision was whom to put in the first row of the presidium. . . . It realized that to push forward now would mean to spoil everything. But unlike the democrats, the apparatus, tempered by years of service, knew how to be patient and wait.

So it proposed for the top roles people who officially had the least possible connection with the apparatus but were still its personnel. Those who had been known in the apparatus as "radicals" before all this began. There had always been such reformist apparatchiks in the apparatus. But the apparatus used to keep these intelligent and bright minds as advisers: at institutes and on editorial boards. Now they were put in the front ranks. . . .

They were radical reformers, but they were still the apparatus. . . .

Then the apparatus began working hard on the democrats who had filled the new posts. It wasn't difficult to prove to them quickly that they didn't have even an approximate notion of the real situation and could not get by without constantly leaning on apparatchiks from "their own" apparatus. While adorning itself with the name of some well-known democrat, the apparatus of one or another ministry or department retained real control over everything. . . .

The restructuring of the apparatus, which had been postponed since 1985, proceeded quickly. But the apparatus also had to prove its ability to conduct reforms in the economy.

Here, too, it demonstrated exceptional skill. Given that it was definitely necessary to do something, and that the people thought that power was in the hands of the democrats, it was best of all to begin implementing the measures that were most painful from a social standpoint—to increase prices, reduce incomes, devalue the population's savings, and so on and so forth. And to postpone the most important matters—first and foremost, the dividing up of property—until the apparatus had established itself more firmly in power. . . .

Only as its positions grew stronger did it, under pressure from the President and the democratic forces, gradually include the problems of privatization in its action program. . . .

[Now] privatization options with a preponderance of apparatus viewpoints are being called a democratic approach. But there is still no agrarian reform. . . .

The apparatchiks [also] used [this] time to form their own political vanguard. At first in the form of individual parties and movements. And then they united them in the Civic Alliance. . . .

Behind the government's outwardly stormy debates with the Civic Alliance and various Deputies' groups made up of apparatchiks, what is really at issue is not a transfer of power from the democrats to the apparatus, as some people are trying to depict the situation. The apparatus never lost power. What is at issue right now is a redistribution of power among individual groups within the apparatus. . . .

The apparatus has thoroughly "purged" its ranks in the past year: It has gotten rid of dogmatists; it has gotten rid of ignoramuses and bunglers. It has shifted the most corrupt people into the ranks of businessmen. It has renewed and rejuvenated itself.

Of course, the conservative group that has its base in the most unpromising parts of the military-industrial complex and of the agrarian sector is still very active in the ranks of the apparatus. Left without the protection of CPSU structures, it is nevertheless still very powerful. . . .

In the past year the apparatus, hiding behind the smoke screen of the illusion that the democrats are in power, has succeeded in preparing itself to take into its own hands, not only in actuality but also officially, the process of transforming Russia into a postindustrial society. What's more, it is already conducting this process. . . .

There is nothing tragic about the fact that, after the CPSU, power remained in the hands of the apparatus. There was no other way to begin reforms. All the other forces in society were unprepared to conduct reforms on their own. . . .

IV.   THE POSITION OF A DEMOCRAT

I always find it puzzling that recognition of the fact that after August 1991 power shifted from the CPSU nomenklatura to the nomenklatura without the CPSU puts some democrats into a state of panic and is perceived by them as a tragedy. . . .

We, the democratic forces, broke the CPSU's back. But we are not in power. We are not ready for it. But we are ready to function actively in the role of an opposition. . . .

A year after the coup we can see that the unprecedented upsurge in the energy of the people, who themselves literally made history in August 1991, has made it possible to accomplish three historic tasks.

One. The dictatorship of the CPSU, with its suppression of the people's initiative, low work efficiency, decreasing prosperity for the masses and increasing prospect of nuclear and ecological catastrophe, a threat that grew greater with every passing year, has been eliminated. . . .

Two. Russia rejected the path of a revolution involving a bloody war between the victorious and vanquished segments of society, accompanied by the danger of a new dictatorship as a reaction to the anarchy that would have been inevitable if events had developed in that way. . . . Russia chose the path of reforms. This was a critically important event in Russian history, and in world history as well. Reforms have begun and have yielded their first important results.

Three. Leadership of the reforms has been concentrated in the hands of the nomenklatura and the apparatus, now cleansed of CPSU control. I think that this is a guarantee that the reforms will be implemented, since Russia has proven unready for the best thing—a democratic version of reforms. . . .

If these three results—the elimination of the CPSU, the beginning of practical reforms, and the consolidation in power of an apparatus that is renewing itself—are augmented by a fourth—the creation of a new democratic opposition—then August 1991 will truly mark not only the end of the past, but the beginning of an era of Russia's transition from totalitarianism to a postindustrial society created by the apparatus under effective pressure from the democratic opposition.

Garviil Popov, "August 1991," *Izvestiia*, August 21, 24, 25, 26, 1992: translated in *Current Digest of the Soviet Press*, XLIV, 34 (September 23, 1992), pp. 1–6.

Yeltsin Dissolves Parliament, Calls Elections
Reply by Ruslan Khasbulatov
September 21, 1993

The confrontation between Yeltsin and the parliament, led by his former ally Ruslan Khasbulatov, exploded in the president's abolition of the parliament—actually two legislative bodies: the Congress of People's Deputies and the Supreme Soviet of the Russian Federation. Yeltsin called for new parliamentary elections to be held in December, as well as ratification of a new constitution. Vice-president Aleksandr Rutskoi declared himself president, and the parliament and its supporters refused to obey Yeltsin's orders. On October 2, barricades once again went up around the White House, now the headquarters of the anti-Yeltsin opposition. The next day, Rutskoi urged pro-parliament forces to seize the national television center at Ostankino. Clashes broke out in the city, and Yeltsin appealed in person to the military to intervene. After initial hesitation, elite divisions of Russian military forces came out for Yeltsin. On October 4, tanks assaulted the White House, setting it on fire, and the resistant parliamentarians surrendered. About 146 people were killed and a thousand wounded in Moscow. The charred hulk of the White House stood as a reminder of the failure of the first democratic experiment in independent Russia. In an unconstitutional way, Yeltsin eventually achieved his constitution.

YELTSIN DISSOLVES PARLIAMENT, CALLS ELECTIONS, SEPTEMBER 21, 1993

On Stage-By-Stage Constitutional Reform in the Russian Federation

Decree of the President of the Russian Federation. The political situation that has come about in the Russian Federation threatens the security of the country as a state and as a society.

Outright opposition to the implementation of social and economic reforms, open and daily obstruction in the Supreme Soviet of the policy of the popularly elected President of the Russian Federation and attempts to directly exercise the functions of the executive branch of government in place of the Council of Ministers are very obvious indications that a majority in the Russian Federation Supreme Soviet and a segment of its leadership have openly set out to directly flout the will of the Russian people as expressed in the referendum of April 25, 1993. This is a flagrant violation of the Law on Referendums, according to which decisions adopted in

Russia-wide referendums have supreme legal force, need no confirmation, and are binding throughout the Russian Federation.

The Congress and the Supreme Soviet are making systematic and increasingly active efforts to usurp not only executive but even judicial functions.

At the same time, to this date not only have they failed to create a legislative basis for implementation of the Federal Treaty, but the decisions they have adopted are often directly at variance with the federal nature of the Russian state.

Constitutional reform in the Russian Federation has come to a standstill, for all practical purposes. The Supreme Soviet is blocking the decisions of Congresses of Russian Federation People's Deputies on the adoption of a new Constitution.

In its everyday work, the Supreme Soviet systematically violates its rules of order and procedures for preparing and adopting decisions. Casting votes for absent Deputies has become a common practice at its sessions, a practice that in effect does away with popular representation.

In this way, the very principles of the Russian Federation's constitutional system—people's rule, separation of powers, federalism—are being destroyed. Without ever having fully emerged or becoming consolidated, the very principle of parliamentarism in the Russian Federation is being discredited.

Under these conditions, the only means, befitting the principles of people's rule, of ending the confrontation between the Congress and the Supreme Soviet, on the one hand, and the President and the government, on the other, as well as of overcoming the paralysis of state power, is to elect a new Russian Federation parliament. Such elections are not early elections for the Congress of Russian Federation People's Deputies or the Russian Federation Supreme Soviet and do not violate the will of the people as expressed in the referendum of April 25, 1993.

The need for elections is also dictated by the fact that the Russian Federation is a new state that has taken the place of the Russian SFSR within the USSR and has become the internationally recognized successor of the USSR.

In view of the fact that the existing Russian Federation Constitution provides no procedure for adopting a new Constitution, political parties and movements, groups of Deputies, participants in the Constitutional Conference and representatives of the public have repeatedly proposed that the President of the Russian Federation immediately schedule elections for a new federal parliament.

> Seeking to eliminate the political obstacle that is preventing the people from deciding their own fate;
>
> in view of the fact that the work of the Supreme Soviet and the Congress of Russian Federation People's Deputies does not meet parliamentary standards;
>
> considering that the security of Russia and its peoples is a higher value than formal conformity to contradictory norms created by the legislative branch of government;
>
> in order to:
>
> preserve the unity and integrity of the Russian Federation;
>
> extricate the country from economic and political crisis;
>
> ensure the security of the Russian Federation as a state and as a society;
>
> restore the authority of state power;

on the basis of Arts. 1, 2, 5 and 121.5 of the Russian Federation Constitution and the results of the referendum of April 25, 1993,

I decree that:

1. The exercise of legislative, administrative and oversight functions by the Congress of Russian Federation People's Deputies and the Russian Federation Supreme Soviet is to stop. Until a new bicameral Russian Federation parliament—the Russian Federation Federal Assembly—begins work and assumes the appropriate powers, the country is to be guided by decrees of the President and resolutions of the Russian Federation government.

The Russian Federation Constitution and the legislation of the Russian Federation and of members of the Russian Federation are to remain in force, insofar as they are not at variance with this decree.

The rights and liberties of Russian Federation citizens as established by the Constitution and laws are to be guaranteed.

2. The Constitutional Commission and the Constitutional Conference are to present, by Dec. 12, 1993, a single agreed-upon draft Russian Federation Constitution in accordance with the recommendations of the Constitutional Commission's working group.

3. Pending the adoption of a Russian Federation Constitution and a Law on Elections to the Russian Federation Federal Assembly and the holding of new elections on the basis of this law, the following interim actions are to be taken:

> • the statute "On Federal Bodies of Power During the Transitional Period," prepared on the basis of the draft Russian Federation Constitution approved by the Constitutional Conference on July 12, 1993, is to be put into effect;

> • the Council of the Federation is to be invested with the functions of a chamber of the Russian Federation Federal Assembly, with all the powers specified in the statute "On Federal Bodies of Power During the Transitional Period."

The exercise of the indicated powers by the Council of the Federation is to begin after elections to the State Duma are held.

4. The statute "On Elections of Deputies to the State Duma," worked out by Russian Federation People's Deputies and the Constitutional Conference, is to be put into effect.

In accordance with the indicated statute, elections to the State Duma of the Russian Federation Federal Assembly are to be held.

The Federal Assembly is to consider the question of an election for President of the Russian Federation.

5. Elections for the State Duma of the Russian Federation Federal Assembly are to be scheduled for Dec. 11–12, 1993.

6. A Central Electoral Commission for Elections to the State Duma of the Russian Federation Federal Assembly is to be formed and is to be instructed, in conjunction with lower-level electoral commissions, within the bounds of their jurisdiction, to organize the elections and to ensure the voting rights of citizens of the Russian

Federation during the elections to the State Duma of the Russian Federation Federal Assembly.

All state agencies and officials are to provide necessary assistance to the electoral commissions for elections to the State Duma of the Russian Federation Federal Assembly and are to put a stop to all acts or actions intended to disrupt the elections to the State Duma, whatever their source.

Persons who obstruct the exercise of the right to vote by citizens of the Russian Federation will have criminal proceedings instituted against them in accordance with Art. 132 of the Russian SFSR Criminal Code.

7. Expenditures associated with holding the elections to the State Duma of the Russian Federation Federal Assembly are to be defrayed by monies in the Russian Federation's Republic Budget.

8. The powers of the representative bodies of power of the members of the Russian Federation are to be preserved.

9 No meetings of the Congress of Russian Federation People's Deputies are to be convened.

The powers of Russian Federation People's Deputies are hereby terminated. The rights of citizens who have served as Russian Federation People's Deputies, including their labor rights, are guaranteed.

The powers of People's Deputies who serve as Russian Federation delegates at plenary meetings of the Interparliamentary Assembly of Member-States of the Commonwealth of Independent States and as representatives on the Assembly's commissions are to be confirmed by the President of the Russian Federation.

Russian Federation People's Deputies who are members of the Constitutional Commission of the Congress of Russian Federation People's Deputies may continue to work for the commission as experts.

Employees of the Russian Federation Supreme Soviet's apparatus and service personnel are to be placed on paid leave until Dec. 13, 1993.

10. The Russian Federation Constitutional Court is to be instructed to convene no meetings pending the beginning of work by the Russian Federation Federal Assembly.

11. The Russian Federation Council of Ministers (government) is to exercise all the powers specified by the Russian Federation Constitution, taking into account the changes and additions made by this decree, as well as by legislation.

The Russian Federation Council of Ministers (government) is to ensure the uninterrupted and coordinated activity of bodies of state administration.

The Russian Federation Council of Ministers (government) is to take under its jurisdiction all organizations and institutions subordinate to the Russian Federation Supreme Soviet and is to conduct their necessary reorganization, the intention being to rule out the duplication of similar governmental structures. Necessary measures are to be taken to find employment for laid-off employees. The Council of Ministers is to exercise legal succession with respect to the powers of the Russian Federation Supreme Soviet as a founder in all spheres in which founder status is specified by existing legislation.

12. The Central Bank of the Russian Federation, pending the beginning of work by the Russian Federation Federal Assembly, is to be guided by decrees of the

President of the Russian Federation and resolutions of the Russian Federation government and is to be accountable to the Russian Federation government.

13. The Russian Federation Prosecutor General is to be appointed by the President of the Russian Federation and is to be accountable to him, pending the beginning of work by the newly elected Russian Federation Federal Assembly.

Agencies of the Russian Federation Prosecutor's Office are to be guided in their activity by the Russian Federation Constitution, as well as by existing legislation, taking into account the changes and additions made by this decree.

14. The Russian Federation Ministry of Internal Affairs, the Russian Federation Ministry of Security and the Russian Federation Ministry of Defense are to take all necessary measures to ensure security in the Russian Federation as a society and as a state, making daily reports on these measures to the President of the Russian Federation.

15. The Russian Federation Ministry of Foreign Affairs is to inform other states and the UN Secretary-General that the holding of elections to the State Duma of the Russian Federation Federal Assembly is dictated by a desire to preserve democratic transformations and economic reforms. This decision is fully in keeping with the principles of the Russian Federation's constitutional system, above all the principles of people's rule, the separation of powers and federalism, and is grounded in the will of the Russian Federation's people as expressed in the referendum of April 25, 1993.

16. The decree "On Stage-by-Stage Constitutional Reform in the Russian Federation" is to be submitted to the Russian Federation Federal Assembly for consideration.

17. This decree is to go into effect the moment it is signed.

I hope that everyone to whom the fate of Russia and the interests of its citizens' prosperity and well-being are dear will understand the need to hold elections to the State Duma of the Federal Assembly in order to extricate the country from its protracted political crisis in a peaceful and legitimate way.

I ask the citizens of Russia to support their President at this crucial moment for the fate of the country.

B. Yeltsin,
President of the Russian Federation.

The Kremlin, Moscow,
Sept. 21, 1993, 8 p.m.
No. 1400.

KHASBULATOV'S REPLY

The President Is Trampling on the Constitution: In the Hour of Trial, Rise to the Defense of Democracy

Speech by Ruslan Khasbulatov, Chairman of the Russian Federation Supreme Soviet. Esteemed fellow citizens! I am speaking to you at a very grave time for our fatherland. You have just heard the televised speech by Boris Nikolayevich Yeltsin, President of the Russian Federation. Ten minutes ago, I received a decree from the President that contains the text he read on television.

In short, what this means is that the numerous threats to overthrow the constitutional system have been carried out in this decree. In accordance with the President's decree, the activity of the Congress of People's Deputies as the supreme body of power in the Russian state has been terminated and eliminated. . . . The activity of the Supreme Soviet has been terminated, and, in accordance with the decree, all power is to be transferred to the hands of the President. This is a coup d'état. A coup that, as I have already said, has been attempted many times, in particular on March 20. . . .

I want to appeal to the Soviets at all levels and to [local] administrations: Convene sessions immediately, assess what is happening, and support the Supreme Soviet in the struggle against the putschists. The President's actions are unconstitutional. Consequently, they are invalid, illegal and unlawful.

I appeal to servicemen and personnel of internal affairs agencies, the police and security agencies, to everyone who has anything to do with the special services: Do not carry out orders based on the President's illegal decree. You know that, in accordance with the laws of the Russian Federation, illegal orders are not to be carried out, and those who do carry them out are not exempt from liability.

The Supreme Soviet guarantees safety for individuals who, after receiving illegal orders, do not carry them out.

As far as the Supreme Soviet is concerned, we are organizing a defense. We have received information that armed detachments are now being moved into Moscow, evidently some sort of units, probably special units of the Ministry of Internal Affairs' troops, possibly in order to intern, right here, the leadership of the Supreme Soviet, the Constitutional Court, the Prosecutor General's Office and the opposition parties, and trade union leaders. In general, all those who have criticized the President's policy in one way or another.

We urge all our fellow citizens to rise to the defense of democracy, for you are now in danger. . . . In this hour of trials that have befallen us, I . . . insistently appeal to you to rise to the defense of the people's elected representatives.

I appeal to the Russian Federation Deputies: Come to Moscow immediately. We will hold an extraordinary Congress.

Rossiiskiie vesti, September 22, 1993, p. 1; *Rossiiskaia gazeta,* September 23, 1993, pp. 1–2; translated in *Current Digest of the Soviet Press,* XLV, 38 (October 20, 1993), pp. 1–5.

═══ Andranik Migranian, "Russia and the Near Abroad" ═══

Careers of bold and clever people were sometimes made quickly in the heady days of glasnost', and one of the more spectacular was that of a young political scientist, Andranik Migranian, educated in Erevan, Armenia, and only recently arrived in Moscow. In a series of provocative articles, Migranian staked out a hard-line political realism, warning Gorbachev and other highly placed officials of the disastrous course they were following in weakening central authority. In the Yeltsin years, he became both a member of the president's circle of advisors and a harsh critic of the policies of Foreign Minister Andrei Kozyrev. In this essay, he surveys the array of problems Russia confronts in the Near Abroad.

. . . [O]ver the course of many decades, Russia had no experience or traditions in establishing interstate relations with the former Union republics, and as a result Moscow has wound up without personnel, traditions or notions about Russia's interests in those regions. However, subjective factors played a rather important role in the amorphousness and vagueness of Russian foreign policy with respect to the near abroad. . . . Neither the Union leadership during the years of perestroika nor the [post-Soviet] Russian Ministry of Foreign Affairs succeeded in formulating, even in its general features, a positive foreign policy taking into account the national and state interests of the USSR or Russia. The attempts that Gorbachev and Shevardnadze made to revise the USSR's old foreign policy, attempts that undoubtedly had important positive significance in terms of their stated goals, during implementation became unilateral concessions that ended in the USSR's disorderly flight from all parts of the world that were critically important for it, areas in which the USSR had had great influence, without the West making proper compensation. As a result, foreign policy, which was supposed to be an important factor creating stability in the political system and facilitating the successful implementation of domestic political reforms, became (in the framework of the policy of perestroika) an additional factor making for destabilization of the domestic political situation in the Soviet Union, gave rise to serious tension in the Army and in society as a whole, and resulted in colossal, irreplaceable losses in the military-political sphere.

The unilateral concessions by Soviet foreign policy were made in hope of receiving economic and political support for Gorbachev's reforms, but these expectations ended in complete failure. Proposals to neutralize the German Democratic Republic and to "Finlandize" Eastern Europe, in particular the proposals I made in 1989, were not heeded by the architects of the policy of perestroika, and as a result the unification of Germany and its departure from Eastern Europe brought only prepaid symbolic sums of assistance, idle talk, noisy applause and friendly pats on the shoulder for Gorbachev and Shevardnadze from the leaders of the US and other Western countries.

Thus, as a result of the inept policy of the Soviet leadership, the one-dimensional superpower—as the USSR was called, with reference to its military aspect, which is what made that state a superpower—was unable to exchange its military might and geopolitical presence in Germany and Eastern Europe for tangible economic and political advantages in implementing reforms in the economic and political system within the country. . . .

The Russian Ministry of Foreign Affairs inherited this foreign policy from the Union ministry, and if one takes into account that Minister Kozyrev and other executives of Russia's Foreign Ministry were "even greater Catholics than the Pope himself" in affirming the existence of unity between Russia's goals and values and those of the US and the Western community as a whole, there is nothing surprising about the fact that the evolution of the foreign policy of the USSR, and then of Russia after the breakup of the Soviet Union, reached its logical conclusion. In effect, Kozyrev and the other Russian leaders replaced one ideological postulate, a Marxist-Leninist one in accordance with which it was necessary to bring about the expansion of the Soviet model everywhere in the world and counteract the policy of the US and the West in all respects, with another ideological postulate, one in accordance with which, following the elimination of the CPSU and the Marxist-Leninist ideology, a complete unity of goals and values exists between the US and the West and Russia. According to this logic, Russia automatically became part of the civilized world community, and therefore there is no longer any need to formulate Russia's specific interests as a nation-state with respect to the far abroad [countries that were never parts of the USSR or under its influence—Trans.]. As far as the near abroad was concerned, it was assumed that the former Union republics and the former socialist countries of Eastern Europe had immediately become completely isolated and independent, that Russia had no specific interests involving them, and that with respect to all problems occurring or reemerging in those regions Russia would act with the US and other Western countries, sharing joint responsibility with them for political and economic stability in those regions.

Among the subjective factors, one should also note the serious miscalculation made by the Russian leadership, which hoped that, following the Belovezhskaya agreements on dissolving the USSR, it would be possible to preserve a single military-political and economic space within the framework of the newly created Commonwealth of Independent States. The Russian leadership also proved unprepared for the fact that a number of republics did not join the CIS at all, while others, especially Ukraine, began to accelerate the organization of their own armies and the process of destroying the single military-political and economic space. . . .

As a result of miscalculations in assessing the role and place of Russia and the deep-seated nature of relations between Russia and the countries of the near abroad, officials of the Russian Foreign Ministry and other political leaders in the country drew the strategically erroneous conclusion that Russia should turn inward, within the borders of the Russian Federation, get out of all the former USSR republics, not interfere in interethnic and regional conflicts in the former Union and not facilitate the internationalization of the process of resolving these conflicts, thereby openly and publicly renouncing any special rights and interests in the post-Soviet space outside the Russian Federation. . . . A significant portion of the political establishment and a good many analysts—certainly not only those who, as Kozyrev put it, represented the "war party," and still represent it—began to realize more and more clearly that a special role in the post-Soviet space belonged to Russia. Russia's deep involvement in military conflicts in the Dnestr region, Abkhazia and Ossetia made obvious the assumption of those analysts that, first of all, Russia would not be able to "sit out" events occurring outside the borders of the Russian Federation without intervening in conflicts along the perimeter of those borders; second, that the international community, burdened with a multitude of problems in the former Yugoslavia, Africa and other parts of the globe, had no burning desire to take an active part in resolving those conflicts on the territory of the former USSR, and that even if it had such a burning desire, it was hardly likely that it would have been able to do anything to resolve those crises without the active participation of Russia itself; and third, that the conflicts along Russia's perimeter, by directly or indirectly drawing that country into them, had begun to exert a serious influence on the domestic political process and on the struggle among various political forces in Russia itself.

The conflicts in the Dnestr region, where ethnic Russians were drawn into military operations for the first time, and then in South Ossetia and Abkhazia, where Russia was drawn directly into military operations, since the related peoples of the North Caucasus living within the Russian Federation had gone to the support of their brothers with weapons in hand, shattered the once uniform notion of Russia's foreign policy in the near abroad. Several centers involved in the process of shaping foreign policy in the near abroad were formed. One might note at least three of these centers that existed up to 1992. They were, first of all, the Foreign Ministry, which tried to keep within the framework of the directives formulated by the Minister with respect to the former [Soviet] republics, something that drew harsh criticism both of the Foreign Ministry and of the Minister himself from many representatives of political and academic circles. For a long time, a major independent factor in the formulation of Russia's foreign policy was Vice-President Rutskoi, who, largely through his support of the actions of the 14th Army in the Dnestr region and a hard line toward the Moldovan leadership, facilitated the stabilization of the situation in the Dnestr region. His numerous statements against the leadership of Ukraine (on the question of Crimea) and against the leadership of Georgia (because of the latter's behavior toward Russian troops) worked to increase the popularity of Rutskoi himself, especially if one considers that this was accompanied by criticism of the Russian Federation Foreign Ministry and was thickly larded with patriotic rhetoric. The third center that was trying to form or at least influence Russia's foreign policy, especially in the near abroad, was the Supreme Soviet. Considering the political views of the overwhelming majority of the corps of Deputies, one should not be surprised that the Supreme Soviet became an irreconcilable opponent of the Yeltsin-Kozyrev policy, missing no opportunity that presented itself to accuse Kozyrev of betraying Russia's national interests and Yeltsin of breaking up the unified Russian state and to say that this had led to millions of Russians' becoming foreigners in what used to be their homeland. Taking into account the sentiments of the corps of Deputies, Supreme Soviet Chairman Ruslan Khasbulatov was the first high-ranking politician, together with opposition Deputies, to begin demanding more resolute actions from the government and the President in conflict zones into which Russia had been directly or indirectly drawn. . . .

In a number of articles in *Rossiiskaya gazeta*, I formulated for the first time the central idea that subsequently became the determining factor in understanding Russia's role and place in the post-Soviet space for all of Russia's leading politicians, from the President to Minister of Foreign Affairs Kozyrev. It comes down to the thesis that the entire geopolitical space of the former Soviet Union is a sphere of Russia's vital interests. So that no one would have any doubts as to what I meant by vital interests, I drew a parallel with the Monroe Doctrine. In a certain sense, I attempted to formulate a Russian Monroe Doctrine that could be applied to the situation that had taken shape following the breakup of the Soviet Union. At first, this concept was criticized in the democratic press and in circles close to the Foreign Ministry; however, it received significant support from a rather large number of politicians and specialists in international relations and—this was very important—the complete support of Yevgeny Ambartsumov, Chairman of the Russian parliament's Joint Committee on International Affairs. I think that by the summer of 1992, despite opposition from the Foreign Ministry, this understanding of Russia's role and place had gradually come to prevail in political and public circles. There was great significance in the fact that not only neo-Communists and national-patriots . . . but also people who had won a reputation in society as responsible and sober analysts and politicians came out in support of this understanding of Russia's place and role. . . .

Only a few months later, Kozyrev, competing with Rutskoi and Khasbulatov in patriotic rhetoric, began to talk about the geopolitical space of the former USSR as a zone of Russia's special interests. In March 1992, this thought was already being voiced by the Russian President himself. . . .

Nezavisimala gazeta, January 12, 18, 1994; translated in *Current Digest of the Post-Soviet Press*, XLVI, 6 (March 9, 1994), pp. 1–4.

Boris Yeltsin, "Appeal to the Citizens of Russia"
December 11, 1994

A small Muslim republic in the North Caucasus, Chechnya has a long history of resistance to Russian rule, both under the tsars and in the first decades of Soviet power. During World War II, Stalin ordered the exile of the Chechens, along with half a dozen other peoples, from their historic homeland to Central Asia. Thousands perished. In the late 1950s, Khrushchev permitted the Chechens to return to the Caucasus, and their state was restored as a joint Chechen-Ingush autonomous republic. With the fall of the Soviet Union, Chechen national- ists under Jokhar Dudaev declared independence and thwarted Moscow's efforts to control the region. After attempts to overthrow Dudaev failed, Yeltsin launched an invasion of the repub- lic in December 1994. In the bloody war that followed, tens of thousands were killed or wounded; hundreds of thousands of others were rendered homeless or became refugees; and the capital city, Groznyi, as well as other towns and villages, were destroyed. The war was un- popular in Russia, and an inconclusive armistice was concluded in May 1997. For several years, local criminals and warlords dominated Chechen society, and Russia's leaders considered the semi-independent region a serious threat. After a series of mysterious explosions in Moscow, which were attributed to Chechen terrorists, the Kremlin began a second war against Chechnya in 1999. Even more vicious than the first war, this brutal campaign was supported by the majority of Russians and helped to propel Yeltsin's chosen successor, Vladimir Putin, to the presidency.

Dear fellow citizens!

Today, Dec. 11, 1994, troop units of the Russian Federation Ministry of Internal Affairs and Ministry of Defense were sent into the Chechen Republic. The govern- ment's actions were prompted by the threat to the integrity of Russia and to the safety of its citizens both in Chechnya and elsewhere, and by the possibility of the destabi- lization of the political and economic situation.

Our goal is to find a political solution to the problems of a member of the Rus- sian Federation—the Chechen Republic—and to protect its citizens from armed ex- tremism. But at present the impending danger of a full-scale civil war in the Chechen Republic is preventing peace talks and the free expression of the Chechen people's will. . . .

The government has been instructed to act in accordance with the Constitution and laws of the Russian Federation, taking the existing situation into account. As Pres- ident, I will monitor the observance of the Constitution and the law. I order all offi- cials responsible for conducting measures to restore constitutional order in the Chechen Republic not to use violence against the civilian population but to take these people under their protection. . . .

I appeal to Russian citizens of Chechen nationality. I am sure that soon, under peaceful conditions, you will be able to decide the fate of your people. I am count- ing on your wisdom.

Fighting men of Russia! Know that, in performing your duty and protecting the integrity of our country and the tranquillity of its citizens, you are under the protection of the Russian state and its Constitution and laws. . . .

B. Yeltsin,
President of the Russian Federation.

The Kremlin, Moscow.
Dec. 11, 1994.

Rossiikie vesti, December 14, 1994; translated in *Current Digest of the Soviet Press,* XLVI, 50 (January 11, 1995), p. 2.

The Russian State Duma Nullifies the Breakup of the Soviet Union

Russia's successive parliaments were generally hostile to President Yeltsin, and a significant bloc of deputies represented the resurrected Communist Party of the Russian Federation. Its leader, Gennadii Ziuganov, born in 1944 in a Russian village, became general secretary of the CPRF at its founding congress in February 1993. He was the principal candidate running against Yeltsin for the presidency in 1996, receiving almost as many votes as Yeltsin in the first round, only to be trounced in the second (Yeltsin, 54 percent; Ziuganov 40 percent). Made up of conservative Communists angry at the collapse of the Soviet Union and the weakening of the "fatherland," the party combined orthodox Soviet-style Marxists with statist nationalists. Its ideology was far from anything resembling Leninism and spoke more often of the humiliated nation than of the working class. Party rhetoric was fiercely anti-Western, not only nationalistic but xenophobic at times, and directed against the new bourgeoisie in Russia. But at the same time, Ziuganov led his party into elections and abided by their results. He was no revolutionary and was careful not to engage in extra-legal acts. In March 1996, the lower house of the parliament, the Duma, passed a resolution, largely symbolic, that rescinded the decision of December 1991 to dissolve the USSR. Yeltsin laughed off the resolution as an empty gesture by people who are "not thinking about Russia," and the liberal leader Grigorii Yavlinskii chided the Communists who, he said, bore as much responsibility for the collapse of the USSR as Yeltsin.

BELIEVE IN YOUR PEOPLE!

Resolution of the State Duma on Deepening the Integration of the Peoples Who Were United in the USSR and Repealing the Russian SFSR Supreme Soviet's Resolution of December 12, 1991. With a view to opening up broad scope for the consistent and voluntary integration of the fraternal peoples who were united in the USSR, and guided by the will of the majority of the country's population as expressed in the nationwide referendum of March 17, 1991, the State Duma of the Russian Federation's Federal Assembly resolves:

1. To declare null and void the RSFSR Supreme Soviet's Dec. 12, 1991, resolution "On Denouncing the Treaty on the Formation of the USSR."

2. To establish that legislative and other legally binding acts stemming from the RSFSR Supreme Soviet's resolution of Dec. 12, 1991, are to be adjusted as the fraternal peoples move toward ever deeper integration and unity.

3. To recommend to the President of the Russian Federation that a system of measures be devised for the further deepening of integration among the Russian Federation, Belarus and the other former republics of the Soviet Union, including the holding of a Russia-wide referendum on the problem of the stage-by-stage strengthening of unity among the peoples who made up the USSR.

4. To propose that the government of the Russian Federation, within the framework of existing accords with the CIS countries, step up monitoring of the implementation of integrative measures in the fields of economics, scientific and technical progress, and social, cultural and defense cooperation among the states created on the territory of the USSR.

5. To instruct the deputation of the Russian Federation Federal Assembly in the Interparliamentary Assembly of the CIS countries to actively promote the deepening and development of ties among the fraternal peoples in the areas of cooperation in matters of state and law and cooperation among nationalities. . . .

FOR A UNION OF PEOPLES, NOT OF RULERS

The Resolution of the Russian Federation Federal Assembly's State Duma 'On the Legal Force for the Russian Federation/Russia of the Results of the March 17, 1991, USSR Referendum on the Question of Preserving the USSR.' Affirming the desire of the peoples of Russia for economic and political integration with the peoples of the states that have been created on the territory of the USSR, . . . the Russian Federation Federal Assembly's State Duma resolves:

1. To confirm that the results of the USSR referendum, held in the Russian SFSR on March 17, 1991, on the question of preserving the USSR have legal force for the Russian Federation/Russia.

2. To note that the RSFSR officials who prepared, signed and ratified the decision on terminating the USSR flagrantly violated the will of the peoples of Russia to preserve the USSR, as expressed in the USSR referendum of March 17, 1991, as well as the Declaration of State Sovereignty of the RSFSR, which proclaimed the desire of Russia's peoples to create a democratic state, based on the rule of law, within a renewed USSR.

3. To affirm that the Dec. 8, 1991, Agreement on the Creation of a Commonwealth of Independent States, which was signed by RSFSR President B. N. Yeltsin and RSFSR State Secretary G. E. Burbulis but was not confirmed by the RSFSR Congress of People's Deputies—the highest body of state power in the RSFSR—did not and does not have legal force insofar as it deals with the termination of the USSR's existence.

4. To proceed from the premise that the interstate and intergovernmental treaties and agreements on political, economic, defense and other questions that have been

concluded within the framework of the Agreement on the Creation of a Commonwealth of Independent States retain their force for the signatory states until these states make a free and voluntary decision to reestablish a single state or a decision to terminate the validity of the indicated treaties and agreements.

5. To propose that the Russian Federation government take the necessary measures to preserve a single economic, political and information space and to develop and strengthen integrative ties among the states that have been created on the territory of the USSR. . . .

7. That, within a month's time, the Council of the Russian Federation Federal Assembly's State Duma is to work out and present to the State Duma for consideration a set of measures to eliminate the consequences of the breakup of the USSR, first of all with respect to its former citizens who have not yet determined what state they belong to. . . .

STATEMENT BY THE PRESIDENT
OF THE RUSSIAN FEDERATION

The Kremlin, Moscow, March 16, 1996. On March 15, 1996, the Russian Federation Federal Assembly's State Duma adopted a resolution "On Deepening the Integration of the Peoples Who Were United in the USSR and Repealing the Dec. 12, 1991, Resolution of the Russian SFSR Supreme Soviet." The main point of this document is to cast doubt on the RSFSR Supreme Soviet's resolution "On Denouncing the Treaty on the Formation of the USSR." The fact that the resolution adopted by the Duma has no legal basis and is directly at variance with the Russian Federation Constitution is plain to see.

Whatever the motives on which the adoption of the resolution was based, its initiators would do well to think about the consequences that it could have for Russia and the Commonwealth of Independent States.

This State Duma resolution, like the resolution "On the Legal Force of the March 17, 1991, USSR Referendum on the Question of Preserving the Union of Soviet Socialist Republics," is in effect aimed at creating a political and legal impasse in Russia.

The agreement on creating the CIS (including the Protocol of Dec. 21, 1991) stated that the USSR no longer existed as a subject of international law or as a geopolitical reality. The resolutions adopted by the Duma are incapable of resurrecting the Soviet Union; they can only give rise to uncertainty with respect to the legal position of the Russian Federation.

Moreover, their adoption can be regarded as an attempt by the Duma to do away with our statehood. They cast doubt on the legitimacy of state bodies, including our present State Duma, and cast doubt on the possibility of holding a presidential election.

If one proceeds from these documents, the Russian state loses its rights as a successor state. There is also a long list of other possible consequences:

- the destruction of international and regional security mechanisms;
- the threat of the uncontrolled proliferation of nuclear weapons;
- an increase in international terrorism and regional conflicts.

Under cover of the guileful thesis of deepening integration among the peoples of the countries belonging to the Commonwealth of Independent States, the Duma resolutions are in fact conducive to precisely the opposite:

- they put obstacles in the way of real integration;
- they give new life to nationalist extremist forces in the CIS countries and the Baltic states;
- they drastically worsen the position of our compatriots in those countries.

Such actions can only be called a betrayal of Russia's interests.

For my part, I assure the citizens of Russia that my position remains unchanged. I resolutely support all proposals for deepening integration among the peoples and states that made up the USSR. But I reject politically explosive and legally unwarranted unilateral decisions.

Integration is a voluntary matter. It must be implemented with the greatest possible respect for one's partners, without pressure from any party, and without unnecessary clamor or declarations. Only then will a firm and lasting foundation for an association of free states be created.

Work to create a single economic, social, technological, scientific, educational, cultural and information space has been under way within the framework of the CIS for several years now.

I guarantee to Russian citizens, the peoples of the countries in the Commonwealth of Independent States and the world community that:

The Russian Federation retains its status and continues to abide by all the treaties it has concluded.

Integration within the framework of the Commonwealth will continue. Breakthrough decisions can be expected in this area before the end of March.

As the guarantor of the Constitution, I will not permit any attempts to undermine the foundations of the Russian state or to destabilize the situation in the country.

—[signed] B. Yeltsin.

Pravda, March 19, 1996, p. 1; March 20, 1996, p. 1; *Rossiiskie vesti,* March 19, 1996, p. 1; translated in *Current Digest of the Soviet Press,* XLVIII, 11 (April 10, 1996), pp. 3–5.

Principles for Determining the Foundations of Relations Between the Russian Federation and the Chechen Republic
August 31, 1996

After a year and a half of war, President Yeltsin vowed to end the unpopular conflict before the presidential election in June 1996. In April, the rebel leader, Dudaev, was killed by a rocket while talking on his cell phone, and a month later a cease-fire was signed. But the agreement did not hold; fighting broke out again, and the Chechens retook their capital. In August, Aleksandr Lebed, Yeltsin's security chief and a critic of his Chechen policy, worked out a new agreement. The Russians agreed to pull out of Chechnya, and a final resolution of the independence question was postponed for five years. The war resumed, however, in 1999, and the

Russians leveled Groznyi and drove the Chechen leaders into the high Caucasus. The war led to hundreds of thousands of refugees, atrocities against civilians, and international condemnation of the Russian policy. But nothing dampened Putin's determination to win in Chechnya, and after the September 11, 2001, terrorist attack against the World Trade Center in New York, he found a more accommodating attitude toward his own "anti-terrorist" campaign than he had enjoyed before.

1. An agreement on the basic principles of relations between the Russian Federation and the Chechen Republic, to be defined in accordance with generally recognized norms of international law, is to be reached by Dec. 31, 2001.

2. A Joint Commission consisting of representatives of bodies of state power of the Russian Federation and the Chechen Republic shall be formed no later than Oct. 1, 1996, and shall have the following tasks:

monitoring the implementation of the Russian Federation President's June 25, 1996, Decree No. 985, and preparing proposals for completing the withdrawal of troops;

preparing coordinated measures for combating crime, terrorism and manifestations of ethnic and religious enmity, and monitoring the implementation of those measures;

preparing proposals on the restoration of monetary, financial and budget relations;

preparing programs for restoring the Chechen Republic's socioeconomic complex and submitting them to the Russian Federation government;

monitoring coordinated interaction between bodies of state power and other relevant organizations in providing the population with food and medicines.

3. Legislation of the Chechen Republic shall be based on the observance of human and civil rights; the right of peoples to self-determination; the principles of equality among peoples; and the ensuring of civil peace, interethnic accord and the safety of citizens living on the territory of the Chechen Republic, regardless of their ethnicity, religion or other differences.

4. The Joint Commission shall terminate its work by mutual agreement.

Izvestiia, September 3, 1996, p. 1; translated in *Current Digest of the Soviet Press,* XLVIII, 35 (September 25, 1996), p. 4.

Boris Yeltsin, "Address to the Russian People"
December 31, 1999

Yeltsin suddenly and unexpectedly resigned on the eve of the new millennium. His successor immediately pardoned him for any improprieties he may have committed, and the ailing former president retired into obscurity. But his legacy was considerable. He had guided the Russian democratic movement through its moments of greatest danger, he had worked to end the entrenched power of the Communist nomenklatura, he had negotiated a new federal relationship between the peoples of the new Russia, he had launched a radical economic transforma-

tion, and he had overseen the peaceful transition from the Soviet empire to a commonwealth of independent states. But his failures were also considerable: the impoverishment of much of the Russian population, a steady erosion of state authority and power, the squandering of resources and human capital, the rise of crime and violence, the brutal wars in Chechnya, and, for many in Russia, the long-term discrediting of democracy. He left the historical stage as gracefully as he had boisterously entered it—with an apology to his weary people.

Dear citizens of Russia!

A magical date in our history is almost upon us. The year 2000 is about to begin. A new century, a new millennium.

We have all measured ourselves against this date. We figured out, first as children and then as adults, how old we would be in the year 2000, how old our mothers would be, how old our children would be. Once upon a time this extraordinary New Year's seemed very far away.

Now it is here.

Dear friends! My dear ones! Today I am wishing you a happy New Year for the last time. But that's not all. Today I am addressing you for the last time as president of Russia.

I have made a decision. I agonized over it for a long time. Today, on the last day of the outgoing century, I am leaving office.

I've heard many times that Yeltsin will hold onto power any way he can, that he'll never give it up to anyone. That's a lie.

The truth is different. I have always said that I would never deviate so much as an inch from the Constitution. That the Duma elections should take place when the Constitution says—and so they did. I also wanted the presidential election to take place on schedule, in June 2000. That was very important for Russia. We are setting an extremely important precedent for the civilized, voluntary transfer of power from one president of Russia to another, newly elected one.

Nevertheless, I have decided differently. I am leaving office. I'm leaving office ahead of schedule.

I realized I had to do this. Russia should enter the new millennium with new politicians, with new faces, with new, intelligent, strong, energetic people. Those of us who have been in power for many years should withdraw.

Seeing the hope and faith with which people voted for a new generation of politicians in the Duma elections, I realized I had accomplished my life's work. Russia will never go back to the past. From now on Russia will only move forward. And I shouldn't stand in the way of the natural course of history. Why should I hold onto power for another six months when the country has a strong man worthy of being president, and when practically every Russian citizen today has pinned his hopes for the future on that man?! Why should I stand in his way? Why should I wait another six months? No, that's not like me! It's not in my nature!

Today, on this extraordinarily important day for me, I want to say a few words of a more personal nature than usual.

I want to ask your forgiveness. Forgiveness for the fact that many of the dreams you and I shared haven't come true, and that what we thought would be easy turned out to be agonizingly difficult. I ask your forgiveness for having failed to live up to some of the hopes of those people who believed that with one surge forward, in a single bound, we could leap from the gray, stagnant, totalitarian past into a bright, rich, civilized future. I believed it myself. It seemed as if we could overcome everything with one surge forward.

It didn't happen. In some ways I was too naïve. Some of the problems facing us turned out to be too difficult. We pressed forward through mistakes and failures. During this difficult time, many people's lives were disrupted.

But I want you to know something. I've never said this, but today it's important for me to tell you. I felt the pain of each of you in my heart. I spent sleepless nights, suffering terribly, wondering what I could do to make people's lives a least a tiny bit, at least a little bit easier and better. Nothing mattered more to me.

I am leaving office. I did all I could. I'm resigning not because of my health, but because of a whole aggregate of problems. A new generation, a generation of people who will be able to do more and do it better, is replacing me.

As the Constitution stipulates, in resigning I have signed a decree appointing chairman of the government Vladimir Vladimirovich Putin acting President of Russia. For three months, as the Constitution stipulates, he will be head of state. And three months from now, also as the Russian Constitution stipulates, a presidential election will be held.

I have always believed in the astonishing wisdom of the people of Russia, so I have no doubt what choice you will make at the end of March 2000.

In parting, I want to say to each of you: Be happy. You deserve happiness. You deserve happiness and peace.

Happy New Year! Happy new century, my dear ones!

Rossiiskaia gazeta, January 5, 2000, Pp. 1–2; translated in *Current Digest of the Post-Soviet Press,* LII, 1 (Feb. 2, 2000), p. 1.

CHAPTER TEN

SUMMING UP

The premise of this collection of articles and documents is that there is no definitive history of the Soviet Union. Rather, there are and will be different narratives with different emphases and evaluations that will flow from the particular experiences, outlooks, and historical contexts of historians. But that does not mean that history is infinitely malleable or that a fair-minded interpretation is not constrained by evidence. The more we learn from archives and "neutral" analyses, the more we allow dispassionate judgment, the more powerful and convincing will be the narratives and interpretations.

This "summing up" is preliminary and provisional. The three essays were all written within seven years, in the same decade during which the Soviet system collapsed and the Soviet Union disintegrated. Martin Malia, a distinguished emeritus professor of Russian history at the University of California, Berkeley, chose to sign his article with the pseudonym "Z," and when his attack on Western Sovietology was published, it stimulated an impassioned debate. Perhaps the most telling critique came from Alexander Dallin, an emeritus political scientist and historian at Stanford University, who challenged the fatalism implied in Malia's analysis. Our concluding essay, by Stephen Holmes, a political philosopher at New York University, locates the mainspring of Russia's post-Soviet problems in the weakness of the state. His claim that freedom requires "a legitimate political authority that enables and sustains it" echoes through the whole history of Russia, the Soviet Union, and their successor states in the twentieth century.

TO THE STALIN MAUSOLEUM

"Z" [Martin Malia]

The most dangerous time for a bad government is when it starts to reform itself.

—ALEXIS DE TOCQUEVILLE, ANENT
TURGOT AND LOUIS XVI

533

I

The Soviet socialist "experiment" has been the great utopian adventure of our century. For more than seventy years, to millions it has meant hope, and to other millions, horror; but for all it has spelled fascination. Nor does age seem to wither its infinite allure.

Never has this fascination been greater than since Mikhail Gorbachev launched *perestroika* in the spring of 1985: a derivative painting in the Paris manner of 1905, a Beatles' vintage rock concert, or a *Moscow News* article revealing some dark episode from the Soviet past known to the rest of the planet for decades could send tremors of expectation throughout the West if it were datelined Moscow. So conservative-to-centrist Margaret Thatcher and Hans-Dietrich Genscher have vied with the liberal-to-radical mainstream of Anglo-American Sovietology in eulogizing Gorbachev's "modernity." Even though after seventy years, the road to the putative "radiant future" of mankind no longer leads through Moscow, the road to world peace still does. And who is against world peace?

But this is not the whole explanation: Moscow is still the focus of a now septuagenarian ideological fixation. On the Right there is the hope that communism may yet repent of its evil totalitarian ways and evolve into a market democracy of sorts (into the bargain putting down the Western Left). On the Left there is the wish that the "experiment" not turn out to be a total loss (if only so as not to comfort the Western Right) and yet acquire something approximating a human face. So on all sides alleged connoisseurs of the *res sovietica* are anxiously asked: Are you optimistic or pessimistic about the chances for perestroika? Can Gorbachev succeed? Will he survive? Should we help him?

These questions, however, presuppose answers with diverse ideological intonations. To what is no doubt a majority in Western opinion, Gorbachev's reforms mean that Stalinism and the Cold War are over and that democracy is at hand in the East, bringing with it the end of global conflict for all. For a smaller but vocal group, the Cold War is indeed over and the West has won, a victory that presages the global triumph of capitalism, the end of communism, indeed even the "end of history." A third group, once large but now a dwindling phalanx, holds that communism remains communism for all Gorbachev's glitter and that *glasnost* is simply a ploy to dupe the West into financing perestroika until Moscow recovers the strength to resume its inveterate expansionism.

Yet the two dominant Western perspectives on Gorbachev have one element in common: the implication that our troubles with the East are over, that we are home free, at the "end of the division of Europe" and on the eve of the Soviet Union's "reintegration into the international order," a prospect first advanced by Gorbachev but eventually taken up by a hesitant President Bush. So in an odd way the perestroika pietism of the Gorbophiles and the free-market triumphalism of the Gorbophobes converge in anticipation of a happy dénouement of a half-century of postwar polarization of the world.

And, indeed, in this avalanche year of 1989 we are surely coming to the end of a historical epoch. It is hardly so clear, however, that we are entering a simpler, serener age: decaying superpowers do not go quietly into the night. It is not even clear that we are asking the right questions at all about Gorbachev. Certainly Western Sovietology, so assiduously fostered over the past four decades, has done nothing to prepare us for the surprises of the past four years.

Nor is the predominant Western question about Gorbachev's chances for success the most pertinent one, or at least the first we should ask. The real question is: Why is it that seventy years after 1917—which was to have been the ultimate revolution, the revolution to end all further need of revolutions—Gorbachev proclaims *urbi et orbi* that Soviet socialism urgently requires a "new revolution," a "rebuilding" of its fundamental fabric? What is so drastically wrong as to require such drastic action? And what, after four and a half years of increasingly frenetic activity, has in fact been accomplished? . . .

If fundamental revolution is now really on the Soviet agenda, then our focus of inquiry ought to be the *longue durée* of deep structures and abiding institutions. And these, as Gorbachev constantly reminds us, were created "sixty years ago," a euphemism for Stalin's "Year of the Great Break," 1929. For this was the beginning of the forced collectivization of agriculture through "de-kulakization," together with "full steam ahead" in industry for a "First Five-Year Plan in four years," policies that created the Soviet system as it exists in its main outlines to the present day. In short, Gorbachev is calling into question the very basis of the Soviet order and the historical matrix of what until now was called "developed" or "real" socialism. Perestroika is thus not just a reform of a basically sound structure, but the manifestation of a systemic crisis of Sovietism per se.

II

It is precisely because during the past twenty-odd years mainline Western Sovietology has concentrated on the sources of Soviet "stability" as a "mature industrial society" with a potential for "pluralist development" that it has prepared us so poorly for the present crisis, not only in the Soviet Union but in communist systems everywhere. Instead of taking the Soviet leadership at its ideological word—that their task was to "build socialism"—Western Sovietology has by and large foisted on Soviet reality social science categories derived from Western realities, with the result that the extraordinary, indeed surreal, Soviet experience has been rendered banal to the point of triviality.

Much of this was done in the name of refuting the alleged simplifications of the post-World War II "totalitarian model," itself deemed to be the product of the ideological passions of the Cold War. Thus, beginning in the mid-1960s successive waves of revisionists have sought to replace the totalitarian model's emphasis on ideology and politics with an emphasis on society and economics, to move from "regime studies" to "social studies," and to displace "history from above" with "history from below." This reversal of the totalitarian model's priorities of explanation has yielded a Soviet Union where the political "superstructure" of the regime derives logically from its "social base" in the proletariat and a peasantry being transformed into urban workers, with a new intelligentsia emerging from both classes. This inversion of the actual roles of state and society obviously gives the Soviet world a normal, almost prosaically Western, character and a democratic cast as well.

At the cost of some simplification, it is possible to say that this social science approach (with a fair admixture of Marxism) has produced a consensus that the Soviet historical trajectory leads "from utopia to development." In this perspective the key to Soviet history is presented as "modernization" through "urbanization" and "universal education"—a process carried out in brutal and costly form, to be sure, especially under Stalin, but the end result of which was the same as in the West. Often this social science reductionism holds that the Stalinist excesses perpetrated during an essentially creative Soviet industrial transformation represented only a passing phase, an "aberration," which under Brezhnev gave way to "normalcy" and "institutional pluralism" expressed through such "interest groups" as the army, industrial managers, or the Academy of Sciences. Indeed, Stalinism itself has been viewed by the more thoroughgoing revisionists not as an aberration at all, but as an essentially democratic phenomenon, stemming from a "cultural revolution" from below, within the Party and the working class, and resulting in a massive "upward mobility" that produced "the Brezhnev generation." In this view the whole revolutionary process may be summed up as "terror, progress, and social mobility," with the modest overall cost in purge victims falling in the "low hundreds of thousands."

A corollary to this revisionist picture is that Gorbachev's "restructuring" will be the crowning of the edifice of Soviet modernity. Thus, all that is required to humanize the Soviet Union is a measure of "reform" in the ordinary sense of reorganization: that is, a "calibrated" decentralization and a gradual debureaucratization of administrative structures, or more specifically, a reduction of the role of the central plan and the *nomenklatura,* or those administrative and managerial posts reserved for appointment by Party committees.

Such, indeed, was the expectation behind Gorbachev's early policies, as in the new Party program (now forgotten) voted at the [Twenty-seventh] Party Congress in February 1986 and expressed in his book *Perestroika and New Thinking* in the fall of the next year. This was still the expectation two years later of the main line of American Sovietology; indeed, this Sovietology to a degree reflected Soviet thinking in the Moscow social science institutes of the Academy of Sciences. But the border nationalities crisis of 1988 and the union-wide economic crisis of 1989 have made these anticipations, though hardly four years old, already superannuated. As for the blatant fantasies—to use a charitable term—about democratic Stalinism, they are clearly destined for that same trashcan of history to which Trotsky once consigned the Provisional Government of 1917. . . .

For if the fact of glasnost demonstrates the Soviet capacity to return to human "normalcy," the revelations of glasnost prove incontrovertibly that for the past seven decades Russia has been anything but just another modernizing country. As we now know, both from Gorbachev's economists and from televised shots of empty shelves in Moscow stores, the Soviet Union, though clearly a failed utopia, is neither a developed nor a modern nation. It is rather something *sui generis,* a phenomenon qualitatively different from all other forms of despotism in this or previous centuries.

It is for this reason that the term *totalitarian,* coined by Mussolini with a positive connotation to designate his new order and first applied in a negative sense to Stalin's Russia by Trotsky, was taken up by Hannah Arendt to produce a general theory of perverse modernity. And she did so because the blander term *authoritarian,* serviceable, say, for a Salazar or a Chiang Kai-shek, simply would not do for the gruesome grandeur of Stalin, Hitler, or Mao. Contrary to current opinion, Jeane Kirkpatrick did not invent but simply continued this distinction, though she added the corollary that totalitarian regimes are far more permanent than authoritarian regimes, a proposition with which the struggling intellectuals of Eastern Europe thoroughly agree, since as yet no country, not even Poland or Hungary, has successfully completed its exit from communism.

The Sovietological revisionists of the West, however, find Kirkpatrick's distinction scandalous, in part because of the conflation it effects between communism and fascism (though the Soviet novelist Vasili Grossman does exactly this in his enormously popular *Fate and Life*) and in part because Stalin must be presented as an aberration from the Leninist main line of Sovietism, for if he is integral to the system, then the prospects for its democratic transformation are dim indeed. But this sanitization of the Soviet regime into mere authoritarianism, at least for the period after Stalin, is achieved only at the cost of a fundamental conceptual confusion, if not an outright caricature of the totalitarian concept. Totalitarianism does not mean that such regimes in fact exercise total control over the population; it means rather that such control is their aspiration. It does not mean they are omnipotent in performance, but instead that they are institutionally omnicompetent. It is not Soviet society that is totalitarian, but the Soviet state.

This conceptual confusion results from taking as the defining criterion of a regime the degree or quantity of repression, not its nature or quality. Thus, since Khrushchev shrank the dimensions of the Gulag and Brezhnev killed or imprisoned far fewer people than did Stalin, the Soviet regime is deemed to have evolved from totalitarianism to authoritarianism (or as some would put it, "post-totalitarianism"), say on the model of Greece under the colonels or of Pinochet's Chile. But this view neglects the central fact that the structures of the Party-state, with its central plan, its police, and its nomenklatura, have remained the same—as Gorbachev's more liberal supporters, such as Sakharov, have constantly complained. Consequently, the milder face of Sovietism after Stalin—and the quantitative change is quite real for those who live under it—simply offers us, in Adam Michnik's phrase, "totalitarianism with its teeth knocked out."

Paradoxically, just as the "T word" was being expunged from Western Sovietology around 1970, it became current in Eastern Europe: Hannah Arendt was translated in *samizdat,* and Soviet intellectuals now routinely refer to the whole system, including its Leninist phase, as totalitarian, and to the Brezhnev period as classical or stable Stalinism. Even more paradoxically, it is when communist totalitarianism began to unravel under Gorbachev that the inner logic of the system became most transparently clear to those who have to live under it. To resort, à la Marx, to a quotation from Hegel: in matters of historical understanding "the owl of Minerva takes flight only as the shades of night are falling." It is this twilight, Eastern view of the evolution of the Soviet experiment from 1917 to Gorbachev that will be adopted here, in an effort to present a historicized update of the original, and in truth too static, totalitarian interpretation.

III

It is impossible to understand anything about Gorbachev and perestroika without taking seriously the origins of the Soviet system in a utopia. The utopia, of course, was never realized, but this is not the point. For applied utopias do not simply fail and fade away; the effort to realize them leads rather, through a perverse cunning of reason, to the creation of a monstrous antireality, or an inverted world. So the great Soviet adventure turned out to be, in the words of an early Polish observer, a grim "mistake of Columbus." This unforeseen landfall led to the creation of a new politics, a new economics, and a new Soviet man, which are at the root of the present crisis of perestroika.

The utopia in which the Soviet system originated is integral revolutionary socialism. This is not to be confused with simple egalitarianism, although this is obviously involved under so protean a label as "socialism." Nor is it to be confused with mere social democracy (a term for which both Marx and Lenin had a distinct aversion), for this is clearly compatible with a mixed economy and constitutional government. Rather, integral revolutionary socialism in the Marxist tradition means full noncapitalism. As the *Manifesto* puts it, "The theory of the Communists may be summed up in the single phrase: Abolition of private property." From this it follows that the product of private property—profit—and the means for realizing this profit—the market—must also be abolished. For property, profit, and the market dehumanize man and fetishize the fruits of his labor by transforming both into reified commodities. It was to end this scandal that the most deprived and dehumanized class, the proletariat, received the world-historical mission of bringing about the socialist revolution, whereby mankind would at last be led out of "prehistory" into genuine human existence in the oneness and unity of a classless society. And all of this is supposed to come about through the inexorable logic of history, operating through the self-enriching alienation of the class struggle. This set of beliefs—the core tenets of marxism—has been characterized by Leszek Kołakowski as "the greatest fantasy of our century."

But the logic of history does not work this way (if indeed it exists at all); and although private property and the market can be abolished, their demise will not come about automatically. Therefore, the hand of history must be forced by the creation of a special instrument, "a party of a new type," with which Lenin declared he "would overturn all Russia." Thus, utopia can be achieved only by an act of political will exercised through revolutionary coercion, in short by quasimilitary means. Utopians of this ruthless temper, however, can get a chance at power only in extreme crisis, amid the collapse of all structures capable of resisting them. Such an exceptional state of affairs came about in Russia in 1917, when under the impact of modern war, the old order unraveled with stunning rapidity to the point where Lenin's Bolsheviks simply "found power lying in the streets and picked it up." True, they enjoyed a significant measure of worker support at the time and their ranks were largely filled with former workers. But this does not mean that what they themselves called, until well into the 1920s, the October overturn (*perevorot*) was any the less a minority coup d'état staged against a background of generalized, particularly peasant, anarchy, and not a "proletarian revolution" in any meaningful sense of that term.

The Bolsheviks then had to confront their utopia with reality in the form of economic collapse and civil war. Under the combined pressure of the military emergency and the logic of their ideology, between 1918 and 1920 they produced the world's first version of noncapitalism, "War Communism." Nor at the time was this viewed as an emergency expedient. For Lenin, socialism would emerge out of the fullness of capitalism; the "imperialist war" was the highest phase of capitalism; General Ludendorff's militarization of the German economy during the struggle was therefore the supreme form of capitalism and by the same token, the matrix of the new socialist order. So nationalizing the entire urban economy under the Supreme Economic Council (the ancestor of the present Soviet industrial ministries and of "Gosplan"), the Bolsheviks amplified Ludendorff's practices in Russia and abolished profit and the market. To this was added the "advanced" American method of Taylorism for the rational organization of work and an ambitious program for building power stations under the conviction that "socialism equals Soviet power plus electrification." At the same time, the Bolsheviks experimented with rural collectives, or *Sovkhozes,* and thereby adumbrated the extension of their statist model to the countryside and the entire population; and in the meantime they simply pillaged alleged "petty bourgeois kulaks" for grain under the policy of "class warfare" in the villages. In fact, during War Communism the Bolsheviks created the first rough draft of what later would be called a planned, or more accurately a command, economy.

Simultaneously, Trotsky hit upon another essential component of the new system, the political commissar. The vocation of the Party is political and ideological, not technical and professional in any of the activities necessary for the functioning of society. Since the Party was at war, the most important professional expertise at the time was military, expertise the Bolsheviks lacked, while most trained officers in the country were former members of the Imperial Army and hence unreliable. So the new people's commissar for war simply conscripted the officers he needed and flanked them with trustworthy Party monitors, such as Stalin, Kirov, Voroshilov, and Orjonikidze, all future leaders of the 1930s. In this way a dual system of administration was created in the army, but one that could easily be adapted to economic and other civilian tasks, where Party figures would supervise industrial managers, collective farm chairmen, educators, scientists, writers—indeed, everybody and everything. This is the earliest origin of the *apparat* and its nomenklatura right of appointment to all functional posts of importance in society. Dual administration thus adumbrates the end of "civil society," by which Central Europeans and Soviets mean social groups capable of self-organization independent of the state. This mode of control is the essence of the Party-state, a system wherein the functional, governmental, or "soviet," bureaucracy is monitored from behind the scenes by a parallel and unaccountable Party administration that has the real power of decision.

The period of War Communism produced a second monitoring apparatus as well, this time for "enemies" of the whole system—the Cheka, or political police. Conceived by Lenin as early as November 1917 to wage class war against those who were certain to resist the Bolsheviks' unilateral seizure of power, the Cheka was originally directed against "feudal" or "bourgeois" parties, but was soon turned against erring, "petty bourgeois" socialist parties as well as recalcitrant workers and peasants who supported them. But there was no structural reason in the system to prevent the Cheka's eventual use against enemies within Bolshevik ranks themselves. For as the Civil War raged on, it became increasingly apparent that the Party and its leadership represented (to use Kołakowski's language again) not the "empirical proletariat," but a "metaphysical proletariat" that had the world-historical mission of leading mankind to socialism. Thus, whenever workers or peasants rejected the Party's power, as in the Kronstadt revolt of 1921, they were automatically revealed as "petty bourgeois" and disposed of *manu militari.*

And so by 1921 all the essential institutions of Sovietism had either been created or sketched in: the Party-state with its monopoly of power, or "leading role," as it is now called; the dual administration of soviet and apparat, both backed by the Cheka; the central plan and the agricultural collective; and a propaganda monopoly in the service of the dictatorship of the proletariat, with its single "correct" ideology and the cult of technological Prometheanism. It is difficult to believe that a system of such internal coherence and logic should be the passing product of military emergency, although this is now the dominant view in Western Sovietology. In any event, it is this model that, in fact, was to become the main line of Soviet development, from Stalin to the eve of perestroika. And this, as the Soviets used to say in their earlier, more ideological days, is surely "no accident."

But War Communism would become the Soviet norm only after what turned out to be the temporary retreat to the mixed economy of the New Economic Policy (NEP) in the 1920s. For War Communism, though it permitted the Bolshevik victory over the Whites, also produced one of the worst social and economic collapses of the twentieth century. In the course of the Civil War, some 15 million to 19 million people perished from war, terror, famine, and epidemic—or more than in all of World War 1. By 1921 industrial production had virtually halted, money had disappeared, and organized exchange had given way to barter. To be sure, a part of this primitivization was due to six years of war; but it was due in even greater part to the ideological extravagance and incompetence of Bolshevik policy, which continued with fanatical grimness for months after the war had been won.

IV

The limited return to the market under the NEP was a success in reviving the country, but not in leading it to socialism. This contradictory circumstance has given rise to endless speculation and controversy about the true nature of the system in the past, and thus about the proper tasks of perestroika in the present. The central questions are these: Is the "hard" communism of War Communism and Stalin the norm or a deviation in Soviet history? Or is the "soft" communism of the NEP this norm and therefore the model for perestroika—a perspective in which Stalinism, together with its Brezhnevite prolongation, becomes the deviation from which perestroika is the hoped-for recovery? Finally, which of these two communisms, the hard or the soft, is the legitimate heir of Lenin and October? Or to put the whole debate in one classic question, Was Stalin necessary?

In strictly temporal terms there is no doubt about the answer to these questions: three years of War Communism, twenty-five of Stalin, and eighteen of Brezhnev clearly add up to the empirical norm of Soviet history, and it is the eight years of the NEP (together with bits and pieces of the Khrushchev period) that are the "aberration," or, if one prefers, the metaphysical norm of "real" Leninism; and this overwhelming preponderance of hard communism must have something to do with the logic, if not of history, then at least of the Soviet system. Yet these questions are not really about chronology; they are about essences, and through these about present attitudes and policies toward Soviet reformability.

The case for the NEP as essential Sovietism rests on the fact that Lenin inaugurated it and did so with the admission that War Communism had been an error, or at least a premature attempt at attaining socialism. In his dying months, moreover, he gave his blessings to "cooperatives" (a concept he did not flesh out) as the means for arriving at socialism. Nikolai Bukharin then developed these hints into something of a system in the mid-1920s and thereby became the true heir of Lenin. Stalin (attacked by name, moreover, in the founder's "Testament") thus rose to power only as an intriguer and a usurper.

In this view the true Leninist-Bukharinist course, which enjoyed majority support in the Party by mid-decade, drew from the horrors and errors of War Communism the lesson that the regime's first priority should be to preserve the "revolutionary alliance of workers and peasants" allegedly forged in October. To this end, the Party was to conciliate the 80 percent of the population that was peasant by orienting the "commanding heights" of state industry to meet rural consumer needs and thereby to accumulate through the market the capital for the industrial development necessary to achieve mature socialism. In this way the socialist sector, since by definition it would be the more efficient, would out-compete the private, peasant sector; the rural cooperatives would be gradually transformed into genuine collective farms; and the whole nation would thus "grow into socialism," in the sense of the full transcendence of capitalism.

There are numerous objections to this view over and above the puerile fetishization of Lenin involved and the bizarre notion that the supreme achievement of October Revolution was the discovery, in 1921, of the virtues of cooperatives and the market. The first major objection is that never during the NEP and Bukharin's brief ascendancy did the Party play the economic game according to market rules: it constantly resorted to "administrative" means to manipulate both supply and demand since it feared the peasants' power over the economy, and hence the state, through their purchasing power, or more simply their freedom to grant or withhold the supply of grain. The second major objection is that the empirical evidence about the resistance of the peasants to the forced requisition of grain during War Communism, and their refusal even to market it under the NEP, especially after 1927, whenever the price ratio was unfavorable, indicates their inveterate distrust of Bolshevik arbitrariness. Never under a Bolshevik monopoly of power would they have entered collective farms voluntarily. Given these circumstances, a collision between the Party and the peasants was at some point inevitable, and the NEP was inherently unstable. Ultimately, either the Party would have to give up on integral socialism and share economic, and eventually political, power with the peasants through the market—in short, opt for mere social democracy—or it would have to crush peasant independence, and along with it the market, and march toward full socialism by coercive, "administrative" methods. . . .

Even when, under Khrushchev, the Soviet Union became the world's "second largest economy," just behind the United States, indeed outstripping it in output of the sinews of modern industry—steel—this number two status was true only in quantitative, not qualitative, terms. Almost all Soviet products were imitative, archaic, crude, or outright defective. Almost nothing the Soviet Union produced, outside of military hardware, was competitive on the international market, and it could sell its products on the internal market only because it had a monopoly that excluded more efficient foreign competition. Even in its most successful decades, therefore, under Stalin and in the early years of Khrushchev, the Soviet Union was never a great industrial power, and still less a "modern" society. The belief that it was such a power is among the great illusions of the century, shared until recently not just by the editorialists of our major newspapers, but by economists of the prominence of John Kenneth Galbraith, and even Wassily Leontiev. In reality, however, the Soviet Union in its prime was never more than a great military-industrial complex and a Party-state superpower. . . .

IX

Against the background of such a history and the highly constraining structural logic underlying it, the task of reform can only be Herculean. But do the system's constraints permit the emergence of the people, and of the vision, necessary for such a staggering task? In this question lies the whole drama, and the dilemma, of the Gorbachev era.

Awareness that something was seriously amiss with Sovietism first came to the surface in 1983 under Andropov. As head of the KGB, he knew far better than his colleagues the true state of affairs; and he took the novel step of calling on intelligentsia specialists, especially economists and sociologists from the Academy of Sciences, to consult on possible remedies, an enterprise in which his protégé Gorbachev was involved. This endeavor produced the *Novosibirsk Report* by the sociologist Tatiana Zaslavskaia, who argued that the Soviet system of centralized planning had become obsolete, a fetter on production, and that Soviet society, far from being a harmonious unity, was riven by the conflicting interests of both the ruling and the ruled—an analysis that implied the necessity of radical restructuring for sheer survival. This document, leaked to the Western press in the once putatively fatal year of 1984, first alerted the world to the impending end of Soviet stability. . . .

When Gorbachev first launched perestroika in April 1985, it had the relatively limited purpose of producing a rapid acceleration, or *uskorenie*, of national economic performance; and his method was similar to Andropov's: reliance on administrative action from above in consultation with intelligentsia experts and operation within the existing structures of the Plan and its attendant ministries. For *perestroika* means, literally and simply, refashioning an existing edifice, or *stroika*, the root also of the Russian term for the "building" of socialism. . . .

An example of the first tack was his 1986 anti-alcohol campaign. This measure backfired, however, by increasing the budget deficit through loss of sizable vodka sales, which now went to the "black" economy. An example of the second tack was the "quality control" of industrial products by state inspectors, whose power to refuse substandard goods, and hence also to lower enterprise revenues, generated insecurity among both managers and workers. In addition, Gorbachev regrouped ministries and replaced cadres on a scale not seen since Stalin. As a result of this, by the fall of 1986 strong resistance emerged among the apparat to further changes, whether of policy or of personnel.

Gorbachev therefore embarked on a second policy, glasnost. In this he was advised by his chief theoretician, Alexander Yakovlev, who had become a connoisseur of modern, Western ways during a decade as ambassador to Canada, an experience that both sharpened his appreciation of Russia's backwardness and acquainted him with the contemporary television techniques required to stimulate innovation. In choosing this new course, Gorbachev was guided by two considerations. As a question of conviction, he recognized that a dynamic economy could not be built with a passive population, isolated from knowledge of the modern world, ignorant even of real conditions within the Soviet Union—a state of affairs that produced Chernobyl, for example. Glasnost was thus intended to energize the nation. Also, as a matter of political tactics, he now made an all-out wager on the "creative intelligentsia" to bring pressure for reform on the recalcitrant apparat.

To signal this change, and to give the intelligentsia assurance that they could speak up without fear, he made a dramatic telephone call to Sakharov in Gorki in December 1986 to summon him back from exile. During the next eighteen months the liberal intelligentsia, in the press and on television, began to criticize society's ills, and to fill in the "blank spots," in Gorbachev's expression, of the Soviet past, with a fervor born of the twenty years of frustration that had built up since the previous thaw under Khrushchev. They did this with all the more passion since it was only by owning up to the errors of the past that they could attack the problems it had created for the present.

In the course of this glasnost explosion, both Gorbachev and his supporters radicalized as they encountered resistance from "conservative" (or more accurately, old socialist) forces under Ligachev. A note of desperation crept into the debate, and on both sides. Ligachev and his allies asserted that the liberal intelligentsia's criticism was leading the country to ruin by undermining the institutions and values that had built socialism and won the Fatherland War. Gorbachev and his supporters answered that the situation was so far gone that there was "no alternative to perestroika": to continue the policies of stagnation would lead to the rapid obsolescence of the economy, loss of superpower status, and ultimately the death of the system. As Yakovlev, in early 1989, put it more bluntly than Gorbachev himself would have dared, "We probably have no more than two to three years to prove that Leninist socialism can work." Thus in 1987 and 1988, the initially self-confident campaign for perestroika of 1985 took on the air of an increasingly desperate gamble, an ever more urgent race against time; and by 1989 matters had acquired the aura of a crisis of survival, which recalled, though in different form, the disaster years of 1921, 1932, and 1941.

The flood of candor under glasnost did indeed produce the consequences of which the conservatives complained, and in a form more radical than during Khrushchev's thaw. For each new revelation about past crimes and disasters did less to stimulate the people to new effort than to desacralize the system in their eyes; it did so all the more thoroughly since the Myth was long since dead, especially among the young. Repressed awareness of the Lie poured forth in a flood progressing from the publication of Anatoli Rybakov's mild novel *Children of the Arbat* in 1986 to that of Solzhenitsyn's outright anti-Soviet *Gulag Archipelago* in 1989. In the process, not only were the long decades of Stalin and Brezhnev swept away, but the very foundations of Sovietism, the economic theories of Marx and the political practices of Lenin, were touched. By 1988 Marxism-Leninism was a shambles; and by 1989 it could be openly denounced by leading intellectuals, such as the historian Iuri Afanasiev, as a dead weight on the mind of the nation.

In the midst of the turmoil unleashed by glasnost, the system was threatened by still another danger: the nationalities crisis and the beginning of the breakup of the empire. The leadership had known from the start of perestroika that it faced an economic problem, but in its Russocentric naiveté was quite unaware it had an equally grave nationalities problem. So the mass strikes of February 1988 in Armenia over the issue of Nagorny-Karabakh came as a total surprise, a "moral Chernobyl," as one Soviet leader put it. But soon autonomist, even separatist, agitation spread to the Baltic states, then to Georgia and Azerbaijan, and by 1989 to the vital Ukraine.

These movements, moreover, everywhere assumed the form of "popular fronts," grouping all classes of the population against the Party apparat (or in the Baltic virtually taking the Party over), a pattern reminiscent of the "dual power" that existed between the original "soviets," or workers' councils, and the Provisional Government in 1917. The cause of this sudden explosion lay in the same process of desacralization that was undermining all Soviet institutions. The fiction that the Party-state was a federal "union" was perhaps the most egregious form of the Lie, for all the border "republics" had in fact been conquered by the Great Russian central region beginning

in 1920, with the Baltic states and the Western Ukraine added only as recently as
1939–1944, and then only after a deal with Hitler. When the freedom to criticize released these border populations from fear, the result was a national as well as an anti-
Party upsurge; for them *perestroika* came to signify "sovereignty," by which they really
meant independence.

With this danger added to the other strains produced by glasnost, the old-line socialists, or conservatives, redoubled their efforts to retain control of the apparat, where
the general secretary still lacked an unquestioned majority, from the Politburo down
to the base. Given the constraints of Party discipline, this resistance could express
itself in public only obliquely, but behind the scenes, what liberals called a bloodless
civil war in fact was raging. Its most open expressions were the firing of Boris
Yeltsin as Moscow Party chief in the fall of 1987 and the national-Communist, anti-
Gorbachev manifesto, known as the "Nina Andreeva Letter," published in much of the
press in the spring of 1988.

In response to these pressures, the general secretary moved to a third and still
more revolutionary policy: democratization. First bruited in early 1987, this meant
double or multiple candidacies in elections and fixed terms of office for all Party and
state, or Soviet, posts. This policy was first applied to the Party by convening a Special Party Conference (in effect, a mini-Congress) in June 1988 in an effort to gain at
last the majority necessary for a renewed attempt at economic reform. Yet this device,
like glasnost, overshot the mark assigned to it, while at the same time it fell short of
achieving its intended positive function. The conference turned out to lack the necessary majority of proreform delegates for a purge of apparat deadwood yet began the
politicization of the hitherto quiescent Russian lower classes, since the partially televised proceedings revealed the once monolithic and mysterious Party to be a fallible
and quarrelsome body of self-seeking interests.

Failing to revitalize the Party, Gorbachev then upped the ante of democratization
by using it the following year to reanimate the hierarchy of state administrative bodies, the soviets. Taking up the 1917 slogan "all power to the soviets," he sought to give
real political life to both halves of the system of dual administration, in which all
power, since Lenin, had belonged to the Party. Again his motives were mixed. There
was first his Leninism—by no means a mere ritual invocation—which he vaunted as
the "pragmatic" capacity to adapt policy rapidly to changing circumstance and the
constant willingness to risk a gamble. Then, too, democracy, like glasnost, was necessary to galvanize the population for perestroika. But above all, Gorbachev sought to
give himself a structure of power parallel to the regular apparat. He sought this in part
so that he could not be deposed by a Central Committee coup as Khrushchev had
been in 1964—a precedent on everyone's mind in the perestroika era—and in part to
give himself an independent instrument for putting through his stalled economic programs. And, as some Soviets noted, this effort to outflank the old guard by a parallel
power was reminiscent, *mutatis mutandis,* of the way Stalin had used the NKVD
against the mainline Party.

This second round of democratization overshot its intended mark far more
widely than the first. This became apparent during the elections in March 1989 to a
Congress of People's Deputies, whose function was to create a strong executive presidency for Gorbachev and to elect a Supreme Soviet, or national parliament, with
some measure of legislative power, unlike its rubber-stamp predecessor. An unintended result of these elections, however, was to produce a resounding defeat not just

for the apparat, as Gorbachev wished, but for the Party as an institution. For the first time in seventy years, the population had the possibility of saying no to official candidates, and did so, at least in the large cities, on a major scale. As a result, the "correlation of forces" within the country changed radically: the Party which had hitherto inspired fear in the people suddenly came to fear the population, and demoralization spread throughout its ranks.

This effect was compounded at the Congress meetings, televised live for two weeks during May and June. To be sure, Gorbachev got himself elected president and thus secured a buffer against a coup by the Party. He also obtained the selection of a new Supreme Soviet—in effect, a consultative assembly, rather than a genuine legislature—which he felt confident would do his bidding. But the authoritarian way he pushed these elections through the Congress caused his popularity, already low because of the economic and ethnic problems engendered by perestroika, to reach its nadir; he, too, was desacralized and made to appear as just a bigger apparatchik. Moreover, the liberal delegates, though a minority, dominated the proceedings with a barrage of exposés of all the ills with which the country is afflicted: the poverty, the abominable health service, the rising crime rate, the ecological disasters, the economic disintegration, the KGB's "secret empire," as one deputy dared call it, and the Party corruption. The net result of the Congress was, in the words of another deputy, "the demystification of power."

As a result, Gorbachev's initially demagogic slogan "all power to the people" began to acquire some real content. The Congress first of all produced an organized Left opposition to Gorbachev in the form of the Interregional Group, led by such figures as Sakharov, Yeltsin, Afanasiev, and the economist Popov, a loyal opposition to be sure, yet one that nonetheless insisted that real perestroika was still in the future. Even more boldly, this group broke the supreme taboo of communism and demanded an end to the leading role of the Party. Simultaneously, the Congress debates produced a politicalization of the Great Russian and Ukrainian populations almost as intense as that of the border nationalities. And since the Congress had come up with no concrete remedies for the ills its debates had exposed, by July the population began to take matters into its own hands. The country was swept with a wave of self-organization from below; popular fronts and embryonic trade union associations appeared in the cities of Russia and the Ukraine. Thus "civil society", as the opposition called these new formations, began to emerge for the first time since it had been suppressed in 1918; and in some areas this movement edged off into a form of "dual power," as some radicals asserted, a phenomenon of which the Kuzbas and Donbas miners' strikes in July 1989 were only the most visible and spectacular manifestations.

X

While all this was going on, what had been accomplished in the economic sphere to produce the hoped-for "acceleration" that had been perestroika's starting point? The short answer is: nothing much. Or more accurately still, those measures that were taken led to an outright deterioration of the situation.

Gorbachev's economic program has thus far consisted of two main components, both formulated in 1987. The first of these is the creation of small "cooperatives," in reality private ventures, in the service sector. But the impact of this cooperative sector has been derisory, since its services are priced far above the purchasing power of the 200-rouble-per-month average wage of the majority of the population. These enterprises have therefore become the focus of popular hostility to economic reform in general, since any form of marketization is perceived by "the people"—as the miners made clear during their strike—to benefit only "speculators" and the privileged—a reaction quite in conformity with the socialist egalitarianism the regime inculcated in the population for decades. Moreover, the cooperatives are harassed by the state bureaucracy, whose monopoly they threaten, and are often either taken over by, or made to pay protection money to, various Mafias from the "black" economy.

The second component of Gorbachev's economic reform is the Law on State Enterprises, providing for "self-management" and "self-financing." If actually applied, these provisions would significantly reduce the role of Gosplan and the central ministries by using self-interest to correct the predominance of administrative directives. This reform is thus an effort to return to the spirit, if not the precise institutions, of the NEP, and to its policy of *khozraschyot*, or businesslike management and accountability under a regime of state enterprise. In other words, it is a variant of the half-measures of soft communism, put forth periodically in Soviet history from Bukharin to Eugene Varga just after World War II to Kosygin, but never really implemented because they threaten the Party apparat's "leading role." And, indeed, this time too, the Law on State Enterprises has remained a dead letter ever since it took effect in January 1988, because the silent resistance of legions of apparatchiki has kept industry operating at 90 percent on "state orders"—that is, on the old Plan.

In still other domains, Gorbachev's economic perestroika has met with failure, but this time without his having really tried to produce a program. In agriculture Gorbachev has spoken repeatedly of long-term leases of land, indeed up to fifty years, for the peasantry. But this proposal has gone nowhere, in part because of the resistance of the huge kolkhoz bureaucracy, in part because the peasantry has seen so many different agrarian reforms imposed from above that it will not trust the regime to respect leases of any duration and hence will not take up the government's half-offer.

Thus, Gorbachev is in a far more difficult position than his predecessors in communist economic reform. He no longer has the option of Lenin in 1921 at the beginning of the NEP, or of Deng Xiaoping in 1979 of reviving agricultural and artisan production rapidly by granting the 80 percent of the population that is peasant a free market. The Russian peasantry, now disproportionately aged and only 35 percent of the population, is too decimated and demoralized by over sixty years of collectivization to respond to any NEP-type initiatives. In consequence, Gorbachev has been obliged to begin his perestroika with industry, where the transition to marketization is far more difficult than in agriculture. Here the very success of Stalin in urbanizing Russia has created a cast-iron block to progress. . . .

And perestroika faces other problems as well; the infrastructure and the capital stock created by decades of extensive development are now approaching exhaustion. In a nationally televised address in October 1989, Prime Minister Ryzhkov warned that the overburdened railway system (Russia still lives basically in the railroad age) was on the verge of collapse. The country's enormous metallurgical plant is outmoded and unprofitable. Housing and administrative buildings are in a state of disrepair often bordering on disintegration. The extraordinary number of industrial "accidents," from Chernobyl to the gas-line and train explosions of June 1989 are usually due to functional breakdown or criminal neglect. All this exhausted equipment must be restored or replaced, and much of the work force retrained and remotivated. . . .

Under such conditions of near breakdown, any transition to real prices, self-management, and self-financing are quite out of the question for the foreseeable future; and the old reflexes of the command-administrative system are sure to persist, if only to ensure a modicum of order. . . .

Overall, then, the balance sheet of more than four years of perestroika has been that the half-reforms introduced so far have unsettled the old economic structures without putting new ones in their place. And in this, perestroika resembles earlier failed halfway-house reforms in Central Europe: General Jaruzelski's reforms of self-management in 1982 and of self-financing in 1987 in Poland, and earlier still the failed, halfway New Economic Mechanism in Hungary. Yet, despite this accumulated evidence of failure, Gorbachev intends to stick to the unnatural hybrid of "market socialism," as his chief economic advisor, Leonid Abalkin, made clear in November 1989 in launching an updated plan of alleged "transition" away from statism.

The current impasse of perestroika, furthermore, resembles the Soviet NEP, but in reverse. The NEP saw the progressive stifling of the surviving prerevolutionary market economy by the nascent ambitions of Party-state power. Gorbachev's perestroika has witnessed the tenacious resistance of an ailing but still massive Party-state structure to a fledgling yet corrosive market. Whereas it proved easy to move brutally from a market to a command economy, it is turning out to be inordinately difficult to make the more delicate reverse transition. Between Gorbachev and a neo-NEP stands the mountainous mass of decaying Stalinist success, whereas between Lenin and the first NEP there stood only the failed wreckage of War Communism. So Gorbachev is left with the worst of two possible worlds: an old one that refuses to die and a new one without the strength to be born.

At the same time, this failure of economic perestroika coincides with the runaway success of glasnost and the progress of democratization and popular politicalization. The result is a new kind of "scissors crisis," to appropriate a metaphor used by Trotsky during the unstable NEP to describe the upward curve of industrial prices when charted against the downward curve of agricultural prices. Similarly, under the unstable neo-NEP of perestroika, the curve of glasnost and politicalization is running alarmingly high, and that of economic restructuring is sinking catastrophically low. So perestroika, like its predecessor, risks being destroyed by the widening gap of the scissors unless energetic emergency measures are taken soon. . . .

In the midst of all this, what of Gorbachev, on whose person the West concentrates its attention and hopes? To the outside world, he passes for a bold and decisive leader, a mover and a shaker of major stature, especially in international affairs. When seen from Moscow, however, after his first initiative in unleashing the perestroika deluge, he has come to look more like a reactive than an active figure, a man increasingly incapable of staking out strong policy positions on the two make-or-break domestic issues of his reign, the economy and the nationalities. Instead, he appears essentially as a political tactician, fully at home only in Party maneuvering, now pruning the Politburo of conservative foes such as the former KGB chief, Chebrikov, or the Ukrainian Party boss, Shcherbitsky, as in the fall of 1989, now tacking from left to right and back again in the debates of the new Supreme Soviet. Indeed, by giving way totally and immediately to the miners' demands in July 1989, he appeared downright weak. And in all things he acts as if his economic problems could be solved by political means. Yet, since the direct road to economic perestroika is closed to him by structural blockage, this easier political route of glasnost and democratization is the only one left open to him.

Nor does he seem to be able to make up his mind whether he is head of state or head of the opposition. As one Soviet commentator put it, he is trying to be both Luther and the pope at the same time. But in such a contradictory situation, for all his political prowess, he may yet turn out to be no more than the ultimate sorcerer's apprentice of Sovietism.

XI

As 1989 draws to a close, it is clear that it will enter history as the beginning of communism's terminal crisis, the year of the Second Great Break, but in the descending, not the ascending, phase of utopia in power; and this not just in Russia, but from the Baltic to the China Sea, and from Berlin to Beijing. It is also clear that perestroika and glasnost, welcome as they are in their intention, have in their application only aggravated the systemic crisis they were intended to alleviate. And they have done so because like all forms of soft communism, they go against the logic of the system they are trying to save. The internal contradiction of perestroika is that Gorbachev has been trying to promote soft communism through structures and a population programmed for hard communism. But the latter is the only variety of Sovietism that is the genuine article for the essence of all varieties of Sovietism is Party supremacy. Thus, the instrument of Gorbachev's reform—the Party—is at the same time the basic cause of Sovietism's troubles. To adapt a diagnosis of Alexander Herzen regarding earlier revolutionaries, the Party is not the doctor; it is the disease. . . .

XII

This grim impasse at the end of utopia in power is the logical outcome of the structures which that power had built. The whole impossible enterprise of Lenin and Stalin was sustainable only as long as the human and material resources on which the system fed retained the vitality to endure the burden of the regime, and as long as some modicum of material success undergirded the Party's monopolistic position. But when these conditions ceased to hold, beginning with Deng Xiaoping's marketization of 1979 and Solidarity's revolt of 1980, the Communist parties' will to power began to flag and their people's habit of fear began to fade. This soon made necessary, for the Soviet Party-state's survival, the recourse to the expedients of perestroika and glasnost. But these are only pale substitutes for the market and democracy, halfway measures designed to square the circle of making the vivifying forces of a resurrected civil society compatible with the Party's leading role.

But this circle cannot be squared. If marketization and privatization are the economic goals of reform in communist countries, then Party planning becomes superfluous, indeed downright parasitical. If multiple parties, elections, and the rule of law are the political goals of reform in communist countries, then the dual administration of the Party-state becomes supernumerary, indeed positively noxious.

The Party is not a party, in the normal sense of an association for contesting elections and alternating in government under the rule of law. The Party is, rather, a self-appointed society for the monopoly of power. It can tolerate normal parties only as temporary expedients, satellites, or fronts when the political weather is stormy. Likewise, the dual administrative body of the Party-state is not a normal state, but a special instrument created by the Party to act as a transmission belt of its policies to the population through the nomenklatura. Such a state cannot therefore be turned into a normal polity simply by legalizing other parties, since they will not have equal access with the Party to the monopolistic facilities of the state apparatus, from its police to its press. Nor is socialist planning an alternative way to organize the economy; it is the negation of the economy, its death as a separate sphere of human activity through its subordination to politics and ideological imperatives. It is this total amalgam, this whole surreal world, that is summed up by the sacrosanct tenet of the leading role.

This role is in its essence inimical to all the professed goals of reform now echoing throughout the Soviet Union and Central Europe, whether glasnost, democratization, or multiparty elections. All these reforms imply that there is a third way, a halfway house between what the ideological call socialism and capitalism, or what the inhabitants of the East think of as Sovietism and a "normal society." But there is no third way between Leninism and the market, between bolshevism and constitutional government. Marketization and democratization lead to the revival of civil society, and such a society requires the rule of law. But civil society under the rule of law is incompatible with the preservation of the lawless leading role.

At some point, therefore, the redline will be reached where reform crosses over into the liquidation of the leading role and all the structures it has created. And both Russia and Central Europe are now reaching that critical line. The false problem of how to restructure Leninism is now giving way to the real problem of how to dismantle the system, how to effect at last an exit from communism Perestroika is not a solution, but a transition to this exit. As Milovan Djilas foresaw early in perestroika: communism is not reforming itself, it is disintegrating. . . .

"Z" (Martin Malia), "To the Stalin Mausoleum." *Daedalus* (January 1990), pp. 295–344.

CAUSES OF THE COLLAPSE OF THE USSR

Alexander Dallin

In awe, amazement, and disbelief, the world witnessed the collapse of the Soviet Union, which swept away the Soviet system of government, the erstwhile superpower, the communist belief system, and the ruling party.

Why did the Soviet system disintegrate? In the first year since its collapse, several conflicting and controversial "theories" have been proposed in explanation. A sharp line may be drawn between explanations that focus on particular aspects of the Soviet system—operations (as indicated by the slowdown of the economy, for example), institutions or personalities—and those which find the cause of the collapse in the essence of the Soviet regime.

ESSENTIALIST ARGUMENTS

The "essentialists," whose moral absolutism was at the root of the famous identification of the Soviet Union, barely ten years ago, as the "evil empire," make three claims regarding the origins of Soviet collapse:

1. The original seizure of power by the Leninists in 1917 was illegitimate, and this illegitimacy and a peculiar "genetic code" remained attached to the ruling party and the regime. And much as a form of original sin, they could not be shed or overcome; thus, the system was in some sense doomed from the start.

2. Throughout its history, the Soviet system was essentially unchangeable; whatever the alterations in institutions, policies, and personalities, these were relatively trivial, as throughout it was and remained an "ideocracy" and a "partocracy."

3. The Soviet system was "intrinsically unreformable": efforts to tinker with it, including those of the Gorbachev era, were intended only to rescue and strengthen it, whereas the system needed to be demolished and a new system built from scratch on a different foundation.

The essentialists themselves break down into those who see the Soviet Union as the quintessence of the worst of Russian political culture and those others who see the source of evil—its totalitarianism—in ideology and organization, that is, in Marxism-Leninism and the Communist Party. In fact, the differences between these two camps are not at all insignificant.

We may take the recent writings of Martin Malia as the most explicit, most elegant, and most systematic exposition of the neo-totalitarian approach, which moreover does claim to provide an explanation for what he calls the "implosion" of the Soviet order. Precisely because this argument risks becoming an ideology of its own—and because it is based on assumptions that this observer considers thoroughly misguided—the following is an attempt to provide a different set of propositions to explain the Soviet collapse.

AGAINST PREDETERMINATION

Identifying the sources of historical events is a notoriously chancy and disputed business. We have no experimental method, nor proof that would stand up in a scientific court of law. Etiology—the search for causes—is not a science, nor is there any reliable technique for weighing the relative importance of different inputs. The archives will reveal no documents that will conveniently spell out the causes of the Soviet collapse. Moreover, the assessment of causes may well change with the distance in time from the events. Finally, as with an earthquake, at times subterranean processes are at work without our being able to track them in advance of their eruption.

Research will help, as will a commitment to making assumptions explicit. At the very least, it is often possible to tell who has gotten it wrong, without being sure who has gotten it right. But, ultimately, we have to rely on an individual analyst's scholarly intuition and empathy, and on his or her implicit philosophy of history. It is only fair to indicate that my own inclination is to distrust both conspiracy theories and flukes, and to be suspicious of all manner of determinism and inevitability, mysterious "essences" and broad a priori philosophical schemes. It is far better, I would maintain, to examine the empirical evidence without prejudging the case.

I find no grounds for arguing that the outcome—the disintegration of the Soviet system—was predetermined, let alone inscribed in the "genetic code" that went back to October 1917 and the origins of that system. How do we know what, if anything, was preordained? More concretely, the system withstood many tests far more severe than what it experienced in the 1980s (for example, in the first Five-Year Plan and in

World War II) and survived: its institutions and controls were scarcely brittle then, and popular attitudes—admittedly, difficult to probe in retrospect—scarcely bore out the neo-totalitarian argument that the regime never had any legitimacy in the eyes of the population.

Of course the seizure of power in 1917 was illegitimate. But it is impossible seriously to derive the events of 1991 from that fact. It is far more sensible and far more persuasive to argue that what we see in the Soviet collapse is the product of unintended results, both of socio-economic development and of earlier policy choices. According to the neo-totalitarian argument, the Soviet Union remained totalitarian after Stalin— not because the reality of Soviet life was so, but because of a continued commitment of the decision-makers to a totalitarian vision. By the same token, it is precisely the extent to which Soviet reality diverged from that vision that provides evidence of social autonomy—of what is properly referred to as unintended consequences.

What we are really puzzling over is how as thoroughly controlled, as tightly disciplined, as rigidly programmed, and as heavily indoctrinated a system as the Soviet managed to fall apart, unravel so easily and so completely, and in the process prompt in its citizenry an utter scorn for authority, and a disregard for laws and regulations.

The answers, I believe, have to go beyond social psychology, for they centrally involve political institutions and behavior. They involve both broad secular changes and particular individual choices. There is, I suggest, a cluster of interrelated developments that together, and in their interaction, formed the essential preconditions—necessary but not sufficient—for what occurred in the 1990s. In brief, they are: (1) the loosening of controls; (2) the spread of corruption; (3) the erosion of ideology; (4) the impact of social change on values and social pathologies; (5) the growing impact of the external environment on Soviet society and politics; and (6) the consequences of economic constraints. Against these background conditions, certain decisions of the Gorbachev regime, in turn, appear decisive as catalysts for collapse.

THE LOOSENING OF CONTROLS

One thing that held the Soviet Union together, exacted obedience and compliance, and provided the framework for its *sui generis* development was the sweeping Stalinist system of controls. Stalin died in 1953. In retrospect, what we see during the following 30 years is a gradual, unheralded loosening and then breakdown of these controls.

An essential part of the control structure and process was the terror that had reached unbelievable proportions and exacted such an incredible cost in the Stalin years. In the Khrushchev years it was the abandonment of mass political terror that provided the conditions for reducing the scope of controls. It ended the atomization, the silencing of that society—with an impact that did not become fully apparent until a generation later. As T. H. Rigby, an astute analyst of the Soviet scene, observed, in differentiating between active and symbolic, covert and overt elements that presaged the emergence of a civil society a generation later:

> The most interesting developments came in the covert active elements. I am not thinking so much of the shadow economy and clientelist networks, although these also thrived mightily, especially during the Brezhnev years. Of far greater importance for the future of the civil society was the profuse blossoming vastly

greater than what was apparent publicly. The key facilitating factor here was the curbing of the political police after Stalin's death. . . . People gradually found they could get away with a great deal in the way of unorthodox opinions and behaviour in private—from rock music to listening to western radio broadcasts, from abstract art to passing on forbidden books or samizdat materials. The re-housing program helped here, because tens of millions of city dwellers now acquired some real privacy as they moved from so-called communal apartments to little family flats. The Soviet population was acquiring "freedom of speech in one kitchen."

At the same time, the post-Stalin years unintentionally conveyed to the Soviet citizen a sense of fallibility and uncertainty in the country's leadership. This was suggested both by the tinkering with institutions—Khrushchev's *sovnarkhozy* and the "bifurcation" of the party, for instance—and by the continuous struggle over power and policy within the elite, which found policy expression in, among other things, the anti-Stalin campaign, and which culminated in the ouster of Khrushchev.

In the Brezhnev years a remarkable change in mood became apparent. Whether or not it accurately reflected reality, Soviet observers began to speak—rather more candidly than before—of stagnation and the leadership's failure to come to grips with urgent problems, and foreigners noted the change. Thus the economist Joseph Berliner was struck by the contrast between 1958 and 1967. By the later date,

there was in fact an air of gloom in the comments of economists I talked to. Perhaps my impression was heightened by the contrast in their tone with that during my earlier visit to the USSR [in 1958] . . . the USSR was riding the crest of a period of rapid economic growth. Consumption levels had risen rapidly following Stalin's death, and rates of investment were high. . . . There was a mood of exuberance and confidence in the vitality of the Soviet economic system. All this had changed by 1967. One found a candid admission that the economy was facing some nasty problems.

This is echoed from the perspective of the 1970s as well, when it had become even more apparent. Soon it went beyond the economy. In a very perceptive analysis, based on his own experience, John Bushnell wrote:

during the 1950s the Soviet middle class became increasingly optimistic about the performance of the Soviet system and about its own prospects for material betterment. . . . In the 1970s it has given way to pessimism. The rise and decline of middle-class optimism can be linked in part to political developments, but the crucial determinant has been the changing perception of Soviet economic performance.

Bushnell detected "mounting skepticism and cynicism about the values and performance of the regime in other areas as well."

And Dusko Doder recalled:

When I arrived in Moscow on temporary duty in the summer of 1978, it was apparent that incremental changes had taken place over the past decade. . . . In the narrow circle of my friends I found something that was new, or at least more pronounced than before—the quest for the comforts of middle-class life: a car, a place in the country, a tiled bathroom, a Japanese stereo, a chance to travel abroad—at least to Bulgaria.

By the early 1980s it was apparent to him that

> Brezhnev's stable regime had produced an amazing proliferation of corruption, a cynicism that undermined all enterprise. An air of stagnation, the timeless inertia of the bureaucracy, a crisis of spirit—all characterized a system that seemed to have accompanied the aging leaders into exhaustion and debility.

These comments touch on the principal arenas in which critical changes were indeed taking place. To what extent the Communist Party itself was affected was not yet apparent, and of course large bureaucratic organizations are capable of conducting routine operations regardless of the morale or enthusiasm, or lack thereof, of their personnel. But something else was becoming evident: what had been aptly described as a "mono-organizational" system was showing cracks. Party, state, and police officials were working the system for their own benefit.

Blair Ruble has suggested that (by analogy with Quebec) what was taking place was a sort of "quiet revolution"—with the informal emergence of a second economy, a second culture, even a second politics alongside, and in full recognition of the continuing limits imposed by the official ones. What added to the toleration of the new ambiguities was the fact that the second economy had its functional aspects insofar as performance was concerned. So, it has been argued, had the crystallization of rival patronage networks cultivated by various Soviet leaders. While the emergence of patron-client relations is a virtually ubiquitous development in all complex societies, John Willerton posits convincingly that, insofar as it promotes individual needs or interests, it undercuts the centrality or priority of government (or party) norms and goals.

THE SPREAD OF CORRUPTION

Far more serious is the massive spread of corruption, in all its many aspects, as a way of life. In a powerful account based on personal experience and replete with well-documented anecdotes, Konstantin Simis, in his *USSR: The Corrupt Society*, is compelled to conclude:

> The Soviet Union is infected from top to bottom with corruption—from the worker who gives the foreman a bottle of vodka to get the best job, to Politburo candidate Mzhavanadze who takes hundreds of thousands of rubles for protecting underground millionaires; from the street prostitute, who pays the policeman ten rubles so that he won't prevent her from soliciting clients, to the former member of the Politburo Ekaterina Furtseva, who built a luxurious suburban villa at the government's expense—each and everyone is afflicted with corruption.
>
> I was born in that country and lived there for almost sixty years. Year after year since childhood and throughout my whole conscious life I watched as corruption ate more deeply into society until it turned the Soviet regime in the sixties and seventies into a land of corrupt rulers, ruling over a corrupted people.

Especially in the late Brezhnev years, scandalous examples multiplied, from the appearance of feudal baronies in Uzbekistan or in the Urals, where high officials were able to operate with impunity, to the involvement of Brezhnev's daughter, Galina, and her lover with a crowd of circus crooks, the theft of jewels, and the entanglement of high secret-police officials.

No doubt, many instances of corruption remained unexposed. But what is known argues strongly that the corruption presupposed a loosening of controls, permitting a wanton violation of law to take place in the interstices. It also implied and fostered a new measure of cynicism about the "radiant heights" of communist morality.

Much of this "quiet revolution" became possible because the end of mass terror also meant an end to the individual's paralyzing fear, and because bureaucratic actors saw opportunities for self-aggrandizement with minimal risk or cost. But in Stalin's time, in addition to both outer constraints and often simply the lack of opportunity for autonomous corruption, there had been psychological inhibitions on many well-placed individuals, rooted in their belief in the system and in the cause in the name of which it was all being done. Later, with a change of generations and apparently a change of values, one began to observe an erosion of ideological commitments and a more single-minded pursuit, and at times also a more explicit articulation, of personal priorities.

Perhaps the most interesting conceptualization of this phenomenon is to be found in Ken Jowitt's writings. Stressing the disappearance of the party's overriding combat task—or transformation agenda—of earlier years, he remarked in the 1980s: "Today what impresses one about the Soviet Union is the party leadership's inability and/or unwillingness to devise a credible and authoritative social combat task capable of sustaining a distinction between the regime elite's particular status interests and the party's general competence and interest. . . ." What is remarkable, he finds, is the increasing tendency of individual members to be "oriented to personal, familial, and material concerns." In Jowitt's post-Weberian vocabulary, "the subordination of office charisma to the incumbents' particular interests" is then identified precisely as "corrupt routinization."

THE EROSION OF IDEOLOGY

Beginning at an earlier point but most explicit and tangible in the post-Stalin years, some of the millions of communists who made up the Soviet elite, and who were slated to become the regime's next generation of leaders, experienced an unadvertised but far-reaching crisis of identity and self-doubt.

One facet of this crisis was the subtle erosion of faith in the future and of the belief that the Bolsheviks alone had all the answers. This disillusionment, greatly intensified by Khrushchev's anti-Stalin campaign, was accompanied by an unheralded transformation in the dominant orientation: a shift from the pursuit of the millennium to compromising with reality. Seweryn Bialer was one of those who remarked on the withering of utopianism in the Brezhnev years. Wherever the faithful looked, the traditional prophecies had failed to come through: world revolution had not occurred, crime had not vanished, nationalism and religion had not disappeared with the passing of capitalism, as had been predicted. To be sure, the orthodox formulae continued to be reprinted *ad nauseam,* but inspiration had turned into ritual, and especially in the Brezhnev years there was no longer any serious effort made to reconcile conflicting articles of faith and observation.

Strikingly, a similar decline may be noted in the rulers' self-confidence concerning their right to rule. Unwittingly, memoirs such as those of Khrushchev's son Sergei and of others close to the leadership testify to this point. A number of former Soviet academics have privately related their difficulties in coming to terms with the Stalin phenomenon. How had it been possible in the first place, and how could Stalinism now be explained to the next generation? What were the implications for the Soviet experiment? Within the limits of the permissible, serious questions were raised from within the Marxist–Leninist tradition: for instance, on the nature of "contradictions" under socialism, and the phenomenon of bureaucracy.

A good example is also provided by General Dmitriy Volkogonov, who recently recalled that in the 1970s

> I was an orthodox Marxist, an officer who knew his duty. I was not part of some liberal current. All my changes came from within, off on my own. I had access to all kinds of literature. . . . I was a Stalinist. I contributed to the strengthening of the system that I am now trying to dismantle. But latently, I had my ideas. I began asking myself questions about Lenin, how, if he was such a genius, none of his predictions came true. The proletarian dictatorship never came to be, the principle of class struggle was discredited, communism was not built in fifteen years as he had promised. None of Lenin's major predictions ever came true! I confess it: I used my position, I began gathering information even though I didn't know yet what I would do with it.

Yet there can be no doubt about the importance of faith for the cohesion of a regime that had chosen to make its ideology so central and weighty a core of the system.

Indeed, it was during the Brezhnev years that we witnessed an unprecedented surge of dissident literature—not from people who had never shared the regime's values or goals but from prominent individuals well within the system's elite. In retrospect, the number of dissidents appears to have been greater than was commonly assumed at the time. In 1970, Andrey Sakharov, Roy Medvedev, and Valeriy Turchin addressed a letter to the Soviet leadership, arguing in favor of far-reaching democratization.

> Over the past decade menacing signs of disorder and stagnation have begun to show themselves in the economy of our country. . . . The population's real income in recent years has hardly grown at all; food supply and medical and consumer services are improving very slowly, and with unevenness between regions. The number of goods in short supply continues to grow. . . . What is the source of all this trouble? The source lies in the antidemocratic traditions and norms of public life established in the Stalin era, which have not been decisively eliminated to this day. Noneconomic coercion, limitations on the exchange of information, restrictions on intellectual freedom, and other examples of the antidemocratic distortion of socialism which took place under Stalin were accepted in our country as an overhead expense in the industrialization process.

Whether or not this had been justified in the first rush of industrialization, they wrote, there is no doubt that these had now become serious handicaps. There is a need, they argued, for free access to information and ideas. Otherwise the Soviet Union will become a second-rate power. They added:

> There are reasons to assume that the point of view expressed in the above theses is shared to one degree or another by a significant part of the Soviet intelli-

gentsia and the advanced section of the working class. This attitude is also reflected in the opinions of student and working youth, as well as in numerous private discussions within small groups of friends.

And in 1983 the famous "Novosibirsk memorandum" found its way abroad. In
it, Tat'yana Zaslavskaya, was telling the authorities:

> Over a number of decades, Soviet society's economic development had been
> characterized by high rates and great stability. . . . However, in the past 12–15
> years a tendency towards a noticeable decline in the rate of growth of the na-
> tional income began to make itself felt in the development of the economy of
> the USSR. . . . This does not provide for either the rate of growth in living
> standards that is required for the people, or for the intensive technical retooling
> of production. . . . In our opinion, [the cause of this is] the inability of this sys-
> tem to make provision for the full and sufficiently effective use of the labour po-
> tential and intellectual resources of society. . . .

SOCIAL CHANGE

The Soviet era witnessed a remarkable process of social change. In some measure it
had begun even before the 1917 revolutions: urbanization and higher educational at-
tainments are the universal by-product of economic development. To a significant degree, this was ideologically welcome to the Leninists as it promoted "proletarianiza-
tion" at the expense of the peasantry. Later, the "liquidation of the kulaks as a class"
was a conscious policy decision buttressed by ideological, economic, and security
considerations (whether spurious or not). Similarly, the massive employment of female labor, the wholesale resettlement and migration, as well as the expansion of labor
camps and forced settlements, were willed by the regime. And to some extent, the
new social stratification was the inevitable by-product of choices made on behalf of
rapid industrialization, bureaucratization, and centralization. But, whether willed or
not, these developments had unforeseen, unintended, and (from the regime's point of
view) often undesirable consequences.

The magnitude of the transformations is suggested by Soviet census figures: the
urban share of the population rose from some 18 percent in 1926 to about 65 percent in 1985. The number of "specialists"—the so-called intelligentsia—grew from
some 2 million before World War II to over 30 million in the 1980s, of whom more
than half had specialized training or higher education. The government, party, police,
and military bureaucracies grew at a comparable pace.

The resulting sociography of the Soviet Union still awaits thorough study. For instance, the attitudes and values of the working class—and regional variations—remain
to be better understood. What is clear, however, is that, in so far as they involved the
formation of a new intelligentsia (the equivalent of an urban middle class), and the
crystallization of new values, priorities, and aspirations within it, these transformations
had profound effects in generating a new sociopolitical force. So, inevitably, did the
appearance of a new, postwar generation of citizens, possessed of rising expectations,
and whose members had not shared in the hopes and sufferings of earlier years.

An additional factor in the 1970s and early 1980s was the (accurate) perception,
spreading in urban society, that the previously axiomatic opportunities for upward social mobility were no longer there. With the slowdown of economic growth, the

more or less stable size of administrative and military cadres, the end of massive purges (and the widespread retention of older officials in office), it was plausible that there should be fewer vacancies to be filled. The resulting effect on morale, especially among ambitious younger people, was obvious.

We find then an unmistakable spread of skepticism and widespread cynicism, particularly in the 1970s. Along with the "weakening belief in ideals," cited above, observers pointed to a career-mindedness and materialism, and a combination of consumerism and consumer pessimism. Moreover, it was pointed out, "because economic performance has been so central to sociopolitical stability, the consequences of this stagnation are potentially serious." There was also a lack of fit between educational opportunities and career needs; and high aspirations combined with a disdain for manual labor to create further tensions. High rates of labor turnover, low productivity, and low worker morale were additional indicators of growing problems.

The loss of optimism and the loss of purpose readily led to a change of attitude. This was reflected, for instance, in the jocular remark, "We pretend to be working, and they pretend to be paying us," as well as in the middle-class view of corruption reported by Bushnell: "It's a crime *not* to steal from them," which is revealing also for the use of "them" for the authorities. It easily spilled over into antisocial behavior. Alcoholism, in particular, became even more of a severe problem than before, with manifest consequences from industrial accidents to family life. Lying and cheating seemed to become pandemic in Soviet society.

One conclusion of particular interest, prompted by studies of Soviet refugees, émigrés, and "displaced persons," concerns variation of grievances by age groups. The so-called Harvard study of Soviet refugees in the 1950s, had concluded that young people were more thoroughly indoctrinated and less critical of the Soviet system than their elders. But in the early 1980s a corresponding study of Brezhnev-era émigrés found evidence that, on the contrary, young people (as well as those with more education) now tended to be more negative and more disenchanted with the performance of the system than their elders.

Students of Soviet society concluded, even prior to the accession of Gorbachev, that the potential for instability was greater then than at any time since World War II.

> Possibly the most dramatic change of recent years, and one with profound implications for the legitimacy and stability of the Soviet system, has been a shift in attitudes within the Soviet population during the two decades [i.e., 1960s and 70s]. Most visible within the middle class and intelligentsia but extending to the working class as well, it involves growing pessimism about the Soviet future, increasing disillusionment with official values, and an accompanying decline in civic morale.

As Geoffrey Hosking, a well-qualified observer, remarked: "There had been evidence for more than two decades that society and politics were out of phase with one another, that society was starting to outgrow the crude and rigid integument of the party-controlled political system."

These attitudes and values need not have been dangerously incongruent with the existing regime. In fact, in large part the new middle class as well as the workers were dependent on that regime for their own advancement and careers, a circumstance that importantly distinguishes Soviet "classes" from their counterparts in liberal-democratic societies. For better or for worse, Soviet citizens had been accustomed—

at whatever price to themselves—to distinguish between their private and their public personae and not to give voice to impolitic desires. Moreover, the existence of unorthodox attitudes does not, and need not, readily translate into political demands or action programs. Yet, it turned out, especially the new middle class—in and out of the Communist Party—provided a fertile breeding ground and, later, a social base, first for the "reformers" and then for the "democrats."

As Zbigniew Brzezinski concluded:

> the Stalinist system endured [in the Brezhnev years] not only because Brezhnev and his immediate comrades benefited from it and remained loyal to it. It survived because it had become a vast structure of overlapping privileges, controls, rewards, and vested interest. . . . Most important, Stalinism both endured and stagnated because it was a political system without real political life within it. That stagnation could not be forever ignored. Already by the later years of the Brezhnev era, a sense of malaise was developing within a portion of the upper Soviet elite. An awareness of decay, of ideological rot, of cultural sterility was setting in. It began not only to permeate the intellectual circles but also to infect some members of the political elite.

THE INTERNATIONAL ENVIRONMENT

There has been discussion in the West, more of it political than scholarly, about the extent to which the international environment, and more explicitly, American policy, can take credit for the collapse of the Soviet system. In regard to explicit policy by Western powers, it is impossible to find direct evidence of its destabilizing impact on Soviet society or polity, though at least three factors can be assumed to have played some role: (1) the unintended consequences of the inclusion of "Basket 3" (on human rights) in the Helsinki accords of 1975; (2) a heightening of the fear of nuclear war; and (3) almost certainly the strains imposed by the defense burden, discussed below. On the other hand, it remains to be studied whether or not a "tough" Western posture tended to reinforce a siege mentality within the Moscow elite. But, quite distinct from Western policy and conduct, there is good evidence of the importance of simply the existence of the outside world as a challenge to and as a reference group for comparisons by Soviet observers.

The years up to 1985, when Gorbachev came to power, saw a significant increase in the Soviet elite's familiarity with alternative political and socioeconomic systems and with life abroad, a result of both technology and détente. While on the surface that early détente was a political failure, it worked certain important changes in information and attitude that are relevant to our discussion, by strengthening pro-reform images.

Thus, after many years of imposed isolation, Soviet specialists were allowed to travel abroad, correspond with professional colleagues, read foreign journals and magazines. Tourists began to visit other countries; we saw Soviet exchange scholars and students in the U.S. wandering through supermarkets and reading books that had been forbidden back home. In fact, at a time of growing middle-class *veshchizm* (crass consumerism), rapidly expanding tourism even to Eastern Europe stimulated provocative comparisons.

What is more, new technology could be enlisted on behalf of the curious citizenry (and not solely, as George Orwell had posited, on behalf of the regime). Direct-dialing telephones put them in easier touch with émigrés and colleagues abroad, gave them a chance to realize how far behind they were, and stimulated questions about regime policies and the assumptions that had prompted them. Audio cassettes, television, and VCRs (video-cassette recorders) made both information and ideas more accessible.

Nor should we dismiss this new acquaintanceship as trivial or marginal. We know the importance of reference groups from numerous studies. And we know of historical instances where exposure to other civilizations wrought havoc, be it China's acquaintance with the West as a result of the Opium Wars, or the intrusion of Islam into the Mediterranean civilization; or for that matter, the impact of television—showing how people lived elsewhere—on the American civil rights movement in the 1960s and on French Quebec.

ECONOMIC DECLINE

Specialists told us that the Soviet economy needed structural reform long before 1985. Above all, the central command economy had failed to keep up its previously impressive growth rate, the GNP plummeting (by Western estimates) from some 6 percent growth rates in the 1960s to perhaps 2 percent or less in the early 1980s. Per capita real income declined as well. One reason was that earlier on, inputs—capital, labor, energy—had been ample and cheap. By the 1970s this was no longer so, and it was necessary to switch from a strategy of extensive development to an intensive one. Moreover, productivity was low, and the system failed to provide adequate incentives for harder work or for technological innovation. If anything, the technological gap and lag behind the West were increasing. Typically, the quality of production and services were substantially below world standards. This reduced Soviet ability to export goods and also added to consumer dissatisfaction, given the rising expectations of the new elite.

This was also the one area where U.S. policy may have had an impact. Given the Soviet leadership's commitment after the Cuban missile crisis of 1962 to catch up with American military might, including R&D in advanced technology, a totally disproportionate share of Soviet GNP (clearly over 15 percent, by some estimates a lot more) was allocated for the arms race—in an economy whose total product was a good deal less than that of the U.S. The result of these investments was to seriously distort the economy at precisely a time when the decline in its growth rate required cuts in allocations to other parts of the economy, including welfare, services, and consumption.

Here then we have a combination of inherent trends and disastrous policy choices by the Soviet leadership. In addition to objective problems that the Soviet economy presented, the trends sketched above were bound to impact subjective perceptions as well. Not only was the unquestioned priority of defense expenditures becoming more apparent, but the resulting "defense burden" no longer went unchallenged. In addition, the implications of the slowdown not only affected other sectors of the economy but also led to questions concerning the axiomatic effect of continued economy growth on the perceived legitimacy of the Soviet system. For some years short-term successes (as well as economic and social problems abroad) had concealed the structural inadequacies of the Soviet economic mechanism, but by the early 1980s profound doubts about it had matured, particularly as Soviet observers increasingly tended to judge the system by its performance rather than by its promises.

INTERACTION AMONG THE VARIABLES

All this adds up to a subtle change in the relationship of state and society on the eve of the Gorbachev years. Society gains greater autonomy, grievances and expectations become more critical and more overt, and there occurs an implicit shift to some expectation of accountability. If there is an increasing inclination to judge the regime by its performance, in the 1980s the regime falls short. And, more immediately important in 1985, it is essentially this perception of the same trends that shaped the conviction of Mikhail Gorbachev and his friends that "things cannot go on like this."

I have argued that none of the trends we have examined was the prime motor in this process of change. It is precisely the interaction among these variables that was critical. While we cannot "replay" the events with one variable left out, some inferences as to relative weights are plausibly strong. Thus, had the whole control structure not loosened up, much of the articulation of grievances could not have occurred, acquaintance with the outside world would have been far more modest, and the assertion of autonomy in various venues could neither have been undertaken nor succeeded to the degree that it did. Similarly, the effect of the loosening up on the spread of corruption, the perception of stagnation, and contact with the West all facilitated the erosion of ideological commitments. So manifestly did the social pathologies, the value shift and the rising expectations among the new urban middle class erode the faith among officials and non-officials alike.

True, the economic constraints alone should have been enough to engender doubts, comparisons, and grievances. However, the true economic facts were not widely known; indeed, some "derogatory" facts were scarcely known even in the highest leadership circles. Furthermore, at earlier times of economic difficulty—be it 1930 or 1946—there had been no such articulation, essentially because both the actors and the political environment had been so different. We must then conclude that the cluster of trends we have focused on provided a set of necessary conditions for the changes that ensued.

THE GORBACHEV FACTOR

Taken together, the trends and developments discussed above suggest a number of serious flaws and fragilities in the Soviet system. But there are no grounds for arguing that they doomed it. If we had seen them as clearly as we do now in, say, 1984, would we have been led to conclude that a collapse of the Soviet Union was inevitable in the foreseeable future? I think the answer has to be "no."

In that case, do we mean to say that, had Gorbachev and his associates *not* come to power, the Soviet Union would have hobbled along, and might have continued to muddle through without overt instability? That is the only possible conclusion. If we reach that conclusion, based on those premises, then we must give serious weight to the proposition that the much-touted "collapse of communism" was perhaps not nearly so inevitable and surely not necessarily so imminent as it has been made out to be.

There is room for counterfactual speculation, and I think the most responsible answer is that, while we cannot be sure, at the very least Moscow might have gained considerable time, might have avoided the destabilization and delegitimation that the Gorbachev years brought, and might have shaped the domestic and international environment very differently from what in fact occurred. What comes to mind as one scenario is something like the evolution of Turkey or Mexico, which experienced radical regimes and transformations in the first quarter of this century, but where revolutionary zeal petered out without an overthrow of governments.

One could point to problems with this sort of scenario, born of differences between the Soviet Union and Mexico or Turkey. Specifically, the Soviet regime propagated an explicit, mandatory ideology based on the notion of two adversary world systems. That ideology, among other things, provided the justification for the inordinately burdensome effort to match the United States in defense expenditures and weapons research. One could argue, therefore, that drastically cutting the military effort—for a nuclear superpower, at that—would have required a fundamental reorientation of the image of the enemy and the whole ideological mind-set. (Moreover, even such a major restructuring of the Soviet budget probably would not have sufficed to address the structural disorders that ailed the Soviet economy.)

This argument is compelling, though not entirely convincing. True, rational policy choices are constrained by dos and don'ts rooted in beliefs. But was this true under Brezhnev? To some extent, yes; but it was becoming less so. Precisely the Brezhnev years had been a great exercise in fudging issues and overtly denying realities. Such behavior both reflected and deepened the disillusionment and uncertainty about ideological verities within the political establishment. But precisely because of that change in perspectives, the doctrine became even more pragmatically malleable. With a little semantic effort, Brezhnev's successors, had they been so inclined, could surely have managed to cut defense without giving up such parts of the residual communist vision as they wished to protect and preserve. Thus, they could have made policy adjustments while continuing to legitimize their right to rule by reference to other components of the ideology. They would have sacrificed some measure of credibility in the process. But that is not the same as losing the ability to maintain elite unity against challenges to the system.

If my argument has merit, the implication is that the Gorbachev years, and what is now called *katastroyka,* are an essential part of the explanation of the collapse. They are not sufficient by themselves to explain it, but they are, ironically or tragically, a vital link in the chain of destabilization, delegitimation, and disintegration that led from the superpower status of the 1970s to the new, shrunken, confused, and impoverished Russian Federation of the 1990s.

Unlike some of the earlier trends that we can label impersonal or secular, in the Gorbachev period we are dealing with the very distinct acts of will, acts that in retrospect should deaden any temptation to agree with those who seek to transform history and politics into mathematical formulae of rational choice. It did make a lot of difference that these particular individuals, beginning with Gorbachev and soon Yakovlev and Shevardnadze, were the ones taking charge in Moscow. Suffice it to contemplate counterfactual scenarios in which, say, Chernenko remained in office for another five years, or was succeeded by Grishin or Romanov: how different would the country have looked?

Those who see the Soviet period and the dominant Leninist ideology as a seamless web have difficulty explaining how a Gorbachev and his cohort could have emerged in charge of such a system in the first place. Whatever happens elsewhere, here personalities have certainly played a significant part. The fact that they, and not any others, came to power in 1985 also serves to torpedo the "inevitable collapse" argument. To claim that the Soviet system was bound to crash amounts to committing what Reinhard Bendix called "the fallacy of retrospective determinism"—denying the choices (however constrained) that the actors had available before acting.

But what was it about the Gorbachev policies—so many of which were brilliant—that contributed to the system's collapse? First and foremost, Gorbachev put an end to the claim that there was one single truth and therefore one single party that was its carrier. In association with this argument, he fostered *glasnost'*, an end to censorship, an end to widespread political repression, and an end to the official monopoly on rewriting the past. In terms of sociopolitical impact, all this brought about a remarkable sense of having been lied to, of having been deprived of what the rest of the world had had access to, a "desacralization" of the system and delegitimation of the authorities, a transformation of the Communist Party from the unchallenged clan of privilege to a hollow institution without a rational task other than self-preservation. This in turn opened the flood-gates to massive and varied grassroots organization and articulation outside the party.

The other major arena in which the new policy of *glasnost'* had an impact was the republics. From Estonia to Azerbaijan, *glasnost'* mobilized opinion around issues of ethnic identity, beginning with language, school, or culture, and ending with national-liberation fronts. And while there had obviously been some sense of national consciousness that had been stifled earlier on, some of its growth was another unintended consequence of the Soviet experience. The organization of the federation by Union republics, each with its dominant nationality, the ethnic identification of all Soviet citizens in their passports, and the promotion of national cultures and histories (in however circumscribed a fashion) all served to nurture memories and identifications that would be mobilized and reshaped later, when conditions permitted.

Yet, one may hypothesize, the big impetus came precisely from the new doubts about, and the newly perceived challengeability of, the Soviet system. For once their identities as Soviet citizens or communists faded, people looked around for alternative loci of loyalty and identity, and the most powerful "imagined communities" were the ethnonational ones. Thus (to oversimplify a complicated process) *glasnost'* made possible the political mobilization of doubting, contemptuous, and newly emboldened publics, and the invention of new organizations. These acquired an additional ethnic coloration because of the discrediting of alternative identities, which brought to the top of the political agenda the question of the future of the Soviet federal system. That transformation did not come soon enough to avoid the polarization between the centralist "coup plotters" of August 1991 and the separatists at the other end of the center/periphery spectrum. A year later, Gorbachev admitted that his failure fully to recognize the seriousness of the "nationality question" had perhaps been his most serious error in office.

In arguing that the liberalization of the system from 1985 to 1991 was part of the explanation for its collapse, I am *not* agreeing with the proposition that the system could not be reformed. That argument comes from both ends of the political spectrum, though it is made with divergent purposes in mind. The Stalinists in Moscow insist that *any* attempt to "reform" the Soviet system—to alter or abandon its Stalinist cast—was bound to subvert it and therefore must at all costs be avoided; Molotov's critique of Khrushchev's policy in the 1950s came close to this view. Likewise, we hear from those at the other extreme that the Soviet system could not be reformed step by step but needed to be totally demolished before a democratic and healthy system could be erected from scratch. The experience of the Gorbachev regime does not answer the question whether its errors—say, on the nationality question or in economic policy—were avoidable or not. I believe they were, as they were errors of individual judgments, not inherent and inescapable trends. While there are many significant differences between the two cases, the "Chinese option" also suggests that—in the regime's own terms—certain reforms could succeed.

Finally we must ask what, in this setting, provided the trigger for the outward collapse of what remained of the Soviet Union. Here Boris Yel'tsin and his successful "second coming" deserve a little credit (or blame). His re-emergence in 1990 in the context of competitive elections was a product of the unraveling of the system and in turn contributed to the shift in the locus of power and popular support away from the old center. His declaration of Russian sovereignty legitimated the other republics' posture against the "center" and momentarily united democrats and nationalists. His election as president of Russia in June 1991 and, two months later, his stand against the "coup plotters" dramatized both his strength and Gorbachev's weakness. Yel'tsin chose to magnify that asymmetry, and in December he decided to torpedo what remained of the "Union" structure and to erect the impoverished "Commonwealth" framework in its place.

Yel'tsin could not have pulled off these changes if the system had not already been badly injured. Still, he made the most of it, for himself as well, and in the process permitted the collapse of the Soviet Union itself. Identifying him as the final catalyst of the collapse may be the easiest part of this exercise.

CONCLUSION

It is perhaps natural for us to seek simple explanations, single causes, and yes–or–no answers. More often than not, in real life, things are far more complex. We must take care not to introduce retrospectively a clarity, let alone inevitability, where there was contingency and complexity. A retrospective view should underscore the dynamic and variable character of many Soviet policies and institutions. While it is no doubt true that "the party" or "the secret police" or "the dictator" was an ever-present power in the Soviet state, the limits of each changed over time. If corruption was a perennial feature, its scope varied greatly. So did dissent and deviance.

And so did legitimacy. From the manifest fact that the Soviet regime, by 1991, was not widely perceived as legitimate by the population, it is important not to draw the inference that the Soviet regime had been perceived as illegitimate at all earlier times—during the NEP, at the end of World War II, or in the 1960s and 1970s, for instance. The recognition of this fact helps us understand why it is not the case that the Soviet system could have collapsed at any given moment during its 74-year history (though, of course, factors other than a lack of legitimacy could have brought about its demise). It turned out that its end required the maturation, as well as the inter-action, of the several trends identified above. It also required the particular, albeit understandable, blind spots in the perceptions and policy choices of the Gorbachev leadership.

Alexander Dallin, "Causes of the Collapse of the USSR," *Post-Soviet Affairs,* VIII, 4(1992), pp. 279–302.

WHAT RUSSIA TEACHES US NOW: HOW WEAK STATES THREATEN FREEDOM

Stephen Holmes

For half a century, the Soviet Union was not only our principal military adversary. It was also our ideological and moral "other." Both left and right in America defended their competing visions of a liberal society in reaction to the Stalinist nightmare. In this sense, the Cold War profoundly shaped our public philosophy. Indeed, we might say that the Cold War was our public philosophy. The demanding contest with Soviet communism guided how we thought about the core principles underlying our basic institutions. For liberalism was, or appeared to be, totalitarianism turned inside out.

What features of the American creed did this master contrast lead us to stress? Freedom of speech and the press, first of all, and freedom of conscience, for these were cruelly repressed under Moscow's sway. In the same spirit, Americans underscored the freedom of movement, the right to form private associations, the right to a fair trial, and the right to vote in competitive elections where incumbents might be toppled from power. Likewise emphasized was the latitude to accumulate private wealth, on the assumption that a decentralized and unplanned economy alone could provide the basis of both prosperity and political freedom.

Revulsion at the Gulag and the thought police encouraged a particular way of construing these classical liberal freedoms. They were styled, in general, as "negative" liberties, as rights against the state, as shields guarding vulnerable individuals from governmental abuse.

Now the Soviet Union has been swept off the map, but all is not well in Russia. Outside of Moscow, living conditions have deteriorated so severely that some Russians have reverted to subsistence agriculture. Ironically, Russians today have more reason to worry about the debility of the state than about its power. Symptoms of internal disarray are ubiquitous: prison outbreaks, railroad bandits, soldiers begging cigarettes in public places, packs of dogs on the streets of provincial cities, unrepaired oil leaks. The state barely has the resources to function as a result of massive tax evasion and the murders of tax inspectors (26 were killed in 1996), the stiff-arming of Moscow by regional leaders, and the eye-popping enrichment of prominent individuals who sit astride public agencies and semiprivatized enterprises.

The debility of the Russian state not only inflicts suffering on Russians, but also is the source of new specters haunting the West: more Chernobyl-style meltdowns, over-the-counter sales of nuclear know-how to rogue states, the proclaimed technical and financial inability to liquidate existing stockpiles of biological and chemical weapons, shamefully maintained oil tankers, a contagious disease crisis that may eventually threaten Europe, organized-crime activity metastasizing alarmingly abroad, the inability of the central government to live up to its obligations (as in the case of NASA's space station), a questionable command-and-control system, and lack of co-ordination among the defense and foreign ministries on questions vital to neighboring states.

Talented young reformers may be welcomed into the Kremlin, but they will not soon resolve their country's grave crisis of governability. While the buses still manage to run, the Russian government is conspicuously unable to enforce its own laws. Total tax revenues as a percentage of gross domestic product hover somewhere below 10 percent (this excludes the vast and untaxable gray economy), compared to roughly 30 percent in the United States and an average of 45 percent in western Europe. The problem liberal reformers face is no longer censorship and the command economy, nor is it frustrated national pride and xenophobia (though these exist), but something quite new: an incoherent state tenuously connected to a demoralized society.

What can we learn from this shocking situation? How should we reassess the celebration of "free markets" and "spontaneous exchange" when we observe totally unregulated markets in ground-to-air missiles and other lethal leftovers of the Soviet arsenal? And what about "pluralism," "decentralization," "countervailing powers," "private associations," and the "independence of society from the state"? Perhaps we have as much to learn about these ideas from communism's aftermath as we once believed we had to learn from communism itself.

During the Cold War, when all political evils seemed to swarm from "too much government," the threat posed by too weak a government played little role in liberal self-understanding. (I use "liberal" in the expansive philosophical sense, embracing both contemporary American conservatives and liberals.) But this was not always so. In Madison's famous formulation in the *Federalist,* constitutional restrictions on government assume that we "first enable the government to control the governed." If the public authorities can be outgunned or bribed, the vibrancy of the private sector can be pathological. For there is no rule of law until the Mafia needs lawyers. Of course, the increased visibility of grave social harms from unregulated markets and cutthroat bands should not prompt us to embrace ironfisted government. But the woes of Russia's politically disorganized society should heighten our appreciation of the role of government in promoting liberal freedoms and serve as a lesson to those among us who see the state only as a threat to liberal values.

NO PUBLIC POWER, NO INDIVIDUAL RIGHTS

Classical liberal theory deemed political authority necessary because individuals are partial to themselves and, left to their own devices, the strong and the deceitful have an irresistible proclivity to exempt themselves from generally valid laws. That old insight is amply confirmed in Russia today. When the state that once owned everything is now so easy to despoil, why play by rules that apply equally to all? Libertarians sometimes argue that the coercive authority of the state extends only to the prevention of harm and the protection of property rights. In the Russian context, the word "only" here strikes a very false note. Limited government, capable of repressing force and fraud, turns out to be mind-bogglingly difficult to erect in a chaotic setting.

Today's Russia makes excruciatingly plain that liberal values are threatened just as thoroughly by state incapacity as by despotic power. "Destatization" is not the solution; it is the problem. For without a well-functioning public power of a certain kind there will be no prevention of mutual harm, no personal security, and no "standing rule to live by," to use a Lockean phrase. The rights inscribed in the 1977 Brezhnev Constitution went unprotected because of a repressive state apparatus. The rights inscribed in the 1993 Yeltsin Constitution go unenforced because the government lacks resources and purpose, and because incumbents are more keen on harvesting kickbacks and insider giveaways than on solving public problems.

Russia's disorder affects both state and civil society. The system of central control and coordination is in shambles, and the citizenry, while resenting political elites, remains passive and inert. Incumbents are venal and incompetent, and social interests are too anemic and diffuse to coalesce into effective collective organizations or constituencies for reform capable of disciplining those in power. While not especially oppressive (with the important exception of Chechnya), the government is fragmented, unaccountable, and seemingly indifferent to the plight of its citizens. Social services atrophy and life expectancy plummets, while ordinary Russians, expecting nothing from politics, eke out a living on their own.

That political fragmentation and the dissipation of authority make it impossible to realize liberal freedoms suggests that liberalism does not aim exclusively, or even principally, at diffusing power. What stands out, in the light of recent Russian experience, is the capacity of liberal government to unify power in accountable hands and to use it effectively.

Russian political dissidents are no longer being jailed, it is true. No one is punished or even threatened for violating the party line, for there is no party line. Journalists are blown to smithereens by suitcase bombs, but only when they rummage indiscreetly into corruption at the Ministry of Defense. No one is being incarcerated for their heretical beliefs, for heresy is not possible in the absence of orthodoxy. Both ideological censorship and indoctrination have disappeared along with ideology itself. No one in power fears, or takes any guidance from, political ideas. The image of the lone refusnik crushed by a remorseless Behemoth reinforced a one-sided interpretation of liberal rights. It placed the accumulated weight of painful experience behind the assumption that rights are essentially "walls" erected against state power. This metaphor no doubt contains an element of truth. But its ultimate inadequacy is disclosed by the Russian situation today, where the defeat of liberal reforms is most clearly visible in the wall of indifference separating state from society. Corrupt incumbents, uninterested in oppression, live in a separate world from depoliticized citizens. Moscow, a sparkling enclave that misleads foreign observers, also symbolizes the total disregard of the Russian rich for the Russian poor. The faltering of Russia's liberal reforms, in other words, suggests that liberalism, best understood, aims not to seal off society from the state but, on the contrary, to keep open robust and transparent channels for consultation and partnership between honest public officials and honest private citizens.

Russia lacks legitimate political authority. But liberal rights depend essentially on the competent exercise of a certain kind of legitimate public power. This is why violating an individual's rights involves disobeying the liberal state. Statelessness is such a deplorable condition because it signals the absence of the sole institution that is capable of extending its protection to the vulnerable. Put differently, the largest and most reliable human rights organization is the liberal state. Beyond the effective reach of such a state, rights will not be consistently protected or enforced. Unless society is politically well organized, there will be no individual liberties and no civil society. It is an obvious lesson, but one that runs counter to what the antitotalitarian ethos induced us to assume.

Why do basic rights to decent treatment go unenforced in pretrial detention cells across Russia? Among the many reasons is a breakdown of the chain of command. The right to be treated decently by policemen, prosecutors, judges, and prison guards presupposes effective systems of monitoring, subordination, and accountability. Custodial personnel behave more decently when monitored. The enforcement of rights, in other words, presupposes stable relations of authority and obedience.

By illustrating vividly the dependence of individual liberty on state power of a certain kind, the new Russia should help us focus more clearly on how authority enhances freedom in our own system. If the state is to have a monopoly of violence, the monopoly must be vested only in officials whom the public can hold accountable for its use. Liberalism demands that people without guns be able to tell people with guns what to do. While any credibly liberal government must be limited in important ways, it must not be so crippled or irresolute that, for example, local military or police or secret service authorities escape centralized civilian control.

In other ways, too, the blockage of liberal reform in Russia can conceivably bring liberal and individualist thought back to basics. The explosive growth there of legally unregulated social sectors should deflate overblown rhetoric about that "autonomous" sphere where American families can keep every penny they earn and from which government is scrupulously barred. Indeed, observing the devastating effects of a genuinely hands-off regime should help us clear up some serious confusions surrounding the words "dependency" and "independence" as they are casually heaved about in our political debate.

The right of a creditor to have a loan repaid is obviously a product of law and state authority. An American who asserts his rights in contract law or tort law must necessarily avail himself of the public power. When I sue, I am neither acting on my own in a coercion-free sphere nor am I trying to get the state off my back. Rather, I am asking the state to perform. A state that leaves loan collection to private thugs and can offer no remedy to victims of aggravated negligence cannot be a liberal state in the most basic sense.

That the same analysis applies to constitutional rights is obscured by the description of our Bill of Rights as a "charter of negative liberties." Constitutional rights are underenforced in Russia today because they, too, require governmental authorities to perform rather than merely to forbear. The right to vote is meaningless if electoral officials take bribes or fail to show up for work. The right to just compensation for confiscated property is empty if the treasury has nothing to disburse. The right to subpoena witnesses in one's own defense is useless if the court's solemn writs are greeted with laughter. The constitutional right to due process presupposes that, at the taxpayers' expense, the state maintains and makes accessible complex legal institutions that perform the cumbersome formalities of fair adjudication. For this reason, a nonperforming state cannot be a liberal state.

TAXES AND LIBERTY

Basic rights go unenforced in Russia not only because the state is distracted and inconsistent, but also because it is insolvent. Chronic underfunding erodes individual liberty for the same reason it damages military preparedness. That rights depend on the efficient use of public resources, as well as on the competent exercise of public authority, becomes clear when we examine the sickening conditions in Russia's correctional facilities, where rampant tuberculosis (2,000 inmates died of the disease in 1996), even among guards, and high mortality rates are due less to custodial abuse than to horrible overcrowding, inedible food, and the absence of basic medical care. Not torture, in this case, but a breakdown of public finances is the principal cause of the violation of inmate rights. So a bankrupt state cannot be a liberal state, whatever the "cultural level" of its citizens.

What I mean by insolvency is not a lack of resources in society at large or the absence of wealthy citizens, for Russia has both. An insolvent state, in the pertinent sense, is one that cannot extract, in a way that is widely deemed to be fair, a modest share of social wealth and then channel the resources extracted into the creation and delivery of public services, rather than into the pockets of incumbents and their cronies. The Russian state is an illiberal state partly because it is insolvent. And it is insolvent because it is corrupt—because norms of public service are weak, and potential taxpayers do not trust the government.

One of the principal lessons of the new Russian illiberalism is that individual rights are unprotectable without the power to tax and spend. To extract resources efficiently, a government must be able to mobilize cooperation. Strong-state liberalism is not ironfisted because "state strength," in a liberal context, depends essentially on the legitimacy of authority, the capacity of the government to enlist voluntary support. Threats of reprisal for nonpayment of taxes, growled by self-enriching state officials, do not elicit honesty about private assets. To raise revenue with relative efficiency, a state must not only be seen to treat citizens fairly, but it must also communicate public purposes in an understandable way and strike partnerships with important social groups and actors in an attempt to solve common problems.

The Russian government cannot protect basic rights for the same reason that it cannot provide such elementary public goods as a nontoxic environment, books in elementary schools, x-ray film in public hospitals, veterans' benefits, a nationwide highway system, railroad maintenance, and potable water. It cannot protect rights because it cannot target extracted resources to the provision of public goods. Courts are working, it is true, but judicial dockets are chronically backlogged because budgetary outlays earmarked for the judiciary are pitiful and often do not arrive. The dependency of basic rights on tax revenues helps us see that rights are public goods. Far from being walls bricking out the meddlesome state, even the so-called negative rights are taxpayer-funded and government-managed social services designed to improve collective and individual well-being.

PROPERTY AND THE STATE

This includes property rights. Soviet Russia drew attention to the way laws and regulations can stifle economic activity. Post-Soviet Russia lends credence to the opposite truth. Without clearly defined, unambiguously assigned, and legally enforceable property rights, ownership does not encourage stewardship, just as privatization does not elicit an entrepreneurial response.

It is not merely that government must supplement and perfect the market. The point is more basic and cuts deeper. The market is created, sustained, and constantly attuned by legislative and adjudicative decisions that prove unenforceable in a politically disorganized society. Just as you cannot have capitalism where everything is planned, so you cannot have capitalism where everything is for sale, not at least if the salable items include employees at the public registry of titles and deeds. Markets presuppose a competent and honest bureaucracy.

My rights to enter, use, exclude from, sell, bequeath, mortgage, and abate nuisances threatening "my" property all palpably depend on something that does not yet exist in Russia: a well-organized, well-funded, authoritative, and relatively honest court system. A liberal legal system does not merely protect and defend my property. It lays down the rules of ownership specifying, for instance, the maintenance and repair obligations of landlords or how jointly owned property is to be sold. It therefore makes no more sense to associate property rights with "freedom from government" than to associate the right to play chess with freedom from the rules of chess.

The contemplation of weak-state capitalism should make plain the hopeless limitations of a libertarian conception of "independence." An autonomous individual cannot create the conditions of his own autonomy autonomously, but only collectively. If the wielders of the police power are not on your side, you will not successfully "assert your right" to enter your own home and make use of its contents, as the Muslims evicted from West Mostar in Bosnia have repeatedly learned. For property is a complex set of rules enforced by the state. Even more dramatically, private property is a sham if the community cannot train and equip an army capable of defending its territory against foreign marauders and predators. That is the lesson of, say, Srebernica.

The implications are worth spelling out: All liberal rights presuppose or imply the dependency of the individual on the collectivity and on the principal instrument of the collectivity, that is, on the coercive-extractive state. This is a truism and a banality. But it is another one of those truisms that Cold War–dominated thought did not fully absorb.

THE DEBILITY OF RUSSIAN CAPITALISM

At the basis of a liberal economy lies the willingness of people to rely on each other's word. Trust, like thrift and industriousness, is a psychological attitude with roots outside the legal order. But while liberal systems elicit and reward such attitudes, illiberal systems asphyxiate them. Because contracts are not reliably enforced in Russia, payment by the installment plan is not an attractive arrangement for creditors. In the autonomous realm, beyond the reach of government, extortion is rampant, but borrowers have a hard time obtaining long-term loans. For one function of the liberal state is to lengthen the time horizons of private actors by predictably enforcing known and stable rules. Property is worthless if you, and potential purchasers, do not believe in the future.

Capitalists know this and tend not to invest in countries, such as Russia, where—to employ a different idiom—the discount rate of economic actors is high. Long-gestation investment in productive facilities, where jobs might be created, is unlikely when fixed assets are difficult to defend against lethally armed extortionists. In such circumstances, capital tends to flow into the removal of natural resources that can be guarded at the site of extraction and during transshipment and that fetch a handsome price on world markets.

Currency stabilization alone is not enough to improve Russia's investment climate because the instability of trade, banking, customs, and tax regulations, too, casts a cloud over the future. While the Russian government is no longer oppressively tyrannical, it is not yet predictable, and therefore remains illiberal. Because the state's capacity to tax is inadequate, authorities have taken to slapping retroactive taxes on foreign firms, which keep honest books and are in no position to refuse. This myopic raiding of potential investors is a fair example of the effects of political disarray on the public welfare.

Moral outrage at weak-state capitalism is not necessarily a reflection of residual socialism or aversion to inequality, as is often assumed. In Russia, the current distribution of ownership—which underlies the market—appears illegitimate to ordinary people because most owners did not work for their wealth or inherit it according to publicly known and accepted rules. Private property is a more troublesome and troubled institution in Russia than in the West because, for obvious reasons, no postcommunist society can consistently implement the rule "give back what is stolen."

Profit seekers also still assume that the most appropriate means for dealing with business competitors are plastic explosives. The unpoliced economy arouses discontent when its principal players are seen as racketeers whose techniques for "dispute resolution" run the gamut from intimidation to contract killings. State incapacity is also revealed in the way new Russians have managed to exploit a pervasive lack of corporate accountability for personal gain. Directors of state-subsidized enterprises buy inputs from friends at inflated prices and sell outputs to friends at bargain prices, thereby decapitalizing their firms and siphoning public wealth into private pockets. They walk away with assets and dump liabilities back into the public debt. They can skim so deftly only because no one with the public interest in mind has the power to stop them.

Dog-eat-dog capitalism also thrives on the absence of enforceable antifraud law. The impunity of con men, although it will surely not last forever, keeps people out of the market today who might otherwise come in. Ordinary Russians are less put off by the act of buying and selling than by their vulnerability to possible scams; hence they cling to suppliers they know personally.

In the West, consumers benefit from a competitive market in restaurants because, as voters and taxpayers, they have created and funded sanitation boards that allow them to range adventurously beyond a restricted circle of personally known and trusted establishments. Thus, the feebleness of markets in Russia, despite economic liberalization, suggests the importance of political organization and state performance for fostering the trust among strangers necessary if the market is to become national and not merely local. A sausage factory in Samara will not sell to a retailer in Nizhnii Novgorod if it is unable to collect debts across oblast borders.

For a punishing percentage, thugs may selectively enforce the repayment of loans. Obligingly, they will also kill your creditors. But the one thing they are not going to do is enforce general rules against fraud or unfair business practices. The reason is obvious. Antifraud law is a common good, based on a biblically simple moral principle (cheating is wrong), the benefits of which cannot be captured by a few but are diffused widely throughout society. So here again, Russian conditions draw attention to the way liberal markets depend, for their moral basis, on a liberal style of governance.

Wild capitalism could nevertheless win public approval—despite its ruthlessness, stunning inequalities, and fondness for fraud—if it produced general prosperity. But

Russians living outside Moscow have not received a booming economy to compensate for their loss of job security. For state incapacity entails not only gangland massacres and pyramid schemes, but also a paucity of investments in infrastructure and skills, feeble enforcement of stockholders' rights, lack of securities-exchange oversight, weak trademark protection, legal unclarity about the status of collateral, and inadequate regulation of the banking sector to ensure a steady flow of credit to businessmen rather than cronies. The nonenforcement of antitrust law may also reduce the shared benefits of economic liberalization. For these reasons—and above all because property rights are not clearly defined and impartially protected—"privatization" in Russia does not foster innovation, encourage investment, boost worker productivity, raise production standards, or stimulate the efficient use of scarce resources.

THE DEMOCRATIC CHARADE

These lessons also apply to the Russian political system. Russia mounts elections and tolerates a free press, but it does not have democracy. Why not? Voting in Russia is not a means by which citizens discipline their rulers. Elections in Russia, in fact, do not create power. For the most part, they mirror the power that already exists. Incumbents find their supporters in hidden networks. They do not draw their power, in any way, from the majority of average voters, which is why the public, although bitterly resenting its rulers, has given up actively opposing the government.

Russian elections do not produce anything even vaguely resembling accountable or responsive government largely because of institutional weakness. Popular cynicism about "democracy" is perfectly understandable: If the state is too weak to enforce its own laws, what is the point of seeking a share of the lawmaking power? Since the bicameral parliament has little knowledge of, and no control over, decisions made in the ministries, electing a deputy does not contribute one iota to governmental accountability.

What Russia's electoral charades bring home is something we already knew: Democratic procedures are of value only if they establish some sort of dependency of public officials on ordinary citizens. While free citizens are dependent on the government for the exercise of their rights, incumbents elected popularly and pro tempore presumably have a reason to behave responsibly, to act as the agent of society, and to produce benefits of palpable value to a majority of voters.

Many Russian officials apparently see no reason to act this way. They live in a secretive bubble, supported—here I exaggerate to make a point—by stolen assets, the International Monetary Fund, and various criminal affiliations. This lack of "dependence on the people" means that incumbents have little incentive to produce public goods that the average voter might find of some value. Just as society is undisciplined by "general and equal laws," so the state is unperturbed by the predicament of ordinary voters. Just as citizens will not cooperate in the enforcement of laws and decrees, so the government seems unable to profit from the decentralized information and intelligence of private individuals.

Contemplating this lack of any discernible partnership between honest public officials and honest private citizens should lead us to reidentify the principal function of liberal constitutionalism. For liberal constitutionalism is valuable not only because it protects us from the tyranny of the minority or the majority, but also because it establishes a mutually beneficial alliance between the many and the few.

The social contract in Russia today can be described as an exchange of unaccountable power for untaxable wealth. This, needless to say, is a contract among "elites," a sleazy deal between political and economic insiders—the so-called criminal-nomenklatura symbiosis—who, in bed with each other, engage in mutually beneficial unpunishable misdeeds. The Russian government's most urgent task today is to decriminalize the economy and stimulate the development of organized rule-of-law constituencies, presumably businessmen who accumulate wealth without force or fraud. But thoroughly compromised incumbents cannot even begin such a process of reform. And where could they find honest businessmen to support them if they tried?

The overriding question in Russia is not: "Who governs?" but rather: "Why govern?" Why take the trouble to govern, if you can feed off the imperial remains and vacation frequently in European resorts? The rest of society, the great mass of citizens, is left out of the contract, left—in extreme cases—to die out in a Darwinian struggle for survival.

Russia seems to be a broken-hourglass society in which the privileged do not exploit or oppress or even govern but simply ignore the majority. Labor quiescence is due to the fact that, roughly speaking, the rich are opportunistic scavengers who have gained their wealth by "cherry picking" and exporting raw materials, not by taking advantage of the working masses. Outside of a few sectors—especially those involving exportable natural resources where workers are paid well and on time—strikes would yield no benefits. Workers cannot credibly threaten to strike at a bankrupt state-owned enterprise, where outputs have a lower market value than the sum of inputs. No one needs their cooperation. You cannot create a "middle class" by handing workers shares in negative-value-added firms that retain their residual welfare functions and will never be able to compete on world markets.

REDISTRIBUTION AS INCLUSION

Communism's unexpected aftermath might also encourage us to reconceptualize our contested social expenditures. Soviet-style regimes made it plausible to conceive of entitlements in liberal societies as a kind of dependency. For what is a recipient of public aid if not the antithesis of an enterprising individual? But the current disorder in Russia—where public officials have taken antipaternalism to the point of child abandonment—might encourage us to view social spending more as a choice between inclusion and exclusion.

The fiscal crisis of the Russian state is not caused principally by pensioners and others clamoring for handouts to which they have become accustomed. The chief impediments to budgetary responsibility (and to responsible governance in general) are the "spoiler elites" who thrive on legal chaos. Budgetary outlays for vulnerable groups have fallen for the same reason that all government expenditures have dropped. The Russian state is unable to tax and spend.

Why are pensioners, veterans, and former Chernobyl cleanup workers infuriated by rumors that their welfare entitlements are soon to be reduced even further for budgetary reasons? Their problem is not (or not only) that seven decades of socialism have weakened their moral fiber. Rather, they do not relish being advised to tighten their belts, to give up, say, their pension benefits on which they counted their whole working lives, by unscrupulous apparatchiks who recently became windfall millionaires through insider-giveaways of assets that once ostensibly belonged to all and who are now surreptitiously stashing Russia's investable resources in Cypriot banks. The roots of postcommunist popular discontent lie less in deplorable habits of dependency than in accurate perceptions of betrayal.

Notice that the pathological disconnect between the Russian government and the Russian people is simultaneously a disturbing insulation of the rich from the poor. The separatism of the privileged, their palpable relief at not being in the same boat with their unfortunate fellow citizens, should force us to specify, by way of contrast, the kinds of rich-poor relations desirable in a liberal regime. During the Cold War, worries about poverty were sometimes, however, implausibly, associated with the road to serfdom. Today, the terms of reference have changed. Should not the spectacular inequity of nomenklatura privatization lead us to ask how much and what kind of distributions are compatible with liberal principles? How unfair can a good society be? How does the liberal social contract—where citizens pay taxes and public officials provide public services—differ from a nomenklatura-criminal swap by which insiders simply wash their hands of the rest?

At the origins of liberalism lay the perception that private property could not be reliably protected by the police power alone, and that only a system of public assistance could moderate the desperation that would drive the poor to theft and arson. Liberalism never aimed at the abolition of classes but at class compromise. In its twentieth-century form, the liberal "mixed regime" honors the property rights of the well-to-do, while guaranteeing procedural fairness, voting rights, the right to strike, entitlement to public education, and various welfare rights to the less advantaged.

Perceptions of gross unfairness severely damage group morale. In order to fight wars, impose law and order, and even promote economic growth, liberal states have found it useful to take the edge off conspicuous economic inequality by relieving desperation and providing a bottom floor beneath which no one might drop. A free economy, where great accumulations of private wealth must be protected from the appetites of foreign and domestic predators, presupposes that the less privileged feel some perceptible stake in the system. A liberal state cannot claim, with any degree of plausibility, to be the impartial agent of society as a whole, unless it emphatically identifies exclusion as a moral problem and responds to it vigorously as a political challenge.

That is our political challenge, not Russia's alone. During the Cold War, the Soviet Union's closed society taught us to value the openness of our own society. In communism's aftermath, Russia's politically disorganized society reminds us of liberalism's deep dependence on efficacious government. The idea that autonomous individuals can enjoy their private liberties if they are simply left unpestered by the public power dissolves before the disturbing realities of the new Russia. To protect our freedom, we had better protect the legitimate political authority that enables and sustains it. And until we have responded more effectively to our own increasingly disturbing forms of social exclusion, we had better spare the world any smug self-congratulation.

Stephen Holmes, "What Russia Teaches Us Now: How Weak States Threaten Freedom." *The American Prospect*, no. 33 (July–August 1997), pp. 30–39.